# 50

## Essays

### *A Portable Anthology*

#### *Sixth Edition*

*Edited by*

## SAMUEL COHEN

*University of Missouri*

**bedford/st.martin's**
Macmillan Learning

Boston | New York

**For Bedford/St. Martin's**
*Vice President, Editorial, Macmillan Learning Humanities*: Edwin Hill
*Executive Program Director for English:* Leasa Burton
*Senior Program Manager, Readers and Literature:* John E. Sullivan III
*Director of Content Development, Humanities:* Jane Knetzger
*Senior Development Manager:* Susan McLaughlin
*Senior Developmental Editor:* Kate George
*Editorial Assistant:* Cari Goldfine
*Executive Marketing Manager:* Joy Fisher Williams
*Content Project Manager:* Pamela Lawson
*Senior Workflow Project Manager:* Lisa McDowell
*Production Supervisor:* Robin Besofsky
*Advanced Media Project Manager:* Rand Thomas
*Associate Media Editor:* Daniel Johnson
*Senior Manager of Publishing Services:* Andrea Cava
*Project Management:* Lumina Datamatics, Inc.
*Composition:* Lumina Datamatics, Inc.
*Text Permissions Manager:* Kalina Ingham
*Text Permissions Researcher:* Kristine Janssens/Elaine Kosta,
  Lumina Datamatics, Inc.
*Photo Permissions Editor:* Angela Boehler
*Director of Design, Content Management:* Diana Blume
*Text Design:* Sandra Rigney; Diana Blume
*Cover Design:* William Boardman
*Cover Image:* pernsanitfoto/Getty Images
*Printing and Binding:* LSC Communications

Copyright © 2020, 2017, 2014, 2011 by Bedford/St. Martin's.

Manufactured in the United States of America.

1   2   3   4   5   6       24   23   22   21   20   19

*For information, write:* Bedford/St. Martin's, 75 Arlington Street,
  Boston, MA 02116

ISBN 978-1-319-19446-8

### Acknowledgments
*Text acknowledgments and copyrights appear at the back of the book on pages 478–79, which constitute an extension of the copyright page. Art acknowledgments and copyrights appear on the same page as the art selections they cover.*

# Preface for Instructors

*50 Essays: A Portable Anthology* is a compact, inexpensive collection of classic and contemporary essays, most of which have already proven popular in hundreds of classrooms and with thousands of students. Learning how to read good writing effectively is crucial to learning how to write and think critically—and *50 Essays* is full of exceptional prose and many opportunities to practice reading, thinking, and writing about it.

*50 Essays* includes a core of classic essays, such as Gloria Anzaldúa's "How to Tame a Wild Tongue," Langston Hughes's "Salvation," and Frederick Douglass's "Learning to Read and Write," accompanied by fresh, recent selections, such as Jenine Holmes's "When Pink Ballet Slippers Won't Do" and Hanya Yanagihara's "A Pet Tortoise Who Will Outlive Us All." For such a compact volume, *50 Essays* represents an extraordinary diversity of voices and genres—from polemical exhortations to personal narratives, from speeches to meditations, and from nuanced arguments to humorous articles of varied length and complexity. The essays should stimulate ideas for students' own writing as they provide sound models for rhetorical analysis.

But *50 Essays* is more than just a selection of good readings: it is a versatile and practical collection designed to prompt critical thinking and writing in the composition classroom. For maximum flexibility and ease of navigation, the essays are arranged alphabetically by author, while alternative tables of contents are provided to help instructors shape courses that meet their teaching preferences. For example, one table of contents is organized by rhetorical mode (narration, description, comparison, and so forth); another by rhetorical purpose (personal, expository, argumentative writing); another by theme (ethics, gender, identity, pop culture, nature and the environment, among others); another by clusters and paired readings (Gloria Anzaldúa, Sandra Cisneros, and Amy Tan on "Language and Identity," James Baldwin, Ta-Nehisi Coates, and Brent Staples on "Men Encountering Racism," and more); another lists the selections chronologically by the date of the essay's composition; and a final new table lists the selections by Lexile level.

For students, an introduction provides advice on the key skills of active reading, critical thinking, and writing. Terms in bold throughout the introduction refer to a glossary at the back of the book, which defines important writing terms, such as audience, evidence, and plagiarism. An annotated model paper shows students how to analyze and work with multiple sources. Headnotes contextualize each reading in its writer's own place and time. As an aid to comprehension, the essays themselves are lightly glossed. Several types of assignments follow each reading and provide multiple avenues into it: questions on meaning, on rhetorical strategy, on connections between and among selections, and on ideas for further analysis and research. A basic sentence guide helps students hone their sentence writing skills, while an MLA-style documentation guide helps students write their own source-based papers.

## NEW TO THIS EDITION

Nineteen readings are new to this edition, including:

- **Essays on contemporary topics** that invite students to confront timely issues, including race relations and the 2016 election in Rahawa Haile's "Going It Alone," grief in the age of the internet in Matthew J. X. Malady's "The Ghosts in Our Machines," and displaced persons in Ai Weiwei's "The Refugee Crisis Isn't About Refugees. It's About Us."
- **Essays that examine everyday culture** to make students aware of the significance of often overlooked things, including Danny Chau's "The Burning Desire for Hot Chicken," which finds truths about urban history in food trends, and Tommy Orange's "Indian Heads," which looks at the history of Native Americans through their representation on things like coins and TV test patterns.

In addition to the new readings, we've added:

- **Sentence Guides for Academic Writers**, which will guide students as they develop their skills as writers both in the classroom and beyond.

- **A new Lexile Level Table of Contents** to help both instructors and students determine the reading levels of the various essays in the book.

## BEDFORD/ST. MARTIN'S PUTS YOU FIRST

From day one, our goal has been simple: to provide inspiring resources that are grounded in best practices for teaching reading and writing. For more than 35 years, Bedford/St. Martin's has partnered with the field, listening to teachers, scholars, and students about the support writers need. We are committed to helping every writing instructor make the most of our resources.

### How Can We Help *You*?

- Our editors can align our resources to your outcomes through correlation and transition guides for your syllabus. Just ask us.
- Our sales representatives specialize in helping you find the right materials to support your course goals.
- Our *Bits* blog on the Bedford/St. Martin's English Community (**community.macmillan.com**) publishes fresh teaching ideas weekly. You'll also find easily downloadable professional resources and links to author webinars on our community site.

Contact your Bedford/St. Martin's sales representative or visit **macmillanlearning.com** to learn more.

### Print and Digital Options for *50 Essays*

Choose the format that works best for your course, and ask about our packaging options that offer savings for students.

#### PRINT

- *Paperback.* To order the sixth edition, use ISBN 978-1-319-19446-8.

#### DIGITAL

- *Innovative digital learning space.* Bedford/St. Martin's suite of digital tools makes it easy to get everyone on the same page by putting student writers at the center. For details, visit **macmillanlearning.com/englishdigital**.

- *Popular e-book formats.* For details about our e-book partners, visit **macmillanlearning.com/ebooks**.
- *Inclusive Access.* Enable every student to receive their course materials through your LMS on the first day of class. Macmillan Learning's Inclusive Access program is the easiest, most affordable way to ensure all students have access to quality educational resources. Find out more at **macmillanlearning .com/inclusiveaccess**.

## Your Course, Your Way

No two writing programs or classrooms are exactly alike. Our Curriculum Solutions team works with you to design custom options that provide the resources your students need. (Options below require enrollment minimums.)

- *ForeWords for English.* Customize any print resource to fit the focus of your course or program by choosing from a range of prepared topics, such as Sentence Guides for Academic Writers.
- *Macmillan Author Program (MAP).* Add excerpts or package acclaimed works from Macmillan's trade imprints to connect students with prominent authors and public conversations. A list of popular examples or academic themes is available upon request.
- *Bedford Select.* Build your own print handbook or anthology from a database of more than 900 selections, and add your own materials to create your ideal text. Package with any Bedford/St. Martin's text for additional savings. Visit **macmillanlearning.com /bedfordselect**.

## Instructor Resources

You have a lot to do in your course. We want to make it easy for you to find the support you need—and to get it quickly.

*Resources for 50 Essays*, Sixth Edition, is available as a PDF that can be downloaded from **macmillanlearning.com**. In addition to chapter overviews and teaching tips, the instructor's manual includes sample syllabi, answers to questions that appear within the book, and suggested classroom activities.

## ACKNOWLEDGMENTS

Many thanks go to the instructors who helped shape this edition of *50 Essays*: Jennifer Annick, El Camino College; Pamela Arlov, Middle Georgia State College; Susan Naomi Bernstein, Arizona State University; Linda Borla, Cypress College; William Carney, Cameron University; Judith Castillo, California State University, Long Beach; Phillip Chamberlin, Hillsborough Community College; Emily Cosper, Delgado Community College; Kathy Cote, Indiana State University; Joseph Couch, Montgomery College; Kevin Degnan, El Camino College; Rigdzin T. Dorje, SUNY College of Technology at Delhi; Diane Flores-Kagan, Antelope Valley College; Christopher S. Glover, El Camino College; Shannon Gramse, University of Alaska Anchorage; Isabel Grayson, Mercy College; Sharon Johnson, Columbus State University; Kristen Keckler, Mercy College; Tim Kelley, Northwest-Shoals Community College; Geri Lawson, California State University, Long Beach; Patti McCarthy, University of the Pacific; David McDevitt, California State University, Long Beach; Elizabeth T. Pardo, California State University, Long Beach; Rachel Prusko, University of Alberta; Lynne Purtle, Western Connecticut State University; Lisa del Rosso, New York University; David Sierk, Cuyahoga Community College; KT Shaver, California State University, Long Beach; S. Andrew Stowe, Anderson University; Maxine Sweeney, Rio Hondo Community College; Alan Michael Trusky, Florence-Darlington Technical College; and Toby Widdicombe, University of Alaska Anchorage.

I would also like to thank the people who have made this book possible, particularly Sherry Mooney for her strong ideas and stronger patience in her work with me on the fifth edition, and Kate George for her enthusiasm and smarts in helping to keep me excited and on track for this edition. Thanks also to Cari Goldfine who ably assisted Kate. I would also like to acknowledge the help of John Sullivan, our senior program manager; Pamela Lawson, who guided the book through production; Kristine Janssens and Elaine Kosta for clearing permissions; and Joy Fisher Williams for her marketing insights. I would like to thank the teachers from whom I was lucky to learn how to read and write, and teach. I would like to thank my Spring 2003 Writing I students at Baruch College, CUNY, who were taught with this book in its early stages and who had a great deal of unflinchingly honest advice for how to put it together. I would also like to thank the sixteen years' worth of students I have had the pleasure to teach since then, most in the English Department at the University of Missouri, for teaching me how to better teach them, in class and in this book. Most of all, I would like to thank Kristin Bowen for everything she has taught me about textbooks and many other things; our boys, Ben and Henry, who have grown up with this book and can now see college ahead of them; and our dog, Azalea, who would like to know when she gets to be on the cover.

# Contents

MAYA ANGELOU, *Graduation*     17

"I was no longer simply a member of the proud graduating class of 1940; I was a proud member of the wonderful, beautiful Negro race."

GLORIA ANZALDÚA, *How to Tame a Wild Tongue*     30

"Ethnic identity is twin skin to linguistic identity—I am my language. Until I can take pride in my language, I cannot take pride in myself."

BARBARA LAZEAR ASCHER, *On Compassion*     43

"Compassion is not a character trait like a sunny disposition. It must be learned, and it is learned by having adversity at our windows. . . ."

ix

together a series of graceful *pensées*; we are talking about
something private, about bits of the mind's string too short to use,
an indiscriminate and erratic assemblage with meaning only for
its maker."

# Table of Contents by Rhetorical Mode

# Table of Contents
# by Purpose

# Table of Contents
# by Theme

# Table of Contents by Clusters and Paired Readings

# Table of Contents by Chronological Order

# Table of Contents
# by Lexile Level

# Sentence Guides for Academic Writers

Being a college student means being a college writer. No matter what field you are studying, your instructors will ask you to make sense of what you are learning through writing. When you work on writing assignments in college, you are, in most cases, being asked to write for an academic audience.

Writing academically means thinking academically—asking a lot of questions, digging into the ideas of others, and entering into scholarly debates and academic conversations. As a college writer, you will be asked to read different kinds of texts; understand and evaluate authors' ideas, arguments, and methods; and contribute your own ideas. In this way, you present yourself as a participant in an academic conversation.

What does it mean to be part of an *academic conversation*? Well, think of it this way: You and your friends may have an ongoing debate about the best film trilogy of all time. During your conversations with one another, you analyze the details of the films, introduce points you want your friends to consider, listen to their ideas, and perhaps cite what the critics have said about a particular trilogy. This kind of conversation is not unlike what happens among scholars in academic writing—except they could be debating the best public policy for a social problem or the most promising new theory in treating disease.

If you are uncertain about what academic writing *sounds like* or if you're not sure you're any good at it, this booklet offers guidance for you at the sentence level. It helps answer questions such as these:

How can I present the ideas of others in a way that demonstrates my understanding of the debate?

How can I agree with someone, but add a new idea?

How can I disagree with a scholar without seeming, well, rude?

How can I make clear in my writing which ideas are mine and which ideas are someone else's?

The following sections offer sentence guides for you to use and adapt to your own writing situations. As in all writing that you do, you will have to think about your purpose (reason for writing) and your audience (readers) before knowing which guides will be most appropriate for a particular piece of writing or for a certain part of your essay.

The guides are organized to help you present background information, the views and claims of others, and your own views and claims — all in the context of your purpose and audience.

## ACADEMIC WRITERS PRESENT INFORMATION AND OTHERS' VIEWS

When you write in academic situations, you may be asked to spend some time giving background information for or setting a context for your main idea or argument. This often requires you to present or summarize what is known or what has already been said in relation to the question you are asking in your writing.

## SG1 Presenting what is known or assumed

When you write, you will find that you occasionally need to present something that is known, such as a specific fact or a statistic. The following structures are useful when you are providing background information.

As we know from history, _____ .

X has shown that _____ .

Research by X and Y suggests that _____ .

According to X, _____ percent of _____ are/favor _____ .

In other situations, you may have the need to present information that is assumed or that is conventional wisdom.

People often believe that _____ .

Conventional wisdom leads us to believe _____ .

Many Americans share the idea that _____ . _____
is a widely held belief.

In order to challenge an assumption or a widely held belief, you have to acknowledge it first. Doing so lets your readers believe that you are placing your ideas in an appropriate context.

Although many people are led to believe X, there is significant benefit to considering the merits of Y.

College students tend to believe that _____ when, in fact, the opposite is much more likely the case.

## SG2  Presenting others' views

As a writer, you build your own *ethos*, or credibility, by being able to fairly and accurately represent the views of others. As an academic writer, you will be expected to demonstrate your understanding of a text by summarizing the views or arguments of its author(s). To do so, you will use language such as the following.

X argues that _____ .

X emphasizes the need for _____ .

In this important article, X and Y claim _____.

X endorses _____ because _____ .

X and Y have recently criticized the idea that _____ .

_____ , according to X, is the most critical cause of _____ .

Although you will create your own variations of these sentences as you draft and revise, the guides can be useful tools for thinking through how best to present another writer's claim or finding clearly and concisely.

## SG3  Presenting direct quotations

When the exact words of a source are important for accuracy, authority, emphasis, or flavor, you will want to use a direct quotation. Ordinarily, you will present direct quotations with language of your own that suggests how you are using the source.

X characterizes the problem this way: " . . . "

According to X, _____ is defined as " . . . "

" . . . ," explains X.

X argues strongly in favor of the policy, pointing out that " . . . "

NOTE: You will generally cite direct quotations according to the documentation style your readers expect. MLA style, often used in English and in other humanities courses, recommends using the author name paired with a page number, if there is one. APA style, used in most social sciences, requires the year of publication generally after the mention of the source, with page numbers after the quoted material. In *Chicago* style, used in history and in some humanities courses, writers use superscript numbers (like this[6]) to refer readers to footnotes or endnotes. In-text citations, like the ones shown below, refer readers to entries in the works cited or reference list.

MLA         Lazarín argues that our overreliance on testing in K-12 schools "does not put students first" (20).

APA         Lazarín (2014) argues that our overreliance on testing in K-12 schools "does not put students first." (p. 20)

*Chicago*    Lazarín argues that our overreliance on testing in K-12 schools "does not put students first."[6]

Many writers use direct quotations to advance an argument of their own:

Standardized testing makes it easier for administrators to measure student performance, but it may not be the best way to measure it. Too much testing wears students out and communicates the idea that recall is the most important skill we want them to develop. Even education policy advisor Melissa Lazarín argues that our overreliance on testing in K-12 schools "does not put students first" (20).

Student writer's idea

Source's idea

## SG4  Presenting alternative views

Most debates, whether they are scholarly or popular, are complex —often with more than two sides to an issue. Sometimes, you will have to synthesize the views of multiple participants in the debate before you introduce your own ideas.

> On the one hand, X reports that _____, but on the other hand, Y insists that _____ .
>
> Even though X endorses the policy, Y refers to it as " . . . "
>
> X, however, isn't convinced and instead argues _____.
>
> X and Y have supported the theory in the past, but new research by Z suggests that _____ .

## ACADEMIC WRITERS PRESENT THEIR OWN VIEWS

When you write for an academic audience, you will indeed have to demonstrate that you are familiar with the views of others who are asking the same kinds of questions as you are. Much writing that is done for academic purposes asks you to put your arguments in the context of existing arguments—in a way asking you to connect the known to the new.

When you are asked to write a summary or an informative text, your own views and arguments are generally not called for. However, much of the writing you will be assigned to do in college asks you to take a persuasive stance and present a reasoned argument—at times in response to a single text, and at other times in response to multiple texts.

## SG5  Presenting your own views: agreement and extension

Sometimes, you agree with the author of a source.

> X's argument is convincing because _____ .
>
> Because X's approach is so _____, it is the best way to _____.
>
> X makes an important point when she says _____ .

Other times you find you agree with the author of a source, but you want to extend the point or go a bit deeper in your own investigation. In a way, you acknowledge the source for getting you so far in the conversation, but then you move the conversation along with a related comment or finding.

> X's proposal for _____ is indeed worth considering. Going one step further, _____.

> X makes the claim that _____. By extension, isn't it also true, then, that _____?

> _____ has been adequately explained by X. Now, let's move beyond that idea and ask whether _____.

## SG6  Presenting your own views: queries and skepticism

You may be intimidated when you're asked to talk back to a source, especially if the source is a well-known scholar or expert or even just a frequent voice in a particular debate. College-level writing asks you to be skeptical, however, and approach academic questions with the mind of an investigator. It is ok to doubt, to question, to challenge—because the end result is often new knowledge or new understanding about a subject.

> Couldn't it also be argued that _____?

> But is everyone willing to agree that this is the case?

> While X insists that _____ is so, he is perhaps asking the wrong question to begin with.

> The claims that X and Y have made, while intelligent and well-meaning, leave many unconvinced because they have failed to consider _____.

## SG7  Presenting your own views: disagreement or correction

You may find that at times the only response you have to a text or to an author is complete disagreement.

> X's claims about _____ are completely misguided.

> X presents a long metaphor comparing _____ to _____; in the end, the comparison is unconvincing because _____.

It can be tempting to disregard a source completely if you detect a piece of information that strikes you as false or that you know to be untrue.

> Although X reports that _____, recent studies indicate that is not the case.

> While X and Y insist that _____ is so, an examination of their figures shows that they have made an important miscalculation.

### A note about using first person "I"

Some disciplines look favorably upon the use of the first person "I" in academic writing. Others do not and instead stick to using third person. If you are given a writing assignment for a class, you are better off asking your instructor what he or she prefers or reading through any samples given than *guessing* what might be expected.

#### First person (I, me, my, we, us, our)

I question Heddinger's methods and small sample size.

Harnessing children's technology obsession in the classroom is, I believe, the key to improving learning.

Lanza's interpretation focuses on circle imagery as symbolic of the family; my analysis leads me in a different direction entirely.

We would, in fact, benefit from looser laws about farming on our personal property.

#### Third person (names and other nouns)

Heddinger's methods and small sample size are questionable.

Harnessing children's technology obsession in the classroom is the key to improving learning.

Lanza's interpretation focuses on circle imagery as symbolic of the family; other readers' analyses may point in a different direction entirely.

Many Americans would, in fact, benefit from looser laws about farming on personal property.

You may feel as if not being able to use "I" in an essay in which you present your ideas about a topic is unfair or will lead to weaker statements. Know that you can make a strong argument even if you write in the third person. Third person writing allows you to sound more assertive, credible, and academic.

## SG8 Presenting and countering objections to your argument

Effective college writers know that their arguments are stronger when they can anticipate objections that others might make.

> Some will object to this proposal on the grounds that _____.

> Not everyone will embrace _____; they may argue instead that _____.

Countering, or responding to, opposing voices fairly and respectfully strengthens your writing and your *ethos*, or credibility.

> X and Y might contend that this interpretation is faulty; however, _____.

> Most _____ believe that there is too much risk in this approach. But what they have failed to take into consideration is _____.

## ACADEMIC WRITERS PERSUADE BY PUTTING IT ALL TOGETHER

Readers of academic writing often want to know what's at stake in a particular debate or text. They want to know why it is that they should care and that they should keep reading. Aside from crafting individual sentences, you must, of course, keep the bigger picture in mind as you attempt to persuade, inform, evaluate, or review.

## SG9 Presenting stakeholders

When you write, you may be doing so as a member of a group affected by the research conversation you have entered. For example, you may be among the thousands of students in your state whose level of debt may change as a result of new laws about financing a college education. In this case, you are a *stakeholder* in the matter. In other words, you have an interest in the matter as a person who could be impacted by the outcome of a decision. On the other hand, you may be writing as an investigator of a topic that interests you but that you aren't directly connected with. You may be persuading your audience on behalf of a group of interested stakeholders—a group of which you yourself are not a member.

You can give your writing some teeth if you make it clear who is being affected by the discussion of the issue and the decisions that have or will be made about the issue. The groups of stakeholders are highlighted in the following sentences.

> Viewers of Kurosawa's films may not agree with X that _____.

> The research will come as a surprise to parents of children with Type 1 diabetes.

> X's claims have the power to offend potentially every low-wage earner in the state.

> Marathoners might want to reconsider their training regimen if stories such as those told by X and Y are validated by the medical community.

## SG10  Presenting the "so what"

For readers to be motivated to read your writing, they have to feel as if you're either addressing something that matters to them or addressing something that matters very much to you or that should matter to us all. Good academic writing often hooks readers with a sense of urgency—a serious response to a reader's "So what?"

> Having a frank discussion about _____ now will put us in a far better position to deal with _____ in the future. If we are unwilling or unable to do so, we risk _____.

> Such a breakthrough will affect _____ in three significant ways.

> It is easy to believe that the stakes aren't high enough to be alarming; in fact, _____ will be affected by _____.

> Widespread disapproval of and censorship of such fiction/films/art will mean _____ for us in the future. Culture should represent _____.

> _____ could bring about unprecedented opportunities for _____ to participate in _____, something never seen before.

> New experimentation in _____ could allow scientists to investigate _____ in ways they couldn't have imagined _____ years ago.

## SG11  Presenting the players and positions in a debate

Some disciplines ask writers to compose a review of the literature as a part of a larger project — or sometimes as a free-standing assignment. In a review of the literature, the writer sets forth a research question, summarizes the key sources that have addressed the question, puts the current research in the context of other voices in the research conversation, and identifies any gaps in the research.

Writing that presents a debate, its players, and their positions can often be lengthy. What follows, however, can give you the sense of the flow of ideas and turns in such a piece of writing.

_____ affects more than 30% of children in America, and signs point to a worsening situation in years to come because of A, B, and C. Solutions to the problem have eluded even the sharpest policy minds and brightest researchers. In an important 2003 study, W found that _____, which pointed to more problems than solutions. [ . . . ] Research by X and Y made strides in our understanding of _____ but still didn't offer specific strategies for children and families struggling to _____. [ . . . ] When Z rejected both the methods and the findings of X and Y, arguing that _____, policymakers and health care experts were optimistic. [ . . . ] Too much discussion of _____, however, and too little discussion of _____, may lead us to solutions that are ultimately too expensive to sustain.

*Student writer states the problem.*

*Student writer summarizes the views of others on the topic.*

*Student writer presents her view in the context of current research.*

## APPENDIX

***Verbs matter***   Using a variety of verbs in your sentences can add strength and clarity as you present others' views and your own views.

### When you want to Present a view fairly neutrally

| | |
|---|---|
| acknowledges | comments |
| adds | contends |
| admits | notes |

| | |
|---|---|
| observes | suggest |
| points out | writes |
| reports | |

X points out that the plan had unintended outcomes.

## When you want to present a stronger view

| | |
|---|---|
| argues | emphasizes |
| asserts | insists |
| declares | |

Y argues in favor of a ban on _____; but Z insists the plan is misguided.

## When you want to show agreement

| | |
|---|---|
| agrees | endorses |
| confirms | |

An endorsement of X's position is smart for a number of reasons.

## When you want to show contrast or disagreement

| | |
|---|---|
| compares | refutes |
| denies | rejects |
| disputes | |

The town must come together and reject X's claims that _____ is in the best interest of the citizens.

## When you want to anticipate an objection

| | |
|---|---|
| admits | concedes |
| acknowledges | |

Y admits that closer study of _____, with a much larger sample size, is necessary for _____.

# Documentation Guide

Engaging with the work of others is an important part of academic writing. When writing formal essays about the works in *50 Essays*, or when you refer in your writing to other outside sources, you need to acknowledge these sources. When you summarize, paraphrase, or quote outside sources in your writing, it is crucial that you properly acknowledge them. It is important for two reasons. First, it demonstrates that you are joining the intellectual discussion, writing not just about your own ideas and about your own experience but in conversation with the ideas and experiences of others. Second, it is your ethical responsibility to acknowledge when the words and ideas that appear in your work do not originate with you; if you don't, you will be guilty of plagiarism, a serious academic offense carrying serious consequences and also an act of dishonesty.

*Documentation* is the word for the activity of acknowledging sources. There are different systems or styles of documentation; the style most often used in English and the humanities is that recommended by the Modern Language Association (MLA). Below are some examples of the most common kinds of documentation in MLA style; consult the *MLA Handbook*, eighth edition, at style.mla.org for additional information and models.

## MLA PARENTHETICAL CITATIONS

MLA style is fairly simple. When you need to cite a source, you do so in a parenthetical in-text citation. Rather than use footnotes or endnotes, you insert, before the period at the end of the sentence, a parenthetical reference that lets readers know the source and, usually, where in the source the particular material can be found. If the source is clear from the sentence itself, you need only include a page number in parentheses; if the source is not clear, including the author's name along with the page number will be enough to allow the reader to find the source in the list of works cited, which you will include at the end of your essay (guidelines for which follow this section). Below are some examples of the most common kinds of parenthetical citations. There are a number of exceptions to these general rules; you'll find these below too.

### ONE AUTHOR

*The Emigrants* begins: "At the end of September 1970, shortly before I took up my position in Norwich, I drove out to Hingham with Clara in search of somewhere to live" (Sebald 3).

### TWO AUTHORS

According to the Enlightenment, "thinking is the creation of unified, scientific order and the derivation of factual knowledge from principles" (Horkheimer and Adorno 83).

### THREE OR MORE AUTHORS

As one letter to the editor of an intellectual journal put it: "Eighteen months later, the CIA is still stonewalling" (Blakey et al. 65).

### UNKNOWN AUTHOR

Of the avian flu, a recent editorial states: "Nobody has the foggiest idea whether a pandemic will arrive in the near future or how severe one might be, but federal officials argue, persuasively, that we have to brace ourselves for the worst" ("Vaccine Capacity" A22).

### SOURCE WITHOUT PAGE NUMBERS

As a recent article on the Web periodical *Inside Higher Education* explains, in many federal agencies, "it is standard practice for external groups to formally ask officials to begin a process to review a specific rule or set of rules" (Lederman).

### INDIRECT SOURCE

In his autobiography, Ford wrote, "If I'm remembered, it will probably be for healing the land" (qtd. in Patterson 94).

## MLA LIST OF WORKS CITED

The works cited list is the place where your reader can go to find out more information about the sources cited in your parenthetical citations. Follow these guidelines for the format for this list, which should be given its own page or pages: it should be organized alphabetically by author's last name or first major word in the title; it should be double-spaced; each entry should begin at the left margin; and the second (and all following) lines of an entry should be indented one tab (or five spaces, or one half inch).

### Books

**ONE AUTHOR**

Cohen, Samuel. *After the End of History: American Fiction in the 1990s*. U of
    Iowa P, 2009.

**TWO AUTHORS**

Mohlenbrock, Robert H., and Paul M. Thomson, Jr. *Flowering Plants:
    Smartweeds to Hazelnuts*. 2nd ed., Southern Illinois UP, 2009.

**THREE OR MORE AUTHORS**

Cunningham, Stewart, et al. *Media Economics*. Palgrave Macmillan, 2015.

**TWO OR MORE BOOKS BY THE SAME AUTHOR**

García, Cristina. *Dreams of Significant Girls*. Simon and Schuster, 2011.

—. *The Lady Matador's Hotel*. Scribner, 2010.

**BOOK WITH AN EDITOR OR TRANSLATOR**

Ullmann, Regina. *The Country Road: Stories*. Translated by Kurt Beals,
    New Directions Publishing, 2015.

**WORK IN AN ANTHOLOGY**

Hughes, Langston. "Salvation." *50 Essays*, edited by Samuel Cohen, 5th ed.,
    Bedford/St. Martin's, 2017, pp. 185–87.

**MULTIVOLUME WORK**

Stark, Freya. *Letters*. Edited by Lucy Moorehead, Compton Press,
    1974–82. 8 vols.

**EDITION OTHER THAN THE FIRST**

Eagleton, Terry. *Literary Theory: An Introduction*. 3rd ed., U of Minnesota P, 2008.

## Periodicals

**ARTICLE IN A JOURNAL**

Matchie, Thomas. "Law versus Love in *The Round House*." *Midwest Quarterly*,
    vol. 56, no. 4, Summer 2015, pp. 353–64.

**ARTICLE IN A MONTHLY MAGAZINE**

Bryan, Christy. "Ivory Worship." *National Geographic*, Oct. 2012, pp. 28–61.

**ARTICLE IN A WEEKLY MAGAZINE**

Grossman, Lev. "A Star Is Born." *Time*, 2 Nov. 2015, pp. 30–39.

**ARTICLE IN A NEWSPAPER**

Bray, Hiawatha. "As Toys Get Smarter, Privacy Issues Emerge." *The Boston
    Globe*, 10 Dec. 2015, p. C1.

**EDITORIAL OR LETTER TO THE EDITOR**

"The Road toward Peace." *The New York Times*, 15 Feb. 1945, p. 18. Editorial.

## Electronic Sources

**ENTIRE WEB SITE**

Transparency International. *Transparency International: The Global Coalition
    against Corruption*. 2015, www.transparency.org/.

**SHORT WORK FROM A WEB SITE**

"Social and Historical Context: Vitality." *Arapesh Grammar and Digital
    Language Archive Project*, Institute for Advanced Technology in the
    Humanities, www.arapesh.org/socio_historical_context_vitality.php.
    Accessed 22 Mar. 2016.

**WORK FROM A SUBSCRIPTION SERVICE**

Fahey, John A. "Recalling the Cuban Missile Crisis." *The Washington Post*, 28
    Oct. 2012, p. A16. Letter. *LexisNexis Library Express*, www.lexisnexis
    .com/hottopics/lnpubliclibraryexpress/.

**ONLINE BOOK**

Piketty, Thomas. *Capital in the Twenty-First Century*. Translated by Arthur
      Goldhammer, Harvard UP, 2014. *Google Books*, books.google.com
      /books?isbn=0674369556.

**ARTICLE IN AN ONLINE PERIODICAL**

Leonard, Andrew. "The Surveillance State High School." *Salon*, 27 Nov. 2012,
      www.salon.com/2012/11/27/the_surveillance_state_high_school/.

**E-MAIL**

Thornbrugh, Caitlin. "Coates Lecture." Received by Rita Anderson, 20 Oct.
      2015. E-mail.

## Other Sources

**ADVERTISEMENT**

AT&T. *National Geographic*, Dec. 2015, p. 14. Advertisement.

**INTERVIEW**

Putin, Vladimir. Interview by Charlie Rose. *Charlie Rose: The Week*, PBS,
      19 June 2015.

**GOVERNMENT DOCUMENT**

United States, Department of Agriculture, Food and Nutrition Service, Child
      Nutrition Programs. *Eligibility Manual for School Meals: Determining
      and Verifying Eligibility. National School Lunch Program*, July 2015,
      www.fns.usda.gov/sites/default/files/cn/SP40_CACFP18_SFSP20-
      2015a1.pdf.

**FILM, VIDEO, OR DVD**

Scott, Ridley, director. *The Martian*. Performances by Matt Damon, Jessica
      Chastain, Kristen Wiig, and Kate Mara, Twentieth Century Fox, 2015.

**TELEVISION OR RADIO PROGRAM**

"Free Speech on College Campuses." *Washington Journal*, narrated by Peter
      Slen, C-SPAN, 27 Nov. 2015.

# Introduction for Students: Active Reading, Critical Thinking, and the Writing Process

## READING, WRITING, 'RITHMETIC

Hard work, preparation, and lots of reading can add up to good writing. That is the arithmetic of writing. We become active, critical, intelligent readers and writers by carefully reading the writing of others and then applying what we have learned to our own writing. Reading and writing are most of what you will do in your college courses. The strongest readers and writers have learned to see these activities as inextricably intertwined. You read, you write, then you read some more, then you write again. And this pattern applies in nearly all of your classes, not just those in English and history and other disciplines that come to mind as reading and writing heavy. Math, biology, and engineering classes require the same skills. Acquiring and strengthening them at the start of your college career will help you all the way to graduation and beyond, as reading and writing are central to so many of the careers you might find yourself in a few years down the road.

This introduction will briefly consider the best ways to approach the kinds of assignments you will encounter in your college writing courses. As you read it, think about the ways you read and write now. Do you do some of these things already? Have you tried them before? Be open to the advice, but remember, it is only the advice of one teacher. Your teacher may have different ideas, just as you may, and these ideas may change. Here's an example: in the first edition of this book, I argued against reading while lying down, saying it was better to sit up so you could pay better attention and stay awake. Students, teachers, and my editor disagreed. I decided they were right. The point? As the introduction will explain, the best thing you can do with the texts you encounter in school and in the world is try both to understand them and to evaluate them, and be open to having your mind changed by them. And if you want, do so while stretched out on a nice comfortable couch.

## ACTIVE READING

We read for a number of reasons. We want the news; we want information; we want to be entertained. We want to hear other people thinking. We want to be taken out of ourselves and live other lives. We also read because it is crucial to learning how to write. The poet Jane Kenyon gave this advice on becoming a better writer: "Have good sentences in your ears." To write well—to express your ideas efficiently and clearly—you need to observe how others do it. You need to see examples of the ways writers write, the techniques and forms they use. Because good writing is about more than correctness, though, you also have to observe the ways writers think. Working with ideas—handling the ideas of others and presenting your own—is the most important thing writers do, and so the most important thing for writers to learn. Because it is so important, of course, it is difficult. Life is like that. But reading examples of good writing gives you access to models: it shows writers engaging with ideas, holding them up to the light, turning them this way and that, and maybe modifying them in some way, adding something, taking something away, taking them apart entirely, offering their own instead.

To learn to do the same, however, you need to do more than simply mimic what good writers do. You need to treat their writing the same way they treat ideas. Hold their writing up to the light, turn it this way and that, figure out how it works and also how it doesn't, think about how it might be wrong—how you might think differently about their subjects. This activity is sometimes called active or critical reading.

The essays in this collection are here to be studied as models; they are also here to be read critically. While you might learn something from every essay, they are not chapters in a chemistry textbook. Your job is not to take what they say as the gospel truth. Instead, you should evaluate what you read. This doesn't mean you should treat these essays as movie critics treat movies or restaurant critics treat food: these essays aren't here for you to simply judge, to give a thumbs up or down to, to savor or spit out. Instead, you should evaluate their ideas and the way they present them as if in conversation with them. Ask questions of them, argue with their assumptions, examine how they connect their ideas, and test these connections. In learning to think this way about what writers create, you will learn to think like a writer.

There are many techniques that can help you read this way. What they boil down to is reading actively rather than passively. Think of passive reading as like watching television. While there are some good, thoughtful programs on TV, most of us watch TV passively—sitting on a couch, maybe eating, maybe doing something else simultaneously (but not our schoolwork, of course), and letting television wash over us. Active reading, in contrast, requires full attention. Posture aside, your mind needs to be sitting up straight, concentrating on the page, ready to reach down into the page and grab the words. Here are some tips to ensure that you get the most out of what you read.

## WAYS TO READ ACTIVELY

**Read consciously.**   In addition to being awake, it is important to be conscious of the situation you are in. Why are you reading? Merely for comprehension, or for observation of the writing itself, or for argument about the ideas? What are you reading? For what purpose or occasion or publication was the piece written, and by whom? Is it a selection from someone's autobiography? Is it an article from a newspaper or an editorial? How has it been contextualized—is it in a chapter on a certain kind of writing or on a certain idea or theme? Keeping these questions in mind as you read makes you notice more, think harder, and make connections among ideas.

**Read critically.**  Always ask yourself what you think about the writer's arguments. Although doing this does not require you to take issue with every or any single thing an author writes, it does ask you to think of reading as conversation: the writer is talking to you, telling you what she thinks about something, and you are free to answer back.

**Read with a pencil in hand.**  This is the best, easiest way to answer back. Many students leave their books untouched, thinking that they will remember what they read or that it is wrong to write in books or that they won't be able to sell them back at the end of the semester if they write in them. These are common objections, but consider this: you won't recall everything (nobody remembers everything he or she reads, and memorizing isn't the only or even the most important thing we do when we read); it's not wrong to write in a book (books don't have feelings, but if they did, they'd like the attention); and bookstores will buy back marked-up books (go check out the used books in the bookstore). Making marks on the page—annotating—is the surest way to read actively. Underline important passages, circle words you haven't heard of, scribble furious rants in the margin, jot down questions about content or writing strategy, use exclamation points and question marks and arrows and Xs. Grab the text with your bare hands. Reading with a highlighter is the passive version of marking your book because it is less suited to annotating and more suited to identifying chunks of text. The result of marking with a highlighter is that you haven't engaged with your reading so much as prioritized parts of it a little bit—used fluorescent yellow or pink or green to say, "Hey, there's something important here." While a highlighter might be more appropriate in your chemistry textbook, even there it can be dangerous: while checking out the used books in the bookstore, notice how often entire paragraphs and even pages are afloat in seas of highlighter ink, and ask yourself how that helped the students whose books these used to be. Pencils are also good for chewing, sticking in your hair to hold your bun together, and sliding behind your ear to make you look smart and industrious.

**Use a notebook or computer.**  Many readers like to take notes in a notebook or computer. Although there are disadvantages to this kind of note taking relative to annotation—your marks are not right in the text and so are less immediately accessible and less immediately tied to the lines on the page—there are also advantages. You can make lengthy notes. You can copy important and well-phrased sentences (making sure to enclose them in quotation marks and to note where they came from). You can **paraphrase**[1] ideas, you can **summarize**, you can note your reactions as you read. Doing these things can make you think more about what you're reading. Some readers use a double-entry system in which they draw a line down the middle of the page, note or reproduce particular passages from the reading in the left column, and respond to those passages in the right column. Many variations on this kind of note taking are possible (and all of them, of course, can be reproduced on a computer).

*An Example of Annotation and Note Taking from Brent Staples, "Just Walk on By: Black Men and Public Space" (p. 345)*

*Strong emotion*

Over the years, I learned to smother the rage I felt at so often being taken for a criminal. Not to do so would surely have led to madness. I now take precautions to make myself less threatening. I move about with care, particularly late in the evening. I give a wide berth to nervous people on subway platforms during the wee hours, particularly when I have exchanged business clothes for jeans. If I happen to be entering a building behind some people who appear skittish, I may walk by, letting them clear the lobby before I return, so as not to seem to be following them. I have been calm and extremely congenial on those rare occasions when I've been pulled over by police.

*Living with rage would make him crazy*

*Echoes the essay's title*

*His tension or other people's?*

*"Everybody"? Seems like a stereotype about white people*

*"rare" implies that he even takes care to behave well when driving*

And on late-evening constitutionals I employ what has proved to be an excellent tension-reducing measure: I whistle melodies from Beethoven and Vivaldi and the more popular classical composers. Even steely New Yorkers hunching toward nighttime destinations seem to relax, and occasionally they even join in the tune. Virtually everybody seems to sense that a mugger wouldn't be warbling bright, sunny selections from Vivaldi's *Four Seasons*. It is my equivalent of the cowbell that hikers wear when they know they are in bear country.

*People are comfortable with what they know*

*Powerful image*

1. Words in boldface are treated in the glossary of writing terms, which starts on page 474.

Notes

*Staples's essay started off making it sound like he was a criminal, but by the end I realized that was his whole point: he's NOT a criminal, yet he's often treated like one because of his race*

*Staples's descriptions of how he copes with people perceiving him as a threat are really illuminating but also really disheartening*

*I found it weird that Staples counteracts the stereotypes people have of him by using other stereotypes—e.g., the idea that cultured people who know classical music can't be criminals (I guess traditionally rap is associated with African Americans? Another stereotype . . .)*

*The last line of this passage is really powerful—Staples feels like he is being viewed as a hunter, when actually he's the one being hunted (he's in "bear country"). That image really emphasizes how the people reacting to him as a threat are, in reality, a threat to him . . .*

Note the different kinds of entries here. The first is about the reader's changing thoughts as he reads. The second is a moment of appreciation. The third and fourth are trains of thought that start from small parts of the essay. None of these sum up the reading, though that is a good thing to do also. Instead, these entries record reactions and thoughts inspired by the essay, and—like the notes made alongside the excerpt—could serve as ways back into the essay when it is time to write about it. See page 7 for a checklist of things you can annotate and make notes about as you read. Also see the sample student paper beginning on page 11. This paper builds on the initial ideas and notes presented here; as you read it, look for ways in which the student develops his preliminary thoughts into an argument.

## CRITICAL THINKING/CRITICAL READING

The previous annotation sample shows how active reading is much more than reading to understand. Summarizing what has been read is important; moving beyond summary to active engagement is something else, and it is crucial to really making use of what you've read. One name for this something else is critical thinking.

## A CHECKLIST FOR ANNOTATING A READING

As you read, consider marking or taking notes on the following:

- ☐ Main topics
- ☐ Secondary topics
- ☐ Main points
- ☐ Supporting points
- ☐ Examples, **evidence**, or other support
- ☐ Ideas or ways of saying things that you like
- ☐ Ideas or ways of saying things that you don't like
- ☐ Ideas you want to think more about later
- ☐ References or words with which you are not familiar

Critical thinking doesn't mean being critical in the everyday sense, that is, being negative. It means being inquisitive, evaluative, even skeptical. When reading, it means thinking not just about what someone says but about the unspoken assumptions that lie behind what she says, the unnamed implications of what she says, and the way she says it. It also means evaluating—asking if you agree with a writer's implicit and explicit **conclusions**, even asking if you agree with the framing of the question asked or the topic addressed, and judging the eloquence and/or effectiveness of the writing. Critical thinking is a catchall term for a number of activities that add up to active, thoughtful engagement with a subject. For many, it is the single most important skill higher education makes possible: it allows people to actively judge and process the things they read and hear rather than passively accept them. For others, it has an arguably more powerful aspect: that of allowing individuals to accept or reject the common wisdom that is all around them, in everyday life, at work, in politics.

When applied to reading, critical thinking might be called critical reading. See page 8 for a checklist of critical reading questions, with follow-up questions, that you can ask yourself when reading critically (that is, always). While they will not all be applicable for every occasion, most will be helpful as you try to understand and evaluate others' writing.

## A CHECKLIST FOR CRITICAL READING

☐ What is the writing situation? Where did the text originally appear?

☐ What is the writer's subject?
  ☐ Is she choosing to focus or not to focus on something important? Is she leaving something out?

☐ What is the writer's main point about her subject?
  ☐ Do you agree? Do you disagree? Why?

☐ What is the writer's purpose in making that point?
  ☐ What do you think of that purpose? Do you think that she achieves it?

☐ To what sort of audience does the writer seem to be addressing herself?
  ☐ Are you part of that audience? Who is, and who is left out?

☐ What are the assumptions behind the writer's treatment of her subject?
  ☐ Do you agree with them? Do you disagree? Why?

☐ What further conclusions could be drawn from the writer's point?
  ☐ Do you agree with them? Do you disagree? Why?

☐ What do you think of the way the writer makes her argument?
  ☐ Is it convincing? Logical? Does she fight fair?

☐ What can you borrow (without plagiarizing)?
  ☐ Are there particular techniques the writer uses to argue, describe, narrate, or just shape a sentence that you want to remember and use in your own writing?

## THE WRITING PROCESS

As the last critical reading question indicates, writers get better by paying attention to how the writing they like works and trying to duplicate those effects in their own work. This is not the same thing as **plagiarism**: you know not to take another's work and pretend it's your own. The very best writers got so good not by copying words and ideas without giving proper credit, but by imitating other writers—their **styles**, their **tones**, their patterns of organization—and using these as starting points for developing their own voices.

Reading actively, critically, and with an eye toward borrowing helps you to become a better writer. However, nothing helps you learn to write like writing itself. While there will be a number of occasions in your academic career when you will be required to hand in formal, typed, proofread essays, take advantage of the times when you have to write informally—in class, in journals, online. Think of times when you don't have to write but could—sitting on the bus, waiting for your computer to boot up—and get out a notebook and write. Like strengthening a muscle through repeated exercise, the more you use your writing skills the stronger they will become.

This strength will help you when it is time to write formal, academic essays, and it can help to lessen anxiety about writing. Every writer, when faced with more demanding assignments, feels some form of dread, trepidation, or nervous excitement. In other words, it is far from rare for writers of all levels of experience to freeze up, space out, or throw in the towel. Many of the best ways writers have found to get past the difficulty of getting started involve recognizing that writing is a process. People often imagine a typical scene when they think of writing: they see the writer, hunched over the blank pad or in front of the blank screen, waiting for inspiration to strike, then, having been struck, finding the exact words to express this inspiration, and then, finishing, leaning back with a sigh of contentment at a job well done. Very few people actually write this way.

Rather than thinking that you must sit down and create a polished piece of work out of thin air, remember that writers can go through many stages when they write and that each stage can help produce a final product. Before you begin to write a first **draft**, try a number of **prewriting** activities, which can help you brainstorm or come up with ideas. You can work up notes or a formal or informal outline before you draft. At this point you can also make use of comments you wrote in the margins of your text. After taking a first stab at a draft, you can **revise**. As important as recognizing that you can break down the writing process into these stages is knowing that they don't have to be followed. After producing a draft, you may return to outlining and brainstorming. You can even do this as you draft: as you see your main point (your **thesis**) changing or your **argument** taking a different course, go back to your notes or outline and modify accordingly. When you get to the revision stage, when you think you might be focusing on correctness and style, you may find not only that you need to rewrite what you wrote in the drafting stage but also that you need to rethink the ideas you came up with during the pre-writing stage. While smoothing out the **transitions** between your **paragraphs**, you may find they are rough because the connections among your ideas are also rough, and so you will need to smooth out your ideas before you can smooth out your expression of them.

This may all sound daunting. It shouldn't. Thinking about writing as a recursive process—one in which you loop back to the starting point as you revise and build on your work—means you don't have to try to get everything perfect the first time. It allows you to get your ideas down on paper as they come to you because you know you can always go back and change them. It allows you to think critically about your work because it never feels like it's too late to improve any aspect of it. Read as a writer reads—critically, actively—and write as a writer writes—in stages, recursively—and pretty soon (that is, before you even know it) you will be a thoughtful, fluid writer who enjoys practicing his or her craft. There is no complicated mathematical formula to explain the interrelation of critical reading, creative brainstorming, careful revision, and all of the other elements that are part of what makes good writing, but the basic arithmetic—reading + hard work = good writing—holds up.

I hope that you enjoy reading the essays in this book, and that you find that they help you with your writing. At the end of this introduction you'll find an example of an essay written in response to readings in *50 Essays*. Annotations have been added to highlight important parts of the essay—elements like the thesis statement, transitions, and a **conclusion**. Read it for ideas about how to put together sentences and paragraphs, how to construct an argument, and how to document sources. This essay is also a good example of **synthesis**—the process of considering a number of different readings, putting them in conversation with each other, and forming your own **claim** or thesis, making your own statement. Remember, though, that there's no one model you should follow, no one way to write about anything. Examples are good, but you need to find your own voice, your own way to say what you want to say.

Schaff 1

Jonathon Schaff
Professor Cohen
English 101
18 February 2019

### Dangerous Duality: How Racism Splits Us in Two
#### By Jonathon Schaff

I have never been told that I am a problem. I have been told that my behavior is problematic, but no one has ever told me that there was something wrong with me just for being me. As a white American, I've never been avoided on the street or denied a meal because of my skin color. Yet many African Americans have faced and continue to face this kind of discrimination in America. Since I am not an African American, I can only try to understand the African American experience of living in this country, both past and present, by submerging myself in the words and ideas of black writers.

Something can happen to the human mind when it is informed that it is a problem. When people are treated differently than the way they see themselves, the human mind creates a kind of divided sense of self. As a result, African Americans who have been victimized by racism oftentimes see themselves in two different, irreconcilable ways, and that divide can have dangerous consequences.

The idea that split identities form as a product of racism may have been first introduced by W. E. B. Du Bois in his important 1903 essay, "Of Our Spiritual Strivings," in which he refers to a state of "double-consciousness." Du Bois argues that blacks, forty years after being legally freed, felt they were black and American at the same time, and yet not both at once. Du Bois wrote:

> It is a peculiar sensation, this double-consciousness, this sense of always looking at one's self through the eyes of others, of measuring one's worth by the tape of a world that looks on in amused contempt and pity. One ever feels his twoness, — an American, a Negro; two souls, two thoughts, two unreconciled strivings; two warring ideals in one dark body, whose dogged strength alone keeps it from being torn asunder. (45)

Du Bois saw himself through the eyes of the white majority, and therefore could not fully separate his own identity from the way he was perceived by other people. Given this, it is easy to understand how his double-consciousness formed. Du Bois suggests that being both black and American, at least in 1903, was not only impossible but was an intersection where violence occurred.

*Author discusses his own **point of view***

*Thesis statement makes the author's claim*

*Use of **quotation** illustrates argument of the original author*

Du Bois's essay has continued to echo in the work of black authors into the twentieth century. His ideas have persisted largely because African Americans continued to suffer indignities long after slavery was abolished. Until the 1960s, Jim Crow laws prevented blacks from having access to the same quality of life that whites enjoyed by means of segregation. Barring blacks from white swimming pools and restaurants, Jim Crow laws had a corrosive effect on the African American psyche. In his essay "Notes of a Native Son," published in 1955, James Baldwin writes about his father, a severe man and the son of a slave. Baldwin's father taught him to hate and mistrust whites because they would inevitably do blacks harm. As he grew up, Baldwin began to understand his father's bitterness and the dangers it posed. Baldwin describes an encounter at a restaurant in New Jersey that had refused to serve him and which ended in his violent attack on the waitress:

> I could not get over two facts, both equally difficult for the imagination to grasp, and one was that I could have been murdered. But the other was that I had been ready to commit murder. I saw nothing very clearly but I did see this: that my life, my real life, was in danger, and not from anything other people might do but from the hatred I carried in my own heart. (p. 56)

Baldwin echoes Du Bois's point that the hatred involved in double-consciousness is destructive for African Americans both externally and internally. In order to curb this hatred, Baldwin says that "[i]t began to seem that one would have to hold in the mind forever two ideas which seemed to be in opposition" (67). These two opposing ideas define the African American struggle between accepting life's injustices and fighting against the corrosive powers of hate that permeated the country in the first half of the twentieth century. Would Baldwin feel the same way if he were alive today?

The work of contemporary African American authors reveals that today's society continues to inform blacks that they are dangerous and frightening. Brent Staples's 1987 essay, "Just Walk on By: Black Men and Public Space," offers a series of poignant anecdotes about his life as a graduate student and an adult. Staples recalls the fear he inspired in others as a habitual nighttime walker. He recollects crossing the street and hearing people in their cars lock their doors. He also remembers the way other people would cross the street if they were on course to pass him on the sidewalk (345). Similarly, John Edgar Wideman, a professor of Africana studies and literary

*Topic sentence* states the *paragraph's main idea*

Schaff 3

arts at Brown University, identifies with being avoided based on his skin color in his 2010 essay "The Seat Not Taken." The seat next to Wideman often remains empty for his entire commute on the Amtrak train from New York City to Providence, Rhode Island. Despite the fact that Wideman is well-dressed and can obviously afford the expensive train ticket, he has observed that "9 times out of 10 people will shun a free seat if it means sitting beside me."

*Author uses evidence from an outside source to support his claim*

Staples and Wideman, both intelligent men and authors for the *New York Times*, seem to be able to keep healthy perspectives on who they are, but this is not easy. Staples remarks that he feels like he travels through "bear country," late at night on the streets (348). People take on the ferociousness of animals when they see him coming around a corner. Wideman, on the other hand, initially claims that the empty seat next to him is a "privilege, conferred upon me by color, to enjoy the luxury of an extra seat to myself." Yet he ultimately "can't accept the bounty of an empty seat without remembering why it's empty, without wondering if its emptiness isn't something quite sad. And quite dangerous, also, if left unexamined." The "danger" represented by the empty seat is the danger of seeing threats where there are none, of judging and avoiding others based solely on skin color.

*Author uses summary to make a point in his own words*

Because of these dangers, pressure is put on African Americans to go out of their way to appear nonthreatening. To alert and pacify the scared strangers he met on the street, Staples would whistle traditionally white classical music by Beethoven and Vivaldi. Viewing himself through white eyes, Staples found a way to avoid causing trouble. But walking down the street without whistling the *Moonlight Sonata* should not instigate an attack. Yet this is the reality for many black Americans. Based on how people react to their skin color, pressure is put upon them from the white majority to behave a certain way, even if that way is senseless, and the consequences for failing to conform to it can result in violence.

*Use of transition "because" connects two ideas*

As a white person, I find it hard to imagine the world reflexively avoiding me. It must be difficult for Staples and Wideman to not feel as though they contribute to how people treat them or not feel as though there is something threatening locked up inside themselves. Neither have I ever felt the hate that Baldwin described with the power to destroy his father nor been compelled to violence because I've experienced injustice. Reading these authors tracing back from over a century ago to present day has made me more conscious of the division race still inserts into our modern lives and

Schaff 4

the emotional and personal consequences of this opposition in the human consciousness. Perhaps this lack of understanding is what enables the divide to continue today.

If blacks throughout our nation's history have suffered from racism, is it realistic to think that there is an end in sight? Circumstances have changed — first slavery gave way to Jim Crow, which has given way to more subtle forms of discrimination, which coexist with the same old-fashioned, street-level racism Du Bois, Baldwin, Staples, and Wideman have all felt — but the underlying duality remains, and remains dangerous. As Baldwin put it, "I imagine that one of the reasons people cling to their hates so stubbornly is because they sense, once hate is gone, that they will be forced to deal with pain" (p. 59). Even though the United States elected an African American president, is the country truly post-racial? There is a lot of pain that this country will have to deal with if and when it lets go of its hate. But if the era of healing lasts half as long as the epoch of prejudice, then we could be in for a better way of living, a way that prefers empathy to ignorance and unity to division.

*Conclusion sums up main point and extends the author's ideas*

*Author uses expressive **diction** and tone in concluding paragraph*

Works Cited

Baldwin, James. "Notes of a Native Son." *50 Essays,* 6th ed., edited by Samuel Cohen, Bedford/St. Martin's, 2017, pp. 47–68.

Du Bois, W. E. B. *The Souls of Black Folk.* 1903. Introduction by Randall Kenan, Signet Books, 1995.

Staples, Brent. "Just Walk on By: Black Men and Public Space." Cohen pp. 345–48.

Wideman, John Edgar. "The Seat Not Taken." *New York Times,* 7 Oct. 2010, www.nytimes.com/2010/10/07/opinion /07Wideman.html?_r=0.

# Readings

MAYA ANGELOU

# Graduation

*Born Marguerite Johnson in St. Louis, Missouri, in 1928, Maya Angelou has been a successful dancer, actor, poet, playwright, fiction writer, producer, director, newspaper editor, civil rights leader, and academic, among other accomplishments. Her autobiographical book* I Know Why the Caged Bird Sings *(1969) was nominated for a National Book Award. In 1993 she delivered her poem, "On the Pulse of Morning," at the inauguration of President Clinton.*

*"Graduation," from* I Know Why the Caged Bird Sings, *tells the story of Angelou's high school graduation in Stamps, Arkansas. Of that day, she writes, "Oh, it was important, all right" (par. 5); as she tells the story, the importance of this day for Angelou grows beyond that of the typical graduation. As you read, note the way she carefully brings the reader along with her as she re-creates the excitement and disappointment of that day and as she reflects on the significance of the moment that allowed her to say, "We were on top again. As always, again. We survived" (par. 61).*

The children in Stamps trembled visibly with anticipation. Some adults were excited too, but to be certain the whole young population had come down with graduation epidemic. Large classes were graduating from both the grammar school and the high school. Even those who were years removed from their own day of glorious release were anxious to help with preparations as a kind of dry run. The junior students who were moving into the vacating classes' chairs were tradition-bound to show their talents for leadership and management. They strutted through the school and around the campus exerting pressure on the lower grades. Their authority was so new that occasionally if they pressed a little too hard it had to be overlooked. After all, next term was coming, and it never hurt a sixth grader to have a play sister in the eighth grade, or a tenth-year student to be able to call

17

a twelfth grader Bubba. So all was endured in a spirit of shared understanding. But the graduating classes themselves were the nobility. Like travelers with exotic destinations on their minds, the graduates were remarkably forgetful. They came to school without their books, or tablets, or even pencils. Volunteers fell over themselves to secure replacements for the missing equip- ment. When accepted, the willing workers might or might not be thanked, and it was of no importance to the pregraduation rites. Even teachers were respectful of the now quiet and aging seniors, and tended to speak to them, if not as equals, as beings only slightly lower than themselves. After tests were returned and grades given, the student body, which acted like an extended family, knew who did well, who excelled, and what piteous ones had failed.

Unlike the white high school, Lafayette County Training School distinguished itself by having neither lawn, nor hedges, nor tennis court, nor climbing ivy. Its two buildings (main classrooms, the grade school, and home economics) were set on a dirt hill with no fence to limit either its boundaries or those of bordering farms. There was a large expanse to the left of the school which was used alternately as a baseball diamond or basketball court. Rusty hoops on swaying poles represented the permanent recreational equipment, although bats and balls could be borrowed from the P.E. teacher if the borrower was qualified and if the diamond wasn't occupied.

Over this rocky area relieved by a few shady tall persimmon trees the graduating class walked. The girls often held hands and no longer bothered to speak to the lower students. There was a sadness about them, as if this old world was not their home and they were bound for higher ground. The boys, on the other hand, had become more friendly, more outgoing. A decided change from the closed attitude they projected while studying for finals. Now they seemed not ready to give up the old school, the familiar paths, and classrooms. Only a small percentage would be continuing on to college—one of the South's A & M (agricultural and mechanical) schools, which trained Negro youths to be carpenters, farmers, handymen, masons, maids, cooks, and baby nurses. Their future rode heavily on their shoulders, and blinded them to the collective joy that had pervaded the lives of the boys and girls in the grammar school graduating class.

Parents who could afford it had ordered new shoes and ready-made clothes for themselves from Sears and Roebuck or Montgomery Ward. They also engaged the best seamstresses to make the floating graduating dresses and to cut down secondhand pants which would be pressed to a military slickness for the important event.

Oh, it was important, all right. Whitefolks would attend the ceremony, and two or three would speak of God and home, and the Southern way of life, and Mrs. Parsons, the principal's wife, would play the graduation march while the lower-grade graduates paraded down the aisles and took their seats below the platform. The high school seniors would wait in empty classrooms to make their dramatic entrance.

In the Store I was the person of the moment. The birthday girl. The center. Bailey had graduated the year before, although to do so he had had to forfeit all pleasures to make up for his time lost in Baton Rouge.

My class was wearing butter-yellow piqué dresses, and Momma launched out on mine. She smocked the yoke into tiny crisscrossing puckers, then shirred the rest of the bodice. Her dark fingers ducked in and out of the lemony cloth as she embroidered raised daisies around the hem. Before she considered herself finished she had added a crocheted cuff on the puff sleeves, and a pointy crocheted collar.

I was going to be lovely. A walking model of all the various styles of fine hand sewing and it didn't worry me that I was only twelve years old and merely graduating from the eighth grade. Besides, many teachers in Arkansas Negro schools had only that diploma and were licensed to impart wisdom.

The days had become longer and more noticeable. The faded beige of former times had been replaced with strong and sure colors. I began to see my classmates' clothes, their skin tones, and the dust that waved off pussy willows. Clouds that lazed across the sky were objects of great concern to me. Their shiftier shapes might have held a message that in my new happiness and with a little bit of time I'd soon decipher. During that period I looked at the arch of heaven so religiously my neck kept a steady ache. I had taken to smiling more often, and my jaws hurt from the unaccustomed activity. Between the two physical sore spots,

I suppose I could have been uncomfortable, but that was not the case. As a member of the winning team (the graduating class of 1940) I had outdistanced unpleasant sensations by miles. I was headed for the freedom of open fields.

Youth and social approval allied themselves with me and we    10
trammeled memories of slights and insults. The wind of our swift passage remodeled my features. Lost tears were pounded to mud and then to dust. Years of withdrawal were brushed aside and left behind, as hanging ropes of parasitic moss.

My work alone had awarded me a top place and I was going to be one of the first called in the graduating ceremonies. On the classroom blackboard, as well as on the bulletin board in the auditorium, there were blue stars and white stars and red stars. No absences, no tardinesses, and my academic work was among the best of the year. I could say the preamble to the Constitution even faster than Bailey. We timed ourselves often: "We the people of the United States in order to form a more perfect union . . ." I had memorized the Presidents of the United States from Washington to Roosevelt in chronological as well as alphabetical order.

My hair pleased me too. Gradually the black mass had lengthened and thickened, so that it kept at last to its braided pattern, and I didn't have to yank my scalp off when I tried to comb it.

Louise and I had rehearsed the exercises until we tired out ourselves. Henry Reed was class valedictorian. He was a small, very black boy with hooded eyes, a long, broad nose and an oddly shaped head. I had admired him for years because each term he and I vied for the best grades in our class. Most often he bested me, but instead of being disappointed I was pleased that we shared top places between us. Like many Southern Black children, he lived with his grandmother, who was as strict as Momma and as kind as she knew how to be. He was courteous, respectful, and soft-spoken to elders, but on the playground he chose to play the roughest games. I admired him. Anyone, I reckoned, sufficiently afraid or sufficiently dull could be polite. But to be able to operate at a top level with both adults and children was admirable.

His valedictory speech was entitled "To Be or Not to Be." The rigid tenth-grade teacher had helped him write it. He'd been working on the dramatic stresses for months.

The weeks until graduation were filled with heady activities.  15
A group of small children were to be presented in a play about
buttercups and daisies and bunny rabbits. They could be heard
throughout the building practicing their hops and their little
songs that sounded like silver bells. The older girls (nongradu-
ates, of course) were assigned the task of making refreshments
for the night's festivities. A tangy scent of ginger, cinnamon, nutmeg, and chocolate wafted around the home economics building as the budding cooks made samples for themselves and their
teachers.

In every corner of the workshop, axes and saws split fresh
timber as the woodshop boys made sets and stage scenery. Only
the graduates were left out of the general bustle. We were free
to sit in the library at the back of the building or look in quite
detachedly, naturally, on the measures being taken for our event.

Even the minister preached on graduation the Sunday before.
His subject was, "Let your light so shine that men will see your
good works and praise your Father, Who is in Heaven." Although
the sermon was purported to be addressed to us, he used the occasion to speak to backsliders, gamblers, and general ne'er-do-wells.
But since he had called our names at the beginning of the service
we were mollified.

Among Negroes the tradition was to give presents to children
going only from one grade to another. How much more important this was when the person was graduating at the top of the
class. Uncle Willie and Momma had sent away for a Mickey
Mouse watch like Bailey's. Louise gave me four embroidered
handkerchiefs. (I gave her crocheted doilies.) Mrs. Sneed, the
minister's wife, made me an undershirt to wear for graduation,
and nearly every customer gave me a nickel or maybe even a
dime with the instruction "Keep on moving to higher ground," or
some such encouragement.

Amazingly the great day finally dawned and I was out of
bed before I knew it. I threw open the back door to see it more
clearly, but Momma said, "Sister, come away from that door and
put your robe on."

I hoped the memory of that morning would never leave me.  20
Sunlight was itself young, and the day had none of the insistence
maturity would bring it in a few hours. In my robe and barefoot

in the backyard, under cover of going to see about my new beans, I gave myself up to the gentle warmth and thanked God that no matter what evil I had done in my life He had allowed me to live to see this day. Somewhere in my fatalism I had expected to die, accidentally, and never have the chance to walk up the stairs in the auditorium and gracefully receive my hard-earned diploma. Out of God's merciful bosom I had won reprieve.

Bailey came out in his robe and gave me a box wrapped in Christmas paper. He said he had saved his money for months to pay for it. It felt like a box of chocolates, but I knew Bailey wouldn't save money to buy candy when we had all we could want under our noses.

He was as proud of the gift as I. It was a soft-leather-bound copy of a collection of poems by Edgar Allan Poe, or, as Bailey and I called him, "Eap." I turned to "Annabel Lee" and we walked up and down the garden rows, the cool dirt between our toes, reciting the beautifully sad lines.

Momma made a Sunday breakfast although it was only Friday. After we finished the blessing, I opened my eyes to find the watch on my plate. It was a dream of a day. Everything went smoothly and to my credit, I didn't have to be reminded or scolded for anything. Near evening I was too jittery to attend to chores, so Bailey volunteered to do all before his bath.

Days before, we had made a sign for the Store, and as we turned out the lights Momma hung the cardboard over the door-knob. It read clearly: CLOSED, GRADUATION.

My dress fitted perfectly and everyone said that I looked like a sunbeam in it. On the hill, going toward the school, Bailey walked behind with Uncle Willie, who muttered, "Go on, Ju." He wanted him to walk ahead with us because it embarrassed him to have to walk so slowly. Bailey said he'd let the ladies walk together, and the men would bring up the rear. We all laughed, nicely.

Little children dashed by out of the dark like fireflies. Their crepe-paper dresses and butterfly wings were not made for running and we heard more than one rip, dryly, and the regretful "uh uh" that followed.

The school blazed without gaiety. The windows seemed cold and unfriendly from the lower hill. A sense of ill-fated timing crept over me, and if Momma hadn't reached for my hand

I would have drifted back to Bailey and Uncle Willie, and possibly beyond. She made a few slow jokes about my feet getting cold, and tugged me along to the now-strange building.

Around the front steps, assurance came back. There were my fellow "greats," the graduating class. Hair brushed back, legs oiled, new dresses and pressed pleats, fresh pocket handkerchiefs and little handbags, all homesewn. Oh, we were up to snuff, all right. I joined my comrades and didn't even see my family go in to find seats in the crowded auditorium.

The school band struck up a march and all classes filed in as had been rehearsed. We stood in front of our seats, as assigned, and on a signal from the choir director, we sat. No sooner had this been accomplished than the band started to play the national anthem. We rose again and sang the song, after which we recited the pledge of allegiance. We remained standing for a brief minute before the choir director and the principal signaled to us, rather desperately I thought, to take our seats. The command was so unusual that our carefully rehearsed and smooth-running machine was thrown off. For a full minute we fumbled for our chairs and bumped into each other awkwardly. Habits change or solidify under pressure, so in our state of nervous tension we had been ready to follow our usual assembly pattern: the American national anthem, then the pledge of allegiance, then the song every Black person I knew called the Negro National Anthem. All done in the same key, with the same passion and most often standing on the same foot.

Finding my seat at last, I was overcome with a presentiment of worse things to come. Something unrehearsed, unplanned, was going to happen, and we were going to be made to look bad. I distinctly remember being explicit in the choice of pronoun. It was "we," the graduating class, the unit, that concerned me then.

The principal welcomed "parents and friends" and asked the Baptist minister to lead us in prayer. His invocation was brief and punchy, and for a second I thought we were getting on the high road to right action. When the principal came back to the dais, however, his voice had changed. Sounds always affected me profoundly and the principal's voice was one of my favorites. During assembly it melted and lowed weakly into the audience. It had not been in my plan to listen to him, but my curiosity was piqued and I straightened up to give him my attention.

He was talking about Booker T. Washington, our "late great leader," who said we can be as close as the fingers on the hand, etc. . . . Then he said a few vague things about friendship and the friendship of kindly people to those less fortunate than themselves. With that his voice nearly faded, thin, away. Like a river diminishing to a stream and then to a trickle. But he cleared his throat and said, "Our speaker tonight, who is also our friend, came from Texarkana to deliver the commencement address, but due to the irregularity of the train schedule, he's going to, as they say, 'speak and run.'" He said that we understood and wanted the man to know that we were most grateful for the time he was able to give us and then something about how we were willing always to adjust to another's program, and without more ado—"I give you Mr. Edward Donleavy."

Not one but two white men came through the door off-stage. The shorter one walked to the speaker's platform, and the tall one moved to the center seat and sat down. But that was our principal's seat, and already occupied. The dislodged gentleman bounced around for a long breath or two before the Baptist minister gave him his chair, then with more dignity than the situation deserved, the minister walked off the stage.

Donleavy looked at the audience once (on reflection, I'm sure that he wanted only to reassure himself that we were really there), adjusted his glasses and began to read from a sheaf of papers.

He was glad "to be here and to see the work going on just as it was in the other schools." [35]

At the first "Amen" from the audience I willed the offender to immediate death by choking on the word. But Amens and Yes, sir's began to fall around the room like rain through a ragged umbrella.

He told us of the wonderful changes we children in Stamps had in store. The Central School (naturally, the white school was Central) had already been granted improvements that would be in use in the fall. A well-known artist was coming from Little Rock to teach art to them. They were going to have the newest microscopes and chemistry equipment for their laboratory. Mr. Donleavy didn't leave us long in the dark over who made these improvements available to Central High. Nor were we to be ignored in the general betterment scheme he had in mind.

He said that he had pointed out to people at a very high level that one of the first-line football tacklers at Arkansas Agricultural and Mechanical College had graduated from good old Lafayette County Training School. Here fewer Amen's were heard. Those few that did break through lay dully in the air with the heaviness of habit.

He went on to praise us. He went on to say how he had bragged that "one of the best basketball players at Fisk sank his first ball right here at Lafayette County Training School."

The white kids were going to have a chance to become Galileos 40 and Madame Curies and Edisons and Gauguins, and our boys (the girls weren't even in on it) would try to be Jesse Owenses and Joe Louises.

Owens and the Brown Bomber were great heroes in our world, but what school official in the white-goddom of Little Rock had the right to decide that those two men must be our only heroes? Who decided that for Henry Reed to become a scientist he had to work like George Washington Carver, as a bootblack, to buy a lousy microscope? Bailey was obviously always going to be too small to be an athlete, so which concrete angel glued to what country seat had decided that if my brother wanted to become a lawyer he had to first pay penance for his skin by picking cotton and hoeing corn and studying correspondence books at night for twenty years?

The man's dead words fell like bricks around the auditorium and too many settled in my belly. Constrained by hard-learned manners I couldn't look behind me, but to my left and right the proud graduating class of 1940 had dropped their heads. Every girl in my row had found something new to do with her handkerchief. Some folded the tiny squares into love knots, some into triangles, but most were wadding them, then pressing them flat on their yellow laps.

On the dais, the ancient tragedy was being replayed. Professor Parsons sat, a sculptor's reject, rigid. His large, heavy body seemed devoid of will or willingness, and his eyes said he was no longer with us. The other teachers examined the flag (which was draped stage right) or their notes, or the windows which opened on our now-famous playing diamond.

Graduation, the hush-hush magic time of frills and gifts and congratulations and diplomas, was finished for me before my name was called. The accomplishment was nothing. The meticulous

maps, drawn in three colors of ink, learning and spelling decasyl-
labic words, memorizing the whole of *The Rape of Lucrece*—it was
for nothing. Donleavy had exposed us.

We were maids and farmers, handymen and washerwomen, and   45
anything higher that we aspired to was farcical and presumptuous.

Then I wished that Gabriel Prosser and Nat Turner had killed
all whitefolks in their beds and that Abraham Lincoln had been
assassinated before the signing of the Emancipation Proclamation, and that Harriet Tubman had been killed by that blow on
her head and Christopher Columbus had drowned in the *Santa
Maria*.

It was awful to be a Negro and have no control over my life.
It was brutal to be young and already trained to sit quietly and
listen to charges brought against my color with no chance of
defense. We should all be dead. I thought I should like to see
us all dead, one on top of the other. A pyramid of flesh with the
whitefolks on the bottom, as the broad base, then the Indians
with their silly tomahawks and teepees and wigwams and trea-
ties, the Negroes with their mops and recipes and cotton sacks
and spirituals sticking out of their mouths. The Dutch children
should all stumble in their wooden shoes and break their necks.
The French should choke to death on the Louisiana Purchase
(1803) while silkworms ate all the Chinese with their stupid pig-
tails. As a species, we were an abomination. All of us.

Donleavy was running for election, and assured our parents
that if he won we could count on having the only colored paved
playing field in that part of Arkansas. Also—he never looked up
to acknowledge the grunts of acceptance—also, we were bound
to get some new equipment for the home economics building
and the workshop.

He finished, and since there was no need to give any more
than the most perfunctory thank-you's, he nodded to the men
on the stage, and the tall white man who was never introduced
joined him at the door. They left with the attitude that now they
were off to something really important. (The graduation ceremonies at Lafayette County Training School had been a mere
preliminary.)

The ugliness they left was palpable. An uninvited guest who   50
wouldn't leave. The choir was summoned and sang a modern
arrangement of "Onward, Christian Soldiers," with new words

pertaining to graduates seeking their place in the world. But it didn't work. Elouise, the daughter of the Baptist minister, recited "Invictus," and I could have cried at the impertinence of "I am the master of my fate, I am the captain of my soul."

My name had lost its ring of familiarity and I had to be nudged to go and receive my diploma. All my preparations had fled. I neither marched up to the stage like a conquering Amazon, nor did I look in the audience for Bailey's nod of approval. Marguerite Johnson, I heard the name again, my honors were read, there were noises in the audience of appreciation, and I took my place on the stage as rehearsed.

I thought about colors I hated: ecru, puce, lavender, beige, and black.

There was shuffling and rustling around me, then Henry Reed was giving his valedictory address, "To Be or Not to Be." Hadn't he heard the whitefolks? We couldn't *be,* so the question was a waste of time. Henry's voice came out clear and strong. I feared to look at him. Hadn't he got the message? There was no "nobler in the mind" for Negroes because the world didn't think we had minds, and they let us know it. "Outrageous fortune"? Now, that was a joke. When the ceremony was over I had to tell Henry Reed some things. That is, if I still cared. Not "rub," Henry, "erase." "Ah, there's the erase." Us.

Henry had been a good student in elocution. His voice rose on tides of promise and fell on waves of warnings. The English teacher had helped him to create a sermon winging through Hamlet's soliloquy. To be a man, a doer, a builder, a leader, or to be a tool, an unfunny joke, a crusher of funky toadstools. I marveled that Henry could go through with the speech as if we had a choice.

I had been listening and silently rebutting each sentence with my eyes closed; then there was a hush, which in an audience warns that something unplanned is happening. I looked up and saw Henry Reed, the conservative, the proper, the A student, turn his back to the audience and turn to us (the proud graduating class of 1940) and sing, nearly speaking,

55

> "Lift ev'ry voice and sing
> Till earth and heaven ring
> Ring with the harmonies of Liberty . . ."

It was the poem written by James Weldon Johnson. It was the music composed by J. Rosamond Johnson. It was the Negro national anthem. Out of habit we were singing it.

Our mothers and fathers stood in the dark hall and joined the hymn of encouragement. A kindergarten teacher led the small children onto the stage and the buttercups and daisies and bunny rabbits marked time and tried to follow:

> "Stony the road we trod
> Bitter the chastening rod
> Felt in the days when hope, unborn, had died.
> Yet with a steady beat
> Have not our weary feet
> Come to the place for which our fathers sighed?"

Each child I knew had learned that song with his ABC's and along with "Jesus Loves Me This I Know." But I personally had never heard it before. Never heard the words, despite the thousands of times I had sung them. Never thought they had anything to do with me.

On the other hand, the words of Patrick Henry had made such an impression on me that I had been able to stretch myself tall and trembling and say, "I know not what course others may take, but as for me, give me liberty or give me death."

And now I heard, really for the first time:

> "We have come over a way that with tears
> has been watered,
> We have come, treading our path through
> the blood of the slaughtered."

While echoes of the song shivered in the air, Henry Reed 60 bowed his head, said "Thank you," and returned to his place in the line. The tears that slipped down many faces were not wiped away in shame.

We were on top again. As always, again. We survived. The depths had been icy and dark, but now a bright sun spoke to our souls. I was no longer simply a member of the proud graduating class of 1940; I was a proud member of the wonderful, beautiful Negro race.

Oh, Black known and unknown poets, how often have your auctioned pains sustained us? Who will compute the lonely nights made less lonely by your songs, or the empty pots made less tragic by your tales?

If we were a people much given to revealing secrets, we might raise monuments and sacrifice to the memories of our poets, but slavery cured us of that weakness. It may be enough, however, to have it said that we survive in exact relationship to the dedication of our poets (include preachers, musicians, and blues singers).

## For Discussion and Writing

1. How do the achievements for which the graduation speaker praises recent graduates from the narrator's school differ from the narrator's hopes for herself and her classmates?

2. How does Angelou use the order in which she relates the background information and events of her story to manipulate the reader's emotions? Why do you think she does this?

3. **connections**   Compare the importance of literature in "Graduation" and in Gloria Anzaldúa's "How to Tame a Wild Tongue" (p. 30). What does poetry mean to Angelou here, and what does it mean to Anzaldúa?

4. Write about a time in your life when expectations and reality didn't match up. What was the situation? How did you react? Did you adjust your expectations? Or were you able to maintain them?

5. **looking further**   Angelou concludes her story by writing about the importance of the African American artistic tradition. Do some research on the writers, musicians, and other artists of this tradition, and then select one person; write a short piece on him or her in the light of Angelou's viewpoint. How is this person's work informed by African American history? Does it reflect the "dedication" Angelou cites? If the work does not do what Angelou describes, then has it in some way failed? Consider the assumptions behind this question.

## GLORIA ANZALDÚA

# How to Tame a Wild Tongue

*Gloria Anzaldúa was born in 1942 in the Rio Grande Valley of South Texas. At age eleven she began working in the fields as a migrant worker; after her father's death, she worked on her family's land. Working her way through school, she eventually became a schoolteacher and then an academic, speaking and writing about feminist, lesbian, and Chicana issues and about autobiography. She is best known for* This Bridge Called My Back: Writings by Radical Women of Color *(1981), which she edited with Cherríe Moraga, and* Borderlands/La Frontera: The New Mestiza *(1987). Anzaldúa died in 2004.*

*"How to Tame a Wild Tongue" is from* Borderlands/La Frontera. *In it, Anzaldúa is concerned with many kinds of borders — between nations, cultures, classes, genders, languages. When she writes, "So, if you want to really hurt me, talk badly about my language" (par. 27), Anzaldúa is arguing for the ways in which identity is intertwined with the way we speak and for the ways in which people can be made to feel ashamed of their own tongues. Keeping hers wild — ignoring the closing of linguistic borders — is Anzaldúa's way of asserting her identity. Pay close attention to the way she writes here, too; her style could be seen as another way in which she keeps her tongue wild.*

"We're going to have to control your tongue," the dentist says, pulling out all the metal from my mouth. Silver bits plop and tinkle into the basin. My mouth is a motherlode.

The dentist is cleaning out my roots. I get a whiff of the stench when I gasp. "I can't cap that tooth yet, you're still draining," he says.

"We're going to have to do something about your tongue," I hear the anger rising in his voice. My tongue keeps pushing out the wads of cotton, pushing back the drills, the long thin needles. "I've never seen anything as strong or as stubborn," he says. And I think, how do you tame a wild tongue, train it to be quiet, how do you bridle and saddle it? How do you make it lie down?

> "Who is to say that robbing a people of
> its language is less violent than war?"
> —RAY GWYN SMITH[1]

I remember being caught speaking Spanish at recess—that was good for three licks on the knuckles with a sharp ruler. I remember being sent to the corner of the classroom for "talking back" to the Anglo teacher when all I was trying to do was tell her how to pronounce my name. "If you want to be American, speak 'American.' If you don't like it, go back to Mexico where you belong."

"I want you to speak English. *Pa' hallar buen trabajo tienes que saber hablar el inglés bien. Qué vale toda tu educación si todavía hablas inglés con un* 'accent,'" my mother would say, mortified that I spoke English like a Mexican. At Pan American University, I and all Chicano students were required to take two speech classes. Their purpose: to get rid of our accents.

Attacks on one's form of expression with the intent to censor are a violation of the First Amendment. *El Anglo con cara de inocente nos arrancó la lengua.* Wild tongues can't be tamed, they can only be cut out.

## OVERCOMING THE TRADITION OF SILENCE

> *Ahogadas, escupimos el oscuro.*
> *Peleando con nuestra propia sombra*
> *el silencio nos sepulta.*

*En boca cerrada no entran moscas.* "Flies don't enter a closed mouth" is a saying I kept hearing when I was a child. *Ser habladora* was to be a gossip and a liar, to talk too much. *Muchachitas bien criadas*, well-bred girls don't answer back. *Es una falta de respeto* to talk back to one's mother or father. I remember one of the sins I'd recite to the priest in the confession box the few times I went to confession: talking back to my mother, *hablar pa' 'tras, repelar. Hocicona, repelona, chismosa*, having a big mouth, questioning, carrying tales are all signs of being *mal criada*. In my culture they are all words that are derogatory if applied to women—I've never heard them applied to men.

*   *   *

The first time I heard two women, a Puerto Rican and a Cuban, say the word *"nosotras,"* I was shocked. I had not known the word existed. Chicanas use *nosotros* whether we're male or female. We are robbed of our female being by the masculine plural. Language is a male discourse.

> And our tongues have become
> dry       the wilderness has
> dried out our tongues        and
> we have forgotten speech.
>           —IRENA KLEPFISZ[2]

Even our own people, other Spanish speakers *nos quieren poner candados en la boca*. They would hold us back with their bag of *reglas de academia*.

## Oyé como ladra: el lenguaje de la frontera

> *Quien tiene boca se equivoca.*
>           —MEXICAN SAYING

"*Pocho*, cultural traitor, you're speaking the oppressor's lan- 10 guage by speaking English, you're ruining the Spanish language," I have been accused by various Latinos and Latinas. Chicano Spanish is considered by the purist and by most Latinos deficient, a mutilation of Spanish.

But Chicano Spanish is a border tongue which developed naturally. Change, *evolución, enriquecimiento de palabras nuevas por invención o adopción* have created variants of Chicano Spanish, *un neuvo lenguaje. Un lenguaje que corresponde a un modo de vivir.* Chicano Spanish is not incorrect, it is a living language.

For a people who are neither Spanish nor live in a country in which Spanish is the first language; for a people who live in a country in which English is the reigning tongue but who are not Anglo; for a people who cannot entirely identify with either standard (formal, Castillian) Spanish nor standard English, what recourse is left to them but to create their own language? A language which they can connect their identity to, one capable of communicating the realities and values true to themselves—a language with terms that are neither *español ni inglés*, but both. We speak a patois, a forked tongue, a variation of two languages.

Chicano Spanish sprang out of the Chicanos' need to identify ourselves as a distinct people. We needed a language with which we could communicate with ourselves, a secret language. For some of us, language is a homeland closer than the Southwest—for many Chicanos today live in the Midwest and the East. And because we are a complex, heterogeneous people, we speak many languages. Some of the languages we speak are:

1. Standard English
2. Working class and slang English
3. Standard Spanish
4. Standard Mexican Spanish
5. North Mexican Spanish dialect
6. Chicano Spanish (Texas, New Mexico, Arizona, and California have regional variations)
7. Tex-Mex
8. *Pachuco* (called *caló*)

My "home" tongues are the languages I speak with my sister and brothers, with my friends. They are the last five listed, with 6 and 7 being closest to my heart. From school, the media, and job situations, I've picked up standard and working class English. From Mamagrande Locha and from reading Spanish and Mexican literature, I've picked up Standard Spanish and Standard Mexican Spanish. From *los recién llegados*, Mexican immigrants, and *braceros*, I learned the North Mexican dialect. With Mexicans I'll try to speak either Standard Mexican Spanish or the North Mexican dialect. From my parents and Chicanos living in the Valley, I picked up Chicano Texas Spanish, and I speak it with my mom, younger brother (who married a Mexican and who rarely mixes Spanish with English), aunts, and older relatives.

With Chicanas from *Nuevo México* or *Arizona* I will speak Chicano Spanish a little, but often they don't understand what I'm saying. With most California Chicanas I speak entirely in English (unless I forget). When I first moved to San Francisco, I'd rattle off something in Spanish, unintentionally embarrassing them. Often it is only with another Chicana *tejana* that I can talk freely.

Words distorted by English are known as anglicisms or *pochismos*. The *pocho* is an anglicized Mexican or American of Mexican origin who speaks Spanish with an accent characteristic of North Americans and who distorts and reconstructs the language according to the influence of English.[3] Tex-Mex, or Spanglish, comes most naturally to me. I may switch back and forth from English to Spanish in the same sentence or in the same word. With my sister and my brother Nune and with Chicano *tejano* contemporaries I speak in Tex-Mex.

From kids and people my own age I picked up *Pachuco*. *Pachuco* (the language of the zoot suiters) is a language of rebellion, both against Standard Spanish and Standard English. It is a secret language. Adults of the culture and outsiders cannot understand it. It is made up of slang words from both English and Spanish. *Ruca* means girl or woman, *vato* means guy or dude, *chale* means no, *simón* means yes, *churro* is sure, talk is *periquiar, pigionear* means petting, *que gacho* means how nerdy, *ponte águila* means watch out, death is called *la pelona*. Through lack of practice and not having others who can speak it, I've lost most of the *Pachuco* tongue.

## CHICANO SPANISH

Chicanos, after 250 years of Spanish/Anglo colonization, have developed significant differences in the Spanish we speak. We collapse two adjacent vowels into a single syllable and sometimes shift the stress in certain words such as *maíz/maiz, cohete/cuete*. We leave out certain consonants when they appear between vowels: *lado/lao, mojado/mojao*. Chicanos from South Texas pronounce *f* as *j* as in *jue (fue)*. Chicanos use "archaisms," words that are no longer in the Spanish language, words that have been evolved out. We say *semos, truje, haiga, ansina*, and *naiden*. We retain the "archaic" *j*, as in *jalar*, that derives from an earlier *h* (the French *halar* or the Germanic *halon* which was lost to standard Spanish in the 16th century), but which is still found in several regional dialects such as the one spoken in South Texas. (Due to geography, Chicanos from the Valley of South Texas were cut off linguistically from other Spanish speakers. We tend to use words that the Spaniards brought over from Medieval Spain. The majority of the Spanish colonizers in Mexico and the Southwest came from Extremadura—Hernán Cortés was one of them—and Andalucía. Andalucians pronounce *ll* like a *y*, and their *d*'s tend to be absorbed by adjacent vowels: *tirado* becomes *tirao*. They brought *el lenguaje popular, dialectos y regionalismos*.[4])

Chicanos and other Spanish speakers also shift *ll* to *y* and *z* to *s*.[5] We leave out initial syllables, saying *tar* for *estar*, *toy* for *estoy*, *hora* for *ahora* (*atinas* and *puertorriqueños* also leave out initial letters of some words). We also leave out the final syllable such as *pa* for *para*. The intervocalic *y*, the *ll* as in *tortilla; ella, botella*, gets replaced by *tortia* or *tortiya*, *ea*, *botea*. We add an additional syllable at the beginning of certain words: *atocar* for *tocar*, *agastar* for *gastar*. Sometimes we'll say *lavaste las vacijas*, other times *lavates* (substituting the *ates* verb endings for the *aste*).

We use anglicisms, words borrowed from English: *bola* from    20 ball, *carpeta* from carpet, *máchina de lavar* (instead of *lavadora*) from washing machine. Tex-Mex argot, created by adding a Spanish sound at the beginning or end of an English word such as *cookiar* for cook, *watchar* for watch, *parkiar* for park, and *rapiar* for rape, is the result of the pressures on Spanish speakers to adapt to English.

We don't use the word *vosotros/as* or its accompanying verb form. We don't say *claro* (to mean yes), *imagínate*, or *me emociona*, unless we picked up Spanish from Latinas, out of a book, or in a classroom. Other Spanish-speaking groups are going through the same, or similar, development in their Spanish.

## LINGUISTIC TERRORISM

> *Deslenguadas. Somos los del español deficiente.* We are your linguistic nightmare, your linguistic aberration, your linguistic *mestisaje*, the subject of your *burla*. Because we speak with tongues of fire we are culturally crucified. Racially, culturally, and linguistically *somos huérfanos—we speak an orphan tongue*.

Chicanas who grew up speaking Chicano Spanish have internalized the belief that we speak poor Spanish. It is illegitimate, a bastard language. And because we internalize how our language has been used against us by the dominant culture, we use our language differences against each other.

Chicana feminists often skirt around each other with suspicion and hesitation. For the longest time I couldn't figure it out. Then it dawned on me. To be close to another Chicana is like looking into the mirror. We are afraid of what we'll see there. *Pena.* Shame. Low estimation of self. In childhood we are told that our language is wrong. Repeated attacks on our native tongue diminish our sense of self. The attacks continue throughout our lives.

Chicanas feel uncomfortable talking in Spanish to Latinas, afraid of their censure. Their language was not outlawed in their countries. They had a whole lifetime of being immersed in their native tongue; generations, centuries in which Spanish was a first language, taught in school, heard on radio and TV, and read in the newspaper.

If a person, Chicana or Latina, has a low estimation of my native tongue, she also has a low estimation of me. Often with *mexicanas y latinas* we'll speak English as a neutral language. Even among Chicanas we tend to speak English at parties or conferences. Yet, at the same time, we're afraid the other will think we're *agringadas* because we don't speak Chicano Spanish. We oppress each other trying to out-Chicano each other, vying to be the "real" Chicanas, to speak like Chicanos. There is no one Chicano language just as there is no one Chicano experience. A monolingual Chicana whose first language is English or Spanish is just as much a Chicana as one who speaks several variants of Spanish. A Chicana from Michigan or Chicago or Detroit is just as much a Chicana as one from the Southwest. Chicano Spanish is as diverse linguistically as it is regionally.

By the end of this century, Spanish speakers will comprise the biggest minority group in the U.S., a country where students in high schools and colleges are encouraged to take French classes because French is considered more "cultured." But for a language to remain alive it must be used.[6] By the end of this century English, and not Spanish, will be the mother tongue of most Chicanos and Latinos.

So, if you want to really hurt me, talk badly about my language. Ethnic identity is twin skin to linguistic identity—I am my language. Until I can take pride in my language, I cannot take pride in myself. Until I can accept as legitimate Chicano Texas Spanish, Tex-Mex, and all the other languages I speak, I cannot accept the legitimacy of myself. Until I am free to write bilingually and to switch codes without having always to translate, while I still have to speak English or Spanish when I would rather speak Spanglish, and as long as I have to accommodate the English speakers rather than having them accommodate me, my tongue will be illegitimate.

I will no longer be made to feel ashamed of existing. I will have my voice: Indian, Spanish, white. I will have my serpent's tongue—my woman's voice, my sexual voice, my poet's voice. I will overcome the tradition of silence.

> My fingers
> move sly against your palm
> Like women everywhere, we speak in code. . . .
> —MELANIE KAYE/KANTROWITZ[7]

### *"Vistas," corridos, y comida:* My Native Tongue

In the 1960s, I read my first Chicano novel. It was *City of Night* by John Rechy, a gay Texan, son of a Scottish father and a Mexican mother. For days I walked around in stunned amazement that a Chicano could write and could get published. When I read *I Am Joaquín*[8] I was surprised to see a bilingual book by a Chicano in print. When I saw poetry written in Tex-Mex for the first time, a feeling of pure joy flashed through me. I felt like we really existed as a people. In 1971, when I started teaching High School English to Chicano students, I tried to supplement the required texts with works by Chicanos, only to be reprimanded and forbidden to do so by the principal. He claimed that I was supposed to teach "American" and English literature. At the risk of being fired, I swore my students to secrecy and slipped in Chicano short stories, poems, a play. In graduate school, while working toward a Ph.D., I had to "argue" with one advisor after the other, semester after semester, before I was allowed to make Chicano literature an area of focus.

Even before I read books by Chicanos or Mexicans, it was    30
the Mexican movies I saw at the drive-in—the Thursday night special of $1.00 a carload—that gave me a sense of belonging. *"Vámonos a las vistas,"* my mother would call out and we'd all—grandmother, brothers, sister, and cousins—squeeze into the car. We'd wolf down cheese and bologna white bread sandwiches while watching Pedro Infante in melodramatic tearjerkers

like *Nosotros los pobres*, the first "real" Mexican movie (that was not an imitation of European movies). I remember seeing *Cuando los hijos se van* and surmising that all Mexican movies played up the love a mother has for her children and what ungrateful sons and daughters suffer when they are not devoted to their mothers. I remember the singing-type "westerns" of Jorge Negrete and Miquel Aceves Mejía. When watching Mexican movies, I felt a sense of homecoming as well as alienation. People who were to amount to something didn't go to Mexican movies, or *bailes*, or tune their radios to *bolero*, *rancherita*, and *corrido* music.

The whole time I was growing up, there was *norteño* music sometimes called North Mexican border music, or Tex-Mex music, or Chicano music, or *cantina* (bar) music. I grew up listening to *conjuntos*, three- or four-piece bands made up of folk musicians playing guitar, *bajo sexto*, drums, and button accordion, which Chicanos had borrowed from the German immigrants who had come to Central Texas and Mexico to farm and build breweries. In the Rio Grande Valley, Steve Jordan and Little Joe Hernández were popular, and Flaco Jiménez was the accordion king. The rhythms of Tex-Mex music are those of the polka, also adapted from the Germans, who in turn had borrowed the polka from the Czechs and Bohemians.

I remember the hot, sultry evenings when *corridos*—songs of love and death on the Texas-Mexican borderlands—reverberated out of cheap amplifiers from the local *cantinas* and wafted in through my bedroom window.

*Corridos* first became widely used along the South Texas/Mexican border during the early conflict between Chicanos and Anglos. The *corridos* are usually about Mexican heroes who do valiant deeds against the Anglo oppressors. Pancho Villa's song, "*La cucaracha*," is the most famous one. *Corridos* of John F. Kennedy and his death are still very popular in the Valley. Older Chicanos remember Lydia Mendoza, one of the great border *corrido* singers who was called *la Gloria de Tejas*. Her "*El tango negro*," sung during the Great Depression, made her a singer of the people. The everpresent *corridos* narrated one hundred years of border history, bringing news of events as well as entertaining. These folk musicians and folk songs are our chief cultural myth-makers, and they made our hard lives seem bearable.

I grew up feeling ambivalent about our music. Country-western and rock-and-roll had more status. In the 50s and 60s, for the slightly educated and *agringado* Chicanos, there existed a sense of shame at being caught listening to our music. Yet I couldn't stop my feet from thumping to the music, could not stop humming the words, nor hide from myself the exhilaration I felt when I heard it.

There are more subtle ways that we internalize identification, 35 especially in the forms of images and emotions. For me food and certain smells are tied to my identity, to my homeland. Wood-smoke curling up to an immense blue sky; woodsmoke perfuming my grandmother's clothes, her skin. The stench of cow manure and the yellow patches on the ground; the crack of a .22 rifle and the reek of cordite. Homemade white cheese sizzling in a pan, melting inside a folded *tortilla*. My sister Hilda's hot, spicy *menudo, chile colorado* making it deep red, pieces of *panza* and hominy floating on top. My brother Carito barbequing *fajitas* in the backyard. Even now and 3,000 miles away, I can see my mother spicing the ground beef, pork, and venison with *chile*. My mouth salivates at the thought of the hot steaming *tamales* I would be eating if I were home.

*Si le preguntas a mi mamá, "¿Qué eres?"*

"Identity is the essential core of who we are as individuals, the conscious experience of the self inside."
—GERSHEN KAUFMAN[9]

*Nosotros los* Chicanos straddle the borderlands. On one side of us, we are constantly exposed to the Spanish of the Mexicans, on the other side we hear the Anglos' incessant clamoring so that we forget our language. Among ourselves we don't say *nosotros los americanos, o nosotros los españoles, o nosotros los hispanos.* We say *nosotros los mexicanos* (by *mexicanos* we do not mean citizens of Mexico; we do not mean a national identity, but a racial one). We distinguish between *mexicanos del otro lado* and *mexicanos de este lado*. Deep in our hearts we believe that being Mexican has nothing to do with which country one lives in. Being Mexican is a state of soul—not one of mind, not one of citizenship. Neither eagle nor serpent, but both. And like the ocean, neither animal respects borders.

> *Dime con quien andas y te dire quien eres.*
> (Tell me who your friends are and I'll tell you who you are.)
> ——MEXICAN SAYING

*Si le preguntas a mi mamá, "¿Qué eres?" te dirá, "Soy mexicana."* My brothers and sister say the same. I sometimes will answer *"soy mexicana"* and at others will say *"soy Chicana" o "soy tejana."* But I identified as *"Raza"* before I ever identified as *"mexicana"* or "Chicana."

As a culture, we call ourselves Spanish when referring to ourselves as a linguistic group and when copping out. It is then that we forget our predominant Indian genes. We are 70–80 percent Indian.[10] We call ourselves Hispanic[11] or Spanish-American or Latin American or Latin when linking ourselves to other Spanish-speaking peoples of the Western hemisphere and when copping out. We call ourselves Mexican-American[12] to signify we are neither Mexican nor American, but more the noun "American" than the adjective "Mexican" (and when copping out).

Chicanos and other people of color suffer economically for not acculturating. This voluntary (yet forced) alienation makes for psychological conflict, a kind of dual identity—we don't identify with the Anglo-American cultural values and we don't totally identify with the Mexican cultural values. We are a synergy of two cultures with various degrees of Mexicanness or Angloness. I have so internalized the borderland conflict that sometimes I feel like one cancels out the other and we are zero, nothing, no one. *A veces no soy nada ni nadie. Pero hasta cuando no lo soy, lo soy.*

When not copping out, when we know we are more than nothing, we call ourselves Mexican, referring to race and ancestry; *mestizo* when affirming both our Indian and Spanish (but we hardly ever own our Black ancestry); Chicano when referring to a politically aware people born and/or raised in the U.S.; *Raza* when referring to Chicanos; *tejanos* when we are Chicanos from Texas.

Chicanos did not know we were a people until 1965 when Ceasar Chavez and the farmworkers united and *I Am Joaquín* was published and *la Raza Unida* party was formed in Texas. With that recognition, we became a distinct people.

Something momentous happened to the Chicano soul—we became aware of our reality and acquired a name and a language (Chicano Spanish) that reflected that reality. Now that we had a name, some of the fragmented pieces began to fall together—who we were, what we were, how we had evolved. We began to get glimpses of what we might eventually become.

Yet the struggle of identities continues, the struggle of borders is our reality still. One day the inner struggle will cease and a true integration take place. In the meantime, *tenémos que hacer la lucha. ¿Quién está protegiendo los ranchos de mi gente? ¿Quién está tratando de cerrar la fisura entre la india y el blanco en nuestra sangre? El Chicano, si, el Chicano que anda como un ladrón en su propia casa.*

*Los Chicanos*, how patient we seem, how very patient. There is the quiet of the Indian about us.[13] We know how to survive. When other races have given up their tongue, we've kept ours. We know what it is to live under the hammer blow of the dominant *norteamericano* culture. But more than we count the blows, we count the days the weeks the years the centuries the eons until the white laws and commerce and customs will rot in the deserts they've created, lie bleached. *Humildes* yet proud, *quietos* yet wild, *nosotros los mexicanos-Chicanos* will walk by the crumbling ashes as we go about our business. Stubborn, persevering, impenetrable as stone, yet possessing a malleability that renders us unbreakable, we, the *mestizas* and *mestizos*, will remain.

## Notes

1. Ray Gwyn Smith, *Moorland Is Cold Country*, unpublished book.

2. Irena Klepfisz, "*Di rayze aheym*/The Journey Home," in *The Tribe of Dina: A Jewish Women's Anthology*, Melanie Kaye/Kantrowitz and Irena Klepfisz, eds. (Montpelier, VT: Sinister Wisdom Books, 1986), 49.

3. R. C. Ortega, *Dialectología Del Barrio*, trans. Hortencia S. Alwan (Los Angeles, CA: R. C. Ortega Publisher & Bookseller, 1977), 132.

4. Eduardo Hernandéz-Chávez, Andrew D. Cohen, and Anthony F. Beltramo, *El Lenguaje de los Chicanos: Regional and Social Characteristics of Language Used by Mexican Americans* (Arlington, VA: Center for Applied Linguistics, 1975), 39.

5. Hernandéz-Chávez, xvii.

6. Irena Klepfisz, "Secular Jewish Identity: Yidishkayt in America," in *The Tribe of Dina*, Kaye/Kantrowitz and Klepfisz, eds., 43.

7. Melanie Kaye/Kantrowitz, "Sign," in *We Speak in Code: Poems and Other Writings* (Pittsburgh, PA: Motheroot Publications, Inc., 1980), 85.

8. Rodolfo Gonzales, *I Am Joaquín/Yo Soy Joaquín* (New York, NY: Bantam Books, 1972). It was first published in 1967.

9. Gershen Kaufman, *Shame: The Power of Caring* (Cambridge, MA: Schenkman Books, Inc., 1980), 68.

10. John R. Chávez, *The Lost Land: The Chicago Images of the Southwest* (Albuquerque, NM: University of New Mexico Press, 1984), 88–90.

11. "Hispanic" is derived from *Hispanis* (*España*, a name given to the Iberian Peninsula in ancient times when it was a part of the Roman Empire) and is a term designated by the U.S. government to make it easier to handle us on paper.

12. The Treaty of Guadalupe Hidalgo created the Mexican-American in 1848.

13. Anglos, in order to alleviate their guilt for dispossessing the Chicano, stressed the Spanish part of us and perpetrated the myth of the Spanish Southwest. We have accepted the fiction that we are Hispanic, that is Spanish, in order to accommodate ourselves to the dominant culture and its abhorrence of Indians. Chávez, 88–91.

## For Discussion and Writing

1. List the different kinds of languages Anzaldúa speaks and organize them according to a principle of your own selection. Explain that principle and what the list it produces tells us about the Chicano/a experience with language.

2. How does Anzaldúa use definition to discuss her experience with language, and to what effect?

3. **connections**   Compare Anzaldúa's sense of herself as an American to Audre Lorde's in "The Fourth of July" (p. 242). In what way does each woman feel American? In what way does each not?

4. In her discussion of moving back and forth between the varieties of languages she speaks, Anzaldúa uses the term "switch codes" (par. 27). Define that term and write about situations in your life in which you switch codes.

5. **looking further**   When the book from which this excerpt comes was published in 1987, much attention was being paid to multiculturalism and reactions against it—a conflict often called the "culture wars." Read up on this controversy and discuss the different political and philosophical visions informing the conflicting positions. Where do you stand on the issues raised by multiculturalism? Do you think our model today should be the melting pot or what then–New York City mayor David Dinkins called the "gorgeous mosaic"?

BARBARA LAZEAR ASCHER

# On Compassion

*Barbara Lazear Ascher, born in 1946, worked as a lawyer for two years before she became a full-time writer. Her essays, which have appeared in newspapers and magazines, have been collected in* Playing after Dark *(1986) and* The Habit of Loving *(1989). She has also written books about her brother's death from AIDS* (Landscape without Gravity: A Memoir of Grief, *1993) and romance* (Dancing in the Dark: Romance, Yearning, and the Search for the Sublime, *1999).*

*A New Yorker, Ascher draws her examples for "On Compassion" from life in that city. The brief scenes she describes—the encounter on the street corner, the moment in the café—allow the reader to imagine the thoughts and feelings of the participants. As you read, take note of how the specific details of the city enliven her examples and the way that specificity helps the examples to illustrate her argument.*

The man's grin is less the result of circumstance than dreams or madness. His buttonless shirt, with one sleeve missing, hangs outside the waist of his baggy trousers. Carefully plaited dreadlocks bespeak a better time, long ago. As he crosses Manhattan's Seventy-ninth Street, his gait is the shuffle of the forgotten ones held in place by gravity rather than plans. On the corner of Madison Avenue, he stops before a blond baby in an Aprica stroller. The baby's mother waits for the light to change and her hands close tighter on the stroller's handle as she sees the man approach.

The others on the corner, five men and women waiting for the crosstown bus, look away. They daydream a bit and gaze into the weak rays of November light. A man with a briefcase lifts and lowers the shiny toe of his right shoe, watching the light reflect, trying to catch and balance it, as if he could hold and make it his, to ease the heavy gray of coming January, February, and March. The winter months that will send snow around the feet, calves, and knees of the grinning man as he heads for the shelter of Grand Central or Pennsylvania Station.

But for now, in this last gasp of autumn warmth, he is still. His eyes fix on the baby. The mother removes her purse from her shoulder and rummages through its contents: lipstick, a lace handkerchief, an address book. She finds what she's looking for and passes a folded dollar over her child's head to the man who stands and stares even though the light has changed and traffic navigates about his hips.

His hands continue to dangle at his sides. He does not know his part. He does not know that acceptance of the gift and gratitude are what make this transaction complete. The baby, weary of the unwavering stare, pulls its blanket over its head. The man does not look away. Like a bridegroom waiting at the altar, his eyes pierce the white veil.

The mother grows impatient and pushes the stroller before her, bearing the dollar like a cross. Finally, a black hand rises and closes around green. 5

Was it fear or compassion that motivated the gift?

Up the avenue, at Ninety-first Street, there is a small French bread shop where you can sit and eat a buttery, overpriced croissant and wash it down with rich cappuccino. Twice when I have stopped here to stave hunger or stay the cold, twice as I have sat and read and felt the warm rush of hot coffee and milk, an old man has wandered in and stood inside the entrance. He wears a stained blanket pulled up to his chin, and a woolen hood pulled down to his gray, bushy eyebrows. As he stands, the scent of stale cigarettes and urine fills the small, overheated room.

The owner of the shop, a moody French woman, emerges from the kitchen with steaming coffee in a Styrofoam cup, and a small paper bag of . . . of what? Yesterday's bread? Today's croissant? He accepts the offering as silently as he came, and is gone.

Twice I have witnessed this, and twice I have wondered, what compels this woman to feed this man? Pity? Care? Compassion? Or does she simply want to rid her shop of his troublesome presence? If expulsion were her motivation she would not reward his arrival with gifts of food. Most proprietors do not. They chase the homeless from their midst with expletives and threats.

As winter approaches, the mayor of New York City is moving     10
the homeless off the streets and into Bellevue Hospital. The New
York Civil Liberties Union is watchful. They question whether
the rights of these people who live in our parks and doorways are
being violated by involuntary hospitalization.

I think the mayor's notion is humane, but I fear it is something
else as well. Raw humanity offends our sensibilities. We want
to protect ourselves from an awareness of rags with voices that
make no sense and scream forth in inarticulate rage. We do not
wish to be reminded of the tentative state of our own well-being
and sanity. And so, the troublesome presence is removed from
the awareness of the electorate.

Like other cities, there is much about Manhattan now that
resembles Dickensian London. Ladies in high-heeled shoes pick
their way through poverty and madness. You hear more cock-
tail party complaints than usual, "I just can't take New York anymore." Our citizens dream of the open spaces of Wyoming, the
manicured exclusivity of Hobe Sound.

And yet, it may be that these are the conditions that finally
give birth to empathy, the mother of compassion. We cannot
deny the existence of the helpless as their presence grows. It is
impossible to insulate ourselves against what is at our very door-
step. I don't believe that one is born compassionate. Compassion is not a character trait like a sunny disposition. It must be
learned, and it is learned by having adversity at our windows,
coming through the gates of our yards, the walls of our towns,
adversity that becomes so familiar that we begin to identify and
empathize with it.

For the ancient Greeks, drama taught and reinforced compassion within a society. The object of Greek tragedy was to inspire
empathy in the audience so that the common response to the
hero's fall was: "There, but for the grace of God, go I." Could
it be that this was the response of the mother who offered the
dollar, the French woman who gave the food? Could it be that
the homeless, like those ancients, are reminding us of our common humanity? Of course, there is a difference. This play doesn't
end—and the players can't go home.

*For Discussion and Writing*

1. What examples of encounters with the homeless does Ascher offer?
2. Imagine and list alternative examples of encounters with the homeless that Ascher might have used. How might their inclusion have changed her essay?
3. **connections**   Both Ascher and Lars Eighner in "On Dumpster Diving" (p. 144) write about people who are down on their luck: Eighner as one who has been down on his luck himself; Ascher from the perspective of the more fortunate. How do their differing perspectives inform their essays?
4. Where does Ascher believe compassion comes from? Do you agree or disagree? Why? Can you illustrate your argument with an example from your own experience?
5. **looking further**   Due to the current economic downturn, our federal and state governments have had to grapple with the question of how much government can and should do to assist citizens who have fallen on hard times. How have these questions been asked and answered across history and across the globe? What informs the answers? What's your answer?

## JAMES BALDWIN

# Notes of a Native Son

*Born in Harlem in 1924, a preacher and a published writer of reviews and essays at a young age, James Baldwin became a noted writer of American prose. Though he lived abroad for much of his adult life, in Paris, Switzerland, and Istanbul, Baldwin wrote incisively and passionately about the experience of being black in America. His first novel,* Go Tell It on the Mountain *(1953), drew on his youth in the church and on his relationship with his preacher father as well as on the rolling, repetitive, swelling language of the sermon. His essay collection* Notes of a Native Son *(1955) reflected further on his own life and on African American experience as well as on the literary and cultural products that have come out of that experience. Baldwin's next novels,* Giovanni's Room *(1956) and* Another Country *(1962), delved into the issue of homosexuality. In his open explorations in fiction and nonfiction of taboo subjects and often hidden but sometimes quite open prejudices, Baldwin became a model of a writer practicing thoughtful yet always heartfelt engagement with the world.*

*"Notes of a Native Son" considers the hatred at the heart of race relations in mid-century America and at the heart of Baldwin's relationship with his father. That Baldwin accepts that hate as neither the totality nor the final destination of these relationships is testament to his sensibility and strength as a writer and as a man. As you read, savor the writing from line to line and paragraph to paragraph, and think about the ways in which these lines and paragraphs add up to such quietly forceful writing.*

## I

On the 29th of July, in 1943, my father died. On the same day, a few hours later, his last child was born. Over a month before this, while all our energies were concentrated in waiting for these events, there had been, in Detroit, one of the bloodiest race riots of the century. A few hours after my father's funeral, while he lay in state in the undertaker's chapel, a race riot broke out in Harlem. On the morning of the 3rd of August, we drove my father to the graveyard through a wilderness of smashed plate glass.

The day of my father's funeral had also been my nineteenth birthday. As we drove him to the graveyard, the spoils of injustice, anarchy, discontent, and hatred were all around us. It seemed to me that God himself had devised, to mark my father's end, the most sustained and brutally dissonant of codas. And it seemed to me, too, that the violence which rose all about us as my father left the world had been devised as a corrective for the pride of his eldest son. I had declined to believe in that apocalypse which had been central to my father's vision; very well, life seemed to be saying, here is something that will certainly pass for an apocalypse until the real thing comes along. I had inclined to be contemptuous of my father for the conditions of his life, for the conditions of our lives. When his life had ended I began to wonder about that life and also, in a new way, to be apprehensive about my own.

I had not known my father very well. We had got on badly, partly because we shared, in our different fashions, the vice of stubborn pride. When he was dead I realized that I had hardly ever spoken to him. When he had been dead a long time I began to wish I had. It seems to be typical of life in America, where opportunities, real and fancied, are thicker than anywhere else on the globe, that the second generation has no time to talk to the first. No one, including my father, seems to have known exactly how old he was, but his mother had been born during slavery. He was of the first generation of free men. He, along with thousands of other Negroes, came North after 1919 and I was part of that generation which had never seen the landscape of what Negroes sometimes call the Old Country.

He had been born in New Orleans and had been a quite young man there during the time that Louis Armstrong, a boy, was running errands for the dives and honky-tonks of what was always presented to me as one of the most wicked of cities—to this day, whenever I think of New Orleans, I also helplessly think of Sodom and Gomorrah. My father never mentioned Louis Armstrong, except to forbid us to play his records; but there was a picture of him on our wall for a long time. One of my father's strong-willed female relatives had placed it there and forbade my father to take it down. He never did, but he eventually maneuvered her out of the house and when, some years later, she was in trouble and near death, he refused to do anything to help her.

He was, I think, very handsome. I gather this from photographs and from my own memories of him, dressed in his Sunday best and on his way to preach a sermon somewhere, when I was little. Handsome, proud, and ingrown, "like a toe-nail," somebody said. But he looked to me, as I grew older, like pictures I had seen of African tribal chieftains: he really should have been naked, with war-paint on and barbaric mementos, standing among spears. He could be chilling in the pulpit and indescribably cruel in his personal life and he was certainly the most bitter man I have ever met; yet it must be said that there was something else in him, buried in him, which lent him his tremendous power and, even, a rather crushing charm. It had something to do with his blackness, I think — he was very black — with his blackness and his beauty, and with the fact that he knew that he was black but did not know that he was beautiful. He claimed to be proud of his blackness but it had also been the cause of much humiliation and it had fixed bleak boundaries to his life. He was not a young man when we were growing up and he had already suffered many kinds of ruin; in his outrageously demanding and protective way he loved his children, who were black like him and menaced, like him; and all these things sometimes showed in his face when he tried, never to my knowledge with any success, to establish contact with any of us. When he took one of his children on his knee to play, the child always became fretful and began to cry; when he tried to help one of us with our homework the absolutely unabating tension which emanated from him caused our minds and our tongues to become paralyzed, so that he, scarcely knowing why, flew into a rage and the child, not knowing why, was punished. If it ever entered his head to bring a surprise home for his children, it was, almost unfailingly, the wrong surprise and even the big watermelons he often brought home on his back in the summertime led to the most appalling scenes. I do not remember, in all those years, that one of his children was ever glad to see him come home. From what I was able to gather of his early life, it seemed that this inability to establish contact with other people had always marked him and had been one of the things which had driven him out of New Orleans. There was something in him,

5

therefore, groping and tentative, which was never expressed and which was buried with him. One saw it most clearly when he was facing new people and hoping to impress them. But he never did, not for long. We went from church to smaller and more improbable church, he found himself in less and less demand as a minister, and by the time he died none of his friends had come to see him for a long time. He had lived and died in an intolerable bitterness of spirit and it frightened me, as we drove him to the graveyard through those unquiet, ruined streets, to see how powerful and overflowing this bitterness could be and to realize that this bitterness now was mine.

When he died I had been away from home for a little over a year. In that year I had had time to become aware of the meaning of all my father's bitter warnings, had discovered the secret of his proudly pursed lips and rigid carriage: I had discovered the weight of white people in the world. I saw that this had been for my ancestors and now would be for me an awful thing to live with and that the bitterness which had helped to kill my father could also kill me.

He had been ill a long time—in the mind, as we now realized, reliving instances of his fantastic intransigence in the new light of his affliction and endeavoring to feel a sorrow for him which never, quite, came true. We had not known that he was being eaten up by paranoia, and the discovery that his cruelty, to our bodies and our minds, had been one of the symptoms of his illness was not, then, enough to enable us to forgive him. The younger children felt, quite simply, relief that he would not be coming home anymore. My mother's observation that it was he, after all, who had kept them alive all these years meant nothing because the problems of keeping children alive are not real for children. The older children felt, with my father gone, that they could invite their friends to the house without fear that their friends would be insulted or, as had sometimes happened with me, being told that their friends were in league with the devil and intended to rob our family of everything we owned. (I didn't fail to wonder, and it made me hate him, what on earth we owned that anybody else would want.)

His illness was beyond all hope of healing before anyone realized that he was ill. He had always been so strange and had lived, like a prophet, in such unimaginably close communion with the Lord that his long silences which were punctuated by moans and hallelujahs and snatches of old songs while he sat at the living-room window never seemed odd to us. It was not until he refused to eat because, he said, his family was trying to poison him that my mother was forced to accept as a fact what had, until then, been only an unwilling suspicion. When he was committed, it was discovered that he had tuberculosis and, as it turned out, the disease of his mind allowed the disease of his body to destroy him. For the doctors could not force him to eat, either, and, though he was fed intravenously, it was clear from the beginning that there was no hope for him.

In my mind's eye I could see him, sitting at the window, locked up in his terrors; hating and fearing every living soul including his children who had betrayed him, too, by reaching towards the world which had despised him. There were nine of us. I began to wonder what it could have felt like for such a man to have had nine children whom he could barely feed. He used to make little jokes about our poverty, which never, of course, seemed very funny to us; they could not have seemed very funny to him, either, or else our all too feeble response to them would never have caused such rages. He spent great energy and achieved, to our chagrin, no small amount of success in keeping us away from the people who surrounded us, people who had all-night rent parties to which we listened when we should have been sleeping, people who cursed and drank and flashed razor blades on Lenox Avenue. He could not understand why, if they had so much energy to spare, they could not use it to make their lives better. He treated almost everybody on our block with a most uncharitable asperity and neither they, nor, of course, their children were slow to reciprocate.

The only white people who came to our house were welfare    10
workers and bill collectors. It was almost always my mother who dealt with them, for my father's temper, which was at the mercy of his pride, was never to be trusted. It was clear that he felt their very presence in his home to be a violation: this was conveyed by his carriage, almost ludicrously stiff, and by his voice, harsh and vindictively polite. When I was around nine or ten I wrote a play which was directed by a young, white schoolteacher, a woman, who then took an interest in me, and gave me books to read and, in order to corroborate my theatrical bent, decided to take me

to see what she somewhat tactlessly referred to as "real" plays. Theatergoing was forbidden in our house, but, with the really cruel intuitiveness of a child, I suspected that the color of this woman's skin would carry the day for me. When, at school, she suggested taking me to the theater, I did not, as I might have done if she had been a Negro, find a way of discouraging her, but agreed that she should pick me up at my house one evening. I then, very cleverly, left all the rest to my mother, who suggested to my father, as I knew she would, that it would not be very nice to let such a kind woman make the trip for nothing. Also, since it was a schoolteacher, I imagine that my mother countered the idea of sin with the idea of "education," which word, even with my father, carried a kind of bitter weight.

Before the teacher came my father took me aside to ask *why* she was coming, what *interest* she could possibly have in our house, in a boy like me. I said I didn't know but I, too, suggested that it had something to do with education. And I understood that my father was waiting for me to say something — I didn't quite know what; perhaps that I wanted his protection against this teacher and her "education." I said none of these things and the teacher came and we went out. It was clear, during the brief interview in our living room, that my father was agreeing very much against his will and that he would have refused permission if he had dared. The fact that he did not dare caused me to despise him: I had no way of knowing that he was facing in that living room a wholly unprecedented and frightening situation.

Later, when my father had been laid off from his job, this woman became very important to us. She was really a very sweet and generous woman and went to a great deal of trouble to be of help to us, particularly during one awful winter. My mother called her by the highest name she knew. She said she was a "christian." My father could scarcely disagree but during the four or five years of our relatively close association he never trusted her and was always trying to surprise in her open, Midwestern face the genuine, cunningly hidden, and hideous motivation. In later years, particularly when it began to be clear that this "education" of mine was going to lead me to perdition, he became more explicit and warned me that my white friends in high school were not really my friends and that I would see, when I was older, how white people would do anything to keep a

Negro down. Some of them could be nice, he admitted, but none of them were to be trusted and most of them were not even nice. The best thing was to have as little to do with them as possible. I did not feel this way and I was certain, in my innocence, that I never would.

But the year which preceded my father's death had made a great change in my life. I had been living in New Jersey, working in defense plants, working and living among southerners, white and black. I knew about the south, of course, and about how southerners treated Negroes and how they expected them to behave, but it had never entered my mind that anyone would look at me and expect *me* to behave that way. I learned in New Jersey that to be a Negro meant, precisely, that one was never looked at but was simply at the mercy of the reflexes the color of one's skin caused in other people. I acted in New Jersey as I had always acted, that is as though I thought a great deal of myself—I had to *act* that way—with results that were, simply, unbelievable. I had scarcely arrived before I had earned the enmity, which was extraordinarily ingenious, of all my superiors and nearly all my coworkers. In the beginning, to make matters worse, I simply did not know what was happening. I did not know what I had done, and I shortly began to wonder what *anyone* could possibly do, to bring about such unanimous, active, and unbearably vocal hostility. I knew about jim-crow but I had never experienced it. I went to the same self-service restaurant three times and stood with all the Princeton boys before the counter, waiting for a hamburger and coffee; it was always an extraordinarily long time before anything was set before me; but it was not until the fourth visit that I learned that, in fact, nothing had ever been set before me: I had simply picked something up. Negroes were not served there, I was told, and they had been waiting for me to realize that I was always the only Negro present. Once I was told this, I determined to go there all the time. But now they were ready for me and, though some dreadful scenes were subsequently enacted in that restaurant, I never ate there again.

It was the same story all over New Jersey, in bars, bowling alleys, diners, places to live. I was always being forced to leave, silently, or with mutual imprecations. I very shortly became notorious and children giggled behind me when I passed and their elders whispered or shouted—they really believed that I was mad.

And it did begin to work on my mind, of course; I began to be afraid to go anywhere and to compensate for this I went places to which I really should not have gone and where, God knows, I had no desire to be. My reputation in town naturally enhanced my reputation at work and my working day became one long series of acrobatics designed to keep me out of trouble. I cannot say that these acrobatics succeeded. It began to seem that the machinery of the organization I worked for was turning over, day and night, with but one aim: to eject me. I was fired once, and contrived, with the aid of a friend from New York, to get back on the payroll; was fired again, and bounced back again. It took a while to fire me for the third time, but the third time took. There were no loopholes anywhere. There was not even any way of getting back inside the gates.

That year in New Jersey lives in my mind as though it were   15
the year during which, having an unsuspected predilection for it, I first contracted some dread, chronic disease, the unfailing symptom of which is a kind of blind fever, a pounding in the skull and fire in the bowels. Once this disease is contracted, one can never be really carefree again, for the fever, without an instant's warning, can recur at any moment. It can wreck more important things than race relations. There is not a Negro alive who does not have this rage in his blood — one has the choice, merely, of living with it consciously or surrendering to it. As for me, this fever has recurred in me, and does, and will until the day I die.

My last night in New Jersey, a white friend from New York took me to the nearest big town, Trenton, to go to the movies and have a few drinks. As it turned out, he also saved me from, at the very least, a violent whipping. Almost every detail of that night stands out very clearly in my memory. I even remember the name of the movie we saw because its title impressed me as being so patly ironical. It was a movie about the German occupation of France, starring Maureen O'Hara and Charles Laughton and called *This Land Is Mine*. I remember the name of the diner we walked into when the movie ended: it was the "American Diner." When we walked in the counterman asked what we wanted and I remember answering with the casual sharpness which had become my habit: "We want a hamburger and a cup of coffee, what do you think we want?" I do not know why, after a year of such rebuffs, I so completely failed to anticipate his answer,

which was, of course, "We don't serve Negroes here." This reply
failed to discompose me, at least for the moment. I made some
sardonic comment about the name of the diner and we walked
out into the streets.

This was the time of what was called the "brown-out," when
the lights in all American cities were very dim. When we reen-
tered the streets something happened to me which had the force
of an optical illusion, or a nightmare. The streets were very
crowded and I was facing north. People were moving in every
direction but it seemed to me, in that instant, that all of the people I could see, and many more than that, were moving toward
me, against me, and that everyone was white. I remember how
their faces gleamed. And I felt, like a physical sensation, a *click*
at the nape of my neck as though some interior string connect-
ing my head to my body had been cut. I began to walk. I heard
my friend call after me, but I ignored him. Heaven only knows
what was going on in his mind, but he had the good sense not
to touch me — I don't know what would have happened if he
had — and to keep me in sight. I don't know what was going on
in my mind, either; I certainly had no conscious plan. I wanted
to do something to crush these white faces, which were crushing
me. I walked for perhaps a block or two until I came to an enormous, glittering, and fashionable restaurant in which I knew not
even the intercession of the Virgin would cause me to be served.
I pushed through the doors and took the first vacant seat I saw,
at a table for two, and waited.

I do not know how long I waited and I rather wonder, until
today, what I could possibly have looked like. Whatever I looked
like, I frightened the waitress who shortly appeared, and the
moment she appeared all of my fury flowed towards her. I hated
her for her white face, and for her great, astounded, frightened
eyes. I felt that if she found a black man so frightening I would
make her fright worthwhile.

She did not ask me what I wanted, but repeated, as though
she had learned it somewhere, "We don't serve Negroes here."
She did not say it with the blunt, derisive hostility to which I had
grown so accustomed, but, rather, with a note of apology in her
voice, and fear. This made me colder and more murderous than
ever. I felt I had to do something with my hands. I wanted her to
come close enough for me to get her neck between my hands.

So I pretended not to have understood her, hoping to draw her    20
closer. And she did step a very short step closer, with her pencil
poised incongruously over her pad, and repeated the formula: ". . .
don't serve Negroes here."

Somehow, with the repetition of that phrase, which was
already ringing in my head like a thousand bells of a nightmare,
I realized that she would never come any closer and that I would
have to strike from a distance. There was nothing on the table
but an ordinary water-mug half full of water, and I picked this
up and hurled it with all my strength at her. She ducked and it
missed her and shattered against the mirror behind the bar. And,
with that sound, my frozen blood abruptly thawed, I returned
from wherever I had been, I *saw*, for the first time, the restaurant,
the people with their mouths open, already, as it seemed to me,
rising as one man, and I realized what I had done, and where I
was, and I was frightened. I rose and began running for the door.
A round, pot-bellied man grabbed me by the nape of the neck
just as I reached the doors and began to beat me about the face.
I kicked him and got loose and ran into the streets. My friend
whispered, *"Run!"* and I ran.

My friend stayed outside the restaurant long enough to mis-
direct my pursuers and the police, who arrived, he told me, at
once. I do not know what I said to him when he came to my
room that night. I could not have said much. I felt, in the oddest,
most awful way, that I had somehow betrayed him. I lived it over
and over and over again, the way one relives an automobile accident after it has happened and one finds oneself alone and safe.
I could not get over two facts, both equally difficult for the imagination to grasp, and one was that I could have been murdered.
But the other was that I had been ready to commit murder. I saw
nothing very clearly but I did see this: that my life, my *real* life,
was in danger, and not from anything other people might do but
from the hatred I carried in my own heart.

## II

I had returned home around the second week in June—in great
haste because it seemed that my father's death and my mother's
confinement were both but a matter of hours. In the case of my

mother, it soon became clear that she had simply made a miscalculation. This had always been her tendency and I don't believe that a single one of us arrived in the world, or has since arrived anywhere else, on time. But none of us dawdled so intolerably about the business of being born as did my baby sister. We sometimes amused ourselves, during those endless, stifling weeks, by picturing the baby sitting within in the safe, warm dark, bitterly regretting the necessity of becoming a part of our chaos and stubbornly putting it off as long as possible. I understood her perfectly and congratulated her on showing such good sense so soon. Death, however, sat as purposefully at my father's bedside as life stirred within my mother's womb and it was harder to understand why he so lingered in that long shadow. It seemed that he had bent, and for a long time, too, all of his energies towards dying. Now death was ready for him but my father held back.

All of Harlem, indeed, seemed to be infected by waiting. I had never before known it to be so violently still. Racial tensions throughout this country were exacerbated during the early years of the war, partly because the labor market brought together hundreds of thousands of ill-prepared people and partly because Negro soldiers, regardless of where they were born, received their military training in the south. What happened in defense plants and army camps had repercussions, naturally, in every Negro ghetto. The situation in Harlem had grown bad enough for clergymen, policemen, educators, politicians, and social workers to assert in one breath that there was no "crime wave" and to offer, in the very next breath, suggestions as to how to combat it. These suggestions always seemed to involve playgrounds, despite the fact that racial skirmishes were occurring in the playgrounds, too. Playground or not, crime wave or not, the Harlem police force had been augmented in March, and the unrest grew—perhaps, in fact, partly as a result of the ghetto's instinctive hatred of policemen. Perhaps the most revealing news item, out of the steady parade of reports of muggings, stabbings, shootings, assaults, gang wars, and accusations of police brutality is the item concerning six Negro girls who set upon a white girl in the subway because, as they all too accurately put it, she was stepping on their toes. Indeed she was, all over the nation.

I had never before been so aware of policemen, on foot, on horseback, on corners, everywhere, always two by two. Nor had I

25

ever been so aware of small knots of people. They were on stoops and on corners and in doorways, and what was striking about them, I think, was that they did not seem to be talking. Never, when I passed these groups, did the usual sound of a curse or a laugh ring out and neither did there seem to be any hum of gossip. There was certainly, on the other hand, occurring between them communication extraordinarily intense. Another thing that was striking was the unexpected diversity of the people who made up these groups. Usually, for example, one would see a group of sharpies standing on the street corner, jiving the passing chicks; or a group of older men, usually, for some reason, in the vicinity of a barber shop, discussing baseball scores, or the numbers or making rather chilling observations about women they had known. Women, in a general way, tended to be seen less often together—unless they were church women, or very young girls, or prostitutes met together for an unprofessional instant. But that summer I saw the strangest combinations: large, respectable, churchly matrons standing on the stoops or the corners with their hair tied up, together with a girl in sleazy satin whose face bore the marks of gin and the razor, or heavy-set, abrupt, no-nonsense older men, in company with the most disreputable and fanatical "race" men, or these same "race" men with the sharpies, or these sharpies with the churchly women. Seventh Day Adventists and Methodists and Spiritualists seemed to be hobnobbing with Holyrollers and they were all, alike, entangled with the most flagrant disbelievers; something heavy in their stance seemed to indicate that they had all, incredibly, seen a common vision, and on each face there seemed to be the same strange, bitter shadow.

The churchly women and the matter-of-fact, no-nonsense men had children in the Army. The sleazy girls they talked to had lovers there, the sharpies and the "race" men had friends and brothers there. It would have demanded an unquestioning patriotism, happily as uncommon in this country as it is undesirable, for these people not to have been disturbed by the bitter letters they received, by the newspaper stories they read, not to have been enraged by the posters, then to be found all over New York, which described the Japanese as "yellow-bellied Japs." It was only the "race" men, to be sure, who spoke ceaselessly of being revenged—how this vengeance was to be exacted was not clear—for the indignities and dangers suffered by Negro boys in uniform; but everybody felt a directionless, hopeless bitterness, as well as that panic which can scarcely be suppressed when one knows that a human being one loves is beyond one's reach, and in danger. This helplessness and this gnawing uneasiness does something, at length, to even the toughest mind. Perhaps the best way to sum all this up is to say that the people I knew felt, mainly, a peculiar kind of relief when they knew that their boys were being shipped out of the south, to do battle overseas. It was, perhaps, like feeling that the most dangerous part of a dangerous journey had been passed and that now, even if death should come, it would come with honor and without the complicity of their countrymen. Such a death would be, in short, a fact with which one could hope to live.

It was on the 28th of July, which I believe was a Wednesday, that I visited my father for the first time during his illness and for the last time in his life. The moment I saw him I knew why I had put off this visit so long. I had told my mother that I did not want to see him because I hated him. But this was not true. It was only that I *had* hated him and I wanted to hold on to this hatred. I did not want to look on him as a ruin: it was not a ruin I had hated. I imagine that one of the reasons people cling to their hates so stubbornly is because they sense, once hate is gone, that they will be forced to deal with pain.

We traveled out to him, his older sister and myself, to what seemed to be the very end of a very Long Island. It was hot and dusty and we wrangled, my aunt and I, all the way out, over the fact that I had recently begun to smoke and, as she said, to give myself airs. But I knew that she wrangled with me because she could not bear to face the fact of her brother's dying. Neither could I endure the reality of her despair, her unstated bafflement as to what had happened to her brother's life, and her own. So we wrangled and I smoked and from time to time she fell into a heavy reverie. Covertly, I watched her face, which was the face of an old woman; it had fallen in, the eyes were sunken and lightless; soon she would be dying, too.

In my childhood—it had not been so long ago—I had thought her beautiful. She had been quick-witted and quick-moving and very generous with all the children, and each of her visits had been an event. At one time one of my brothers and myself had thought of running away to live with her. Now she could no longer produce out of her handbag some unexpected and yet familiar delight. She made me feel pity and revulsion and fear. It was awful to realize that she no longer caused me to feel affection. The closer we came to the hospital the more querulous she became and at the same time, naturally, grew more dependent on me. Between pity and guilt and fear I began to feel that there was another me trapped in my skull like a jack-in-the-box who might escape my control at any moment and fill the air with screaming.

She began to cry the moment we entered the room and she    30 saw him lying there, all shriveled and still, like a little black monkey. The great, gleaming apparatus which fed him and would have compelled him to be still even if he had been able to move brought to mind, not beneficence, but torture; the tubes entering his arm made me think of pictures I had seen when a child, of Gulliver, tied down by the pygmies on that island. My aunt wept and wept; there was a whistling sound in my father's throat; nothing was said; he could not speak. I wanted to take his hand, to say something. But I do not know what I could have said, even if he could have heard me. He was not really in that room with us, he had at last really embarked on his journey; and though my aunt told me that he said he was going to meet Jesus, I did not hear anything except that whistling in his throat. The doctor came back and we left, into that unbearable train again, and home. In the morning came the telegram saying that he was dead. Then the house was suddenly full of relatives, friends, hysteria, and confusion and I quickly left my mother and the children to the care of those impressive women, who, in Negro communities at least, automatically appear at times of bereavement armed with lotions, proverbs, and patience, and an ability to cook. I went downtown. By the time I returned, later the same day, my mother had been carried to the hospital and the baby had been born.

## III

For my father's funeral I had nothing black to wear and this posed a nagging problem all day long. It was one of those problems, simple, or impossible of solution, to which the mind insanely clings in order to avoid the mind's real trouble. I spent most of that day at the downtown apartment of a girl I knew, celebrating my birthday with whiskey and wondering what to wear that night. When planning a birthday celebration one naturally does not expect that it will be up against competition from a funeral and this girl had anticipated taking me out that night, for a big dinner and a night club afterwards. Sometime during the course of that long day we decided that we would go out anyway, when my father's funeral service was over. I imagine *I* decided it, since, as the funeral hour approached, it became clearer and clearer to me that I would not know what to do with myself when it was over. The girl, stifling her very lively concern as to the possible effects of the whiskey on one of my father's chief mourners, concentrated on being conciliatory and practically helpful. She found a black shirt for me somewhere and ironed it and, dressed in the darkest pants and jacket I owned, and slightly drunk, I made my way to my father's funeral.

The chapel was full, but not packed, and very quiet. There were, mainly, my father's relatives, and his children, and here and there I saw faces I had not seen since childhood, the faces of my father's one-time friends. They were very dark and solemn now, seeming somehow to suggest that they had known all along that something like this would happen. Chief among the mourners was my aunt, who had quarreled with my father all his life; by which I do not mean to suggest that her mourning was insincere or that she had not loved him. I suppose that she was one of the few people in the world who had, and their incessant quarreling proved precisely the strength of the tie that bound them. The only other person in the world, as far as I knew, whose relationship to my father rivaled my aunt's in depth was my mother, who was not there.

It seemed to me, of course, that it was a very long funeral. But it was, if anything, a rather shorter funeral than most, nor, since there were no overwhelming, uncontrollable expressions of grief, could it be called—if I dare to use the word—successful. The minister who preached my father's funeral sermon was one of the few my father had still been seeing as he neared his end. He presented to us in his sermon a man whom none of us had ever seen—a man thoughtful, patient, and forbearing, a Christian inspiration to all who knew him, and a model for his children. And no doubt the children, in their disturbed and guilty state, were almost ready to believe this; he had been remote enough to be anything and, anyway, the shock of the incontrovertible, that it was really our father lying up there in that casket, prepared the mind for anything. His sister moaned and this grief-stricken moaning was taken as corroboration. The other faces held a dark, non-committal thoughtfulness. This was not the man they had known, but they had scarcely expected to be confronted with *him*; this was, in a sense deeper than questions of fact, the man they had not known, and the man they had not known may have been the real one. The real man, whoever he had been, had suffered and now he was dead: this was all that was sure and all that mattered now. Every man in the chapel hoped that when his hour came he, too, would be eulogized, which is to say forgiven, and that all of his lapses, greeds, errors, and strayings from the truth would be invested with coherence and looked upon with charity. This was perhaps the last thing human beings could give each other and it was what they demanded, after all, of the Lord. Only the Lord saw the midnight tears, only He was present when one of His children, moaning and wringing hands, paced up and down the room. When one slapped one's child in anger the recoil in the heart reverberated through heaven and became part of the pain of the universe. And when the children were hungry and sullen and distrustful and one watched them, daily, growing wilder, and further away, and running headlong into danger, it was the Lord who knew what the charged heart endured as the strap was laid to the backside; the Lord alone who knew what one *would* have said if one had had, like the Lord, the gift of the living word. It was the Lord who knew of the impossibility every parent in that room faced: how to prepare the child for the day when the child would be despised and how to *create* in the child—by what means?—a stronger antidote to this poison than one had found for oneself. The avenues, side streets, bars, billiard halls, hospitals, police stations, and even the playgrounds of Harlem—not to mention the houses of correction, the jails, and the morgue—testified to the potency of the poison while remaining silent as to the efficacy of whatever antidote, irresistibly raising the question of whether or not such an antidote existed; raising, which was worse, the question of whether or not an antidote was desirable; perhaps poison should be fought with poison. With these several schisms in the mind and with more terrors in the heart than could be named, it was better not to judge the man who had gone down under an impossible burden. It was better to remember. *Thou knowest this man's fall; but thou knowest not his wrassling.*

While the preacher talked and I watched the children—years of changing their diapers, scrubbing them, slapping them, taking them to school, and scolding them had had the perhaps inevitable result of making me love them, though I am not sure I knew this then—my mind was busily breaking out with a rash of disconnected impressions. Snatches of popular songs, indecent jokes, bits of books I had read, movie sequences, faces, voices, political issues—I thought I was going mad; all these impressions suspended, as it were, in the solution of the faint nausea produced in me by the heat and liquor. For a moment I had the impression that my alcoholic breath, inefficiently disguised with chewing gum, filled the entire chapel. Then someone began singing one of my father's favorite songs and, abruptly, I was with him, sitting on his knee, in the hot, enormous, crowded church which was the first church we attended. It was the Abyssinia Baptist Church on 138th Street. We had not gone there long. With this image, a host of others came. I had forgotten, in the rage of my growing up, how proud my father had been of me when I was little. Apparently, I had had a voice and my father had liked to show me off before the members of the church. I had forgotten what he had looked like when he was pleased but now I remembered that he had always been grinning with pleasure when my solos ended. I even remembered certain expressions on his face when he teased my mother—had he loved her? I would never know. And when had it all begun to change? For now it seemed that he had not always been cruel. I remembered being taken for a haircut and scraping my knee on the footrest of the barber's chair and I remembered my father's face as he soothed my crying and applied the stinging iodine. Then I remembered our fights, fights which had been of the worst possible kind because my technique had been silence.

I remembered the one time in all our life together when we had really spoken to each other.

It was on a Sunday and it must have been shortly before I left home. We were walking, just the two of us, in our usual silence, to or from church. I was in high school and had been doing a lot of writing and I was, at about this time, the editor of the high school magazine. But I had also been a Young Minister and had been preaching from the pulpit. Lately, I had been taking fewer engagements and preached as rarely as possible. It was said in the church, quite truthfully, that I was "cooling off."

My father asked me abruptly, "You'd rather write than preach, wouldn't you?"

I was astonished at his question—because it was a real question. I answered, "Yes."

That was all we said. It was awful to remember that that was all we had *ever* said.

The casket now was opened and mourners were being led up 40 the aisle to look for the last time on the deceased. The assumption was that the family was too overcome with grief to be allowed to make this journey alone and I watched while my aunt was led to the casket and, muffled in black, and shaking, led back to her seat. I disapproved of forcing the children to look on their dead father, considering that the shock of his death, or, more truthfully, the shock of death as a reality, was already a little more than a child could bear, but my judgment in this matter had been overruled and there they were, bewildered and frightened and very small, being led, one by one, to the casket. But there is also something very gallant about children at such moments. It has something to do with their silence and gravity and with the fact that one cannot help them. Their legs, somehow, seem *exposed*, so that it is at once incredible and terribly clear that their legs are all they have to hold them up.

I had not wanted to go to the casket myself and I certainly had not wished to be led there, but there was no way of avoiding either of these forms. One of the deacons led me up and I looked on my father's face. I cannot say that it looked like him at all. His blackness had been equivocated by powder and there was no suggestion in that casket of what his power had or could have been. He was simply an old man dead, and it was hard to believe that he had ever given anyone either joy or pain. Yet, his life filled that room. Further up the avenue his wife was holding his newborn child. Life and death so close together, and love and hatred, and right and wrong, said something to me which I did not want to hear concerning man, concerning the life of man.

After the funeral, while I was downtown desperately cele-brating my birthday, a Negro soldier, in the lobby of the Hotel Braddock, got into a fight with a white policeman over a Negro girl. Negro girls, white policemen, in or out of uniform, and Negro males—in or out of uniform—were part of the furniture of the lobby of the Hotel Braddock and this was certainly not the first time such an incident had occurred. It was destined, how-ever, to receive an unprecedented publicity, for the fight between the policeman and the soldier ended with the shooting of the sol-dier. Rumor, flowing immediately to the streets outside, stated that the soldier had been shot in the back, an instantaneous and revealing invention, and that the soldier had died protecting a Negro woman. The facts were somewhat different—for example, the soldier had not been shot in the back, and was not dead, and the girl seems to have been as dubious a symbol of womanhood as her white counterpart in Georgia usually is, but no one was interested in the facts. They preferred the invention because this invention expressed and corroborated their hates and fears so perfectly. It is just as well to remember that people are always doing this. Perhaps many of those legends, including Christian-ity, to which the world clings began their conquest of the world with just some such concerted surrender to distortion. The effect, in Harlem, of this particular legend was like the effect of a lit match in a tin of gasoline. The mob gathered before the doors of the Hotel Braddock simply began to swell and to spread in every direction, and Harlem exploded.

The mob did not cross the ghetto lines. It would have been easy, for example, to have gone over Morningside Park on the west side or to have crossed the Grand Central railroad tracks at 125th Street on the east side, to wreak havoc in white neigh-borhoods. The mob seems to have been mainly interested in something more potent and real than the white face, that is, in white power, and the principal damage done during the riot of the summer of 1943 was to white business establishments in Harlem. It might have been a far bloodier story, of course, if, at the hour the riot began, these establishments had still been open. From the Hotel Braddock the mob fanned out, east and west along 125th Street, and for the entire length of Lenox, Seventh, and Eighth avenues. Along each of these avenues, and along each major side street—116th, 125th, 135th, and so on—bars, stores, pawnshops, restaurants, even little luncheonettes had been smashed open and entered and looted—looted, it might be added, with more haste than efficiency. The shelves really looked as though a bomb had struck them. Cans of beans and soup and dog food, along with toilet paper, corn flakes, sardines and milk tumbled every which way, and abandoned cash registers and cases of beer leaned crazily out of the splintered windows and were strewn along the avenues. Sheets, blankets, and clothing of every description formed a kind of path, as though people had dropped them while running. I truly had not realized that Harlem *had* so many stores until I saw them all smashed open; the first time the word *wealth* ever entered my mind in relation to Harlem was when I saw it scattered in the streets. But one's first, incongruous impression of plenty was countered immediately by an impression of waste. None of this was doing anybody any good. It would have been better to have left the plate glass as it had been and the goods lying in the stores.

It would have been better, but it would also have been intolerable, for Harlem had needed something to smash. To smash something is the ghetto's chronic need. Most of the time it is the members of the ghetto who smash each other, and themselves. But as long as the ghetto walls are standing there will always come a moment when these outlets do not work. That summer, for example, it was not enough to get into a fight on Lenox Avenue, or curse out one's cronies in the barber shops. If ever, indeed, the violence which fills Harlem's churches, pool halls, and bars erupts outward in a more direct fashion, Harlem and its citizens are likely to vanish in an apocalyptic flood. That this is not likely to happen is due to a great many reasons, most hidden and powerful among them the Negro's real relation to the white American. This relation prohibits, simply, anything as uncomplicated and satisfactory as pure hatred. In order really to hate white people, one has to blot so much out of the mind—and the heart—that this hatred itself becomes an exhausting and self-destructive pose. But this does not mean, on the other hand, that love comes easily: the white world is too powerful, too complacent, too ready with gratuitous humiliation, and, above all, too ignorant and too innocent for that. One is absolutely forced to make perpetual qualifications and one's own reactions are always canceling each other out. It is this, really, which has driven so many people mad, both white and black. One is always in the position of having to decide between amputation and gangrene. Amputation is swift but time may prove that the amputation was not necessary—or one may delay the amputation too long. Gangrene is slow, but it is impossible to be sure that one is reading one's symptoms right. The idea of going through life as a cripple is more than one can bear, and equally unbearable is the risk of swelling up slowly, in agony, with poison. And the trouble, finally, is that the risks are real even if the choices do not exist.

"But as for me and my house," my father had said, "we will    45 serve the Lord." I wondered, as we drove him to his resting place, what this line had meant for him. I had heard him preach it many times. I had preached it once myself, proudly giving it an interpretation different from my father's. Now the whole thing came back to me, as though my father and I were on our way to Sunday school and I were memorizing the golden text: *And if it seem evil unto you to serve the Lord, choose you this day whom you will serve; whether the gods which your fathers served that were on the other side of the flood, or the gods of the Amorites, in whose land ye dwell: but as for me and my house, we will serve the Lord.* I suspected in these familiar lines a meaning which had never been there for me before. All of my father's texts and songs, which I had decided were meaningless, were arranged before me at his death like empty bottles, waiting to hold the meaning which life would give them for me. This was his legacy: nothing is ever escaped. That bleakly memorable morning I hated the unbelievable streets and the Negroes and whites who had, equally, made them that way. But I knew that it was folly, as my father would have said, this bitterness was folly. It was necessary to hold on to the things that mattered. The dead man mattered, the new life mattered; blackness and whiteness did not matter; to believe that they did was to acquiesce in one's own destruction. Hatred, which could destroy so much, never failed to destroy the man who hated and this was an immutable law.

It began to seem that one would have to hold in the mind forever two ideas which seemed to be in opposition. The first idea was acceptance, the acceptance, totally without rancor, of life as it is, and men as they are: in the light of this idea, it goes without saying that injustice is a commonplace. But this did not mean that one could be complacent, for the second idea was of equal power: that one must never, in one's own life, accept these injustices as commonplace but must fight them with all one's strength. This fight begins, however, in the heart and it now had been laid to my charge to keep my own heart free of hatred and despair. This intimation made my heart heavy and, now that my father was irrecoverable, I wished that he had been beside me so that I could have searched his face for the answers which only the future would give me now.

### For Discussion and Writing

1. Identify all of the different stories Baldwin tells in "Notes of a Native Son."

2. How does Baldwin relate the story of his relationship with his father to the story of the relationship between black and white America?

3. **connections**   When Ta-Nehisi Coates's book *Letter to My Son* was published, reviewers often compared his writing to Baldwin's. Read Coates's "The Paranoid Style of American Policing" (p. 106) alongside "Notes of a Native Son." Compare the word choice, the structure and rhythm of the sentences, and the use of rhetorical devices. Do you see similarities in the way the two authors write? Do you see differences?

4. Write about a moment in your life when you were extremely angry. How did you handle it, and what does the experience tell you about yourself now?

5. **looking further**   It is one thing to handle yourself well when you are angry; it is another thing for a large group of people to handle itself well in the face of extreme provocation and injustice. Research the history of nonviolent protest. What has enabled such movements to avoid letting their anger lead them to meet violence with violence?

# WILLIAM F. BUCKLEY JR.

# Why Don't We Complain?

*William F. Buckley Jr. (1925–2008), born in New York City, was one of the leading voices of conservative politics. Best known as founder and longtime editor of the opinion journal* National Review *and host of the PBS political talk show* Firing Line, *Buckley also wrote a syndicated column, contributed to many magazines, and authored more than forty fiction and nonfiction books.*

*"Why Don't We Complain?" originally appeared in* Esquire *in 1960. Buckley's connection of political apathy to failures to act in other parts of life is still timely today. As you read, though, think about all that has happened in America since the writing of this article.*

It was the very last coach and the only empty seat on the entire train, so there was no turning back. The problem was to breathe. Outside the temperature was below freezing. Inside the railroad car, the temperature must have been about 85 degrees. I took off my overcoat, and a few minutes later my jacket, and noticed that the car was flecked with the white shirts of passengers. I soon found my hand moving to loosen my tie. From one end of the car to the other, as we rattled through Westchester County, we sweated; but we did not moan.

I watched the train conductor appear at the head of the car. "Tickets, all tickets, please!" In a more virile age, I thought, the passengers would seize the conductor and strap him down on a seat over the radiator to share the fate of his patrons. He shuffled down the aisle, picking up tickets, punching commutation cards. *No one addressed a word to him.* He approached my seat, and I drew a deep breath of resolution. "Conductor," I began with a considerable edge to my voice. . . . Instantly the doleful eyes of my seatmate turned tiredly from his newspaper to fix me with a resentful stare: what question could be so important as to justify my sibilant intrusion into his stupor? I was shaken by those eyes. I am incapable of making a discreet fuss, so I mumbled a question about what time were we due in Stamford (I didn't even ask whether it would be before or after dehydration could be expected to set in), got my reply, and went back to my newspaper and to wiping my brow.

The conductor had nonchalantly walked down the gauntlet of eighty sweating American freemen, and not one of them had asked him to explain why the passengers in that car had been consigned to suffer. There is nothing to be done when the temperature *outdoors* is 85 degrees, and indoors the air conditioner has broken down; obviously when that happens there is nothing to do, except perhaps curse the day that one was born. But when the temperature outdoors is below freezing, it takes a positive act of will on somebody's part to set the temperature *indoors* at 85. Somewhere a valve was turned too far, a furnace overstoked, a thermostat maladjusted: something that could easily be remedied by turning off the heat and allowing the great outdoors to come indoors. All this is so obvious. What is not obvious is what has happened to the American people.

It isn't just the commuters, whom we have come to visualize as a supine breed who have got onto the trick of suspending their sensory faculties twice a day while they submit to the creeping dissolution of the railroad industry. It isn't just they who have given up trying to rectify irrational vexations. It is the American people everywhere.

A few weeks ago at a large movie theatre I turned to my wife 5 and said, "The picture is out of focus." "Be quiet," she answered. I obeyed. But a few minutes later I raised the point again, with mounting impatience. "It will be all right in a minute," she said apprehensively. (She would rather lose her eyesight than be around when I make one of my infrequent scenes.) I waited. It was *just* out of focus—not glaringly out, but out. My vision is 20–20, and I assume that is the vision, adjusted, of most people in the movie house. So, after hectoring my wife throughout the first reel, I finally prevailed upon her to admit that it *was* off, and very annoying. We then settled down, coming to rest on the presumption that: a) someone connected with the management of the theatre must soon notice the blur and make the correction; or b) that someone seated near the rear of the house would make the complaint in behalf of those of us up front; or c) that—any minute now — the entire house would explode into catcalls and foot stamping, calling dramatic attention to the irksome distortion.

What happened was nothing. The movie ended, as it had begun, just out of focus, and as we trooped out, we stretched our faces in a variety of contortions to accustom the eye to the shock of normal focus.

I think it is safe to say that everybody suffered on that occasion. And I think it is safe to assume that everyone was expecting someone else to take the initiative in going back to speak to the manager. And it is probably true even that if we had supposed the movie would run right through with the blurred image, someone surely would have summoned up the purposive indignation to get up out of his seat and file his complaint.

But notice that no one did. And the reason no one did is because we are all increasingly anxious in America to be unobtrusive, we are reluctant to make our voices heard, hesitant about claiming our rights; we are afraid that our cause is unjust, or that if it is not unjust, that it is ambiguous; or if not even that, that it is too trivial to justify the horrors of a confrontation with Authority; we will sit in an oven or endure a racking headache before undertaking a head-on, I'm-here-to-tell-you complaint. That tendency to passive compliance, to a heedless endurance is something to keep one's eyes on — in sharp focus.

I myself can occasionally summon the courage to complain, but I cannot, as I have intimated, complain softly. My own instinct is so strong to let the thing ride, to forget about it — to expect that someone will take the matter up, when the grievance is collective, in my behalf — that it is only when the provocation is at a very special key, whose vibrations touch simultaneously a complexus of nerves, allergies, and passions, that I catch fire and find the reserves of courage and assertiveness to speak up. When that happens, I get quite carried away. My blood gets hot, my brow wet, I become unbearably and unconscionably sarcastic and bellicose: I am girded for a total showdown.

Why should that be? Why could not I (or anyone else) on that railroad coach have said simply to the conductor, "Sir," — I take that back: that sounds sarcastic — "Conductor, would you be good enough to turn down the heat? I am extremely hot. In fact,

10

I tend to get hot every time the temperature reaches 85 degr—"
Strike that last sentence. Just end it with the simple statement
that you are extremely hot, and let the conductor infer the cause.

Every New Year's Eve I resolve to do something about the
Milquetoast in me and vow to speak up, calmly, for my rights,
and for the betterment of our society, on every appropriate occasion. Entering last New Year's Eve I was fortified in my resolve
because that morning at breakfast I had had to ask the waitress
three times for a glass of milk. She finally brought it—after I had
finished my eggs, which is when I don't want it any more. I did
not have the manliness to order her to take the milk back, but
settled instead for a cowardly sulk, and ostentatiously refused
to drink the milk—though I later paid for it—rather than state
plainly to the hostess, as I should have, why I had not drunk it,
and would not pay for it.

So by the time the New Year ushered out the Old, riding in on
my morning's indignation and stimulated by the gastric juices of
resolution that flow so faithfully on New Year's Eve, I rendered
my vow. Henceforward I would conquer my shyness, my despi-
cable disposition to supineness. I would speak out like a man
against the unnecessary annoyances of our time.

Forty-eight hours later, I was standing in line at the ski-repair
store in Pico Peak, Vermont. All I needed, to get on with my
skiing, was the loan, for one minute, of a small screwdriver, to
tighten a loose binding. Behind the counter in the workshop
were two men. One was industriously engaged in servicing the
complicated requirements of a young lady at the head of the
line, and obviously he would be tied up for quite a while. The
other—"Jiggs," his workmate called him—was a middle-aged
man, who sat in a chair puffing a pipe, exchanging small talk
with his working partner. My pulse began its telltale acceleration.
The minutes ticked on. I stared at the idle shopkeeper, hoping to
shame him into action, but he was impervious to my telepathic
reproof and continued his small talk with his friend, brazenly
insensitive to the nervous demands of six good men who were
raring to ski.

Suddenly my New Year's Eve resolution struck me. It was
now or never. I broke from my place in line and marched to the
counter. I was going to control myself. I dug my nails into my
palms. My effort was only partially successful:

"If you are not too busy," I said icily, "would you mind handing    15
me a screwdriver?"

Work stopped and everyone turned his eyes on me, and I experienced that mortification I always feel when I am the center of
centripetal shafts of curiosity, resentment, perplexity.

But the worst was yet to come. "I am sorry, sir," said Jiggs def-
erentially, moving the pipe from his mouth. "I am not supposed
to move. I have just had a heart attack." That was the signal for
a great whirring noise that descended from heaven. We looked,
stricken, out the window, and it appeared as though a cyclone
had suddenly focused on the snowy courtyard between the shop
and the ski lift. Suddenly a gigantic Army helicopter materialized,
and hovered down to a landing. Two men jumped out of the plane
carrying a stretcher, tore into the ski shop, and lifted the shopkeeper onto the stretcher. Jiggs bade his companion good-by, was
whisked out the door, into the plane, up to the heavens, down—we
learned—to a nearby Army hospital. I looked up manfully—into a
score of man-eating eyes. I put the experience down as a reversal.

As I write this, on an airplane, I have run out of paper and
need to reach into my briefcase under my legs for more. I cannot do this until my empty lunch tray is removed from my lap.
I arrested the stewardess as she passed empty-handed down the
aisle on the way to the kitchen to fetch the lunch trays for the
passengers up forward who haven't been served yet. "Would you
please take my tray?" "Just a *moment*, sir," she said, and marched
on sternly. Shall I tell her that since she is headed for the kitchen
*anyway*, it cannot delay the feeding of the other passengers by the
two seconds necessary to stash away my empty tray? Or remind
her that not fifteen minutes ago she spoke unctuously into the
loud-speaker the words undoubtedly devised by the airline's
highly paid public-relations counselor: "If there is anything I or
Miss French can do for you to make your trip more enjoyable,
*please* let us—" I have run out of paper.

I think the observable reluctance of the majority of Americans
to assert themselves in minor matters is related to our increased
sense of helplessness in an age of technology and centralized
political and economic power. For generations, Americans who
were too hot, or too cold, got up and did something about it. Now
we call the plumber, or the electrician, or the furnace man. The
habit of looking after our own needs obviously had something to

do with the assertiveness that characterized the American family familiar to readers of American literature. With the technification of life goes our direct responsibility for our material environment, and we are conditioned to adopt a position of helplessness not only as regards the broken air conditioner, but as regards the overheated train. It takes an expert to fix the former, but not the latter: yet these distinctions, as we withdraw into helplessness, tend to fade away.

Our notorious political apathy is a related phenomenon. 20 Every year, whether the Republican or the Democratic Party is in office, more and more power drains away from the individual to feed vast reservoirs in far-off places; and we have less and less say about the shape of events which shape our future. From this aberration of personal power comes the sense of resignation with which we accept the political dispensations of a powerful government whose hold upon us continues to increase.

An editor of a national weekly news magazine told me a few years ago that as few as a dozen letters of protest against an editorial stance of his magazine was enough to convene a plenipotentiary meeting of the board of editors to review policy. "So few people complain, or make their voices heard," he explained to me, "that we assume a dozen letters represent the inarticulated views of thousands of readers." In the past ten years, he said, the volume of mail has noticeably decreased, even though the circulation of his magazine has risen.

When our voices are finally mute, when we have finally suppressed the natural instinct to complain, whether the vexation is trivial or grave, we shall have become automatons, incapable of feeling. When Premier Khrushchev first came to this country late in 1959 he was primed, we are informed, to experience the bitter resentment of the American people against his tyranny, against his persecutions, against the movement which is responsible for the then great number of American deaths in Korea, for billions in taxes every year, and for life everlasting on the brink of disasters; but Khrushchev was pleasantly surprised, and reported back to the Russian people that he had been met with overwhelming cordiality (read: apathy), except, to be sure, for "a few fascists who followed me around with their wretched posters, and should be . . . horsewhipped."

I may be crazy, but I say there would have been lots more posters in a society where train temperatures in the dead of winter are not allowed to climb up to 85 degrees without complaint.

## For Discussion and Writing

1. What are Buckley's three examples of situations in which one might complain?

2. What does Buckley argue is the relationship between our failure to complain and our failure to care about politics? How does he attempt to convince us of that relationship?

3. **connections** Compare Buckley's argument about our behavior as citizens with Barbara Lazear Ascher's in "On Compassion" (p. 43). Do they focus on the same kinds of behaviors? How do their differences in subject relate to the differences in their essays?

4. Write an essay in which you reflect on your own political feelings and orientation. What do you care about, and why? How do you demonstrate your beliefs?

5. **looking further** Research one of your political ideals. Where does it come from, historically? How is it relevant in contemporary politics? Are there ways in which this ideal has been realized? Ways in which it has not? Are there things you think government should/could do to move closer to it?

DANNY CHAU

# The Burning Desire for Hot Chicken

*Danny Chau is a born and bred Los Angeles sportswriter who also writes about food. He worked as an editorial assistant, assistant editor, and associate editor for* Grantland, *a now-defunct website focusing on long-form journalism about popular culture and sports. He is now an associate editor at* Grantland's *successor,* The Ringer, *for which he writes about basketball and food. This essay originally appeared in* The Ringer.

*In his work at* Grantland *and* The Ringer, *Chau has often taken an eclectic approach to his subject, whether it is a particular dish or a basketball player, finding various ways of approaching his subject. In his essay "The Burning Desire for Hot Chicken," Chau writes about hot chicken the dish, but also about the chemistry of heat, about local culture, and about his childhood. As you read, pay attention to the ways in which his account strays from the straightforward, circling his central concern until he captures it.*

Years ago, when he was still the mayor of Nashville, Bill Purcell received a call from England. The son of Prince Charles's girlfriend wanted to meet him. *I don't know if that's something I need to do,* he thought to himself. The voice on the other line clarified the purpose of the meeting: He wanted to eat hot chicken. "Well, then I'm in," Purcell blurted out.

Purcell is a man who, while serving as majority leader in the Tennessee House of Representatives, declared Prince's Hot Chicken Shack to be the best restaurant in Tennessee. In 2005, the mayor and his royalty-adjacent guest met at Prince's and sat down to chat. Purcell's guest immediately said, "I will have the extra hot."

"Oh, don't do that," Purcell said. "You should have the hot chicken." He pointed to the window art that greets visitors on their way in. "See? Prince's *Hot* Chicken Shack. That's what they serve."

The men walked up to the counter to place their order through a little square opening in the wall which conceals the kitchen from civilians. The exchange feels like a negotiation at a box office.

"One quarter chicken, brown and white, extra hot," the guest said.     5

Prince's owner Andre Prince Jeffries attempted to talk him off the ledge, but extra hot is what he got. Purcell walked back to the table with a smile. He knew what was coming.

The Brit was Tom Parker Bowles, the son of Camilla, (now) duchess of Cornwall. Parker Bowles, a prominent food writer, was on a research trip for his book, *The Year of Eating Dangerously: A Global Adventure in Search of Culinary Extremes*. He got what he wanted, and he loved his first bite. Then it started to hurt. Then came the tears. Bowles would dedicate two pages in his book to describing the misery the Prince's extra-hot chicken put him through. "The only thing willing me on is pure, pig-headed pride," Bowles wrote. "Each mouthful becomes more and more painful and numbing until I'm uncertain as to whether I'm swallowing my saliva or just dribbling it out of my mouth."

"He thought he was going to die," Purcell told me.

Chicken was a dish created for the express purpose of bringing a man to his knees. Its origin myth wasn't the result of a mistake, like chocolate chip cookies, Coca-Cola, or the French dip sandwich. Hot chicken was premeditated; to this day, every bite of Nashville hot chicken is touched by the spectral presence of a betrayed lover.

The story remains such a foundational part of hot chicken's allure that it bears repeating (and, frankly, it never gets old):     10 Back in the 1930s, there was a man named Thornton Prince, who had a reputation around town as a serial philanderer. His girlfriend at the time, sick of his shit and spending her nights alone, decided to do something about it. After a long night out, Prince came home to breakfast. His girlfriend made fried chicken, his favorite. But before serving it, she caked on the most volatile spices she had in the pantry—presumably cayenne pepper and mustard seed, among other things. If it didn't kill him, at least he would reevaluate his life choices. He didn't do either—Prince fell harder for the over-spiced piece of chicken than he did for any woman he'd ever courted. Prince implored her to make it for his family and friends—they all loved it, too.

An act of revenge became a neighborhood treasure, and Nashville's one true indigenous food. The identity of Prince's girlfriend (the real innovator here) has been lost to time, but the fearful flashes of mortality that hot chicken eaters have experienced for more than 80 years gives a particular angel in heaven her wings.

Technically, hot chicken is straightforward. The flavor profile has likely evolved since Thornton Prince took his first bite, and every restaurant claims to have a secret preparation. But in essence, it is fried chicken coated in a paste largely consisting of cayenne and other dried spices with a splash of hot oil from the fryer. Because the paste is oil-based and searingly hot, the skin stays crisp, unlike buffalo wings, which are prone to either drying out or getting gloppy in a hurry. (Hot chicken predates the first buffalo wing by three decades.) The finished product has a lurid, reddish hue that, depending on the spice level, ranges from California sunset to the bowels of hell. Hot chicken is served with two mandatory accompaniments: a slice of plain old white bread upon which the bird is perched and a few pickle chips skewered to the chicken with a toothpick.

That's it. It is, in my opinion, a damn-near perfect dish. The lines that separate love and hate, pleasure and pain, expectation and reality—they dissolve when you eat hot chicken. If you do it right, it will hurt. You might cry. And you will spend the next week thinking about when you might have it again.

Hot chicken has become one of the biggest national food trends of the last few years, but I didn't come to Nashville to Columbus a dish that has existed for nearly a century. I did come to see, from the source, why America's fascination with hot chicken is exploding at this particular moment. As recently as 10 years ago, hot chicken wasn't a universally acknowledged dish, even in its birthplace. For the majority of its existence, it was largely contained within the predominantly black East Nashville neighborhoods that created it, kept out of view under the shroud of lawful segregation.

Prince's old location was close to the Ryman Auditorium,    15
where the Grand Ole Opry performed for more than three
decades. Its late-night hours were perfect for performers, and
early adopters like Country Music Hall of Famer George Morgan
helped build a devout following. But in the segregation era, to
get their fix, they had to walk through a side door. Prince's was
operated like a white establishment in reverse: blacks order in
front, whites out back.

Even after desegregation, hot chicken remained hidden in
plain sight for much of Nashville, due to what Purcell described
as "comfort" on both sides of the racial divide.

"I think in terms of the first 50 years or more, there was a
satisfaction by the family and families that were making hot
chicken that they were doing something special and worthwhile,"
Purcell said. "But they had no particular inclination or desire in
those days to franchise it, or move it beyond their own capacity
to ensure its quality. And it satisfied them to be that way, and
that's how they proceeded. Not unlike in some ways, aspects of
Nashville at that time."

Nashville appears to be growing into itself, and growing to
accommodate strangers; you can tell from the afternoon con-
gestion on the interstate, where the gridlock is beginning to
resemble the kind you'd experience in Atlanta or Austin. "There
are a lot of people moving here from California," Andrew, an
Uber driver, told me. "And the traffic is as bad as Los Angeles."
Nashville is different now.

There's 2,000 miles between us, but Nashville and I have
mutual interests.

My favorite restaurants could double as a Medieval Times-    20
esque show for misandrists, where the male tears flow like wine.
In high school, a group of friends and I ventured to a traditional
Sichuanese restaurant just up the street from my school in the
city of San Gabriel, a suburb east of Los Angeles where more
than 60 percent of residents were Asian as of the 2010 census. We
ordered a traditional hot pot full of meats and vegetables covered
in a bubbling broth, loaded with dried whole chili pods and anes-
thetic Sichuan peppercorns, and topped off with what looked
like a tanker explosion of crimson chili oil. On a count of three,
we all agreed to lean in and inhale deeply. Instantly, everyone at
the table broke out into a fit of uncontrollable coughing. It was

the most demanding meal any of us had ever eaten. It wasn't just a memorable lunch, it was one of the best I'll ever have. These are the kinds of restaurants I'm in constant search of, where what's being served challenges sensory norms and forces you to reckon with food's capacity to change you in the moment — not just emotionally, but physically.

My search brought me to Prince's, but it didn't stop there. In planning my journey, I found inspiration in Anthony Bourdain, who had tweeted earlier this year that eating hot chicken was a "three day commitment." And so that's what I did. I committed myself to eating at three hot chicken joints in three days, ordering the highest spice level available at each one.

I realize now that isn't what Bourdain meant.

### THURSDAY, 9:28 P.M. // PRINCE'S HOT CHICKEN SHACK

*Spice Level: XXXHot*

"Boy, I want to see you eat this," the woman taking my order said.

Those who order the highest spice level at Prince's — usually tourists, as there seems to be an unwritten rule as a Nashvillian to never order the extra hot — are almost always discouraged by the staff. Maybe it was the crazed grin I had walking up the counter, but I was met with minimal resistance. "You must have been convincing," Purcell told me. "Because they will normally not just question the order, but attempt to talk you down." All I got was an offer of ranch dressing, free of charge. I politely declined.

Nothing could have surprised me upon first bite, except for what happened: nothing. No tears, no sweat, minimal pain. Maybe I should've seen that coming.    25

Before career aspirations, before standardized testing — hell, before first grade — I was fixated on increasing my spice tolerance, on fulfilling a family hallmark. As a 4-year-old, I cautiously began dipping my food into sriracha; as a 10-year-old, I was my brother's sous-chef and designated taste tester, helping him chop habaneros for a salsa at his first college house party; last year, I ate a Carolina Reaper, the hottest chili on the planet, in front of a camera. Two decades of pushing my boundaries had culminated in eating the XXXHot at Prince's, in front of a petrified couple visiting from Chicago, without a hitch.

Desensitizing oneself to the burn of chilies broadens the palate. When the sting is no longer a hindrance, it's easier to focus on actual flavor. Prince's spice blend is heavily weighted toward cayenne and paprika, among other spices; the earthiness almost reminiscent of nuclear Oaxacan *mole*. It's hard to overstate how beautiful this fried chicken is. It glows, with a sheen emanating from every crevice. The flesh itself is perfect; Prince's specifically is lauded for a clandestine marination technique that begins before the bird ever hits the fryer. Whatever they do in their preparation made that fried chicken the best I've ever had, hot or not.

Was I a little disappointed by the initial heat of Prince's? Sure. But Jeffries, the great-niece of Thornton Prince, calls her chicken a 24-hour chicken, and she tells no lies. My mouth may not have minded all the cayenne, but my stomach was under siege. The pain wasn't sharp, like a knife stabbing through you. It was round and blunt, but incessant, like blows from a hammer tenderizing you from the inside. It can do strange things to a person, as my hallucinatory dreams that night would attest. Even I hadn't escaped the wrath of Prince's mythic heat.

There are photos on Yelp of people passed out on Prince's tables trying to finish their food. Purcell once took a coworker to the restaurant for lunch. The woman behind the window shook her head. His coworker was visibly pregnant. "She can't have hot chicken," the employee said. "She'll have to come back after the baby is born." Of course, there are also tales of pregnant women who have asked their partners to fetch Prince's hot chicken for takeout in hopes of expediting the delivering process. Pain is pain, I suppose.

But the strange mysticism surrounding the business doesn't end with its alleged childbirth-inducing properties. Prince's calls a small, bumpy strip mall just off the Dickerson Pike in East Nashville its home, in an area known to be a hotbed for prostitution. And there are countless stories about the role hot chicken plays as an aphrodisiac for locals. Andre Prince Jeffries has seen firsthand the rabid sexual appetite hot chicken can cast upon diners.

30

"We do have a lady that comes and she's been coming for about as long as I've been in business, she and others," Jeffries told the Southern Foodways Alliance in 2006. "And she gets it hot. She brings her suitors down here, different suitors. She comes always on the weekend and she gets it hot. One night, she just couldn't wait to get out, so the finale was on the hood of a car parked in front of the chicken shack. She's not the only one. . . . We just shut our eyes and continue to do our work, what we're good at. Hey, different things turn different people on."

But why? And, more importantly, how? For those answers, we'll need a quick science lesson. Capsaicin, the compound in chilis that causes a burning sensation, activates a receptor in the body called TRPV1, the same receptor activated when the body comes in contact with anything hotter than 109 degrees Fahrenheit. Capsaicin is a fat-soluble compound, which is normally a tidbit used to tell you to drink milk, not water to quell the heat. But in hot chicken's case, it explains why the dish is so damn hot. All the capsaicin in the spice mix is drawn out in the oil-based application, so with every bite, the compound floods the receptors in your mouth, effectively signalling to your body that you've committed self-immolation.

The rest of the body responds accordingly. Your temperature increases. You start sweating profusely. The blood vessels in your face begin to dilate to rush blood in and out of the problem site, causing swelling and redness. Snot is dripping from your nose. But then you start to feel loopy. The body thinks it's on fire, so it unleashes a wave of endorphins to help quell the burning. You start to feel something akin to a runner's high. The sharp stinging pain will subside, but the rush — and subsequent sense of tranquility — lasts a bit longer.

But that's taking into account only one biological process that goes into eating hot chicken. As an imaginary fire envelops the senses, the body processes the fact that you're eating some of the best fried chicken in the country. "Palatable foods are working on similar reward centers in the brain [compared to drugs like cocaine, amphetamine, and heroin]," said Matthew Young, a neuroscientist who spent three years researching the effects of MDMA at Emory University. "That's what makes us like certain foods more than others." The pleasure and pain of hot chicken comes in layers — in waves. It is a simple dish, but what it inspires in the body is as multivalent as a designer drug.

All that science still doesn't explain impulsive sex on the hood    35
of a car in front of an entire restaurant full of people.

"Based on what I know about the brain and what I know about people, first of all, there are obvious environmental factors involved," Young said. "I assume people are eating this stuff late at night. I'm assuming they're eating this stuff after being out and drinking. So if you're already kind of drunk and your inhibitions are down, and you're increasing your perceived body temperature by eating this very spicy chicken — all of these things, environmental as well as biological, probably work together to increase the likelihood of two people looking across the table at each other and wanting to get down."

Hot chicken's mythology has grown immensely in the past decade, but it's hard to divorce the dish's allure from the over-the-top experiences Prince's has fostered over its nearly 80 years.

"It's funny," Purcell, the former mayor, said. "It's a place where nothing seems particularly crazy. It doesn't matter, somehow, whatever people are saying or doing, it all seems just fine."

## FRIDAY, 10:20 P.M. // BOLTON'S SPICY CHICKEN & FISH

### Spice level: Extra Hot

After chatting with people at Nashville bars and restaurants, it seemed that Bolton's Spicy Chicken & Fish was more often the site of out-of-body experiences. "Yeah, you have to try Prince's, but I died at Bolton's," a bartender told me. "And if you're going there, get the hot fish."

Nashville was recently rated the friendliest city in America,    40
according to *Travel + Leisure,* so I wasn't going to ignore the kindness and wisdom of locals. Along with the extra-hot chicken leg, I ordered an extra-hot fried catfish sandwich.

Bolton's co-owner Dollye Ingram-Matthews included fish on the menu as a way of preserving one of her cherished childhood memories: the backyard fish fry in her neighborhood, which began to disappear as she grew older. What is placed before you at Bolton's might seem a bit unorthodox to an outsider: a whole filet breaded and deep-fried, with a healthy dousing of cayenne, raw onion slivers, pickle chips, and a squeeze of French's yellow mustard between two pieces of plain white sandwich bread, the filet overflowing the sides to a comical degree. It may be a humble dish of humble origin, but it weaves a web of interconnected flavors, textures, and sensations: the cayenne is boosted by the acidic components surrounding it, the delicate crisp of the fish is embraced by the pillowy nature of the bread. After a few beers, and the mile walk from Dino's in which Gallatin Avenue curves into Main Street, the fish sandwich at Bolton's feels like destiny.

The chicken is good, too, though less cosmically aligned. The spice application in Bolton's is dryer than what you'll find at Prince's, akin to a Memphis barbecue dry rub. The individual granules of the spice mixture are visible on a piece of Bolton's chicken; the residual shake glitters the piece of white bread beneath. The cayenne mixture itself has a brighter heat than Prince's, and, to my tongue, hotter, too.

Ingram-Matthews walked by to check on me. "Is that hot enough for you?"

It would've been nice to have a few tears fall out of my eyes, but, yes. I told her it's hotter than what I ate at Prince's. "Of course it is," she replied, with calm certitude. "It's what we put in it."

Bolton's is a celebration of Bolton Polk, the uncle of    45 Ingram-Matthews's husband, Bolton Matthews, and his contributions to the proliferation of hot chicken. Polk was the owner of Columbo's, a hot chicken shack, that, for a time, was Prince's only worthy competition to the throne. The two businesses shared roots. Polk was the former fry cook at Prince's before a quarrel with the Prince family had him jumping ship and starting his own business. Grand Ole Opry singer George Morgan was a frequent customer and loved Polk's chicken so much he had a chemist analyze the spice blend so he'd be able to replicate it at home.

Purcell remembers Columbo's well. It was where he had his first bite of hot chicken. "I can actually look out the window of my office and see where it was," he said. The former mayor generally speaks in measured, gentle tones, but is often consumed by his own emotions talking about the city and its food staple.

"I remember at that moment thinking that I'd never had any-thing like this, I don't think there is anything like this—I think this might be the best thing I've ever had. And that's a memory you hopefully never lose. I haven't."

Purcell's devotion to the dish over the years led him to plan a Nashville hot chicken festival in 2006 while he was still mayor. It was Nashville's bicentennial year, and Purcell could think of no better way to celebrate the city than by paying a tribute to one of its great delicacies. Without a tinge of haughtiness in his voice, Purcell credits the hot chicken festival for the dish's propulsion into a Nashville mainstream cultural hallmark. "I think that the festival itself made it clear to people who haven't focused on it, or had it, or understood it before, just how unique and special it is—that it is ours," he said. "That it started here and it will always be ours, as long as we support it and keep it alive."

Music City Hot Chicken Festival celebrated its 10th year this summer. It's held on the Fourth of July every year, and while it may seem strange to want to share a day with the greatest celebration of America, Purcell figured there was no better set-ting. "It's one of those times when people are celebrating the nature of their civic relationships," Purcell said. "[It is] the one day of the year where you could be sure that everybody would be thinking about what it meant to be a person in Nashville, in America."

## SATURDAY, 11:40 A.M. // HATTIE B's

*Spice level: Shut the Cluck Up*

It was strange, yet reassuring, to hear Purcell talk about hot chicken as an affirmation of the American spirit. Hot chicken reflects certain attitudes and values about food and culture that I didn't associate as American. It was certainly an America I'd longed for, but one I wasn't sure existed—an America that didn't always process extremes as pure gimmickry. The idea of a "challenging" food bringing people together in an immer-sive experience was always something I attributed more to my Southeast Asian upbringing.

It's not that America doesn't have a history of chili consumption: 50
The Hatch chili is a staple of New Mexico, and we'll always have

people experimenting with new weapons-grade sauces, but New Mexico chilies aren't cultivated specifically for heat, and toying with capsaicin extract is more of a sub-subcultural pastime. Hot chicken is an anomaly, a kind of extreme so rarely celebrated by Americans en masse. It's a dish that outlasted the Great Depression and segregation in America, and lived long enough to see itself become a modern American food trend and symbol of gentrification.

Just around the corner from Prince's and a short walk down Dickerson Pike is a KFC. Earlier this year, the chain took hot chicken and ran it through the Colonel's Transmutation Chamber, delivering KFC's Nashville Hot Chicken, a castrated product that, by mere mention of the word "Nashville," is meant to reinforce their modern branding: *vaguely Southern, vaguely something*.

Tuesday is hot chicken night at Zingerman's in Ann Arbor, Michigan. New hot chicken specialists have opened in the New York City, Seattle, and Chicago metropolitan areas this year alone. My first bite of hot chicken came courtesy of Howlin' Ray's in Los Angeles. Owner Johnny Ray Zone has worked for Gordon Ramsay, Joël Robuchon, and Nobu Matsuhisa, but found his calling during a brief stint with Sean Brock's Southern bastion Husk in Nashville, where he was first exposed to hot chicken. Together with his wife, Amanda, he decided to bring a souvenir back to his hometown, initially as a food truck. Now, it's a limited-hours storefront in a shopping complex in L.A.'s rapidly gentrifying Chinatown.

Stylistically, the chicken at Howlin' Ray's is highly influenced by Bolton's dry application. It's a spiritually faithful recreation: Howlin', the hottest option on their menu, is at least as hot as anything I've had from the source. I choked on my first bite of Howlin' Ray's hot chicken. My eyes geysered. I lost control of my body. I was in love.

Hot chicken's widespread popularity suggests a shift in the national palate. But it's a dish rooted in a strong sense of place; you'll always know how to go directly to the source. The most celebrated and emblematic dish of one of the 25 most populous cities in the country is something designed to hurt you. I'd never felt more American than when I was eating hot chicken in Nashville.

I wanted to make one last stop before boarding my flight back    55
home. Hattie B's, established in 2012, is one of the newer hot
chicken joints in the city; its location in midtown Nashville makes
it a tourist-friendly alternative to many other iconic hot chicken
shacks. I was skeptical. Hattie B's was a topic of discussion in
nearly all of my Uber rides. On my way to Prince's, my driver,
Hicham, wondered why I wasn't going to Hattie B's, which he
heard was the best. (Hicham had never tried hot chicken before).

On my way back from Prince's, my driver Eugene and I
exchanged our versions of the Thornton Prince fable, and he,
too, wondered why, as a tourist, I didn't try Hattie B's first. "Well,
I'm glad you went to Prince's," Eugene said. "The guys at Hattie
B's once sent their workers out to Prince's to try to steal their
marination recipe, try to get that flavor. But they obviously
couldn't."

Hattie B's had been open only 30 minutes, but the line—mostly
white, mostly tourists—bent around the restaurant and ran down
the street. While there are a few tables in the store itself, most ate
from the trendy, raised patio deck. At Prince's and Bolton's, there
was a sense of familial warmth, the product of years, maybe even
generations, of patronage. Hugs were exchanged by members of
the community who just happened to stop in for a bite at the
same time. Considering that Hattie B's hasn't even made to a
half-decade of existence, it might be unfair to pit the restaurant
against that standard, but in its four years, Hattie B's already has
three locations in two states; Prince's, after nearly eight decades
of serving hot chicken, only recently announced an upcoming
second location. Same product, different ethos—though the
enterprising spirit Hattie B's has demonstrated in its franchising
is American, too.

I'll cop to being a little discriminatory. I'd assumed this third
wave of hot chicken purveyors would dilute the product, at least
a bit. When it was time to order, I asked the Hattie B's cashier
how their hottest (regrettably named "Shut the Cluck Up")
stacked up to Prince's and Bolton's. "Well, it's a different flavor
profile entirely," she said. "We use ghost peppers. You'll enjoy it."

*Fuck.* It wasn't that I couldn't handle that—one of my favorite snacks is McDonald's fries with a sprinkle of pulverized ghost
peppers—but I was well aware of the kind of havoc *bhut jolokia*
can wreak on a stomach. My flight was in four hours.

The exterior of the chicken at Hattie B's is darker than what    60
I had at either Prince's or Bolton's. Apparently at the Shut the
Cluck Up level, the spice blend incorporates habanero, ghost
pepper, and Trinidad Scorpion. The cashier was right; the flavor profile is markedly different from a cayenne-centric piece of
hot chicken. The higher up you go on the Scoville unit scale, the
more the pungency of a chili registers as acidic. Thai bird's eye
chilies, habaneros, ghost peppers—they all release a fresh, floral
essence that razors through other flavors as a trigger warning
for the pain you're about to experience. That bracing sensation—not pain, but the liminal back and forth between the brain
and the palate signaling that you're in for trouble—is, to me, one
of the best feelings in the world. I ate on the back patio, overlook-
ing the line to get through the door. Unlike the intimate scenes
at Prince's and Bolton's, the Hattie B's experience is broadcast.
I invited people to watch me and my trembling fingers, completely fine with the idea of people noticing my trembling fingers and heavy breathing. I asked strangers to take pictures of
my busted face; my experience became theirs.

There have been fascinating studies in recent years linking
body temperature and mood. While he was at the University of
Arizona, Dr. Charles Raison began experimenting with whole-
body hyperthermia (essentially toasting people from the neck
down at high temperatures). Raison's study was inspired
by Tibetan monks up in the Himalayan mountains who used
special breathing techniques in their meditation, which studies have shown were able to increase the temperature of their
extremities by 15 degrees Fahrenheit. Coincidentally, the capsaicin that binds itself to receptors on the tongue and other parts
of the mouth can trick the mind into thinking that something is
15 degrees hotter than it is.

"Capsaicin-containing foods have the potential, like heat, to
activate sensory fibers and function of brain areas involved in
affect and cognition," said Christopher A. Lowry, an associate
professor of integrative physiology at the University of Colorado
Boulder, who worked alongside Raison in the heat studies. "So,
the infrastructure is there for hot chicken to affect mood and
higher order brain function."

The hot chicken shack, then, becomes more than just a restaurant. It is a sweat lodge, a hot yoga studio, a sauna; it is a safe

space to cry among strangers. There is no pretense; we all know the forces at work, beckoning those tears and beads of sweat. I once saw an old Chinese man at Chengdu Taste, my favorite Sichuan restaurant in Los Angeles, crying into his bowl of rice. I caught myself staring, and so did he. The man let out a nervous smile, and shrugged. My three days in Nashville were full of those moments. It struck me how the hot chicken trend has mirrored a recent boom in Sichuan restaurants in L.A.'s eastern suburbs over the last three years. The hot chicken shack in Nashville, not unlike the restaurants I frequent in the strange Asian bubble of the San Gabriel Valley, gathers a community, and, gimmick or not, everyone is there for the same reason: to feel the great relief of succumbing.

Last month, Jack White and his Nashville-based Third Man Records successfully launched the Icarus Craft, a space-proof vessel housing a turntable attached to a high-altitude balloon that floated out into the void. Sound, as perceived by humans, cannot be carried in the vast emptiness of deep space. Walking out of Hattie B's, my face and arms went numb, tingling as I glided in the cool, post-drizzle breeze. I stumbled down the road, hearing only the faint ringing of my own body fighting an imaginary fire as I floated along the sidewalk and into what might've been oncoming traffic. Hours later, encased in a high-altitude vessel myself, 25,000 feet in the air and climbing, the hammers began to descend. I was Icarus.

## For Discussion and Writing

1. What makes eating spicy food enjoyable?

2. Chau structures his essay around visits to different restaurants, but the restaurants themselves are not the main subject of his essay. What is? How does he use his structure to explore it?

3. **connections**  In writing about his subject, Chau delves into history, science, and personal writing in addition to the food writing you might expect. Another essay in this book that roams across a range of areas of inquiry and genres of writing is Gloria Anzaldúa's "How to Tame a Wild Tongue" (p. 30). What is Anzaldúa's subject, and into what realms does her essay roam to examine it? Compare the way the two essays use a number of different approaches to get at their subjects. Are there commonalities in the way they combine these approaches, and in their effectiveness? Are their differences?

4. Write about your own eating experiences—one in particular or one kind. Are there foods you've been scared of or drawn to? Are there foods that you identify with your family or background that others might not appreciate in the same way? In your writing, make sure to focus both on your descriptions of the food and on its personal or cultural significance.

5. **looking further**   Chau uses the verb "Columbus," a slang term drawn from the explorer's name that means to "discover" or "claim as one's own" something that is already known by others. He uses it to distance his essay from that criticism. Try to find some examples of this kind of activity from contemporary culture, and write about what it means to refer to it as "Columbusing." Is all use or appreciation of things originating in other communities or cultures appropriation? What makes it so, or not so? Who decides?

# SANDRA CISNEROS

# Only Daughter

*Sandra Cisneros is a Mexican American writer. Born in 1954 in Chicago, Cisneros grew up in both Mexico and the United States, attending high school in Chicago and earning her BA at Loyola University Chicago. She earned an MFA from the Iowa Writers' Workshop and has taught writing at both the high school and college levels. Best known as the author of the novel* The House on Mango Street *(1984), Cisneros is also author of many other books, including the poetry collection* My Wicked, Wicked Ways *(1987), the short story collection* Woman Hollering Creek and Other Stories *(1991), and the autobiographical* A House of My Own *(2015).*

Once, several years ago, when I was just starting out my writing career, I was asked to write my own contributor's note for an anthology I was part of. I wrote: "I am the only daughter in a family of six sons. *That* explains everything."

Well, I've thought about that ever since, and yes, it explains a lot to me, but for the reader's sake I should have written: "I am the only daughter in a *Mexican* family of six sons." Or even: "I am the only daughter of a Mexican father and a Mexican-American mother." Or: "I am the only daughter of a working-class family of nine." All of these had everything to do with who I am today.

I was/am the only daughter and *only* a daughter. Being an only daughter in a family of six sons forced me by circumstance to spend a lot of time by myself because my brothers felt it beneath them to play with a *girl* in public. But that aloneness, that loneliness, was good for a would-be writer—it allowed me time to think and think, to imagine, to read and prepare myself.

Being only a daughter for my father meant my destiny would lead me to become someone's wife. That's what he believed. But when I was in the fifth grade and shared my plans for college with him, I was sure he understood. I remember my father saying, "*Que bueno, ni'ja,* that's good." That meant a lot to me, especially since my brothers thought the idea hilarious. What I

91

didn't realize was that my father thought college was good for girls — good for finding a husband. After four years in college and two more in graduate school, and still no husband, my father shakes his head even now and says I wasted all that education.

In retrospect, I'm lucky my father believed daughters were     5
meant for husbands. It meant it didn't matter if I majored in something silly like English. After all, I'd find a nice professional eventually, right? This allowed me the liberty to putter about embroidering my little poems and stories without my father interrupting with so much as a "What's that you're writing?"

But the truth is, I wanted him to interrupt. I wanted my father to understand what it was I was scribbling, to introduce me as "My only daughter, the writer." Not as "This is only my daughter. She teaches." *Es maestra* — teacher. Not even *profesora*.

In a sense, everything I have ever written has been for him, to win his approval even though I know my father can't read English words, even though my father's only reading includes the brown-ink *Esto* sports magazines from Mexico City and the bloody *¡Alarma!* magazines that feature yet another sighting of *La Virgen de Guadalupe* on a tortilla or a wife's revenge on her philandering husband by bashing his skull in with a *molcajete* (a kitchen mortar made of volcanic rock). Or the *fotonovelas*, the little picture paperbacks with tragedy and trauma erupting from the characters' mouths in bubbles.

My father represents, then, the public majority. A public who is uninterested in reading, and yet one whom I am writing about and for, and privately trying to woo.

When we were growing up in Chicago, we moved a lot because of my father. He suffered bouts of nostalgia. Then we'd have to let go of our flat, store the furniture with mother's relatives, load the station wagon with baggage and bologna sandwiches, and head south. To Mexico City.

We came back, of course. To yet another Chicago flat, another     10
Chicago neighborhood, another Catholic school. Each time, my father would seek out the parish priest in order to get a tuition break, and complain or boast: "I have seven sons."

He meant *siete hijos*, seven children, but he translated it as "sons." "I have seven sons." To anyone who would listen. The Sears Roebuck employee who sold us the washing machine. The short-order cook where my father ate his ham-and-eggs breakfasts. "I have seven sons." As if he deserved a medal from the state.

My papa. He didn't mean anything by that mistranslation, I'm sure. But somehow I could feel myself being erased. I'd tug my father's sleeve and whisper: "Not seven sons. Six! and *one daughter.*"

When my oldest brother graduated from medical school, he fulfilled my father's dream that we study hard and use this—our heads, instead of this—our hands. Even now my father's hands are thick and yellow, stubbed by a history of hammer and nails and twine and coils and springs. "Use this," my father said, tapping his head, "and not this," showing us those hands. He always looked tired when he said it.

Wasn't college an investment? And hadn't I spent all those years in college? And if I didn't marry, what was it all for? Why would anyone go to college and then choose to be poor? Especially someone who had always been poor.

Last year, after ten years of writing professionally, the financial rewards started to trickle in. My second National Endowment for the Arts Fellowship. A guest professorship at the University of California, Berkeley. My book, which sold to a major New York publishing house.

At Christmas, I flew home to Chicago. The house was throbbing, same as always; hot *tamales* and sweet *tamales* hissing in my mother's pressure cooker, and everybody—my mother, six brothers, wives, babies, aunts, cousins—talking too loud and at the same time, like in a Fellini film, because that's just how we are.

I went upstairs to my father's room. One of my stories had just been translated into Spanish and published in an anthology of Chicano writing, and I wanted to show it to him. Ever since he recovered from a stroke two years ago, my father likes to spend his leisure hours horizontally. And that's how I found him, watching a Pedro Infante movie on Galavisión and eating rice pudding.

There was a glass filmed with milk on the bedside table. There were several vials of pills and balled Kleenex. And on the floor, one black sock and a plastic urinal that I didn't want to look at but looked at anyway. Pedro Infante was about to burst into song, and my father was laughing.

I'm not sure if it was because my story was translated into Spanish, or because it was published in Mexico, or perhaps because the story dealt with Tepeyac, the *colonia* my father was raised in and the house he grew up in, but at any rate, my father punched the mute button on his remote control and read my story.

I sat on the bed next to my father and waited. He read it very    20 slowly. As if he were reading each line over and over. He laughed at all the right places and read lines he liked out loud. He pointed and asked questions: "Is this So-and-so?" "Yes," I said. He kept reading.

When he was finally finished, after what seemed like hours, my father looked up and asked: "Where can we get more copies of this for the relatives?"

Of all the wonderful things that happened to me last year, that was the most wonderful.

### *For Discussion and Writing*

1. What does it mean to be a daughter in the author's family?
2. Cisneros tells the story of her childhood in this essay, but the essay is not structured chronologically, as might be expected. How is it struc- tured? Why do you think Cisneros chose to order the elements of her narrative in the way that she did?
3. **connections** In "Professions for Women" (p. 447), Virginia Woolf also examines what it is like to be a woman writer. Compare the two essays: do Cisneros and Woolf focus on the same aspects life as a woman writer? Where do they differ?
4. Think about whether there is something about your family situation that shapes who you are—number of siblings, birth order, gender, or something else. What about this situation has had an effect on you, and how? Do you think it will help determine your future career?
5. **looking further** When Cisneros recounts bringing a translated copy of a story to show to her father, she describes the kinds of writing he usually reads. How does she reflect on what this reading material means? How does she generalize about reading beyond her father? Do some research into reading patterns and write about their larger social ramifications. What might reading habits mean for society?

ELI CLARE

# Clearcut: Explaining the Distance

*Eli Clare is a writer, activist, and public speaker who grew up in the Pacific Northwest and now lives in Vermont. His subjects include disability, queerness, peace, and social justice. He is the author of two works of creative nonfiction,* Brilliant Imperfection: Grappling with Cure *(2017) and* Exile and Pride: Disability, Queerness, and Liberation *(1999), and a poetry collection,* The Marrow's Telling: Words in Motion *(2007). "Clearcut" was included in* Exile and Pride; *as you read it, think about the various ways in which its author is an exile, and how this affects his worldview.*

*1979.* Each day after school I run the six miles from highway 101 to my house. The road follows Elk River. I pass the dairy farm, the plywood mill that burned down three years ago, the valley's volunteer fire department station, the boat landing where recreational fishermen put in their boats during salmon season. I have the curves and hills memorized, tick the miles off, skin salty with sweat, lungs working a hard rhythm. I know most of the people who drive by. They wave and swerve into the other lane. The logging trucks honk as they rumble by loaded with 10 or 15 skinny logs. I remember when one or two huge logs made a load. Pushing up the last big hill, my lungs and legs begin to ache. Two curves before my house, I pass a yellow and brown sign. It reads: "United States Forest Service. Entering the Siskiyou National Forest."

*1994.* I live now in southeast Michigan on the edge of corn country. Book-browsing I happen upon *Clearcut: The Tragedy of Industrial Forestry*.[1] The book documents clearcut logging throughout the United States and Canada. I glance at the big, full-color photos of new clearcuts, second growth forests, old

---

1. *Clearcut: The Tragedy of Industrial Forestry*, ed. Bill Deval. Sierra Club Books, 1995.

95

growth forests, and tree farms; read the captions and descriptions. The book is divided by state and province. I look for Oregon and suddenly find myself in the Siskiyous, the photograph overwhelmingly familiar. The ground is bare, heaps of branches, stumps, and half logs hanging to the slope. There are no standing trees, only snatches of green, the new sprouts of huckleberry, greasewood, gorse, and tansy ragwort.

I used to cut firewood on clearcuts like this one. Upriver near Butler Basin and Bald Mountain after the last logs were driven away, loggers bulldozed the remains—branches, shattered logs, trees too small to buck into logs, stumps—into one enormous pile. Rather than burn these remains, the US Forest Service issued firewood-cutting permits. My father and I would spend the whole month of October on these clearcuts, gathering our winter's supply of firewood. He'd cut the logs into rounds, silver bar of chainsaw slicing through the wood, spewing sawdust. I'd watch his hands holding the saw steady, knowing its vibrations were climbing his arms, my ears full of the idle and roar.

I turn from the photo to the accompanying text. Photographer Elizabeth Feryl writes:

> While in the Port Orford, Oregon area, I'd heard of a slide along Bear Creek, so I decided to investigate. Nothing could have prepared me for the estimated 40,000 tons of mud, rock, and logging debris that had been dumped on the road and littered in the waterway. This "blowout," caused by the headwall of the drainage giving way, had also carved a swath through the hillside thirty feet deep, sixty feet across, and a half mile long taking the drainage down to the bedrock. We followed this carnage about a quarter of a mile to the "belly of the beast," the clearcut pictured here.[2]

Forty thousand tons of rock, mud, and logging debris to be    5
washed downstream from Disaster Creek to Bear Creek to Bald Mountain Creek to Elk River to the Pacific Ocean. Elk River: river of my poems, real and metaphor; river of my childhood where I swam, skipped rocks, watched heron and salmon, learned to paddle a canoe. I read and reread the place names and the explanation. On steep slopes, trees literally hold the earth in place, and thus, clearcutting can destabilize whole mountainsides, inviting catastrophic slides called blowouts. I know all this but can't stop reading.

2. From *Clearcut: The Tragedy of Industrial Forestry*, ed. Bill Deval. Sierra Club Books, 1995.

Later, I tell a friend about finding this photo. She has never walked a logging road, listened to the idle and roar of a chainsaw, or counted growth rings on an old growth stump, but we share a sensibility about environmental destruction. I describe the photo, explain blowouts, talk about watershed. What I don't say is how homesick I feel for those place names, plant names, bare slopes, not nostalgic, but lonely for a particular kind of familiarity, a loneliness that reaches deep under my skin, infuses my muscles and tendons. How do I explain the distance, the tension, the disjunction between my politics and my loneliness? She asks, "If you went for a walk along Elk River now, what changes would you notice?" I try to describe the images that have rumbled around my head for days. That winter, the river must have flooded chalky brown over the gravel bars. The next summer, the kids who lived near the river must have found their swimming holes changed, the deep pools shallower, current running faster. I describe spawning season at the confluence of Elk River and Anvil Creek. Salmon flounder into the creek, thrash up the shallows, dig nests in the gravel, flood the water with spawn. They are almost dead, bodies covered with white rot, the gravel bars littered with their carcasses. The following summer the river teems with coho and chinook fingerlings, three inches long, as they head downstream to the ocean. I can barely register that the spawning bed at Anvil Creek might be silted in with rock, mud, and logging debris, might not exist anymore.

For years I have wanted to write this story, have tried poems, diatribes, and theories. I've failed mostly because I haven't been able to bridge the chasm between my homesickness for a place thousands of miles away in the middle of logging country and my urban-created politics that have me raging at environmental destruction. I have felt lonely and frustrated. Without the words for this story, I lose part of myself into the chasm.

I am the child who grew up in the Siskiyou National Forest, in second growth woods that won't be logged again for a long time. The hills weren't replanted in the '40s and '50s when they were first clearcut and so grew back in a mix of alder, tan oak, myrtle, and madrone, trees the timber industry considers worthless. I played endlessly in this second growth forest.

Followed the stream from our house uphill to the little dam where we siphoned water off to the holding tanks that supplied our house with water year-round. I loved taking the covers off the tanks, listening to the trickle of water, watching the reflection of trees waver in the cool dark surface. I drank big gulps straight from the tanks, my cheeks and chin growing cold and wet. Then continued uphill, kicking through the alder and tan oak leaves, scrambling up slippery shale slides. I pulled the bark off madrone trees in curly red strips, crumpled myrtle leaves to smell their pungent bay leaf odor. I knew where the few remaining old growth firs still stood. Had my favorite climbing trees—white fir, grand fir, myrtle. I'd wrap my hands around their branches, skin against bark, and pull my body up, clambering toward sky, resting in the cradles where branch met trunk. Or I'd stay on the ground, lean back into the unmovable tower of trees. I walked out onto rotten logs that spanned the stream, crouched down to examine moss, liverwort, lichen, shelf mushrooms, tried to name the dozen shades of green, tan, and brown, poked at snails and banana slugs. In the summer the hills were hot and dry, the sun reaching easily through the trees. I scrambled across clearings tangled in berry brambles and gorse, through and around undergrowth, uphill to the rock out of which the stream dripped.

I grew up to the high whine of diesel donkeys and chainsaws, yarders and cats next ridge over, the endless clatter of plywood mill two miles downstream. When the warning whistle squealed through the valley, I knew that logs were being pulled up out of the gullies toward the loading areas where empty logging trucks waited. I grew up to the sweet smell of damp wood chips being hauled north on Highway 101 to the port in Coos Bay or the paper mill in Gardiner. I watched for hours as gigantic blowing machines loaded mountains of wood chips onto freighters bound for Japan. I reveled in plant names: huckleberry, salmonberry, blackberry, salal, greasewood, manzanita, scotch broom, foxglove, lupine, rhododendron, vine maple, alder, tan oak, red cedar, white cedar, Port Orford cedar. I wanted a name for everything. I still have a topographical map of the Elk River watershed, each quadrant carefully taped to the next.

I am the backpacker whose favorite trails now wind through old growth rain forest, trees standing so tall I can't find their tops, bark deeply grooved, ropy, fire-scarred. The sun barely reaches through the canopy, leaving small pools of light on the forest floor layered inches deep in fir and spruce needles. Everything cascades green, moss upon moss, swordtail ferns sprouting from rotten logs. The trail bends again and again around Sitka spruce, their roots sticking up high above ground, knobby and twisted. There is no undergrowth, only a thousand shades of green. Among these trees, I find a quiet.

I am the activist who has never poured sugar into a cat's gas tank but knows how. The activist who has never spent a night in the top of a Douglas fir slated for felling the next morning but would. The activist who has never blockaded a logging site or a logging executive's office as I have military complexes. I am the socialist with anarchist leanings who believes the big private timber corporations, like Weyerhaeuser and Georgia-Pacific, are corrupt, and the government agencies, like the US Forest Service, that control public land are complicit. I am the adult who still loves the smell of wood chips, the roar of a lumber mill, who knows out-of-work loggers and dying logging towns. Living now on the edge of corn country, I am the writer who wants to make sense.

In the white, Western world view that I learned as a child, trees, fish, and water were renewable resources. Only 50 years prior, they were conceived of as endless resources, a myth white people brought west into the "frontier." Sometimes when I hiked upriver toward Butler Bar and saw ridge after ridge covered with alder and tan oak, mixed with Douglas fir and Sitka spruce, I believed trees were endless. Or when I went to the cannery and saw a day's catch of coho and chinook, I thought fish were endless. Particularly in the middle of winter when rain drenched the valley every day, I knew water was endless.

But in the 1960s and 70s, the powers-that-be in the public schools, government, and industry taught us that trees and fish, rather than being endless, were renewable. If clearcuts were diligently replanted, we would never run out of trees, paper, or lumber. If the salmon runs were carefully maintained by hatcheries, we would never run out of salmon. No one even bothered to explain about water.

Clearcuts, our teachers said, were good. They encouraged the growth of fir and pine, the so-called good—meaning profitable— trees that as seedlings need direct sunlight to grow. The practice of replanting and the superiority of tree farms were placed at the center of these lessons. But our teachers went far beyond trees in their defense of clearcut logging. Clearcuts, my classmates and I were told, provided bountiful browsing for deer and other wildlife. Hunters and their supporters quickly added that because this abundance of food, coupled with the disappearance of predators, led to a cycle of overpopulation, deer hunting was not just a sport, but a necessity. And so our worldview developed, layer upon layer. How did the forest and its wildlife ever survive before clearcutting, replanting, and sport hunting? We didn't ask because we were children taught not to question. We believed the propaganda.

No one told us about old growth forest. They didn't say, 15 "Understand, a tree farm differs from an old growth forest." We didn't study the cycle of an ecosystem that depends upon rotting logs on the forest floor and a tree canopy hundreds of feet high—a cycle neither static nor altogether predictable, interrupted sometimes by fire, climate changes, or major volcanic activity, but nonetheless a cycle. I knew big, old trees existed. I remember the winter my favorite fir blew down. After we cut it into firewood, I hunkered down by the stump and counted its growth rings, one for every year of its life. It was 400 years old. But I didn't know about thousands of acres of big old trees. Nor did I know about animals, like the northern spotted owl, that live in old growth forests. No one told us, and the logging industry had quite a stake in the silence.

*1979.* I am part of the Youth Conservation Corps, a summer work program for teenagers. All summer we have made trails, picked up trash, maintained campgrounds, and built fences in the Siuslaw National Forest. This week we are camped east of Mapleton, near a ten-year-old tree farm, thinning the trees. Each morning we fan out into the woods to cut down all the trees four inches or less in diameter. The remaining trees will grow faster and bigger. In 30 or 40 years the US Forest Service will bid these acres out to some private company to clearcut and then replant. I am learning to swing an ax, to know what angle to start a cut at, when to stop chopping and let gravity do the rest, how to pull a tree all the way down to the ground so it won't lean against neighboring trees and kill them. It's hot, dirty work. A girl on my crew went back to camp early yesterday after she stumbled into a bees' nest and was stung 30 times. Everyone thinks I'm nuts for liking this job. At lunch I sharpen my ax, the file flat against the beveled cutting edge. I like the weight of its wooden handle balanced on my shoulder as I trudge up and down the hills. I like touching the trees as I walk by, hands growing dark with pitch. I like the way my arms feel, aching but loose, at the end of the day. The sun is hot against my hard hat. Sweat collects under its band. I can smell the woods on my skin.

Along with trees, I studied salmon, fascinated with their three-year life cycle from spawning bed to ocean back to spawning bed. Most of what I knew came from the salmon hatchery two miles upriver of my house. In the winter I stood at the fish ladder waiting for fish to come leaping up the cascading stairs of water, then went to count the big scarred animals in their holding tanks. Sometimes I visited the lab where the biologists held the spawn and incubated the fertilized eggs. In the summer I rode my bike around the holding ponds and watched Glen and Paul feed the fingerlings, their hands dipping into five gallon buckets of feed, sweeping through the air, water coming alive as the fish jumped to catch the pellets. Other times I went across the river to the spawning bed at Anvil Creek. I knew two kinds of salmon existed, hatchery salmon and wild salmon. I thought they were the same, just as I thought a tree farm and an old growth forest were the same.

I didn't know why hatchery salmon needed to be grown in Elk River. I knew dams on the Columbia and urban pollution in the Willamette had nearly destroyed the salmon runs in those rivers, but there were no dams and minimal pollution on Elk River. The propaganda that passed as outdoor education didn't speak of the effects of clearcutting on salmon habitat. No one explained that as spawning beds silt up with logging debris and disappear, fewer and fewer wild salmon can spawn. I never heard that if the trees shading a creek are cut, the direct sunlight warms the water. And if the water temperature rises enough in a watershed, salmon, which require relatively cold water to survive, are put at risk. Nor did the propaganda speak of over-fishing. The commercial salmon fishermen who made their livelihoods fishing the summer salmon runs off the coast of California, Oregon, Washington, British Columbia, and Alaska hadn't yet heard of sustainable yield. The salmon runs seemed endless.

The powers-that-be didn't teach us that hatchery salmon differ from wild salmon, that they are genetically more homogeneous,

more susceptible to disease, and less hardy once at sea. To raise
salmon year after year in a hatchery, biologists use formalde-
hyde and other chemicals each summer to combat recurring diseases that kill thousands of hatchery fingerlings. The continuous
pumping of water from the river into the hatchery's complex of
tanks and back to the river washes these chemicals into the ecosystem. And each winter when hatchery salmon don't return to
the hatchery in large enough numbers, biologists go to natural
spawning beds and net wild salmon, taking them to the hatchery
to augment their supply of spawn. Soon wild salmon might not
exist. The propaganda neglected these details.

My classmates and I were taught by teachers who worked for      20
schools funded largely with timber taxes; by US Forest Service
rangers and their brochures; and by industry-supported textbooks, displays, slide shows, and tours. The point isn't simply
that we, like schoolchildren across the country, were taught half-
truths about trees and salmon. Rather we learned even more fundamental lessons, that trees and salmon are endlessly renewable
commodities. This view of the natural world, which puts clearcutting, replanting, and hatcheries at its center, conveniently
supported the two industries, logging and fishing, that sustained
the towns we lived in.

Not until I left Port Orford did I come into contact with other
worldviews. Living in a city for the first time, I met people who
knew salmon only as frozen patties, who used paper but had
never been to a paper mill. For them trees were the tall, skinny
maples, oaks, and beeches that grew along sidewalks. They navi-
gated the seemingly impossible parking structures and bus stops
with ease and comfort. Some of them believed that trees and
salmon were more than commodities.

They created a fuzzy, romanticized version of nature, combining memories of Walt Disney nature movies with their occasional summer vacations to overcrowded national parks. Or they
believed in a white urban version of tree spirits and Mother Earth.
Either way, my new acquaintances held trees and fish in an awe-
struck reverence as they talked about the dangers of nuclear power
and the destruction of rain forests in Brazil, about clearcutting as
rape. I simply listened. Surrounded by concrete and high-rises,
I slowly stopped taking the familiar plants and animals of the
Siskiyou National Forest for granted. When I returned home to

visit, I caught glimpses of what was beautiful and extraordinary about the place I grew up in, and what was ugly and heartbreaking. I started to believe that trees and salmon weren't just harvestable crops. I read Sierra Club literature, the *Earth First! Journal*, Dave Foreman's ecotage manual; learned about Love Canal, Three Mile Island, the Nevada Test Site, Big Mountain; and started to turn from a right-wing, Libertarian-influenced childhood Coward a progressive adulthood. I never grew into the white urban reverence of tree spirits and Mother Earth, a reverence often stolen from Native spiritual traditions and changed from a demanding, reciprocal relationship with the world into something naive and shallow that still places human life and form at its center. Nor did I ever grow comfortable with the metaphor of clearcutting as rape, the specificity of both acts too vivid for me to ever compare or conflate them. But I did come to believe that trees and fish are their own beings, important in and of themselves, and that I—as activist, consumer, and human being among the many beings on this planet—have a deeply complex relationship with them.

The people in Port Orford who had known me since I was born—Les Smith, the retired logger who ran the Port and Starboard Pizza Parlor; Venita Marstall, the cashier at True Value Hardware; Gerla Marsh, the teller at First Interstate Bank—no longer really knew me. I treasured the anonymity of the city and relished the multitude of cultures, ideas, and differences I encountered there. But still I ached for the trees, the river, the steep, quiet Siskiyous.

*1989.* I am backpacking alone on Washington's Olympic Peninsula. I have spent the last week camping on the beach near Hole-in-the-Wall, reading and writing, letting high and low tide shape my days. Now I am camped at a state park, amidst new clearcuts. I replenished my food supply at Forks, a familiar little logging town, five or six one-ton pickups parked outside the chainsaw shop. I caught a ride to this campground with a man who works as a hoedad, replanting clearcuts. I am planning a three-day hike in the old growth rain forest before I head back to Seattle. I can never get enough of the big, old trees.

In the morning I set out for the trailhead. The logging road I'm on follows the Bogacheil River, winding through rolling pastures and second growth forest, that familiar mix of alder,

25

tan oak, and fir. I hear chainsaws idle and roar the next ridge over. For a time I hear the logging trucks on Highway tot downshift as they chug up a hill. I hear the high whine of the warning whistle. I haven't heard these sounds in years. They mean home even as I remind myself about Weyerhaeuser, their union-busting tactics, their language of timber management, their defense of environmental destruction. A great blue heron startles me as it lifts off, flapping downstream on dusky blue wings. Home is also the damp, rotting log smell, the fog lifting to broken sun and wind. I am climbing steadily now, the two-lane shale road narrowing.

I round the next bend and am suddenly in a new clearcut: stumps as far as I can see, the great heap of tree parts left behind, bulldozer tracks frozen into the dry mud. I don't want this to mean destruction but rather to be home. I strain toward the memories of happy, exhausting trips to Butler Basin to cut firewood, sweat-drenched days east of Mapleton learning to swing an ax. Instead I see a graveyard, a war zone, the earth looking naked and torn. I imagine tree ghosts as real as crows. Whatever metaphor I use, this is what white people have done to North America for 500 years—laid the land bare in the name of profit and progress. I walk a mile, then two, knowing that I am seeing for the first time, seeing not as an outsider, a tourist horrified by some surface ugliness, but as someone who grew up in this graveyard, seeing with both my adult politics and my childhood loyalties, seeing through a lens of tension and contradiction. I climb up onto a stump and count its growth rings, trace the drought seasons marked by tight rings wrapped close together, the wet seasons marked by loose rings spaced farther apart. I want to rage and mourn, but instead I feel ordinary, matter-of-fact, as if the war zone can't touch my heart. I walk, waiting for my bone marrow to catch up to my politics. I walk numb, no longer in my body, unable to contain the tug-of-war between what is home and what is war zone. I round another bend, and am suddenly back in second growth forest.

I find the trailhead. These trees are marked every 50 feet with neon pink ribbon. Markers for a new road? A profit assessment? I tear the ribbon off each tree, stuff the plastic into a pocket, raging now at the impending destruction, at the audacity of neon pink amidst all the green. I cross a stream on a narrow moss-grown bridge. And then I am in old growth forest, national park land. It has started to rain softly. I sit, sheltered under a western red cedar, and eat my lunch, press my back into the thick, gray bark. The lines between old growth, second growth, and clearcut are sudden and unmistakable.

I live in a very different landscape now. The land is flat and open. The trees lose their leaves in an explosion of red, yellow, and orange every fall; regrow them in a burst of green every spring. In winter the snow comes wet and heavy, lining all the trees, or light and dry, drifting in billows. The green here isn't layered and shaded in a thousand varieties. Often I hunger for the ocean, the spawning beds, Douglas fir, rain that blows horizontally across the hills. I have filled my house with photographs, maps, stones, shells, sand dollars, fir cones, and wood to remind me of the landscape I still call home, a landscape that includes the sights, sounds, and smells of logging and commercial fishing.

## For Discussion and Writing

1. What is the "distance" of the essay's subtitle?

2. Description is crucial to this essay. Make a list of the different kinds of things Clare describes and the kinds of words he uses to describe them. Can you see any patterns? Do certain kinds of adjectives go with certain kinds of nouns?

3. **connections**   Read "Clearcut" next to Stephanie Ericsson's "The Ways We Lie" (p. 157). What role does lying play in this essay? Which of the many different ways to lie appear in "Clearcut"? How do they appear? Is there anything in Clare's essay that might speak to Ericsson's larger ideas about untruth—anything that complicates, refutes, or extends her account of the roles the telling of lies plays in our lives?

4. Clare describes himself as "the writer who wants to make sense." Is there something in your life that you would like to make sense of—some tension between beliefs and loves, or between different sets of beliefs? Pick one and describe an essay in which you might do what Clare attempts here, which is to make sense of the tension between two things by writing about them. What might your essay look like?

5. **looking further**   Clare describes what he learned in school about logging and fishing as "propaganda." Research propaganda. What is it? Find a contemporary example of propaganda and write about it. What makes it propaganda? How does it work? Who produces it? Who consumes it? Is anyone fighting to expose it?

# The Paranoid Style of American Policing

*Ta-Nehisi Coates, born in Baltimore, Maryland, in 1975, began his career in journalism at the* Washington City Paper *and contributed to the* Village Voice *and* Time *before becoming an editor and national correspondent at the* Atlantic. *In 2015, he received both the National Book Award for Nonfiction for his autobiography,* Between the World and Me *(2015), and a visiting fellowship at the American Library in Paris.*

*Coates's essay, "The Paranoid Style of American Policing," was first published in the* Atlantic *on December 30, 2015. In it, he addresses the rise in police violence against the black community and the loss of trust that many have in the police as an agent of order and justice. As you read, think about your own interactions with the police—either casual or perhaps more formal. Does what Coates says ring true for your experience?*

When I was around 10 years old, my father confronted a young man who was said to be "crazy." The young man was always too quick to want to fight. A foul in a game of 21 was an insult to his honor. A cross word was cause for a duel, and you never knew what that cross word might be. One day, the young man got into it with one of my older brother's friends. The young man pulled a metal stake out of the ground (there was some work being done nearby) and began swinging it wildly in a threatening manner. My father, my mother, or my older brother—I don't recall which—told the other boy to go inside of our house. My dad then came outside. I don't really remember what my father said to the young man. Perhaps he said something like "Go home," or maybe something like, "Son, it's over." I don't really recall. But what I do recall is that my dad did not shoot and kill the young man.

That wasn't the first time I'd seen my father confront the violence of young people without resorting to killing them. This was not remarkable. When you live in communities like ours — or perhaps any community — mediating violence between young people is part of being an adult. Sometimes the young people are involved in scary behavior — like threatening people with metal objects. And yet the notion that it is permissible, wise, moral, or advisable to kill such a person as a method of de-escalation, to kill because one was afraid, did not really exist among parents in my community.

The same could not be said for those who came from outside of the community.

This weekend, after a Chicago police officer killed her 19-year-old son Quintonio LeGrier, Janet Cooksey struggled to understand the mentality of the people she pays to keep her community safe:

> "What happened to Tasers? Seven times my son was shot," Cooksey said.

> "The police are supposed to serve and protect us and yet they take the lives," Cooksey said.

> "Where do we get our help?" she asked.

LeGrier had struggled with mental illness. When LeGrier attempted to break down his father's door, his father called the police, who apparently arrived to find the 19-year-old wielding a bat. Interpreting this as a lethal threat, one of the officers shot and killed LeGrier and somehow managed to shoot and kill one of his neighbors, Bettie Jones. Cooksey did not merely have a problem with how the police acted, but with the fact that the police were even called in the first place. "He should have called me," Cooksey said of LeGrier's father.

Instead, the father called the Chicago Police Department. Likely he called them because he invested them with some measure of legitimacy. This is understandable. In America, police officers are agents of the state and thus bound by the social contract in a way that criminals, and even random citizens, are not. Criminals and random citizens are not paid to protect other citizens. Police officers are. By that logic, one might surmise that the police would be better able to mediate conflicts than community members. In Chicago, this appears, very often, not to be the case.

It will not do to note that 99 percent of the time the police mediate conflicts without killing people anymore than it will do for a restaurant to note that 99 percent of the time rats don't run through the dining room. Nor will it do to point out that most black citizens are killed by other black citizens, not police officers, anymore than it will do to point out that most American citizens are killed by other American citizens, not terrorists. If officers cannot be expected to act any better than ordinary citizens, why call them in the first place? Why invest them with any more power?

Legitimacy is what is ultimately at stake here. When Cooksey says that her son's father should not have called the police, when she says that they "are supposed to serve and protect us and yet they take the lives," she is saying that police in Chicago are police in name only. This opinion is widely shared. Asked about the possibility of an investigation, Melvin Jones, the brother of Bettie Jones, could muster no confidence. "I already know how that will turn out," he scoffed. "We all know how that will turn out."

Indeed, we probably do. Two days after Jones and LeGrier were killed, a district attorney in Ohio declined to prosecute the two officers who drove up, and within two seconds of arriving, killed the 12-year-old Tamir Rice. No one should be surprised by this. In America, we have decided that it is permissible, that it is wise, that it is moral for the police to de-escalate through killing. A standard which would not have held for my father in West Baltimore, which did not hold for me in Harlem, is reserved for those who have the maximum power—the right to kill on behalf of the state. When police can not adhere to the standards of the neighborhood, of citizens, or of parents, what are they beyond a bigger gun and a sharper sword? By what right do they enforce their will, save force itself?

When policing is delegitimized, when it becomes an occupying 10 force, the community suffers. The neighbor-on-neighbor violence in Chicago, and in black communities around the country, is not an optical illusion. Policing is (one) part of the solution to that violence. But if citizens don't trust officers, then policing can't actually work. And in Chicago, it is very hard to muster reasons for trust.

When Bettie Jones's brother displays zero confidence in an investigation into the killing of his sister, he is not being cynical.

He is shrewdly observing a government that executed a young man and sought to hide that fact from citizens. He is intelligently assessing a local government which, for two decades, ran a torture ring. What we have made of our police departments [in] America, what we have ordered them to do, is a direct challenge to any usable definition of democracy. A state that allows its agents to kill, to beat, to tase, without any real sanction, has ceased to govern and has commenced to simply rule.

*For Discussion and Writing*

1. Why does Coates begin with a story from his childhood that has nothing directly to do with policing?

2. Coates uses variations on the phrase "it will not do" more than once in this essay. How does he use it? Why does he repeat it? Imagine other phrases he could have used to serve the same purpose; why did he not use those?

3. **connections**   Coates, in "The Paranoid Style of American Policing," and Audre Lorde, in "The Fourth of July" (p. 242), focus on racism in America, but in very different ways. Compare and contrast the two essays in terms of their subjects and their methods. What kinds of stories do Lorde and Coates tell, and to what ends? What kind of evidence does each use? How do the kinds of narratives and evidence fit each author's subject and argument?

4. As Coates writes, "99 percent of the time the police mediate conflicts without killing people" (par. 7). Write a reflection about one or more interactions you have had with the police, from the serious to the casual; how did the interaction(s) make you feel? How do you feel about the police in general? Did the interaction(s) confirm your opinion or change it? (If you've had no direct dealings with a police officer of any kind, write about things you've witnessed or read about.)

5. **looking further**   List Coates's objections to the use of what he deems excessive force by police. Many connect to larger political questions about the nature of the relationship between the state and the citizen. Extrapolate, from these objections, Coates's theory of government. Why does it exist? What is it for? Then, with the help of a little reading, connect this theory to contemporary thinking about government's role in American life.

JUDITH ORTIZ COFER

# The Myth of the Latin Woman: I Just Met a Girl Named María

*Judith Ortiz Cofer was born in Puerto Rico in 1952 and grew up there and in New Jersey. She is a poet, fiction writer, and autobiographer, and teaches literature and writing at the University of Georgia. In 2010, Cofer was inducted into the Georgia Writers Hall of Fame. Much of her work, such as her novel* The Line of the Sun *(1989) and* The Latin Deli: Prose and Poetry *(1993), explores her experiences as a Puerto Rican émigré and a Latina. Her most recent books include a novel,* If I Could Fly *(2011), and three children's books,* Animal Jamboree: Latino Folktales *(2012),* The Poet Upstairs *(2012), and* ¡A bailar! *(2011).*

*"The Myth of the Latin Woman: I Just Met a Girl Named María" considers the stereotypes Americans hold about Latinas, and it does so through narrative and reflection. At the end of one of the stories she tells in her essay, dealing with an offensive man, Cofer writes, "My friend complimented me on my cool handling of the situation" (par. 10) and then notes that what she really wanted to do was push the man into the pool. Notice, as you read, the ways in which Cofer is able in this essay, as in that incident, to strike a balance between anger and analysis.*

On a bus trip to London from Oxford University where I was earning some graduate credits one summer, a young man, obviously fresh from a pub, spotted me and as if struck by inspiration went down on his knees in the aisle. With both hands over his heart he broke into an Irish tenor's rendition of "María" from *West Side Story*. My politely amused fellow passengers gave his lovely voice the round of gentle applause it deserved. Though I was not quite as amused, I managed my version of an English smile: no show of teeth, no extreme contortions of the facial muscles—I was at this time of my life practicing reserve and cool. Oh, that British

110

control, how I coveted it. But María had followed me to London, reminding me of a prime fact of my life: you can leave the Island, master the English language, and travel as far as you can, but if you are a Latina, especially one like me who so obviously belongs to Rita Moreno's gene pool, the Island travels with you.

This is sometimes a very good thing—it may win you that extra minute of someone's attention. But with some people, the same things can make *you* an island—not so much a tropical paradise as an Alcatraz, a place nobody wants to visit. As a Puerto Rican girl growing up in the United States and wanting like most children to "belong," I resented the stereotype that my Hispanic appearance called forth from many people I met.

Our family lived in a large urban center in New Jersey during the sixties, where life was designed as a microcosm of my parents' casas on the island. We spoke in Spanish, we ate Puerto Rican food bought at the bodega, and we practiced strict Catholicism complete with Saturday confession and Sunday mass at a church where our parents were accommodated into a one-hour Spanish mass slot, performed by a Chinese priest trained as a missionary for Latin America.

As a girl I was kept under strict surveillance, since virtue and modesty were, by cultural equation, the same as family honor. As a teenager I was instructed on how to behave as a proper señorita. But it was a conflicting message girls got, since the Puerto Rican mothers also encouraged their daughters to look and act like women and to dress in clothes our Anglo friends and their mothers found too "mature" for our age. It was, and is, cultural, yet I often felt humiliated when I appeared at an American friend's party wearing a dress more suitable to a semiformal than to a playroom birthday celebration. At Puerto Rican festivities, neither the music nor the colors we wore could be too loud. I still experience a vague sense of letdown when I'm invited to a "party" and it turns out to be a marathon conversation in hushed tones rather than a fiesta with salsa, laughter, and dancing—the kind of celebration I remember from my childhood.

I remember Career Day in our high school, when teachers told    5
us to come dressed as if for a job interview. It quickly became obvious that to the barrio girls, "dressing up" sometimes meant wearing ornate jewelry and clothing that would be more appropriate (by mainstream standards) for the company Christmas

party than as daily office attire. That morning I had agonized in front of my closet, trying to figure out what a "career girl" would wear because, essentially, except for Marlo Thomas on TV, I had no models on which to base my decision. I knew how to dress for school: at the Catholic school I attended we all wore uniforms; I knew how to dress for Sunday mass, and I knew what dresses to wear for parties at my relatives' homes. Though I do not recall the precise details of my Career Day outfit, it must have been a composite of the above choices. But I remember a comment my friend (an Italian-American) made in later years that coalesced my impressions of that day. She said that at the business school she was attending the Puerto Rican girls always stood out for wearing "everything at once." She meant, of course, too much jewelry, too many accessories. On that day at school, we were simply made the negative models by the nuns who were themselves not credible fashion experts to any of us. But it was painfully obvious to me that to the others, in their tailored skirts and silk blouses, we must have seemed "hopeless" and "vulgar." Though I now know that most adolescents feel out of step much of the time, I also know that for the Puerto Rican girls of my generation that sense was intensified. The way our teachers and classmates looked at us that day in school was just a taste of the culture clash that awaited us in the real world, where prospective employers and men on the street would often misinterpret our tight skirts and jingling bracelets as a come-on.

Mixed cultural signals have perpetuated certain stereotypes — for example, that of the Hispanic woman as the "Hot Tamale" or sexual firebrand. It is a one-dimensional view that the media have found easy to promote. In their special vocabulary, advertisers have designated "sizzling" and "smoldering" as the adjectives of choice for describing not only the foods but also the women of Latin America. From conversations in my house I recall hearing about the harassment that Puerto Rican women endured in factories where the "boss men" talked to them as if sexual innuendo was all they understood and, worse, often gave them the choice of submitting to advances or being fired.

It is custom, however, not chromosomes, that leads us to choose scarlet over pale pink. As young girls, we were influenced in our decisions about clothes and colors by the women — older sisters and mothers who had grown up on a tropical island where the natural environment was a riot of primary colors, where showing your skin was one way to keep cool as well as to look sexy. Most important of all, on the island, women perhaps felt freer to dress and move more provocatively, since, in most cases, they were protected by the traditions, mores, and laws of a Spanish/Catholic system of morality and machismo whose main rule was: *You may look at my sister, but if you touch her I will kill you.* The extended family and church structure could provide a young woman with a circle of safety in her small pueblo on the island; if a man "wronged" a girl, everyone would close in to save her family honor.

This is what I have gleaned from my discussions as an adult with older Puerto Rican women. They have told me about dressing in their best party clothes on Saturday nights and going to the town's plaza to promenade with their girlfriends in front of the boys they liked. The males were thus given an opportunity to admire the women and to express their admiration in the form of *piropos*: erotically charged street poems they composed on the spot. I have been subjected to a few piropos while visiting the Island, and they can be outrageous, although custom dictates that they must never cross into obscenity. This ritual, as I understand it, also entails a show of studied indifference on the woman's part; if she is "decent," she must not acknowledge the man's impassioned words. So I do understand how things can be lost in translation. When a Puerto Rican girl dressed in her idea of what is attractive meets a man from the mainstream culture who has been trained to react to certain types of clothing as a sexual signal, a clash is likely to take place. The line I first heard based on this aspect of the myth happened when the boy who took me to my first formal dance leaned over to plant a sloppy overeager kiss painfully on my mouth, and when I didn't respond with sufficient passion said in a resentful tone: "I thought you Latin girls were supposed to mature early"—my first instance of being thought of as a fruit or vegetable—I was supposed to *ripen*, not just grow into womanhood like other girls.

It is surprising to some of my professional friends that some people, including those who should know better, still put others "in their place." Though rarer, these incidents are still commonplace in my life. It happened to me most recently during a stay at a very classy metropolitan hotel favored by young professional couples for their weddings. Late one evening after the theater, as I walked toward my room with my new colleague (a woman with whom I was coordinating an arts program), a middle-aged man in a tuxedo, a young girl in satin and lace on his arm, stepped directly into our path. With his champagne glass extended toward me, he exclaimed, "Evita!"

Our way blocked, my companion and I listened as the man half-recited, half-bellowed "Don't Cry for Me, Argentina." When he finished, the young girl said: "How about a round of applause for my daddy?" We complied, hoping this would bring the silly spectacle to a close. I was becoming aware that our little group was attracting the attention of the other guests. "Daddy" must have perceived this too, and he once more barred the way as we tried to walk past him. He began to shout-sing a ditty to the tune of "La Bamba"—except the lyrics were about a girl named María whose exploits all rhymed with her name and gonorrhea. The girl kept saying "Oh, Daddy" and looking at me with pleading eyes. She wanted me to laugh along with the others. My companion and I stood silently waiting for the man to end his offensive song. When he finished, I looked not at him but at his daughter. I advised her calmly never to ask her father what he had done in the army. Then I walked between them and to my room. My friend complimented me on my cool handling of the situation. I confessed to her that I really had wanted to push the jerk into the swimming pool. I knew that this same man—probably a corporate executive, well educated, even worldly by most standards—would not have been likely to regale a white woman with a dirty song in public. He would perhaps have checked his impulse by assuming that she could be somebody's wife or mother, or at least *somebody* who might take offense. But to him, I was just an Evita or a María: merely a character in his cartoon-populated universe.

Because of my education and my proficiency with the English language, I have acquired many mechanisms for dealing with the anger I experience. This was not true for my parents, nor is it true for the many Latin women working at menial jobs who must put up with stereotypes about our ethnic group such as: "They make good domestics." This is another facet of the myth of the Latin woman in the United States. Its origin is simple to deduce. Work as domestics, waitressing, and factory jobs are all that's available to women with little English and few skills. The myth of the Hispanic menial has been sustained by the same media phenomenon that made "Mammy" from *Gone with the Wind* America's idea of the black woman for generations: María, the housemaid or counter girl, is now indelibly etched into the national psyche. The big and the little screens have presented us with the picture of the funny Hispanic maid, mispronouncing words and cooking up a spicy storm in a shiny California kitchen.

This media-engendered image of the Latina in the United States has been documented by feminist Hispanic scholars, who claim that such portrayals are partially responsible for the denial of opportunities for upward mobility among Latinas in the professions. I have a Chicana friend working on a Ph.D. in philosophy at a major university. She says her doctor still shakes his head in puzzled amazement at all the "big words" she uses. Since I do not wear my diplomas around my neck for all to see, I too have on occasion been sent to that "kitchen," where some think I obviously belong.

One such incident that has stayed with me, though I recognize it as a minor offense, happened on the day of my first public poetry reading. It took place in Miami in a boat-restaurant where we were having lunch before the event. I was nervous and excited as I walked in with my notebook in my hand. An older woman motioned me to her table. Thinking (foolish me) that she wanted me to autograph a copy of my brand-new slender volume of verse, I went over. She ordered a cup of coffee from me, assuming that I was the waitress. Easy enough to mistake my poems for menus, I suppose. I know that it wasn't an intentional act of cruelty, yet of all the good things that happened that day, I remember that scene most clearly, because it reminded me of what I had to overcome before anyone would take me seriously. In retrospect I understand that my anger gave my reading fire, that I have almost always taken doubts in my abilities as a challenge—and that the result is, most times, a feeling of satisfaction at having won a convert when I see the cold, appraising eyes warm to my words, the body language change, the smile that indicates that I have opened some avenue for communication. That day I read to that woman and her lowered eyes told me that she was embarrassed at her little faux pas, and when I willed her to look up at me, it was my victory, and she graciously allowed me to punish her with my full attention. We shook hands at the end of the reading, and I never saw her again. She has probably forgotten the whole thing but maybe not.

Yet I am one of the lucky ones. My parents made it possible for me to acquire a stronger footing in the mainstream culture by giving me the chance at an education. And books and art have saved me from the harsher forms of ethnic and racial prejudice that many of my Hispanic *compañeras* have had to endure. I travel a lot around the United States, reading from my books of poetry and my novel, and the reception I most often receive is one of positive interest by people who want to know more about my culture. There are, however, thousands of Latinas without the privilege of an education or the entrée into society that I have. For them life is a struggle against the misconceptions perpetuated by the myth of the Latina as whore, domestic, or criminal. We cannot change this by legislating the way people look at us. The transformation, as I see it, has to occur at a much more individual level. My personal goal in my public life is to try to replace the old pervasive stereotypes and myths about Latinas with a much more interesting set of realities. Every time I give a reading, I hope the stories I tell, the dreams and fears I examine in my work, can achieve some universal truth which will get my audience past the particulars of my skin color, my accent, or my clothes.

I once wrote a poem in which I called us Latinas "God's brown   15 daughters." This poem is really a prayer of sorts, offered upward, but also, through the human-to-human channel of art, outward. It is a prayer for communication, and for respect. In it, Latin women pray "in Spanish to an Anglo God / with a Jewish heritage," and they are "fervently hoping / that if not omnipotent, / at least He be bilingual."

### For Discussion and Writing

1. What do the incidents on the bus, in the hotel, and at the poetry reading have in common?

2. What are the different kinds of Latinas Cofer says are recognized in mainstream Anglo-American culture? By making explicit her observations of how others classify people like her, what point does she make about classification in general?

3. **connections**   Compare Cofer's feelings about those who react to her based on her ethnicity, and her reactions to them as she relates them to us, to Nancy Mairs's feelings about those who react to her based on her disability, and her reactions to them, in "On Being a Cripple" (p. 247). How do their feelings compare? How do their reactions compare? Are there any differences? If so, how might they connect to the nature of the characteristics for which each is viewed as different?

4. Write about how you perceive others in certain ways because of something about them—how they look, where they live, what they do for a living. Can we live without these kinds of snap judgments? Can we live with them? Be sure to use specific examples as you write.

5. **looking further**   Do some research into the changing demographic picture of the United States. What is the current racial and ethnic breakdown of the U.S. population? By what year is it predicted that whites will no longer be the majority? Do you think this will affect the way "minorities" are thought of and treated? How, or how not?

## JOAN DIDION

# On Keeping a Notebook

*Joan Didion, a fifth-generation Californian born in 1934, has been an essayist since her undergraduate days. Known for a reflexive, self-conscious, yet cool style and a sharp political eye, Didion has, in essays and novels, carved out a unique place in American letters. Best known for her essay collections* Slouching Towards Bethlehem *(1968) and* The White Album *(1979), her novels, including* Play It as It Lays *(1970) and* The Last Thing He Wanted *(1996), are also widely read. Her latest book,* Blue Nights *(2011), is a memoir about her life with her late daughter, aging, and parenthood.*

*In "On Keeping a Notebook," Didion writes about writing, or about the work that she does prior to the writing of her published prose. As you read, think about whether her notebook-keeping is entirely in the service of preparation for her writing or if it is also about other things and, if so, how these other goals might connect to her work.*

"'That woman Estelle,'" the note reads, "'is partly the reason why George Sharp and I are separated today.' *Dirty crepe-de-Chine wrapper, hotel bar, Wilmington RR, 9:45 A.M. August Monday morning.*"

Since the note is in my notebook, it presumably has some meaning to me. I study it for a long while. At first I have only the most general notion of what I was doing on an August Monday morning in the bar of the hotel across from the Pennsylvania Railroad station in Wilmington, Delaware (waiting for a train? missing one? 1960? 1961? why Wilmington?), but I do remember being there. The woman in the dirty crepe-de-Chine wrapper had come down from her room for a beer, and the bartender had heard before the reason why George Sharp and she were separated today. "Sure," he said, and went on mopping the floor. "You told me." At the other end of the bar is a girl. She is talking, pointedly, not to the man beside her but to a cat lying in the

118

triangle of sunlight cast through the open door. She is wearing a plaid silk dress from Peck & Peck, and the hem is coming down.

Here is what it is: the girl has been on the Eastern Shore, and now she is going back to the city, leaving the man beside her, and all she can see ahead are the viscous summer sidewalks and the 3 A.M. long-distance calls that will make her lie awake and then sleep drugged through all the steaming mornings left in August (1960? 1961?). Because she must go directly from the train to lunch in New York, she wishes that she had a safety pin for the hem of the plaid silk dress, and she also wishes that she could forget about the hem and the lunch and stay in the cool bar that smells of disinfectant and malt and make friends with the woman in the crepe-de-Chine wrapper. She is afflicted by a little self-pity, and she wants to compare Estelles. That is what that was all about.

Why did I write it down? In order to remember, of course, but exactly what was it I wanted to remember? How much of it actually happened? Did any of it? Why do I keep a notebook at all? It is easy to deceive oneself on all those scores. The impulse to write things down is a peculiarly compulsive one, inexplicable to those who do not share it, useful only accidentally, only secondarily, in the way that any compulsion tries to justify itself. I suppose that it begins or does not begin in the cradle. Although I have felt compelled to write things down since I was five years old, I doubt that my daughter ever will, for she is a singularly blessed and accepting child, delighted with life exactly as life presents itself to her, unafraid to go to sleep and unafraid to wake up. Keepers of private notebooks are a different breed altogether, lonely and resistant rearrangers of things, anxious malcontents, children afflicted apparently at birth with some presentiment of loss.

My first notebook was a Big Five tablet, given to me by my mother with the sensible suggestion that I stop whining and learn to amuse myself by writing down my thoughts. She returned the tablet to me a few years ago; the first entry is an account of a woman who believed herself to be freezing to death in the Arctic night, only to find, when day broke, that she had stumbled onto the Sahara Desert, where she would die of the heat before lunch. I have no idea what turn of a five-year-old's mind could have prompted so insistently "ironic" and exotic a story, but it does reveal a certain predilection for the extreme which has dogged me into adult life; perhaps if I were analytically inclined I would

5

find it a truer story than any I might have told about Donald Johnson's birthday party or the day my cousin Brenda put Kitty Litter in the aquarium.

So the point of my keeping a notebook has never been, nor is it now, to have an accurate factual record of what I have been doing or thinking. That would be a different impulse entirely, an instinct for reality which I sometimes envy but do not possess. At no point have I ever been able successfully to keep a diary; my approach to daily life ranges from the grossly negligent to the merely absent, and on those few occasions when I have tried dutifully to record a day's events, boredom has so overcome me that the results are mysterious at best. What is this business about "shopping, typing piece, dinner with E, depressed"? Shopping for what? Typing what piece? Who is E? Was this "E" depressed, or was I depressed? Who cares?

In fact I have abandoned altogether that kind of pointless entry; instead I tell what some would call lies. "That's simply not true," the members of my family frequently tell me when they come up against my memory of a shared event. "The party was *not* for you, the spider was *not* a black widow, *it wasn't that way at all.*" Very likely they are right, for not only have I always had trouble distinguishing between what happened and what merely might have happened, but I remain unconvinced that the distinction, for my purposes, matters. The cracked crab that I recall having for lunch the day my father came home from Detroit in 1945 must certainly be embroidery, worked into the day's pattern to lend verisimilitude; I was ten years old and would not now remember the cracked crab. The day's events did not turn on cracked crab. And yet it is precisely that fictitious crab that makes me see the afternoon all over again, a home movie run all too often, the father bearing gifts, the child weeping, an exercise in family love and guilt. Or that is what it was to me. Similarly, perhaps it never did snow that August in Vermont; perhaps there never were flurries in the night wind, and maybe no one else felt the ground hardening and summer already dead even as we pretended to bask in it, but that was how it felt to me, and it might as well have snowed, could have snowed, did snow.

*How it felt to me:* that is getting closer to the truth about a notebook. I sometimes delude myself about why I keep a notebook,

imagine that some thrifty virtue derives from preserving everything observed. See enough and write it down, I tell myself, and
then some morning when the world seems drained of wonder,
some day when I am only going through the motions of doing
what I am supposed to do, which is write—on that bankrupt
morning I will simply open my notebook and there it will all be, a
forgotten account with accumulated interest, paid passage back
to the world out there: dialogue overheard in hotels and elevators
and at the hat-check counter in Pavillon (one middle-aged man
shows his hat check to another and says, "That's my old football
number"); impressions of Bettina Aptheker and Benjamin Son-
nenberg and Teddy ("Mr. Acapulco") Stauffer; careful *aperçus*[1]
about tennis burns and failed fashion models and Greek shipping
heiresses, one of whom taught me a significant lesson (a lesson
I could have learned from F. Scott Fitzgerald, but perhaps we all
must meet the very rich for ourselves) by asking, when I arrived to
interview her in her orchid-filled sitting room on the second day of
a paralyzing New York blizzard, whether it was snowing outside.

I imagine, in other words, that the notebook is about other
people. But of course it is not. I have no real business with what
one stranger said to another at the hat-check counter in Pavillon;
in fact I suspect that the line "That's my old football number"
touched not my own imagination at all, but merely some memory of something once read, probably "The Eighty-Yard Run."
Nor is my concern with a woman in a dirty crepe-de-Chine wrapper in a Wilmington bar. My stake is always, of course, in the
unmentioned girl in the plaid silk dress. *Remember what it was to
be me:* that is always the point.

It is a difficult point to admit. We are brought up in the ethic     10
that others, any others, all others, are by definition more interesting than ourselves; taught to be diffident, just this side of
self-effacing. ("You're the least important person in the room
and don't forget it," Jessica Mitford's governess would hiss in
her ear on the advent of any social occasion; I copied that into
my notebook because it is only recently that I have been able to
enter a room without hearing some such phrase in my inner ear.)
Only the very young and the very old may recount their dreams

1. **aperçus:** Insights (French). [Ed.]

at breakfast, dwell upon self, interrupt with memories of beach picnics and favorite Liberty lawn dresses and the rainbow trout in a creek near Colorado Springs. The rest of us are expected, rightly, to affect absorption in other people's favorite dresses, other people's trout.

And so we do. But our notebooks give us away, for however dutifully we record what we see around us, the common denominator of all we see is always, transparently, shamelessly, the implacable "I." We are not talking here about the kind of notebook that is patently for public consumption, a structural conceit for binding together a series of graceful *pensées*;[2] we are talking about something private, about bits of the mind's string too short to use, an indiscriminate and erratic assemblage with meaning only for its maker.

And sometimes even the maker has difficulty with the meaning. There does not seem to be, for example, any point in my knowing for the rest of my life that, during 1964, 720 tons of soot fell on every square mile of New York City, yet there it is in my notebook labeled "FACT." Nor do I really need to remember that Ambrose Bierce liked to spell Leland Stanford's name "£eland $tanford" or that "smart women almost always wear black in Cuba," a fashion hint without much potential for practical application. And does not the relevance of these notes seem marginal at best?:

> In the basement museum of the Inyo County Courthouse in Independence, California, sign pinned to a mandarin coat: "This MANDARIN COAT was often worn by Mrs. Minnie S. Brooks when giving lectures on her TEAPOT COLLECTION."

> Redhead getting out of car in front of Beverly Wilshire Hotel, chinchilla stole, Vuitton bags with tags reading:

> MRS LOU FOX
> HOTEL SAHARA
> VEGAS

Well, perhaps not entirely marginal. As a matter of fact, Mrs. Minnie S. Brooks and her MANDARIN COAT pull me back into my own childhood, for although I never knew Mrs. Brooks and did not visit Inyo County until I was thirty, I grew up in just such

2. **pensées:** Thoughts, reflections (French). [Ed.]

a world, in houses cluttered with Indian relics and bits of gold ore and ambergris and the souvenirs my Aunt Mercy Farnsworth brought back from the Orient. It is a long way from that world to Mrs. Lou Fox's world, where we all live now, and is it not just as well to remember that? Might not Mrs. Minnie S. Brooks help me to remember what I am? Might not Mrs. Lou Fox help me to remember what I am not?

But sometimes the point is harder to discern. What exactly did I have in mind when I noted down that it cost the father of someone I know $650 a month to light the place on the Hudson in which he lived before the Crash? What use was I planning to make of this line by Jimmy Hoffa: "I may have my faults, but being wrong ain't one of them"? And although I think it interesting to know where the girls who travel with the Syndicate have their hair done when they find themselves on the West Coast, will I ever make suitable use of it? Might I not be better off just passing it on to John O'Hara? What is a recipe for sauerkraut doing in my notebook? What kind of magpie keeps this notebook? *"He was born the night the Titanic went down."* That seems a nice enough line, and I even recall who said it, but is it not really a better line in life than it could ever be in fiction?

But of course that is exactly it: not that I should ever use the line, but that I should remember the woman who said it and the afternoon I heard it. We were on her terrace by the sea, and we were finishing the wine left from lunch, trying to get what sun there was, a California winter sun. The woman whose husband was born the night the *Titanic* went down wanted to rent her house, wanted to go back to her children in Paris. I remember wishing that I could afford the house, which cost $1,000 a month. "Someday you will," she said lazily. "Someday it all comes." There in the sun on her terrace it seemed easy to believe in someday, but later I had a low-grade afternoon hangover and ran over a black snake on the way to the supermarket and was flooded with inexplicable fear when I heard the checkout clerk explaining to the man ahead of me why she was finally divorcing her husband. "He left me no choice," she said over and over as she punched the register. "He has a little seven-month-old baby by her, he left me no choice." I would like to believe that my dread then was for the human condition, but of course it was for me, because I wanted a baby and did not then have one and because I wanted to own the house that cost $1,000 a month to rent and because I had a hangover.

It all comes back. Perhaps it is difficult to see the value in having one's self back in that kind of mood, but I do see it; I think we are well advised to keep on nodding terms with the people we used to be whether we find them attractive company or not. Otherwise they turn up unannounced and surprise us, come hammering on the mind's door at 4 A.M. of a bad night and demand to know who deserted them, who betrayed them, who is going to make amends. We forget all too soon the things we thought we could never forget. We forget the loves and the betrayals alike, forget what we whispered and what we screamed, forget who we were. I have already lost touch with a couple of people I used to be; one of them, a seventeen-year-old, presents little threat, although it would be of some interest to me to know again what it feels like to sit on a river levee drinking vodka-and-orange-juice and listening to Les Paul and Mary Ford and their echoes sing "How High the Moon" on the car radio. (You see I still have the scenes, but I no longer perceive myself among those present, no longer could even improvise the dialogue.) The other one, a twenty-three-year-old, bothers me more. She was always a good deal of trouble, and I suspect she will reappear when I least want to see her, skirts too long, shy to the point of aggravation, always the injured party, full of recriminations and little hurts and stories I do not want to hear again, at once saddening me and angering me with her vulnerability and ignorance, an apparition all the more insistent for being so long banished.

It is a good idea, then, to keep in touch, and I suppose that keeping in touch is what notebooks are all about. And we are all on our own when it comes to keeping those lines open to ourselves: your notebook will never help me, nor mine you. *"So what's new in the whiskey business?"* What could that possibly mean to you? To me it means a blonde in a Pucci bathing suit sitting with a couple of fat men by the pool at the Beverly Hills Hotel. Another man approaches, and they all regard one another in silence for a while. "So what's new in the whiskey business?" one of the fat men finally says by way of welcome, and the blonde stands up, arches one foot and dips it in the pool, looking all the while at the cabaña where Baby Pignatari is talking on the telephone. That is all there is to that, except that several years later I saw the blonde coming out of Saks Fifth Avenue in New York with her California complexion and a voluminous mink coat. In the harsh wind that day she looked old and irrevocably tired to me, and even the skins in the mink coat were not worked the way they were doing them that year, not the way she would have wanted them done, and there is the point of the story. For a while after that I did not like to look in the mirror, and my eyes would skim the newspapers and pick out only the deaths, the cancer victims, the premature coronaries, the suicides, and I stopped riding the Lexington Avenue IRT because I noticed for the first time that all the strangers I had seen for years— the man with the seeing-eye dog, the spinster who read the classified pages every day, the fat girl who always got off with me at Grand Central—looked older than they once had.

It all comes back. Even that recipe for sauerkraut: even that brings it back. I was on Fire Island when I first made that sauerkraut, and it was raining, and we drank a lot of bourbon and ate the sauerkraut and went to bed at ten, and I listened to the rain and the Atlantic and felt safe. I made the sauerkraut again last night and it did not make me feel any safer, but that is, as they say, another story.

## For Discussion and Writing

1. What are the reasons that Didion keeps a notebook? What are reasons that other people might keep them that are not her reasons?

2. Didion is known as a master stylist. Find five sentences you think are stylish — unusual, or well constructed, or somehow striking. What makes them each good? Imagine how another writer might have written them—what would be different? What would be missing?

3. **connections**   Read Didion's essay alongside E. B. White's "Once More to the Lake" (p. 432). Both essays are concerned with aging, with the past, and with memory. In what ways are the methods by which Didion and White recollect and re-create the past similar? How do they differ? What do you make of the comparison, in terms of the difference between the two authors' writing styles, or projects, or implicit beliefs about the nature of selfhood and memory?

4. Are you on "nodding terms" with the person you used to be, to borrow Didion's line (par. 16)? Pick a time in your life, a few to many years ago, and reflect on your relationship to the person you were then. What kinds of things about that time do you remember, from the small to the large? Do you remember how they made you feel or what you thought about them? Do the events you remember and the reactions you remember tell you something about who you were then? Do you find that person "attractive company"?

5. **looking further**   Do some research into Joan Didion's career, looking closely at the collection this essay was published in (*Slouching Towards Bethlehem*) or more broadly at the range of work—essays, novels, memoir—she has written. How do you think the ideas about writing and life Didion describes in "On Keeping a Notebook" are reflected in this work?

# Learning to Read and Write

*Frederick Douglass was born a slave in 1818 in Maryland. He learned to read and write, escaped to New York, and became a leader in the abolitionist movement. He engaged in speaking tours and edited* North Star, *a newspaper named for the one guide escaping Southern slaves could rely on to find their way to freedom. Douglass is best known for his autobiography,* Narrative of the Life of Frederick Douglass *(1845), from which "Learning to Read and Write" is excerpted. In this selection, Douglass tells the story of his coming to literacy. As you read, keep your eye on the ways in which Douglass describes the world opening up for him as he learns his letters and the range of emotions this process evokes in him.*

I lived in Master Hugh's family about seven years. During this time, I succeeded in learning to read and write. In accomplishing this, I was compelled to resort to various stratagems. I had no regular teacher. My mistress, who had kindly commenced to instruct me, had, in compliance with the advice and direction of her husband, not only ceased to instruct, but had set her face against my being instructed by any one else. It is due, however, to my mistress to say of her, that she did not adopt this course of treatment immediately. She at first lacked the depravity indispensable to shutting me up in mental darkness. It was at least necessary for her to have some training in the exercise of irresponsible power, to make her equal to the task of treating me as though I were a brute.

My mistress was, as I have said, a kind and tender-hearted woman; and in the simplicity of her soul she commenced, when I first went to live with her, to treat me as she supposed one human being ought to treat another. In entering upon the duties of a slaveholder, she did not seem to perceive that I sustained to her the relation of a mere chattel, and that for her to treat me as a human being was not only wrong, but dangerously so.

Slavery proved as injurious to her as it did to me. When I went there, she was a pious, warm, and tender-hearted woman. There was no sorrow or suffering for which she had not a tear. She had bread for the hungry, clothes for the naked, and comfort for every mourner that came within her reach. Slavery soon proved its ability to divest her of these heavenly qualities. Under its influence, the tender heart became stone, and the lamb-like disposition gave way to one of tiger-like fierceness. The first step in her downward course was in her ceasing to instruct me. She now commenced to practice her husband's precepts. She finally became even more violent in her opposition than her husband himself. She was not satisfied with simply doing as well as he had commanded; she seemed anxious to do better. Nothing seemed to make her more angry than to see me with a newspaper. She seemed to think that here lay the danger. I have had her rush at me with a face made all up of fury, and snatch from me a newspaper, in a manner that fully revealed her apprehension. She was an apt woman; and a little experience soon demonstrated, to her satisfaction, that education and slavery were incompatible with each other.

From this time I was most narrowly watched. If I was in a separate room any considerable length of time, I was sure to be suspected of having a book, and was at once called to give an account of myself. All this, however, was too late. The first step had been taken. Mistress, in teaching me the alphabet, had given me the *inch*, and no precaution could prevent me from taking the *ell*.

The plan which I adopted, and the one by which I was most successful, was that of making friends of all the little white boys whom I met in the street. As many of these as I could, I converted into teachers. With their kindly aid, obtained at different times and in different places, I finally succeeded in learning to read. When I was sent of errands, I always took my book with me, and by going one part of my errand quickly, I found time to get a lesson before my return. I used also to carry bread with me, enough of which was always in the house, and to which I was always welcome; for I was much better off in this regard than many of the poor white children in our neighborhood. This bread I used to bestow upon the hungry little urchins, who, in return, would give me that more valuable bread of knowledge. I am strongly tempted to give the names of two or three of those little boys, as a testimonial of the gratitude and affection I bear them; but prudence forbids:—not that it would injure me, but it might embarrass them; for it is almost an unpardonable offence to teach slaves to read in this Christian country. It is enough to say of the dear little fellows, that they lived on Philpot Street, very near Durgin and Bailey's ship-yard. I used to talk this matter of slavery over with them. I would sometimes say to them, I wished I could be as free as they would be when they got to be men. "You will be free as soon as you are twenty-one, *but I am a slave for life!* Have not I as good a right to be free as you have?" These words used to trouble them; they would express for me the liveliest sympathy, and console me with the hope that something would occur by which I might be free.

I was now about twelve years old, and the thought of being *a slave for life* began to bear heavily upon my heart. Just about this time, I got hold of a book entitled "The Columbian Orator." Every opportunity I got, I used to read this book. Among much of other interesting matter, I found in it a dialogue between a master and his slave. The slave was represented as having run away from his master three times. The dialogue represented the conversation which took place between them, when the slave was retaken the third time. In this dialogue, the whole argument in behalf of slavery was brought forward by the master, all of which was disposed of by the slave. The slave was made to say some very smart as well as impressive things in reply to his master—things which had the desired though unexpected effect; for the conversation resulted in the voluntary emancipation of the slave on the part of the master.

In the same book, I met with one of Sheridan's mighty speeches on and in behalf of Catholic emancipation. These were choice documents to me. I read them over and over again with unabated interest. They gave tongue to interesting thoughts of my own soul, which had frequently lashed through my mind, and died away for want of utterance. The moral which I gained from the dialogue was the power of truth over the conscience of even a slaveholder. What I got from Sheridan was a bold denunciation of slavery, and a powerful vindication of human rights. The reading of these documents enabled me to utter my thoughts, and to meet the arguments brought forward to sustain slavery; but while they relieved me of one difficulty, they brought on another

5

even more painful than the one of which I was relieved. The more I read, the more I was led to abhor and detest my enslavers. I could regard them in no other light than a band of successful robbers, who had left their homes, and gone to Africa, and stolen us from our homes, and in a strange land reduced us to slavery. I loathed them as being the meanest as well as the most wicked of men. As I read and contemplated the subject, behold! that very discontentment which Master Hugh had predicted would follow my learning to read had already come, to torment and sting my soul to unutterable anguish. As I writhed under it, I would at times feel that learning to read had been a curse rather than a blessing. It had given me a view of my wretched condition, without the remedy. It opened my eyes to the horrible pit, but to no ladder upon which to get out. In moments of agony, I envied my fellow-slaves for their stupidity. I have often wished myself a beast. I preferred the condition of the meanest reptile to my own. Any thing, no matter what, to get rid of thinking! It was this everlasting thinking of my condition that tormented me. There was no getting rid of it. It was pressed upon me by every object within sight or hearing, animate or inanimate. The silver trump of freedom had roused my soul to eternal wakefulness. Freedom now appeared, to disappear no more forever. It was heard in every sound, and seen in every thing. It was ever present to torment me with a sense of my wretched condition. I saw nothing without seeing it, I heard nothing without hearing it, and felt nothing without feeling it. It looked from every star, it smiled in every calm, breathed in every wind, and moved in every storm.

I often found myself regretting my own existence, and wishing myself dead; and but for the hope of being free, I have no doubt but that I should have killed myself, or done something for which I should have been killed. While in this state of mind, I was eager to hear any one speak of slavery. I was a ready listener. Every little while, I could hear something about the abolitionists. It was some time before I found what the word meant. It was always used in such connections as to make it an interesting word to me. If a slave ran away and succeeded in getting clear, or if a slave killed his master, set fire to a barn, or did any thing very wrong in the mind of a slaveholder, it was spoken of as the fruit of *abolition*. Hearing the word in this connection very often, I set about learning what it meant. The dictionary afforded me little or no help. I found it was "the act of abolishing"; but then I did not know what was to be abolished. Here I was perplexed. I did not dare to ask any one about its meaning, for I was satisfied that it was something they wanted me to know very little about. After a patient waiting, I got one of our city papers, containing an account of the number of petitions from the north, praying for the abolition of slavery in the District of Columbia, and of the slave trade between the States. From this time I understood the words *abolition* and *abolitionist*, and always drew near when that word was spoken, expecting to hear something of importance to myself and fellow-slaves. The light broke in upon me by degrees. I went one day down on the wharf of Mr. Waters; and seeing two Irishmen unloading a scow of stone, I went, unasked, and helped them. When we had finished, one of them came to me and asked me if I were a slave. I told him I was. He asked, "Are ye a slave for life?" I told him that I was. The good Irishman seemed to be deeply affected by the statement. He said to the other that it was a pity so fine a little fellow as myself should be a slave for life. He said it was a shame to hold me. They both advised me to run away to the north; that I should find friends there, and that I should be free. I pretended not to be interested in what they said, and treated them as if I did not understand them; for I feared they might be treacherous. White men have been known to encourage slaves to escape, and then, to get the reward, catch them and return them to their masters. I was afraid that these seemingly good men might use me so; but I nevertheless remembered their advice, and from that time I resolved to run away. I looked forward to a time at which it would be safe for me to escape. I was too young to think of doing so immediately; besides, I wished to learn how to write, as I might have occasion to write my own pass. I consoled myself with the hope that I should one day find a good chance. Meanwhile, I would learn to write.

The idea as to how I might learn to write was suggested to me by being in Durgin and Bailey's ship-yard, and frequently seeing the ship carpenters, after hewing, and getting a piece of timber ready for use, write on the timber the name of that part of the ship for which it was intended. When a piece of timber was intended for the larboard side, it would be marked thus—"L." When a piece was for the starboard side, it would be marked thus—"S." A piece for the larboard side forward, would be marked thus—"L. F." When a piece was for starboard side forward, it would be marked thus—"S. F." For larboard aft, it would be marked thus—"L. A." For starboard aft, it would be marked thus—"S. A." I soon learned the names of these letters, and for what they were intended when placed upon a piece of timber in the ship-yard. I immediately commenced copying them, and in a short time was able to make the four letters named. After that, when I met with any boy who I knew could write, I would tell him I could write as well as he. The next word would be, "I don't believe you. Let me see you try it." I would then make the letters which I had been so fortunate as to learn, and ask him to beat that. In this way I got a good many lessons in writing, which it is quite possible I should never have gotten in any other way. During this time, my copy-book was the board fence, brick wall, and pavement; my pen and ink was a lump of chalk. With these, I learned mainly how to write. I then commenced and continued copying the Italics in Webster's Spelling Book, until I could make them all without looking on the book. By this time, my little Master Thomas had gone to school, and learned how to write, and had written over a number of copy-books. These had been brought home, and shown to some of our near neighbors, and then laid aside. My mistress used to go to class meeting at the Wilk Street meetinghouse every Monday afternoon, and leave me to take care of the house. When left thus, I used to spend the time in writing in the spaces left in Master Thomas's copy-book, copying what he had written. I continued to do this until I could write a hand very similar to that of Master Thomas. Thus, after a long, tedious effort for years, I finally succeeded in learning how to write.

*For Discussion and Writing*

1. List the different ways Douglass taught himself to read and write. What other things did he learn?
2. The main focus of this passage is the process by which Douglass began to become literate. Who else in the passage undergoes a "learning" process, and what are the results?
3. **connections**   Douglass teaches himself to read and write in a society that condemns literacy for people like him. Sandra Cisneros, in "Only Daughter" (p. 91) tells a story about her own writing, a story set in a very different time and place and under a very different set of

circumstances. What connections do you see between the experiences related by Douglass and by Cisneros?

4. Douglass's education is presented as both pleasurable and painful, opening up new worlds to him at the same time as it helps him to understand painful facts. Describe something you have learned — a new subject, a new fact about the world — that has been similarly double-edged for you.

5. **looking further**   A common topic of conversation among educators concerns the ultimate goal of learning. One version of this conversation is about the tension between instrumentalist goals — you learn to prepare yourself to do certain things, such as a particular job — and the goal of knowledge for its own sake. Read up on this debate and think about what Douglass has to say about education in that light. How does this distinction make sense in his situation? What do you think about the distinction in this context and in itself?

BARBARA EHRENREICH

# Serving in Florida

*Born in 1941 and raised in Butte, Montana, Barbara Ehrenreich earned a doctorate in biology before devoting herself to writing about culture and politics. She has written extensively on social class, work, gender, and politics in columns and in books, including* The Worst Years of Our Lives: Irreverent Notes on a Decade of Greed *(1990),* Blood Rites: The Origins and History of the Passions for War *(1997),* Nickel and Dimed: On (Not) Getting By in America *(2001),* Bright-Sided: How the Relentless Promotion of Positive Thinking Has Undermined America *(2009), and her newest book,* Living with a Wild God: A Nonbeliever's Search for the Truth about Everything *(2014).*

*"Serving in Florida" comes from* Nickel and Dimed. *In the book, Ehrenreich recounts her experiences trying to live on the income earned working a number of low-paying jobs. While these stories are engrossing, that is not the only reason they are in the book. As you read the stories in "Serving in Florida," keep an eye out for the ways in which Ehrenreich uses these stories to make a number of points about contemporary American life.*


I could drift along like this, in some dreamy proletarian idyll, except for two things. One is management. If I have kept this subject to the margins so far it is because I still flinch to think that I spent all those weeks under the surveillance of men (and later women) whose job it was to monitor my behavior for signs of sloth, theft, drug abuse, or worse. Not that managers and especially "assistant managers" in low-wage settings like this are exactly the class enemy. Mostly, in the restaurant business, they are former cooks still capable of pinch-hitting in the kitchen, just as in hotels they are likely to be former clerks, and paid a salary of only about $400 a week. But everyone knows they have crossed over to the other side, which is, crudely put, corporate as opposed to human. Cooks want to prepare tasty meals, servers want to serve them graciously, but managers are there for only one reason—to make sure that money is made for some theoretical entity, the corporation, which exists far away in Chicago or New York, if a corporation can be said to have a physical existence at all. Reflecting on her career, Gail tells me ruefully that she swore, years ago, never to work for a corporation again. "They don't cut you no slack. You give and you give and they take."

Managers can sit—for hours at a time if they want—but it's their job to see that no one else ever does, even when there's nothing to do, and this is why, for servers, slow times can be as exhausting as rushes. You start dragging out each little chore because if the manager on duty catches you in an idle moment he will give you something far nastier to do. So I wipe, I clean, I consolidate catsup bottles and recheck the cheesecake supply, even tour the tables to make sure the customer evaluation forms are all standing perkily in their places—wondering all the time how many calories I burn in these strictly theatrical exercises. In desperation, I even take the desserts out of their glass display case and freshen them up with whipped cream and bright new maraschino cherries; anything to look busy. When, on a particularly dead afternoon, Stu finds me glancing at a *USA Today* a customer has left behind, he assigns me to vacuum the entire floor with the broken vacuum cleaner, which has a handle only two feet long, and the only way to do that without incurring orthopedic damage is to proceed from spot to spot on your knees.

On my first Friday at Hearthside there is a "mandatory meeting for all restaurant employees," which I attend, eager for insight into our overall marketing strategy and the niche (your basic Ohio cuisine with a tropical twist?) we aim to inhabit. But there is no "we" at this meeting. Phillip, our top manager except for an occasional "consultant" sent out by corporate headquarters, opens it with a sneer: "The break room—it's disgusting. Butts in the ashtrays, newspapers lying around, crumbs." This window-less little room, which also houses the time clock for the entire hotel, is where we stash our bags and civilian clothes and take our half-hour meal breaks. But a break room is not a right, he tells us, it can be taken away. We should also know that the lockers in the break room and whatever is in them can be searched at any time. Then comes gossip; there has been gossip; gossip (which seems to mean employees talking among themselves) must stop. Off-duty employees are henceforth barred from eating at the restaurant, because "other servers gather around them and gossip." When Phillip has exhausted his agenda of rebukes, Joan complains about the condition of the ladies' room and I throw in my two bits about the vacuum cleaner. But I don't see any backup coming from my fellow servers, each of whom has slipped into her own personal funk; Gail, my role model, stares sorrowfully at a point six inches from her nose. The meeting ends when Andy, one of the cooks, gets up, muttering about breaking up his day off for this almighty bullshit.

Just four days later we are suddenly summoned into the kitchen at 3:30 P.M., even though there are live tables on the floor. We all—about ten of us—stand around Phillip, who announces grimly that there has been a report of some "drug activity" on the night shift and that, as a result, we are now to be a "drug-free" workplace, meaning that all new hires will be tested and possibly also current employees on a random basis. I am glad that this part of the kitchen is so dark because I find myself blushing as hard as if I had been caught toking up in the ladies' room myself: I haven't been treated this way—lined up in the corridor, threatened with locker searches, peppered with carelessly aimed accusations—since at least junior high school. Back on the floor, Joan cracks, "Next they'll be telling us we can't have *sex* on the job." When I ask Stu what happened to inspire the crackdown, he just mutters about "management decisions" and takes the opportunity to upbraid Gail and me for being too generous with the rolls. From now on there's to be only one per customer and it goes out with the dinner, not with the salad. He's also been riding the cooks, prompting Andy to come out of the kitchen and observe—with the serenity of a man whose customary implement is a butcher knife—that "Stu has a death wish today."

Later in the evening, the gossip crystallizes around the theory   5
that Stu is himself the drug culprit, that he uses the restaurant phone to order up marijuana and sends one of the late servers out to fetch it for him. The server was caught and she may have ratted out Stu, at least enough to cast some suspicion on him, thus accounting for his pissy behavior. Who knows? Personally,

I'm ready to believe anything bad about Stu, who serves no evident function and presumes too much on our common ethnicity, sidling up to me one night to engage in a little nativism directed at the Haitian immigrants: "I feel like I'm the foreigner here. They're taking over the country." Still later that evening, the drug in question escalates to crack. Lionel, the busboy, entertains us for the rest of the shift by standing just behind Stu's back and sucking deliriously on an imaginary joint or maybe a pipe.

The other problem, in addition to the less-than-nurturing management style, is that this job shows no sign of being financially viable. You might imagine, from a comfortable distance, that people who live, year in and year out, on $6 to $10 an hour have discovered some survival stratagems unknown to the middle class. But no. It's not hard to get my coworkers talking about their living situations, because housing, in almost every case, is the principal source of disruption in their lives, the first thing they fill you in on when they arrive for their shifts. After a week, I have compiled the following survey:

Gail is sharing a room in a well-known downtown flophouse for $250 a week. Her roommate, a male friend, has begun hitting on her, driving her nuts, but the rent would be impossible alone.

Claude, the Haitian cook, is desperate to get out of the two-room apartment he shares with his girlfriend and two other, unrelated people. As far as I can determine, the other Haitian men live in similarly crowded situations.

Annette, a twenty-year-old server who is six months pregnant and abandoned by her boyfriend, lives with her mother, a postal clerk.

Marianne, who is a breakfast server, and her boyfriend are paying $170 a week for a one-person trailer.

Billy, who at $10 an hour is the wealthiest of us, lives in the trailer he owns, paying only the $400-a-month lot fee.

The other white cook, Andy, lives on his dry-docked boat, which, as far as I can tell from his loving descriptions, can't be more than twenty feet long. He offers to take me out on it once it's repaired, but the offer comes with inquiries as to my marital status, so I do not follow up on it.

Tina, another server, and her husband are paying $60 a night for a room in the Days Inn. This is because they have no car and the Days Inn is in walking distance of the Hearthside. When Marianne is tossed out of her trailer for subletting (which is against trailer park rules), she leaves her boyfriend and moves in with Tina and her husband.

Joan, who had fooled me with her numerous and tasteful outfits (hostesses wear their own clothes), lives in a van parked behind a shopping center at night and showers in Tina's motel room. The clothes are from thrift shops.[1]

It strikes me, in my middle-class solipsism, that there is gross improvidence in some of these arrangements. When Gail and I are wrapping silverware in napkins—the only task for which we are permitted to sit—she tells me she is thinking of escaping from her roommate by moving into the Days Inn herself. I am astounded: how she can even think of paying $40 to $60 a day? But if I was afraid of sounding like a social worker, I have come out just sounding like a fool. She squints at me in disbelief: "And where am I supposed to get a month's rent and a month's deposit for an apartment?" I'd been feeling pretty smug about my $500 efficiency, but of course it was made possible only by the $1,300 I had allotted myself for start-up costs when I began my low-wage life: $1,000 for the first month's rent and deposit, $100 for initial groceries and cash in my pocket, $200 stuffed away for emergencies. In poverty, as in certain propositions in physics, starting conditions are everything.

There are no secret economies that nourish the poor; on the contrary, there are a host of special costs. If you can't put up the two months' rent you need to secure an apartment, you end up paying through the nose for a room by the week. If you have only a room, with a hot plate at best, you can't save by cooking up huge lentil stews that can be frozen for the week ahead. You eat fast food or the hot dogs and Styrofoam cups of soup that can be microwaved in a convenience store. If you have no money for health insurance—and the Hearthside's niggardly plan kicks in only after three months—you go without routine care or prescription drugs and end up paying the price. Gail, for example, was doing fine, healthwise anyway, until she ran out of money for estrogen pills. She is supposed to be on the company health plan by now, but they claim to have lost her application form and to be beginning the paperwork all over again. So she spends

1. I could find no statistics on the number of employed people living in cars or vans, but according to a 1997 report of the National Coalition for the Homeless, "Myths and Facts about Homelessness," nearly one-fifth of all homeless people (in twenty-nine cities across the nation) are employed in full- or part-time jobs. [Ehrenreich's note.]

$9 a pop for pills to control the migraines she wouldn't have, she insists, if her estrogen supplements were covered. Similarly, Marianne's boyfriend lost his job as a roofer because he missed so much time after getting a cut on his foot for which he couldn't afford the prescribed antibiotic.

My own situation, when I sit down to assess it after two weeks of work, would not be much better if this were my actual life. The seductive thing about waitressing is that you don't have to wait for payday to feel a few bills in your pocket, and my tips usually cover meals and gas, plus something left over to stuff into the kitchen drawer I use as a bank. But as the tourist business slows in the summer heat, I sometimes leave work with only $20 in tips (the gross is higher, but servers share about 15 percent of their tips with the busboys and bartenders). With wages included, this amounts to about the minimum wage of $5.15 an hour. The sum in the drawer is piling up but at the present rate of accumulation will be more than $100 short of my rent when the end of the month comes around. Nor can I see any expenses to cut. True, I haven't gone the lentil stew route yet, but that's because I don't have a large cooking pot, potholders, or a ladle to stir with (which would cost a total of about $30 at Kmart, somewhat less at a thrift store), not to mention onions, carrots, and the indispensable bay leaf. I do make my lunch almost every day—usually some slow-burning, high-protein combo like frozen chicken patties with melted cheese on top and canned pinto beans on the side. Dinner is at the Hearthside, which offers its employees a choice of BLT, fish sandwich, or hamburger for only $2. The burger lasts longest, especially if it's heaped with gut-puckering jalapeños, but by midnight my stomach is growling again.

So unless I want to start using my car as a residence, I have to find a second or an alternative job. I call all the hotels I'd filled out housekeeping applications at weeks ago—the Hyatt, Holiday Inn, Econo Lodge, HoJo's, Best Western, plus a half dozen locally run guest houses. Nothing. Then I start making the rounds again, wasting whole mornings waiting for some assistant manager to show up, even dipping into places so creepy that the front-desk clerk greets you from behind bullet-proof glass and sells pints of liquor over the counter. But either someone has exposed my real-life housekeeping habits—which are, shall we say, mellow—or I am at the wrong end of some infallible ethnic equation: most, but by no means all, of the working housekeepers I see on my job searches are African Americans, Spanish-speaking, or refugees from the Central European post-Communist world, while servers are almost invariably white and monolingually English-speaking. When I finally get a positive response, I have been identified once again as server material. Jerry's—again, not the real name—which is part of a well-known national chain and physically attached here to another budget hotel, is ready to use me at once. The prospect is both exciting and terrifying because, with about the same number of tables and counter seats, Jerry's attracts three or four times the volume of customers as the gloomy old Hearthside.

Picture a fat person's hell, and I don't mean a place with no food. Instead there is everything you might eat if eating had no bodily consequences—the cheese fries, the chicken-fried steaks, the fudge-laden desserts—only here every bit must be paid for, one way or another, in human discomfort. The kitchen is a cavern, a stomach leading to the lower intestine that is the garbage and dishwashing area, from which issue bizarre smells combining the edible and the offal: creamy carrion, pizza barf, and that unique and enigmatic Jerry's scent, citrus fart. The floor is slick with spills, forcing us to walk through the kitchen with tiny steps, like Susan McDougal in leg irons. Sinks everywhere are clogged with scraps of lettuce, decomposing lemon wedges, water-logged toast crusts. Put your hand down on any counter and you risk being stuck to it by the film of ancient syrup spills, and this is unfortunate because hands are utensils here, used for scooping up lettuce onto the salad plates, lifting out pie slices, and even moving hash browns from one plate to another. The regulation poster in the single unisex rest room admonishes us to wash our hands thoroughly, and even offers instructions for doing so, but there is always some vital substance missing—soap, paper towels, toilet paper—and I never found all three at once. You learn to stuff your pockets with napkins before going in there, and too bad about the customers, who must eat, although they don't realize it, almost literally out of our hands.

The break room summarizes the whole situation: there is none, because there are no breaks at Jerry's. For six to eight hours in a row, you never sit except to pee. Actually, there are three folding chairs at a table immediately adjacent to the bathroom, but

hardly anyone ever sits in this, the very rectum of the gastroar-
chitectural system. Rather, the function of the peri-toilet area is
to house the ashtrays in which servers and dishwashers leave
their cigarettes burning at all times, like votive candles, so they
don't have to waste time lighting up again when they dash back
here for a puff. Almost everyone smokes as if their pulmonary
well-being depended on it—the multinational mélange of cooks;
the dishwashers, who are all Czechs here; the servers, who are
American natives—creating an atmosphere in which oxygen is
only an occasional pollutant. My first morning at Jerry's, when
the hypoglycemic shakes set in, I complain to one of my fellow
servers that I don't understand how she can go so long without
food. "Well, I don't understand how *you* can go so long without a
cigarette," she responds in a tone of reproach. Because work is
what you do for others; smoking is what you do for yourself. I don't
know why the antismoking crusaders have never grasped the element of defiant self-nurturance that makes the habit so endear-
ing to its victims—as if, in the American workplace, the only
thing people have to call their own is the tumors they are nourishing and the spare moments they devote to feeding them.

Now, the Industrial Revolution is not an easy transition, especially, in my experience, when you have to zip through it in just a
couple of days. I have gone from craft work straight into the factory, from the air-conditioned morgue of the Hearthside directly
into the flames. Customers arrive in human waves, sometimes
disgorged fifty at a time from their tour buses, puckish and
whiny. Instead of two "girls" on the floor at once, there can be
as many as six of us running around in our brilliant pink-and-
orange Hawaiian shirts. Conversations, either with customers or
with fellow employees, seldom last more than twenty seconds at
a time. On my first day, in fact, I am hurt by my sister servers'
coldness. My mentor for the day is a supremely competent, emotionally uninflected twenty-three-year-old, and the others, who
gossip a little among themselves about the real reason someone is
out sick today and the size of the bail bond someone else has had
to pay, ignore me completely. On my second day, I find out why.
"Well, it's good to see *you* again," one of them says in greeting.
"Hardly anyone comes back after the first day." I feel powerfully
vindicated—a survivor—but it would take a long time, probably
months, before I could hope to be accepted into this sorority.

I start out with the beautiful, heroic idea of handling the two jobs at once, and for two days I almost do it: working the breakfast/lunch shift at Jerry's from 8:00 till 2:00, arriving at the Hearthside a few minutes late, at 2:10, and attempting to hold out until 10:00. In the few minutes I have between jobs, I pick up a spicy chicken sandwich at the Wendy's drive-through window, gobble it down in the car, and change from khaki slacks to black, from Hawaiian to rust-colored polo. There is a problem, though. When, during the 3:00–4:00 o'clock dead time, I finally sit down to wrap silver, my flesh seems to bond to the seat. I try to refuel with a purloined cup of clam chowder, as I've seen Gail and Joan do dozens of times, but Stu catches me and hisses "No *eating!*" although there's not a customer around to be offended by the sight of food making contact with a server's lips. So I tell Gail I'm going to quit, and she hugs me and says she might just follow me to Jerry's herself.

But the chances of this are minuscule. She has left the flophouse and her annoying roommate and is back to living in her truck. But, guess what, she reports to me excitedly later that evening. Phillip has given her permission to park overnight in the hotel parking lot, as long as she keeps out of sight, and the parking lot should be totally safe since it's patrolled by a hotel security guard! With the Hearthside offering benefits like that, how could anyone think of leaving? This must be Phillip's theory, anyway. He accepts my resignation with a shrug, his main concern being that I return my two polo shirts and aprons. 15

Gail would have triumphed at Jerry's, I'm sure, but for me it's a crash course in exhaustion management. Years ago, the kindly fry cook who trained me to waitress at a Los Angeles truck stop used to say: Never make an unnecessary trip; if you don't have to walk fast, walk slow; if you don't have to walk, stand. But at Jerry's the effort of distinguishing necessary from unnecessary and urgent from whenever would itself be too much of an energy drain. The only thing to do is to treat each shift as a one-time-only emergency: you've got fifty starving people out there, lying scattered on the battlefield, so get out there and feed them! Forget that you will have to do this again tomorrow, forget that you will have to be alert enough to dodge the drunks on the drive home tonight—just burn, burn, burn! Ideally, at some point you enter what servers call a "rhythm" and psychologists term a "flow state," where signals pass from the sense organs directly to the muscles, bypassing the cerebral cortex, and a Zen-like emptiness sets in. I'm on a 2:00–10:00 P.M. shift now, and a male server from the morning shift tells me about the time he "pulled a triple"—three shifts in a row, all the way around the clock—and then got off and had a drink and met this girl, and maybe he shouldn't tell me this, but they had sex right then and there and it was like *beautiful.* . . .

## For Discussion and Writing

1. Why is Ehrenreich working as a waitress?
2. Ehrenreich builds her argument about the difficulties of living on minimum or near-minimum wage through her use of examples. Her argument is well constructed and her examples plentiful, but the effectiveness of many of her examples comes from their being part of a story. By looking closely at one of the stories she tells about her experiences and the experiences of the men and women she works with, describe how Ehrenreich embeds examples in stories about individuals.
3. **connections**    Lars Eighner's "On Dumpster Diving" (p. 144) makes most of its readers rethink homelessness. Similarly, Ehrenreich's piece makes us rethink employment: contrary to what many comfortable middle- or upper-class people might think, it is clear from "Serving in Florida" that employed people can be homeless or at least in a precarious financial position. With regard to the way in which these pieces make us rethink ways of life, how are Ehrenreich's and Eighner's pieces similar? How are they different?
4. One of the key points of comparison between "Serving in Florida" and Lars Eighner's "On Dumpster Diving" (p. 144) is the position of the writer in relation to the life he or she is describing. It is also a point of contrast, as Eighner was homeless when he wrote his book, while Ehrenreich was only living as a wage worker in order to write her book. Write a dialogue between the two authors in which they discuss this difference. Might Eighner challenge Ehrenreich? Or praise her? How might she defend herself?
5. **looking further**    The first sentence of "Serving in Florida" includes the term *proletarian*. Outside of Roman law, the term is best known from its appearance in Marxist theory. Do a little research on Marxist political theory. Though Ehrenreich doesn't discuss larger economic systems, there is certainly a critique of capitalism here. Do you think this critique is informed by Marxist thought? Do you agree with the implicit critique of capitalism Ehrenreich makes here? Based on your limited research, do you agree with the explicit critique Marx made?

LARS EIGHNER

# On Dumpster Diving

*Born in Texas in 1948, Lars Eighner became famous with the publi-
cation of his memoir* Travels with Lizbeth: Three Years on the Road
and on the Streets *(1993). The memoir of his (and his dog's) homelessness,* Travels with Lizbeth, *was a great success but was not enough to
keep Eighner and Lizbeth off the streets. Eventually with the support
of friends, new housing was found for them, but Lizbeth died in 1998.
Eighner continues to write fiction, essays, and erotica and has a new
dog named Wilma.*

*"On Dumpster Diving" is the essay that led to the writing of what
was to become the rest of* Travels with Lizbeth. *In it Eighner explains
one aspect of his life during the three hard years that are the subject of
his memoir—the process of feeding himself from the refuse of others.
The clear-eyed way in which he describes this process and the manner
in which he situates it in the larger culture make this essay worthy of
careful reading.*

Long before I began Dumpster diving I was impressed with
Dumpsters, enough so that I wrote the Merriam-Webster research
service to discover what I could about the word "Dumpster."
I learned from them that "Dumpster" is a proprietary word
belonging to the Dempster Dumpster company.

Since then I have dutifully capitalized the word although it
was lowercased in almost all of the citations Merriam-Webster
photocopied for me. Dempster's word is too apt. I have never
heard these things called anything but Dumpsters. I do not know
anyone who knows the generic name for these objects. From
time to time, however, I hear a wino or hobo give some corrupted
credit to the original and call them Dipsy Dumpsters.

I began Dumpster diving about a year before I became homeless.

I prefer the term "scavenging" and use the word "scrounging"
when I mean to be obscure. I have heard people, evidently meaning to be polite, using the word "foraging," but I prefer to reserve

144

that word for gathering nuts and berries and such which I do also according to the season and the opportunity. "Dumpster diving" seems to me to be a little too cute and, in my case, inaccurate because I lack the athletic ability to lower myself into the Dumpsters as the true divers do, much to their increased profit.

I like the frankness of the word "scavenging," which I can   5 hardly think of without picturing a big black snail on an aquarium wall. I live from the refuse of others. I am a scavenger. I think it a sound and honorable niche, although if I could I would naturally prefer to live the comfortable consumer life, perhaps—and only perhaps—as a slightly less wasteful consumer owing to what I have learned as a scavenger.

While my dog Lizbeth and I were still living in the house on Avenue B in Austin, as my savings ran out, I put almost all my sporadic income into rent. The necessities of daily life I began to extract from Dumpsters. Yes, we ate from Dumpsters. Except for jeans, all my clothes came from Dumpsters. Boom boxes, candles, bedding, toilet paper, medicine, books, a typewriter, a virgin male love doll, change sometimes amounting to many dollars: I acquired many things from the Dumpsters.

I have learned much as a scavenger. I mean to put some of what I have learned down here, beginning with the practical art of Dumpster diving and proceeding to the abstract.

What is safe to eat?

After all, the finding of objects is becoming something of an urban art. Even respectable employed people will sometimes find something tempting sticking out of a Dumpster or standing beside one. Quite a number of people, not all of them of the bohemian type, are willing to brag that they found this or that piece in the trash. But eating from Dumpsters is the thing that separates the dilettanti from the professionals.

Eating safely from the Dumpsters involves three principles:   10 using the senses and common sense to evaluate the condition of the found materials, knowing the Dumpsters of a given area and checking them regularly, and seeking always to answer the question "Why was this discarded?"

Perhaps everyone who has a kitchen and a regular supply of groceries has, at one time or another, made a sandwich and eaten half of it before discovering mold on the bread or got a mouthful of milk before realizing the milk had turned. Nothing of the sort is likely to happen to a Dumpster diver because he is constantly reminded that most food is discarded for a reason. Yet a lot of perfectly good food can be found in Dumpsters.

Canned goods, for example, turn up fairly often in the Dumpsters I frequent. All except the most phobic people would be willing to eat from a can even if it came from a Dumpster. Canned goods are among the safest of foods to be found in Dumpsters, but are not utterly foolproof.

Although very rare with modern canning methods, botulism is a possibility. Most other forms of food poisoning seldom do lasting harm to a healthy person. But botulism is almost certainly fatal and often the first symptom is death. Except for carbonated beverages, all canned goods should contain a slight vacuum and suck air when first punctured. Bulging, rusty, dented cans and cans that spew when punctured should be avoided, especially when the contents are not very acidic or syrupy.

Heat can break down the botulin, but this requires much more cooking than most people do to canned goods. To the extent that botulism occurs at all, of course, it can occur in cans on pantry shelves as well as in cans from Dumpsters. Need I say that home-canned goods found in Dumpsters are simply too risky to be recommended.

From time to time one of my companions, aware of the source of my provisions, will ask, "Do you think these crackers are really safe to eat?" For some reason it is most often the crackers they ask about.

This question always makes me angry. Of course I would not offer my companion anything I had doubts about. But more than that I wonder why he cannot evaluate the condition of the crackers for himself. I have no special knowledge and I have been wrong before. Since he knows where the food comes from, it seems to me he ought to assume some of the responsibility for deciding what he will put in his mouth.

For myself I have few qualms about dry foods such as crackers, cookies, cereal, chips, and pasta if they are free of visible contaminates and still dry and crisp. Most often such things are found in the original packaging, which is not so much a positive sign as it is the absence of a negative one.

Raw fruits and vegetables with intact skins seem perfectly safe to me, excluding of course the obviously rotten. Many are discarded for minor imperfections which can be pared away. Leafy vegetables, grapes, cauliflower, broccoli, and similar things may be contaminated by liquids and may be impractical to wash.

Candy, especially hard candy, is usually safe if it has not drawn ants. Chocolate is often discarded only because it has become discolored as the cocoa butter de-emulsified. Candying after all is one method of food preservation because pathogens do not like very sugary substances.

All of these foods might be found in any Dumpster and 20 can be evaluated with some confidence largely on the basis of appearance. Beyond these are foods which cannot be correctly evaluated without additional information.

I began scavenging by pulling pizzas out of the Dumpster behind a pizza delivery shop. In general prepared food requires caution, but in this case I knew when the shop closed and went to the Dumpster as soon as the last of the help left.

Such shops often get prank orders, called "bogus." Because help seldom stays long at these places pizzas are often made with the wrong topping, refused on delivery for being cold, or baked incorrectly. The products to be discarded are boxed up because inventory is kept by counting boxes: a boxed pizza can be written off; an unboxed pizza does not exist.

I never placed a bogus order to increase the supply of pizzas and I believe no one else was scavenging in this Dumpster. But the people in the shop became suspicious and began to retain their garbage in the shop overnight.

While it lasted I had a steady supply of fresh, sometimes warm pizza. Because I knew the Dumpster I knew the source of the pizza, and because I visited the Dumpster regularly I knew what was fresh and what was yesterday's.

The area I frequent is inhabited by many affluent college stu- 25 dents. I am not here by chance; the Dumpsters in this area are very rich. Students throw out many good things, including food. In particular they tend to throw everything out when they move at the end of a semester, before and after breaks, and around midterm when many of them despair of college. So I find it advantageous to keep an eye on the academic calendar.

The students throw food away around the breaks because they do not know whether it has spoiled or will spoil before they return. A typical discard is a half jar of peanut butter. In fact nonorganic peanut butter does not require refrigeration and is unlikely to spoil in any reasonable time. The student does not know that, and since it is Daddy's money, the student decides not to take a chance.

Opened containers require caution and some attention to the question "Why was this discarded?" But in the case of discards from student apartments, the answer may be that the item was discarded through carelessness, ignorance, or wastefulness. This can sometimes be deduced when the item is found with many others, including some that are obviously perfectly good.

Some students, and others, approach defrosting a freezer by chucking out the whole lot. Not only do the circumstances of such a find tell the story, but also the mass of frozen goods stays cold for a long time and items may be found still frozen or freshly thawed.

Yogurt, cheese, and sour cream are items that are often thrown out while they are still good. Occasionally I find a cheese with a spot of mold, which of course I just pare off, and because it is obvious why such a cheese was discarded, I treat it with less suspicion than an apparently perfect cheese found in similar circumstances. Yogurt is often discarded, still sealed, only because the expiration date on the carton had passed. This is one of my favorite finds because yogurt will keep for several days, even in warm weather.

Students throw out canned goods and staples at the end of semesters and when they give up college at midterm. Drugs, pornography, spirits, and the like are often discarded when parents are expected — Dad's day, for example. And spirits also turn up after big party weekends, presumably discarded by the newly reformed. Wine and spirits, of course, keep perfectly well even once opened.

My test for carbonated soft drinks is whether they still fizz vigorously. Many juices or other beverages are too acid or too syrupy to cause much concern provided they are not visibly contaminated. Liquids, however, require some care.

One hot day I found a large jug of Pat O'Brien's Hurricane mix. The jug had been opened, but it was still ice cold. I drank three large glasses before it became apparent to me that someone had added the rum to the mix, and not a little rum. I never tasted the rum and by the time I began to feel the effects I had already ingested a very large quantity of the beverage. Some divers would have considered this a boon, but being suddenly and thoroughly intoxicated in a public place in the early afternoon is not my idea of a good time.

I have heard of people maliciously contaminating discarded food and even handouts, but mostly I have heard of this from people with vivid imaginations who have had no experience with the Dumpsters themselves. Just before the pizza shop stopped discarding its garbage at night, jalapeños began showing up on most of the discarded pizzas. If indeed this was meant to discourage me it was a wasted effort because I am native Texan.

For myself, I avoid game, poultry, pork, and egg-based foods whether I find them raw or cooked. I seldom have the means to cook what I find, but when I do I avail myself of plentiful supplies of beef which is often in very good condition. I suppose fish becomes disagreeable before it becomes dangerous. The dog is happy to have any such thing that is past its prime and, in fact, does not recognize fish as food until it is quite strong.

Home leftovers, as opposed to surpluses from restaurants, are very often bad. Evidently, especially among students, there is a common type of personality that carefully wraps up even the smallest leftover and shoves it into the back of the refrigerator for six months or so before discarding it. Characteristic of this type are the reused jars and margarine tubs which house the remains.

I avoid ethnic foods I am unfamiliar with. If I do not know what it is supposed to look like when it is good, I cannot be certain I will be able to tell if it is bad.

No matter how careful I am I still get dysentery at least once a month, oftener in warm weather. I do not want to paint too romantic a picture. Dumpster diving has serious drawbacks as a way of life.

I learned to scavenge gradually, on my own. Since then I have initiated several companions into the trade. I have learned that there is a predictable series of stages a person goes through in learning to scavenge.

At first the new scavenger is filled with disgust and self-loathing. He is ashamed of being seen and may lurk around, trying to duck behind things, or he may try to dive at night.

(In fact, most people instinctively look away from a scavenger. By skulking around, the novice calls attention to himself and arouses suspicion. Diving at night is ineffective and needlessly messy.)

Every grain of rice seems to be a maggot. Everything seems to stink. He can wipe the egg yolk off the found can, but he cannot erase the stigma of eating garbage out of his mind.

That stage passes with experience. The scavenger finds a pair of running shoes that fit and look and smell brand new. He finds a pocket calculator in perfect working order. He finds pristine ice cream, still frozen, more than he can eat or keep. He begins to understand: people do throw away perfectly good stuff, a lot of perfectly good stuff.

At this stage, Dumpster shyness begins to dissipate. The diver, after all, has the last laugh. He is finding all manner of good things which are his for the taking. Those who disparage his profession are the fools, not he.

He may begin to hang onto some perfectly good things for which he has neither a use nor a market. Then he begins to take note of the things which are not perfectly good but are nearly so. He mates a Walkman with broken earphones and one that is missing a battery cover. He picks up things which he can repair.

At this stage he may become lost and never recover. Dumpsters   45 are full of things of some potential value to someone and also of things which never have much intrinsic value but are interesting. All the Dumpster divers I have known come to the point of trying to acquire everything they touch. Why not take it, they reason, since it is all free.

This is, of course, hopeless. Most divers come to realize that they must restrict themselves to items of relatively immediate utility. But in some cases the diver simply cannot control himself. I have met several of these pack-rat types. Their ideas of the values of various pieces of junk verge on the psychotic. Every bit of glass may be a diamond, they think, and all that glistens, gold.

I tend to gain weight when I am scavenging. Partly this is because I always find far more pizza and doughnuts than water-packed tuna, nonfat yogurt, and fresh vegetables. Also I have not developed much faith in the reliability of Dumpsters as a food source, although it has been proven to me many times. I tend to eat as if I have no idea where my next meal is coming from. But mostly I just hate to see food go to waste and so I eat much more than I should. Something like this drives the obsession to collect junk.

As for collecting objects, I usually restrict myself to collecting one kind of small object at a time, such as pocket calculators, sunglasses, or campaign buttons. To live on the street I must anticipate my needs to a certain extent: I must pick up and save warm bedding I find in August because it will not be found in Dumpsters in November. But even if I had a home with extensive storage space I could not save everything that might be valuable in some contingency.

I have proprietary feelings about my Dumpsters. As I have suggested, it is no accident that I scavenge from Dumpsters where good finds are common. But my limited experience with Dumpsters in other areas suggests to me that it is the population of competitors rather than the affluence of the dumpers that most affects the feasibility of survival by scavenging. The large number of competitors is what puts me off the idea of trying to scavenge in places like Los Angeles.

Curiously, I do not mind my direct competition, other scaven-   50
gers, so much as I hate the can scroungers.

People scrounge cans because they have to have a little cash. I have tried scrounging cans with an able-bodied companion. Afoot a can scrounger simply cannot make more than a few dollars a day. One can extract the necessities of life from the Dumpsters directly with far less effort than would be required to accumulate the equivalent value in cans.

Can scroungers, then, are people who *must* have small amounts of cash. These are drug addicts and winos, mostly the latter because the amounts of cash are so small.

Spirits and drugs do, like all other commodities, turn up in Dumpsters and the scavenger will from time to time have a half bottle of a rather good wine with his dinner. But the wino cannot survive on these occasional finds; he must have his daily dose to stave off the DTs. All the cans he can carry will buy about three bottles of Wild Irish Rose.

I do not begrudge them the cans, but can scroungers tend to tear up the Dumpsters, mixing the contents and littering the area. They become so specialized that they can see only cans. They earn my contempt by passing up change, canned goods, and readily hockable items.

There are precious few courtesies among scavengers. But it   55
is a common practice to set aside surplus items: pairs of shoes, clothing, canned goods, and such. A true scavenger hates to see good stuff go to waste and what he cannot use he leaves in good condition in plain sight.

Can scroungers lay waste to everything in their path and will stir one of a pair of good shoes to the bottom of a Dumpster, to be lost or ruined in the muck. Can scroungers will even go through individual garbage cans, something I have never seen a scavenger do.

Individual garbage cans are set out on the public easement only on garbage days. On other days going through them requires trespassing close to a dwelling. Going through individual garbage cans without scattering litter is almost impossible. Litter is likely to reduce the public's tolerance of scavenging. Individual garbage cans are simply not as productive as Dumpsters; people in houses and duplexes do not move as often and for some reason do not tend to discard as much useful material. Moreover, the time required to go through one garbage can that serves one household is not much less than the time required to go through a Dumpster that contains the refuse of twenty apartments.

But my strongest reservation about going through individual garbage cans is that this seems to me a very personal kind of invasion to which I would object if I were a householder. Although many things in Dumpsters are obviously meant never to come to light, a Dumpster is somehow less personal.

I avoid trying to draw conclusions about the people who dump in the Dumpsters I frequent. I think it would be unethical to do so, although I know many people will find the idea of scavenger ethics too funny for words.

Dumpsters contain bank statements, bills, correspondence, and 60 other documents, just as anyone might expect. But there are also less obvious sources of information. Pill bottles, for example. The labels on pill bottles contain the name of the patient, the name of the doctor, and the name of the drug. AIDS drugs and antipsychotic medicines, to name but two groups, are specific and are seldom prescribed for any other disorders. The plastic compacts for birth control pills usually have complete label information.

Despite all of this sensitive information, I have had only one apartment resident object to my going through the Dumpster. In that case it turned out the resident was a university athlete who was taking bets and who was afraid I would turn up his wager slips.

Occasionally a find tells a story. I once found a small paper bag containing some unused condoms, several partial tubes of flavored sexual lubricant, a partially used compact of birth control pills, and the torn pieces of a picture of a young man. Clearly she was through with him and planning to give up sex altogether.

Dumpster things are often sad — abandoned teddy bears, shredded wedding books, despaired-of sales kits. I find many pets lying in state in Dumpsters. Although I hope to get off the streets so that Lizbeth can have a long and comfortable old age, I know this hope is not very realistic. So I suppose when her time comes she too will go into a Dumpster. I will have no better place for her. And after all, for most of her life her livelihood has come from the Dumpster. When she finds something I think is safe that has been spilled from the Dumpster I let her have it. She already knows the route around the best Dumpsters. I like to think that if she survives me she will have a chance of evading the dog catcher and of finding her sustenance on the route.

Silly vanities also come to rest in the Dumpsters. I am a rather accomplished needleworker. I get a lot of materials from the Dumpsters. Evidently sorority girls, hoping to impress someone, perhaps themselves, with their mastery of a womanly art, buy a lot of embroider-by-number kits, work a few stitches horribly, and eventually discard the whole mess. I pull out their stitches, turn the canvas over, and work an original design. Do not think I refrain from chuckling as I make original gifts from these kits.

I find diaries and journals. I have often thought of compiling a   65
book of literary found objects. And perhaps I will one day. But what I find is hopelessly commonplace and bad without being, even unconsciously, camp. College students also discard their papers. I am horrified to discover the kind of paper which now merits an A in an undergraduate course. I am grateful, however, for the number of good books and magazines the students throw out.

In the area I know best I have never discovered vermin in the Dumpsters, but there are two kinds of kitty surprise. One is alley cats which I meet as they leap, claws first, out of Dumpsters. This is especially thrilling when I have Lizbeth in tow. The other kind of kitty surprise is a plastic garbage bag filled with some ponderous, amorphous mass. This always proves to be used cat litter.

City bees harvest doughnut glaze and this makes the Dumpster at the doughnut shop more interesting. My faith in the instinctive wisdom of animals is always shaken whenever I see Lizbeth attempt to catch a bee in her mouth, which she does whenever bees are present. Evidently some birds find Dumpsters profitable, for birdie surprise is almost as common as kitty surprise of the first kind. In hunting season all kinds of small game turn up in Dumpsters, some of it, sadly, not entirely dead. Curiously, summer and winter, maggots are uncommon.

The worst of the living and near-living hazards of the Dumpsters are the fire ants. The food that they claim is not much of a loss, but they are vicious and aggressive. It is very easy to brush against some surface of the Dumpster and pick up half a dozen or more fire ants, usually in some sensitive area such as the underarm. One advantage of bringing Lizbeth along as I make Dumpster rounds is that, for obvious reasons, she is very alert to ground-based fire ants. When Lizbeth recognizes the signs of fire ant infestation around our feet she does the Dance of the Zillion Fire Ants. I have learned not to ignore this warning from Lizbeth, whether I perceive the tiny ants or not, but to remove ourselves at Lizbeth's first pas de bourrée.[1] All the more so because the ants are the worst in the months I wear flip-flops, if I have them.

(Perhaps someone will misunderstand the above. Lizbeth does the Dance of the Zillion Fire Ants when she recognizes more fire ants than she cares to eat, not when she is being bitten. Since I have learned to react promptly, she does not get bitten at all. It is the isolated patrol of fire ants that falls in Lizbeth's range that deserves pity. Lizbeth finds them quite tasty.)

By far the best way to go through a Dumpster is to lower yourself into it. Most of the good stuff tends to settle at the bottom because it is usually weightier than the rubbish. My more athletic companions have often demonstrated to me that they can extract much good material from a Dumpster I have already been over. 70

To those psychologically or physically unprepared to enter a Dumpster, I recommend a stout stick, preferably with some barb or hook at one end. The hook can be used to grab plastic garbage bags. When I find canned goods or other objects loose at the bottom of a Dumpster I usually can roll them into a small bag that I can then hoist up. Much Dumpster diving is a matter of experience for which nothing will do except practice.

Dumpster diving is outdoor work, often surprisingly pleasant. It is not entirely predictable; things of interest turn up every day and some days there are finds of great value. I am always very

---

1. **pas de bourrée:** A ballet step (French). [Ed.]

pleased when I can turn up exactly the thing I most wanted to find. Yet in spite of the element of chance, scavenging more than most other pursuits tends to yield returns in some proportion to the effort and intelligence brought to bear. It is very sweet to turn up a few dollars in change from a Dumpster that has just been gone over by a wino.

The land is now covered with cities. The cities are full of Dumpsters. I think of scavenging as a modern form of self-reliance. In any event, after ten years of government service, where everything is geared to the lowest common denominator, I find work that rewards initiative and effort refreshing. Certainly I would be happy to have a sinecure again, but I am not heartbroken not to have one anymore.

I find from the experience of scavenging two rather deep lessons. The first is to take what I can use and let the rest go by. I have come to think that there is no value in the abstract. A thing I cannot use or make useful, perhaps by trading, has no value however fine or rare it may be. I mean useful in a broad sense — so, for example, some art I would think useful and valuable, but other art might be otherwise for me.

I was shocked to realize that some things are not worth acquiring, but now I think it is so. Some material things are white elephants that eat up the possessor's substance.                         75

The second lesson is of the transience of material being. This has not quite converted me to a dualist, but it has made some headway in that direction. I do not suppose that ideas are immortal, but certainly mental things are longer-lived than other material things.

Once I was the sort of person who invests material objects with sentimental value. Now I no longer have those things, but I have the sentiments yet.

Many times in my travels I have lost everything but the clothes I was wearing and Lizbeth. The things I find in Dumpsters, the love letters and ragdolls of so many lives, remind me of this lesson. Now I hardly pick up a thing without envisioning the time I will cast it away. This I think is a healthy state of mind. Almost everything I have now has already been cast out at least once, proving that what I own is valueless to someone.

Anyway, I find my desire to grab for the gaudy bauble has been largely sated. I think this is an attitude I share with the very wealthy—we both know there is plenty more where what we have came from. Between us are the rat-race millions who have confounded their selves with the objects they grasp and who nightly scavenge the cable channels looking for they know not what.

I am sorry for them.                                                          80

*For Discussion and Writing*

1. Eighner is careful to offer definitions of the key terms he uses. List those key terms and their definitions.

2. Summarize Eighner's analysis of the practical stages through which a beginning Dumpster diver goes. What does his analysis tell us about the larger experience of having to scavenge for food? What does his writing style tell you about his views on his way of life?

3. **connections**   Read William F. Buckley Jr.'s "Why Don't We Complain?" (p. 69) alongside Eighner's essay. Compare the two essayists' attitudes about their daily lives. Compare their lives, using the evidence presented in their essays. Who sees his life as more difficult? Who complains more? What do you make of the differences between their lives and their attitudes toward them?

4. How does reading Eighner make you feel about your own material values? How do you relate to Dumpster diving and to what he calls the "grab for the gaudy bauble" (par. 79)?

5. **looking further**   "On Dumpster Diving" is a classic example of the rhetorical mode known as process analysis. Eighner takes readers through all of the things involved in Dumpster diving, sharing descriptive details and step-by-step accounts. Rarely does he step back and talk about what living in this way has taught him about how the larger world works. Do you think his close attention to the process of Dumpster diving helps him make a larger argument about how the world is or should be, or do you think it obscures any larger point he might want to press? Further, do you think his attention to the process is less effective as an exposé because it makes something that could be seen as the degrading result of larger forces seem more acceptable?

STEPHANIE ERICSSON

# The Ways We Lie

*A screenwriter and advertising copywriter, Stephanie Ericsson, born in 1953 and raised in San Francisco, is also an author of self-help books, including* Companion through the Darkness: Inner Dialogues on Grief *(1993). "The Ways We Lie" originally appeared in the* Utne Reader. *Consider, as you read, how Ericsson breaks down the activity of lying into the different kinds of lies we tell but also manages to pull together the different sections of her essay to make a larger point about the role lying plays in our lives and our culture.*

The bank called today and I told them my deposit was in the mail, even though I hadn't written a check yet. It'd been a rough day. The baby I'm pregnant with decided to do aerobics on my lungs for two hours, our three-year-old daughter painted the living-room couch with lipstick, the IRS put me on hold for an hour, and I was late to a business meeting because I was tired.

I told my client that traffic had been bad. When my partner came home, his haggard face told me his day hadn't gone any better than mine, so when he asked, "How was your day?" I said, "Oh, fine," knowing that one more straw might break his back. A friend called and wanted to take me to lunch. I said I was busy. Four lies in the course of a day, none of which I felt the least bit guilty about.

We lie. We all do. We exaggerate, we minimize, we avoid confrontation, we spare people's feelings, we conveniently forget, we keep secrets, we justify lying to the big-guy institutions. Like most people, I indulge in small falsehoods and still think of myself as an honest person. Sure I lie, but it doesn't hurt anything. Or does it?

I once tried going a whole week without telling a lie, and it was paralyzing. I discovered that telling the truth all the time is nearly impossible. It means living with some serious consequences:

the bank charges me $60 in overdraft fees, my partner keels over when I tell him about my travails, my client fires me for telling her I didn't feel like being on time, and my friend takes it personally when I say I'm not hungry. There must be some merit to lying.

But if I justify lying, what makes me any different from slick politicians or the corporate robbers who raided the S&L industry? Saying it's okay to lie one way and not another is hedging. I cannot seem to escape the voice deep inside me that tells me: when someone lies, someone loses. 5

What far-reaching consequences will I, or others, pay as a result of my lie? Will someone's trust be destroyed? Will someone else pay *my* penance because I ducked out? We must consider the *meaning of our actions*. Deception, lies, capital crimes, and misdemeanors all carry meanings. *Webster's* definition of *lie* is specific:

1. a false statement or action especially made with the intent to deceive;
2. anything that gives or is meant to give a false impression.

A definition like this implies that there are many, many ways to tell a lie. Here are just a few.

## THE WHITE LIE

*A man who won't lie to a woman has very little consideration for her feelings.*

— BERGEN EVANS

The white lie assumes that the truth will cause more damage than a simple, harmless untruth. Telling a friend he looks great when he looks like hell can be based on a decision that the friend needs a compliment more than a frank opinion. But, in effect, it is the liar deciding what is best for the lied to. Ultimately, it is a vote of no confidence. It is an act of subtle arrogance for anyone to decide what is best for someone else.

Yet not all circumstances are quite so cut-and-dried. Take, for instance, the sergeant in Vietnam who knew one of his men was killed in action but listed him as missing so that the man's family would receive indefinite compensation instead of the lump-sum pittance the military gives widows and children. His intent was honorable. Yet for twenty years this family kept their hopes alive, unable to move on to a new life.

## FAÇADES

*Et tu, Brute?*
— CAESAR

We all put up façades to one degree or another. When I put on a suit to go to see a client, I feel as though I am putting on another face, obeying the expectation that serious businesspeople wear suits rather than sweatpants. But I'm a writer. Normally, I get up, get the kid off to school, and sit at my computer in my pajamas until four in the afternoon. When I answer the phone, the caller thinks I'm wearing a suit (though the UPS man knows better).

But façades can be destructive because they are used to seduce others into an illusion. For instance, I recently realized that a former friend was a liar. He presented himself with all the right looks and the right words and offered lots of new consciousness theories, fabulous books to read, and fascinating insights. Then I did some business with him, and the time came for him to pay me. He turned out to be all talk and no walk. I heard a plethora of reasonable excuses, including in-depth descriptions of the big break around the corner. In six months of work, I saw less than a hundred bucks. When I confronted him, he raised both eyebrows and tried to convince me that I'd heard him wrong, that he'd made no commitment to me. A simple investigation into his past revealed a crowded graveyard of disenchanted former friends.

## IGNORING THE PLAIN FACTS

*Well, you must understand that Father Porter is only human.*
— A MASSACHUSETTS PRIEST

In the '60s, the Catholic Church in Massachusetts began hearing complaints that Father James Porter was sexually molesting children. Rather than relieving him of his duties, the ecclesiastical authorities simply moved him from one parish to another between 1960 and 1967, actually providing him with a fresh supply of unsuspecting families and innocent children to abuse. After treatment in 1967 for pedophilia, he went back to work, this time in Minnesota. The new diocese was aware of Father Porter's obsession with children, but they needed priests and recklessly believed treatment had cured him. More children were abused until he was relieved of his duties a year later. By his own admission, Porter may have abused as many as a hundred children.

Ignoring the facts may not in and of itself be a form of lying, but consider the context of this situation. If a lie is *a false action done with the intent to deceive*, then the Catholic Church's conscious covering for Porter created irreparable consequences. The church became a co-perpetrator with Porter.

## DEFLECTING

> *When you have no basis for an argument, abuse the plaintiff.*
> —CICERO

I've discovered that I can keep anyone from seeing the true me by being selectively blatant. I set a precedent of being up-front about intimate issues, but I never bring up the things I truly want to hide; I just let people assume I'm revealing everything. It's an effective way of hiding.

Any good liar knows that the way to perpetuate an untruth is to deflect attention from it. When Clarence Thomas exploded with accusations that the Senate hearings were a "high-tech lynching," he simply switched the focus from a highly charged subject to a radioactive subject. Rather than defending himself, he took the offensive and accused the country of racism. It was a brilliant maneuver. Racism is now politically incorrect in official circles—unlike sexual harassment, which still rewards those who can get away with it.

Some of the most skilled deflectors are passive-aggressive people who, when accused of inappropriate behavior, refuse to respond to the accusations. This you-don't-exist stance infuriates the accuser, who, understandably, screams something obscene out of frustration. The trap is sprung and the act of deflection successful, because now the passive-aggressive person can indignantly say, "Who can talk to someone as unreasonable as you?" The real issue is forgotten and the sins of the original victim become the focus. Feeling guilty of name-calling, the victim is fully tamed and crawls into a hole, ashamed. I have watched this fighting technique work thousands of times in disputes between men and women, and what I've learned is that the real culprit is not necessarily the one who swears the loudest.

## OMISSION

*The cruelest lies are often told in silence.*
— R. L. STEVENSON

Omission involves telling most of the truth minus one or two key facts whose absence changes the story completely. You break a pair of glasses that are guaranteed under normal use and get a new pair, without mentioning that the first pair broke during a rowdy game of basketball. Who hasn't tried something like that? But what about omission of information that could make a difference in how a person lives his or her life?

For instance, one day I found out that rabbinical legends tell of another woman in the Garden of Eden before Eve. I was stunned. The omission of the Sumerian goddess Lilith from Genesis—as well as her demonization by ancient misogynists as an embodiment of female evil—felt like spiritual robbery. I felt like I'd just found out my mother was really my stepmother. To take seriously the tradition that Adam was created out of the same mud as his equal counterpart, Lilith, redefines all of Judeo-Christian history.

Some renegade Catholic feminists introduced me to a view of Lilith that had been suppressed during the many centuries when this strong goddess was seen only as a spirit of evil. Lilith was a proud goddess who defied Adam's need to control her, attempted negotiations, and when this failed, said adios and left the Garden of Eden.

This omission of Lilith from the Bible was a patriarchal strategy to keep women weak. Omitting the strong-woman archetype of Lilith from Western religions and starting the story with Eve    20 the Rib has helped keep Christian and Jewish women believing they were the lesser sex for thousands of years.

## STEREOTYPES AND CLICHÉS

*Where opinion does not exist, the status quo becomes stereotyped and all originality is discouraged.*

— BERTRAND RUSSELL

Stereotype and cliché serve a purpose as a form of shorthand. Our need for vast amounts of information in nanoseconds has made the stereotype vital to modern communication. Unfortunately, it often shuts down original thinking, giving those hungry for the truth a candy bar of misinformation instead of a balanced meal. The stereotype explains a situation with just enough truth to seem unquestionable.

All the "isms" — racism, sexism, ageism, et al. — are founded on and fueled by the stereotype and the cliché, which are lies of exaggeration, omission, and ignorance. They are always dangerous. They take a single tree and make it a landscape. They destroy curiosity. They close minds and separate people. The single mother on welfare is assumed to be cheating. Any black male could tell you how much of his identity is obliterated daily by stereotypes. Fat people, ugly people, beautiful people, old people, large-breasted women, short men, the mentally ill, and the homeless all could tell you how much more they are like us than we want to think. I once admitted to a group of people that I had a mouth like a truck driver. Much to my surprise, a man stood up and said, "I'm a truck driver, and I never cuss." Needless to say, I was humbled.

## GROUPTHINK

*Who is more foolish, the child afraid of the dark, or the man afraid of the light?*

— MAURICE FREEHILL

Irving Janis, in *Victims of Group Think*, defines this sort of lie as a psychological phenomenon within decision-making groups in which loyalty to the group has become more important than any other value, with the result that dissent and the appraisal of alternatives are suppressed. If you've ever worked on a committee or in a corporation, you've encountered groupthink. It requires a combination of other forms of lying—ignoring facts, selective memory, omission, and denial, to name a few.

The textbook example of groupthink came on December 7, 1941. From as early as the fall of 1941, the warnings came in, one after another, that Japan was preparing for a massive military operation. The navy command in Hawaii assumed Pearl Harbor was invulnerable—the Japanese weren't stupid enough to attack the United States' most important base. On the other hand, racist stereotypes said the Japanese weren't smart enough to invent a torpedo effective in less than 60 feet of water (the fleet was docked in 30 feet); after all, US technology hadn't been able to do it.

On Friday, December 5, normal weekend leave was granted to all the commanders at Pearl Harbor, even though the Japanese consulate in Hawaii was busy burning papers. Within the tight, good-ole-boy cohesiveness of the US command in Hawaii, the myth of invulnerability stayed well entrenched. No one in the group considered the alternatives. The rest is history.   25

## OUT-AND-OUT LIES

*The only form of lying that is beyond reproach is lying for its own sake.*

— OSCAR WILDE

Of all the ways to lie, I like this one the best, probably because I get tired of trying to figure out the real meanings behind things. At least I can trust the bald-faced lie. I once asked my five-year-old nephew, "Who broke the fence?" (I had seen him do it.) He answered, "The murderers." Who could argue?

At least when this sort of lie is told it can be easily confronted. As the person who is lied to, I know where I stand. The bald-faced lie doesn't toy with my perceptions—it argues with them. It doesn't try to refashion reality, it tries to refute it. *Read my lips. . . .* No sleight of hand. No guessing. If this were the only form of lying, there would be no such things as floating anxiety or the adult-children-of-alcoholics movement.

## DISMISSAL

*Pay no attention to that man behind the curtain!*
*I am the Great Oz!*
— THE WIZARD OF OZ

Dismissal is perhaps the slipperiest of all lies. Dismissing feelings, perceptions, or even the raw facts of a situation ranks as a kind of lie that can do as much damage to a person as any other kind of lie.

The roots of many mental disorders can be traced back to the dismissal of reality. Imagine that a person is told from the time she is a tot that her perceptions are inaccurate. *"Mommy, I'm scared."* *"No you're not, darling."* *"I don't like that man next door, he makes me feel icky."* "Johnny, that's a terrible thing to say, of course you like him. You go over there right now and be nice to him."

I've often mused over the idea that madness is actually a sane    30
reaction to an insane world. Psychologist R. D. Laing supports this hypothesis in *Sanity, Madness and the Family*, an account of his investigation into the families of schizophrenics. The common thread that ran through all of the families he studied was a deliberate, staunch dismissal of the patient's perceptions from a very early age. Each of the patients started out with an accurate grasp of reality, which, through meticulous and methodical dismissal, was demolished until the only reality the patient could trust was catatonia.

Dismissal runs the gamut. Mild dismissal can be quite handy for forgiving the foibles of others in our day-to-day lives. Toddlers who have just learned to manipulate their parents' attention sometimes are dismissed out of necessity. Absolute attention from the parents would require so much energy that no one would get to eat dinner. But we must be careful and attentive about how far we take our "necessary" dismissals. Dismissal is a dangerous tool, because it's nothing less than a lie.

## DELUSION

*We lie loudest when we lie to ourselves.*
— ERIC HOFFER

I could write the book on this one. Delusion, a cousin of dismissal, is the tendency to see excuses as facts. It's a powerful lying tool because it filters out information that contradicts what we want to believe. Alcoholics who believe that the problems in their lives are legitimate reasons for drinking rather than results of the drinking offer the classic example of deluded thinking. Delusion uses the mind's ability to see things in myriad ways to support what it wants to be the truth.

But delusion is also a survival mechanism we all use. If we were to fully contemplate the consequences of our stockpiles of nuclear weapons or global warming, we could hardly function on a day-to-day level. We don't want to incorporate that much reality into our lives because to do so would be paralyzing.

Delusion acts as an adhesive to keep the status quo intact. It shamelessly employs dismissal, omission, and amnesia, among other sorts of lies. Its most cunning defense is that it cannot see itself.

> The liar's punishment [ . . . ] is that he cannot believe anyone else.
>
> —GEORGE BERNARD SHAW

These are only a few of the ways we lie. Or are lied to. As I said earlier, it's not easy to entirely eliminate lies from our lives. No matter how pious we may try to be, we will still embellish, hedge, and omit to lubricate the daily machinery of living. But there is a world of difference between telling functional lies and living a lie. Martin Buber once said, "The lie is the spirit committing treason against itself." Our acceptance of lies becomes a cultural cancer that eventually shrouds and reorders reality until moral garbage becomes as invisible to us as water is to a fish.

How much do we tolerate before we become sick and tired of being sick and tired? When will we stand up and declare our *right* to trust? When do we stop accepting that the real truth is in the fine print? Whose lips do we read this year when we vote for president? When will we stop being so reticent about making judgments? When do we stop turning over our personal power and responsibility to liars?

Maybe if I don't tell the bank the check's in the mail I'll be less tolerant of the lies told me every day. A country song I once heard said it all for me: "You've got to stand for something or you'll fall for anything."

## For Discussion and Writing

1. What are the different kinds of lies Ericsson catalogs?

2. How many kinds of lies does Ericsson describe? How does the number of kinds of lies help her make her larger point about lying?

3. **connections** What might Ericsson have to say about what William F. Buckley Jr. describes in "Why Don't We Complain?" (p. 69).

4. Imagine a day in which you told no lies of any kind. Write a narrative telling the story of that day and the consequences of your total honesty.

5. **looking further** Is there, as Ericsson writes, "a world of difference between telling functional lies and living a lie" (par. 35)? Regardless of your opinion of Ericsson's claim, write a counterargument to that claim. What is the strongest argument you can come up with against untruth? How can you use it to counter her argument? Where does your counterargument come from—that is, on what moral or ethical system or belief does it depend?

## JEN GANN

# Wrongful Birth

*Jen Gann has worked as an editor, writer, and copyeditor. She earned her BA from Sarah Lawrence College and her MFA from the University of Montana. Gann is Parenting Editor for* The Cut, *a website launched by* New York *magazine that focuses on women's issues. This essay, which originally appeared in* New York, *is about parenting, but it is also about issues that touch on women's experience, medicine, law, insurance, and a number of other things. Like much of the best long-form journalism, it is about an immediate subject and also about a variety of other broader, significant things to which the author connects it. As you read "Wrongful Birth," watch for the ways Gann brings up these different areas, and how she makes one woman's story—her own—a story that touches on many important parts of contemporary life.*

Twice a day in our house, we turn on a projector that casts cartoon music videos on a blank stretch of wall. The songs are catchy and bright and usually keep our toddler captivated for the amount of time we need him to hold still. "There are no monsters who live in our home," goes one of my favorites. "There's only me and my family who live in our home / 'Cause there are no monsters that live here." Up on the wall, two healthy-looking cartoon children learn not to be scared of the dark, while my son clutches my forearm and breathes dutifully into a mask. Sometimes he spots something familiar—an animal with a noise he can make, a color he knows how to say—and rushes to point it out, only to have his voice muffled by medical equipment. Unlike the home in the song, ours does have a monster, one that doesn't hide under the bed or in the closet. Half of it lives in my husband's DNA, half in mine. We're still figuring out what the whole thing looks like, but we do know it's coming for our son. In lots of ways, it's already here.

167

In the most basic sense, this is why: Tag and I are both healthy carriers of mutations that cause the genetic disease cystic fibrosis. Dudley inherited two mutations, one from each of us, and this means he has the disease, which results from the body's mishandling of chloride and sodium. On the outside, this means CF patients have extra-salty skin. On the inside, it means they have thick, sticky mucus in their lungs, pancreas, and other organs, leading to digestive problems and low weight gain, clogged airways and trapped bacteria. The excess mucus causes persistent lung infections, severely limiting patients' abilities to breathe until, eventually, they no longer can. People who have CF must treat it vigilantly, with physical therapy to clear airways, inhaled medications, and fistfuls of pills. Doing so takes lots of money and staggering amounts of time.

Time is important in describing life with cystic fibrosis: how many hours each day you spend on treatments (for my toddler son, two; for adults, up to four), how many weeks at a time you spend in the hospital (a couple, if you're having a "tune-up" for a lung infection), how many months since you last saw a doctor (during periods of relative health, three). How many years you can expect to live: In 2016, half of all reported deaths occurred before the age of 30. In the later stages of the disease, you might measure time between incidents of coughing up blood, keep track of how long you've been on oxygen full time, or, should you qualify for one, count the number of years you're expected to live after a double lung transplant (about five). Most patients with CF die in a hospital setting, after a long, steady decline, of overwhelming lung infections. The first time more adults than children were living with cystic fibrosis was just three years ago, in 2014.

My son has always had CF and always will. We first learned it was a possibility in April of 2016, when Dudley was a week old. The hospital called to tell us that his newborn screening—a blood test that checks for various disorders not immediately apparent after birth—had come back abnormal. Dudley needed something called a sweat test, the woman on the phone said, to see whether he had cystic fibrosis. I told her this had to be a mistake. "If there were something wrong," I insisted, "we would already know." In a tone attempting to be gentle, she explained that this was not necessarily the case.

5

In an educational video about newborn screenings Tag and
I watched soon after that phone call, people perching on stools
described what it means when a baby needs a sweat test, which
is exactly what it sounds like: an examination of an infant's
sweat. Babies like Dudley, we learned, need the test because their
newborn screenings indicate they *might* have cystic fibrosis.
A woman with long hair told the camera that only a very small
number of these babies actually have CF, holding her forefinger
and thumb a hair's width apart to demonstrate just how few.
I was impatient for my family to be safely outside that woman's
fingers, but because very young babies don't make enough sweat
to test, we had to wait another two weeks.

On the day of Dudley's sweat test, the genetic counselor who
took down our information was upbeat. We sat across from her
in a dim room kept warm; already, before the test started, I could
feel Dudley overheating from the clothes we'd been instructed
to dress him in—a hat, a sweater, thick socks. The counselor
repeated what our pediatrician had already explained: how his
newborn screening had shown just one mutation, how there
were plenty of reasons besides cystic fibrosis (a long, jagged
labor, a touch of jaundice) that could be responsible for the
abnormal result. Also, she pointed out, I'd said I remembered
having genetic tests during pregnancy. Unless I had an extremely
rare genetic mutation, a prenatal test would have caught mine.

Later that day, when I called her back after a beer at our
favorite bar, the genetic counselor sounded different. She'd been
wrong about when the results would be ready for her to read.
They wouldn't be in until the next day, she said, her voice newly
hesitant. *Annoying* is what I think Tag called that information.
We stopped by the grocery store; I probably nursed once we got
home. Dudley must have gone down for a nap, because my hands
were free when the counselor called again and asked whether
I was alone.

I put the phone on speaker, and Tag sat down next to me on
the couch, our heads bent underneath a shelf I realized later I'd
always hated. The counselor claimed she'd gone back and was
now able to read the results—which must have been a lie, one I
almost wish I'd called her out on, if it hadn't been so hilariously
and heartbreakingly kind in its intention. I've seen the results for
myself, and the numbers could not be clearer. The normal range

for chloride in an infant's sweat is about 29 millimoles or less per liter. The sweat on Dudley's left arm came back at 68, his right at 71.

"I know this is not what we were expecting," the counselor said, choking up. My own voice rose; I asked the same question once, twice, three times. Our dog trotted over and peed on the rug, as if to express his own disbelief. I repeated myself again: How could this have happened? The counselor explained her theory, which we found out later was not quite right.

All theories aside, ten years ago, when Tag and I walked toward    10 each other in a dark bar off the side of a highway in Montana, this is what we had no idea we were walking toward: the one-in-four chance of creating a child permanently unwell. Because we both carry a CF mutation, there is a 50 percent chance any child of ours will be born a healthy carrier, like we are. There's a 25 percent chance of a baby with no mutations at all. And there's a 25 percent chance of a baby with two disease-causing mutations, like Dudley.

*But if you had known, what then?* a woman asked me earlier this year, shaking her head, her smile soft with pity. If I responded at all, and I'm not sure I did, I can't remember what I said. But I know I did not use the word *abortion*, or bring up our legal situation, or explain the concept of "wrongful birth." In a roomful of people I barely knew, with Dudley pushing a plastic car back and forth over the carpet nearby, I did not tell her that I do know exactly what it is I would have done.

During my first pregnancy appointment, at eight weeks along, it was Tag who asked the midwife whether most people did genetic testing. She told us most people did. We agreed to the tests; the midwife wrote up the order. We were laying the foundation of a plan we'd discussed before I'd even gotten pregnant: If something were wrong, we'd decided, we wouldn't continue the pregnancy.

Before we left that appointment, the midwife reminded us of the practice's policy on test results. *No news is good news.* Unless tests showed something negative, no one would call us. No one did. Until Dudley was diagnosed, we did not know the nature of my results. Somewhere between the hospital that processed the results and the midwives who handled my care, something went awry, and the answer to the question we'd asked was never delivered. I saw the midwives at least once a month for the rest of my pregnancy. At every appointment, we were told how well everything was going.

At first, we couldn't imagine suing them.

But then, we could. I could. Dudley was diagnosed in May; I contacted a lawyer in June. I remember being so proud of myself for the way I did not cry when I explained everything over the phone—not even once. I cut off our lawyer, Martha McBrayer, as she led up to the question and stopped her from asking it all the way: I would have had an abortion, I told her.   15

You can't discuss what happened to me without discussing abortion. In what's called a wrongful-birth case, plaintiffs sue a medical practitioner for the failure to diagnose or inform them of a disease or disability possible to detect in utero; it is understood that in almost all cases, the plaintiff would have aborted the pregnancy had she been able to make an informed decision. The money awarded in wrongful-birth cases goes toward the cost—usually astronomically high—of the child's medical care. In other words, a mother desperate to help her child declares that she would not have had that child.

Tag, Dudley, and I met Martha for the first time at the diner across from our apartment. Between explaining the particulars of medical malpractice, she stopped to smile at our baby. "He is just so present," she exclaimed. "Look at him—he's like, I'm *here*" I grinned back at her as hard as I could, as if the strength of a smile could eclipse why we were sitting in front of pancakes: the assertion that we would not have had him be here, or anywhere, had we known.

For the pro-lifers who oppose wrongful-birth suits, this paradox—what does it mean to fight for someone when what you're fighting for is a missed chance at that person's not existing?—is reason enough to eliminate the legal pathway altogether. Anti-abortion crusaders paint wrongful birth as an attack on those living with disability or disease; they accuse mothers like me of wishing our children had never been born, of seeking flawless "designer babies" free of health issues. The language probably doesn't help: No birth is *wrong*, those against wrongful birth love to point out.

Not long after we met with Martha, I went to gather my medical records from the midwives. I told myself to wait until

I got home, but instead I opened the envelope a block from my house, with Dudley in the carrier and his face against my chest. I remember holding the papers above his head to see the text:

*Results: Positive for one copy of F508del mutation.*

*Interpretation: This individual is a carrier of CF.*

*Genetic counseling is recommended to discuss the potential clinical and/ or reproductive implications of this result, as well as recommendations for testing other family members and, when applicable, this individual's partner.*

Because we'd been under the impression that nothing had come    20 up on my prenatal genetic tests, the genetic counselor we saw the day of Dudley's sweat test had posited that I had a mutation too rare to be detected by the newborn screening. I don't; Tag does. Mine isn't just common—it's the most common cystic-fibrosis gene mutation, capable of being detected by a basic genetic screening. In the sunlight, the recommendation grew starker, the distance widening between what could have happened and what did. The reproductive implication, meanwhile, continued his nap.

Usually, people need a little bit of time to understand the conditions that created our situation in the first place. The summer after Dudley was born, my sister-in-law came to visit; we were talking in the kitchen while he slept in the other room. "But," she said, trying to figure out what it would mean to sue over a disease that can't be prevented or fixed, "if you had known—" I interrupted her, wanting to rush ahead but promptly bursting into tears when I said it: "There would be no Dudley." I remember the look that crossed her face, how she nodded slowly and said, twice, "That's a lot."

The more I discuss the abortion I didn't have, the easier that part gets to say aloud: *I would have ended the pregnancy. I would have terminated. I would have had an abortion.* That's firmly in the past, and it is how I would have rearranged my actions, given all the information. It's moving a piece of furniture from one place to another before anything can go wrong, the way we got rid of our wobbly side tables once Dudley learned to walk. What's so acutely painful is what I didn't quite mean to say to my sister-in-law, what all that past rearranging would mean right now: no Dudley.

Parents like me often feel betrayed by their child's cystic-fibrosis diagnosis: Maybe there was medical malpractice, maybe an inherited mutation so rare it wasn't detected prenatally. Other parents have chosen to avoid any kind of testing, believing it's their destiny to embrace whatever God or fate or genetics deals them. I'm horrified by the sanctimony that often accompanies this acceptance, especially when it's admired, especially when it's offered up by mothers who don't "believe" in prenatal testing or who have more than one child with cystic fibrosis. The women who willingly made choices that were never presented to me and chose a child's suffering: Sometimes I hate them.

I also hate the women who were supposed to care for me. I hate the faceless people at the lab. I hate them ferociously, the way you hate a family member or the closest of friends. I hate them the way you hate a spouse, for all the bad they caused, and how closely tied that bad is with good. I hate them for what feels like the slyest of deals: While my family's life is now shaped around a disease I would never willingly bring into the world, we are a family because of them—unwittingly, they gave me my most precious gift. I hate them for making me a mother whose biggest mistake was becoming one.

My son has blue eyes, curly blond hair, slightly crooked teeth. 25 He's daring, most of the time. He's afraid of doctors and any-one in a flapping coat. I want the people I hate to know these details about him. I want them to be able to smell his soft breath in the morning, just before I strap a mask over his face so he can inhale medication. I want them to fathom telling a child no amount of treatment can make his disease go away, that people with CF are so likely to pass bacteria between each other they can't be in the same room, that most men with CF are infertile, that every drinking fountain holds the risk of a lung infection. I want them to feel all the moments in a life affected by this disease and experience what it's going to be like, to be Dudley. I want to take all the pain and disappointment he'll have and drown them in it.

But no matter whose fault it is, giving birth to a child with a terminal disease is something I did do. This is just as obvious as it is important: I am the one who was pregnant and gave birth to Dudley. That I continued my pregnancy under mistaken pretenses feels like an irreparable violation, one that I don't think any man—including the one who loves Dudley as much as I do—is capable of understanding. A woman once described the grief of her miscarriage to me as a "biological loneliness"; that's something close to what wrongful birth feels like. A biological remorse. Logically, I know the guilt belongs elsewhere. But biologically, I feel a deep responsibility, a primal and uniquely female pain.

In 1975, a woman named Dortha Biggs, then Dortha Jacobs, successfully sued her doctor for not diagnosing her with rubella—known to cause a host of birth defects—while she was pregnant with her daughter Lesli. Hers was the case that established the legal concept of wrongful birth, paving the way for families like mine.

Lesli, who's now in her late 40s, lives in an assisted-living home; because of the rubella that infected her cells in utero, Lesli cannot see, hear, talk, or walk. She has severe intellectual disabilities and has had over 20 surgeries. I was afraid of what her mother might think of me, with a son like mine, who looks relatively okay between treatments. But Dortha was easy to find and readily willing to speak with me, insistent on asking about my child before talking about her own.

Dortha's voice was calm during most of our talk, but it did speed up once, after I brought up anger. "Oh, yeah," she said. "Oh, *yeah*." The last time Dortha saw the doctor she sued, the now-deceased Louis Theimer, was at a deposition more than 40 years ago. In some ways, she respects him because he didn't try to lie his way out of anything. He never denied that Dortha asked about rubella while she was pregnant.

"I don't hate him," she said, taking half a pause. "I don't *like* him." We both laughed a little before she grew serious again: "I don't like what he did to me." She told me about going back to Dr. Theimer to inform him Lesli had been born with the rubella virus in her body. "I'll always remember," she said, her voice full of fresh wonder even after all this time, "him looking at me and saying, 'I'm just going to have to be more careful.'"

The conversation turned back to Dudley, and I tried explaining our situation—the similarities, the differences—ending with a sideways apology for having a child with much more of a chance than hers ever did. "But it's *your* child," she interrupted, "and when it's your child, it's the worst."

30

Wobblingly, I asked Dortha what she felt after the ruling and subsequent settlement agreement with Dr. Theimer (about $120,000, which was placed in a fund for Lesli), explaining I'd been thinking about what might happen if we got a settlement. "It didn't make her well," she said. It did not help her own pain. It helped her get out of debt. It gave her some money for her daughter.

Dortha's glad her case ended the way it did, but she's not happy about the name the action ended up with: "I don't like it!" she told me. "I just think it's horrible." If she could rename it, she'd do away with the words *wrongful* and *birth* in favor of something like "parental choice." For whatever reason, the language, controversial as it is, doesn't bother me. It's clumsy and raw, and I do think it's horrible—just like the circumstances.

Toward the end of our talk, Dortha gently helped me with a question, reframing it to let me know I could ask her about guilt. She said she does feel guilty, sometimes. She'll go back and think about what she might have done differently. Her doctor was a general practitioner; maybe she should have seen a gynecologist. She did call one—but he was too busy to see her, she said, in the voice of someone who's told herself the same complicated, circular story many times over.

Similar decisions I made when I was pregnant continue to haunt me. A friend had recommended I see her midwife over the ones I chose; I didn't take her advice. For my son's sake, I wish I'd chosen differently—the last half of that sentence swiftly yanking away the first. Dortha thinks it's only natural for mothers like us to rove over the possibilities of what could have been, what we did or didn't do. "It's a life sentence," she said simply, 47 years ahead of me in serving hers. 35

When I first started writing about Dudley, his treatments took 30 minutes in the morning, 30 more in the evening. That's since changed. This summer, he tested positive for the bacteria *Pseudomonas* and was prescribed an additional treatment, the antibiotic Tobramycin, which takes 20 to 30 minutes to administer via a nebulizer, a drug-delivery device that diffuses liquid medication into a fine spray so it can be inhaled. When he sits in front of cartoons with a mask on, he's inhaling the antibiotics that work to kill the bacteria. But *Pseudomonas* is likely to return—it's an "opportunistic infection" that, eventually, becomes immune to antibiotics. For cystic-fibrosis patients, it's one of the factors associated with an earlier death.

Lately, Dudley's favorite word is *more*. The meaning seems to blur at the edges—sometimes I can tell he wants more milk, other times he seems to mean something akin to "again." But whatever he means, when he says the word, he stares off into the distance, repeating himself as his voice grows quieter and quieter, until it's more of a plaintive murmur than a demand. He's a toddler, and between treatments, he's a busy, capable little boy. He interacts with the world more and more each day, and he wants things from it.

I'm afraid of what he might want from me someday, of the kinds of questions he'll want answered. He's not dumb: He'll figure out that his disease should have been detected before he was born, not after. The prenatal results should have been communicated to me by the midwives. A genetic counselor should have explained that being a carrier doesn't necessarily mean an unhealthy fetus. She should have recommended that my husband be tested, just in case. She should have explained that in the U.S., one in 29 Caucasians carry a CF mutation. And even if Tag were also a carrier, a counselor should have told us, there was still a 75 percent chance of the fetus being fine. I would have had an amniocentesis or chorionic villus sampling to know for sure.

But none of those results would have been the ones we wanted, and we'd be up against the last *should*: I should have had an abortion. And that's where my conviction crumples, because I don't know how I'm supposed to tell Dudley that someday. It's one thing to watch a loved one suffer. It's another to watch and know it's your fault, even if only because of the way your body is made. And it's something almost beyond me to imagine, looking into Dudley's eyes and saying, *I'm sorry I didn't save you, from your own life.*

It's true that the outlook for a cystic-fibrosis patient has 40 improved greatly, especially over the past 20 years. In the 1950s, most children with cystic fibrosis died before getting the chance to attend kindergarten. This progress was something emphasized to us, over and over again, after Dudley was diagnosed. *We've got adult patients!* our clinic kept saying. It took me a little while to figure out why I was supposed to feel grateful to hear about them, these full-grown strangers whose disease I'd once known nothing about. These days, adulthood is a big part of what I fear most for Dudley—what that must feel like, to be 25 and not sure what 30 will look like, if you might see 40. Our clinic recently added a new member to its staff: a psychologist specially trained to focus on the mental health of cystic-fibrosis patients, who suffer from depression and anxiety at alarmingly high rates.

Right now, Dudley does not look ill in a way that would startle anyone. No one knows he's unwell unless we tell them. A time will come, I know, when the decision to tell others about his disease will belong to him. Young adults with CF sometimes discuss this in the context of dating, how and at what point in a new relationship to explain what I've heard described as a "long-term terminal" disease.

When we moved forward with our lawyer, I first pictured the money we might obtain in a settlement like the crassest of apologies. I could give it to young-adult Dudley if his health seemed to be taking a turn for the worse, and he could use it to travel the world and see places I've never been, in a glamorous rush to fill his shortened life. But this is a silly thought—he'd almost certainly be too sick to travel. And we need that money for his medical expenses.

Recently, the FDA approved Dudley's particular genetic mutations for treatment with a "miracle" cystic-fibrosis drug called Kalydeco—the first drug to fight the disease's underlying cause. It's a stunning change, one that could potentially add years to his life. The news does not come without complications—Kalydeco costs about $300,000 a year. If everything stays the same for our family, with employment and health-care politics, insurance will pay for most of its cost. But the enormity of that burden makes me scared for us, for Dudley. It's such a looming need. And not even the millions and millions of dollars we'd need to purchase this drug outright can buy what I truly want for my son: the chance to look ahead and see the same bright mystery that healthy young people see, brimming in their perfect idiot youth.

Of the bond between motherhood and mortality, the novelist Samantha Hunt has written, "No one has ever looked at my kids and said, 'Wow. You made three deaths. You must really understand life.'" When I made Dudley, I made a particularly brutal death, one that starts in his cells, which don't work quite right. I don't know how to be sorry, only that I am. If I had received my test results, and gotten pregnant using IVF to ensure a healthy embryo, would I still have made Dudley, this exact son, only without his disease? That possibility is agonizing to think of—all the years of life I can't give him.

*I love my child just the way he is* is a sentiment often put forth, 45 fiercely, by the parents of sick or disabled kids. It's not hard to understand the intention—every parent wants to make it clear that no challenge renders their love conditional. But given the choice, if one existed, I would have Dudley another way: healthy. Wrongful birth doesn't grant anyone that choice; like Dortha said, no legal outcome can ever make your child well.

Having to put this kind of pain into words is, to me, the hardest part of wrongful birth. To have to specify what would make me terminate a pregnancy, to imagine my life today without a toddler. There's no escape from knowing that the opportunity for mercy quietly slipped by and that something as idiotic as a clerical error is responsible. But the most consuming, language-defying pain is just the other side of the most overwhelming joy. There are no words for the feeling of walking down the street with the person I love most, no words to describe why I wanted to have a child in the first place. After all this pain and humiliation and anger boiled down to records and money and who did what, the love I have for my son feels like the one thing that can't be taken from me. It's what I know more than anything in this world.

## For Discussion and Writing

1. What is meant by the term "wrongful birth"? Why is it important to the author?

2. One of the hard things to do when writing about emotionally difficult subjects is to manage tone—to navigate middle paths between maudlin and dry, melodramatic and effecting. Read through "Wrongful Birth" again and keep a log separately or in the margins of the book, noting the tones she uses and when she switches from one to another. Then reflect: how does she do it? To what effect?

3. **connections**  Like Gann, Nancy Mairs, "On Being a Cripple" (p. 247), writes about the physical and emotional effects of disease. But the situations described in each essay are very different. What

are the differences between the two essays' handling of disease? What are the similarities? Mairs's essay ends with her writing that if a cure existed for her disease, she'd take it "in a minute." How does this relate to Gann's feelings about her son's "wrongful birth"?

4. Gann relates how it feels to be her in the situation she writes about. Try to imagine yourself into the thoughts and feelings of another person involved in this story. What would it be like to be her husband, Tag? Her child, Dudley? The midwife or the genetic counselor? What would you have to say about the situation? What reactions might you have to Gann's essay?

5. **looking further**   This essay's central concern touches on a question that runs through many contemporary controversial social issues, such as euthanasia, abortion, and the death penalty. Read up on these and other issues you feel might be connected to these kinds of questions. What are the central concerns? What issues of values or morality or other philosophical or metaphysical belief systems inform the different positions people take on these controversies?

MALCOLM GLADWELL

# Small Change: Why the Revolution Will Not Be Tweeted

*Born in England in 1963 and raised there and in Ontario, Canada, Malcolm Gladwell is a staff writer for the* New Yorker *and author of* The Tipping Point: How Little Things Make a Big Difference *(2000),* Blink: The Power of Thinking without Thinking *(2005),* Outliers: The Story of Success *(2008),* What the Dog Saw: And Other Adventures *(2009), and* David and Goliath: Underdogs, Misfits, and the Art of Battling Giants *(2014).*

*Gladwell's work usually takes the broad view, looking for explanations for cultural phenomena so widespread that they are often overlooked as things not needing or susceptible to explanation. Here, in "Small Change: Why the Revolution Will Not Be Tweeted," he takes on a phenomenon that is far from unnoticed—the development of social media—and a possible effect of its growth: the recent spate of revolutionary movements. However, Gladwell uses many of the same techniques and ways of thinking to make his argument. As you read, keep an eye out for the ways in which he makes connections.*

At four-thirty in the afternoon on Monday, February 1, 1960, four college students sat down at the lunch counter at the Woolworth's in downtown Greensboro, North Carolina. They were freshmen at North Carolina A. & T., a black college a mile or so away.

"I'd like a cup of coffee, please," one of the four, Ezell Blair, said to the waitress.

"We don't serve Negroes here," she replied.

The Woolworth's lunch counter was a long L-shaped bar that could seat sixty-six people, with a standup snack bar at one end. The seats were for whites. The snack bar was for blacks. Another employee, a black woman who worked at the steam table, approached the students and tried to warn them away.

"You're acting stupid, ignorant!" she said. They didn't move. Around five-thirty, the front doors to the store were locked. The four still didn't move. Finally, they left by a side door. Outside, a small crowd had gathered, including a photographer from the Greensboro *Record*. "I'll be back tomorrow with A. & T. College," one of the students said.

By next morning, the protest had grown to twenty-seven men    5
and four women, most from the same dormitory as the original four. The men were dressed in suits and ties. The students had brought their schoolwork, and studied as they sat at the counter. On Wednesday, students from Greensboro's "Negro" secondary school, Dudley High, joined in, and the number of protesters swelled to eighty. By Thursday, the protesters numbered three hundred, including three white women, from the Greensboro campus of the University of North Carolina. By Saturday, the sit-in had reached six hundred. People spilled out onto the street. White teenagers waved Confederate flags. Someone threw a fire-cracker. At noon, the A. & T. football team arrived. "Here comes the wrecking crew," one of the white students shouted.

By the following Monday, sit-ins had spread to Winston-Salem, twenty-five miles away, and Durham, fifty miles away. The day after that, students at Fayetteville State Teachers College and at Johnson C. Smith College, in Charlotte, joined in, followed on Wednesday by students at St. Augustine's College and Shaw University, in Raleigh. On Thursday and Friday, the protest crossed state lines, surfacing in Hampton and Portsmouth, Virginia, in Rock Hill, South Carolina, and in Chattanooga, Tennessee. By the end of the month, there were sit-ins through-out the South, as far west as Texas. "I asked every student I met what the first day of the sitdowns had been like on his cam-pus," the political theorist Michael Walzer wrote in *Dissent*. "The answer was always the same: 'It was like a fever. Everyone wanted to go.' " Some seventy thousand students eventually took part. Thousands were arrested and untold thousands more radicalized. These events in the early sixties became a civil-rights war that engulfed the South for the rest of the decade — and it happened without e-mail, texting, Facebook, or Twitter.

The world, we are told, is in the midst of a revolution. The new tools of social media have reinvented social activism. With Facebook and Twitter and the like, the traditional relationship between political authority and popular will has been upended, making it easier for the powerless to collaborate, coordinate, and give voice to their concerns. When ten thousand protesters took to the streets in Moldova in the spring of 2009 to protest against their country's Communist government, the action was dubbed the Twitter Revolution, because of the means by which the demonstrators had been brought together. A few months after that, when student protests rocked Tehran, the State Department took the unusual step of asking Twitter to suspend scheduled maintenance of its Web site, because the Administration didn't want such a critical organizing tool out of service at the height of the demonstrations. "Without Twitter the people of Iran would not have felt empowered and confident to stand up for freedom and democracy," Mark Pfeifle, a former national-security adviser, later wrote, calling for Twitter to be nominated for the Nobel Peace Prize. Where activists were once defined by their causes, they are now defined by their tools. Facebook warriors go online to push for change. "You are the best hope for us all," James K. Glassman, a former senior State Department official, told a crowd of cyber activists at a recent conference sponsored by Facebook, A. T. & T., Howcast, MTV, and Google. Sites like Facebook, Glassman said, "give the U.S. a significant competitive advantage over terrorists. Some time ago, I said that Al Qaeda was 'eating our lunch on the Internet.' That is no longer the case. Al Qaeda is stuck in Web 1.0. The Internet is now about interactivity and conversation."

These are strong, and puzzling, claims. Why does it matter who is eating whose lunch on the Internet? Are people who log on to their Facebook page really the best hope for us all? As for Moldova's so-called Twitter Revolution, Evgeny Morozov, a scholar at Stanford who has been the most persistent of digital evangelism's critics, points out that Twitter had scant internal significance in Moldova, a country where very few Twitter accounts exist. Nor does it seem to have been a revolution, not least because the protests—as Anne Applebaum suggested in the *Washington Post*—may well have been a bit of stagecraft cooked up by the government. (In a country paranoid about Romanian revanchism,[1]

---

1. **revanchism** (from the French: revanche, "revenge"): A political policy of a nation or an ethnic group, intended to regain lost territory or standing. [Ed.]

the protesters flew a Romanian flag over the Parliament building.) In the Iranian case, meanwhile, the people tweeting about the demonstrations were almost all in the West. "It is time to get Twitter's role in the events in Iran right," Golnaz Esfandiari wrote, this past summer, in *Foreign Policy*. "Simply put: There was no Twitter Revolution inside Iran." The cadre of prominent bloggers, like Andrew Sullivan, who championed the role of social media in Iran, Esfandiari continued, misunderstood the situation. "Western journalists who couldn't reach — or didn't bother reaching? — people on the ground in Iran simply scrolled through the English-language tweets post with tag #iranelection," she wrote. "Through it all, no one seemed to wonder why people trying to coordinate protests in Iran would be writing in any language other than Farsi."

Some of this grandiosity is to be expected. Innovators tend to be solipsists. They often want to cram every stray fact and experience into their new model. As the historian Robert Darnton has written, "The marvels of communication technology in the present have produced a false consciousness about the past — even a sense that communication has no history, or had nothing of importance to consider before the days of television and the Internet." But there is something else at work here, in the outsized enthusiasm for social media. Fifty years after one of the most extraordinary episodes of social upheaval in American history, we seem to have forgotten what activism is.

Greensboro in the early nineteen-sixties was the kind of place   10
where racial insubordination was routinely met with violence. The four students who first sat down at the lunch counter were terrified. "I suppose if anyone had come up behind me and yelled 'Boo,' I think I would have fallen off my seat," one of them said later. On the first day, the store manager notified the police chief, who immediately sent two officers to the store. On the third day, a gang of white toughs showed up at the lunch counter and stood ostentatiously behind the protesters, ominously muttering epithets such as "burr-head nigger." A local Ku Klux Klan leader made an appearance. On Saturday, as tensions grew, someone called in a bomb threat, and the entire store had to be evacuated. The dangers were even clearer in the Mississippi Freedom Summer Project of 1964, another of the sentinel campaigns of

the civil-rights movement. The Student Nonviolent Coordinating Committee recruited hundreds of Northern, largely white unpaid volunteers to run Freedom Schools, register black voters, and raise civil-rights awareness in the Deep South. "No one should go *anywhere* alone, but certainly not in an automobile and certainly not at night," they were instructed. Within days of arriving in Mississippi, three volunteers—Michael Schwerner, James Chaney, and Andrew Goodman—were kidnapped and killed, and, during the rest of the summer, thirty-seven black churches were set on fire and dozens of safe houses were bombed; volunteers were beaten, shot at, arrested, and trailed by pickup trucks full of armed men. A quarter of those in the program dropped out. Activism that challenges the status quo—that attacks deeply rooted problems—is not for the faint of heart.

What makes people capable of this kind of activism? The Stanford sociologist Doug McAdam compared the Freedom Summer dropouts with the participants who stayed, and discovered that the key difference wasn't, as might be expected, ideological fervor. "*All* of the applicants—participants and withdrawals alike—emerge as highly committed, articulate supporters of the goals and values of the summer program," he concluded. What mattered more was an applicant's degree of personal connection to the civil-rights movement. All the volunteers were required to provide a list of personal contacts—the people they wanted kept apprised of their activities—and participants were far more likely than dropouts to have close friends who were also going to Mississippi. High-risk activism, McAdam concluded, is a "strong-tie" phenomenon.

This pattern shows up again and again. One study of the Red Brigades, the Italian terrorist group of the nineteen-seventies, found that seventy percent of recruits had at least one good friend already in the organization. The same is true of the men who joined the mujahideen in Afghanistan. Even revolutionary actions that look spontaneous, like the demonstrations in East Germany that led to the fall of the Berlin Wall, are, at core, strong-tie phenomena. The opposition movement in East Germany consisted of several hundred groups, each with roughly a dozen members. Each group was in limited contact with the others: at the time, only thirteen percent of East Germans even had a phone. All they knew was that on Monday nights, outside

St. Nicholas Church in downtown Leipzig, people gathered to voice their anger at the state. And the primary determinant of who showed up was "critical friends"—the more friends you had who were critical of the regime the more likely you were to join the protest.

So one crucial fact about the four freshmen at the Greensboro lunch counter—David Richmond, Franklin McCain, Ezell Blair, and Joseph McNeil—was their relationship with one another. McNeil was a roommate of Blair's in A. & T.'s Scott Hall dormitory. Richmond roomed with McCain one floor up, and Blair, Richmond, and McCain had all gone to Dudley High School. The four would smuggle beer into the dorm and talk late into the night in Blair and McNeil's room. They would all have remembered the murder of Emmett Till in 1955, the Montgomery bus boycott that same year, and the showdown in Little Rock in 1957. It was McNeil who brought up the idea of a sit-in at Woolworth's. They'd discussed it for nearly a month. Then McNeil came into the dorm room and asked the others if they were ready. There was a pause, and McCain said, in a way that works only with people who talk late into the night with one another, "Are you guys chicken or not?" Ezell Blair worked up the courage the next day to ask for a cup of coffee because he was flanked by his roommate and two good friends from high school.

The kind of activism associated with social media isn't like this at all. The platforms of social media are built around weak ties. Twitter is a way of following (or being followed by) people you may never have met. Facebook is a tool for efficiently managing your acquaintances, for keeping up with the people you would not otherwise be able to stay in touch with. That's why you can have a thousand "friends" on Facebook, as you never could in real life.   15

This is in many ways a wonderful thing. There is strength in weak ties, as the sociologist Mark Granovetter has observed. Our acquaintances—not our friends—are our greatest source of new ideas and information. The Internet lets us exploit the power of these kinds of distant connections with marvellous efficiency. It's terrific at the diffusion of innovation, interdisciplinary collaboration, seamlessly matching up buyers and sellers, and the logistical functions of the dating world. But weak ties seldom lead to high-risk activism.

In a new book called *The Dragonfly Effect: Quick, Effective, and Powerful Ways to Use Social Media to Drive Social Change*, the business consultant Andy Smith and the Stanford Business School professor Jennifer Aaker tell the story of Sameer Bhatia, a young Silicon Valley entrepreneur who came down with acute myelogenous leukemia. It's a perfect illustration of social media's strengths. Bhatia needed a bone-marrow transplant, but he could not find a match among his relatives and friends. The odds were best with a donor of his ethnicity, and there were few South Asians in the national bone-marrow database. So Bhatia's business partner sent out an e-mail explaining Bhatia's plight to more than four hundred of their acquaintances, who forwarded the e-mail to their personal contacts; Facebook pages and YouTube videos were devoted to the Help Sameer campaign. Eventually, nearly twenty-five thousand new people were registered in the bone-marrow database, and Bhatia found a match.

But how did the campaign get so many people to sign up? By not asking too much of them. That's the only way you can get someone you don't really know to do something on your behalf. You can get thousands of people to sign up for a donor registry, because doing so is pretty easy. You have to send in a cheek swab and — in the highly unlikely event that your bone marrow is a good match for someone in need — spend a few hours at the hospital. Donating bone marrow isn't a trivial matter. But it doesn't involve financial or personal risk; it doesn't mean spending a summer being chased by armed men in pickup trucks. It doesn't require that you confront socially entrenched norms and practices. In fact, it's the kind of commitment that will bring only social acknowledgment and praise.

The evangelists of social media don't understand this distinction; they seem to believe that a Facebook friend is the same as a real friend and that signing up for a donor registry in Silicon Valley today is activism in the same sense as sitting at a segregated lunch counter in Greensboro in 1960. "Social networks are particularly effective at increasing motivation," Aaker and Smith write. But that's not true. Social networks are effective at increasing *participation* — by lessening the level of motivation that participation requires. The Facebook page of the Save Darfur Coalition has 1,282,339 members, who have donated an average of nine cents apiece. The next biggest Darfur charity on

Facebook has 22,073 members, who have donated an average of thirty-five cents. Help Save Darfur has 2,797 members, who have given, on average, fifteen cents. A spokesperson for the Save Darfur Coalition told *Newsweek*, "We wouldn't necessarily gauge someone's value to the advocacy movement based on what they've given. This is a powerful mechanism to engage this critical population. They inform their community, attend events, volunteer. It's not something you can measure by looking at a ledger." In other words, Facebook activism succeeds not by motivating people to make a real sacrifice but by motivating them to do the things that people do when they are not motivated enough to make a real sacrifice. We are a long way from the lunch counters of Greensboro.

The students who joined the sit-ins across the South during the winter of 1960 described the movement as a "fever." But the civil-rights movement was more like a military campaign than like a contagion. In the late nineteen-fifties, there had been sixteen sit-ins in various cities throughout the South, fifteen of which were formally organized by civil-rights organizations like the NAACP and CORE. Possible locations for activism were scouted. Plans were drawn up. Movement activists held training sessions and retreats for would-be protesters. The Greensboro Four were a product of this groundwork: all were members of the NAACP Youth Council. They had close ties with the head of the local NAACP chapter. They had been briefed on the earlier wave of sit-ins in Durham, and had been part of a series of movement meetings in activist churches. When the sit-in movement spread from Greensboro throughout the South, it did not spread indiscriminately. It spread to those cities which had preexisting "movement centers"—a core of dedicated and trained activists ready to turn the "fever" into action.

The civil-rights movement was high-risk activism. It was also, crucially, strategic activism: a challenge to the establishment mounted with precision and discipline. The NAACP was a centralized organization, run from New York according to highly formalized operating procedures. At the Southern Christian Leadership Conference, Martin Luther King, Jr., was the unquestioned authority. At the center of the movement was the black church, which had, as Aldon D. Morris points out in his superb

20

1984 study, "The Origins of the Civil Rights Movement," a carefully demarcated division of labor, with various standing committees and disciplined groups. "Each group was task-oriented and coordinated its activities through authority structures," Morris writes. "Individuals were held accountable for their assigned duties, and important conflicts were resolved by the minister, who usually exercised ultimate authority over the congregation."

This is the second crucial distinction between traditional activism and its online variant: social media are not about this kind of hierarchical organization. Facebook and the like are tools for building *networks*, which are the opposite, in structure and character, of hierarchies. Unlike hierarchies, with their rules and procedures, networks aren't controlled by a single central authority. Decisions are made through consensus, and the ties that bind people to the group are loose.

This structure makes networks enormously resilient and adaptable in low-risk situations. Wikipedia is a perfect example. It doesn't have an editor, sitting in New York, who directs and corrects each entry. The effort of putting together each entry is self-organized. If every entry in Wikipedia were to be erased tomorrow, the content would swiftly be restored, because that's what happens when a network of thousands spontaneously devote their time to a task.

There are many things, though, that networks don't do well. Car companies sensibly use a network to organize their hundreds of suppliers, but not to design their cars. No one believes that the articulation of a coherent design philosophy is best handled by a sprawling, leaderless organizational system. Because networks don't have a centralized leadership structure and clear lines of authority, they have real difficulty reaching consensus and setting goals. They can't think strategically; they are chronically prone to conflict and error. How do you make difficult choices about tactics or strategy or philosophical direction when everyone has an equal say?

The Palestine Liberation Organization originated as a 25 network, and the international-relations scholars Mette Eilstrup-Sangiovanni and Calvert Jones argue in a recent essay in *International Security* that this is why it ran into such trouble as it grew: "Structural features typical of networks—the absence of central authority, the unchecked autonomy of rival groups, and the inability to arbitrate quarrels through formal mechanisms—made the P.L.O. excessively vulnerable to outside manipulation and internal strife."

In Germany in the nineteen-seventies, they go on, "the far more unified and successful left-wing terrorists tended to organize hierarchically, with professional management and clear divisions of labor. They were concentrated geographically in universities, where they could establish central leadership, trust, and camaraderie through regular, face-to-face meetings." They seldom betrayed their comrades in arms during police interrogations. Their counterparts on the right were organized as decentralized networks, and had no such discipline. These groups were regularly infiltrated, and members, once arrested, easily gave up their comrades. Similarly, Al Qaeda was most dangerous when it was a unified hierarchy. Now that it has dissipated into a network, it has proved far less effective.

The drawbacks of networks scarcely matter if the network isn't interested in systemic change—if it just wants to frighten or humiliate or make a splash—or if it doesn't need to think strategically. But if you're taking on a powerful and organized establishment you have to be a hierarchy. The Montgomery bus boycott required the participation of tens of thousands of people who depended on public transit to get to and from work each day. It lasted a *year*. In order to persuade those people to stay true to the cause, the boycott's organizers tasked each local black church with maintaining morale, and put together a free alternative private carpool service, with forty-eight dispatchers and forty-two pickup stations. Even the White Citizens Council, King later said, conceded that the carpool system moved with "military precision." By the time King came to Birmingham, for the climactic showdown with Police Commissioner Eugene (Bull) Connor, he had a budget of a million dollars, and a hundred full-time staff members on the ground, divided into operational units. The operation itself was divided into steadily escalating phases, mapped out in advance. Support was maintained through consecutive mass meetings rotating from church to church around the city.

Boycotts and sit-ins and nonviolent confrontations—which were the weapons of choice for the civil-rights movement—are high-risk strategies. They leave little room for conflict and error. The moment even one protester deviates from the script and

responds to provocation, the moral legitimacy of the entire protest is compromised. Enthusiasts for social media would no
doubt have us believe that King's task in Birmingham would
have been made infinitely easier had he been able to communicate with his followers through Facebook, and contented himself
with tweets from a Birmingham jail. But networks are messy:
think of the ceaseless pattern of correction and revision, amendment and debate, that characterizes Wikipedia. If Martin Luther
King, Jr., had tried to do a wiki-boycott in Montgomery, he would
have been steamrollered by the white power structure. And of
what use would a digital communication tool be in a town where
ninety-eight percent of the black community could be reached
every Sunday morning at church? The things that King needed in
Birmingham—discipline and strategy—were things that online
social media cannot provide.

The bible of the social-media movement is Clay Shirky's *Here
Comes Everybody*. Shirky, who teaches at New York University,
sets out to demonstrate the organizing power of the Internet, and
he begins with the story of Evan, who worked on Wall Street,
and his friend Ivanna, after she left her smart phone, an expensive Sidekick, on the back seat of a New York City taxicab. The
telephone company transferred the data on Ivanna's lost phone
to a new phone, whereupon she and Evan discovered that the
Sidekick was now in the hands of a teenager from Queens, who
was using it to take photographs of herself and her friends.

When Evan e-mailed the teenager, Sasha, asking for the phone    30
back, she replied that his "white ass" didn't deserve to have it
back. Miffed, he set up a Web page with her picture and a
description of what had happened. He forwarded the link to his
friends, and they forwarded it to their friends. Someone found
the MySpace page of Sasha's boyfriend, and a link to it found its
way onto the site. Someone found her address online and took
a video of her home while driving by; Evan posted the video on
the site. The story was picked up by the news filter Digg. Evan
was now up to ten e-mails a minute. He created a bulletin board
for his readers to share their stories, but it crashed under the
weight of responses. Evan and Ivanna went to the police, but the
police filed the report under "lost," rather than "stolen," which
essentially closed the case. "By this point millions of readers

were watching," Shirky writes, "and dozens of mainstream news outlets had covered the story." Bowing to the pressure, the NYPD reclassified the item as "stolen." Sasha was arrested, and Evan got his friend's Sidekick back.

Shirky's argument is that this is the kind of thing that could never have happened in the pre-Internet age—and he's right. Evan could never have tracked down Sasha. The story of the Sidekick would never have been publicized. An army of people could never have been assembled to wage this fight. The police wouldn't have bowed to the pressure of a lone person who had misplaced something as trivial as a cell phone. The story, to Shirky, illustrates "the ease and speed with which a group can be mobilized for the right kind of cause" in the Internet age.

Shirky considers this model of activism an upgrade. But it is simply a form of organizing which favors the weak-tie connections that give us access to information over the strong-tie connections that help us persevere in the face of danger. It shifts our energies from organizations that promote strategic and disciplined activity and toward those which promote resilience and adaptability. It makes it easier for activists to express themselves, and harder for that expression to have any impact. The instruments of social media are well suited to making the existing social order more efficient. They are not a natural enemy of the status quo. If you are of the opinion that all the world needs is a little buffing around the edges, this should not trouble you. But if you think that there are still lunch counters out there that need integrating it ought to give you pause.

Shirky ends the story of the lost Sidekick by asking, portentously, "What happens next?"—no doubt imagining future waves of digital protesters. But he has already answered the question. What happens next is more of the same. A networked, weak-tie world is good at things like helping Wall Streeters get phones back from teenage girls. *Viva la revolución.*

### For Discussion and Writing

1. What idea about social media is Gladwell arguing against?
2. The most important comparison Gladwell makes here is between revolutionary moments pre- and post-Internet. How does he use this comparison not only to make his point but also to structure his essay?

Imagine other ways in which he could have structured it. How would they have differed? Would they have been less effective?

3. **connections**   Compare Gladwell on social media to Malcolm X. J. Malady, in "The Ghosts in Our Machines," on the internet (p. 261). In connection to what nontechnological phenomenon does each discuss his technological topic? What does each have to say about the connection? Ultimately, how does each essay reconsider the nature of both elements of the connection?

4. Reconsider Gladwell's argument from the point of view of someone who believes in the possibility of social media–enabled revolutions. Make your argument both in response to Gladwell's points and examples and with your own. What evidence or proof or logical point supports the case for Twitter revolutions?

5. **looking further**   Gladwell wrote this essay before Occupy Wall Street. Research the Occupy movement, describe social media's role(s), and consider whether including Occupy, if Gladwell had written this essay after its inception, would bolster or undermine his argument.

JONATHAN GOLD

# What Is a Burrito? A Primer

*Born and raised in Los Angeles, Jonathan Gold was a music and food critic closely identified with L.A. He had columns in* LA Weekly *and the* Los Angeles Times *and was the restaurant critic for* Gourmet *magazine. He was known for focusing on L.A.'s small, immigrant-owned restaurants rather than the traditional subjects of restaurant reviews — fancy, white-tablecloth establishments. Gold was the first food writer to win the Pulitzer Prize for criticism. He is the subject of a 2015 documentary,* City of Gold; *when he died in 2018 at the age of fifty-eight, a number of buildings and landmarks in Los Angeles were illuminated as part of a "city of gold" tribute.*

I have never been able to change a Taiwanese woman's mind when I tilt against her favorite soy milk, and there is no arguing rigatoni with a certain kind of Italian-American, at least unless your opinion is that his mother makes the single best version in the world. When I praise one kind of ramen at the expense of another, I half expect to end the evening with a brace of feathered banderillas stuck into my flanks, as if I were a panting bull. Discussing the finer points of fried clams with a New Englander has all the charm of sticking a fork into a wall socket.

But to talk about burritos is to charge down a road lined with IEDs, every bump potentially the charge that is going to send you flying into a ditch, every screeching curve potentially your last. Tell me what kind of burrito you like and I will tell you who you are, but tell me what kind of burrito you really think I should like and I start looking for the next escape route out of town. The last time we casually described the moist, overstuffed monstrosity that San Francisco calls a burrito, it was almost enough to prod the weepy, black bean–craving citizens to ride their fixies down here to picket. Do we dare insult the oozing tubes of melted cheese that pass for burritos in San Diego, the deep-fried mail bombs in Arizona, or the suppurating man-purses you find in Colorado? Need we even address the fungus-munching, DF-bred snobs who claim the burrito is as un-Mexican as duck *à l'orange?*

On a late summer day when the mountains were in flames and the temperature soared into the hundreds, Anne Fishbein, the photographer whose pictures have illustrated this column since the late 1980s, decided that she wanted to go on an extended Eastside burrito run, a journey through the heart of darkness that is beans fried with *manteca* as the good Lord intended, tortillas crisped on overheated griddles, molten cheese running through its veins. Because it's never too hot for a good burrito.

A burrito is the crackly skinned marvel at Lupe's #2, filled to order while the tortilla is still on the griddle so that it develops both intense toasted-grain flavor and spurting fumaroles of spicy beef stew if you are so bold as to slide it out of its paper wrapper as you eat. A burrito is the slender, home-style product of Tonia's, a burrito stand that has been holding down its corner of Pico Rivera for half of forever. A burrito is the suave, lard-scented creation slid out from the barred windows at Al & Bea's, a burrito so tasty that recently sprung cons squeeze into line behind the uniformed denizens of the police station down the block, and the green-chile salsa is practically a sacrament. A burrito is the fat, oozing block desultorily assembled at the Pico Rivera Lupe's that may or may not have had a primordial relationship to Lupe's #2 40 years ago, but not so you'd know it. (Lupe's #2 has been owned since the early 1970s by Tuche, a burrito master who apprenticed under the late founder of Tonia's—even some 20-year customers don't know that her real name isn't Lupe.) After midnight, a burrito is the bean-and-cheese specialty of J&S in Montebello, a stand that looks like a relic of the Eisenhower administration.

L.A.'s most authentic taquerias think they serve burritos as a     5
public service to their dumb Northern cousins who don't know that you're supposed to eat *al pastor* in a taco. Taqueria burritos are filled with stewed beans instead of refried beans, with grilled chicken instead of gristly beef, and often with unholy supplements of rice.

Certain purists would like to tell you otherwise, but in Los Angeles and other regions of Northern Mexico, the burrito came into being as the rough equivalent of a hardhat's lunch pail, a method of constructing a filling, portable meal from a tortilla, last night's beans and a spoonful of stew if there was one. A burrito is a Chicano thing, a Los Angeles thing, proudly Mexican-American. It is the food of mom.

## For Discussion and Writing

1. What does the first paragraph, which is not about burritos, have to do with the rest of the essay?

2. Gold uses many terms that may be unfamiliar to you because you may not be a food critic, you may not be from Los Angeles, and/or you may not know Spanish. Make a list of the terms you don't know and find definitions for them. Then reflect on the effects of Gold's choice to include them without defining them. What is it like for you as a reader?

3. **connections**   "What Is a Burrito?" could not, in many ways, be more different from Danny Chau's "The Burning Desire for Hot Chicken" (p. 76). They are different in form and content, from their lengths and styles to their subjects. Yet they both belong to the same genre of writing, food writing, and both treat food as important in itself and as meaningful in other ways. Compare these two essays along these lines and reflect on the underlying similarities amid the differences.

4. Write your own piece of food criticism. It can be about the fanciest meal you ever had, something you eat at home all the time, or, following Gold's lead, a dish you enjoy at a local strip mall, gas station, or food truck. Remember to describe the food and the experience of eating it as specifically as possible, and also to try to reflect on why you like it or what it means to you in terms other than strictly gustatory.

5. **looking further**   Do some research into the food you wrote about in #4 (or another if you wish). Regardless of whether you think it might be interesting, look into the history of the dish, cuisine, or restaurant (or, if the restaurant is your kitchen at home, the history of the person who cooked it) and see what you uncover. There might be a surprising story about how the main ingredient came to the country of the food's origin, or a funny story about how it came to be called what it's called (no Earl of Sandwich stories, please), or a revealing story about how your mom came to think it was okay to melt marshmallows on top of sweet potatoes.

RAHAWA HAILE

# Going It Alone

*Rahawa Haile is an Eritrean American writer who grew up in South Florida. She writes short stories and essays; her work has appeared in many places including* Pacific Standard, Buzzfeed, Brooklyn Magazine, *and* Best American Travel Writing 2018. *One of the things the* Best American Travel Writing *series shows about travel writing is that the best is about much more than the places to which travel writers journey or even than the journeys to those places—it's about the traveling writer and the cultures from which they come and in which they travel. As you read "Going It Alone," keep an eye out for the things its author is interested in that go beyond the journey and the destination.*

It's the spring of 2016, and I'm ten miles south of Damascus, Virginia, where an annual celebration called Trail Days has just wrapped up. Last night, temperatures plummeted into the thirties. Today, long-distance Appalachian Trail hikers who'd slept in hammocks and mailed their underquilts home too soon were groaning into their morning coffee. A few small fires shot wood-smoke at the sun as thousands of tent stakes were dislodged. Over the next 24 hours, most of the hikers in attendance would pack up and hit the 554-mile stretch of the AT that runs north through Virginia.

I've used the Trail Days layover as an opportunity to stash most of my belongings with friends and complete a short section of the AT I'd missed, near the Tennessee-Virginia border. As I'm moving along, a day hiker heading in the opposite direction stops me for a chat. He's affable and inquisitive. He asks what many have asked before: "Where are you from?" I tell him Miami.

He laughs and says, "No, but really. Where are you from from?" He mentions something about my features, my thin nose, and then trails off. I tell him my family is from Eritrea, a country in the Horn of Africa, next to Ethiopia. He looks relieved.

"I knew it," he says. "You're not black."

I say that of course I am. "None more black," I weakly joke.    5

"Not really," he says. "You're African, not black-black. Blacks don't hike."

I'm tired of this man. His from-froms and black-blacks. He wishes me good luck and leaves. He means it, too; he isn't malicious. To him there's nothing abnormal about our conversation. He has categorized me, and the world makes sense again. Not black-black. I hike the remaining miles back to my tent and don't emerge for hours.

Heading north from Springer Mountain in Georgia, the Appalachian Trail class of 2017 would have to walk 670 miles before reaching the first county that did not vote for Donald Trump. The average percentage of voters who did vote for Trump—a xenophobic candidate who was supported by David Duke—in those miles?

Seventy-six. Approximately 30 miles farther away, they'd come to a hiker hostel that proudly flies a Confederate flag. Later they would reach the Lewis Mountain campground in Shenandoah National Park—created in Virginia in 1935, during the Jim Crow era—and read plaques acknowledging its former history as the segregated Lewis Mountain Negro Area. The campground was swarming with RVs flying Confederate flags when I hiked through. This flag would haunt the hikers all the way to Mount Katahdin, the trail's end point, in northern Maine. They would see it in every state, feeling the tendrils of hatred that rooted it to the land they walked upon.

During the early part of my through-hike, I arrive in Gatlinburg,    10
Tennessee, one afternoon, a little later than I planned. I was one of many thirtysomethings who'd ended their relationships, quit their jobs, left their pets with best friends, and flown to Georgia. By this point, I'm 200 miles into my arduous, rain-soaked trek. Everything aches. The bluets and wildflowers have emerged, and I've taken a break in town to resupply, midway through my biggest challenge thus far, the Smokies.

It isn't until I'm about to leave town that I see it: blackface soap, a joke item that supposedly will turn a white person black if you can trick them into using it. I'm in a general store opposite the Nantahala Outdoor Center. The soap is in a discount bin next to the cash register. I'd popped in to buy chocolate milk and was instead reminded of a line from Claudia Rankine's book *Citizen*: "The past is a life sentence, a blunt instrument aimed at tomorrow."

There's a shuttle back to the trail at Newfound Gap leaving in 15 minutes. I fumble to take a photograph of the cartoon white woman on the packaging, standing in front of her bathroom sink. She can't believe it. How could this happen? Her face and hands are black. She scrubs to no avail.

I leave. Cars honk. I'm standing at an intersection and straining to return to the world. The shuttle arrives to take us from town to trailhead. The van leads us up, up into the mountains. It's a clear day. Hikers are laughing, rejuvenated. "Did you have fun in town?" a friend I met on the trail asks. "This visibility is unreal," says another, nose against the window. He thinks he has spotted a bear. The sun has lifted spirits. The van spills us out, but I can barely see a thing.

Two days later, a stream of texts hit my phone. Prince has died. I feel my vision blur, sit down on the first rock I see, and don't move for a while. The hikers who walk past ask if I'm hurt. "I'm sorry to tell you this," I'll hear myself say. "Prince just died." No one knows who I'm talking about. I will see variations of the same vacant expression for the rest of the day. "The Prince of Wales?" one hiker asks.

I'm losing light. I have to get to the next shelter. The afternoon 15 has been a learning experience: the trail is no place to share black grief. Later, when Beyoncé releases *Lemonade*, an album that speaks powerfully to black women, I won't permit myself to hear it out here. I'm lonely enough as it is, without feeling additional isolation. I keep it from myself, and I follow the blazes north. I tell the trees the truth of it: some days I feel like breaking.

The National Park Service celebrated its centennial last year. In one brochure, a white man stands boldly, precariously, in Rocky Mountain National Park, gazing at a massive rock face. He wears a full pack. He is ready to tackle the impossible. The poster salutes "100 years of getting away from it all." The parenthetical is implied if not obvious: for some.

In a *Backpacker* interview from 2000, a black man named Robert Taylor was asked about the hardest things he faced during his through-hike of the Appalachian Trail. He'd recently completed both the AT and the Pacific Crest Trail. "My problems were mainly with people," he said. "In towns, people yelled racist threats at me in just about every state I went through. They'd say, 'We don't like you,' and 'You're a nigger.' Once when I stopped at a mail drop, the postmaster said, 'Boy, get out of here. We got no mail drop for you.'"

It will be several months before I realize that most AT hikers in 2016 are unaware of the clear division that exists between what hikers of color experience on the trail (generally positive) and in town (not so much). While fellow through-hikers and trail angels are some of the kindest and most generous people I'll ever encounter, many trail towns have no idea what to make of people who look like me. They say they don't see much of "my kind" around here and leave the rest hanging in the air.

The rule is you don't talk about politics on the trail. The truth is you can't talk about diversity in the outdoors without talking about politics, since politics is a big reason why the outdoors look the way they do. From the park system's inception, Jim Crow laws and Native American removal campaigns limited access to recreation by race. From the mountains to the beaches, outdoor leisure was often accompanied by the words whites only. The repercussions for disobedience were grave.

"For me, the fear is like a heartbeat, always present, while at the same time, intangible, elusive, and difficult to define," Evelyn C. White wrote in her 1999 essay "Black Women and the Wilderness." In it she explains why the thought of hiking in Oregon, which some writer friends invited her to do, fills her with dread. In wilderness, White does not see freedom but a portal to the past. It is a trigger. The history of suffering is too much for her to overcome. This fear has conjured a similar paralysis nationwide. It says to the minority: Be in this place and someone might seize the opportunity to end you. Nature itself is the least of White's concerns. Bear paws have harmed fewer black bodies in the wild than human hands. She does not wish to be the only one who looks like her in a place with history like this.

Perspective is everything.

There are 11 cats at Bob Peoples's Kincora Hiking Hostel in Hampton, Tennessee. When I ask Peoples how he keeps track of them, he responds, "They keep track of me." We talk about the places he's hiked and the people he's met. "Germans have the best hiking culture of any country," he says. "If there was a trail to hell, Germans would be on it." The chance of precipitation the next day is 100 percent. When it drizzles the rain plays me, producing different sounds as it strikes hat, jacket, and pack cover. Of the many reasons to pause while hiking, this remains my favorite. The smell and sound of the dampening forest is a sensory gift, a time for reflection.

The first bumper sticker I see in Hot Springs, North Carolina, says that April is Confederate History Month. A week later, I stay in a hostel near Roan Mountain, Tennessee, next to a house that's flying a Confederate flag. Hikers who've hitched into town tell me that the rides they got were all from drunk white men. Be careful, they warn.

I reconsider going into town at all. It's near freezing. Two days ago, I woke up on Roan Mountain itself in a field of frozen mayapples. Today I wear my Buff headband like a head scarf under my fleece hat. When I walk a third of a mile back to the trailhead alone the next morning, I look at the neighbor's flag and wonder if someone will assume I'm Muslim, whether I'm putting myself at risk. I lower the Buff to my neck and worry that I'm being paranoid. Six months later, the San Francisco Chronicle will report on a woman of color who was hiking in Fremont, California, while wearing a Buff like a bandana and returned to find her car's rear window smashed, along with a note. "Hijab wearing bitch," it said. "This is our nation now get the fuck out." She wasn't Muslim, but that's not the point. The point is the ease with which a person becomes a "them" in the woods.

Two weeks later, at Trail Days, there's a parade celebrating current and past hikers. A black man with the trail name Exterminator aims a water gun at a white crowd as he moves along. He shoots their white children. They laugh and shoot back with their own water guns. This goes on for 30 yards. I pause to corral my galloping anxiety. He is safe, I tell myself. This event is one of the few places in America where I don't fear for a black man with a toy gun in a public setting. 25

The Southern Poverty Law Center tracked more than 1,000 hate crimes and bias incidents that occurred in the month after the election. On November 16, 2016, the Appalachian Trail Conservancy posted information about racist trail graffiti on its

Facebook page. It showed up along the trail corridor in Pennsylvania. The group was encouraging anyone who encountered "offensive graffiti or vandalism" to report it via e-mail.

Starting in 1936, amid the violence of Jim Crow, a publication known as the *Green Book* functioned as a guide for getting black motorists from point A to point B safely. It told you which gas stations would fill your tank, which restaurants would seat you, and where you could lay your head at night without fear. It remained in print for 30 years. As recently as 50 years ago, black families needed a guide just to travel through America unharmed.

There is nothing approximating a *Green Book* for minorities navigating the American wilderness. How could there be? You simply step outside and hope for the best. One of the first questions asked of many women who solo-hike the Appalachian Trail is whether they brought a gun. Some find it preposterous. But one hiker of color I spoke to insisted on carrying a machete, an unnecessarily heavy piece of gear. "You can never be too sure," he told me.

As a queer black woman, I'm among the last people anyone expects to see on a through-hike. But nature is a place I've always belonged. My home in South Florida spanned the swamp, the Keys, and the dredged land in between. My father and I explored them all, waving at everything from egrets to purple gallinules and paddling by the bowed roots of mangroves. This was before Burmese pythons overran the Everglades, when the rustling of leaves in the canopy above our canoe still veered mammalian.

Throughout my youth, my grandmother and I took walks in Miami, where I'd hear her say the words tuum nifas. It meant a delicious wind, a nourishing wind. These experiences shaped how I viewed movement throughout the natural world. How I view it still. The elements, I thought, could end my hunger.

Little has changed since. Now the rocks gnaw at my shins. I thud against the ground, my tongue coated in dirt. I pick myself back up and start again.

Every day I eat the mountains, and the mountains, they eat me. "Less to carry," I tell the others: this skin, America, the weight of that past self. My hiking partners are concerned and unconvinced. There is a weight to you still, they tell me. They are not wrong. My footing has been off for days. There were things I had braced for at the beginning of this journey that have finally started to undo me. We were all hurtling through the unfamiliar,

30

aching, choppy, destroyed by weather, trying not to tear apart. But some of us were looking around as well. By the time I made it through Maryland, it was hard not to think of the Appalachian Trail as a 2,190-mile trek through Trump lawn signs. In July, I read the names of more black men killed by police: Philando Castile, Alton Sterling. Never did I imagine that the constant of the woods would be my friends urging, pleading, that I never return home.

That was then. Back home in Oakland, California, now, my knees hurt. I struggle with the stairs. I wonder if it's Lyme disease from an unseen tick bite. The weight I lost has come back. My arms, the blackest I ever saw them after weeks in the summer sun, have faded to their usual dark brown. The bruises on my collarbones from my pack straps are no more. My legs aren't oozing blood. My feet haven't throbbed in four months. I am once again soft and unblemished and pleading with my anxiety every day for a few hours of peace. My timing couldn't be worse. The news is relentless. Facts mean nothing. The truth is, I don't know how to move through the world these days. Everything feels like it needs saving. I can barely keep up.

Who is wilderness for? It depends on who you ask. In 2013, Trail Life USA, a faith-based organization, was established as a direct response to the Boy Scouts of America's decision to allow openly gay kids into their program. A statement by the group made the rules clear: Trail Life USA "will not admit youth who are open or avowed about their homosexuality, and it will not admit boys who are not 'biologically male' or boys who wish to dress and act like girls."

Roughly two years later, news outlets profiled the Radical 35 Monarchs, a group for children of color between the ages of eight and twelve, intended as a Girl Scouts for social activists. Headlines like "Radical Brownies Are Yelling 'Black Lives Matter,' Not Hawking Girl Scout Cookies" highlighted what an intersectional approach to youth activism could look like. Organizations such as Trail Life USA and Radical Monarchs show opposite ends of the outdoor spectrum. For conservative Christian men, religion is used as a means of tying exclusionary practices to outdoor participation. For people of color, the wilderness is everywhere they look. They don't need mountains. Wilderness lives outside their front doors. Orienteering skills mean navigating white anxiety about them. They are belaying to effect change. And even then, their efforts might not be enough.

"People on the trail, overwhelmingly, are good people, but it isn't advertised for us," says Bryan Winckler, a black AT through-hiker who went by the trail name Boomer. "If you see a commercial for anything outdoor related, it's always a white person on it. I think if people saw someone who looked like them they would be interested. It's not advertised, so people think, That's not for me."

Brittany Leavitt, an Outdoor Afro trip leader based in Washington, D.C., echoed this sentiment. "You don't see it in the media," she told me recently. "You don't see it advertised when you go into outdoor stores. When I do a hike, I talk about what's historically in the area. Nature has always been part of black history."

She's right. Outdoor skills were a matter of survival for black people before they became a form of exclusion. Harriet Tubman is rarely celebrated as one of the most important outdoor figures in American history, despite traversing thousands of miles over the same mountains I walked this year.

"How can we make being in the outdoors a conduit for helping people realize, understand, and become comfortable with the space they occupy in the world?" says Krystal Williams, a black woman who through-hiked the AT in 2011. The change is happening slowly, in large part because of public figures bringing attention to the outdoors. Barack Obama designated more national monuments than any president before him. Oprah has called 2017 her year of adventure. "My favorite thing on earth is a tree," she told ranger Shelton Johnson, an advocate for diversity in the national parks, when she met him in Yosemite in 2010. A recent photo of Oprah at the Grand Canyon shows her carrying a full pack. "Hiking requires no particular skill, only two feet and a sturdy pair of shoes," she said. "You set the pace. You choose the trail. You lock into a certain rhythm with the road, and that rhythm becomes your clarion song."

Halfway through the descent into Daleville, Virginia, I found    40
myself lying on the trail floor, wincing up at the canopy. I had taken a sudden tumble and was dazed. My right ankle ached badly, though my trekking poles had saved me from a truly nasty sprain. It was not a difficult stretch of trail—some packed dirt,

a few small rocks, plenty of switchbacks. I felt betrayed and then ashamed. I could feel my confidence evaporating. If I couldn't walk a well-groomed trail, what in the world was I going to do with the boulder scrambles awaiting me in the north? Falls could be fatal. At worst this one was a slight embarrassment, but it marked the first time I needed to forgive myself for what I could not control.

Every inch of my being by that point had been shaped by an explicit choice. In pursuit of Katahdin—which I reached on October 1, after six months of hiking—I had wept and chopped off the long, natural hair, so politicized in America, that my grandmother had told me to always treasure. My afro was no more. I had left my skin to ash, my lips to crack. I wore my transmission-tower-print bandana like an electric prayer. The Appalachian Trail was the longest conversation I'd ever had with my body, both where I fit in it and where it fits in the world.

One of the popular Appalachian Trail books I read while preparing for my trek asked readers to make a short list of reasons why they wanted to do it. The author suggested we understand these reasons, down to our core, before embarking, coming up with something deeper than "I like nature." I took out this document often when things felt overwhelming on the AT, when the enormity of the pursuit threatened to swallow me whole. Looking back, the list is a series of unrealized hopes. One line reads: "I have always been the token in a group; I have never chosen how I want to lead." Another says: "It will be the first time I get to discover not whether I will succeed but who I am becoming." The last line is a declaration: "I want to be a role model to black women who are interested in the outdoors, including myself."

There were days when the only thing that kept me going was knowing that each step was one toward progress, a boot to the granite face of white supremacy. I belong here, I told the trail. It rewarded me in lasting ways. The weight I carried as a black woman paled in comparison with the joy I felt daily among my peers in that wilderness. They shaped my heart into what it will be for the rest of my life.

One of the most common sentiments one hears about the Appalachian Trail is how it restores a person's faith in humanity. It is no understatement to say that the friends I made, and the experiences I had with strangers who, at times, literally gave me the shirt off their back, saved my life. I owe a great debt to the through-hiking community that welcomed me with open arms, that showed me what I could be and helped me when I faltered. There is no impossible, they taught me: only good ideas of extraordinary magnitude.

## For Discussion and Writing

1. What is the connection between Haile's hike and the presidential election of 2016?

2. "Going It Alone" tells a story, but it is not structured in a linear fashion, retelling events chronologically one after the other like successive segments of a trail. How is it structured? To what effect? Why do you think Haile chose to structure it in this way?

3. **connections**   The essay asks the question, "What is wilderness for?" Another essay that asks this question is Eli Clare's "Clearcut: Explaining the Distance" (p. 95). How does each essay ask this question? Does each essay answer it? How?

4. "Perspective is everything," Haile writes in her essay. Pick a place you go or have been or an activity you do or have done that you think would look different from the perspective of someone different from you. How does this place look (or this experience feel) to you? How does it look or feel different to this other person? What about the difference between the two of you explains the difference between your experiences?

5. **looking further**   Although racial discrimination and political division figure prominently from the essay's start, community becomes increasingly important over the course of the essay. Strangers, often seen as threats, are also by the end of the essay what the author values most highly about her time on the Appalachian Trail. Given the essay's focus on the presidential election of 2016 and its aftermath, how would you characterize the state of the American community today? Base your answer on research. What numbers support your conclusions? What historical trends? What landmark events?

JENINE HOLMES

# When Pink Ballet Slippers Won't Do

*Jenine Holmes is a nonfiction writer who also works as a copy writer and
creative director in advertising. In her nonfiction work, she writes about
parenting and being a single mother. She earned her BA from Parsons
School of Design and her MFA from Spalding University. "When Pink
Ballet Slippers Won't Do" demonstrates its author's eye for the details of
contemporary life that concern appearance, perception, and identity, an
eye that certainly serves her well in her day job. As you read, watch out
for the ways in which Holmes shows her understanding of the connections between how people see the world and how they see themselves.*

As an African-American mother of a brown-skinned 7-year-old
girl, I seek empowering examples for my daughter.

After seven years of infertility and one horrendous miscarriage, I adopted my daughter, Julia, from Ethiopia at 8 months
old and made motherhood my mission. She plays with dolls that
look like her, reads books that feature brown children and had
the "Sesame Street" video of a muppet proclaiming that she loves
her kinky-curly hair in steady rotation. Yet our most powerful
experience of racial identity came through a pair of ballet tights.

Julia longed to attend classes at the Dance Theater of Harlem
with her older pal, Jade. Her audition this winter, held behind
closed doors, ran an hour. Two weeks later, the results arrived.
Julia, thanks to her preschool ballet lessons, had made the cut.

We headed to the school store to purchase her gear. A saleswoman pulled a pair of tan tights from a basket and held them
against Julia's forearm.

"Umm, too bright."                                                      5

She returned to the basket. My curiosity followed. Inside, I
spied an assortment of legwear—from nutmeg to milk chocolate
to espresso—in neat packaging. She tried a cognac-colored pair.

206

"Now that's a match."

"*Match?*"

"To her skin tone."

My eyes widened. I'd given ballet, and its uniform, little    10
thought since I studied the form as an 8-year-old in a Detroit
studio, decades ago. I wore an inky black leotard paired with
snowy white tights. The pairing made a bold graphic statement,
much like a Franz Kline painting, or a penguin, or a grand
piano. Back then no one considered my skin tone. Ballet tights
were typically white, just as the ballet dancers typically were.
Now, 40 years later, my daughter's ballet school protocol peeled
back my brain.

Next the saleswoman held up a pair of cotton-candy colored
slippers and explained that I would need to dye them to match
the tights, so the line of Julia's leg "would be continuous to the
eye. That's the look we want to create."

I nodded, studying my assignment.

Arthur Mitchell, a professional African-American dancer with
the New York City Ballet, founded the Dance Theater of Harlem,
along with Karel Shook, in 1969. Mr. Mitchell wanted to create
opportunities in the Harlem community where he grew up. With
funding from Alva Gimbel, wife of the board chairman of Gimbel
Brothers, the Ford Foundation, and his own savings, Mr. Mitchell
opened his school. Next he set out to open minds.

"Initially, Dance Theater of Harlem dancers wore pink tights
and toe shoes," Anna Glass, the executive director of the school,
is quoted as saying in a 40-year retrospective.

"But Arthur Mitchell changed course as he believed pink tights    15
visually interrupted his dancer's lines. The wardrobe staff worked
with each dancer to combine the correct amount of Rit dyes to
match their individual skin tone, then applied pressed powder
to their ribbons and shoes to seamlessly blend the color. Now,
matching tights and toe shoes to skin tone became a trademark
of Dance Theater of Harlem."

And with that, Mr. Mitchell broke a 300-year-old tradition.

In 1971, the neoclassical company debuted at the Guggenheim
Museum in New York City, wearing custom, skin-toned shoes
and tights, which, nearly 50 years later, remains the company's
signature.

To have a beloved art form reflected back in body shapes and hues that mirror yours is powerful. That was part of the magic behind the success of the blockbuster "Black Panther" when it opened in February. For African-Americans to see actors of color reflected as the protagonist, antagonist, scientist, even the queen, created a revelry of humanity that resulted in over $1 billion in ticket sales.

But that familiarity wasn't waiting in the wings when Debra Austin first slipped on her slippers. She would become the first black principal dancer with a major American company, the Pennsylvania Ballet, in 1982, decades before Misty Copeland.

How is such a drive born without a basket of brown-hued   20
tights? Perhaps, Freud found the key. "Beauty has no obvious use; nor is there any clear cultural necessity for it. Yet civilization could not do without it."

Ms. Austin couldn't, either.

I wish we lived in a world where brown-hued ballet tights didn't matter so much. Perhaps, one day we'll achieve it. But for now, it matters, deeply. It matters in Kenya, at the Kibera Ballet School where teachers bring that beauty and resilience to students who live in the slums, helping create the next generation of dancers for the national company. It mattered to Michaela DePrince, a soloist in the Dutch National Ballet who discovered her connection to dance at a young age. She wrote in her memoir, "Hope in a Ballet Shoe," about being a child in an orphanage in Sierra Leone when she spotted a magazine with the image of a ballerina on the cover blowing against the gate.

She dreamed of becoming a ballerina and carried that dream to stardom. Not every brown girl who loves classical dance will be a star, of course, but many can find inspiration through their tights, their bodies, their being. I want that opportunity for my daughter, that unique confidence code.

Some professional dancers have taken to social media to protest the lack of toe shoes mass-produced beyond the range of pink and black. But as a woman of color who has for years mixed foundation to match my skin tone as an act of self-love, I view tinting ballet shoes as an act of love for my daughter.

On the first day of classes, I helped Julia get dressed and line   25
up with the other students. The girls admired their forms. There's an inherent sweetness to tiny ballerinas. As I studied the tableau of dark chocolate, cinnamon and café au lait legs, the sense of racial pride, self-identity and belonging set me glowing.

But not everyone seemed to fall under the same spell: Beside me, a mom with long, thin braids perused her Facebook feed on her iPhone.

"Time to go!" the teacher announced.

Moms and dads stood. We checked the girls' upswept buns once more. We planted kisses on their smooth foreheads. We watched our daughters troop down the hall, toward the studio, in a conga line of cuteness. My eyes glossed over.

"Really beautiful, right?" I heard from behind.

I turned. The Facebook addict.                                                30

"Sure is."

She sighed. "Those brown tights get me every single time. I had to look at Facebook, so I wouldn't start crying."

## For Discussion and Writing

1. Why does the author tint her daughter's ballet shoes?

2. Holmes begins her essay in the personal, writing, as she says, "as an African-American mother of a brown-skinned seven-year-old girl," and brings in interviews and historical facts over the course of her essay. She ends with a scene focusing on an individual, but not herself. Why do you think she does this? What is the effect on you as a reader?

3. **connections**    Read Sandra Cisneros's "Only Daughter" (p. 91) next to Holmes's essay. Though we don't know if Holmes's daughter will become a professional ballet dancer, she has models available and new traditions ready to accept her. Would the path to Cisneros's writing career have been easier if she had had examples of people like her pursuing it?

4. Think of an activity—sports, arts, even school—for which a parent or guardian prepared you, and reflect on it in the way Holmes reflects on her preparing her own child for ballet. List the ways in which they did so, from buying equipment to picking out clothes to telling you how to act. What kinds of things do you think they were thinking about when they got you ready? Were they concerned with how you (and they) might be perceived? Did they do the same that had been done for them when they were young, in the same way, or was the situation, and so the preparation, somehow different?

5. **looking further**    Read up on the sociological concept called socialization. What are the different kinds of socialization? What are the different groups or categories into which individuals are socialized? Reflect on Holmes's story and/or your story in Question 4 in light of what you learn.

# LANGSTON HUGHES

# Salvation

*Born in 1902 in Joplin, Missouri, Langston Hughes became a major figure in the Harlem Renaissance, a flowering of African American literature, art, music, and scholarship in the 1920s and 1930s. He was first and foremost a poet, incorporating the vernacular of the streets and the rhythms of the jazz clubs into his voice. He was also a playwright, a fiction writer, an essayist, and an autobiographer. In "Salvation" we can see the skills with which Hughes created imaginative literature; here, in nonfiction, he both tells the story of an important point in his life and makes his readers think about significant ideas, doing so poetically and with great economy and expressiveness. As you read, keep the essay's title in the back of your head, and think about why Hughes might have chosen it.*

I was saved from sin when I was going on thirteen. But not really saved. It happened like this. There was a big revival at my Auntie Reed's church. Every night for weeks there had been much preaching, singing, praying, and shouting, and some very hardened sinners had been brought to Christ, and the membership of the church had grown by leaps and bounds. Then just before the revival ended, they held a special meeting for children, "to bring the young lambs to the fold." My aunt spoke of it for days ahead. That night I was escorted to the front row and placed on the mourners' bench with all the other young sinners, who had not yet been brought to Jesus.

My aunt told me that when you were saved you saw a light, and something happened to you inside! And Jesus came into your life! And God was with you from then on! She said you could see and hear and feel Jesus in your soul. I believed her. I had heard a great many old people say the same thing and it seemed to me they ought to know. So I sat there calmly in the hot, crowded church, waiting for Jesus to come to me.

The preacher preached a wonderful rhythmical sermon, all moans and shouts and lonely cries and dire pictures of hell, and then he sang a song about the ninety and nine safe in the fold, but one little lamb was left out in the cold. Then he said: "Won't you come? Won't you come to Jesus? Young lambs, won't you come?" And he held out his arms to all us young sinners there on the mourners' bench. And the little girls cried. And some of them jumped up and went to Jesus right away. But most of us just sat there.

A great many old people came and knelt around us and prayed, old women with jet-black faces and braided hair, old men with work-gnarled hands. And the church sang a song about the lower lights are burning, some poor sinners to be saved. And the whole building rocked with prayer and song.

Still I kept waiting to *see* Jesus.                                    5

Finally all the young people had gone to the altar and were saved, but one boy and me. He was a rounder's son named Westley. Westley and I were surrounded by sisters and deacons praying. It was very hot in the church, and getting late now. Finally Westley said to me in a whisper: "God damn! I'm tired o' sitting here. Let's get up and be saved." So he got up and was saved.

Then I was left all alone on the mourners' bench. My aunt came and knelt at my knees and cried, while prayers and songs swirled all around me in the little church. The whole congregation prayed for me alone, in a mighty wail of moans and voices. And I kept waiting serenely for Jesus, waiting, waiting—but he didn't come. I wanted to see him, but nothing happened to me. Nothing! I wanted something to happen to me, but nothing happened.

I heard the songs and the minister saying: "Why don't you come? My dear child, why don't you come to Jesus? Jesus is waiting for you. He wants you. Why don't you come? Sister Reed, what is this child's name?"

"Langston," my aunt sobbed.

"Langston, why don't you come? Why don't you come and be    10
saved? Oh, Lamb of God! Why don't you come?"

Now it was really getting late. I began to be ashamed of myself, holding everything up so long. I began to wonder what God thought about Westley, who certainly hadn't seen Jesus either, but who was now sitting proudly on the platform, swinging his knickerbockered legs and grinning down at me, surrounded by deacons and old women on their knees praying. God had not struck Westley dead for taking his name in vain or for lying in the temple. So I decided that maybe to save further trouble, I'd better lie, too, and say that Jesus had come, and get up and be saved.

So I got up.

Suddenly the whole room broke into a sea of shouting, as they saw me rise. Waves of rejoicing swept the place. Women leaped in the air. My aunt threw her arms around me. The minister took me by the hand and led me to the platform.

When things quieted down, in a hushed silence, punctuated by a few ecstatic "Amens," all the new young lambs were blessed in the name of God. Then joyous singing filled the room.

That night, for the last time in my life but one—for I was a big    15 boy twelve years old—I cried. I cried, in bed alone, and couldn't stop. I buried my head under the quilts, but my aunt heard me. She woke up and told my uncle I was crying because the Holy Ghost had come into my life, and because I had seen Jesus. But I was really crying because I couldn't bear to tell her that I had lied, that I had deceived everybody in the church, and I hadn't seen Jesus, and that now I didn't believe there was a Jesus any more, since he didn't come to help me.

### For Discussion and Writing

1. Why does Hughes cry that night?

2. Hughes's story is told very briefly; how does that brevity make it more powerful? How might a longer version have been less affecting?

3. **connections**   Compare the feeling the young Hughes has when he is the last child on the bench to the feeling George Orwell has when the crowd follows him in "Shooting an Elephant" (p. 279). What are the effects of being watched on each?

4. Write about a time when you felt your family held certain expectations for you. Was it a positive experience, a negative one, or both? Why?

5. **looking further**   There are people today who profess what some refer to as secular religion. Research this topic, then describe it. If you could speak to the twelve-year-old Langston Hughes, or to the adult Hughes who wrote "Salvation," what might you say to him about it? How would you relate it to the experience he writes about?

# How It Feels to Be Colored Me

*Born in 1891 in rural Alabama and raised in Florida, Zora Neale Hurston arrived in New York at the height of the Harlem Renaissance, a flowering of African American literature, art, music, and scholarship in the 1920s and 1930s, and became an active participant, writing stories and coauthoring a play with Langston Hughes. Her interest in the folk culture of the South, influenced by her studies with noted anthropologist Franz Boas, led to her return to Florida to study her native community and, eventually, to the work for which she is best known, the novel* Their Eyes Were Watching God *(1937). When reading "How It Feels to Be Colored Me," it is interesting to think about Hurston's statements about race and identity—such as her image of people of different races as different-colored bags stuffed with similar contents—in the context of this anthropological training.*

I am colored but I offer nothing in the way of extenuating circumstances except the fact that I am the only Negro in the United States whose grandfather on the mother's side was *not* an Indian chief.

I remember the very day that I became colored. Up to my thirteenth year I lived in the little Negro town of Eatonville, Florida. It is exclusively a colored town. The only white people I knew passed through the town going to or coming from Orlando. The native whites rode dusty horses, the Northern tourists chugged down the sandy village road in automobiles. The town knew the Southerners and never stopped cane chewing when they passed. But the Northerners were something else again. They were peered at cautiously from behind curtains by the timid. The more venturesome would come out on the porch to watch them go past and got just as much pleasure out of the tourists as the tourists got out of the village.

The front porch might seem a daring place for the rest of the town, but it was a gallery seat for me. My favorite place was atop the gate-post. Proscenium box for a born first-nighter. Not only did I enjoy the show, but I didn't mind the actors knowing that I liked it. I usually spoke to them in passing. I'd wave at them and when they returned my salute, I would say something like this: "Howdy-do-well-I-thank-you-where-you-goin'?" Usually automobile or the horse paused at this, and after a queer exchange of compliments, I would probably "go a piece of the way" with them, as we say in farthest Florida. If one of my family happened to come to the front in time to see me, of course negotiations would be rudely broken off. But even so, it is clear that I was the first "welcome-to-our-state" Floridian, and I hope the Miami Chamber of Commerce will please take notice.

During this period, white people differed from colored to me only in that they rode through town and never lived there. They liked to hear me "speak pieces" and sing and wanted to see me dance the parse-me-la, and gave me generously of their small silver for doing these things, which seemed strange to me for I wanted to do them so much that I needed bribing to stop. Only they didn't know it. The colored people gave no dimes. They deplored any joyful tendencies in me, but I was their Zora nevertheless. I belonged to them, to the nearby hotels, to the county—everybody's Zora.

But changes came in the family when I was thirteen, and I was 5 sent to school in Jacksonville. I left Eatonville, the town of the oleanders, as Zora. When I disembarked from the river-boat at Jacksonville, she was no more. It seemed that I had suffered a sea change. I was not Zora of Orange County any more, I was now a little colored girl. I found it out in certain ways. In my heart as well as in the mirror, I became a fast brown—warranted not to rub nor run.

But I am not tragically colored. There is no great sorrow dammed up in my soul, nor lurking behind my eyes. I do not mind at all. I do not belong to the sobbing school of Negrohood who hold that nature somehow has given them a lowdown dirty deal and whose feelings are all hurt about it. Even in the helter-skelter skirmish that is my life, I have seen that the world is to the strong regardless of a little pigmentation more or less. No, I do not weep at the world—I am too busy sharpening my oyster knife.

Someone is always at my elbow reminding me that I am the granddaughter of slaves. It fails to register depression with me. Slavery is sixty years in the past. The operation was successful and the patient is doing well, thank you. The terrible struggle that made me an American out of a potential slave said "On the line!" The Reconstruction said "Get set!"; and the generation before said "Go!" I am off to a flying start and I must not halt in the stretch to look behind and weep. Slavery is the price I paid for civilization, and the choice was not with me. It is a bully adventure and worth all that I have paid through my ancestors for it. No one on earth ever had a greater chance for glory. The world to be won and nothing to be lost. It is thrilling to think—to know that for any act of mine, I shall get twice as much praise or twice as much blame. It is quite exciting to hold the center of the national stage, with the spectators not knowing whether to laugh or to weep.

The position of my white neighbor is much more difficult. No brown specter pulls up a chair beside me when I sit down to eat. No dark ghost thrusts its leg against mine in bed. The game of keeping what one has is never so exciting as the game of getting.

I do not always feel colored. Even now I often achieve the unconscious Zora of Eatonville before the Hegira.[1] I feel most colored when I am thrown against a sharp white background.

For instance at Barnard. "Beside the waters of the Hudson" I feel my race. Among the thousand white persons, I am a dark rock surged upon, and overswept, but through it all, I remain myself. When covered by the waters, I am; and the ebb but reveals me again.

Sometimes it is the other way around. A white person is set down in our midst, but the contrast is just as sharp for me. For instance, when I sit in the drafty basement that is The New World Cabaret with a white person, my color comes. We enter chatting about any little nothing that we have in common and are seated by the jazz waiters. In the abrupt way that jazz orchestras have, this one plunges into a number. It loses no time in circumlocutions, but gets right down to business. It constricts the thorax and splits the heart with its tempo and narcotic harmonies. This orchestra grows rambunctious, rears on its hind legs

10

1. **Hegira:** A flight to escape danger. [Ed.]

and attacks the tonal veil with primitive fury, rending it, clawing it until it breaks through to the jungle beyond. I follow those heathen—follow them exultingly. I dance wildly inside myself; I yell within, I whoop; I shake my assegai[2] above my head, I hurl it true to the mark *yeeeeooww!* I am in the jungle and living in the jungle way. My face is painted red and yellow and my body is painted blue. My pulse is throbbing like a war drum. I want to slaughter something—give pain, give death to what, I do not know. But the piece ends. The men of the orchestra wipe their lips and rest their fingers. I creep back slowly to the veneer we call civilization with the last tone and find the white friend sitting motionless in his seat, smoking calmly.

"Good music they have here," he remarks, drumming the table with his fingertips.

Music. The great blobs of purple and red emotion have not touched him. He has only heard what I felt. He is far away and I see him but dimly across the ocean and the continent that have fallen between us. He is so pale with his whiteness then and I am *so* colored.

At certain times I have no race, I am *me*. When I set my hat at a certain angle and saunter down Seventh Avenue, Harlem City, feeling as snooty as the lions in front of the Forty-Second Street Library, for instance. So far as my feelings are concerned, Peggy Hopkins Joyce on the Boule Mich with her gorgeous raiment, stately carriage, knees knocking together in a most aristocratic manner, has nothing on me. The cosmic Zora emerges. I belong to no race nor time. I am the eternal feminine with its string of beads.

I have no separate feeling about being an American citizen and    15
colored. I am merely a fragment of the Great Soul that surges within the boundaries. My country, right or wrong.

Sometimes, I feel discriminated against, but it does not make me angry. It merely astonishes me. How *can* any deny themselves the pleasure of my company? It's beyond me.

But in the main, I feel like a brown bag of miscellany propped against a wall. Against a wall in company with other bags, white, red, and yellow. Pour out the contents, and there is discovered a jumble of small things priceless and worthless. A first-water

2. **assegai:** A spear. [Ed.]

diamond, an empty spool, bits of broken glass, lengths of string, a key to a door long since crumbled away, a rusty knife-blade, old shoes saved for a road that never was and never will be, a nail bent under the weight of things too heavy for any nail, a dried flower or two still a little fragrant. In your hand is the brown bag. On the ground before you is the jumble it held—so much like the jumble in the bags, could they be emptied, that all might be dumped in a single heap and the bags refilled without altering the content of any greatly. A bit of colored glass more or less would not matter. Perhaps that is how the Great Stuffer of Bags filled them in the first place—who knows?

### For Discussion and Writing

1. What point is Hurston trying to make in her first paragraph? *Is* she "the only Negro in the United States whose grandfather on the mother's side was *not* an Indian chief"?

2. Consider Hurston's use of imagination in her descriptions of the white neighbor, her experience at the jazz club, and in the final paragraph. How does she use specific details to ground these flights of imagination? How does she use these imaginative moments to make her points?

3. **connections**   Name an African American writer in this book whom you think Hurston might include in what she calls "the sobbing school of Negrohood" (par. 6). How might he or she answer Hurston's criticism?

4. How do you respond to the conception of race with which Hurston ends her essay? Does it agree with how you understand race?

5. **looking further**   Hurston's reference to "the Great Stuffer of Bags" is not meant to be a serious engagement with religion, but it can be taken as more than a throwaway line. Think (and maybe do a little research) about how conceptions of race have been tied to larger systems of belief, both religious and secular. How have different ideas about the nature of race depended on varying systems of belief about how human beings came to be? Why and in what ways are they different from each other? What do you believe, and why?

# THOMAS JEFFERSON

# The Declaration of Independence

*Born in 1743 in the British colony that is now the state of Virginia, Thomas Jefferson, descendant of one of the first families of Virginia, went on to become a founding father of the nation born out of thirteen united colonies. In addition to being the primary writer of the Declaration of Independence, Jefferson was governor of Virginia, vice president, president (from 1801 to 1809), and founder of the University of Virginia.*

*The Declaration is more than a historical document. It is a clear and effective piece of writing. We present both an early version and the final document. As you read, note the choices that were made in its writing, in particular the revisions evident in the final draft.*

## DRAFT OF THE DECLARATION OF INDEPENDENCE

A Declaration of the Representatives
of the UNITED STATES OF AMERICA,
in General Congress Assembled.

When in the course of human events it becomes necessary for a people to advance from that subordination in which they have hitherto remained, & to assume among the powers of the earth the equal & independant station to which the laws of nature & of nature's god entitle them, a decent respect to the opinions of mankind requires that they should declare the causes which impel them to the change.

We hold these truths to be sacred & undeniable; that all men are created equal & independant, that from that equal creation they derive rights inherent & inalienable, among which are the preservation of life, & liberty, & the spirit of happiness; that to secure these ends, governments are instituted among men, deriving their just powers from the consent of the governed; that whenever any form of government shall become destructive of these ends, it is the right of the people to alter or to abolish it, & to institute new government, laying its foundation on such principles & organizing its powers in such form, as to them shall seem most likely to effect their safety & happiness. prudence indeed will dictate that governments long established should not be changed for light & transient causes: and accordingly all experience hath shewn that mankind are more disposed to suffer while evils are sufferable, than to right themselves by abolishing the forms to which they are accustomed. but when a long train of abuses & usurpations, begun at a distinguished period, & pursuing invariably the same object, evinces a design to subject them to arbitrary power, it is their right, it is their duty, to throw off such government & to provide new guards for their future security. such has been the patient sufferance of these colonies; & such is now the necessity which constrains them to expunge their former systems of government. The history of his present majesty, is a history of unremitting injuries and usurpations, among which no one fact stands single or solitary to contradict the uniform tenor of the rest, all of which have in direct object the establishment of an absolute tyranny over these states. to prove this, let facts be submitted to a candid world, for the truth of which we pledge a faith yet unsullied by falsehood.

he has refused his assent to laws the most wholesome and necessary for the public good:

he has forbidden his governors to pass laws of immediate & pressing importance, unless suspended in their operation till his assent should be obtained: and when so suspended, he has neglected utterly to attend to them:

he has refused to pass other laws for the accommodation of large districts of people unless those people would relinquish the right of representation, a right inestimable to them, & formidable to tyrants alone:

he has dissolved Representative houses repeatedly & continually, for opposing with manly firmness his invasions on the rights of the people:

he has refused for a long space of time to cause others to be elected, whereby the legislative powers, incapable of annihilation, have returned to the people at large for their exercise, the state remaining in the mean time exposed to all the dangers of invasion from without, &, convulsions within:

he has suffered the administration of justice totally to cease in some of these colonies, refusing his assent to laws for establishing judiciary powers:

he has made our judges dependant on his will alone, for the tenure of their offices, and amount of their salaries:

he has erected a multitude of new offices by a self-assumed power, & sent hither swarms of officers to harrass our people & eat out their substance: he has kept among us in times of peace standing armies & ships of war:

he has affected to render the military, independent of & superior to the civil power:

he has combined with others to subject us to a jurisdiction foreign to our constitutions and unacknowledged by our laws; giving his assent to their pretended acts of legislation, for quartering large bodies of armed troops among us:

for protecting them by a mock-trial from punishment for any murders they should commit on the inhabitants of these states;

for cutting off our trade with all parts of the world;

for imposing taxes on us without our consent;

for depriving us of the benefits of trial by jury

he has endeavored to prevent the population of these states; for that purpose obstructing the laws for naturalization of foreigners; refusing to pass others to encourage their migrations hither; & raising the conditions of new appropriations of lands;

for transporting us beyond seas to be tried for pretended offences;

for taking away our charters & altering fundamentally the forms of our governments;

for suspending our own legislatures & declaring themselves invested with power to legislate for us in all cases whatsoever;

he has abdicated government here, withdrawing his governors, & declaring us out of his allegiance & protection:

he has plundered our seas, ravaged our coasts, burnt our towns & destroyed the lives of our people:

he is at this time transporting large armies of foreign mercenaries to compleat the works of death, desolation & tyranny, already begun with circumstances of cruelty & perfidy unworthy the head of a civilized nation:

he has endeavored to bring on the inhabitants of our frontiers the merciless Indian savages, whose known rule of warfare is an undistinguished destruction of all ages, sexes, & conditions of existence:

he has incited treasonable insurrections of our fellow-citizens, with the allurements of forfeiture & confiscation of our property:

he has waged cruel war against human nature itself, violating its most sacred rights of life & liberty in the persons of a distant people who never offended him, captivating & carrying them into slavery in another hemisphere, or to incur miserable death in their transportation thither. this piratical warfare, the opprobrium of *infidel* powers, is the warfare of the CHRISTIAN king of Great Britain, determined to keep open a market where MEN should be bought & sold; he has prostituted his negative for suppressing every legislative attempt to prohibit or to restrain this execrable commerce: and that this assemblage of horrors might want no fact of distinguished die, he is now exciting those very people to rise in arms among us, and to purchase that liberty of which *he* has deprived them, by murdering the people upon whom *he* also obtruded them; thus paying off former crimes committed against the *liberties* of one people, with crimes which he urges them to commit against the *lives* of another.

in every stage of these oppressions we have petitioned for redress in the most humble terms; our repeated petitions have been answered by repeated injury. a prince whose character is thus marked by every act which may define a tyrant, is unfit to be the ruler of a people who mean to be free. future ages will scarce believe that the hardiness of one man, adventured within the short compass of twelve years only, on so many acts of tyranny without a mask, over a people fostered & fixed in principles of liberty.

Nor have we been wanting in attentions to our British brethren. we have warned them from time to time of attempts by their legislature to extend a jurisdiction over these our states. we have reminded them of the circumstances of our emigration & settlement here, no one of which could warrant so strange a pretension: that these were effected at the expence of our own blood & treasure, unassisted by the wealth or the strength of Great Britain: that in constituting indeed our several forms of government, we had adopted one common king, thereby laying a foundation for perpetual league & amity with them; but that submission to their [Parliament, was no Part of our Constitution, nor ever in Idea, if History may be] credited: and we appealed to their native justice & magnanimity, as to the ties of our common kindred to disavow these usurpations which were likely to interrupt our correspondence & connection. they too have been deaf to the voice of justice & of consanguinity, & when occasions have been given them, by the regular course of their laws, of removing from their councils the disturbers of our harmony, they have by their free election re-established them in power. at this very time too they are permitting their chief magistrate to send over not only soldiers of our common blood, but Scotch & foreign mercenaries to invade & deluge us in blood. these facts have given the last stab to agonizing affection, and manly spirit bids us to renounce for ever these unfeeling brethren. we must endeavor to forget our former love for them, and to hold them as we hold the rest of mankind, enemies in war, in peace friends. we might have been a free & a great people together; but a communication of grandeur & of freedom it seems is below their dignity. be it so, since they will have it: the road to glory & happiness is open to us too; we will climb it in a separate state, and acquiesce in the necessity which pronounces our everlasting Adieu!

We therefore the representatives of the United States of America in General Congress assembled do, in the name & by authority of the good people of these states, reject and renounce all allegiance & subjection to the kings of Great Britain & all others who may hereafter claim by, through, or under them; we utterly dissolve & break off all political connection which may have heretofore subsisted between us & the people or parliament of Great Britain; and finally we do assert and declare these colonies to be free and independant states, and that as free & independant states they shall hereafter have power to levy war, conclude peace, contract alliances, establish commerce, & to do all other acts and things which independant states may of right do. And for the support of this declaration we mutually pledge to each other our lives, our fortunes, & our sacred honor.

## THE DECLARATION OF INDEPENDENCE

In Congress, July 4, 1776
The Unanimous Declaration of the
Thirteen United States of America

When in the Course of human events it becomes necessary for 5
one people to dissolve the political bands which have connected them with another, and to assume among the powers of the earth, the separate and equal station to which the Laws of Nature and

of Nature's God entitle them, a decent respect to the opinions of mankind requires that they should declare the causes which impel them to the separation.

We hold these truths to be self-evident, that all men are created equal, that they are endowed by their Creator with certain unalienable Rights, that among these are Life, Liberty, and the pursuit of Happiness. That to secure these rights, Governments are instituted among Men, deriving their just powers from the consent of the governed. That whenever any Form of Government becomes destructive of these ends, it is the Right of the People to alter or to abolish it, and to institute new Government, laying its foundation on such principles and organizing its powers in such form, as to them shall seem most likely to effect their Safety and Happiness. Prudence, indeed, will dictate that Governments long established should not be changed for light and transient causes; and accordingly all experience hath shewn that mankind are more disposed to suffer, while evils are sufferable, than right themselves by abolishing the forms to which they are accustomed. But when a long train of abuses and usurpations, pursuing invariably the same Object evinces a design to reduce them under absolute Despotism, it is their right, it is their duty, to throw off such Government, and to provide new Guards for their future security. Such has been the patient sufferance of these Colonies; and such is now the necessity which constrains them to alter their former Systems of Government. The history of the present King of Great Britain is a history of repeated injuries and usurpations, all having in direct object the establishment of an absolute Tyranny over these States. To prove this, let Facts be submitted to a candid world.

He has refused his Assent to Laws, the most wholesome and necessary for the public good.

He has forbidden his Government to pass laws of immediate and pressing importance, unless suspended in their operation till his Assent should be obtained; and when so suspended, he has utterly neglected to attend to them.

He has refused to pass other Laws for the accommodation of large districts of people, unless those people would relinquish the right of Representation in the Legislature, a right inestimable to them and formidable to tyrants only.

He has called together legislative bodies at places unusual, uncomfortable, and distant from the depository of their Public

10

Records, for the sole purpose of fatiguing them into compliance with his measures.

He has dissolved Representative Houses repeatedly, for opposing with manly firmness his invasions on the rights of the people.

He has refused for a long time, after such dissolutions, to cause others to be elected; whereby the Legislative Powers, incapable of Annihilation, have returned to the People at large for their exercise; the State remaining in the mean time exposed to all the dangers of invasion from without, and convulsions within.

He has endeavored to prevent the population of these States; for that purpose obstructing the Laws for Naturalization of Foreigners; refusing to pass others to encourage their migration hither, and raising the conditions of new Appropriations of Lands.

He has obstructed the Administration of Justice, by refusing his Assent to Laws for establishing Judiciary Powers.

He has made Judges dependent on his Will alone, for the tenure of their offices, and the amount and payment of their salaries. 15

He has erected a multitude of New Offices, and sent hither swarms of Officers to harass our people, and eat out their substance.

He has kept among us, in times of peace, Standing Armies without the Consent of our legislatures.

He has affected to render the Military independent of and superior to the Civil Power.

He has combined with others to subject us to a jurisdiction foreign to our constitution, and unacknowledged by our laws; giving his Assent to their Acts of pretended Legislation: For quartering large bodies of armed troops among us: For protecting them, by a mock Trial, from punishment for any Murders which they should commit on the Inhabitants of these States: For cutting off our Trade with all parts of the world: For imposing Taxes on us without our Consent: For depriving us in many cases, of the benefits of Trial by Jury: For transporting us beyond Seas to be tried for pretended offenses: For abolishing the free System of English Laws in a neighboring Province, establishing therein an Arbitrary government, and enlarging its Boundaries so as to render it at once an example and fit instrument for introducing the same absolute rule into these Colonies: For taking away our Charters, abolishing our most valuable Laws and altering fundamentally the Forms of our Governments: For suspending our own Legislatures, and declaring themselves invested with power to legislate for us in all cases whatsoever.

He has abdicated Government here, by declaring us out of his    20
Protection and waging War against us.

He has plundered our seas, ravaged our Coasts, burnt our towns, and destroyed the lives of our people.

He is at this time transporting large Armies of foreign Mercenaries to complete the works of death, desolation and tyranny, already begun with circumstances of Cruelty & Perfidy scarcely paralleled in the most barbarous ages, and totally unworthy the Head of a civilized nation.

He has constrained our fellow Citizens taken Captive on the high Seas to bear Arms against their Country, to become the executioners of their friends and Brethren, or to fall themselves by their Hands.

He has excited domestic insurrections amongst us, and has endeavored to bring on the inhabitants of our frontiers, the merciless Indian Savages, whose known rule of warfare, is an undistinguished destruction of all ages, sexes, and conditions.

In every stage of these Oppressions We have Petitioned for    25
Redress in the most humble terms: Our repeated Petitions have been answered only by repeated injury. A Prince, whose character is thus marked by every act which may define a Tyrant, is unfit to be the ruler of a free people.

Nor have We been wanting in attention to our British brethren. We have warned them from time to time of attempts by their legislature to extend an unwarrantable jurisdiction over us. We have reminded them of the circumstances of our emigration and settlement here. We have appealed to their native justice and magnanimity, and we have conjured them by the ties of our common kindred to disavow these usurpations, which would inevitably interrupt our connections and correspondence. They too have been deaf to the voice of justice and of consanguinity. We must, therefore, acquiesce in the necessity, which denounces our Separation, and hold them, as we hold the rest of mankind, Enemies in War, in Peace Friends.

We, THEREFORE the Representatives of the UNITED STATES OF AMERICA, in General Congress, Assembled, appealing to the Supreme Judge of the world for the rectitude of our intentions, do, in the Name, and by Authority of the good People of these

Colonies, solemnly publish and declare, That these United Colonies are, and of Right ought to be FREE AND INDEPENDENT STATES; that they are Absolved from all Allegiance to the British Crown, and that all political connection between them and the State of Great Britain, is and ought to be totally dissolved; and that as Free and Independent States, they have full Power to levy War, conclude Peace, contract Alliances, establish Commerce, and to do all other Acts and Things which Independent States may of right do. And for the support of this Declaration, with a firm reliance on the protection of Divine Providence, we mutually pledge to each other our Lives, our Fortunes, and our sacred Honor.

### For Discussion and Writing

1. How many examples of wrongs done by the Crown to the colonies are offered here? What is the effect of this list?

2. In small groups, compile lists of all of the differences between the first and second drafts of the Declaration. Write up a summary of these changes and an analysis of how they make the final document more effective.

3. **connections**   Compare the Declaration and George Orwell's "Shooting an Elephant" (p. 279). How do these two condemnations of the British Empire differ?

4. Think about America today. From your personal experience and observations, discuss how it meets the promise of the opening of the Declaration's second paragraph, and how it does not.

5. **looking further**   One of the stated rationales behind American intervention in the affairs of other nations, historically, has been the idea that other peoples want to live under the same kind of system of government that the Declaration helped establish in the United States. Keeping in mind the many, far-flung places where this dynamic has played out (and doing some research if you need to), which elements of the Declaration might have appealed to these peoples? Which elements might be more problematic?

JAMAICA KINCAID

# The Ugly Tourist

*Jamaica Kincaid was born Elaine Potter Richardson in Antigua in 1949 and raised there until she left for New York when she was seventeen. Working as a domestic, she returned to school, earned her high school and college degrees, and returned to New York to write, where under her new name she eventually became a staff writer for the* New Yorker. *She is the author of fifteen books of poetry, fiction, and nonfiction about her Caribbean home, her family, and gardening, among other topics, including* At the Bottom of the River *(1983),* Annie John *(1985),* Lucy *(1990),* The Autobiography of My Mother *(1996),* My Brother *(1997), and* See Now Then *(2013).*

*"The Ugly Tourist," which originally appeared in* Harper's *in 1988, became the opening chapter of* A Small Place. *The editor of the* New Yorker *rejected the essay as "too angry," and when the full book appeared many of the reviews agreed. However, many did not, finding the book's tone appropriate to its subject. As you read, put yourself in the shoes of these editors and reviewers. Would you have accepted "The Ugly Tourist" for publication? What kind of review would you have given it?*

The thing you have always suspected about yourself the minute you become a tourist is true: a tourist is an ugly human being. You are not an ugly person all the time; you are not an ugly person ordinarily; you are not an ugly person day to day. From day to day, you are a nice person. From day to day, all the people who are supposed to love you on the whole do. From day to day, as you walk down a busy street in the large and modern and prosperous city in which you work and live, dismayed, puzzled (a cliché, but only a cliché can explain you) at how alone you feel in this crowd, how awful it is to go unnoticed, how awful it is to go unloved, even as you are surrounded by more people than you could possibly get to know in a lifetime that lasted for

millennia, and then out of the corner of your eye you see someone looking at you and absolute pleasure is written all over that
person's face, and then you realise that you are not as revolting a
presence as you think you are (for that look just told you so). And
so, ordinarily, you are a nice person, an attractive person, a person capable of drawing to yourself the affection of other people
(people just like you), a person at home in your own skin (sort of;
I mean, in a way; I mean, your dismay and puzzlement are natural to you, because people like you just seem to be like that, and
so many of the things people like you find admirable about yourselves—the things you think about, the things you think really
define you—seem rooted in these feelings): a person at home
in your own house (and all its nice house things), with its nice
back yard (and its nice back-yard things), at home on your street,
your church, in community activities, your job, at home with
your family, your relatives, your friends—you are a whole person. But one day, when you are sitting somewhere, alone in that
crowd, and that awful feeling of displacedness comes over you,
and really, as an ordinary person you are not well equipped to
look too far inward and set yourself aright, because being ordinary is already so taxing, and being ordinary takes all you have
out of you, and though the words "I must get away" do not actually pass across your lips, you make a leap from being that nice
blob just sitting like a boob in your amniotic sac of the modern
experience to being a person visiting heaps of death and ruin and
feeling alive and inspired at the sight of it; to being a person lying
on some faraway beach, your stilled body stinking and glistening
in the sand, looking like something first forgotten, then remembered, then not important enough to go back for; to being a person marvelling at the harmony (ordinarily, what you would say
is the backwardness) and the union these other people (and they
are other people) have with nature. And you look at the things
they can do with a piece of ordinary cloth, the things they fashion out of cheap, vulgarly colored (to you) twine, the way they
squat down over a hole they have made in the ground, the hole
itself is something to marvel at, and since you are being an ugly
person this ugly but joyful thought will swell inside you: their
ancestors were not clever in the way yours were and not ruthless
in the way yours were, for then would it not be you who would be
in harmony with nature and backwards in that charming way?

An ugly thing, that is what you are when you become a tourist, an ugly, empty thing, a stupid thing, a piece of rubbish pausing here and there to gaze at this and taste that, and it will never occur to you that the people who inhabit the place in which you have just passed cannot stand you, that behind their closed doors they laugh at your strangeness (you do not look the way they look); the physical sight of you does not please them; you have bad manners (it is their custom to eat their food with their hands; you try eating their way, you look silly; you try eating the way you always eat, you look silly); they do not like the way you speak (you have an accent); they collapse helpless from laughter, mimicking the way they imagine you must look as you carry out some everyday bodily function. They do not like you. *They do not like me!* That thought never actually occurs to you. Still, you feel a little uneasy. Still, you feel a little foolish. Still, you feel a little out of place. But the banality of your own life is very real to you; it drove you to this extreme, spending your days and your nights in the company of people who despise you, people you do not like really, people you would not want to have as your actual neighbour. And so you must devote yourself to puzzling out how much of what you are told is really, really true (Is ground-up bottle glass in peanut sauce really a delicacy around here, or will it do just what you think ground-up bottle glass will do? Is this rare, multicoloured, snout-mouthed fish really an aphrodisiac, or will it cause you to fall asleep permanently?). Oh, the hard work all of this is, and is it any wonder, then, that on your return home you feel the need of a long rest, so that you can recover from your life as a tourist?

That the native does not like the tourist is not hard to explain. For every native of every place is a potential tourist, and every tourist is a native of somewhere. Every native everywhere lives a life of overwhelming and crushing banality and boredom and desperation and depression, and every deed, good and bad, is an attempt to forget this. Every native would like to find a way out, every native would like a rest, every native would like a tour. But some natives—most natives in the world—cannot go anywhere. They are too poor. They are too poor to go anywhere. They are too poor to escape the reality of their lives; and they are too poor to live properly in the place where they live, which is the very place you, the tourist, want to go—so when the natives see you, the tourist, they envy you, they envy your ability to leave your own banality and boredom, they envy your ability to turn their own banality and boredom into a source of pleasure for yourself.

## For Discussion and Writing

1. What does Kincaid argue is wrong with how tourists think of natives?
2. In addition to its brevity, what is notable about "The Ugly Tourist" is the length of its first paragraph. What is the effect of reading such a long paragraph? Why do you think Kincaid chose to write it that way?
3. **connections** Read Kincaid's essay next to Barbara Ehrenreich's "Serving in Florida" (p. 134). How are both about tourism? How are both about class? What can the differences between the two tell us about each?
4. Write about a trip you have taken; it can be to another town or state, or even another part of your town—it doesn't have to be to another country. How did it feel to be a tourist? Did anything in your experience relate to Kincaid's description of tourism? Alternatively, write about a time when you have felt like a native in the presence of people from elsewhere visiting your home.
5. **looking further** Kincaid argues that it is a recognition of the "banality and boredom" (par. 2) of their lives that leads people to visit other parts of the world. Imagine a counterargument to Kincaid's. Are there other reasons to want to see the rest of the world? How would you compare them to the one Kincaid assumes?

STEPHEN KING

# Reading to Write

*Stephen King was born in 1947 in Portland, Maine, and raised in Maine, Wisconsin, Indiana, and Connecticut. He has authored dozens of novels of horror, suspense, and science fiction, nine collections' worth of short stories, and five books of nonfiction; many of his novels and stories have been made into films, including* Carrie *(1976),* The Shining *(1980),* Stand by Me *(1986),* Misery *(1990),* The Shawshank Redemption *(1994), and* The Green Mile *(1999). While often thought of as a genre writer—someone who writes the kinds of popular stories (like horror or science fiction, in his case) that are not quite considered literary fiction—his work has increasingly been met with critical praise.*

*"Reading to Write" is taken from King's book* On Writing: A Memoir of the Craft *(2000). In it, this amazingly prolific writer gives advice about writing that ends up being as much about how to use one's time as it is about specific recommended activities. As you read, see if you can extract an underlying philosophy of life from King's essay.*

If you want to be a writer, you must do two things above all others: read a lot and write a lot. There's no way around these two things that I'm aware of, no shortcut.

I'm a slow reader, but I usually get through seventy or eighty books a year, mostly fiction. I don't read in order to study the craft; I read because I like to read. It's what I do at night, kicked back in my blue chair. Similarly, I don't read fiction to study the art of fiction, but simply because I like stories. Yet there is a learning process going on. Every book you pick up has its own lesson or lessons, and quite often the bad books have more to teach than the good ones.

When I was in the eighth grade, I happened upon a paperback novel by Murray Leinster, a science fiction pulp writer who did most of his work during the forties and fifties, when magazines

231

like *Amazing Stories* paid a penny a word. I had read other books by Mr. Leinster, enough to know that the quality of his writing was uneven. This particular tale, which was about mining in the asteroid belt, was one of his less successful efforts. Only that's too kind. It was terrible, actually, a story populated by paper-thin characters and driven by outlandish plot developments. Worst of all (or so it seemed to me at the time), Leinster had fallen in love with the word *zestful*. Characters watched the approach of ore-bearing asteroids with *zestful smiles*. Characters sat down to supper aboard their mining ship with *zestful anticipation*. Near the end of the book, the hero swept the large-breasted, blonde heroine into a *zestful embrace*. For me, it was the literary equivalent of a smallpox vaccination: I have never, so far as I know, used the word *zestful* in a novel or a story. God willing, I never will.

*Asteroid Miners* (which wasn't the title, but that's close enough) was an important book in my life as a reader. Almost everyone can remember losing his or her virginity, and most writers can remember the first book he/she put down thinking: *I can do better than this, Hell, I am doing better than this!* What could be more encouraging to the struggling writer than to realize his/her work is unquestionably better than that of someone who actually got paid for his/her stuff?

One learns most clearly what not to do by reading bad prose—one novel like *Asteroid Miners* (or *Valley of the Dolls*, *Flowers in the Attic*, and *The Bridges of Madison County*, to name just a few) is worth a semester at a good writing school, even with the superstar guest lecturers thrown in.  5

Good writing, on the other hand, teaches the learning writer about style, graceful narration, plot development, the creation of believable characters, and truth-telling. A novel like *The Grapes of Wrath* may fill a new writer with feelings of despair and good old-fashioned jealousy—"I'll never be able to write anything that good, not if I live to be a thousand"—but such feelings can also serve as a spur, goading the writer to work harder and aim higher. Being swept away by a combination of great story and great writing—of being flattened, in fact—is part of every writer's necessary formation. You cannot hope to sweep someone else away by the force of your writing until it has been done to you.

So we read to experience the mediocre and the outright rotten; such experience helps us to recognize those things when they begin to creep into our own work, and to steer clear of them. We also read in order to measure ourselves against the good and the great, to get a sense of all that can be done. And we read in order to experience different styles.

You may find yourself adopting a style you find particularly exciting, and there's nothing wrong with that. When I read Ray Bradbury as a kid, I wrote like Ray Bradbury—everything green and wondrous and seen through a lens smeared with the grease of nostalgia. When I read James M. Cain, everything I wrote came out clipped and stripped and hard-boiled. When I read Lovecraft, my prose became luxurious and Byzantine. I wrote stories in my teenage years where all these styles merged, creating a kind of hilarious stew. This sort of stylistic blending is a necessary part of developing one's own style, but it doesn't occur in a vacuum. You have to read widely, constantly refining (and redefining) your own work as you do so. It's hard for me to believe that people who read very little (or not at all in some cases) should presume to write and expect people to like what they have written, but I know it's true. If I had a nickel for every person who ever told me he/she wanted to become a writer but "didn't have time to read," I could buy myself a pretty good steak dinner. Can I be blunt on this subject? If you don't have time to read, you don't have the time (or the tools) to write. Simple as that.

Reading is the creative center of a writer's life. I take a book with me everywhere I go, and find there are all sorts of opportunities to dip in. The trick is to teach yourself to read in small sips as well as in long swallows. Waiting rooms were made for books—of course! But so are theater lobbies before the show, long and boring checkout lines, and everyone's favorite, the john. You can even read while you're driving, thanks to the audiobook revolution. Of the books I read each year, anywhere from six to a dozen are on tape. As for all the wonderful radio you will be missing, come on—how many times can you listen to Deep Purple sing "Highway Star"?

Reading at meals is considered rude in polite society, but 10 if you expect to succeed as a writer, rudeness should be the second-to-least of your concerns. The least of all should be polite society and what it expects. If you intend to write as truthfully as you can, your days as a member of polite society are numbered, anyway.

Where else can you read? There's always the treadmill, or whatever you use down at the local health club to get aerobic. I try to spend an hour doing that every day, and I think I'd go mad without a good novel to keep me company. Most exercise facilities (at home as well as outside it) are now equipped with TVs, but TV—while working out or anywhere else—really is about the last thing an aspiring writer needs. If you feel you must have the news analyst blowhards on CNN while you exercise, or the stock market blowhards on MSNBC, or the sports blowhards on ESPN, it's time for you to question how serious you really are about becoming a writer. You must be prepared to do some serious turning inward toward the life of the imagination, and that means, I'm afraid, that Geraldo, Keith Olbermann, and Jay Leno must go. Reading takes time, and the glass teat takes too much of it.

Once weaned from the ephemeral craving for TV, most people will find they enjoy the time they spend reading. I'd like to suggest that turning off that endlessly quacking box is apt to improve the quality of your life as well as the quality of your writing. And how much of a sacrifice are we talking about here? How many *Frasier* and *ER* reruns does it take to make one American life complete? How many Richard Simmons infomercials? How many whiteboy/fatboy Beltway insiders on CNN? Oh man, don't get me started. Jerry-Springer-Dr.-Dre-Judge-Judy-Jerry-Falwell-Donny-and-Marie, I rest my case.

When my son Owen was seven or so, he fell in love with Bruce Springsteen's E Street Band, particularly with Clarence Clemons, the band's burly sax player. Owen decided he wanted to learn to play like Clarence. My wife and I were amused and delighted by this ambition. We were also hopeful, as any parent would be, that our kid would turn out to be talented, perhaps even some sort of prodigy. We got Owen a tenor saxophone for Christmas and lessons with Gordon Bowie, one of the local music men. Then we crossed our fingers and hoped for the best.

Seven months later I suggested to my wife that it was time to discontinue the sax lessons, if Owen concurred. Owen did, and with palpable relief—he hadn't wanted to say it himself, especially not after asking for the sax in the first place, but seven months had been long enough for him to realize that, while he might love Clarence Clemons's big sound, the saxophone was simply not for him — God had not given him that particular talent.

I knew, not because Owen stopped practicing, but because he was practicing only during the periods Mr. Bowie had set for him: half an hour after school four days a week, plus an hour on the weekends. Owen mastered the scales and the notes — nothing wrong with his memory, his lungs, or his eye-hand coordination — but we never heard him taking off, surprising himself with something new, blissing himself out. And as soon as his practice time was over, it was back into the case with the horn, and there it stayed until the next lesson or practice time. What this suggested to me was that when it came to the sax and my son, there was never going to be any real playtime; it was all going to be rehearsal. That's no good. If there's no joy in it, it's just no good. It's best to go on to some other area, where the deposits of talent may be richer and the fun quotient higher.

Talent renders the whole idea of rehearsal meaningless; when you find something at which you are talented, you do it (whatever *it* is) until your fingers bleed or your eyes are ready to fall out of your head. Even when no one is listening (or reading, or watching), every outing is a bravura performance, because you as the creator are happy. Perhaps even ecstatic. That goes for reading and writing as well as for playing a musical instrument, hitting a baseball, or running the four-forty. The sort of strenuous reading and writing program I advocate — four to six hours a day, every day — will not seem strenuous if you really enjoy doing these things and have an aptitude for them; in fact, you may be following such a program already. If you feel you need permission to do all the reading and writing your little heart desires, however, consider it hereby granted by yours truly.

The real importance of reading is that it creates an ease and intimacy with the process of writing; one comes to the country of the writer with one's papers and identification pretty much in order. Constant reading will pull you into a place (a mind-set, if you like the phrase) where you can write eagerly and without self-consciousness. It also offers you a constantly growing knowledge of what has been done and what hasn't, what is trite and

15

what is fresh, what works and what just lies there dying (or dead) on the page. The more you read, the less apt you are to make a fool of yourself with your pen or word processor.

*For Discussion and Writing*

1. Why does King say that people who want to be writers should read?

2. "Reading to Write" might not seem to be literature — it's nonfiction and informational rather than creative — but it is well written. Make some observations about the way it is written — King's word choices, the kinds of voice he uses, the kinds of stories he tells — and consider what you might learn, as a budding writer, from reading it.

3. **connections** Compare King's essay to Frederick Douglass's "Learning to Read and Write" (p. 127). In some ways, these essays are very different: one is a reflection by a writer on achieving literacy despite his enslavement and the effect of this on his life, the other an offering of advice on one important part of learning to write. In what ways are they similar? Are there points of comparison between the authors' motivations? Between the ways they pursue their shared goal? Between the ways they feel about pursuing it?

4. Write a piece inspired by King's essay. It can be about writing, if you are passionate about that, or about some other pursuit — academic, creative, or neither. Try to include elements inspired by King's essay: tell a story or two about yourself, offer observations about something important to that pursuit (maybe one that others might overlook), and convey the sense of dedication that King conveys in "Reading to Write."

5. **looking further** In urging aspiring writers to turn off their televisions when exercising so they might use that time for reading, King calls TV "the glass teat" (par. 11). Write a response informed by research on contemporary television, which argues that writers have something to learn from television. How might you argue that TV is not a glass teat but a source of information about the world, as well as a place where good writing can also be found?

## VERLYN KLINKENBORG

# Our Vanishing Night

Most city skies have become virtually empty of stars

*Born in 1952 in Colorado and raised in Iowa and California, Verlyn Klinkenborg has a Ph.D. in English from Princeton University and has taught literature and creative writing at a number of colleges and universities. He is on the editorial board of the* New York Times *and is the author of* Making Hay *(1986),* The Last Fine Time *(1991), and* The Rural Life *(2003). He has written for the* New Yorker, National Geographic, Harper's, *and many other magazines.*

*"Our Vanishing Night," which first appeared in* National Geographic, *shows Klinkenborg doing more than writing about the rural life he has captured so evocatively in his pieces for the* New York Times. *As you read, observe how he deftly incorporates history and science into his writing.*

If humans were truly at home under the light of the moon and stars, we would go in darkness happily, the midnight world as visible to us as it is to the vast number of nocturnal species on this planet. Instead, we are diurnal creatures, with eyes adapted to living in the sun's light. This is a basic evolutionary fact, even though most of us don't think of ourselves as diurnal beings any more than we think of ourselves as primates or mammals or Earthlings. Yet it's the only way to explain what we've done to the night: we've engineered it to receive us by filling it with light.

This kind of engineering is no different than damming a river. Its benefits come with consequences—called light pollution—whose effects scientists are only now beginning to study. Light pollution is largely the result of bad lighting design, which allows artificial light to shine outward and upward into the sky, where it's not wanted, instead of focusing it downward, where it is. Ill-designed lighting washes out the darkness of night and radically alters the light levels—and light rhythms—to which many forms of life, including ourselves, have adapted. Wherever human light spills into the natural world, some aspect of life—migration, reproduction, feeding—is affected.

For most of human history, the phrase "light pollution" would have made no sense. Imagine walking toward London on a moonlit night around 1800, when it was Earth's most populous city. Nearly a million people lived there, making do, as they always had, with candles and rushlights and torches and lanterns. Only a few houses were lit by gas, and there would be no public gaslights in the streets or squares for another seven years. From a few miles away, you would have been as likely to *smell* London as to see its dim collective glow.

Now most of humanity lives under intersecting domes of reflected, refracted light, of scattering rays from overlit cities and suburbs, from light-flooded highways and factories. Nearly all of nighttime Europe is a nebula of light, as is most of the United States and all of Japan. In the south Atlantic the glow from a single fishing fleet—squid fishermen luring their prey with metal halide lamps—can be seen from space, burning brighter, in fact, than Buenos Aires or Rio de Janeiro.

In most cities the sky looks as though it has been emptied of 5 stars, leaving behind a vacant haze that mirrors our fear of the dark and resembles the urban glow of dystopian science fiction. We've grown so used to this pervasive orange haze that the original glory of an unlit night—dark enough for the planet Venus to throw shadows on Earth—is wholly beyond our experience, beyond memory almost. And yet above the city's pale ceiling lies the rest of the universe, utterly undiminished by the light we waste—a bright shoal of stars and planets and galaxies, shining in seemingly infinite darkness.

We've lit up the night as if it were an unoccupied country, when nothing could be further from the truth. Among mammals alone, the number of nocturnal species is astonishing. Light is a powerful biological force, and on many species it acts as a magnet, a process being studied by researchers such as Travis Longcore and Catherine Rich, co-founders of the Los Angeles–based Urban Wildlands Group. The effect is so powerful that scientists speak of songbirds and seabirds being "captured" by searchlights on land or by the light from gas flares on marine oil platforms, circling and circling in the thousands until they drop. Migrating at night, birds are apt to collide with brightly lit tall buildings; immature birds on their first journey suffer disproportionately.

Insects, of course, cluster around streetlights, and feeding at those insect clusters is now ingrained in the lives of many bat species. In some Swiss valleys the European lesser horseshoe bat began to vanish after streetlights were installed, perhaps because those valleys were suddenly filled with light-feeding pipistrelle bats. Other nocturnal mammals—including desert rodents, fruit bats, opossums, and badgers—forage more cautiously under the permanent full moon of light pollution because they've become easier targets for predators.

Some birds—blackbirds and nightingales, among others—sing at unnatural hours in the presence of artificial light. Scientists have determined that long artificial days—and artificially short nights—induce early breeding in a wide range of birds. And because a longer day allows for longer feeding, it can also affect migration schedules. One population of Bewick's swans wintering in England put on fat more rapidly than usual, priming them to begin their Siberian migration early. The problem, of course, is that migration, like most other aspects of bird behavior, is a precisely timed biological behavior. Leaving early may mean arriving too soon for nesting conditions to be right.

Nesting sea turtles, which show a natural predisposition for dark beaches, find fewer and fewer of them to nest on. Their hatchlings, which gravitate toward the brighter, more reflective sea horizon, find themselves confused by artificial lighting behind the beach. In Florida alone, hatchling losses number in the hundreds of thousands every year. Frogs and toads living near brightly lit highways suffer nocturnal light levels that are as much as a million times brighter than normal, throwing nearly every aspect of their behavior out of joint, including their nighttime breeding choruses.

Of all the pollutions we face, light pollution is perhaps the most easily remedied. Simple changes in lighting design and installation yield immediate changes in the amount of light spilled into the atmosphere and, often, immediate energy savings.

10

It was once thought that light pollution only affected astronomers, who need to see the night sky in all its glorious clarity. And, in fact, some of the earliest civic efforts to control light pollution—in Flagstaff, Arizona, half a century ago—were made to protect the view from Lowell Observatory, which sits high above that city. Flagstaff has tightened its regulations since then, and in 2001 it was declared the first International Dark Sky City. By now the effort to control light pollution has spread around the globe. More and more cities and even entire countries, such as the Czech Republic, have committed themselves to reducing unwanted glare.

Unlike astronomers, most of us may not need an undiminished view of the night sky for our work, but like most other creatures we do need darkness. Darkness is as essential to our biological welfare, to our internal clockwork, as light itself. The regular oscillation of waking and sleep in our lives—one of our circadian rhythms—is nothing less than a biological expression of the regular oscillation of light on Earth. So fundamental are these rhythms to our being that altering them is like altering gravity.

For the past century or so, we've been performing an open-ended experiment on ourselves, extending the day, shortening the night, and short-circuiting the human body's sensitive response to light. The consequences of our bright new world are more readily perceptible in less adaptable creatures living in the peripheral glow of our prosperity. But for humans, too, light pollution may take a biological toll. At least one new study has suggested a direct correlation between higher rates of breast cancer in women and the nighttime brightness of their neighborhoods.

In the end, humans are no less trapped by light pollution than the frogs in a pond near a brightly lit highway. Living in a glare of our own making, we have cut ourselves off from our evolutionary and cultural patrimony—the light of the stars and the rhythms of day and night. In a very real sense, light pollution causes us to lose sight of our true place in the universe, to forget the scale of our being, which is best measured against the dimensions of a deep night with the Milky Way—the edge of our galaxy—arching overhead.

## For Discussion and Writing

1. "We've lit up the night as if it were an unoccupied country, when nothing could be further from the truth," Klinkenborg writes (par. 6). How have we done this? By what is the night occupied?

2. Klinkenborg makes an argument in "Our Vanishing Night," but he does so through the use of precise, evocative descriptions. Often these descriptions are of phenomena readers may not have known about or realized. How do these kinds of descriptions help Klinkenborg to make his argument?

3. **connections**   In "Small Change: Why the Revolution Will Not Be Tweeted" (p. 180), Malcolm Gladwell is pessimistic about the potential of current social movements (or at least those rooted in social media) to bring about real change. Does "Our Vanishing Night" believe in the possibility of change? Does it consider the differences between individual action and social movements in bringing about change?

4. Klinkenborg describes the shortening of the night and lighting up of the night sky as an experiment we've been performing on ourselves. Think about your own life in these terms, about the amount of sleep you get and the amount of night light you experience. Do you think the modern experiment with light pollution has had effects on you?

5. **looking further**   Doing some research, think about light pollution and other ways in which humans have changed the planet we live on. Follow your thinking and see where it takes you: how does the way we have changed other things compare to this? Have we changed any things for the better? Is it our place to worry about the effect of the way we live? What will the planet look like in a hundred years? In a thousand?

AUDRE LORDE

# The Fourth of July

*Audre Lorde (1934–1992) was a poet and nonfiction writer. Born in New York City to Caribbean immigrants, Lorde trained and worked as a librarian and became a widely published poet in the 1960s, when she also became politically active. Her poetry collections include* The First Cities *(1968),* Cables to Rage *(1970), and* The Black Unicorn *(1978); her other books were memoir and political and social theory, including* The Cancer Journals *(1980) and* Zami: A New Spelling of My Name *(1982).*

*"The Fourth of July" is a beautifully spare yet forceful piece of writing. In it, readers can see the anger that spurred much of Lorde's writing, whether about racism, as in this essay, or about sexism or homophobia, but they can also see the control with which Lorde expressed her ideas and the honesty with which she implicated herself and her family in her writing.*

The first time I went to Washington, D.C., was on the edge of the summer when I was supposed to stop being a child. At least that's what they said to us all at graduation from the eighth grade. My sister Phyllis graduated at the same time from high school. I don't know what she was supposed to stop being. But as graduation presents for us both, the whole family took a Fourth of July trip to Washington, D.C., the fabled and famous capital of our country.

It was the first time I'd ever been on a railroad train during the day. When I was little, and we used to go to the Connecticut shore, we always went at night on the milk train, because it was cheaper.

Preparations were in the air around our house before school was even over. We packed for a week. There were two very large suitcases that my father carried, and a box filled with food. In fact, my first trip to Washington was a mobile feast; I started eating as soon as we were comfortably ensconced in our seats, and did not stop until somewhere after Philadelphia. I remember it was Philadelphia because I was disappointed not to have passed by the Liberty Bell.

My mother had roasted two chickens and cut them up into dainty bite-size pieces. She packed slices of brown bread and butter and green pepper and carrot sticks. There were little violently yellow iced cakes with scalloped edges called "marigolds," that came from Cushman's Bakery. There was a spice bun and rock-cakes from Newton's, the West Indian bakery across Lenox Avenue from St. Mark's School, and iced tea in a wrapped mayonnaise jar. There were sweet pickles for us and dill pickles for my father, and peaches with the fuzz still on them, individually wrapped to keep them from bruising. And, for neatness, there were piles of napkins and a little tin box with a washcloth dampened with rosewater and glycerine for wiping sticky mouths.

I wanted to eat in the dining car because I had read all about them, but my mother reminded me for the umpteenth time that dining car food always cost too much money and besides, you never could tell whose hands had been playing all over that food, nor where those same hands had been just before. My mother never mentioned that black people were not allowed into railroad dining cars headed south in 1947. As usual, whatever my mother did not like and could not change, she ignored. Perhaps it would go away, deprived of her attention. 5

I learned later that Phyllis's high school senior class trip had been to Washington, but the nuns had given her back her deposit in private, explaining to her that the class, all of whom were white, except Phyllis, would be staying in a hotel where Phyllis "would not be happy," meaning, Daddy explained to her, also in private, that they did not rent rooms to Negroes. "We will take you to Washington, ourselves," my father had avowed, "and not just for an overnight in some measly fleabag hotel."

American racism was a new and crushing reality that my parents had to deal with every day of their lives once they came to this country. They handled it as a private woe. My mother and father believed that they could best protect their children from the realities of race in America and the fact of American racism by never giving them name, much less discussing their nature. We were told we must never trust white people, but *why* was never explained, nor the nature of their ill will. Like so many other vital pieces of information in my childhood, I was supposed to know without being told. It always seemed like a very strange injunction coming from my mother, who looked so much like one of those people we were never supposed to trust. But something always warned me not to ask my mother why she wasn't white, and why Auntie Lillah and Auntie Etta weren't, even though they were all that same problematic color so different from my father and me, even from my sisters, who were somewhere in-between.

In Washington, D.C., we had one large room with two double beds and an extra cot for me. It was a back-street hotel that belonged to a friend of my father's who was in real estate, and I spent the whole next day after Mass squinting up at the Lincoln Memorial where Marian Anderson had sung after the D.A.R. refused to allow her to sing in their auditorium because she was black. Or because she was "Colored," my father said as he told us the story. Except that what he probably said was "Negro," because for his times, my father was quite progressive.

I was squinting because I was in that silent agony that characterized all of my childhood summers, from the time school let out in June to the end of July, brought about by my dilated and vulnerable eyes exposed to the summer brightness.

I viewed Julys through an agonizing corolla of dazzling whiteness and I always hated the Fourth of July, even before I came to realize the travesty such a celebration was for black people in this country.

My parents did not approve of sunglasses, nor of their expense.

I spent the afternoon squinting up at monuments to freedom and past presidencies and democracy, and wondering why the light and heat were both so much stronger in Washington, D.C., than back home in New York City. Even the pavement on the streets was a shade lighter in color than back home.

Late that Washington afternoon my family and I walked back down Pennsylvania Avenue. We were a proper caravan, mother bright and father brown, the three of us girls step-standards in-between. Moved by our historical surroundings and the heat of early evening, my father decreed yet another treat. He had a great sense of history, a flair for the quietly dramatic and the sense of specialness of an occasion and a trip.

"Shall we stop and have a little something to cool off, Lin?"

Two blocks away from our hotel, the family stopped for a dish    15 of vanilla ice cream at a Breyer's ice cream and soda fountain. Indoors, the soda fountain was dim and fan-cooled, deliciously relieving to my scorched eyes.

Corded and crisp and pinafored, the five of us seated ourselves one by one at the counter. There was I between my mother and father, and my two sisters on the other side of my mother. We settled ourselves along the white mottled marble counter, and when the waitress spoke at first no one understood what she was saying, and so the five of us just sat there.

The waitress moved along the line of us closer to my father and spoke again. "I said I kin give you to take out, but you can't eat here. Sorry." Then she dropped her eyes looking very embarrassed, and suddenly we heard what it was she was saying all at the same time, loud and clear.

Straight-backed and indignant, one by one, my family and I got down from the counter stools and turned around and marched out of the store, quiet and outraged, as if we had never been black before. No one would answer my emphatic questions with anything other than a guilty silence. "But we hadn't done anything!" This wasn't right or fair! Hadn't I written poems about Bataan and freedom and democracy for all?

My parents wouldn't speak of this injustice, not because they had contributed to it, but because they felt they should have anticipated it and avoided it. This made me even angrier. My fury was not going to be acknowledged by a like fury. Even my two sisters copied my parents' pretense that nothing unusual and anti-American had occurred. I was left to write my angry letter to the president of the United States all by myself, although my father did promise I could type it out on the office typewriter next week, after I showed it to him in my copybook diary.

The waitress was white, and the counter was white, and the    20 ice cream I never ate in Washington, D.C., that summer I left childhood was white, and the white heat and the white pavement and the white stone monuments of my first Washington summer made me sick to my stomach for the whole rest of that trip and it wasn't much of a graduation present after all.

*For Discussion and Writing*

1. What adjective does Lorde use six times in the essay's one-sentence final paragraph? Why do you think she chose to use it so many times?

2. Though Lorde says that the story she tells here really happened to her, it is as carefully constructed as any short story. One aspect of story construction she pays special attention to is setting things up in such a way that the dramatic moment will have its greatest impact. What is the dramatic moment in "The Fourth of July"? How does Lorde tell the story in a way that makes that moment especially effective?

3. **connections** Jamaica Kincaid's "The Ugly Tourist" (p. 227) is in many ways quite different from Lorde's essay, from its narrative voice to its setting, but both essays are about tourists and race. Compare and contrast these two essays: What are their concerns? How do they explore them? How do they use point of view, scene and setting, and narrative to get their points across? Finally, how are their topics related? Is there any way in which one could be made to speak to the other?

4. Reflect on Lorde's use of irony in this essay. On one level, irony is simply when you say one thing but mean another, or when people in a narrative perceive a situation one way while readers know they're wrong; on another, deeper level, irony is about how things in the world are widely said to be one way when in fact they are not that way at all. How does Lorde use the surface ironies available to narrative—the ways in which things aren't what they seem—to write about the deeper ironies of American society?

5. **looking further** What might Audre Lorde have to say about this childhood experience if she were still alive today? How might the election of Barack Obama as president have changed the way she looked back on this visit to Washington, D.C.? Imagine her possible reactions, and not just in a "things sure have changed" kind of way; try to consider ways in which her reactions might be mixed and even contradictory.

# NANCY MAIRS

# On Being a Cripple

*Born in 1943 in Long Beach, California, and raised north of Boston, Massachusetts, Nancy Mairs is a poet, essayist, and teacher. She has written memoirs and personal essays about women's issues, disability, and death in contemporary culture. In "On Being a Cripple," Mairs demonstrates the power of writing that confronts social issues through personal narrative as well as impersonal analysis. Starting with her blunt title, the piece offers an extended consideration of how we choose to name disability, and how that definition affects how we think about it. "I am not a disease," she writes (par. 23). Note other powerful moments in her essay when these two strands cross.*

> *To escape is nothing. Not to escape is nothing.*
> —LOUISE BOGAN

The other day I was thinking of writing an essay on being a cripple. I was thinking hard in one of the stalls of the women's room in my office building, as I was shoving my shirt into my jeans and tugging up my zipper. Preoccupied, I flushed, picked up my book bag, took my cane down from the hook, and unlatched the door. So many movements unbalanced me, and as I pulled the door open I fell over backward, landing fully clothed on the toilet seat with my legs splayed in front of me: the old beetle-on-its-back routine. Saturday afternoon, the building deserted, I was free to laugh aloud as I wriggled back to my feet, my voice bouncing off the yellowish tiles from all directions. Had anyone been there with me, I'd have been still and faint and hot with chagrin. I decided that it was high time to write the essay.

First, the matter of semantics. I am a cripple. I choose this word to name me. I choose from among several possibilities, the most common of which are "handicapped" and "disabled." I made the choice a number of years ago, without thinking, unaware of my motives for doing so. Even now, I'm not sure what those motives are, but I recognize that they are complex and not entirely flattering. People—crippled or not—wince at the word "cripple," as they do not at "handicapped" or "disabled." Perhaps I want them to wince. I want them to see me as a tough customer, one to whom the fates/gods/viruses have not been kind, but who can face the brutal truth of her existence squarely. As a cripple, I swagger.

But, to be fair to myself, a certain amount of honesty underlies my choice. "Cripple" seems to me a clean word, straightforward and precise. It has an honorable history, having made its first appearance in the Lindisfarne Gospel in the tenth century. As a lover of words, I like the accuracy with which it describes my condition: I have lost the full use of my limbs. "Disabled," by contrast, suggests any incapacity, physical or mental. And I certainly don't like "handicapped," which implies that I have deliberately been put at a disadvantage, by whom I can't imagine (my God is not a Handicapper General), in order to equalize chances in the great race of life. These words seem to me to be moving away from my condition, to be widening the gap between word and reality. Most remote is the recently coined euphemism "differently abled," which partakes of the same semantic hopefulness that transformed countries from "undeveloped" to "underdeveloped," then to "less developed," and finally to "developing" nations. People have continued to starve in those countries during the shift. Some realities do not obey the dictates of language.

Mine is one of them. Whatever you call me, I remain crippled. But I don't care what you call me, so long as it isn't "differently abled," which strikes me as pure verbal garbage designed, by its ability to describe anyone, to describe no one. I subscribe to George Orwell's thesis that "the slovenliness of our language makes it easier for us to have foolish thoughts." And I refuse to participate in the degeneration of the language to the extent that I deny that I have lost anything in the course of this calamitous disease; I refuse to pretend that the only differences between you and me are the various ordinary ones that distinguish any one person from another. But call me "disabled" or "handicapped" if you like. I have long since grown accustomed to them; and if they are vague, at least they hint at the truth. Moreover, I use them myself. Society is no readier to accept crippledness than to accept death, war, sex, sweat, or wrinkles. I would never refer to another person as a cripple. It is the word I use to name only myself.

I haven't always been crippled, a fact for which I am soundly grateful. To be whole of limb is, I know from experience, infinitely more pleasant and useful than to be crippled; and if that knowledge leaves one open to bitterness at my loss, the physical soundness I once enjoyed (though I did not enjoy it half enough) is well worth the occasional stab of regret. Though never any good at sports, I was a normally active child and young adult. I climbed trees, played hopscotch, jumped rope, skated, swam, rode my bicycle, sailed. I despised team sports, spending some of the wretchedest afternoons of my life, sweaty and humiliated, behind a field-hockey stick and under a basketball hoop. I tramped alone for miles along the bridle paths that webbed the woods behind the house I grew up in. I swayed through countless dim hours in the arms of one man or another under the scattered shot of light from mirrored balls, and gyrated through countless more as Tab Hunter and Johnny Mathis gave way to the Rolling Stones, Creedence Clearwater Revival, Cream. I walked down the aisle. I pushed baby carriages, changed tires in the rain, marched for peace.

When I was twenty-eight I started to trip and drop things. What at first seemed my natural clumsiness soon became too pronounced to shrug off. I consulted a neurologist, who told me that I had a brain tumor. A battery of tests, increasingly disagreeable, revealed no tumor. About a year and a half later I developed a blurred spot in one eye. I had, at last, the episodes "disseminated in space and time" requisite for a diagnosis: multiple sclerosis. I have never been sorry for the doctor's initial misdiagnosis, however. For almost a week, until the negative results of the tests were in, I thought that I was going to die right away. Every day for the past nearly ten years, then, has been a kind of gift. I accept all gifts.

Multiple sclerosis is a chronic degenerative disease of the central nervous system, in which the myelin that sheathes the nerves is somehow eaten away and scar tissue forms in its place, interrupting the nerves' signals. During its course, which is unpredictable and uncontrollable, one may lose vision, hearing, speech, the ability to walk, control of bladder and/or bowels, strength in any or all extremities, sensitivity to touch, vibration, and/or pain, potency, coordination of movements—the list of possibilities is lengthy and, yes, horrifying. One may also lose one's sense of humor. That's the easiest to lose and the hardest to survive without.

In the past ten years, I have sustained some of these losses. Characteristic of MS are sudden attacks, called exacerbations, followed by remissions, and these I have not had. Instead, my disease has been slowly progressive. My left leg is now so weak that I walk with the aid of a brace and a cane; and for distances I use an Amigo, a variation on the electric wheelchair that looks rather like an electrified kiddie car. I no longer have much use of my left hand. Now my right side is weakening as well. I still have the blurred spot in my right eye. Overall, though, I've been lucky so far. My world has, of necessity, been circumscribed by my losses, but the terrain left me has been ample enough for me to continue many of the activities that absorb me: writing, teaching, raising children and cats and plants and snakes, reading, speaking publicly about MS and depression, even playing bridge with people patient and honorable enough to let me scatter cards every which way without sneaking a peek.

Lest I begin to sound like Pollyanna, however, let me say that I don't like having MS. I hate it. My life holds realities—harsh ones, some of them—that no right-minded human being ought to accept without grumbling. One of them is fatigue. I know of no one with MS who does not complain of bone-weariness; in a disease that presents an astonishing variety of symptoms, fatigue seems to be a common factor. I wake up in the morning feeling the way most people do at the end of a bad day, and I take it from there. As a result, I spend a lot of time *in extremis* and, impatient with limitation, I tend to ignore my fatigue until my body breaks down in some way and forces rest. Then I miss picnics, dinner parties, poetry readings, the brief visits of old friends from out of town. The offspring of a puritanical tradition of exceptional venerability, I cannot view these lapses without shame. My life often seems a series of small failures to do as I ought.

I lead, on the whole, an ordinary life, probably rather like the one I would have led had I not had MS. I am lucky that my predilections were already solitary, sedentary, and bookish—unlike the world-famous French cellist I have read about, or the young

10

woman I talked with one long afternoon who wanted only to be a
jockey. I had just begun graduate school when I found out something was wrong with me, and I have remained, interminably,
a graduate student. Perhaps I would not have if I'd thought I had
the stamina to return to a full-time job as a technical editor; but
I've enjoyed my studies.

In addition to studying, I teach writing courses. I also teach
medical students how to give neurological examinations. I pick
up freelance editing jobs here and there. I have raised a fos-
ter son and sent him into the world, where he has made me
two grandbabies, and I am still escorting my daughter and son
through adolescence. I go to Mass every Saturday. I am a superb,
if messy, cook. I am also an enthusiastic laundress, capable of
sorting a hamper full of clothes into five subtly differentiated
piles, but a terrible housekeeper. I can do italic writing and, in
an emergency, bathe an oil-soaked cat. I play a fiendish game of
Scrabble. When I have the time and the money, I like to sit on
my front steps with my husband drinking Amaretto and smoking
a cigar, as we imagine our counterparts in Leningrad and make
sure that the sun gets down once more behind the sharp childish
scrawl of the Tucson Mountains.

This lively plenty has its bleak complement, of course, in all
the things I can no longer do. I will never run again, except in
dreams, and one day I may have to write that I will never walk
again. I like to go camping, but I can't follow George and the
children along the trails that wander out of a campsite through
the desert or into the mountains. In fact, even on the level I've
learned never to check the weather or try to hold a coherent conversation: I need all my attention for my wayward feet. Of late,
I have begun to catch myself wondering how people can propel
themselves without canes. With only one usable hand, I have to
select my clothing with care not so much for style as for ease of
ingress and egress, and even so, dressing can be laborious. I can
no longer do fine stitchery, pick up babies, play the piano, braid
my hair. I am immobilized by acute attacks of depression, which
may or may not be physiologically related to MS but are certainly
its logical concomitant.

These two elements, the plenty and the privation, are never
pure, nor are the delight and wretchedness that accompany them.
Almost every pickle that I get into as a result of my weakness

and clumsiness—and I get into plenty—is funny as well as maddening and sometimes painful. I recall one May afternoon when a friend and I were going out for a drink after finishing up at school. As we were climbing into opposite sides of my car, chatting, I tripped and fell, flat and hard, onto the asphalt parking lot, my abrupt departure interrupting him in mid-sentence. "Where'd you go?" he called as he came around the back of the car to find me hauling myself up by the door frame. "Are you all right?" Yes, I told him, I was fine, just a bit rattly, and we drove off to find a shady patio and some beer. When I got home an hour or so later, my daughter greeted me with "What have you done to yourself?" I looked down. One elbow of my white turtleneck with the green froggies, one knee of my white trousers, one white kneesock were bloodsoaked. We peeled off the clothes and inspected the damage, which was nasty enough but not alarming. That part wasn't funny: the abrasions took a long time to heal, and one got a little infected. Even so, when I think of my friend talking earnestly, suddenly, to the hot thin air while I dropped from his view as though through a trap door, I find the image as silly as something from a Marx Brothers movie.

I may find it easier than other cripples to amuse myself because I live propped by the acceptance and the assistance and, sometimes, the amusement of those around me. Grocery clerks tear my checks out of my checkbook for me, and sales clerks find chairs to put into dressing rooms when I want to try on clothes. The people I work with make sure I teach at times when I am least likely to be fatigued, in places I can get to, with the materials I need. My students, with one anonymous exception (in an end-of-the-semester evaluation), have been unperturbed by my disability. Some even like it. One was immensely cheered by the information that I paint my own fingernails; she decided, she told me, that if I could go to such trouble over fine details, she could keep on writing essays. I suppose I became some sort of bright-fingered muse. She wrote good essays, too.

The most important struts in the framework of my existence, of course, are my husband and children. Dismayingly few marriages survive the MS test, and why should they? Most twenty-two- and nineteen-year-olds, like George and me, can vow in clear conscience, after a childhood of chicken pox and summer colds, to keep one another in sickness and in health so long as they both shall live. Not many are equipped for catastrophe: the dismay, the depression, the extra work, the boredom that a degenerative disease can insinuate into a relationship. And our society, with its emphasis on fun and its association of fun with physical performance, offers little encouragement for a whole spouse to stay with a crippled partner. Children experience similar stresses when faced with a crippled parent, and they are more helpless, since parents and children can't usually get divorced. They hate, of course, to be different from their peers, and the child whose mother is tacking down the aisle of a school auditorium packed with proud parents like a Cape Cod dinghy in a stiff breeze jolly well stands out in a crowd. Deprived of legal divorce, the child can at least deny the mother's disability, even her existence, forgetting to tell her about recitals and PTA meetings, refusing to accompany her to stores or church or the movies, never inviting friends to the house. Many do.

But I've been limping along for ten years now, and so far George and the children are still at my left elbow, holding tight. Anne and Matthew vacuum floors and dust furniture and haul trash and rake up dog droppings and button my cuffs and bake lasagna and Toll House cookies with just enough grumbling so I know that they don't have brain fever. And far from hiding me, they're forever dragging me by racks of fancy clothes or through teeming school corridors, or welcoming gaggles of friends while I'm wandering through the house in Anne's filmy pink babydoll pajamas. George generally calls before he brings someone home, but he does just as many dumb thankless chores as the children. And they all yell at me, laugh at some of my jokes, write me funny letters when we're apart—in short, treat me as an ordinary human being for whom they have some use. I think they like me. Unless they're faking. . . .

Faking. There's the rub. Tugging at the fringes of my consciousness always is the terror that people are kind to me only because I'm a cripple. My mother almost shattered me once, with that instinct mothers have—blind, I think, in this case, but unerring nonetheless—for striking blows along the fault-lines of their children's hearts, by telling me, in an attack on my selfishness, "We all have to make allowances for you, of course, because of the way you are." From the distance of a couple of years, I have to admit that I haven't any idea just what she meant, and I'm not sure that she knew either. She was awfully angry. But at the time, as the words thudded home, I felt my worst fear, suddenly realized. I could bear being called selfish: I am. But I couldn't bear the corroboration that those around me were doing in fact what I'd always suspected them of doing, professing fondness while silently putting up with me because of the way I am. A cripple. I've been a little cracked ever since.

Along with this fear that people are secretly accepting shoddy goods comes a relentless pressure to please — to prove myself worth the burdens I impose, I guess, or to build a substantial account of goodwill against which I may write drafts in times of need. Part of the pressure arises from social expectations. In our society, anyone who deviates from the norm had better find some way to compensate. Like fat people, who are expected to be jolly, cripples must bear their lot meekly and cheerfully. A grumpy cripple isn't playing by the rules. And much of pressure is self-generated. Early on I vowed that, if I had to have MS, by God I was going to do it well. This is a class act, ladies and gentlemen. No tears, no recriminations, no faint-heartedness.

One way and another, then, I wind up feeling like Tiny Tim, peering over the edge of the table at the Christmas goose, waving my crutch, piping down God's blessing on us all. Only sometimes I don't want to play Tiny Tim. I'd rather be Caliban, a most scurvy monster. Fortunately, at home no one much cares whether I'm a good cripple or a bad cripple as long as I make vichyssoise with fair regularity. One evening several years ago, Anne was reading at the dining-room table while I cooked dinner. As I opened a can of tomatoes, the can slipped in my left hand and juice spattered me and the counter with bloody spots. Fatigued and infuriated, I bellowed, "I'm so sick of being crippled!" Anne glanced at me over the top of her book. "There now," she said, "do you feel better?" "Yes," I said, "yes, I do." She went back to her reading. I felt better. That's about all the attention my scurviness ever gets.

Because I hate being crippled, I sometimes hate myself for 20 being a cripple. Over the years I have come to expect — even accept — attacks of violent self-loathing. Luckily, in general our society no longer connects deformity and disease directly with evil (though a charismatic once told me that I have MS because a devil is in me) and so I'm allowed to move largely at will, even among small children. But I'm not sure that this revision of attitude has been particularly helpful. Physical imperfection, even freed of moral disapprobation, still defies and violates the ideal, especially for women, whose confinement in their bodies as objects of desire is far from over. Each age, of course, has its ideal, and I doubt that ours is any better or worse than any other. Today's ideal woman, who lives on the glossy pages of dozens of magazines, seems to be between the ages of eighteen and twenty-five; her hair has body, her teeth flash white, her breath smells minty, her underarms are dry; she has a career but is still a fabulous cook, especially of meals that take less than twenty minutes to prepare; she does not ordinarily appear to have a husband or children; she is trim and deeply tanned; she jogs, swims, plays tennis, rides a bicycle, sails, but does not bowl; she travels widely, even to out-of-the-way places like Finland and Samoa, always in the company of the ideal man, who possesses a nearly identical set of characteristics. There are a few exceptions. Though usually white and often blonde, she may be black, Hispanic, Asian, or Native American, so long as she is unusually sleek. She may be old, provided she is selling a laxative or is Lauren Bacall. If she is selling a detergent, she may be married and have a flock of strikingly messy children. But she is never a cripple.

Like many women I know, I have always had an uneasy relationship with my body. I was not a popular child, largely, I think now, because I was peculiar: intelligent, intense, moody, shy, given to unexpected actions and inexplicable notions and emotions. But as I entered adolescence, I believed myself unpopular because I was homely: my breasts too flat, my mouth too wide, my hips too narrow, my clothing never quite right in fit or style. I was not, in fact, particularly ugly, old photographs inform me, though I was well off the ideal; but I carried this sense of self-alienation with me into adulthood, where it regenerated in response to the depredations of MS. Even with my brace I walk with a limp so pronounced that, seeing myself on the videotape of a television program on the disabled, I couldn't believe that anything but an inchworm could make progress humping along like that. My shoulders droop and my pelvis thrusts forward as I try to balance myself upright, throwing my frame into a bony S. As a result of contractures, one shoulder is higher than the other and I carry one arm bent in front of me, the fingers curled into a claw. My left arm and leg have wasted into pipestems, and I try always to keep them covered. When I think about how my body must look to others, especially to men, to whom I have been trained to display myself, I feel ludicrous, even loathsome.

At my age, however, I don't spend much time thinking about my appearance. The burning egocentricity of adolescence, which assures one that all the world is looking all the time, has passed, thank God, and I'm generally too caught up in what I'm doing to step back, as I used to, and watch myself as though upon a stage. I'm also too old to believe in the accuracy of self-image. I know that I'm not a hideous crone, that in fact, when I'm rested, well dressed, and well made up, I look fine. The self-loathing I feel is neither physically nor intellectually substantial. What I hate is not me but a disease.

I am not a disease.

And a disease is not — at least not singlehandedly — going to determine who I am, though at first it seemed to be going to. Adjusting to a chronic incurable illness, I have moved through a process similar to that outlined by Elisabeth Kübler-Ross in *On Death and Dying*. The major difference — and it is far more significant than most people recognize — is that I can't be sure of the outcome, as the terminally ill cancer patient can. Research studies indicate that, with proper medical care, I may achieve a "normal" life span. And in our society, with its vision of death as the ultimate evil, worse even than decrepitude, the response to such news is, "Oh well, at least you're not going to *die*." Are there worse things than dying? I think that there may be.

I think of two women I know, both with MS, both enough older than I to have served me as models. One took to her bed several years ago and has been there ever since. Although she can sit in a high-backed wheelchair, because she is incontinent she refuses to go out at all, even though incontinence pants, which are readily available at any pharmacy, could protect her from embarrassment. Instead, she stays at home and insists that her husband, a small quiet man, a retired civil servant, stay there with her except for a quick weekly foray to the supermarket. The other woman, whose illness was diagnosed when she was eighteen, a nursing student engaged to a young doctor, finished her training, married her doctor, accompanied him to Germany when he was in the service, bore three sons and a daughter, now grown and gone. When she can, she travels with her husband;

she plays bridge, embroiders, swims regularly; she works, like me, as a symptomatic-patient instructor of medical students in neurology. Guess which woman I hope to be.

At the beginning, I thought about having MS almost incessantly and because of the unpredictable course of the disease, my thoughts were always terrified. Each night I'd get into bed wondering whether I'd get out again the next morning, whether I'd be able to see, to speak, to hold a pen between my fingers. Knowing that the day might come when I'd be physically incapable of killing myself, I thought perhaps I ought to do so right away, while I still had the strength. Gradually I came to understand that the Nancy who might one day lie inert under a bedsheet, arms and legs paralyzed, unable to feed or bathe herself, unable to reach out for a gun, a bottle of pills, was not the Nancy I was at present, and that I could not presume to make decisions for that future Nancy, who might well not want in the least to die. Now the only provision I've made for the future Nancy is that when the time comes—and it is likely to come in the form of pneumonia, friend to the weak and the old—I am not to be treated with machines and medications. If she is unable to communicate by then, I hope she will be satisfied with these terms.

Thinking all the time about having MS grew tiresome and intrusive, especially in the large and tragic mode in which I was accustomed to considering my plight. Months and even years went by without catastrophe (at least without one related to MS), and really I was awfully busy, what with George and children and snakes and students and poems, and I hadn't the time, let alone the inclination, to devote myself to being a disease. Too, the richer my life became, the funnier it seemed, as though there were some connection between largesse and laughter, and so my tragic stance began to waver until, even with the aid of a brace and a cane, I couldn't hold it for very long at a time.

After several years I was satisfied with my adjustment. I had suffered my grief and fury and terror, I thought, but now I was at ease with my lot. Then one summer day I set out with George and the children across the desert for a vacation in California. Part way to Yuma I became aware that my right leg felt funny. "I think I've had an exacerbation," I told George. "What shall we do?" he asked. "I think we'd better get the hell to California," I said, "because I don't know whether I'll ever make it again."

So we went on to San Diego and then to Orange, up the Pacific Coast Highway to Santa Cruz, across to Yosemite, down to Sequoia and Joshua Tree, and so back over the desert to home. It was a fine two-week trip, filled with friends and fair weather, and I wouldn't have missed it for the world, though I did in fact make it back to California two years later. Nor would there have been any point in missing it, since in MS, once the symptoms have appeared, the neurological damage has been done, and there's no way to predict or prevent that damage.

The incident spoiled my self-satisfaction, however. It renewed my grief and fury and terror, and I learned that one never finishes adjusting to MS. I don't know now why I thought one would. One does not, after all, finish adjusting to life, and MS is simply a fact of my life—not my favorite fact, of course—but as ordinary as my nose and my tropical fish and my yellow Mazda station wagon. It may at any time get worse, but no amount of worry, or anticipation can prepare me for a new loss. My life is a lesson in losses. I learn one at a time.

And I had best be patient in the learning, since I'll have to do    30 it like it or not. As any rock fan knows, you can't always get what you want. Particularly when you have MS. You can't, for example, get cured. In recent years researchers and the organizations that fund research have started to pay MS some attention even though it isn't fatal; perhaps they have begun to see that life is something other than a quantitative phenomenon, that one may be very much alive for a very long time in a life that isn't worth living. The researchers have made some progress toward understanding the mechanism of the disease: it may well be an auto-immune reaction triggered by a slow-acting virus. But they are nowhere near its prevention, control, or cure. And most of us want to be cured. Some, unable to accept incurability, grasp at one treatment after another, no matter how bizarre: megavitamin therapy, gluten-free diet, injections of cobra venom, hypothermal suits, lymphocytopharesis, hyperbaric chambers. Many treatments are probably harmless enough, but none are curative.

The absence of a cure often makes MS patients bitter toward their doctors. Doctors are, after all, the priests of modern society, the new shamans, whose business is to heal, and many an MS patient roves from one to another, searching for the "good" doctor who will make him well. Doctors too think of themselves as healers, and for this reason many have trouble dealing with MS patients, whose disease in its intransigence defeats their aims and mocks their skills. Too few doctors, it is true, treat their patients as whole human beings, but the reverse is also true. I have always tried to be gentle with my doctors, who often have more at stake in terms of ego than I do. I may be frustrated, maddened, depressed by the incurability of my disease, but I am not diminished by it, and they are. When I push myself up from my seat in the waiting room and stumble toward them, I incarnate the limitation of their powers. The least I can do is refuse to press on their tenderest spots.

This gentleness is part of the reason that I'm not sorry to be a cripple. I didn't have it before. Perhaps I'd have developed it anyway—how could I know such a thing?—and I wish I had more of it, but I'm glad of what I have. It has opened and enriched my life enormously, this sense that my frailty and need must be mirrored in others, that in searching for and shaping a stable core in a life wrenched by change and loss, change and loss, I must recognize the same process, under individual conditions, in the lives around me. I do not deprecate such knowledge, however I've come by it.

All the same, if a cure were found, would I take it? In a minute. I may be a cripple, but I'm only occasionally a loony and never a saint. Anyway, in my brand of theology God doesn't give bonus points for a limp. I'd take a cure; I just don't need one. A friend who also has MS startled me once by asking, "Do you ever say to yourself, 'Why me, Lord?'" "No, Michael, I don't," I told him, "because whenever I try, the only response I can think of is 'Why not?'" If I could make a cosmic deal, who would I put in my place? What in my life would I give up in exchange for sound limbs and a thrilling rush of energy? No one. Nothing. I might as well do the job myself. Now that I'm getting the hang of it.

### For Discussion and Writing

1. Make two lists, one of Mairs's talents and one of the activities her MS makes difficult or impossible.
2. "As a cripple, I swagger," Mairs writes (par. 2). What does this mean? More generally, what is Mairs saying about her MS in this essay? How does this use of the word *cripple* help her say it?

3. **connections**   Mairs rejects the labels "handicapped" and "disabled," preferring "crippled," even though many see it as offensive. Compare Mairs's attention to words in this essay to Gloria Anzaldúa's in "How to Tame a Wild Tongue" (p. 30). What power does Anzaldúa see words having? What can words do and undo? Are there moments when Anzaldúa harnesses that power for herself in ways analogous to what Mairs does in "On Being a Cripple"?

4. Think about the way others see you and the way you see yourself. How would you correct their perception of you if it were possible?

5. **looking further**   Read up on Franklin Delano Roosevelt's physical disability. While some attitudes and laws have changed since the 1940s, do you think they have changed enough that if he were president today, he could (or would) act differently about his disability? Make an argument based on evidence including current laws and current politicians.

MATTHEW J. X. MALADY

# The Ghosts in Our Machines

*Matthew J. X. Malady is a writer, editor, and attorney living in Berkeley.*
*He earned his undergraduate degree from Syracuse University and his*
*law degree from the University of Michigan Law School. He is a col-*
*umnist for* Slate *and* The Awl *and has written for other magazines,*
*including the* New Republic, *the* New Yorker, *and the* New York Times
Magazine. *He has been editor of* Columbia Law School Magazine,
AVENUE, *and* Strong Magazine.

*"The Ghosts in Our Machines" first appeared on the* New Yorker
*website's "Culture Desk," which it describes as including "conversa-*
*tions about movies, television, theatre, music, and other cultural*
*events." When you read this essay, think about why the Culture*
*Desk editor wanted it for the Culture Desk. What cultural event,*
*phenomenon, or development is it about that earned it its placement?*

Every now and again, when I've been working for too many hours
without a break or have spent an entire day writing something,
I jump on Google Maps Street View and get lost in my past.

The images on Street View, taken by fancy cameras that are
usually—though not always—strapped to the tops of cars, are
a boon for basement-dwelling architecture buffs and those who
want to see the world without going broke. I use the site for far
less cosmopolitan purposes. I track down baseball diamonds
and bike trails I played on as a kid. I locate comic-book shops
from back in the day, old college dorms, hotels my family stayed
in during summer vacations back when we took summer vacations as a family. I plop down in places I've been, places that have
meant something to me, and look around. Then I compare the
contemporary to what's in my memory. It's a way to unwind,
a respite from more taxing laptop-based endeavors.

In some cases, the ball field or building I remember no longer
exists. (I would never call the crummy two-story house I lived in

261

during the summer between undergrad and law school paradise, but it was, in fact, knocked down, paved over, and turned into a parking lot.) Other times, I've happened upon more pleasant changes—beautiful flowerbeds that weren't there in 1992, a new in-ground swimming pool at the rec center, better paint choices. When I really want to dig in, I'll treat these Street View adventures as mini treasure hunts, attempting to come up with the most obscure and faintly held memory of a place, to make my search for that location as difficult as possible. Earlier this year, I remembered a weird middle-school trip I took to somewhere in Georgia for what amounted to a national convention of nerdy kids. (Its official name was Academic Games.) I was twelve at the time, and all I recalled about the event was that it was held at some gigantic 4-H-type place in the woods and that I lost the fishing rod I had brought all the way from Pennsylvania when I was showing off for some girls. (My grip slipped while casting, and I accidentally chucked it into the lake.) Anyway, I found that place on Street View. The campground is just north of Eatonton, Georgia. My fishing rod is somewhere at the bottom of Rock Eagle Lake.

That was a tough one. It took me a while to find.

More recently, on a late night after a long day of writing, I picked a Street View target that was much simpler, so I could take a quick mental jaunt and then go to bed. I decided to check out a house I lived in during my late teens, and that my mother continued to live in until she passed away, unexpectedly, right around this time two years ago. I currently live 2,578 miles from that home, and I hadn't been there since a few years before my mom died. I mainly wanted to see how the street and neighborhood had changed. 5

I started at the top of the street and worked my way down toward her house. The Google Maps car had apparently passed by on the most glorious of spring days. The sky, in the pictures, is a brilliant shade of blue. Yards teem with bright crimson Japanese maples and well-manicured shrubbery. As I moved the cursor down the street, I noticed all sorts of newly constructed picket fences that I'd never seen before. Trees had sprouted up in the yards of my former neighbors.

According to the Web site, the images had been taken in April of 2012, and I was glad to see that my old street was doing just fine. That was no great surprise, though; my mom lived on a suburban block in a middle-class neighborhood with lots of trees. What I saw was pretty much what I had expected to see.

When I reached my mother's house, that all changed. First, I noticed that a gigantic American flag had been affixed to the mailbox post at the corner of the driveway. That was new. Then I spotted the fire pit in the front yard that my mom and her husband, my stepfather, used for block parties, and the grill on the patio, and my mom's car. And then there she was, out front, walking on the path that leads from the driveway to the home's front door. My mom.

At first I was convinced that it couldn't be her, that I was just seeing things. When's the last time you've spotted someone you know on Google Maps? I never had. And my mother, besides, is no longer alive. It couldn't be her.

That feeling passed quickly. Because it *was* her. In the photo,    10
my mom is wearing a pair of black slacks and a floral-print blouse. Her hair is exactly as I always remember it. She's carrying what appears to be a small grocery bag.

The confluence of emotions, when I registered what I was looking at, was unlike anything I had ever experienced—something akin to the simultaneous rush of a million overlapping feelings. There was joy, certainly—"Mom! I found you! Can you believe it?"—but also deep, deep sadness. There was heartbreak and hurt, curiosity and wonder, and everything, seemingly, in between.

I cried for a minute. Then I chuckled. I shook my head. It was as though my mind and body had no clue how to appropriately respond, so I was made to do a little bit of everything all at once. But almost immediately I realized how fortunate I was to have made the discovery: at some point in the future, and probably quite soon, Google will update the pictures of my mom's old street, and those images of her will disappear from the Internet.

I bit my lip and started clicking around. By moving the camera position up and down the street, and using the zoom function, I could trace my mom's movements on that day as the Google car drove by. In the first frame, she's a few paces from the door, with her back to the street; she was probably just returning from work. Then she veers from the path, toward the neighbor's house—you can see, in another photo, that neighbor out front, picking up a newspaper; I'm pretty certain my mom briefly stopped to say hello.

Then, in the next couple of frames, she reaches the front door, opens it, and goes inside. In that last one, you can barely see my mom, as the door closes behind her.

It took me a while to fall asleep that night, and the whole next day I walked around in a daze. All I could think about was my mom. It was impossible to concentrate on anything else for more than a few moments. Reeling, I shared the experience with a close friend, a woman who, unlike me, is quite religious, and who lost her father to cancer a few years ago. She had helped me get through the pain and sorrow I felt after my mom died. When my friend heard about the Street View discovery, she was thrilled. "These things happen," she told me. "And they'll sneak up on you at the oddest times." She said she calls unexpected connections with lost loved ones "winks," and that they happen to her often. Certain songs will come on the radio when she is thinking of her father, or she'll find something on the beach with his initials on it, stuff like that. I don't generally think about things in the intensely spiritual way this friend does, but finding these Google Maps photos of my mother felt like a wink of monumental proportions.

It is now a few weeks later, and that late-night discovery still occupies my mind for long stretches of each day. It has also prompted me to pay more attention to the expanding, multifaceted role technology plays in the experience of grief. Facebook is awash in memorials and posts paying tribute to deceased loved ones, of course, and scores of Web sites are in the online obituary business. But in most instances, people have to seek out that content in one way or another. It doesn't sneak up on you. Not so for the ambush-style online reminders that began arriving shortly after my mom's death and still throw me for a loop every single time.

Each year, I receive automated Facebook reminders urging me not to forget to wish my mom a happy birthday. During the weeks leading up to Mother's Day, the flower company FTD, without fail, sends between five and ten e-mails to my old Yahoo account telling me that I should not wait any longer before ordering flowers for mom. I didn't even realize that my mother had joined LinkedIn until January 2nd of this year, when I received one of those maddening, computer-generated e-mails informing me that her job anniversary was coming up.

15

These fleeting online occurrences can make an already difficult grieving process even more complicated and bizarre—mainly because it's more difficult than you might expect to decide, finally, what to make of these things, or what to do about them. My Street View discovery was the best, but it was also the worst. Those Facebook pings about my deceased mom's birthday bother me, but I don't think I'd want them to go away forever.

In some ways, these sorrowful little blips feel like a reboot of an old, low-tech phenomenon: the way that, after the loss of a loved one, people pop up at every turn to either ask you how you are doing or urge you to "think of all the good times."

At my mom's funeral, several people I hadn't seen in years, or barely knew, came up to me and, mid-hug, said things like, "Do you remember that time we all went to such-and-such place together?" or "Remember when your mom said such-and-such, and it was just so wonderful?" In each case, I did remember the times being referenced, and for the most part I was happy to have been reminded of them. They also made the sadness hit even harder, though, and interactions like that continue for weeks after someone close to you dies.

The unexpected tech taps I've experienced during the past few years feel similarly welcome and unwelcome, heartwarming and grief exacerbating, much appreciated and yet still somehow pretty terrible. 20

If you were to ask me right now whether I'm looking forward to receiving the e-mails that are sure to appear in my inbox during the first few weeks of December, inquiring whether I'd like to send another holiday wreath to my mom this year, or whether my mother might want another framed photo from Art.com, I would answer without any hedging or hesitation: absolutely not.

But, truth be told, when those e-mails arrive, in addition to becoming very sad, I will also be reminded of my mom, and will be glad for that. Until those branded mortality reminders start rolling in, later this year, I'll still have the Miracle on Google Street View to recall. I took screenshots of my mom from every angle available on the site, saved them to my hard drive, and e-mailed copies to myself, just in case my hard drive crashes at some point. Then, like a living, breathing grief-complicating cliché, I e-mailed the images to family and friends, in order to simultaneously brighten and ruin their days.

## For Discussion and Writing

1. The phrase "ghost in the machine" originated in philosophy and refers to the idea that the mind and the physical body are separate and independent things. It has also come to be used to refer to the phenomenon of computers seeming to do other than what they are supposed to, as if possessing or possessed by an independent consciousness. What is Malady referring to when he uses the phrase in his title? Why do you think he might have wanted to use this phrase?

2. How would you characterize tone in this essay? How does it express what its author seems to be trying to communicate?

3. **connections**   Think about Malady's essay in relation to Malcolm Gladwell's "Small Change: Why the Revolution Will Not Be Tweeted" (p. 180). How does each essay reflect on the presence of the digital in our lives? What role does each author think computers play in our lives?

4. Write about grief—your experience of it, your observations of others' experiences, your thoughts about how different cultures grieve. How do we do it? Why? What does it mean? What can it tell us about what we value and about our world?

5. **looking further**   Use Google Maps to investigate places from your past and write about what you find. Do things look as you remember them? Has anything changed? What is it like to see them again?

BHARATI MUKHERJEE

# Two Ways to Belong in America

*Born in 1940 and raised in Calcutta, India, Bharati Mukherjee immigrated to the United States in 1961 and earned an MFA and a Ph.D. in literature. Mukherjee is the author of several novels, including* Tiger's Daughter *(1972),* Jasmine *(1989),* Desirable Daughters *(2002), and* The Tree Bride *(2004). She has also written short story collections, such as* The Middleman and Other Stories *(1988). She is a professor emerita at the University of California, Berkeley.*

*"Two Ways to Belong in America" first appeared in the* New York Times. *It was written to address a movement in Congress to take away government benefits from resident aliens. Like her fiction, though, it is about the issues that confront immigrants in America.*

This is a tale of two sisters from Calcutta, Mira and Bharati, who have lived in the United States for some 35 years, but who find themselves on different sides in the current debate over the status of immigrants. I am an American citizen and she is not. I am moved that thousands of long-term residents are finally taking the oath of citizenship. She is not.

Mira arrived in Detroit in 1960 to study child psychology and pre-school education. I followed her a year later to study creative writing at the University of Iowa. When we left India, we were almost identical in appearance and attitude. We dressed alike, in saris; we expressed identical views on politics, social issues, love, and marriage in the same Calcutta convent-school accent. We would endure our two years in America, secure our degrees, then return to India to marry the grooms of our father's choosing.

Instead, Mira married an Indian student in 1962 who was getting his business administration degree at Wayne State University. They soon acquired the labor certifications necessary for the green card of hassle-free residence and employment.

267

Mira still lives in Detroit, works in the Southfield, Mich., school system, and has become nationally recognized for her contributions in the fields of pre-school education and parent-teacher relationships. After 36 years as a legal immigrant in this country, she clings passionately to her Indian citizenship and hopes to go home to India when she retires.

In Iowa City in 1963, I married a fellow student, an American      5
of Canadian parentage. Because of the accident of his North Dakota birth, I bypassed labor-certification requirements and the race-related "quota" system that favored the applicant's country of origin over his or her merit. I was prepared for (and even welcomed) the emotional strain that came with marrying outside my ethnic community. In 33 years of marriage, we have lived in every part of North America. By choosing a husband who was not my father's selection, I was opting for fluidity, self-invention, blue jeans, and T-shirts, and renouncing 3,000 years (at least) of caste-observant, "pure culture" marriage in the Mukherjee family. My books have often been read as unapologetic (and in some quarters overenthusiastic) texts for cultural and psychological "mongrelization." It's a word I celebrate.

Mira and I have stayed sisterly close by phone. In our regular Sunday morning conversations, we are unguardedly affectionate. I am her only blood relative on this continent. We expect to see each other through the looming crises of aging and ill health without being asked. Long before Vice President Gore's "Citizenship U.S.A." drive, we'd had our polite arguments over the ethics of retaining an overseas citizenship while expecting the permanent protection and economic benefits that come with living and working in America.

Like well-raised sisters, we never said what was really on our minds, but we probably pitied one another. She, for the lack of structure in my life, the erasure of Indianness, the absence of an unvarying daily core. I, for the narrowness of her perspective, her uninvolvement with the mythic depths or the superficial pop culture of this society. But, now, with the scapegoatings of "aliens" (documented or illegal) on the increase, and the targeting of long-term legal immigrants like Mira for new scrutiny and new self-consciousness, she and

I find ourselves unable to maintain the same polite discretion. We were always unacknowledged adversaries, and we are now, more than ever, sisters.

"I feel used," Mira raged on the phone the other night. "I feel manipulated and discarded. This is such an unfair way to treat a person who was invited to stay and work here because of her talent. My employer went to the I.N.S. and petitioned for the labor certification. For over 30 years, I've invested my creativity and professional skills into the improvement of *this* country's pre-school system. I've obeyed all the rules, I've paid my taxes, I love my work, I love my students, I love the friends I've made. How dare America now change its rules in midstream? If America wants to make new rules curtailing benefits of legal immigrants, they should apply only to immigrants who arrive after those rules are already in place."

To my ears, it sounded like the description of a long-enduring, comfortable yet loveless marriage, without risk or recklessness. Have we the right to demand, and to expect, that we be loved? (That, to me, is the subtext of the arguments by immigration advocates.) My sister is an expatriate, professionally generous and creative, socially courteous and gracious, and that's as far as her Americanization can go. She is here to maintain an identity, not to transform it.

I asked her if she would follow the example of others 10 who have decided to become citizens because of the anti-immigration bills in Congress. And here, she surprised me. "If America wants to play the manipulative game, I'll play it, too," she snapped. "I'll become a U.S. citizen for now, then change back to India when I'm ready to go home. I feel some kind of irrational attachment to India that I don't to America. Until all this hysteria against legal immigrants, I was totally happy. Having my green card meant I could visit any place in the world I wanted to and then come back to a job that's satisfying and that I do very well."

In one family, from two sisters alike as peas in a pod, there could not be a wider divergence of immigrant experience. America spoke to me—I married it—I embraced the demotion from expatriate aristocrat to immigrant nobody, surrendering those thousands of years of "pure culture," the saris, the delightfully accented English. She retained them all. Which of us is the freak?

Mira's voice, I realize, is the voice not just of the immigrant South Asian community but of an immigrant community of the millions who have stayed rooted in one job, one city, one house, one ancestral culture, one cuisine, for the entirety of their productive years. She speaks for greater numbers than I possibly can. Only the fluency of her English and the anger, rather than fear, born of confidence from her education, differentiate her from the seamstresses, the domestics, the technicians, the shop owners, the millions of hard-working but effectively silenced documented immigrants as well as their less fortunate "illegal" brothers and sisters.

Nearly 20 years ago, when I was living in my husband's ancestral homeland of Canada, I was always well-employed but never allowed to feel part of the local Quebec or larger Canadian society. Then, through a Green Paper that invited a national referendum on the unwanted side effects of "nontraditional" immigration, the government officially turned against its immigrant communities, particularly those from South Asia.

I felt then the same sense of betrayal that Mira feels now. I will never forget the pain of that sudden turning, and the casual racist outbursts the Green Paper elicited. That sense of betrayal had its desired effect and drove me, and thousands like me, from the country.

Mira and I differ, however, in the ways in which we hope to   15 interact with the country that we have chosen to live in. She is happier to live in America as expatriate Indian than as an immigrant American. I need to feel like a part of the community I have adopted (as I tried to feel in Canada as well). I need to put roots down, to vote and make the difference that I can. The price that the immigrant willingly pays, and that the exile avoids, is the trauma of self-transformation.

## For Discussion and Writing

1. Make a list of specific qualities, behaviors, and beliefs for each of the two sisters. What similarities and differences are evident?
2. Mukherjee spends much of this essay comparing herself to her sister. What larger comparison does this analysis support?

3. **connections**   Mukherjee's essay contains a lot of background information (about politics and history), which she skillfully weaves into the story she tells about herself and her sister. Compare the way she weaves together these two strands of the narrative with the methods employed by Rahawa Haile in "Going It Alone" (p. 196).

4. Think of a sibling or friend with whom you disagree vehemently over some issue or idea. Describe your arguments about it. Are they "polite," as Mukherjee says hers are with her sister?

5. **looking further**   Mukherjee quotes her sister as describing her own allegiance to her native culture as "some kind of irrational attachment" (par. 10). Would you describe it as irrational, as some critics of multiculturalism do? Or do you find it a natural result of her identity, as advocates of multiculturalism do? Research multiculturalism and discuss "Two Ways to Belong in America" in the light of multiculturalism as both demographic fact and political philosophy.

TOMMY ORANGE

# Indian Heads

*Tommy Orange is a writer and an enrolled member of the Cheyenne and Arapahoe tribes. He was born and raised in Oakland, California. Orange earned a BS in sound engineering and an MFA from the Institute of American Indian Arts, where he now teaches. This essay is the prologue of Orange's debut novel* There, There *(2018). As you read, think about it in itself but also as it appeared in Orange's novel. Without having read the novel, how do you think the prologue might prepare readers for what follows? What kinds of characters, themes, and settings do you expect? What questions might it ask?*

## INDIAN HEAD

There was an Indian head, the head of an Indian, the drawing of the head of a headdressed, long-haired Indian depicted, drawn by an unknown artist in 1939, broadcast until the late 1970s to American TVs everywhere after all the shows ran out. It's called the Indian Head test pattern. If you left the TV on, you'd hear a tone at 440 hertz—the tone used to tune instruments—and you'd see that Indian, surrounded by circles that looked like sights through riflescopes. There was what looked like a bull's-eye in the middle of the screen, with numbers like coordinates.

The Indian head was just above the bullseye, like all you'd need to do was nod up in agreement to set the sights on the target. This was just a test.

In 1621, colonists invited Massasoit, chief of the Wampanoags, to a feast after a recent land deal. Massasoit came with ninety of his men. That meal is why we still eat a meal together in November. Celebrate it as a nation. But that one wasn't a thanksgiving meal. It was a land deal meal. Two years later there was another, similar meal, meant to symbolize eternal friendship. Two hundred Indians dropped dead that night from supposed unknown poison.

272

By the time Massasoit's son Metacomet became chief, there were no Indian-Pilgrim meals being eaten together. Metacomet, also known as King Phillip, was forced to sign a peace treaty to give up all Indian guns. Three of his men were hanged. His brother Wamsutta was let's say very likely poisoned after being summoned and seized by the Plymouth court. All of which lead to the first official Indian war. The first war with Indians. King Phillip's War. Three years later the war was over and Metacomet was on the run. He was caught by Benjamin Church, Captain of the very first American Ranger force and an Indian by the name of John Alderman. Metacomet was beheaded and dismembered. Quartered. They tied his four body sections to nearby trees for the birds to pluck. John Alderman was given Metacomet's hand, which he kept in a jar of rum and for years took it around with him—charged people to see it. Metacomet's head was sold to the Plymouth Colony for thirty shillings—the going rate for an Indian head at the time. The head was spiked and carried through the streets of Plymouth before it was put on display at Plymouth Colony Fort for the next twenty five years.

In 1637, anywhere from four to seven hundred Pequot were gathered for their annual green corn dance. Colonists surrounded the Pequot village, set it on fire, and shot any Pequot who tried to escape. The next day the Massachusetts Bay Colony had a feast in celebration, and the governor declared it a day of thanksgiving. Thanksgivings like these happened everywhere, whenever there were, what we have to call: successful massacres. At one such celebration in Manhattan, people were said to have celebrated by kicking the heads of Pequot people through the streets like soccer balls.

The first novel ever written by a Native person, and the first novel written in California, was written in 1854, by a Cherokee guy named John Rollin Ridge. His novel, The Life and Adventures of Joaquin Murieta, was based on a supposed real-life Mexican bandit from California by the same name, who, in 1853, was killed by a group of Texas rangers. To prove they'd killed Murrieta and collect the five thousand dollar reward put on his head—they cut it off. Kept it in a jar of whiskey. They also took the hand of his fellow bandit Three Fingered Jack. The rangers took Joaquin's head and the hand on a tour throughout California, charged a dollar for the show.

5

The Indian head in the jar, the Indian head on a pike were like flags flown, to be seen, cast broadly. Just like the Indian head test pattern was broadcast to sleeping Americans as we set sail from our living rooms, over the ocean blue-green glowing air-waves, to the shores, the screens of the New World.

## ROLLING HEAD

There's an old Cheyenne story about a rolling head. We heard it said there was a family who moved away from their camp, moved near a lake—husband, wife, daughter, son. In the morning when the husband finished dancing, he would brush his wife's hair and paint her face red, then go off to hunt. When he came back her face would be clean. After this happened a few times he decided to follow her and hide, see what she did while he was gone. He found her in the lake, with a water monster, some kind of snake thing, wrapped around her in an embrace. The man cut the monster up and killed his wife. He brought the meat home to his son and daughter. They noticed it tasted different. The son, who was still nursing, said, My mother tastes just like this. His older sister told him it's just deer meat. While they ate, a head rolled in. They ran and the head followed them. The sister remembered where they played, how thick the thorns were there, and she brought the thorns to life behind them with her words. But the head broke through, kept coming. Then she remembered where rocks used to be piled in a difficult way. The rocks appeared when she spoke of them but didn't stop the head, so she drew a hard line in the ground, which made a deep chasm the head couldn't cross. But after a long heavy rain, the chasm filled with water. The head crossed the water, and when it reached the other side, it turned around and drank all that water up. The rolling head became confused and drunk. It wanted more. More of anything. More of everything. And it just kept rolling.

One thing we should keep in mind, moving forward, is that no one ever rolled heads down temple stairs. Mel Gibson made that up. But we do have in our minds, those of us who saw the movie, the heads rolling down temple stairs in a world meant to resemble the real Indian world in the 1500s in Mexico. Mexicans before they were Mexicans. Before Spain came.

We've been defined by everyone else and continue to be slan-  10
dered despite easy-to-look-up-on-the-internet facts about the
realities of our histories and current state as a people. We have
the sad, defeated Indian silhouette, and the heads rolling down
temple stairs, we have it in our heads, Kevin Costner saving
us, John Wayne's six-shooter slaying us, an Italian guy named
Iron Eyes Cody playing our parts in movies. We have the litter-
mourning, tear-ridden Indian in the commercial (also Iron Eyes
Cody), and the sink-tossing, crazy Indian who was the narrator
in the novel, the voice of *One Flew Over the Cuckoo's Nest*. We
have all the logos and mascots. The copy of a copy of the image
of an Indian in a textbook. All the way from the top of Canada,
the top of Alaska, down to the bottom of South America, Indians
were removed, then reduced to a feathered image. Our heads are
on flags, jerseys, and coins. Our heads were on the penny first,
of course, the Indian cent, and then on the buffalo nickel, both
before we could even vote as a people—which, like the truth of
what happened in history all over the world, and like all that
spilled blood from slaughter, are now out of circulation.

## MASSACRE AS PROLOGUE

Some of us grew up with stories about massacres. Stories about
what happened to our people not so long ago. How we came
out of it. At Sand Creek, we heard it said that they mowed us
down with their howitzers. Volunteer militia under Colonel John
Chivington came to kill us—we were mostly women, children,
and elders. The men were away to hunt. They'd told us to fly
the American flag. We flew that and a white flag too. Surrender,
the white flag waved. We stood under both flags as they came
at us. They did more than kill us. They tore us up. Mutilated us.
Broke our fingers to take our rings, cut off our ears to take our
silver, scalped us for our hair. We hid in the hollows of tree
trunks, buried ourselves in sand by the riverbank. That same
sand ran red with blood. They tore unborn babies out of bellies,
took what we intended to be, our children before they were
children, babies before they were babies, they ripped them out
of our bellies. They broke soft baby heads against trees. Then
they took our body parts as trophies and displayed them on a

stage in downtown Denver. Colonel Chivington danced with dismembered parts of us in his hands, with women's pubic hair, drunk, he danced, and the crowd gathered there before him was all the worse for cheering and laughing along with him. It was a celebration.

## HARD, FAST

Getting us to cities was supposed to be the final, necessary step in our assimilation, absorption, erasure, the completion of a five-hundred-year-old genocidal campaign. But the city made us new, and we made it ours. We didn't get lost amid the sprawl of tall buildings, the stream of anonymous masses, the ceaseless din of traffic. We found one another, started up Indian Centers, brought out our families and powwows, our dances, our songs, our bead-work. We bought and rented homes, slept on the streets, under freeways; we went to school, joined the armed forces, populated Indian bars in the Fruitvale in Oakland and in the Mission in San Francisco. We lived in boxcar villages in Richmond. We made art and we made babies and we made way for our people to go back and forth between reservation and city. We did not move to cities to die. The sidewalks and streets, the concrete, absorbed our heaviness. The glass, metal, rubber, and wires, the speed, the hurtling masses—the city took us in. We were not Urban Indians then. This was part of the Indian Relocation Act, which was part of the Indian Termination Policy, which was and is exactly what it sounds like. Make them look and act like us. Become us. And so disappear. But it wasn't just like that. Plenty of us came by choice, to start over, to make money, or for a new experience. Some of us came to cities to escape the reservation. We stayed after fighting in the Second World War. After Vietnam too. We stayed because the city sounds like a war, and you can't leave a war once you've been, you can only keep it at bay—which is easier when you can see and hear it near you, that fast metal, that constant firing around you, cars up and down the streets and freeways like bullets. The quiet of the reservation, the side-of-the-highway towns, rural communities, that kind of silence just makes the sound of your brain on fire that much more pronounced.

Plenty of us are urban now. If not because we live in cities, then because we live on the internet. Inside the high-rise of multiple browser windows. They used to call us sidewalk Indians. Called us citified, superficial, inauthentic, cultureless refugees, apples. An apple is red on the outside and white on the inside. But what we are is what our ancestors did. How they survived. We are the memories we don't remember, which live in us, which we feel, which make us sing and dance and pray the way we do, feelings from memories that flare and bloom unexpectedly in our lives like blood through a blanket from a wound made by a bullet fired by a man shooting us in the back for our hair, for our heads, for a bounty, or just to get rid of us.

When they first came for us with their bullets, we didn't stop moving even though the bullets moved twice as fast as the sound of our screams, and even when their heat and speed broke our skin, shattered our bones, skulls, pierced our hearts, we kept on, even when we saw the bullets send our bodies flailing through the air like flags, like the many flags and buildings that went up in place of everything we knew this land to be before. The bullets were premonitions, ghosts from dreams of a hard, fast future. The bullets moved on after moving through us, became the promise of what was to come, the speed and the killing, the hard, fast lines of borders and buildings. They took everything and ground it down to dust as fine as gunpowder, they fired their guns into the air in victory and the strays flew out into the nothingness of histories written wrong and meant to be forgotten. Stray bullets and consequences are landing on our unsuspecting bodies even now.

## URBANITY

Urban Indians were the generation born in the city. We've been moving for a long time, but the land moves with you like memory. An Urban Indian belongs to the city, and cities belong to the earth. Everything here is formed in relation to every other living and nonliving thing from the earth. All our relations. The process that brings anything to its current form—chemical, synthetic, technological, or otherwise—doesn't make the product not a product of the living earth. Buildings, freeways, cars—are these not of the earth? Were they shipped in from Mars, the moon? Is it because they're processed, manufactured, or that we handle them? Are we so different? Were we at one time not something else entirely, *Homo sapiens*, single-celled organisms, space dust, unidentifiable pre-bang quantum theory? Cities form in the same way as galaxies. Urban Indians feel at home walking in the shadow of a downtown building. We came to know the downtown Oakland skyline better than we did any sacred mountain range, the redwoods in the Oakland hills better than any other deep wild forest. We know the sound of the freeway better than we do rivers, the howl of distant trains better than wolf howls, we know the smell of gas and freshly wet concrete and burned rubber better than we do the smell of cedar or sage or even fry bread—which isn't traditional, like reservations aren't traditional, but nothing is original, everything comes from something that came before, which was once nothing. Everything is new and doomed. We ride buses, trains, and cars across, over, and under concrete plains. Being Indian has never been about returning to the land. The land is everywhere or nowhere.

### For Discussion and Writing

1. Why is this piece titled "Indian Heads"? To what does it refer?
2. What might at first seem like a disjointed collection of anecdotes is actually a complicated, carefully structured essay. What are the different threads that run through "Indian Heads"?
3. **connections**  "We've been defined by everyone else and continue to be slandered," Orange writes. Read Judith Ortiz Cofer's "The Myth of the Latin Woman" (p. 110) in light of this phrase. How do each of these writers confront this phenomenon? What does the act of their writing about it mean?
4. Orange writes, "what we are is what our ancestors did." Reflect on what he means by this, and then write about who you—understood however you wish—are, in the same terms. What did your ancestors do that made you who you are?
5. **looking further**  Ancestry and identity are complicated things. Think about one of the ways in which you identify—using the "you" of Question 4 or another way of understanding identity, born into or raised in or chosen—and do some research into the history of the group with which you identify. What happened in the past of that group—what was done to them and by them—that informs who you are now?

# GEORGE ORWELL

# Shooting an Elephant

*Born in India in 1903, Eric Blair was the son of an English civil servant in the British Raj, the rule of India by the British, as was his father. Educated in England, Blair was an imperial policeman in India for five years, but he resigned and returned to England to pursue his dream of becoming a writer—complete with a pen name, George Orwell. Known best for his novels* Animal Farm *(1945) and* 1984 *(1949), Orwell's political concerns were expressed in nonfiction as well, in works such as his chronicle of life among the poor,* Down and Out in Paris and London *(1933). Because of his stands against economic injustice and totalitarianism, Orwell remains an influential figure, as the "adjectivization" of his pen name shows—*Orwellian *has entered the vernacular as a term to describe the violence done to language and common sense by totalitarianism. "Shooting an Elephant" tells the story of a moment early in Orwell's life when his sense of injustice surfaced. As you read, watch for the ways in which Orwell uses the tools of narrative writing to dramatize the moment.*

In Moulmein, in Lower Burma, I was hated by large numbers of people—the only time in my life that I have been important enough for this to happen to me. I was sub-divisional police officer of the town, and in an aimless, petty kind of way anti-European feeling was very bitter. No one had the guts to raise a riot, but if a European woman went through the bazaars alone somebody would probably spit betel juice over her dress. As a police officer I was an obvious target and was baited whenever it seemed safe to do so. When a nimble Burman tripped me up on the football field and the referee (another Burman) looked the other way, the crowd yelled with hideous laughter. This happened more than once. In the end the sneering yellow faces of young men that met me everywhere, the insults hooted after me when I was at a safe distance, got badly on my nerves. The young Buddhist priests were the worst of all. There were several thousands of them in the town and none of them seemed to have anything to do except stand on street corners and jeer at Europeans.

All this was perplexing and upsetting. For at that time I had already made up my mind that imperialism was an evil thing and the sooner I chucked up my job and got out of it the better. Theoretically—and secretly, of course—I was all for the Burmese and all against their oppressors, the British. As for the job I was doing, I hated it more bitterly than I can perhaps make clear. In a job like that you see the dirty work of Empire at close quarters. The wretched prisoners huddling in the stinking cages of the lock-ups, the grey, cowed faces of the long-term convicts, the scarred buttocks of the men who had been flogged with bamboos—all these oppressed me with an intolerable sense of guilt. But I could get nothing into perspective. I was young and ill-educated and I had had to think out my problems in the utter silence that is imposed on every Englishman in the East. I did not even know that the British Empire is dying, still less did I know that it is a great deal better than the younger empires that are going to supplant it. All I knew was that I was stuck between my hatred of the empire I served and my rage against the evil-spirited little beasts who tried to make my job impossible. With one part of my mind I thought of the British Raj as an unbreakable tyranny, as something clamped down, in *saecula saeculorum* upon the will of prostrate peoples; with another part I thought that the greatest joy in the world would be to drive a bayonet into a Buddhist priest's guts. Feelings like these are the normal by-products of imperialism; ask any Anglo-Indian official, if you can catch him off duty.

One day something happened which in a roundabout way was enlightening. It was a tiny incident in itself, but it gave me a better glimpse than I had had before of the real nature of imperialism—the real motives for which despotic governments act. Early one morning the sub-inspector at a police station the other end of the town rang me up on the phone and said that an elephant was ravaging the bazaar. Would I please come and do something about it? I did not know what I could do, but I wanted to see what was happening and I got on to a pony and started out. I took my rifle, an old .44 Winchester and much too small to kill an elephant, but I thought the noise might be useful *in terrorem*. Various Burmans stopped me on the way and told me about the elephant's doings. It was not, of course, a wild elephant, but a tame one which had gone "must." It had been chained up, as tame elephants always are when their attack of "must" is due, but on the previous night it had broken its chain and escaped. Its mahout, the only person who could manage it when it was in that state, had set out in pursuit, but had taken the wrong direction and was now twelve hours' journey away, and in the morning the elephant had suddenly reappeared in the town. The Burmese population had no weapons and were quite helpless against it. It had already destroyed somebody's bamboo hut, killed a cow and raided some fruit-stalls and devoured the stock; also it had met the municipal rubbish van and, when the driver jumped out and took to his heels, had turned the van over and inflicted violences upon it.

The Burmese sub-inspector and some Indian constables were waiting for me in the quarter where the elephant had been seen. It was a very poor quarter, a labyrinth of squalid bamboo huts, thatched with palm-leaf, winding all over a steep hillside. I remember that it was a cloudy, stuffy morning at the beginning of the rains. We began questioning the people as to where the elephant had gone and, as usual, failed to get any definite information. That is invariably the case in the East; a story always sounds clear enough at a distance, but the nearer you get to the scene of events the vaguer it becomes. Some of the people said that the elephant had gone in one direction, some said that he had gone in another, some professed not even to have heard of any elephant. I had almost made up my mind that the whole story was a pack of lies, when we heard yells a little distance away. There was a loud, scandalized cry of "Go away, child! Go away this instant!" and an old woman with a switch in her hand came round the corner of a hut, violently shooing away a crowd of naked children. Some more women followed, clicking their tongues and exclaiming; evidently there was something that the children ought not to have seen. I rounded the hut and saw a man's dead body sprawling in the mud. He was an Indian, a black Dravidian coolie, almost naked, and he could not have been dead many minutes. The people said that the elephant had come suddenly upon him round the corner of the hut, caught him with its trunk, put its foot on his back and ground him into the earth. This was the rainy season and the ground was soft, and his face had scored a trench a foot deep and a couple of yards long. He was lying on his belly with arms crucified and head sharply twisted to one side. His face was coated with mud, the eyes wide open, the teeth bared and grinning with an expression of unendurable agony. (Never tell me, by the way, that the dead look peaceful. Most of the corpses I have seen looked devilish.) The friction of the great beast's foot had stripped the skin from his back as neatly as one skins a rabbit. As soon as I saw the dead man I sent an orderly to a friend's house nearby to borrow an elephant rifle. I had already sent back the pony, not wanting it to go mad with fright and throw me if it smelt the elephant.

The orderly came back in a few minutes with a rifle and five    5 cartridges, and meanwhile some Burmans had arrived and told us that the elephant was in the paddy fields below, only a few hundred yards away. As I started forward practically the whole population of the quarter flocked out of the houses and followed me. They had seen the rifle and were all shouting excitedly that I was going to shoot the elephant. They had not shown much interest in the elephant when he was merely ravaging their homes, but it was different now that he was going to be shot. It was a bit of fun to them, as it would be to an English crowd; besides they wanted the meat. It made me vaguely uneasy. I had no intention of shooting the elephant—I had merely sent for the rifle to defend myself if necessary—and it is always unnerving to have a crowd following you. I marched down the hill, looking and feeling a fool, with the rifle over my shoulder and an ever-growing army of people jostling at my heels. At the bottom, when you got away from the huts, there was a metalled road and beyond that a miry waste of paddy fields a thousand yards across, not yet ploughed but soggy from the first rains and dotted with coarse grass. The elephant was standing eight yards from the road, his left side towards us. He took not the slightest notice of the crowd's approach. He was tearing up bunches of grass, beating them against his knees to clean them and stuffing them into his mouth.

I had halted on the road. As soon as I saw the elephant I knew with perfect certainty that I ought not to shoot him. It is a serious matter to shoot a working elephant—it is comparable to destroying a huge and costly piece of machinery—and obviously one ought not to do it if it can possibly be avoided. And at that distance, peacefully eating, the elephant looked no more dangerous than a cow. I thought then and I think now that his attack of "must" was already passing off; in which case he would merely wander harmlessly about until the mahout came back and caught him. Moreover, I did not in the least want to shoot him. I decided that I would watch him for a little while to make sure that he did not turn savage again, and then go home.

But at that moment I glanced round at the crowd that had followed me. It was an immense crowd, two thousand at the least and growing every minute. It blocked the road for a long distance on either side. I looked at the sea of yellow faces above the garish clothes—faces all happy and excited over this bit of fun, all certain that the elephant was going to be shot. They were watching me as they would watch a conjurer about to perform a trick. They did not like me, but with the magical rifle in my hands I was momentarily worth watching. And suddenly I realized that I should have to shoot the elephant after all. The people expected it of me and I had got to do it; I could feel their two thousand wills pressing me forward, irresistibly. And it was at this moment, as I stood there with the rifle in my hands, that I first grasped the hollowness, the futility of the white man's dominion in the East. Here was I, the white man with his gun, standing in front of the unarmed native crowd—seemingly the leading actor of the piece; but in reality I was only an absurd puppet pushed to and fro by the will of those yellow faces behind. I perceived in this moment that when the white man turns tyrant it is his own freedom that he destroys. He becomes a sort of hollow, posing dummy, the conventionalized figure of a sahib. For it is the condition of his rule that he shall spend his life in trying to impress the "natives," and so in every crisis he has got to do what the "natives" expect of him. He wears a mask, and his face grows to fit it. I had got to shoot the elephant. I had committed myself to doing it when I sent for the rifle. A sahib has got to act like a sahib; he has got to appear resolute, to know his own mind and do definite things. To come all that way, rifle in hand, with two thousand people marching at my heels, and then to trail feebly away, having done nothing—no, that was impossible. The crowd would laugh at me. And my whole life, every white man's life in the East, was one long struggle not to be laughed at.

But I did not want to shoot the elephant. I watched him beating his bunch of grass against his knees, with that preoccupied grandmotherly air that elephants have. It seemed to me that it would be murder to shoot him. At that age I was not squeamish about killing animals, but I had never shot an elephant and never wanted to. (Somehow it always seems worse to kill a *large* animal.) Besides, there was the beast's owner to be considered. Alive, the elephant was worth at least a hundred pounds; dead, he would only be worth the value of his tusks, five pounds, possibly. But I had got to act quickly. I turned to some experienced-looking Burmans who had been there when we arrived, and asked them how the elephant had been behaving. They all said the same thing: he took no notice of you if you left him alone, but he might charge if you went too close to him.

It was perfectly clear to me what I ought to do. I ought to walk up to within, say, twenty-five yards of the elephant and test his behavior. If he charged, I could shoot; if he took no notice of me, it would be safe to leave him until the mahout came back. But also I knew that I was going to do no such thing. I was a poor shot with a rifle and the ground was soft mud into which one would sink at every step. If the elephant charged and I missed him, I should have about as much chance as a toad under a steam-roller. But even then I was not thinking particularly of my own skin, only of the watchful yellow faces behind. For at that moment, with the crowd watching me, I was not afraid in the ordinary sense, as I would have been if I had been alone. A white man mustn't be frightened in front of "natives"; and so, in general, he isn't frightened. The sole thought in my mind was that if anything went wrong those two thousand Burmans would see me pursued, caught, trampled on and reduced to a grinning corpse like that Indian up the hill. And if that happened it was quite probable that some of them would laugh. That would never do. There was only one alternative. I shoved the cartridges into the magazine and lay down on the road to get a better aim.

The crowd grew very still, and a deep, low, happy sigh, as of    10 people who see the theater curtain go up at last, breathed from innumerable throats. They were going to have their bit of fun after all. The rifle was a beautiful German thing with cross-hair sights. I did not then know that in shooting an elephant one would shoot to cut an imaginary bar running from ear-hole to ear-hole. I ought, therefore, as the elephant was sideways on, to have aimed straight at his ear-hole; actually I aimed several inches in front of this, thinking the brain would be further forward.

When I pulled the trigger I did not hear the bang or feel the kick—one never does when a shot goes home—but I heard the devilish roar of glee that went up from the crowd. In that instant, in too short a time, one would have thought, even for the bullet to get there, a mysterious, terrible change had come over the elephant. He neither stirred nor fell, but every line of his body had altered. He looked suddenly stricken, shrunken, immensely old, as though the frightful impact of the bullet had paralyzed him without knocking him down. At last, after what seemed a long time—it might have been five seconds, I dare say—he sagged flabbily to his knees. His mouth slobbered. An enormous senility seemed to have settled upon him. One could have imagined him thousands of years old. I fired again into the same spot. At the second shot he did not collapse but climbed with desperate slowness to his feet and stood weakly upright, with legs sagging and head drooping. I fired a third time. That was the shot that did for him. You could see the agony of it jolt his whole body and knock the last remnant of strength from his legs. But in falling he seemed for a moment to rise, for as his hind legs collapsed beneath him he seemed to tower upward like a huge rock toppling, his trunk reaching skywards like a tree. He trumpeted, for the first and only time. And then down he came, his belly towards me, with a crash that seemed to shake the ground even where I lay.

I got up. The Burmans were already racing past me across the mud. It was obvious that the elephant would never rise again, but he was not dead. He was breathing very rhythmically with long rattling gasps, his great mound of a side painfully rising and falling. His mouth was wide open—I could see far down into caverns of pale pink throat. I waited a long time for him to die, but his breathing did not weaken. Finally I fired my two remaining shots into the spot where I thought his heart must be. The thick blood welled out of him like red velvet, but still he did not die. His body did not even jerk when the shots hit him, the tortured breathing continued without a pause. He was dying, very slowly and in great agony, but in some world remote from me where not even a bullet could damage him further. I felt that I had got to put an end to that dreadful noise. It seemed dreadful to see the great beast lying there, powerless to move and yet powerless to die, and not even to be able to finish him. I sent back for my small rifle and poured shot after shot into his heart and down his throat. They seemed to make no impression. The tortured gasps continued as steadily as the ticking of a clock.

In the end I could not stand it any longer and went away. I heard later that it took him half an hour to die. Burmans were bringing dahs and baskets even before I left, and I was told they had stripped his body almost to the bones by the afternoon.

Afterwards, of course, there were endless discussions about the shooting of the elephant. The owner was furious, but he was only an Indian and could do nothing. Besides, legally I had done the right thing, for a mad elephant has to be killed, like a mad dog, if its owner fails to control it. Among the Europeans opinion was divided. The older men said I was right, the younger men said it was a damn shame to shoot an elephant for killing a coolie, because an elephant was worth more than any damn Coringhee coolie. And afterwards I was very glad that the coolie had been killed; it put me legally in the right and it gave me a sufficient pretext for shooting the elephant. I often wondered whether any of the others grasped that I had done it solely to avoid looking a fool.

## For Discussion and Writing

1. Why does Orwell shoot the elephant?

2. Orwell uses the anecdote of his shooting an elephant to illustrate his feelings about imperialism. What are those feelings, and how does the anecdote illustrate them?

3. **connections**   Read Orwell's essay against a very different one — Jonathan Swift's "A Modest Proposal" (p. 370). These pieces are deeply political, yet in very different ways, both in terms of the points they make and the ways in which they make them. How do these differences relate to each other? Do the strategies serve the messages?

4. What would you have done if you had been in Orwell's place? Why?

5. **looking further**   Research the historical situation out of which Orwell was writing. Though we are now said to be in a postcolonial age, situations like the one Orwell describes still exist in the world. Can you imagine a similar story being told from somewhere in today's world? Where? Describe this second situation and compare it to Orwell's. Can the exact same story be told? How might it differ?

# PLATO

# The Allegory of the Cave

*Plato was born in 428 BCE in Athens, Greece. He is known as a student of Socrates and teacher of Aristotle. Most of what we know about Socrates, in fact, comes from Plato's writings, many of which are constructed as philosophical dialogues between Socrates and his students. Plato is best known for the* Republic, *a work of political philosophy based in metaphysics (which examines the nature of reality), ethics (the study of right conduct), and epistemology (the study of knowledge itself); as in his other works, he is not concerned only with how we should act but also with how we know, who we are, and what is true.*

*"The Allegory of the Cave," taken from the* Republic, *demonstrates this mixture of concerns in Plato's work. (An allegory is a representation — a story or image — that dramatizes abstract ideas.) As you read, note the ways in which his thoughts about politics are grounded in his understanding of the nature of human experience and knowledge.*

And now, I said, let me show in a figure how far our nature is enlightened or unenlightened: — Behold! human beings living in an underground den, which has a mouth open towards the light and reaching all along the den; here they have been from their childhood, and have their legs and necks chained so that they cannot move, and can only see before them, being prevented by the chains from turning round their heads. Above and behind them a fire is blazing at a distance, and between the fire and the prisoners there is a raised way; and you will see, if you look, a low wall built along the way, like the screen which marionette players have in front of them, over which they show the puppets.

I see.

And do you see, I said, men passing along the wall carrying all sorts of vessels, and statues and figures of animals made of wood and stone and various materials, which appear over the wall? Some of them are talking, others silent.

You have shown me a strange image, and they are strange prisoners.

Like ourselves, I replied; and they see only their own shad-   5
ows, or the shadows of one another, which the fire throws on the opposite wall of the cave?

True, he said; how could they see anything but the shadows if they were never allowed to move their heads?

And of the objects which are being carried in like manner they would only see the shadows?

Yes, he said.

And if they were able to converse with one another, would they not suppose that they were naming what was actually before them?

Very true.   10

And suppose further that the prison had an echo which came from the other side, would they not be sure to fancy when one of the passers-by spoke that the voice which they heard came from the passing shadow?

No question, he replied.

To them, I said, the truth would be literally nothing but the shadows of the images.

That is certain.

And now look again, and see what will naturally follow if the   15
prisoners are released and disabused of their error. At first, when any of them is liberated and compelled suddenly to stand up and turn his neck round and walk and look towards the light, he will suffer sharp pains; the glare will distress him, and he will be unable to see the realities of which in his former state he had seen the shadows; and then conceive someone saying to him, that what he saw before was an illusion, but that now, when he is approach-ing nearer to being and his eye is turned towards more real exis-tence, he has a clearer vision—what will be his reply? And you may further imagine that his instructor is pointing to the objects as they pass and requiring him to name them,—will he not be perplexed? Will he not fancy that the shadows which he formerly saw are truer than the objects which are now shown to him?

Far truer.

And if he is compelled to look straight at the light, will he not have a pain in his eyes which will make him turn away to take refuge in the objects of vision which he can see, and which he will conceive to be in reality clearer than the things which are now being shown to him?

True, he said.

And suppose once more, that he is reluctantly dragged up a steep and rugged ascent, and held fast until he is forced into the presence of the sun himself, is he not likely to be pained and irritated? When he approaches the light his eyes will be dazzled, and he will not be able to see anything at all of what are now called realities.

Not all in a moment, he said.  20

He will require to grow accustomed to the sight of the upper world. And first he will see the shadows best, next the reflections of men and other objects in the water, and then the objects themselves; then he will gaze upon the light of the moon and the stars and the spangled heaven; and he will see the sky and the stars by night better than the sun or the light of the sun by day?

Certainly.

Last of all he will be able to see the sun, and not mere reflections of him in the water, but he will see him in his own proper place, and not in another; and he will contemplate him as he is.

Certainly.

He will then proceed to argue that this is he who gives the sea-  25
son and the years, and is the guardian of all that is in the visible world, and in a certain way the cause of all things which he and his fellows have been accustomed to behold?

Clearly, he said, he would first see the sun and then reason about him.

And when he remembered his old habitation, and the wisdom of the den and his fellow prisoners, do you not suppose that he would felicitate himself on the change, and pity them?

Certainly, he would.

And if they were in the habit of conferring honors among themselves on those who were quickest to observe the passing shadows and to remark which of them went before, and which followed after, and which were together; and who were therefore best able to draw conclusions as to the future, do you think that he would care for such honors and glories, or envy the possessors of them? Would he not say with Homer,

> Better to be the poor servant of a poor master,

and to endure anything, rather than think as they do and live after their manner?

Yes, he said, I think that he would rather suffer anything than  30
entertain these false notions and live in this miserable manner.

Imagine once more, I said, such an one coming suddenly out of the sun to be replaced in his old situation; would he not be certain to have his eyes full of darkness?

To be sure, he said.

And if there were a contest, and he had to compete in measuring the shadows with the prisoners who had never moved out of the den, while his sight was still weak, and before his eyes had become steady (and the time which would be needed to acquire this new habit of sight might be very considerable), would he not be ridiculous? Men would say of him that up he went and down he came without his eyes; and that it was better not even to think of ascending; and if any one tried to loose another and lead him up to the light, let them only catch the offender, and they would put him to death.

No question, he said.

This entire allegory, I said, you may now append, dear Glaucon,      35
to the previous argument; the prison house is the world of sight, the light of the fire is the sun, and you will not misapprehend me if you interpret the journey upwards to be the ascent of the soul into the intellectual world according to my poor belief, which, at your desire, I have expressed — whether rightly or wrongly God knows. But, whether true or false, my opinion is that in the world of knowledge the idea of good appears last of all, and is seen only with an effort; and, when seen, is also inferred to be the universal author of all things beautiful and right, parent of light and of the lord of light in this visible world, and the immediate source of reason and truth in the intellectual; and that this is the power upon which he who would act rationally either in public or private life must have his eye fixed.

I agree, he said, as far as I am able to understand you.

Moreover, I said, you must not wonder that those who attain to this beatific vision are unwilling to descend to human affairs; for their souls are ever hastening into the upper world where they desire to dwell; which desire of theirs is very natural, if our allegory may be trusted.

Yes, very natural.

And is there anything surprising in one who passes from divine contemplations to the evil state of man, misbehaving himself in a ridiculous manner; if, while his eyes are blinking and before he has become accustomed to the surrounding darkness, he is compelled to fight in courts of law, or in other places, about the images or the shadows of images of justice, and is endeavoring to meet the conceptions of those who have never yet seen absolute justice?

Anything but surprising, he replied.                                    40

Anyone who has common sense will remember that the bewilderments of the eyes are of two kinds, and arise from two causes, either from coming out of the light or from going into the light, which is true of the mind's eye, quite as much as of the bodily eye; and he who remembers this when he sees anyone whose vision is perplexed and weak, will not be too ready to laugh; he will first ask whether that soul of man has come out of the brighter life, and is unable to see because unaccustomed to the dark, or having turned from darkness to the day is dazzled by excess of light. And he will count the one happy in his condition and state of being, and he will pity the other; or, if he have a mind to laugh at the soul which comes from below into the light, there will be more reason in this than in the laugh which greets him who returns from above out of the light into the den.

That, he said, is a very just distinction.

But then, if I am right, certain professors of education must be wrong when they say that they can put a knowledge into the soul which was not there before, like sight into blind eyes.

They undoubtedly say this, he replied.

Whereas, our argument shows that the power and capacity of    45
learning exists in the soul already; and that just as the eye was unable to turn from darkness to light without the whole body, so too the instrument of knowledge can only by the movement of the whole soul be turned from the world of becoming into that of being, and learn by degrees to endure the sight of being, and of the brightest and best of being, or in other words, of the good.

Very true.

And must there not be some art which will effect conversion in the easiest and quickest manner; not implanting the faculty of sight, for that exists already, but has been turned in the wrong direction, and is looking away from the truth?

Yes, he said, such an art may be presumed.

And whereas the other so-called virtues of the soul seem to be akin to bodily qualities, for even when they are not originally innate they can be implanted later by habit and exercise, the virtue of wisdom more than anything else contains a divine element which always remains, and by this conversion is rendered useful and profitable; or, on the other hand, hurtful and useless. Did you never observe the narrow intelligence flashing from the keen eye of a clever rogue—how eager he is, how clearly his paltry soul sees the way to his end; he is the reverse of blind, but his keen eyesight is forced into the service of evil, and he is mischievous in proportion to his cleverness?

Very true, he said.                                                                              50

But what if there had been a circumcision of such natures in the days of their youth; and they had been severed from those sensual pleasures, such as eating and drinking, which, like leaden weights, were attached to them at their birth, and which drag them down and turn the vision of their souls upon the things that are below—if, I say, they had been released from these impediments and turned in the opposite direction, the very same faculty in them would have seen the truth as keenly as they see what their eyes are turned to now.

Very likely.

Yes, I said; and there is another thing which is likely, or rather a necessary inference from what has preceded, that neither the uneducated and uninformed of the truth, nor yet those who never make an end of their education, will be able ministers of State; not the former, because they have no single aim of duty which is the rule of all their actions, private as well as public; nor the latter, because they will not act at all except upon compulsion, fancying that they are already dwelling apart in the islands of the blessed.

Very true, he replied.

Then, I said, the business of us who are the founders of the        55
State will be to compel the best minds to attain that knowledge which we have already shown to be the greatest of all—they must continue to ascend until they arrive at the good; but when they have ascended and seen enough we must not allow them to do as they do now.

What do you mean?

I mean that they remain in the upper world: but this must not be allowed; they must be made to descend again among the prisoners in the den, and partake of their labors and honors, whether they are worth having or not.

But is not this unjust? he said; ought we to give them a worse life, when they might have a better?

You have again forgotten, my friend, I said, the intention of the legislator, who did not aim at making any one class in the State happy above the rest; the happiness was to be in the whole State, and he held the citizens together by persuasion and necessity, making them benefactors of the State, and therefore benefactors of one another; to this end he created them, not to please themselves, but to be his instruments in binding up the State.

True, he said, I had forgotten.

Observe, Glaucon, that there will be no injustice in compelling our philosophers to have a care and providence of others; we shall explain to them that in other States, men of their class are not obliged to share in the toils of politics: and this is reasonable, for they grow up at their own sweet will, and the government would rather not have them. Being self-taught, they cannot be expected to show any gratitude for a culture which they have never received. But we have brought you into the world to be rulers of the hive, kings of yourselves and of the other citizens, and have educated you far better and more perfectly than they have been educated, and you are better able to share in the double duty. Wherefore each of you, when his turn comes, must go down to the general underground abode, and get the habit of seeing in the dark. When you have acquired the habit, you will see ten thousand times better than the inhabitants of the den, and you will know what the several images are, and what they represent, because you have seen the beautiful and just and good in their truth. And thus our State, which is also yours, will be a reality, and not a dream only, and will be administered in a spirit unlike that of other States, in which men fight with one another about shadows only and are distracted in the struggle for power, which in their eyes is a great good. Whereas the truth is that the State in which the rulers are most reluctant to govern is always the best and most quietly governed, and the State in which they are most eager, the worst.

Quite true, he replied.

And will our pupils, when they hear this, refuse to take their turn at the toils of State, when they are allowed to spend the greater part of their time with one another in the heavenly light?

Impossible, he answered; for they are just men, and the commands which we impose upon them are just; there can be no doubt that every one of them will take office as a stern necessity, and not after the fashion of our present rulers of State.

Yes, my friend, I said; and there lies the point. You must con-    65
trive for your future rulers another and a better life than that of
a ruler, and then you may have a well-ordered State; for only in
the State which offers this, will they rule who are truly rich, not
in silver and gold, but in virtue and wisdom, which are the true
blessings of life. Whereas if they go to the administration of public affairs, poor and hungering after their own private advantage,
thinking that hence they are to snatch the chief good, order there
can never be; for they will be fighting about office, and the civil
and domestic broils which thus arise will be the ruin of the rulers
themselves and of the whole State.

Most true, he replied.

And the only life which looks down upon the life of political
ambition is that of true philosophy. Do you know of any other?

Indeed, I do not, he said.

### For Discussion and Writing

1. What does the cave stand for in Plato's allegory? Make a list of the
   other elements in the allegory—chains, light, darkness, and so
   on—and explain what they represent.

2. Plato compares a number of things in this essay—the material world
   to the world of ideas, the life of the mind to the work of governing,
   silver and gold to virtue and wisdom. How does he use his comparisons to make his argument?

3. **connections**  Though George Orwell, in "Shooting an Elephant"
   (p. 279), is a different kind of leader than the rulers in Plato's allegory,
   he is in a position of authority. Do you think there points of connection between the two essays in this area? Can you consider Orwell's
   reflection on his actions, and the tangle of motivations behind them,
   in light of Plato's discussion of the potentially conflicting motivations
   of rulers?

4. Plato argues that working in public affairs and working for one's own
   private advantage cannot mix. How might contemporary politics
   bear out this assertion or contradict it?

5. **looking further**  In "The Allegory of the Cave," legislators are
   described as aiming not "at making any one class in the State happy
   above the rest; the happiness was to be in the whole State" (par. 59).
   Consider contemporary politics through this statement. In what ways
   do you find the aim here ascribed to legislators to be shared by contemporary elected officials? In what ways do you not?

MIKE ROSE

# "I Just Wanna Be Average"

*Born in 1944 to Italian immigrants and raised in South Central Los Angeles, Mike Rose is a professor of education at UCLA and an advocate for the democratization of the university and for creative teaching. His* Lives on the Boundary: The Struggles and Achievements of America's Underprepared *(1989) investigated remedial education, and* Possible Lives: The Promise of Public Education in America *(1995) was the product of four years of research into teaching in America.*

*"I Just Wanna Be Average," taken from* Lives on the Boundary, *examines learning, knowledge, and expectations and is drawn from Rose's own experiences in school. Of knowledge, Rose writes, "It enabled me to do things in the world" (par. 37)—an idea at once simple and profound. Consider, as you read, the kinds of things that your education has allowed you to do. What else do you need to learn to "do things in the world"?*

It took two buses to get to Our Lady of Mercy. The first started deep in South Los Angeles and caught me at midpoint. The second drifted through neighborhoods with trees, parks, big lawns, and lots of flowers. The rides were long but were livened up by a group of South L.A. veterans whose parents also thought that Hope had set up shop in the west end of the county. There was Christy Biggars, who, at sixteen, was dealing and was, according to rumor, a pimp as well. There were Bill Cobb and Johnny Gonzales, grease-pencil artists extraordinaire, who left Nembutal-enhanced swirls of "Cobb" and "Johnny" on the corrugated walls of the bus. And then there was Tyrrell Wilson. Tyrrell was the coolest kid I knew. He ran the dozens like a metric halfback, laid down a rap that outrhymed and outpointed Cobb, whose rap was good but not great—the curse of a moderately soulful kid trapped in white skin. But it was Cobb who would sneak a radio onto the bus, and thus underwrote his

295

patter with Little Richard, Fats Domino, Chuck Berry, the Coasters, and Ernie K. Doe's mother-in-law, an awful woman who was "sent from down below." And so it was that Christy and Cobb and Johnny G. and Tyrrell and I and assorted others picked up along the way passed our days in the back of the bus, a funny mix brought together by geography and parental desire.

Entrance to school brings with it forms and releases and assessments. Mercy relied on a series of tests, mostly the Stanford-Binet, for placement, and somehow the results of my tests got confused with those of another student named Rose. The other Rose apparently didn't do very well, for I was placed in the vocational track, a euphemism for the bottom level. Neither I nor my parents realized what this meant. We had no sense that Business Math, Typing, and English–Level D were dead ends. The current spate of reports on the schools criticizes parents for not involving themselves in the education of their children. But how would someone like Tommy Rose, with his two years of Italian schooling, know what to ask? And what sort of pressure could an exhausted waitress apply? The error went undetected, and I remained in the vocational track for two years. What a place.

My homeroom was supervised by Brother Dill, a troubled and unstable man who also taught freshman English. When his class drifted away from him, which was often, his voice would rise in paranoid accusations, and occasionally he would lose control and shake or smack us. I hadn't been there two months when one of his brisk, face-turning slaps had my glasses sliding down the aisle. Physical education was also pretty harsh. Our teacher was a stubby ex-lineman who had played old-time pro ball in the Midwest. He routinely had us grabbing our ankles to receive his stinging paddle across our butts. He did that, he said, to make men of us. "Rose," he bellowed on our first encounter; me standing geeky in line in my baggy shorts. " 'Rose'? What the hell kind of name is that?"

"Italian, sir," I squeaked.

"Italian! Ho. Rose, do you know the sound a bag of shit makes   5 when it hits the wall?"

"No, sir."

"Wop!"

Sophomore English was taught by Mr. Mitropetros. He was a large, bejeweled man who managed the parking lot at the

Shrine Auditorium. He would crow and preen and list for us the stars he'd brushed against. We'd ask questions and glance knowingly and snicker, and all that fueled the poor guy to brag some more. Parking cars was his night job. He had little training in English, so his lesson plan for his day work had us reading the district's required text, *Julius Caesar*, aloud for the semester. We'd finished the play way before the twenty weeks was up, so he'd have us switch parts again and again and start again: Dave Snyder, the fastest guy at Mercy, muscling through Caesar to the breathless squeals of Calpurnia, as interpreted by Steve Fusco, a surfer who owned the school's most envied paneled wagon. Week ten and Dave and Steve would take on new roles, as would we all, and render a water-logged Cassius and a Brutus that are beyond my powers of description.

Spanish I—taken in the second year—fell into the hands of a new recruit. Mr. Montez was a tiny man, slight, five foot six at the most, soft-spoken and delicate. Spanish was a particularly rowdy class, and Mr. Montez was as prepared for it as a doily maker at a hammer throw. He would tap his pencil to a room in which Steve Fusco was propelling spitballs from his heavy lips, in which Mike Dweetz was taunting Billy Hawk, a half-Indian, half-Spanish, reed-thin, quietly explosive boy. The vocational track at Our Lady of Mercy mixed kids traveling in from South L.A. with South Bay surfers and a few Slavs and Chicanos from the harbors of San Pedro. This was a dangerous miscellany: surfers and hodads and South-Central blacks all ablaze to the metronomic tapping of Hector Montez's pencil.

One day Billy lost it. Out of the corner of my eye I saw him strike out with his right arm and catch Dweetz across the neck. Quick as a spasm, Dweetz was out of his seat, scattering desks, cracking Billy on the side of the head, right behind the eye. Snyder and Fusco and others broke it up, but the room felt hot and close and naked. Mr. Montez's tenuous authority was finally ripped to shreds, and I think everyone felt a little strange about that. The charade was over, and when it came down to it, I don't think any of the kids really wanted it to end this way. They had pushed and pushed and bullied their way into a freedom that both scared and embarrassed them.

Students will float to the mark you set. I and the others in the vocational classes were bobbing in pretty shallow water.

10

Vocational education has aimed at increasing the economic opportunities of students who do not do well in our schools. Some serious programs succeed in doing that, and through exceptional teachers — like Mr. Gross in *Horace's Compromise* — students learn to develop hypotheses and troubleshoot, reason through a problem, and communicate effectively — the true job skills. The vocational track, however, is most often a place for those who are just not making it, a dumping ground for the disaffected. There were a few teachers who worked hard at education; young Brother Slattery, for example, combined a stern voice with weekly quizzes to try to pass along to us a skeletal outline of world history. But mostly the teachers had no idea of how to engage the imaginations of us kids who were scuttling along at the bottom of the pond.

And the teachers would have needed some inventiveness, for none of us was groomed for the classroom. It wasn't just that I didn't know things — didn't know how to simplify algebraic fractions, couldn't identify different kinds of clauses, bungled Spanish translations — but that I had developed various faulty and inadequate ways of doing algebra and making sense of Spanish. Worse yet, the years of defensive tuning out in elementary school had given me a way to escape quickly while seeming at least half alert. During my time in Voc. Ed., I developed further into a mediocre student and a somnambulant problem solver, and that affected the subjects I did have the wherewithal to handle: I detested Shakespeare; I got bored with history. My attention flitted here and there. I fooled around in class and read my books indifferently — the intellectual equivalent of playing with your food. I did what I had to do to get by, and I did it with half a mind.

But I did learn things about people and eventually came into my own socially. I liked the guys in Voc. Ed. Growing up where I did, I understood and admired physical prowess, and there was an abundance of muscle here. There was Dave Snyder, a sprinter and halfback of true quality. Dave's ability and his quick wit gave him a natural appeal, and he was welcome in any clique, though he always kept a little independent. He enjoyed acting the fool and could care less about studies, but he possessed a certain maturity and never caused the faculty much trouble. It was a testament to his independence that he included me among his friends — I eventually went out for track, but I was no jock. Owing to the Latin alphabet and a dearth of *R*s and *S*s, Snyder sat behind Rose, and we started exchanging one-liners and became friends.

There was Ted Richard, a much-touted Little League pitcher. He was chunky and had a baby face and came to Our Lady of Mercy as a seasoned street fighter. Ted was quick to laugh and he had a loud, jolly laugh, but when he got angry he'd smile a little smile, the kind that simply raises the corner of the mouth a quarter of an inch. For those who knew, it was an eerie signal. Those who didn't found themselves in big trouble, for Ted was very quick. He loved to carry on what we would come to call philosophical discussions: What is courage? Does God exist? He also loved words, enjoyed picking up big ones like *salubrious* and *equivocal* and using them in our conversations—laughing at himself as the word hit a chuckhole rolling off his tongue. Ted didn't do all that well in school—baseball and parties and testing the courage he'd speculated about took up his time. His textbooks were *Argosy* and *Field and Stream*, whatever newspapers he'd find on the bus stop—from the *Daily Worker* to pornography—conversations with uncles or hobos or businessmen he'd meet in a coffee shop, *The Old Man and the Sea*. With hindsight, I can see that Ted was developing into one of those rough-hewn intellectuals whose sources are a mix of the learned and the apocryphal, whose discussions are both assured and sad.

And then there was Ken Harvey. Ken was good-looking in a puffy way and had a full and oily ducktail and was a car enthusiast . . . a hodad. One day in religion class, he said the sentence that turned out to be one of the most memorable of the hundreds of thousands I heard in those Voc. Ed. years. We were talking about the parable of the talents, about achievement, working hard, doing the best you can do, blah-blah-blah, when the teacher called on the restive Ken Harvey for an opinion. Ken thought about it, but just for a second, and said (with studied, minimal affect), "I just wanna be average." That woke me up. Average? Who wants to be average? Then the athletes chimed in with the clichés that make you want to laryngectomize them, and the exchange became a platitudinous melee. At the time, I thought Ken's assertion was stupid, and I wrote him off. But his sentence has stayed with me all these years, and I think I am finally coming to understand it.

15

Ken Harvey was gasping for air. School can be a tremendously disorienting place. No matter how bad the school, you're going to encounter notions that don't fit with the assumptions and beliefs that you grew up with—maybe you'll hear these dissonant notions from teachers, maybe from the other students, and maybe you'll read them. You'll also be thrown in with all kinds of kids from all kinds of backgrounds, and that can be unsettling—this is especially true in places of rich ethnic and linguistic mix, like the L.A. basin. You'll see a handful of students far excel you in courses that sound exotic and that are only in the curriculum of the elite: French, physics, trigonometry. And all this is happening while you're trying to shape an identity, your body is changing, and your emotions are running wild. If you're a working-class kid in the vocational track, the options you'll have to deal with this will be constrained in certain ways: you're defined by your school as "slow"; you're placed in a curriculum that isn't designed to liberate you but to occupy you, or, if you're lucky, train you, though the training is for work the society does not esteem; other students are picking up the cues from your school and your curriculum and interacting with you in particular ways. If you're a kid like Ted Richard, you turn your back on all this and let your mind roam where it may. But youngsters like Ted are rare. What Ken and so many others do is protect themselves from such suffocating madness by taking on with a vengeance the identity implied in the vocational track. Reject the confusion and frustration by openly defining yourself as the Common Joe. Champion the average. Rely on your own good sense. Fuck this bullshit. Bullshit, of course, is everything you—and the others—fear is beyond you: books, essays, tests, academic scrambling, complexity, scientific reasoning, philosophical inquiry.

The tragedy is that you have to twist the knife in your own gray matter to make this defense work. You'll have to shut down, have to reject intellectual stimuli or diffuse them with sarcasm, have to cultivate stupidity, have to convert boredom from a malady into a way of confronting the world. Keep your vocabulary simple, act stoned when you're not or act more stoned than you are, flaunt ignorance, materialize your dreams. It is a powerful and effective defense—it neutralizes the insult and the frustration of being a vocational kid and, when perfected, it drives teachers up the wall, a delightful secondary effect. But like all strong magic, it exacts a price.

My own deliverance from the Voc. Ed. world began with sophomore biology. Every student, college prep to vocational, had to take biology, and unlike the other courses, the same person taught all sections. When teaching the vocational group, Brother Clint probably slowed down a bit or omitted a little of the fundamental biochemistry, but he used the same book and more or less the same syllabus across the board. If one class got tough, he could get tougher. He was young and powerful and very handsome, and looks and physical strength were high currency. No one gave him any trouble.

I was pretty bad at the dissecting table, but the lectures and the textbook were interesting: plastic overlays that, with each turned page, peeled away skin, then veins and muscle, then organs, down to the very bones that Brother Clint, pointer in hand, would tap out on our hanging skeleton. Dave Snyder was in big trouble, for the study of life—versus the living of it—was sticking in his craw. We worked out a code for our multiple-choice exams. He'd poke me in the back: once for the answer under *A*, twice for *B*, and so on; and when he'd hit the right one, I'd look up to the ceiling as though I were lost in thought. Poke: cytoplasm. Poke, poke: methane. Poke, poke, poke: William Harvey. Poke, poke, poke, poke: islets of Langerhans. This didn't work out perfectly, but Dave passed the course, and I mastered the dreamy look of a guy on a record jacket. And something else happened. Brother Clint puzzled over this Voc. Ed. kid who was racking up 98s and 99s on his tests. He checked the school's records and discovered the error. He recommended that I begin my junior year in the College Prep program. According to all I've read since, such a shift, as one report put it, is virtually impossible. Kids at that level rarely cross tracks. The telling thing is how chancy both my placement into and exit from Voc. Ed. was; neither I nor my parents had anything to do with it. I lived in one world during spring semester, and when I came back to school in the fall, I was living in another.

Switching to College Prep was a mixed blessing. I was an erratic student. I was undisciplined. And I hadn't caught onto the rules of the game: why work hard in a class that didn't grab my fancy? I was also hopelessly behind in math. Chemistry was

20

hard; toying with my chemistry set years before hadn't prepared me for the chemist's equations. Fortunately, the priest who taught both chemistry and second-year algebra was also the school's athletic director. Membership on the track team covered me; I knew I wouldn't get lower than a C. U.S. history was taught pretty well, and I did okay. But civics was taken over by a football coach who had trouble reading the textbook aloud—and reading aloud was the centerpiece of his pedagogy. College Prep at Mercy was certainly an improvement over the vocational program—at least it carried some status—but the social science curriculum was weak, and the mathematics and physical sciences were simply beyond me. I had a miserable quantitative background and ended up copying some assignments and finessing the rest as best I could. Let me try to explain how it feels to see again and again material you should once have learned but didn't.

You are given a problem. It requires you to simplify algebraic fractions or to multiply expressions containing square roots. You know this is pretty basic material because you've seen it for years. Once a teacher took some time with you, and you learned how to carry out these operations. Simple versions, anyway. But that was a year or two or more in the past, and these are more complex versions, and now you're not sure. And this, you keep telling yourself, is ninth- or even eighth-grade stuff.

Next it's a word problem. This is also old hat. The basic elements are as familiar as story characters: trains speeding so many miles per hour or shadows of buildings angling so many degrees. Maybe you know enough, have sat through enough explanations, to be able to begin setting up the problem: "If one train is going this fast . . ." or "This shadow is really one line of a triangle. . . ." Then: "Let's see . . ." "How did Jones do this?" "Hmmmm." "No." "No, that won't work." Your attention wavers. You wonder about other things: a football game, a dance, that cute new checker at the market. You try to focus on the problem again. You scribble on paper for a while, but the tension wins out and your attention flits elsewhere. You crumple the paper and begin daydreaming to ease the frustration.

The particulars will vary, but in essence this is what a number of students go through, especially those in so-called remedial classes. They open their textbooks and see once again the familiar and impenetrable formulas and diagrams and terms that have stumped them for years. There is no excitement here. *No excitement.* Regardless of what the teacher says, this is not a new challenge. There is, rather, embarrassment and frustration and, not surprisingly, some anger in being reminded once again of long-standing inadequacies. No wonder so many students finally attribute their difficulties to something inborn, organic: "That part of my brain just doesn't work." Given the troubling histories many of these students have, it's miraculous that any of them can lift the shroud of hopelessness sufficiently to make deliverance from these classes possible.

Through this entire period, my father's health was deteriorating with cruel momentum. His arteriosclerosis progressed to the point where a simple nick on his shin wouldn't heal. Eventually it ulcerated and widened. Lou Minton would come by daily to change the dressing. We tried renting an oscillating bed — which we placed in the front room — to force blood through the constricted arteries in my father's legs. The bed hummed through the night, moving in place to ward off the inevitable. The ulcer continued to spread, and the doctors finally had to amputate. My grandfather had lost his leg in a stockyard accident. Now my father too was crippled. His convalescence was slow but steady, and the doctors placed him in the Santa Monica Rehabilitation Center, a sun-bleached building that opened out onto the warm spray of the Pacific. The place gave him some strength and some color and some training in walking with an artificial leg. He did pretty well for a year or so until he slipped and broke his hip. He was confined to a wheelchair after that, and the confinement contributed to the diminishing of his body and spirit.

I am holding a picture of him. He is sitting in his wheelchair 25 and smiling at the camera. The smile appears forced, unsteady, seems to quaver, though it is frozen in silver nitrate. He is in his mid-sixties and looks eighty. Late in my junior year, he had a stroke and never came out of the resulting coma. After that, I would see him only in dreams, and to this day that is how I join him. Sometimes the dreams are sad and grisly and primal: my father lying in a bed soaked with his suppuration, holding me, rocking me. But sometimes the dreams bring him back to me healthy: him talking to me on an empty street, or buying some pictures to decorate our old house, or transformed somehow into someone strong and adept with tools and the physical.

Jack MacFarland couldn't have come into my life at a better time. My father was dead, and I had logged up too many years of scholastic indifference. Mr. MacFarland had a master's degree from Columbia and decided, at twenty-six, to find a little school and teach his heart out. He never took any credentialing courses, couldn't bear to, he said, so he had to find employment in a private system. He ended up at Our Lady of Mercy teaching five sections of senior English. He was a beatnik who was born too late. His teeth were stained, he tucked his sorry tie in between the third and fourth buttons of his shirt, and his pants were chronically wrinkled. At first, we couldn't believe this guy, thought he slept in his car. But within no time, he had us so startled with work that we didn't much worry about where he slept or if he slept at all. We wrote three or four essays a month. We read a book every two to three weeks, starting with the *Iliad* and ending up with Hemingway. He gave us a quiz on the reading every other day. He brought a prep school curriculum to Mercy High.

MacFarland's lectures were crafted, and as he delivered them he would pace the room jiggling a piece of chalk in his cupped hand, using it to scribble on the board the names of all the writers and philosophers and plays and novels he was weaving into his discussion. He asked questions often, raised everything from Zeno's paradox to the repeated last line of Frost's "Stopping by Woods on a Snowy Evening." He slowly and carefully built up our knowledge of Western intellectual history — with facts, with connections, with speculations. We learned about Greek philosophy, about Dante, the Elizabethan worldview, the Age of Reason, existentialism. He analyzed poems with us, had us reading sections from John Ciardi's *How Does a Poem Mean?*, making a potentially difficult book accessible with his own explanations. We gave oral reports on poems Ciardi didn't cover. We imitated the styles of Conrad, Hemingway, and *Time* magazine. We wrote and talked, wrote and talked. The man immersed us in language.

Even MacFarland's barbs were literary. If Jim Fitzsimmons, hung over and irritable, tried to smart-ass him, he'd rejoin with a flourish that would spark the indomitable Skip Madison — who'd lost his front teeth in a hapless tackle — to flick his tongue through the gap and opine, "good chop," drawing out the single "o" in stinging indictment. Jack MacFarland, this tobacco-stained intellectual, brandished linguistic weapons of a kind

I hadn't encountered before. Here was this *egghead*, for God's sake, keeping some pretty difficult people in line. And from what I heard, Mike Dweetz and Steve Fusco and all the notorious Voc. Ed. crowd settled down as well when MacFarland took the podium. Though a lot of guys groused in the schoolyard, it just seemed that giving trouble to this particular teacher was a silly thing to do. Tomfoolery, not to mention assault, had no place in the world he was trying to create for us, and instinctively everyone knew that. If nothing else, we all recognized MacFarland's considerable intelligence and respected the hours he put into his work. It came to this: the troublemaker would look foolish rather than daring. Even Jim Fitzsimmons was reading *On the Road* and turning his incipient alcoholism to literary ends.

There were some lives that were already beyond Jack MacFarland's ministrations, but mine was not. I started reading again as I hadn't since elementary school. I would go into our gloomy little bedroom or sit at the dinner table while, on the television, Danny McShane was paralyzing Mr. Moto with the atomic drop, and work slowly back through *Heart of Darkness*, trying to catch the words in Conrad's sentences. I certainly was not MacFarland's best student; most of the other guys in College Prep, even my fellow slackers, had better backgrounds than I did. But I worked very hard, for MacFarland had hooked me. He tapped my old interest in reading and creating stories. He gave me a way to feel special by using my mind. And he provided a role model that wasn't shaped on physical prowess alone, and something inside me that I wasn't quite aware of responded to that. Jack MacFarland established a literacy club, to borrow a phrase of Frank Smith's, and invited me — invited all of us — to join.

There's been a good deal of research and speculation suggesting that the acknowledgment of school performance with extrinsic rewards — smiling faces, stars, numbers, grades — diminishes the intrinsic satisfaction children experience by engaging in reading or writing or problem solving. While it's certainly true that we've created an educational system that encourages our best and brightest to become cynical grade collectors and, in general, have developed an obsession with evaluation and assessment, I must tell you that venal though it may have been, I loved getting good grades from MacFarland. I now know how subjective grades can be, but then they came tucked in the back of essays

30

like bits of scientific data, some sort of spectroscopic readout that said, objectively and publicly, that I had made something of value. I suppose I'd been mediocre for too long and enjoyed a public redefinition. And I suppose the workings of my mind, such as they were, had been private for too long. My linguistic play moved into the world; . . . these papers with their circled, red B-pluses and A-minuses linked my mind to something outside it. I carried them around like a club emblem.

One day in the December of my senior year, Mr. MacFarland asked me where I was going to go to college. I hadn't thought much about it. Many of the students I teach today spent their last year in high school with a physics text in one hand and the Stanford catalog in the other, but I wasn't even aware of what "entrance requirements" were. My folks would say that they wanted me to go to college and be a doctor, but I don't know how seriously I ever took that; it seemed a sweet thing to say, a bit of supportive family chatter, like telling a gangly daughter she's graceful. The reality of higher education wasn't in my scheme of things: no one in the family had gone to college; only two of my uncles had completed high school. I figured I'd get a night job and go to the local junior college because I knew that Snyder and Company were going there to play ball. But I hadn't even prepared for that. When I finally said, "I don't know," MacFarland looked down at me—I was seated in his office—and said, "Listen, you can write."

My grades stank. I had A's in biology and a handful of B's in a few English and social science classes. All the rest were C's—or worse. MacFarland said I would do well in his class and laid down the law about doing well in the others. Still, the record for my first three years wouldn't have been acceptable to any four-year school. To nobody's surprise, I was turned down flat by USC and UCLA. But Jack MacFarland was on the case. He had received his bachelor's degree from Loyola University, so he made calls to old professors and talked to somebody in admissions and wrote me a strong letter. Loyola finally accepted me as a probationary student. I would be on trial for the first year, and if I did okay, I would be granted regular status. MacFarland also intervened to get me a loan, for I could never have afforded a private college without it. Four more years of religion classes and four more years of boys at one school, girls at another. But at least I was going to college. Amazing.

In my last semester of high school, I elected a special English course fashioned by Mr. MacFarland, and it was through this elective that there arose at Mercy a fledgling literati. Art Mitz, the editor of the school newspaper and a very smart guy, was the kingpin. He was joined by me and by Mark Dever, a quiet boy who wrote beautifully and who would die before he was forty. MacFarland occasionally invited us to his apartment, and those visits became the high point of our apprenticeship: we'd clamp on our training wheels and drive to his salon.

He lived in a cramped and cluttered place near the airport, tucked away in the kind of building that architectural critic Reyner Banham calls a *dingbat*. Books were all over: stacked, piled, tossed, and crated, underlined and dog eared, well worn and new. Cigarette ashes crusted with coffee in saucers or spilling over the sides of motel ashtrays. The little bedroom had, along two of its walls, bricks and boards loaded with notes, magazines, and oversized books. The kitchen joined the living room, and there was a stack of German newspapers under the sink. I had never seen anything like it: a great flophouse of language furnished by City Lights and Café le Metro. I read every title. I flipped through paperbacks and scanned jackets and memorized names: Gogol, *Finnegans Wake*, Djuna Barnes, Jackson Pollock, *A Coney Island of the Mind*, F. O. Matthiessen's *American Renaissance*, all sorts of Freud, *Troubled Sleep*, Man Ray, *The Education of Henry Adams*, Richard Wright, *Film as Art*, William Butler Yeats, Marguerite Duras, *Redburn, A Season in Hell, Kapital*. On the cover of Alain-Fournier's *The Wanderer* was an Edward Gorey drawing of a young man on a road winding into dark trees. By the hotplate sat a strange Kafka novel called *Amerika*, in which an adolescent hero crosses the Atlantic to find the Nature Theater of Oklahoma. Art and Mark would be talking about a movie or the school newspaper, and I would be consuming my English teacher's library. It was heady stuff. I felt like a Pop Warner athlete on steroids.

Art, Mark, and I would buy stogies and triangulate from MacFarland's apartment to the Cinema, which now shows X-rated films but was then L.A.'s premier art theater, and then to the musty Cherokee Bookstore in Hollywood to hobnob with beatnik homosexuals — smoking, drinking bourbon and coffee, and trying out awkward phrases we'd gleaned from our mentor's

35

bookshelves. I was happy and precocious and a little scared as well, for Hollywood Boulevard was thick with a kind of decadence that was foreign to the South Side. After the Cherokee, we would head back to the security of MacFarland's apartment, slaphappy with hipness.

Let me be the first to admit that there was a good deal of adolescent passion in this embrace of the avant-garde: self-absorption, sexually charged pedantry, an elevation of the odd and abandoned. Still it was a time during which I absorbed an awful lot of information: long lists of titles, images from expressionist paintings, new wave shibboleths, snippets of philosophy, and names that read like Steve Fusco's misspellings—Goethe, Nietzsche, Kierkegaard. Now this is hardly the stuff of deep understanding. But it was an introduction, a phrase book, a Baedeker to a vocabulary of ideas, and it felt good at the time to know all these words. With hindsight I realize how layered and important that knowledge was.

It enabled me to do things in the world. I could browse bohemian bookstores in far-off, mysterious Hollywood; I could go to the Cinema and see events through the lenses of European directors; and, most of all, I could share an evening, talk that talk, with Jack MacFarland, the man I most admired at the time. Knowledge was becoming a bonding agent. Within a year or two, the persona of the disaffected hipster would prove too cynical, too alienated to last. But for a time it was new and exciting: it provided a critical perspective on society, and it allowed me to act as though I were living beyond the limiting boundaries of South Vermont.

*For Discussion and Writing*

1. List the different teachers Rose writes about in this essay, adding a sentence to each name, describing his significance for Rose.

2. This essay is from Rose's powerful book *Lives on the Boundary*. What boundaries does Rose write about here? What acts of classification do these boundaries serve?

3. **connections**   Rose is put on the vocational track accidentally and remains there for two years; while there, he learns how profound the effect of environment on identity can be. He also learns how important the intervention of one teacher can be. How can you connect Rose's essay to Gloria Anzaldúa's "How to Tame a Wild

Tongue" (p. 30) on the subject of education and identity? What kind of teacher does Anzaldúa try to be for her students? How do her methods compare to Jack MacFarland's? What are the aims of each and the strategies for achieving them?

4. "Students will float to the mark you set," Rose writes (par. 11). Write about a time in your life when this was true of you, and reflect more generally on your life as a student. Have you found that your educational experiences thus far have pushed you to exceed what you originally thought was possible? What kinds of motivation are built into our educational system? Has traditional motivation (such as getting good grades) worked for you? What kind of an educational system might motivate *all* students?

5. **looking further**   Research the recent emphasis on standardized testing in public education through initiatives such as No Child Left Behind. What are the arguments for and against the increased use of testing? Do you find one set of arguments more compelling? If so, for what reasons? If not, are there further studies you think need to be done on the issue? Describe them.

CARL SAGAN

# Does Truth Matter?

*Carl Sagan (1934–1996) was an astronomer best known for his popular science writing and for the 1980 television series* Cosmos: A Personal Voyage, *which he co-wrote and narrated. Sagan worked in astrophysics, astrobiology, and cosmology; was on the faculty at Harvard University and Cornell University, where he served as director of the Laboratory for Planetary Studies; and was an advisor to the U.S. Air Force and NASA. Sagan was also devoted to the search for intelligent extraterrestrial life. His books included the 1977* Dragons of Eden: Speculations on the Evolution of Human Intelligence *(which won the Pulitzer Prize);* Broca's Brain: Reflections on the Romance of Science *(1979);* Cosmos *(1980), a book based on and extending the television series; and a sequel to* Cosmos, Pale Blue Dot: A Vision of the Human Future in Space *(1994). Sagan was a devoted reader of science fiction in his youth, and wrote a novel about intelligent extraterrestrial life,* Contact *(1985), which in 1997 was made into a movie of the same name.*

*Sagan's many interests included the promotion of critical thinking—of the employment of scientific skepticism against superstition and pseudoscience. As you read "Does Truth Matter?" look for ways this belief appears.*

Do we care what's true? Does it matter?

> *... where ignorance is bliss,*
> *'Tis folly to be wise*

wrote the poet Thomas Gray. But is it? Edwin Way Teale in his 1950 book *Circle of the Seasons* understood the dilemma better:

> It is morally as bad not to care whether a thing is true or not, so long as it makes you feel good, as it is not to care how you got your money as long as you have got it.

It's disheartening to discover government corruption and incompetence, for example; but is it better *not* to know about it? Whose interest does ignorance serve? If we humans bear, say, hereditary propensities toward the hatred of strangers, isn't self-knowledge the only antidote? If we long to believe that the stars rise and set for us, that we are the reason there *is* a Universe, does science do us a disservice in deflating our conceits?

In *The Genealogy of Morals,* Friedrich Nietzsche, as so many before and after, decries the "unbroken progress in the self-belittling of man" brought about by the scientific revolution. Nietzsche mourns the loss of "man's belief in his dignity, his uniqueness, his irreplaceability in the scheme of existence." For me, it is far better to grasp the Universe as it really is than to persist in delusion, however satisfying and reassuring. Which attitude is better geared for our long-term survival? Which gives us more leverage on our future? And if our naive self-confidence is a little undermined in the process, is that altogether such a loss? Is there not cause to welcome it as a maturing and character-building experience?

To discover that the universe is some 8 to 15 billion and not 6 to 12 thousand years old[1] improves our appreciation of its sweep and grandeur; to entertain the notion that we are a particularly complex arrangement of atoms, and not some breath of divinity, at the very least enhances our respect for atoms; to discover, as now seems probable, that our planet is one of billions of other worlds in the Milky Way Galaxy and that our galaxy is one of billions more, majestically expands the arena of what is possible; to find that our ancestors were also the ancestors of apes ties us to the rest of life and makes possible important—if occasionally rueful—reflections on human nature.

Plainly there is no way back. Like it or not, we are stuck with science. We had better make the best of it. When we finally come to terms with it and fully recognize its beauty and its power, we will find, in spiritual as well as in practical matters, that we have made a bargain strongly in our favor. But superstition and pseudoscience keep getting in the way, distracting us, providing easy

1. "No thinking religious person believes this. Old hat," writes one of the referees of this book. But many "scientific creationists" not only believe it, but are making increasingly aggressive and successful efforts to have it taught in the schools, museums, zoos, and textbooks. Why? Because adding up the "begats," the ages of patriarchs and others in the Bible, gives such a figure, and the Bible is "inerrant."

answers, dodging skeptical scrutiny, casually pressing our awe buttons and cheapening the experience, making us routine and comfortable practitioners as well as victims of credulity. Yes, the world *would be* a more interesting place if there were UFOs lurking in the deep waters off Bermuda and eating ships and planes, or if dead people could take control of our hands and write us messages. It would be fascinating if adolescents were able to make telephone handsets rocket off their cradles just by thinking at them, or if our dreams could, more often than can be explained by chance and our knowledge of the world, accurately foretell the future.

---

### Science as a Source of Spirituality

In its encounter with Nature, science invariably elicits a sense of reverence and awe. The very act of understanding is a celebration of joining, merging, even if on a very modest scale, with the magnificence of the Cosmos. And the cumulative worldwide buildup of knowledge over time converts science into something only a little short of a transnational, transgenerational metamind.

"Spirit" comes from the Latin word "to breathe." What we breathe is air, which is certainly matter, however thin. Despite usage to the contrary, there is no necessary implication in the word "spiritual" that we are talking of anything other than matter (including the matter of which the brain is made), or anything outside the realm of science. On occasion, I will feel free to use the word. Science is not only compatible with spirituality; it is a profound source of spirituality. When we recognize our place in an immensity of light-years and in the passage of ages, when we grasp the intricacy, beauty, and subtlety of life, then that soaring feeling, that sense of elation and humility combined, is surely spiritual. So are our emotions in the presence of great art or music or literature, or of acts of exemplary selfless courage such as those of Mohandas Gandhi or Martin Luther King, Jr. The notion that science and spirituality are somehow mutually exclusive does a disservice to both.

---

These are all instances of pseudoscience. They purport to use the methods and findings of science, while in fact they are faithless to its nature—often because they are based on insufficient evidence or because they ignore clues that point the other way. They ripple with gullibility. With the uninformed cooperation (and often the cynical connivance) of newspapers, magazines, book publishers, radio, television, movie producers, and the like, such ideas are easily and widely available. Far more difficult to come upon are the alternative, more challenging, and even more dazzling findings of science.

Pseudoscience is easier to contrive than science because distracting confrontations with reality—where we cannot control the outcome of the comparison—are more readily avoided. The standards of argument, what passes for evidence, are much more relaxed. In part for these same reasons, it is much easier to present pseudoscience to the general public than science. But this isn't enough to explain its popularity.

Naturally people try various belief systems on for size, to see if they help. And if we're desperate enough, we become all too willing to abandon what may be perceived as the heavy burden of skepticism. Pseudoscience speaks to powerful emotional needs that science often leaves unfulfilled. It caters to fantasies about personal powers we lack and long for (like those attributed to comic book superheroes today, and earlier, to the gods). In some of its manifestations, it offers satisfaction of spiritual hungers, cures for disease, promises that death is not the end. It reassures us of our cosmic centrality and importance. It vouchsafes that we are hooked up with, tied to, the universe.[2] Sometimes it's a kind of halfway house between old religion and new science, mistrusted by both.

At the heart of some pseudoscience (and some religion also, New Age and Old) is the idea that wishing makes it so. How satisfying it would be, as in folklore and children's stories, to fulfill our heart's desire just by wishing. How seductive this notion is, especially when compared with the hard work and good luck usually required to achieve our hopes. The enchanted fish or the genie from the lamp will grant us three wishes—anything we want except more wishes. Who has not pondered—just to be on the safe side, just in case we ever come upon and accidentally rub an old, squat brass oil lamp—what to ask for?

I remember, from childhood comic strips and books, a top-hatted, mustachioed magician who brandished an ebony walking stick. His name was Zatara. He could make anything happen,

10

---

2. Although it's hard for me to see a more profound cosmic connection than the astonishing findings of modern nuclear astrophysics: Except for hydrogen, all the atoms that make each of us up—the iron in our blood, the calcium in our bones, the carbon in our brains—were manufactured in red giant stars thousands of light-years away in space and billions of years ago in time. We are, as I like to say, starstuff.

anything at all. How did he do it? Easy. He uttered his commands backwards. So if he wanted a million dollars, he would say "srallod noillim a em evig." That's all there was to it. It was something like prayer, but much surer of results.

I spent a lot of time at age eight experimenting in this vein, commanding stones to levitate: "esir, enots." It never worked. I blamed my pronunciation.

---

**The Metaphysicist Has No Laboratory**

The truth may be puzzling or counterintuitive. It may contradict deeply held beliefs. Experiment is how we get a handle on it. At a dinner many decades ago, the physicist Robert W. Wood was asked to respond to the toast, "To physics and metaphysics." By "metaphysics," people then meant something like philosophy, or truths you could recognize just by thinking about them. They could also have included pseudoscience. Wood answered along these lines:

The physicist has an idea. The more he thinks it through, the more sense it seems to make. He consults the scientific literature. The more he reads, the more promising the idea becomes. Thus prepared, he goes to the laboratory and devises an experiment to test it. The experiment is painstaking. Many possibilities are checked. The accuracy of measurement is refined, the error bars reduced. He lets the chips fall where they may. He is devoted only to what the experiment teaches. At the end of all this work, through careful experimentation, the idea is found to be worthless. So the physicist discards it, frees his mind from the clutter of error, and moves on to something else.[3]

The difference between physics and metaphysics, Wood concluded as he raised his glass high, is not that the practitioners of one are smarter than the practitioners of the other. The difference is that the metaphysicist has no laboratory.

---

Pseudoscience is embraced, it might be argued, in exact proportion as real science is misunderstood—except that the language breaks down here. If you've never heard of science (to say nothing of how it works), you can hardly be aware you're

---

3. As the pioneering physicist Benjamin Franklin put it, "In going on with these experiments, how many pretty systems do we build, which we soon find ourselves obliged to destroy?" At the very least, he thought, the experience sufficed to "help to make a vain Man humble."

embracing pseudoscience. You're simply thinking in one of the ways that humans always have. Religions are often the state-protected nurseries of pseudoscience, although there's no reason why religions have to play that role. In a way, it's an artifact from times long gone. In some countries nearly everyone believes in astrology and precognition, including government leaders. But this is not simply drummed into them by religion; it is drawn out of the enveloping culture in which everyone is comfortable with these practices, and affirming testimonials are everywhere.

Most of the case histories I will relate are American—because these are the cases I know best, not because pseudoscience and mysticism are more prominent in the United States than elsewhere. But the psychic spoonbender and extraterrestrial channeler Uri Geller hails from Israel. As tensions rise between Algerian secularists and Moslem fundamentalists, more and more people are discreetly consulting the country's 10,000 soothsayers and clairvoyants (about half of whom operate with a license from the government). High French officials, including a former president of France, arranged for millions of dollars to be invested in a scam (the Elf-Aquitaine scandal) to find new petroleum reserves from the air. In Germany, there is concern about carcinogenic "Earth rays" undetectable by science; they can be sensed only by experienced dowsers brandishing forked sticks. "Psychic surgery" flourishes in the Philippines. Ghosts are something of a national obsession in Britain. Since World War II, Japan has spawned enormous numbers of new religions featuring the supernatural. An estimated 100,000 fortunetellers flourish in Japan; the clientele are mainly young women. Aum Shinrikyo, a sect thought to be involved in the release of the nerve gas sarin in the Tokyo subway system in March 1995, features levitation, faith healing, and ESP among its main tenets. Followers, at a high price, drank the "miracle pond" water—from the bath of Asaraha, their leader. In Thailand, diseases are treated with pills manufactured from pulverized sacred Scripture. "Witches" are today being burned in South Africa. Australian peacekeeping forces in Haiti rescue a woman tied to a tree; she is accused of flying from rooftop to rooftop, and sucking the blood of children. Astrology is rife in India, geomancy widespread in China.

Perhaps the most successful recent global pseudoscience—by many criteria, already a religion—is the Hindu doctrine of transcendental meditation (TM). The soporific homilies of its founder and spiritual leader, the Maharishi Mahesh Yogi, can be seen on television. Seated in the yogi position, his white hair here and there flecked with black, surrounded by garlands and floral offerings, he has a *look*. One day while channel surfing we came upon this visage. "You know who that is?" asked our four-year-old son. "God." The worldwide TM organization has an estimated valuation of 3 billion. For a fee they promise through meditation to be able to walk you through walls, to make you invisible, to enable you to fly. By thinking in unison they have, they say, diminished the crime rate in Washington, D.C., and caused the collapse of the Soviet Union, among other secular miracles. Not one smattering of real evidence has been offered for any such claims. TM sells folk medicine, runs trading companies, medical clinics and "research" universities, and has unsuccessfully entered politics. In its oddly charismatic leader, its promise of community, and the offer of magical powers in exchange for money and fervent belief, it is typical of many pseudosciences marketed for sacerdotal export.

At each relinquishing of civil controls and scientific education another little spun in pseudoscience occurs. Leon Trotsky described it for Germany on the eve of the Hider takeover (but in a description that might equally have applied to the Soviet Union of 1933): 15

> Not only in peasant homes, but also in city skyscrapers, there lives along side the twentieth century the thirteenth. A hundred million people use electricity and still believe in the magic powers of signs and exorcisms. . . . Movie stars go to mediums. Aviators who pilot miraculous mechanisms created by man's genius wear amulets on their sweaters. What inexhaustible reserves they possess of darkness, ignorance and savagery!

Russia is an instructive case. Under the tsars, religious superstition was encouraged, but scientific and skeptical thinking—except by a few tame scientists—was ruthlessly expunged. Under Communism, both religion and pseudoscience were systematically suppressed—except for the superstition of the state ideological religion. It was advertised as scientific, but fell as far short of this ideal as the most unself-critical mystery cult. Critical thinking—except by scientists in hermetically sealed compartments of knowledge—was recognized as dangerous, was not taught in the schools, and was punished where expressed. As a result, post-Communism, many

Russians view science with suspicion. When the lid was lifted, as was also true of virulent ethnic hatreds, what had all along been bubbling subsurface was exposed to view. The region is now awash in UFOs, poltergeists, faith healers, quack medicines, magic waters, and old-rime superstition. A stunning decline in life expectancy, increasing infant mortality, rampant epidemic disease, subminimal medical standards, and ignorance of preventative medicine all work to raise the threshold at which skepticism is triggered in an increasingly desperate population. As I write, the electorally most popular member of the Duma, a leading supporter of the ultranationalist Vladimir Zhirinovsky, is one Anatoly Kashpirovsky—a faith healer who remotely cures diseases ranging from hernias to AIDS by glaring at you out of your television set. His face starts stopped clocks.

A somewhat analogous situation exists in China. After the death of Mao Zedong and the gradual emergence of a market economy, UFOs, channeling, and other examples of Western pseudoscience emerged, along with such ancient Chinese practices as ancestor worship, astrology, and fortune telling—especially that version that involves throwing yarrow sticks and working through the hoary tetragrams of the *I Ching*. The government newspaper lamented that "the superstition of feudal ideology is reviving in our countryside." It was (and remains) a rural, not primarily an urban, affliction.

Individuals with "special powers" gained enormous followings. They could, they said, project Qi, the "energy field of the universe," out of their bodies to change the molecular structure of a chemical 2000 kilometers away, to communicate with aliens, to cure diseases. Some patients died under the ministrations of one of these "masters of Qi Gong" who was arrested and convicted in 1993. Wang Hongcheng, an amateur chemist, claimed to have synthesized a liquid, small amounts of which, when added to water, would convert it to gasoline or the equivalent. For a time he was funded by the army and the secret police, but when his invention was found to be a scam he was arrested and imprisoned. Naturally the story spread that his misfortune resulted not from fraud, but from his unwillingness to reveal his "secret formula" to the government. (Similar stories have circulated in America for decades, usually with the government role replaced by a major oil or auto company.) Asian rhinos are being driven to extinction because their horns, when pulverized, are said to prevent impotence; the market encompasses all of East Asia.

The government of China and the Chinese Communist Party were alarmed by certain of these developments. On December 5, 1994, they issued a joint proclamation that read in part:

[P]ublic education in science has been withering in recent years. At the same time, activities of superstition and ignorance have been growing, and anti-science and pseudoscience cases have become frequent. Therefore, effective measures must be applied as soon as possible to strengthen public education in science. The level of public education in science and technology is an important sign of the national scientific accomplishment. It is a matter of overall importance in economic development, scientific advance, and the progress of society. We must be attentive and implement such public education as part of the strategy to modernize our socialist country and to make our nation powerful and prosperous. Ignorance is never socialist, nor is poverty.

So pseudoscience in America is part of a global trend. Its causes, 20 dangers, diagnosis, and treatment are likely to be similar everywhere. Here, psychics ply their wares on extended television commercials, personally endorsed by entertainers. They have their own channel, the "Psychic Friends Network"; a million people a year sign on and use such guidance in their everyday lives. For the CEOs of major corporations, for financial analysts, for lawyers and bankers there is a species of astrologer/ soothsayer/psychic ready to advise on any matter. "If people knew how many people, especially the very rich and powerful ones, went to psychics, their jaws would drop through the floor," says a psychic from Cleveland, Ohio. Royalty has traditionally been vulnerable to psychic frauds. In ancient China and Rome astrology was the exclusive property of the emperor; any private use of this potent art was considered a capital offense. Emerging from a particularly credulous Southern California culture, Nancy and Ronald Reagan relied on an astrologer in private and public matters—unknown to the voting public. Some portion of the decision-making that influences the future of our civilization is plainly in the hands of charlatans. If anything, the practice is comparatively muted in America; its venue is worldwide.

As amusing as some of pseudoscience may seem, as confident as we may be that we would never be so gullible as to be swept up by such a doctrine, we know it's happening all around us. Transcendental Meditation and Aum Shinrikyo seem to have attracted a large number of accomplished people, some with advanced degrees in physics or engineering. These are not doctrines for nitwits. Something else is going on.

What's more, no one interested in what religions are and how they begin can ignore them. While vast barriers may seem to stretch between a local, single-focus contention of pseudoscience and something like a world religion, the partitions are very thin. The world presents us with nearly insurmountable problems. A wide variety of solutions are offered, some of very limited worldview, some of portentous sweep. In the usual Darwinian natural selection of doctrines, some thrive for a time, while most quickly vanish. But a few—sometimes, as history has shown, the most scruffy and least prepossessing among them—may have the power to profoundly change the history of the world.

The continuum stretching from ill-practiced science, pseudoscience, and superstition (New Age or Old), all the way to respectable mystery religion, based on revelation, is indistinct. I try not to use the word "cult" in its usual meaning of a religion the speaker dislikes, but try to reach for the headstone of knowledge—do they really know what they claim to know? Everyone, it turns out, has relevant expertise.

I am critical of the excesses of theology, because at the extremes it is difficult to distinguish pseudoscience from rigid, doctrinaire religion. Nevertheless, I want to acknowledge at the outset the prodigious diversity and complexity of religious thought and practice over the millennia; the growth of liberal religion and ecumenical fellowship during the last century, and the fact that—as in the Protestant Reformation, the rise of Reform Judaism, Vatican II, and the so-called higher criticism of the Bible—religion has fought (with varying degrees of success) its own excesses. But in parallel to the many scientists who seem reluctant to debate or even publicly discuss pseudoscience, many proponents of mainstream religions are reluctant to take on extreme conservatives and fundamentalists. If the trend continues, eventually the field is theirs; they can win the debate by default.

One religious leader writes to me of his longing for "disciplined integrity" in religion: 25

> We have grown far too sentimental. . . . Devotionalism and cheap psychology on one side, and arrogance and dogmatic intolerance on the other distort authentic religious life almost beyond recognition. Sometimes I come close to despair, but then I live tenaciously and always with hope. . . . Honest religion, more familiar than its critics with the

distortions and absurdities perpetrated in its name, has an active interest in encouraging a healthy skepticism for its own purposes. . . . There is the possibility for religion and science to forge a potent partnership against pseudoscience. Strangely, I think it would soon be engaged also in opposing pseudo-religion.

---

### The Siren Song of Unreason

*A Candle in the Dark* is the title of a courageous, largely Biblically based book by Thomas Ady, published in London in 1656, attacking the witch-hunts then in progress as a scam "to delude the people." Any illness or storm, anything out of the ordinary, was popularly attributed to witch-craft. Witches must exist, Ady quoted the "witchmongers" as arguing—"else how should these things be, or come to pass?" For much of our history, we were so fearful of the outside world, with its unpredictable dangers, that we gladly embraced anything that promised to soften or explain away the terror. Science is an attempt, largely successful, to understand the world, to get a grip on things, to get hold of ourselves, to steer a safe course. Microbiology and meteorology now explain what only a few centuries ago was considered sufficient cause to burn women to death.

Ady also warned of the danger that "the Nations [will] perish for lack of knowledge." Avoidable human misery is more often caused not so much by stupidity as by ignorance, particularly our ignorance about ourselves. I worry that, especially as the Millennium edges nearer, pseudoscience and superstition will seem year by year more tempting, the siren song of unreason more sonorous and attractive. Where have we heard it before? Whenever our ethnic or national prejudices are aroused, in times of scarcity, during challenges to national self-esteem or nerve, when we agonize about our diminished cosmic place and purpose, or when fanaticism is bubbling up around us—men, habits of thought familiar from ages past reach for the controls.

The candle flame gutters. Its little pool of light trembles. Darkness gathers. The demons begin to stir.

---

Pseudoscience differs from erroneous science. Science thrives on errors, cutting them away one by one. False conclusions are drawn all the time, but they are drawn tentatively. Hypotheses are framed so they are capable of being disproved. A succession of alternative hypotheses is confronted by experiment and observation. Science gropes and staggers toward improved understanding. Proprietary feelings are of course offended when a scientific hypothesis is disproved, but such disproofs are recognized as central to the scientific enterprise.

Pseudoscience is just the opposite. Hypotheses are often framed precisely so they are invulnerable to any experiment that offers a prospect of disproof, so even in principle they cannot be invalidated. Practitioners are defensive and wary. Skeptical scrutiny is opposed. When the pseudoscientific hypothesis fails to catch fire with scientists, conspiracies to suppress it are deduced.

Motor ability in healthy people is almost perfect. We rarely stumble and fall, except in young and old age. We can learn tasks such as riding a bicycle or skating or skipping, jumping rope or driving a car, and retain that mastery for the rest of our lives. Even if we've gone a decade without doing it, it comes back to us effortlessly. The precision and retention of our motor skills may, however, give us a false sense of confidence in our other talents. Our perceptions are fallible. We sometimes see what isn't there. We are prey to optical illusions. Occasionally we hallucinate. We are error-prone. A most illuminating book called *How We Know What Isn't So: The Fallibility of Human Reason in Everyday Life*, by Thomas Gilovich, shows how people systematically err in understanding numbers, in rejecting unpleasant evidence, in being influenced by the opinions of others. We're good in some things, but not in everything. Wisdom lies in understanding our limitations. "For Man is a giddy thing," teaches William Shakespeare. That's where the stuffy skeptical rigor of science comes in.

Perhaps the sharpest distinction between science and pseudoscience is that science has a far keener appreciation of human imperfections and fallibility than does pseudoscience (or "inerrant" revelation). If we resolutely refuse to acknowledge where we are liable to fall into error, then we can confidently expect that error—even serious error, profound mistakes—will be our companion forever. But if we are capable of a little courageous self-assessment, whatever rueful reflections they may engender, our chances improve enormously.

If we teach only the findings and products of science—no matter how useful and even inspiring they may be—without communicating its critical method, how can the average person possibly distinguish science from pseudoscience? Both then are presented as unsupported assertion. In Russia and China, it used to be easy. Authoritative science was what the authorities taught. The distinction between science and pseudoscience was made *for* you. No perplexities needed to be muddled through. But when profound political changes occurred and strictures on free thought were loosened, a host of confident or charismatic claims — especially those that told us what we wanted to hear — gained a vast following. Every notion, however improbable, became authoritative.

It is a supreme challenge for the popularizer of science to make clear the actual, tortuous history of its great discoveries and the misapprehensions and occasional stubborn refusal by its practitioners to change course. Many, perhaps most, science textbooks for budding scientists tread lightly here. It is enormously easier to present in an appealing way the wisdom distilled from centuries of patient and collective interrogation of Nature than to detail the messy distillation apparatus. The method of science, as stodgy and grumpy as it may seem, is far more important than the findings of science.

---

**An Absence of Alien Artifacts**

Some [alleged UFO] abductees say that tiny implants, perhaps metallic, were inserted into their bodies — high up their nostrils, for example. These implants, alien abduction therapists tell us, sometimes accidentally fall out, but "in all but a few of the cases the artifact has been lost or discarded." These abductees seem stupefyingly incurious. A strange object — possibly a transmitter sending telemetered data about the state of your body to an alien spaceship somewhere above the Earth — drops out of your nose; you idly examine it and then throw it in the garbage. Something like this is true, we are told, of the majority of abduction cases.

A few such "implants" have been produced and examined by experts. None has been confirmed as of unearthly manufacture. No components are made of unusual isotopes, despite the fact that other stars and other worlds are known to be constituted of different isotopic proportions than the Earth. There are no metals from the transuranic "island of stability," where physicists think there should be a new family of nonradioactive chemical elements unknown on Earth.

What abduction enthusiasts considered the best case was that of Richard Price, who claims that aliens abducted him when he was eight years old and implanted a small artifact in his penis. A quarter century later a physician confirmed a "foreign body" embedded there. After eight more years, it fell out. Roughly a millimeter in

diameter and 4 millimeters long, it was carefully examined by scientists from MIT and Massachusetts General Hospital. Their conclusion? Collagen formed by the body at sites of inflammation plus
cotton fibers from Price's underpants.

On August 28, 1995, television stations owned by Rupert Murdoch
ran what was purported to be an autopsy of a dead alien, shot on
16-millimeter film. Masked pathologists in vintage radiation-
protection suits (with rectangular glass windows to see out of)
cut up a large-eyed 12-fingered figure and examined the internal
organs. While the film was sometimes out of focus, and the view of
the cadaver often blocked by the humans crowding around it, some
viewers found the effect chilling. The *Times* of London, also owned
by Murdoch, didn't know what to make of it, although it did quote
one pathologist who thought the autopsy performed with unseemly
and unrealistic haste (ideal, though, for television viewing). It was
said to have been shot in New Mexico in 1947 by a participant, now
in his eighties, who wished to remain anonymous. What appeared to
be the clincher was the announcement that the leader of the film (its
first few feet) contained coded information that Kodak, the manufacturer, dated to 1947. However, it turns out that the full film magazine was not presented to Kodak, but at most the cut leader. For all
we know, the leader could have been cut from a 1947 newsreel, abundantly archived in America, and the "autopsy" staged and filmed
separately and recently. There's a dragon footprint all right—but
a fakable one. If this is a hoax, it requires not much more cleverness
than crop circles and the MJ-12 document.

In none of these stories is there anything strongly suggestive of
extraterrestrial origin. There is certainly no retrieval of cunning
machinery far beyond current technology.

No abductee has filched a page from the captain's logbook, or an
examining instrument, or taken an authentic photograph of the interior of the ship, or come back with detailed and verifiable scientific
information not hitherto available on Earth. Why not? These failures
must tell us something.

Since the middle of the twentieth century, we've been assured
by proponents of the extraterrestrial hypothesis that physical
evidence—not star maps remembered from years ago, not scars,
not disturbed soil, but real alien technology—was in hand. The
analysis would be released momentarily. These claims go back
to the earliest crashed saucer scam of Newton and GeBauer.

Now it's decades later and we're still waiting. Where are the articles published in the refereed scientific literature, in the metallurgical and ceramics journals, in publications of the Institute of Electrical and Electronic Engineers, in *Science* or *Nature*?

Such a discovery would be momentous. If there were real artifacts, physicists and chemists would be fighting for the privilege of discovering that there are aliens among us — who use, say, unknown alloys, or materials of extraordinary tensile strength or ductility or conductivity. The practical implications of such a finding — never mind the confirmation of an alien invasion — would be immense. Discoveries like this are what scientists live for. Their absence must tell us something.

### For Discussion and Writing

1. What is the difference between pseudoscience and erroneous science?

2. Sagan uses many examples in making his argument. Look back through the essay and make a list of his examples. What different kinds of examples does he use, and how does he use them? What formal qualities characterize them?

3. **connections**   Look at Sagan's essay next to Stephanie Ericsson's "The Ways We Lie" (p. 157). Which of the "ways" Ericsson describes might be relevant to Sagan's discussion? What does it mean to talk about the subjects of Sagan's skepticism as lies?

4. Sagan cites a religious leader as promoting "honest religion," religion that engages with "healthy skepticism." What are your thoughts on this idea? Are religious faith and adherence to scientific skepticism mutually exclusive, or can they coexist?

5. **looking further**   Write about your own religious beliefs (including nonbelief or agnosticism). What role does scientific skepticism play in the way you think about the existence or nonexistence of a deity or deities or a spiritual or supernatural dimension of life? Is the nature of your beliefs shaped in some way by your knowledge of science or your employment of scientific skepticism? If so, how?

# MARIA MICHELA SASSI

# The Sea Was Never Blue

*Maria Michela Sassi teaches ancient philosophy at the University of Pisa in Italy. She is the author of many books on the ancient world, including* The Science of Man in Ancient Greece *(2001),* The Beginnings of Philosophy in Greece *(2009), and books on Democritus and Socrates.*

*In her preface to the English translation of* The Science of Man in Ancient Greece, *Sassi writes about the opening up in classical studies of interest in previously neglected works—for example, the attention that started being paid around the turn of the 21st century to Aristotle's zoological treatises rather than only to his* Essays on Metaphysics and Ethics. *As you read "The Sea Was Never Blue," keep an eye out for this inclination by Sassi to look at things other people might not have looked at as much or as closely, including looking itself.*

Homer used two adjectives to describe aspects of the colour blue: *kuaneos,* to denote a dark shade of blue merging into black; and *glaukos,* to describe a sort of 'blue-grey', notably used in Athena's epithet *glaukopis,* her 'grey-gleaming eyes'. He describes the sky as big, starry, or of iron or bronze (because of its solid fixity). The tints of a rough sea range from 'whitish' (*polios*) and 'blue-grey' (*glaukos*) to deep blue and almost black (*kuaneos, melas*). The sea in its calm expanse is said to be 'pansy-like' (*ioeides*), 'wine-like' (*oinops*), or purple (*porphureos*). But whether sea or sky, it is never just 'blue'. In fact, within the entirety of Ancient Greek literature you cannot find a single pure blue sea or sky.

Yellow, too, seems strangely absent from the Greek lexicon. The simple word *xanthos* covers the most various shades of yellow, from the shining blond hair of the gods, to amber, to the reddish blaze of fire. *Chloros,* since it's related to *chloe* (grass), suggests the colour green but can also itself convey a vivid yellow, like honey.

The Ancient Greek experience of colour does not seem to match our own. In a well-known aphorism, Friedrich Nietzsche captures the strangeness of the Greek colour vocabulary:

> How differently the Greeks must have viewed their natural world, since their eyes were blind to blue and green, and they would see instead of the former a deeper brown, and yellow instead of the latter (and for instance they also would use the same word for the colour of dark hair, that of the corn-flower, and that of the southern sea; and again, they would employ exactly the same word for the colour of the greenest plants and of the human skin, of honey and of the yellow resins: so that their greatest painters reproduced the world they lived in only in black, white, red, and yellow).
> [My translation]

How is this possible? Did the Greeks really see the colours of the world differently from the way we do?

Johann Wolfgang von Goethe, too, observed these features of Greek chromatic vision. The versatility of *xanthos* and *chloros* led him to infer a peculiar fluidity of Greek colour vocabulary. The Greeks, he said, were not interested in defining the different hues. Goethe underpinned his judgment through a careful examination of the theories on vision and colours elaborated by the Greek philosophers, such as Empedocles, Plato and Aristotle, who attributed an active role to the visual organ, equipped with light coming *out* of the eye and interacting with daylight so as to generate the complete range of colours.

Goethe also noted that ancient colour theorists tended to derive colours from a mixture of black and white, which are placed on the two opposite poles of light and dark, and yet are still called 'colours'. The ancient conception of black and white as colours—often primary colours—is remarkable when compared with Isaac Newton's experiments on the decomposition of light by refraction through a prism. The common view today is that white light is colourless and arises from the sum of all the hues of the spectrum, whereas black is its absence.

Goethe considered the Newtonian theory to be a mathematical abstraction in contrast with the testimony of the eyes, and thus downright absurd. In fact, he claimed that light is the most simple and homogeneous substance, and the variety of colours arise at the edges where dark and light meet. Goethe set the Greeks' approach to colour *against* Newton's for their having caught the subjective side of colour perception. The Greeks already knew, Goethe wrote, that: 'If the eye were not Sun-like, it could never see the Sun.'

Another explanation for the apparent oddness of Greek perception came from the eminent politician and Hellenist William Gladstone, who devoted a chapter of his *Studies on Homer and the Homeric Age* (1858) to 'perceptions and use of colour'. He too noticed the vagueness of the green and blue designations in Homer, as well as the absence of words covering the centre of the 'blue' area. Where Gladstone differed was in taking as normative the Newtonian list of colours (red, orange, yellow, green, blue, indigo, violet). He interpreted the Greeks' supposed linguistic poverty as deriving from an imperfect discrimination of prismatic colours. The visual organ of the ancients was still in its *infancy*, hence their strong sensitivity to light rather than hue, and the related inability to clearly distinguish one hue from another. This argument fit well with the post-Darwinian climate of the late 19th century, and came to be widely believed. Indeed, it prompted Nietzsche's own judgment, and led to a series of investigations that sought to prove that the Greek chromatic categories do not fit in with modern taxonomies.

Today, no one thinks that there has been a stage in the history of humanity when some colours were 'not yet' being perceived. But thanks to our modern 'anthropological gaze' it is accepted that every culture has its own way of naming and categorising colours. This is not due to varying anatomical structures of the human eye, but to the fact that different ocular areas are stimulated, which triggers different emotional responses, all according to different cultural contexts.

So was Goethe right that the Greek *experience* of colours is quite peculiar? Yes, he was. There is a specific Greek chromatic culture, just as there is an Egyptian one, an Indian one, a European one, and the like, each of them being reflected in a vocabulary that has its own peculiarity, and not to be measured only by the scientific meter of the Newtonian paradigm. The question then is: how can we hope to understand how the Greeks saw their world?

Let's begin with the colourimetric system, based on the Color Sphere created in 1898 by an American artist named Albert Henry Munsell. According to this model, any colour sensation can be defined through three interacting aspects: the *hue*, determined by the position in the Newtonian spectrum, by which we discriminate one colour from another; the *value* or lightness, ranging from white to black; and the *chroma*, which corresponds to the purity or saturation of the colour, depending on the wavelength distribution of light. Fire-red and sky-blue are highly saturated, whereas grey is not at all.

Add to these the concept of *saliency*, that is, the capacity of a colour to catch visual attention, and the defective definition of blue and green that Gladstone interpreted as a symptom of colour-blindness can be explained since the linguistic definition of hue is proportionate to the saliency of a colour. That is why red, the most salient colour, is the first to be defined in terms of hue in any culture (*eruthros* in Greek), while green and blue are generally first perceived as brightness because they are less salient colours, and are slowly focused as hues later. This means that in some contexts the Greek adjective *chloros* should be translated as 'fresh' instead of 'green', or *leukos* as 'shining' rather than 'white'. The Greeks were perfectly able to *perceive* the blue tint, but were not particularly interested in *describing* the blue tone of sky or sea—at least not in the same way as we are, with our modern sensibility.

This model is helpful for describing the different ways in which a chromatic culture can segment the huge range of possible combinations of the three dimensions by privileging one or the other. A culture might emphasise hue or chroma or value, each with varying intensity. And so the Munsell model is useful in that it helps to demonstrate the remarkable Greek predilection for *brightness*, and the fact that the Greeks experienced colours in degrees of lightness and darkness rather than in terms of hue.

However, the Munsell model doesn't completely explain how the Greeks perceived colour since it leaves out the richness of the 'colour *event*'—the subjective, felt perspective of colour that Goethe so valued. For the Greeks, colour was a basic unit of information necessary to understanding the world, above all the social world. One's complexion was a major criterion of social identity, so much so that contrasting light women and dark men was a widespread *cliché* in Greek literature and iconography, rooted in the prejudice that the pale complexion of women is due to their living in the darkness of the domestic sphere, whereas men are tanned and strengthened by physical exertion and outdoor sports. So the Greek word *chroa/chroiá* means both the coloured surface of a thing and the colour itself, and is significantly related to *chros*, which means 'skin' and 'skin colour'. The emotional and ethical values of colour cannot be forgotten in trying to discern Greek chromatic culture.

Of use are two further parameters, in addition to the Munsell   15
model and the subjective value of colour. There is the *glitter effect*
of colour, which is produced by the interplay of the texture of the
object and the light conditions, and there is the *material* or *technological process* by which a certain colour is obtained in the practice of painters and dyers. With these in hand, the full range of
Greek colours will come into view—even the notorious 'curious
case' of *porphureos*, the chromatic term most difficult to grasp.

Not only does *porphureos* not correspond to any definite
hue, placed as it is on the borderline between red and blue (in
Newtonian terms), but it is often applied to objects that do not
appear straightforwardly 'purple', as in the case of the sea. (The
fact that the sea can appear purple at sunset is not sufficient to
explain the frequency of this epithet in Greek literature.) When
the sea is called *porphureos*, what is described is a mix of brightness and movement, changing according to the light conditions at
different hours of the day and with different weather, which was
the aspect of the sea that most attracted Greek sensitivity. This is
why Homer calls the sea 'winey', which alludes not so much to
the wine tint of the water as to the shine of the liquid inside the
cups used to drink out of at a symposium. As shown by the naval
friezes and the aquatic animals painted inside many drinking vessels, vase painters turned the image around, so that the surface of
the drink suggested the waving of the sea. *Porphureos* conveys this
combination of brightness and movement—a chromatic term
impossible to understand without considering the glimmer effect.

The material effect of shimmering under the light rays is wellcaught by Aristotle within a discussion on the colours of the
rainbow (one of them being violet). In his *Meteorology*, he states:

> The same effect [as in the rainbow] can also be seen in dyes: for there is
> an indescribable difference in the appearance of the colours in woven
> and embroidered materials when they are differently arranged; for
> instance, purple is quite different on a white or a black background, and
> variations of light can make a similar difference. So embroiderers say
> they often make mistakes in their colours when they work by lamplight,
> picking out one colour in mistake for another.

The luminous quality of purple textiles is due to the particular
manufacturing of *porphura*, the *material* from which the dye
was drawn. Purple dye was produced as early as 1200 BCE in

Phoenicia from urine, sea water, and ink from the bladder of *murex* snails. To extract the snails, the shells were put in a vat where their putrefying bodies excreted a yellowish liquid that would be boiled (the verb *porphurō* means 'swirling' besides 'growing/dying purple'). Various nuances from yellow to green, to blue, to red could be obtained, depending on how much water was added and when the boiling process was stopped. The red and purple tones were greatly prized in antiquity because of the costliness of the process (one mollusc providing just a few drops of undiluted juice) and the colour did not easily fade—on the contrary, it became brighter with weathering and sunlight. This is why purple was associated throughout antiquity—and beyond—with power, prestige and glorious beauty, worn for centuries by Emperors and kings, cardinals and Popes.

So the curious case of *porphura* shows how the effects of movement, variation and luminosity went along with resonances of preciousness. (Gold was also appreciated for similar reasons, and it is not by chance that the heroes and gods from Homer to Philostratus are often attired in gold and *porphura*.) By moving beyond the Newtonian model, a clearer picture of the Greek chromatic world emerges. However, there is one lingering question about the Greek perception of colour: why, after all, did the Greeks value brightness so much? The philosophers that inspired Goethe offer a clue.

The first pre-Socratic philosopher to mention colour was Parmenides, who wrote in the fifth century BCE that 'changing place and altering in bright colour' are among the characteristics that mortals ascribe to reality, 'trusting them to be true'. Then came Empedocles, with a fragment that compares the mixing of the four elements that build the sensible world to the work that painters do when mixing different pigments in variable proportions: [20]

> As when painters decorate votive offerings—
> men through cunning well-taught in their skill—
> who when they take the many-coloured pigments in their hands,
> mixing in harmony more of these and less of those,
> out of them they produce shapes similar to all things,
> creating trees and men and women
> and beasts and birds and fishes nurtured in water
> and long-lived gods highest in honours

The effect of splendour was likely important to Empedocles' concept of colour, as he explained the production of all colours through the mixture of two elements, fire and water, which correspond respectively to white (light) and black (darkness), and are considered the two extremes in the chromatic continuum.

During the second half of the fifth century BCE, Democritus argued that the nature of colours depends on the interaction between visual rays, daylight and the atomic structure of objects. He considered brilliance to be a factor as important as hue for defining colours. Moreover, in explaining the various colours as mixtures of a basic set of four (white, black, red and green), or as mixtures of the primary mixtures, he considered the mixture of red and white (corresponding to the golden and copper-colour) plus a small amount of green (adding a sense of freshness and life) to give 'the most beautiful colour' (probably gold). He regarded purple as a particularly 'delightful' colour, on the grounds that it comes from white, black and red, the presence of white being indicated by its brilliance and luminosity. The same appreciation of brilliance is found in Plato, whose account of vision in *Timaeus* is centred on the interaction of three factors, namely: the fire internal to the observer's eye; daylight; and the 'flame' (that is, again, the light) transmitted by the coloured object. Plato's list of primary colours includes white, black, red and, most remarkably, the 'brilliant and shining', which to us is not a colour at all.

Aristotle differs from Plato on crucial points in metaphysics and psychology. Nevertheless, he shares Plato's predilection for brilliant colours. In *On Sense and the Sensible*, he devotes a chapter to colour where he argues that the various colours arise from different proportions in the mixtures of white and black. These last two, moreover, correspond in his view to the fire and the water in the physical bodies, and determine the transparent medium as light and darkness respectively. Red, purple, green and *dark* blue, *kuanoun*, are primary mixtures of white and black, the remaining colours resulting from mixtures of the primary ones. Purple, red and green are 'most pleasant' to the eye as they are endowed with a peculiar reflectivity, which is due to the neat proportion of light and darkness in their composition.

Aristotle elaborates on the aesthetic assumptions of his predecessors and makes explicit statements on colour being an indicator of vitality and vigour, *both* in the world and in painting (which recalls the need to take into account the emotional meaning of a colour). Indeed, Aristotle describes the embryo's development in his biological work *On the Generation of Animals* by an analogy with painting practice:

> In the early stages [of the embryo's formation] the parts are all traced out in outline; later on, they get their various colours and softnesses and hardnesses, quite as if a painter were at work on them, the painter being nature. Painters, as we know, first of all outline the figure of the animal and after that go on to apply the colours.

What is more visible in painting to Aristotle's eyes, so as to    25 help to explain the embryo's growth, is how the pairing of line and colour works: first the drawing of an outline provides the essential features of an image, then comes colour to add 'flesh' and the beauty of life. It is most noteworthy that a similar attitude emerges from a number of ancient descriptions of the aesthetic effect produced by the colouring of statues, pervaded by the celebration of the brightening and enlivening properties of colour. For instance, the character of Helen in Euripides' tragedy, in complaining about the devastating events caused by her beauty, wishes for her colours to be erased from a statue, so as to eliminate her fatal charm. The literary evidence has recently received striking corroboration on this subject from important archaeological reconstructions of ancient sculptural polychromy. The effect sought by applying the most brilliant (and saturated) colours was exactly one of splendour, along with energy, movement and life.

So Goethe was right. In trying to see the world through Greek eyes, the Newtonian view is only somewhat useful. We need to supplement it with the Greeks' own colour theories, and to examine the way in which they actually tried to describe their world. Without this, the crucial role of light and brightness in their chromatic vision would be lost, as would any chance to make sense of the mobility and fluidity of their chromatic vocabulary. If we rely only on the mathematical abstractions of Newton's optics, it will be impossible to imagine what the Greeks saw when they stood on their shores, gazing out upon the *porphureos* sea stretching into the distant horizon.

*This Essay was originally published in* Aeon *(aeon.co).*

## For Discussion and Writing

1. What does Sassi mean by "saliency"? Why is it an important concept in her essay?

2. Some essays set out to prove a point that they name at the start; others, like "The Sea Was Never Blue," are constructed more like a detective story, asking questions that they strive to answer over the course of the essay. Annotate this essay with "Q"s and "A"s in the margins. Looking back over the essay, can you say anything about its form from the placement of these annotations? Where does the author ask questions, and where does she answer them?

3. **connections**   Sassi cites Goethe's preference of the Greeks' way of seeing color over Newton's, saying that Goethe favored the subjective side of color perception. Compare this treatment of science to Carl Sagan's treatment of it in "Does Truth Matter?" (p. 310). Is Sassi disagreeing with Sagan? What does she think the importance of science is, in the context of her topic?

4. One of the difficulties that arises in reading literature from another time and place is the difficulty of imagining how the author and the characters depicted in the work saw their world. Every image, feeling, and observation in any short story, novel, poem, or play is shaped by the conventional ways of understanding and perceiving things inherent in the historical period and culture out of which the work came. What about life today might leave future students scratching their heads?

5. **looking further**   Thinking of works of literature and nonfiction you've read, what kinds of differences are important to recognize when reading something ancient or something from another culture? Pick something you've read that is from another time or place, and research the historical context. What do you have to understand about how they saw (or see) the world to fully understand the piece?

## DAVID SEDARIS

# I Like Guys

*Born in 1956 in Johnston City, New York, David Sedaris grew up in Raleigh, North Carolina. He is a playwright (in collaboration with his sister Amy) and an essayist whose work has been featured regularly on National Public Radio and in the essay collections* Naked *(1997),* Dress Your Family in Corduroy and Denim *(2004),* When You Are Engulfed in Flames *(2008), and* Let's Explore Diabetes with Owls *(2013), as well as the short story collection* Squirrel Seeks Chipmunk: A Modest Bestiary *(2010). His most recent books include 2017's* Theft by Finding: Diaries (1977–2002) *and the essay collection* Calypso *(2018). Sedaris's work tends toward the satiric, but even the most wickedly pointed of his pieces are marked by an ironic stance that includes the author among those humans whose folly must be satirized. As you read "I Like Guys," note how even when the main object of his scorn is other people and their attitudes, he takes pains to consider his own folly.*

Shortly before I graduated from eighth grade, it was announced that, come fall, our county school system would adopt a policy of racial integration by way of forced busing. My Spanish teacher broke the news in a way she hoped might lead us to a greater understanding of her beauty and generosity.

"I remember the time I was at the state fair, standing in line for a Sno-Kone," she said, fingering the kiss curls that framed her squat, compact face. "And a little colored girl ran up and tugged at my skirt, asking if she could touch my hair. 'Just once,' she said. 'Just one time for good luck.'"

"Now, I don't know about the rest of you, but my hair means a lot to me." The members of my class nodded to signify that their hair meant a lot to them as well. They inched forward in their seats, eager to know where this story might be going. Perhaps the little Negro girl was holding a concealed razor blade. Maybe she was one of the troublemakers out for a fresh white scalp.

I sat marveling at their naïveté. Like all her previous anecdotes, this woman's story was headed straight up her ass.

"I checked to make sure she didn't have any candy on her hands, 5 and then I bent down and let this little colored girl touch my hair." The teacher's eyes assumed the dewy, faraway look she reserved for such Hallmark moments. "Then this little fudge-colored girl put her hand on my cheek and said, 'Oh,' she said, 'I wish I could be white and pretty like you.'" She paused, positioning herself on the edge of the desk as though she were posing for a portrait the federal government might use on a stamp commemorating gallantry. "The thing to remember," she said, "is that more than anything in this world, those colored people wish they were white."

I wasn't buying it. This was the same teacher who when announcing her pregnancy said, "I just pray that my firstborn is a boy. I'll have a boy and then maybe later I'll have a girl, because when you do it the other way round, there's a good chance the boy will turn out to be funny."

"'Funny,' as in having no arms and legs?" I asked.

"That," the teacher said, "is far from funny. That is tragic, and you, sir, should have your lips sewn shut for saying such a cruel and ugly thing. When I say 'funny,' I mean funny as in . . ." She relaxed her wrist, allowing her hand to dangle and flop. "I mean 'funny,' as in *that* kind of funny." She minced across the room, but it failed to illustrate her point, as this was more or less her natural walk, a series of gamboling little steps, her back held straight, giving the impression she was balancing something of value atop her empty head. My seventh-period math teacher did a much better version. Snatching a purse off the back of a student's chair, he would prance about the room, batting his eyes and blowing kisses at the boys seated in the front row. "So fairy nice to meet you," he'd say.

Fearful of drawing any attention to myself, I hooted and squawked along with the rest of the class, all the while thinking, *That's me he's talking about.* If I was going to make fun of people, I had to expect a little something in return, that seemed only fair. Still, though, it bothered me that they'd found such an easy way to get a laugh. As entertainers, these teachers were nothing, zero. They could barely impersonate themselves. "Look at you!" my second-period gym teacher would shout, his sneakers squealing against the basketball court. "You're a group of ladies, a pack of tap-dancing queers."

The other boys shrugged their shoulders or smiled down at   10
their shoes. They reacted as if they had been called Buddhists or
vampires; sure, it was an insult, but no one would ever mistake
them for the real thing. Had they ever chanted in the privacy of
their backyard temple or slept in a coffin, they would have felt
the sting of recognition and shared my fear of discovery.

I had never done anything with another guy and literally
prayed that I never would. As much as I fantasized about it, I
understood that there could be nothing worse than making it official. You'd seen them on television from time to time, the homosexuals, maybe on one of the afternoon talk shows. No one ever
came out and called them a queer, but you could just tell by their
voices as they flattered the host and proclaimed great respect for
their fellow guests. These were the celebrities never asked about
their home life, the comedians running scarves beneath their
toupees or framing their puffy faces with their open palms in an
effort to eliminate the circles beneath their eyes. "The poor man's
face lift," my mother called it. Regardless of their natty attire,
these men appeared sweaty and desperate, willing to play the
fool in exchange for the studio applause they seemed to mistake
for love and acceptance. I saw something of myself in their mock
weary delivery, in the way they crossed their legs and laughed at
their own jokes. I pictured their homes: the finicky placement
of their throw rugs and sectional sofas, the magazines carefully
fanned just so upon the coffee tables with no wives or children
to disturb their order. I imagined the pornography hidden in
their closets and envisioned them powerless and sobbing as the
police led them away in shackles, past the teenage boy who stood
bathed in the light of the television news camera and shouted,
"That's him! He's the one who touched my hair!"

It was my hope to win a contest, cash in the prizes, and use the
money to visit a psychiatrist who might cure me of having homosexual thoughts. Electroshock, brain surgery, hypnotism—I was
willing to try anything. Under a doctor's supervision, I would
buckle down and really change, I swore I would.

My parents knew a couple whose son had killed a Presbyterian minister while driving drunk. They had friends whose eldest
daughter had sprinkled a Bundt cake with Comet, and knew of
a child who, high on spray paint, had set fire to the family's cocker
spaniel. Yet, they spoke of no one whose son was a homosexual.

The odds struck me as bizarre, but the message was the same: this was clearly the worst thing that could happen to a person. The day-to-day anxiety was bad enough without my instructors taking their feeble little potshots. If my math teacher were able to subtract the alcohol from his diet, he'd still be on the football field where he belonged; and my Spanish teacher's credentials were based on nothing more than a long weekend in Tijuana, as far as I could tell. I quit taking their tests and completing their homework assignments, accepting Fs rather than delivering the grades I thought might promote their reputations as good teachers. It was a strategy that hurt only me, but I thought it cunning. We each had our self-defeating schemes, all the boys I had come to identify as homosexuals. Except for a few transfer students, I had known most of them since the third grade. We'd spent years gathered together in cinder-block offices as one speech therapist after another tried to cure us of our lisps. Had there been a walking specialist, we probably would have met there, too. These were the same boys who carried poorly forged notes to gym class and were the first to raise their hands when the English teacher asked for a volunteer to read aloud from *The Yearling* or *Lord of the Flies*. We had long ago identified one another and understood that because of everything we had in common, we could never be friends. To socialize would have drawn too much attention to ourselves. We were members of a secret society founded on self-loathing. When a teacher or classmate made fun of a real homosexual, I made certain my laugh was louder than anyone else's. When a club member's clothing was thrown into the locker-room toilet, I was always the first to cheer. When it was my clothing, I watched as the faces of my fellows broke into recognizable expressions of relief. *Faggots*, I thought. *This should have been you.*

Several of my teachers, when discussing the upcoming school integration, would scratch at the damp stains beneath their arms, pulling back their lips to reveal every bit of tooth and gum. They made monkey noises, a manic succession of ohhs and ahhs meant to suggest that soon our school would be no different than a jungle. Had a genuine ape been seated in the room, I guessed he might have identified their calls as a cry of panic. Anything that caused them suffering brought me joy, but I doubted they would talk this way come fall. From everything I'd seen on television, the Negros would never stand for such foolishness. As a people, they seemed to stick together. They knew how to fight, and I hoped that once they arrived, the battle might come down to the gladiators, leaving the rest of us alone.

At the end of the school year, my sister Lisa and I were excused 15 from our volunteer jobs and sent to Greece to attend a month-long summer camp advertised as "the Crown Jewel of the Ionian Sea." The camp was reserved exclusively for Greek Americans and featured instruction in such topics as folk singing and something called "religious prayer and flag." I despised the idea of summer camp but longed to boast that I had been to Europe. "It changes people!" our neighbor had said. Following a visit to Saint-Tropez, she had marked her garden with a series of tissue-sized international flags. A once discreet and modest woman, she now paraded about her yard wearing nothing but clogs and a flame-stitched bikini. "Europe is the best thing that can happen to a person, especially if you like wine!"

I saw Europe as an opportunity to re-invent myself. I might still look and speak the same way, but having walked those cobblestoned streets, I would be identified as Continental. "He has a passport," my classmates would whisper. "Quick, let's run before he judges us!"

I told myself that I would find a girlfriend in Greece. She would be a French tourist wandering the beach with a loaf of bread beneath her arm. Lisette would prove that I wasn't a homosexual, but a man with refined tastes. I saw us holding hands against the silhouette of the Acropolis, the girl begging me to take her accordion as a memento of our love. "Silly you," I would say, brushing the tears from her eyes, "just give me the beret, that will be enough to hold you in my heart until the end of time."

In case no one believed me, I would have my sister as a witness. Lisa and I weren't getting along very well, but I hoped that the warm Mediterranean waters might melt the icicle she seemed to have mistaken for a rectal thermometer. Faced with a country of strangers, she would have no choice but to appreciate my company.

Our father accompanied us to New York, where we met our fellow campers for the charter flight to Athens. There were hundreds of them, each one confident and celebratory. They tossed their complimentary Aegean Airlines tote bags across the room, shouting and jostling one another. This would be the way I'd act once we'd finally returned from camp, but not one moment before. Were it an all-girl's camp, I would have been able to work up some enthusiasm. Had they sent me alone to pry leeches off the backs of bloodthirsty Pygmies, I might have gone bravely — but spending a month in a dormitory full of boys, that was asking too much. I'd tried to put it out of my mind, but faced with their boisterous presence, I found myself growing progressively more hysterical. My nervous tics shifted into their highest gear, and a small crowd gathered to watch what they believed to be an exotic folk dance. If my sister was anxious about our trip, she certainly didn't show it. Prying my fingers off her wrist, she crossed the room and introduced herself to a girl who stood picking salvage-able butts out of the standing ashtray. This was a tough-looking Queens native named Stefani Heartattackus or Testicockules. I recall only that her last name had granted her a lifelong supply of resentment. Stefani wore mirrored aviator sunglasses and carried an oversized comb in the back pocket of her hiphugger jeans. Of all the girls in the room, she seemed the least likely candidate for my sister's friendship. They sat beside each other on the plane, and by the time we disembarked in Athens, Lisa was speaking in a very bad Queens accent. During the long flight, while I sat cowering beside a boy named Seamen, my sister had undergone a complete physical and cultural transformation. Her shoulder-length hair was now parted on the side, covering the left half of her face as if to conceal a nasty scar. She cursed and spat, scowling out the window of the chartered bus as if she'd come to Greece with the sole intention of kicking its dusty ass. "What a shithole," she yelled. "Jeez, if I'd knowed it was gonna be dis hot, I woulda stayed home wit my headdin da oven, right, girls!"

It shamed me to hear my sister struggle so hard with an accent    20
that did nothing but demean her, yet I silently congratulated her on the attempt. I approached her once we reached the camp, a cluster of whitewashed buildings hugging the desolate coast, far from any neighboring village.

"Listen, asshole," she said, "as far as this place is concerned, I don't know you and you sure as shit don't know me, you got that?" She spoke as if she were auditioning for a touring company of *West Side Story*, one hand on her hip and the other fingering her pocket comb as if it were a switchblade.

"Hey, Carolina!" one of her new friends called.

"A righta ready," she brayed. "I'm comin', I'm comin'."

That was the last time we spoke before returning home. Lisa had adjusted with remarkable ease, but something deep in my stomach suggested I wouldn't thrive nearly as well. Camp lasted a month, during which time I never once had a bowel movement. I was used to having a semiprivate bathroom and could not bring myself to occupy one of the men's room stalls, fearful that someone might recognize my shoes or, even worse, not see my shoes at all and walk in on me. Sitting down three times a day for a heavy Greek meal became an exercise akin to packing a musket. I told myself I'd sneak off during one of our field trips, but those toilets were nothing more than a hole in the floor, a hole I could have filled with no problem whatsoever. I considered using the Ionian Sea, but for some unexplained reason, we were not allowed to swim in those waters. The camp had an Olympic-size pool that was fed from the sea and soon grew murky with stray bits of jellyfish that had been pulverized by the pump. The tiny tentacles raised welts on campers' skin, so shortly after arriving, it was announced that we could photograph both the pool *and* the ocean but could swim in neither. The Greeks had invented democracy, built the Acropolis, and then called it a day. Our swimming period was converted into "contemplation hour" for the girls and an extended soccer practice for the boys.

"I really think I'd be better off contemplating," I told the coach, massaging my distended stomach. "I've got a personal problem that's sort of weighing me down."        25

Because we were first and foremost Americans, the camp was basically an extension of junior high school except that here everyone had an excess of moles or a single eyebrow. The attractive sports-minded boys ran the show, currying favor from the staff and ruining our weekly outdoor movie with their inane heckling. From time to time the rented tour buses would carry us to view one of the country's many splendors, and we would raid the gift shops, stealing anything that wasn't chained to the shelf or locked in a guarded case. These were cheap, plated puzzle rings and pint-size vases, little pom-pommed shoes, and coffee mugs reading SPARTA IS FOR A LOVER. My shoplifting experience was the only thing that gave me an edge over the popular boys. "Hold it like this," I'd whisper. "Then swivel around and slip the statue of Diana down the back of your shorts, covering it with your T-shirt. Remember to back out the door while leaving and never forget to wave good-bye."

There was one boy at camp I felt I might get along with, a Detroit native named Jason who slept on the bunk beneath mine. Jason tended to look away when talking to the other boys, shifting his eyes as though he were studying the weather conditions. Like me, he used his free time to curl into a fetal position, staring at the bedside calendar upon which he'd x-ed out all the days he had endured so far. We were finishing our 7:15 to 7:45 wash-and-rinse segment one morning when our dormitory counselor arrived for inspection shouting, "What are you, a bunch of goddamned faggots who can't make your beds?"

I giggled out loud at his stupidity. If anyone knew how to make a bed, it was a faggot. It was the others he needed to worry about. I saw Jason laughing, too, and soon we took to mocking this counselor, referring to each other first as "faggots" and then as "stinking faggots." We were "lazy faggots" and "sunburned faggots" before we eventually became "faggoty faggots." We couldn't protest the word, as that would have meant acknowledging the truth of it. The most we could do was embrace it as a joke. Embodying the term in all its clichéd glory, we minced and pranced about the room for each other's entertainment when the others weren't looking. I found myself easily outperforming my teachers, who had failed to capture the proper spirit of loopy bravado inherent in the role. *Faggot*, as a word, was always delivered in a harsh, unforgiving tone befitting those weak or stupid enough to act upon their impulses. We used it as a joke, an accusation, and finally as a dare. Late at night I'd feel my bunk buck and sway, knowing that Jason was either masturbating or beating eggs for an omelette. *Is it me he's thinking about?* I'd follow his lead and wake the next morning to find our entire iron-frame unit had wandered a good eighteen inches away from the wall. Our love had the power to move bunks.

Having no willpower, we depended on circumstances to keep us apart. *This cannot happen* was accompanied by the sound of bedsprings whining, *Oh, but maybe just this once.* There came an afternoon when, running late for flag worship, we found ourselves alone in the dormitory. What started off as name-calling escalated into a series of mock angry slaps. We wrestled each other onto one of the lower bunks, both of us longing to be pinned. "You kids think you invented sex," my mother was fond of saying. But hadn't we? With no instruction manual or federally enforced training period, didn't we all come away feeling we'd discovered something unspeakably modern? What produced in others a feeling of exhilaration left Jason and me with a mortifying sense of guilt. We fled the room as if, in our fumblings, we had uncapped some virus we still might escape if we ran fast enough. Had one of the counselors not caught me scaling the fence, I felt certain I could have made it back to Raleigh by morning, skittering across the surface of the ocean like one of those lizards often featured on television wildlife programs.

When discovered making out with one of the Greek bus drivers, a sixteen-year-old camper was forced to stand beside the flagpole dressed in long pants and thick sweaters. We watched her cook in the hot sun until, fully roasted, she crumpled to the pavement and passed out.

"That," the chief counselor said, "is what happens to people who play around."

If this was the punishment for a boy and a girl, I felt certain the penalty for two boys somehow involved barbed wire, a team of donkeys, and the nearest volcano. Nothing, however, could match the cruelty and humiliation Jason and I soon practiced upon each other. He started a rumor that I had stolen an athletic supporter from another camper and secretly wore it over my mouth like a surgical mask. I retaliated, claiming he had expressed a desire to become a dancer. "That's nothing," he said to the assembled crowd, "take a look at what I found on David's bed!" He reached into the pocket of his tennis shorts and withdrew a sheet of notebook paper upon which were written the words I LIKE GUYS. Presented as an indictment, the document was both pathetic and comic. Would I supposedly have written the note to remind myself of that fact, lest I forget? Had I intended to wear it taped to my back, advertising my preference the next time our rented buses carried us off to yet another swinging sexual playground?

I LIKE GUYS. He held the paper above his head, turning a slow circle so that everyone might get a chance to see. I supposed he had originally intended to plant the paper on my bunk for one of the counselors to find. Presenting it himself had foiled the note's intended effect. Rather than beating me with sticks and heavy shoes, the other boys simply groaned and looked away, wondering why he'd picked the thing up and carried it around in his pants pocket. He might as well have hoisted a glistening turd, shouting, "Look what he did!" Touching such a foul document made him suspect and guilty by association. In attempting to discredit each other, we wound up alienating ourselves even further.

*Jason*—even his name seemed affected. During meals I studied him from across the room. Here I was, sweating onto my plate, my stomach knotted and cramped, when *he* was the one full of shit. Clearly he had tricked me, cast a spell or slipped something into my food. I watched as he befriended a girl named Theodora and held her hand during a screening of *A Lovely Way to Die,* one of the cave paintings the head counselor offered as a weekly movie.

She wasn't a bad person, Theodora. Someday the doctors    35 might find a way to transplant a calf's brain into a human skull, and then she'd be just as lively and intelligent as he was. I tried to find a girlfriend of my own, but my one possible candidate was sent back home when she tumbled down the steps of the Parthenon, causing serious damage to her leg brace.

Jason looked convincing enough in the company of his girlfriend. They scrambled about the various ruins, snapping each other's pictures while I hung back fuming, watching them nuzzle and coo. My jealousy stemmed from the belief that he had been cured. One fistful of my flesh and he had lost all symptoms of the disease.

Camp ended and I flew home with my legs crossed, dropping my bag of stolen souvenirs and racing to the bathroom, where I spent the next several days sitting on the toilet and studying my face in a hand mirror. *I like guys.* The words had settled themselves into my features. I was a professional now, and it showed.

I returned to my volunteer job at the mental hospital, carrying harsh Greek cigarettes as an incentive to some of the more difficult patients.

"Faggot!" a woman shouted, stooping to protect her collection of pinecones. "Get your faggoty hands away from my radio transmitters."

"Don't mind Mary Elizabeth," the orderly said. "She's crazy."    40

Maybe not, I thought, holding a pinecone up against my ear. She's gotten the faggot part right, so maybe she was onto something.

The moment we boarded our return flight from Kennedy to Raleigh, Lisa re-arranged her hair, dropped her accent, and turned to me saying, "Well, I thought that was very nice, how about you?" Over the course of five minutes, she had eliminated all traces of her reckless European self. Why couldn't I do the same?

In late August my class schedule arrived along with the news that I would not be bused. There had been violence in other towns and counties, trouble as far away as Boston; but in Raleigh the transition was peaceful. Not only students but many of the teachers had been shifted from one school to another. My new science teacher was a black man very adept at swishing his way across the room, mocking everyone from Albert Einstein to the dweebish host of a popular children's television program. Black and white, the teachers offered their ridicule as though it were an olive branch. "Here," they said, "this is something we each have in common, proof that we're all brothers under the skin."

### For Discussion and Writing

1. Why does Sedaris tell the story of his school's impending integration in an essay about his sexuality?

2. Of all the rhetorical devices, irony is the one most employed by satire because it is a mode well-suited to showing the distance between the way things are and the way they should be. It is also the mode most employed by Sedaris in this essay, for the same reason. Find three examples of irony in the essay and explain how each of them works in itself and in the larger context of the essay.

3. **connections**   The last sentence of Audre Lorde's "The Fourth of July" starts, "The Waitress was white, and the counter was white, and the ice cream I never ate in Washington, D.C., that summer I left childhood was white" (p. 245). Read "I Like Guys" next to Lorde's essay. Could Sedaris describe the summer that is the setting of this essay using the same language? In what ways might he be said to be telling the story of the summer he left childhood?

4. Can you think of a time when you have ridiculed someone else because of some feature of their identity? If not, can you think of a time when you were the object of such ridicule? Tell the story, including details of the kind that Sedaris uses to paint scene, further exposition, and create tone.

5. **looking further**   One way to think about the phenomenon of individuals looking down on themselves because of the way others look down on them is what W.E.B. DuBois called "double consciousness." Research DuBois and his creation and use of the term. Then apply the term to "I Like Guys." Who suffers from this condition? How?

BRENT STAPLES

# Just Walk on By: Black Men and Public Space

*Brent Staples, born in 1951 in Chester, Pennsylvania, has a doctorate in psychology and has taught, but he has built a career as a reporter and columnist. He is on the editorial board of the* New York Times, *where he writes on education, culture, and politics. He has also contributed to* Ms., Harper's, *and other magazines. Staples's memoir,* Parallel Time: Growing Up in Black and White *(1994), tells the story of his youth and that of his younger brother, whose violent life followed a very different path.*

*"Just Walk on By" originally appeared in* Ms. *As you read, think about why this piece might be appropriate for a publication intended primarily for women.*

My first victim was a woman—white, well dressed, probably in her early twenties. I came upon her late one evening on a deserted street in Hyde Park, a relatively affluent neighborhood in an otherwise mean, impoverished section of Chicago. As I swung onto the avenue behind her, there seemed to be a discreet, uninflammatory distance between us. Not so. She cast back a worried glance. To her, the youngish black man—a broad six feet two inches with a beard and billowing hair, both hands shoved into the pockets of a bulky military jacket—seemed menacingly close. After a few more quick glimpses, she picked up her pace and was soon running in earnest. Within seconds she disappeared into a cross street.

That was more than a decade ago, I was twenty-two years old, a graduate student newly arrived at the University of Chicago. It was in the echo of that terrified woman's footfalls that I first began to know the unwieldy inheritance I'd come into—the ability to alter public space in ugly ways. It was clear that she thought herself the quarry of a mugger, a rapist, or worse. Suffering a bout of insomnia, however, I was stalking sleep, not defenseless wayfarers. As a softy who is scarcely able to take a knife to a raw chicken—let alone hold one to a person's throat—I was surprised, embarrassed, and dismayed all at once. Her flight made me feel like an accomplice in tyranny. It also made it clear that I was indistinguishable from the muggers who occasionally seeped into the area from the surrounding ghetto. That first encounter, and those that followed, signified that a vast, unnerving gulf lay between nighttime pedestrians—particularly women—and me. And I soon gathered that being perceived as dangerous is a hazard in itself. I only needed to turn a corner into a dicey situation, or crowd some frightened, armed person in a foyer somewhere, or make an errant move after being pulled over by a policeman. Where fear and weapons meet—and they often do in urban America—there is always the possibility of death.

In that first year, my first away from my hometown, I was to become thoroughly familiar with the language of fear. At dark, shadowy intersections, I could cross in front of a car stopped at a traffic light and elicit the *thunk, thunk, thunk, thunk* of the driver—black, white, male, or female—hammering down the door locks. On less traveled streets after dark, I grew accustomed to but never comfortable with people crossing to the other side of the street rather than pass me. Then there were the standard unpleasantries with policemen, doormen, bouncers, cabdrivers, and others whose business it is to screen out troublesome individuals *before* there is any nastiness.

I moved to New York nearly two years ago and I have remained an avid night walker. In central Manhattan, the near-constant crowd cover minimizes tense one-on-one street encounters. Elsewhere—in SoHo, for example, where sidewalks are narrow and tightly spaced buildings shut out the sky—things can get very taut indeed.

After dark, on the warrenlike streets of Brooklyn where I live, I often see women who fear the worst from me. They seem to have set their faces on neutral, and with their purse straps strung across their chests bandolier-style, they forge ahead as though bracing themselves against being tackled. I understand, of course, that the danger they perceive is not a hallucination. Women are particularly vulnerable to street violence, and young black males are drastically overrepresented among the perpetrators of that violence. Yet these truths are no solace against the kind of alienation that comes of being ever the suspect, a fearsome entity with whom pedestrians avoid making eye contact. 5

It is not altogether clear to me how I reached the ripe old age of twenty-two without being conscious of the lethality nighttime pedestrians attributed to me. Perhaps it was because in Chester, Pennsylvania, the small, angry industrial town where I came of age in the 1960s, I was scarcely noticeable against a backdrop of gang warfare, street knifings, and murders. I grew up one of the good boys, had perhaps a half-dozen fistfights. In retrospect, my shyness of combat has clear sources.

As a boy, I saw countless tough guys locked away; I have since buried several, too. They were babies, really—a teenage cousin, a brother of twenty-two, a childhood friend in his mid-twenties—all gone down in episodes of bravado played out in the streets. I came to doubt the virtues of intimidation early on. I chose, perhaps unconsciously, to remain a shadow—timid, but a survivor.

The fearsomeness mistakenly attributed to me in public places often has a perilous flavor. The most frightening of these confusions occurred in the late 1970s and early 1980s, when I worked as a journalist in Chicago. One day, rushing into the office of a magazine I was writing for with a deadline story in hand, I was mistaken for a burglar. The office manager called security and, with an ad hoc posse, pursued me through the labyrinthine halls, nearly to my editor's door. I had no way of proving who I was. I could only move briskly toward the company of someone who knew me.

Another time I was on assignment for a local paper and killing time before an interview. I entered a jewelry store on the city's affluent Near North Side. The proprietor excused herself and returned with an enormous red Doberman pinscher straining at the end of a leash. She stood, the dog extended toward me, silent to my questions, her eyes bulging nearly out of her head. I took a cursory look around, nodded, and bade her good night.

Relatively speaking, however, I never fared as badly as another   10
black male journalist. He went to nearby Waukegan, Illinois, a couple of summers ago to work on a story about a murderer who was born there. Mistaking the reporter for the killer, police officers hauled him from his car at gunpoint and but for his press credentials would probably have tried to book him. Such episodes are not uncommon. Black men trade tales like this all the time.

Over the years, I learned to smother the rage I felt at so often being taken for a criminal. Not to do so would surely have led to madness. I now take precautions to make myself less threatening.

I move about with care, particularly late in the evening. I give a wide berth to nervous people on subway platforms during the wee hours, particularly when I have exchanged business clothes for jeans. If I happen to be entering a building behind some people who appear skittish, I may walk by, letting them clear the lobby before I return, so as not to seem to be following them. I have been calm and extremely congenial on those rare occasions when I've been pulled over by the police.

And on late-evening constitutionals I employ what has proved to be an excellent tension-reducing measure: I whistle melodies from Beethoven and Vivaldi and the more popular classical composers. Even steely New Yorkers hunching toward nighttime destinations seem to relax, and occasionally they even join in the tune. Virtually everybody seems to sense that a mugger wouldn't be warbling bright, sunny selections from Vivaldi's *Four Seasons*. It is my equivalent of the cowbell that hikers wear when they know they are in bear country.

## For Discussion and Writing

1. How does Staples describe himself? How is he sometimes seen by others?

2. Staples begins his essay by discussing the effect of his presence on another person. However, others' reactions to his presence affect him in return, and he spends much of the essay explaining the emotional and practical effects he experiences as a consequence of his interactions. How are the complication and paradox of these situations expressed by the last sentence about Staples's whistling classical music being the "equivalent of the cowbell that hikers wear when they know they are in bear country" (par. 12)?

3. **connections**   Compare Staples's reaction to race-inflected encounters to James Baldwin's reaction to the encounter in the restaurant in "Notes of a Native Son" (p. 47). What might the differences tell us about the individuals and their respective times?

4. The person with whom you find yourself identifying in a story sometimes depends on your own identity. With whom did you identify at the start of Staples's essay, and how did it affect your reading of the full piece?

5. **looking further**   Imagine a response to "Just Walk on By" that takes issue with the tactics Staples employs in order to avoid frightening people with his mere presence. What arguments might someone make against his choice to accommodate the irrational fears of others? On what basis might objections to this practice be raised?

GLORIA STEINEM

# Sex, Lies, and Advertising

*Gloria Steinem is a journalist and political activist. Born and raised in Toledo, Ohio, Steinem attended Smith College. After getting her work published as a freelance writer, including a piece on contraception in* Esquire *(1962), and a now well-known 1963 article for which she worked as a waitress in the New York Playboy Club in order to chronicle the mistreatment of the waitresses, known as "bunnies," she was hired as a columnist at* New York *magazine. In 1972, Steinem cofounded the groundbreaking feminist magazine* Ms.*, which began as a special issue of* New York. *She has been active in women's and other social causes and in politics for six decades, working from within the political process to change it in ways that promote the things she believes in. As you read "Sex, Lies, and Advertising," note how Steinem works from within the magazine industry to change it.*

About three years ago, as *glasnost* was beginning and *Ms.* seemed to be ending I was invited to a press lunch for a Soviet official. He entertained us with anecdotes about new problems of democracy in his country. Local Communist leaders were being criticized in their media for the first time, he explained, and they were angry.

"So I'll have to ask my American friends," he finished pointedly, "how more subtly to control the press." In the silence that followed, I said, "Advertising."

The reporters laughed, but later, one of them took me aside: How dare I suggest that freedom of the press was limited? How dare I imply that his newsweekly could be influenced by ads?

I explained that I was thinking of advertising's mediawide influence on most of what we read. Even newsmagazines use "soft" cover stories to sell ads, confuse readers with "advertorials," and occasionally self-censor on subjects known to be a problem with big advertisers.

But, I also explained, I was thinking especially of women's magazines. There, it isn't just a little content that's devoted to attracting 5

349

ads, it's almost all of it. That's why advertisers—not readers—have always been the problem for *Ms*. As the only women's magazine that didn't supply what the ad world euphemistically describes as "supportive editorial atmosphere" or "complementary copy" (for instance, articles that praise food/ fashion/beauty subjects to "support" and "complement" food/fashion/beauty ads), *Ms*. could never attract enough advertising to break even.

"Oh, *women's* magazines," the journalist said with contempt. "Everybody knows they're catalogs—but who cares? They have nothing to do with journalism."

I can't tell you how many times I've had this argument in 25 years of working for many kinds of publications. Except as moneymaking machines—"cash cows" as they are so elegantly called in the trade—women's magazines are rarely taken seriously. Though changes being made by women have been called more far-reaching than the industrial revolution—and though many editors try hard to reflect some of them in the few pages left to them after all the ad-related subjects have been covered—the magazines serving the female half of this country are still far below the journalistic and ethical standards of news and general interest publications. Most depressing of all, this doesn't even rate an expose.

If *Time* and *Newsweek* had to lavish praise on cars in general and credit General Motors in particular to get GM ads, there would be a scandal—maybe a criminal investigation. When women's magazines from *Seventeen* to *Lear's* praise beauty products in general and credit Revlon in particular to get ads, it's just business as usual.

I.

When *Ms*. began, we didn't consider not taking ads. The most important reason was keeping the price of a feminist magazine low enough for most women to afford. But the second and almost equal reason was providing a forum where women and advertisers could talk to each other and improve advertising itself. After all, it was (and still is) as potent a source of information in this country as news or TV and movie dramas.

We decided to proceed in two stages. First, we would con-  10 vince makers of "people products" used by both men and women but advertised mostly to men—cars, credit cards, insurance, sound equipment, financial services, and the like—that their ads should be placed in a women's magazine. Since they were accustomed to the division between editorial and advertising in news and general interest magazines, this would allow our editorial content to be free and diverse. Second, we would add the best ads for whatever traditional "women's products" (clothes, shampoo, fragrance, food, and so on) that surveys showed *Ms.* readers used. But we would ask them to come in *without* the usual quid pro quo of "complementary copy."

We knew the second step might be harder. Food advertisers have always demanded that women's magazines publish recipes and articles on entertaining (preferably ones that name their products) in return for their ads; clothing advertisers expect to be surrounded by fashion spreads (especially ones that credit their designers); and shampoo, fragrance, and beauty products in general usually insist on positive editorial coverage of beauty subjects, plus photo credits besides. That's why women's magazines look the way they do. But if we could break this link between ads and editorial content, then we wanted good ads for "women's products," too.

By playing their part in this unprecedented mix of all the things our readers need and use, advertisers also would be rewarded: ads for products like cars and mutual funds would find a new growth market; the best ads for women's products would no longer be lost in Oceans of ads for the same category; and both would have access to a laboratory of smart and caring readers whose response would help create effective ads for other media as well.

I thought then that our main problem would be the imagery in ads themselves. Car-makers were still draping blondes in evening gowns over the hoods like ornaments. Authority figures were almost always male, even in ads for products that only women used. Sadistic, he-man campaigns even won industry praise. (For instance, *Advertising Age* had hailed the infamous Silva Thin cigarette theme, "How to Get a Woman's Attention: Ignore Her," as "brilliant.") Even in medical journals, tranquilizer ads showed depressed housewives standing beside piles of dirty dishes and promised to get them back to Work.

Obviously *Ms.* would have to avoid such ads and seek out the best ones—but this didn't seem impossible. *The New Yorker* had been selecting ads for aesthetic reasons for years, a practice that only seemed to make advertisers more eager to be in its pages. *Ebony* and *Essence* were asking for ads with positive black images, and though their struggle was hard, they weren't being called unreasonable.

Clearly, what *Ms.* needed was a very special publisher and ad 15 sales staff. I could think of only one woman with experience on the business side of magazines—Patricia Carbine, who recently had become a vice president of *McCall's* as well as its editor in chief—and the reason I knew her name was a good omen. She had been managing editor at *Look* (really *the* editor, but its owner refused to put a female name at the top of his masthead) when I was writing a column there. After I did an early interview with Cesar Chavez, then just emerging as a leader of migrant labor, and the publisher turned it down because he was worried about ads from Sunkist, Pat was the one who intervened. As I learned later, she had told the publisher she would resign if the interview wasn't published. Mainly because *Look* couldn't afford to lose Pat, it was published (and the ads from Sunkist never arrived).

Though I barely knew this woman, she had done two things I always remembered: put her job on the line in a way that editors often talk about but rarely do and been so loyal to her colleagues that she never told me or anyone outside *Look* that she had done so.

Fortunately Pat did agree to leave *McCall's* and take a huge cut in salary to become publisher of *Ms.* She became responsible for training and inspiring generations of young women who joined the *Ms.* ad sales force many of whom went on to become "firsts" at the top of publishing. When *Ms.* first started, however, there were so few women with experience selling space that Pat and I made the rounds of ad agencies ourselves. Later the fact that *Ms.* was asking companies to do business in a different way meant our saleswomen had to make many times the usual number of calls—first to convince agencies and then client companies beside—and to present endless amounts of research. I was often asked to do a final ad presentation, or see some higher decision-maker or speak to women employees so executives could see the interest of women they worked with. That's why I spent more time persuading advertisers than editing or writing for *Ms.* and why I ended up with an unsentimental education in the seamy underside of publishing that few writers see (and even fewer magazines can publish).

Let me take you with us through some experiences, just as they happened:

- Cheered on by early support from Volkswagen and one or two other car companies, we scrape together time and money to put on a major reception in Detroit. We know U.S. car-makers firmly believe that women choose the upholstery not the car, but we are armed with statistics and reader mail to prove the contrary: a car is an important purchase for women, one that symbolizes mobility and freedom.

  But almost nobody comes. We are left with many pounds of shrimp on the table, and quite a lot of egg on our face. We blame ourselves for not guessing that there would be a baseball pennant play-off on the same day, but executives go out of their way to explain they wouldn't have come anyway. Thus begins ten years of knocking on hostile doors, presenting endless documentation, and hiring a full-time saleswoman in Detroit; all necessary before *Ms.* gets any real results.

  This long saga has a semihappy ending: foreign and, later, domestic car makers eventually provided *Ms.* with enough advertising to make cars one of our top sources of ad revenue. Slowly, Detroit began to take the women's market seriously enough to put car ads in other women's magazines, too, thus freeing a few pages from the hothouse of fashion-beauty-food ads.

  But long after figures showed a third, even a half, of many car models being bought by women, U.S. makers continued to be uncomfortable addressing women. Unlike foreign car makers, Detroit never quite learned the secret of creating intelligent ads that exclude no one, and then placing them in women's magazines to overcome past exclusion. (*Ms.* readers were so grateful for a routine Honda ad featuring rack and pinion steering, for instance, that they sent fan mail.) Even now, Detroit continues to ask, "Should we make special ads for women?" Perhaps that's why some foreign cars still have a disproportionate share of the U.S. women's market.

- In the *Ms.* Gazette, we do a brief report on a congressional hearing into chemicals used in hair dyes that are absorbed through the skin and may be carcinogenic. Newspapers report this too, but Clairol, a Bristol-Myers subsidiary that makes dozens of products—a few of which have just begun to advertise in *Ms.*—is outraged. Not at newspapers or newsmagazines, just at us. It's bad enough that *Ms.* is the only women's magazine refusing to provide the usual "complementary" articles and beauty photos, but to criticize one of their categories—*that* is going too far.

We offer to publish a letter from Clairol telling its side of the story. In an excess of solicitousness, we even put this letter in the Gazette, not in Letters to the Editors where it belongs. Nonetheless—and in spite of surveys that show *Ms.* readers are active women who use more of almost everything Clairol makes than do the readers of any other women's magazine—*Ms.* gets almost none of these ads for the rest of its natural life.

Meanwhile, Clairol changes its hair coloring formula, apparently in response to the hearings we reported.

Our saleswomen set out early to attract ads for consumer electronics: sound equipment, calculators, computers, VCRs, and the like. We know that our readers are determined to be included in the technological revolution. We know from reader surveys that *Ms.* readers are buying this stuff in numbers as high as those of magazines like *Playboy;* or "men 18 to 34," the prime targets of the consumer electronics industry. Moreover, unlike traditional women's products that our readers buy but don't need to read articles about, these are subjects they want covered in our pages. There actually is a supportive editorial atmosphere.

"But women don't understand technology," say executives at the end of ad presentations. "Maybe not," we respond, "but neither do men—and we all buy it."

"If women do buy it," say the decision-makers, "they're asking their husbands and boyfriends what to buy first." We produce letters from *Ms.* readers saying how turned off they are when salesmen say things like "Let me know when your husband can come in."

After several years of this, we get a few ads for compact sound systems. Some of them come from JVC, whose vice president, Harry Elias, is trying to convince his Japanese bosses that there is something called a women's market. At his invitation, I find myself speaking at huge trade shows in Chicago and Las Vegas, trying to persuade JVC dealers that showrooms don't have to be locker rooms where women are made to feel unwelcome. But as it turns out, the shows themselves are part of the problem. In Las Vegas, the only women around the technology displays are seminude models serving champagne. In Chicago, the big attraction is Marilyn Chambers, who followed Linda Lovelace of *Deep Throat* fame as Chuck

Traynor's captive and/or employee. VCRs are being demonstrated with her porn videos.

In the end, we get ads for a car stereo now and then, but no
VCRs; some IBM personal computers, but no Apple or Japanese
ones. We notice that office magazines like *Working Woman* and
*Savvy* don't benefit as much as they should from office equipment
ads either. In the electronics world, women and technology seem
mutually exclusive. It remains a decade behind even Detroit.

- Because we get letters from little girls who love toy trains, and
who ask our help in changing ads and box-top photos that feature
little boys only, we try to get toy-train ads from Lionel. It turns
out that Lionel executives have been concerned about little girls.
They made a pink train, and were surprised when it didn't sell.

Lionel bows to consumer pressure with a photograph of a
boy *and* a girl—but only on some of their boxes. They fear
that, if trains are associated with girls, they will be devalued
in the minds of boys. Needless to say, *Ms.* gets no train ads;
and little girls remain a mostly unexplored market. By 1986,
Lionel is put up for sale.

But for different reasons, we haven't had much luck with
other kinds of toys either. In spite of many articles on child-
rearing; an annual listing of nonsexist, multi-racial toys by
Letty Cottin Pogrebin; Stories for Free Children, a regular
feature also edited by Letty; and other prizewinning features
for or about children, we get virtually no toy ads. Generations
of *Ms.* saleswomen explain to toy manufacturers that a larger
proportion of *Ms.* readers have preschool children than do the
readers of other women's magazines, but this industry can't
believe feminists have or care about children.

- When *Ms.* begins, the staff decides not to accept ads for feminine hygiene sprays or cigarettes: they are damaging and
carry no appropriate health warnings. Though we don't think
we should tell our readers what to do, we do think we should
provide facts so they can decide for themselves. Since the antismoking lobby has been pressing for health warnings on cigarette ads, we decide to take them only as they comply.

Philip Morris is among the first to do so. One of its brands,
Virginia Slims, is also sponsoring women's tennis and the
first national polls of women's opinions. On the other hand,
the Virginia Slims theme, "You've come a long way, baby," has

more than a "baby" problem. It makes smoking a symbol of progress for women.

We explain to Philip Morris that this slogan won't do well in our pages, but they are convinced its success with some women means it will work with *all* women. Finally, we agree to publish an ad for a Virginia Slims calendar as a test. The letters from readers are critical—and smart. For instance: Would you show a black man picking cotton, the same man in a Cardin suit, and symbolize the antislavery and civil rights movements by smoking? Of course not. But instead of honoring the test results, the Philip Morris people seem angry to be proven wrong. They take away ads for *all* their many brands.

This costs *Ms.* about $250,000 the first year. After five years, we can no longer keep track. Occasionally, a new set of executives listens to *Ms.* saleswomen, but because we won't take Virginia Slims, not one Philip Morris product returns to our pages for the next 16 years.

Gradually, we also realize our naiveté in thinking we could decide against taking cigarette ads. They became a disproportionate support of magazines the moment they were banned on television, and few magazines could compete and survive without them; certainly not Ms., which lacks so many other categories. By the time statistics in the 1980s showed that women's rate of lung cancer was approaching men's, the necessity of taking cigarette ads has become a kind of prison.

- General Mills, Pillsbury, Carnation, DelMonte, Dole, Kraft, Stouffer, Hormel, Nabisco: you name the food giant, we try it. But no matter how desirable the *Ms.* readership, our lack of recipes is lethal.

We explain to them that placing food ads only next to recipes associates food with work. For many women, it is a negative that works against the ads. Why not place food ads in diverse media without recipes (thus reaching more men, who are now a third of the shoppers in supermarkets anyway), and leave the recipes to specialty magazines like *Gourmet* (a third of whose readers are also men)?

These arguments elicit interest, but except for an occasional ad for a convenience food, instant coffee, diet drinks, yogurt, or such extras as avocados and almonds, this mainstay of the publishing industry stays closed to us. Period.

- Traditionally, wines and liquors didn't advertise to women: men were thought to make the brand decisions, even if women did the buying. But after endless presentations, we begin to make a dent in this category. Thanks to the unconventional Michel Roux of Carillon Importers (distributors of Grand Marnier, Absolut Vodka, and others), who assumes that food and drink have no gender, some ads are leaving their men's club.

  Beermakers are still selling masculinity. It takes *Ms.* fully eight years to get its first beer ad (Michelob). In general, however, liquor ads are less stereotyped in their imagery—and far less controlling of the editorial content around them—than are women's products. But given the underrepresentation of other categories, these very facts tend to create a disproportionate number of alcohol ads in the pages of *Ms.* This in turn dismays readers worried about women and alcoholism.

- We hear in 1980 that women in the Soviet Union have been producing feminist *samizdat* (underground, self-published books) and circulating them throughout the country. As punishment, four of the leaders have been exiled. Though we are operating on our usual shoe string, we solicit individual contributions to send Robin Morgan to interview these women in Vienna.

  The result is an exclusive cover story that includes the first news of a populist peace movement against the Afghanistan occupation, a prediction of *glasnost* to come, and a grassroots, intimate view of Soviet women's lives. From the popular press to women's studies courses, the response is great. The story wins a Front Page award.

  Nonetheless, this journalistic coup undoes years of efforts to get an ad schedule from Revlon. Why? Because the Soviet women on our cover *are not wearing makeup.*

- Four years of research and presentations go into convincing airlines that women now make travel choices and business trips. United, the first airline to advertise in *Ms.*, is so impressed with the response from our readers that one of its executives appears in a film for our ad presentations. As usual, good ads get great results.

  But we have problems unrelated to such results. For instance: because American Airlines flight attendants include among their labor demands the stipulation that they could choose to have their last names preceded by "*Ms.*" on their name tags — in a long-delayed revolt against the standard, "I am your pilot, Captain Rothgart, and this is your flight attendant, Cindy Sue" — American officials seem to hold the magazine responsible. We get no ads.

There is still a different problem at Eastern. A vice president cancels subscriptions for thousands of copies on Eastern flights. Why? Because he is offended by ads for lesbian poetry journals in the *Ms.* Classified. A "family airline," as he explains to me coldly on the phone, has to "draw the line somewhere."

It's obvious that *Ms.* can't exclude lesbians and serve women. We've been trying to make that point ever since our first issue included an article by and about lesbians, and both Suzanne Levine, our managing editor, and I were lectured by such heavy hitters as Ed Kosner, then editor of *Newsweek* (and now of *New York Magazine*), who insisted that *Ms.* should "position" itself *against* lesbians. But our advertisers have paid to reach a guaranteed number of readers, and soliciting new subscriptions to compensate for Eastern would cost $150,000, plus rebating money in the meantime.

Like almost everything ad-related, this presents an elaborate organizing problem. After days of searching for sympathetic members of the Eastern board, Frank Thomas, president of the Ford Foundation, kindly offers to call Roswell Gilpatrick, a director of Eastern. I talk with Mr. Gilpatrick, who calls Frank Borman, then the president of Eastern. Frank Borman calls me to say that his airline is not in the business of censoring magazines: *Ms.* will be returned to Eastern flights.

- Women's access to insurance and credit is vital, but with the exception of Equitable and a few other ad pioneers, such financial services address men. For almost a decade after the Equal Credit Opportunity Act passes in 1974, we try to convince American Express that women are a growth market — but nothing works.

  Finally a former professor of Russian named Jerry Welsh becomes head of marketing. He assumes that women should be cardholders, and persuades his colleagues to feature women in a campaign. Thanks to this 1980s series, the growth rate for female cardholders surpasses that for men.

  For this article, I asked Jerry Welsh if he would explain why American Express waited so long. "Sure," he said, "they were afraid of having a 'pink' card."

- Women of color read *Ms.* in disproportionate numbers. This is a source of pride to *Ms.* staffers, who are also more racially representative than the editors of other women's magazines. But this reality is obscured by ads filled with enough white women to make a reader snow-blind.

  Pat Carbine remembers mostly "astonishment" when she requested African American, Hispanic, Asian, and other diverse images. Marcia Ann Gillespie, a *Ms.* editor who was previously the editor in chief of *Essence*, witnesses ad bias a second time: having tried for *Essence* to get white advertisers to use black images (Revlon did so eventually, but L'Oréal, Lauder, Chanel, and other companies never did), she sees similar problems getting integrated ads for an integrated magazine. Indeed, the ad world often creates black and Hispanic ads only for black and Hispanic media. In an exact parallel of the fear that marketing a product to women will endanger its appeal to men, the response is usually, "But your [white] readers won't identify"

  In fact, those we are able to get—for instance, a Max Factor ad made for *Essence* that Linda Wachner gives us after she becomes president—are praised by white readers, too. But there are pathetically few such images.

- By the end of 1986, production and mailing costs have risen astronomically, ad income is flat, and competition for ads is stiffer than ever. The 60/40 preponderance of edit over ads that we promised to readers becomes 50/50; children's stories, most poetry, and some fiction are casualties of less space; in order to get variety into limited pages, the length (and sometimes the depth) of articles suffers; and, though we do refuse most of the ads that would look like a parody in our pages, we get so worn down that some slip through. . . . Still, readers perform miracles. Though we haven't been able to afford a subscription mailing in two years, they maintain our guaranteed circulation of 450,000.

Nonetheless, media reports on *Ms.* often insist that our unprofitability "must be due to reader disinterest." The myth that advertisers simply follow readers is very strong. Not one reporter notes that other comparable magazines our size (say, *Vanity Fair* or *The Atlantic*) have been losing more money in one year than *Ms.* has lost in 16 years. No matter how much never-to-be-recovered cash is poured into starting a magazine or keeping one going, appearances seem to be all that matter (which is why we haven't been able to explain our fragile state in public. Nothing causes ad-flight like the smell of nonsuccess.)

My healthy response is anger. My not-so-healthy response is   20 constant worry—also an obsession with finding one more rescue. There is hardly a night when I don't wake up with sweaty palms and pounding heart, scared that we won't be able to pay the printer or the post office; scared most of all that closing our doors will hurt the women's movement.

Out of chutzpah and desperation, I arrange a lunch with Leonard Lauder, president of Estee Lauder. With the exception of Clinique (the brainchild of Carol Phillips), none of Lauder's hundreds of products has been advertised in *Ms*. A year's schedule of ads for just three or four of them could save us. Indeed, as the scion of a family-owned company whose ad practices are followed by the beauty industry he is one of the few men who could liberate many pages in all women's magazines just by changing his mind about "complementary copy."

Over a lunch that costs more than we can pay for some articles, I explain the need for his leadership. I also lay out the record of *Ms.*: more literary and journalistic prizes won, more new issues introduced into the main-stream, new writers discovered, and impact on society than any other magazine; more articles that became books, stories that became movies, ideas that became television series, and newly advertised products that became profitable; and, most important for him, a place for his ads to reach women who aren't reachable through any other women's magazine. Indeed, if there is one constant characteristic of the ever-changing *Ms*. readership, it is their impact as leaders. Whether it's waiting until later to have first babies, or pioneering PABA as sun protection in cosmetics, whatever they are doing today a third to a half of American women will be doing three to five years from now. It's never failed.

But, he says, *Ms*. readers are not *our* women. They're not interested in things like fragrance and blush-on. If they were, *Ms*. would write articles about them.

On the contrary, I explain, surveys show they are more likely to buy such things than the readers of, say, *Cosmopolitan* or *Vogue*. They're good customers because they're out in the world enough to need several sets of everything home, work, purse, travel, gym, and so on. They just don't need to read articles about these things. Would he ask a men's magazine to publish monthly columns on how to shave before he advertised Aramis products (his line for men)?

He concedes that beauty features are often concocted more for advertisers than readers. But *Ms.* isn't appropriate for his ads anyway, he explains. Why? Because Estee Lauder is selling "a kept-woman mentality."

I can't quite believe this. Sixty percent of the users of his products are salaried, and generally resemble *Ms.* readers. Besides, his company has the appeal of having been started by a creative and hardworking woman, his mother, Estee Lauder.

That doesn't matter, he says. He knows his customers, and they would *like* to be kept women. That's why he will never advertise in *Ms.*

In November 1987, by vote of the *Ms.* Foundation for Education and Communication (*Ms.*'s owner and publisher, the media subsidiary of the *Ms.* Foundation for Women), *Ms.* was sold to a company whose officers, Australian feminists Sandra Yates and Anne Summers, raised the investment money in their country that *Ms.* couldn't find in its own. They also started *Sassy* for teenage women.

In their two-year tenure, circulation was raised to 550,000 by investment in circulation mailings, and, to the dismay of some readers, editorial features on clothes and new products made a more traditional bid for ads. Nonetheless, ad pages fell below previous levels. In addition, *Sassy*, whose fresh voice and sexual frankness were an unprecedented success with young readers, was targeted by two mothers from Indiana who began, as one of them put it, "calling every Christian organization I could think of." In response to this controversy, several crucial advertisers pulled out.

Such links between ads and editorial content was a problem in Australia, too, but to a lesser degree. "Our readers pay two times more for their magazines," Anne explained, "so advertisers have less power to threaten a magazine's viability."

"I was shocked," said Sandra Yates with characteristic directness. "In Australia, we think you have freedom of the press—but you don't."

Since Anne and Sandra had not met their budget's projections for ad revenue, their investors forced a sale. In October 1989, *Ms.* and *Sassy* were bought by Dale Lang, owner of *Working Mother, Working Woman,* and one of the few independent publishing companies left among the conglomerates. In response to a request from the original *Ms.* staff—as well as to reader letters urging that *Ms.* continue, plus his own belief that *Ms.* would benefit his other magazines by blazing a trail—he agreed to try the ad-free, reader-supported *Ms.* you hold now and to give us complete editorial control.

## II.

Do you think, as I once did, that advertisers make decisions based on solid research? Well, think again. "Broadly speaking," says Joseph Smith of Oxtoby-Smith Inc., a consumer research firm, "there is no persuasive evidence that the editorial context of an ad matters."

Advertisers who demand such "complementary copy," even in the absence of respectable studies, clearly are operating under a double standard. The same food companies place ads in *People* with no recipes. Cosmetic companies support the *New Yorker* with no regular beauty columns. So where does this habit of controlling the content of women's magazines come from?

Tradition. Ever since *Ladies Magazine* debuted in Boston in 1828, 35 editorial copy directed to women has been informed by something other than its readers' wishes. There were no ads then, but in an age when married women were legal minors with no right to their own money, there was another revenue source to be kept in mind: husbands. "Husbands may rest assured," wrote editor Sarah Josepha Hale, "that nothing found in these pages shall cause her [his wife] to be less assiduous in preparing for his reception or encourage her to 'usurp station' or encroach upon prerogatives of men."

Hale went on to become the editor of *Godey's Lady's Book*, a magazine featuring "fashion plates": engraving of dresses for readers to take to their seamstresses or copy themselves. Hale added "how to" articles, which set the tone for women's service magazines for years to come, how to write politely, avoid sunburn, and—in no fewer than 1,200 words—how to maintain a goose quill pen. She advocated education for women but avoided controversy. Just as most women's magazines now avoid politics, poll their readers on issues like abortion but rarely take a stand, and praise socially approved lifestyles, Hale saw to it that *Godey's* avoided the hot topics of its day: slavery abolition, and women's suffrage.

What definitively turned women's magazines, into catalogs, however, were two events: Ellen Butterick's invention of the clothing pattern in 1863 and the mass manufacture of patent medicines containing everything from colored water to cocaine. For the first time, readers could purchase what magazines encouraged them to want. As such magazines became more profitable, they also began to attract men as editors. (Most women's magazines continued to have men as top editors until the feminist 1970s.) Edward Bok, who became editor of the *Ladies' Home Journal* in 1889, discovered the power of advertisers when he rejected ads for patent medicines and found that other advertisers canceled in retribution. In the early 20th century, *Good Housekeeping* started its Institute to "test and approve" products. Its Seal of Approval became the grandfather of current "value added" programs that offer advertisers such bonuses as product sampling and department store promotions.

By the time suffragists finally won the vote in 1920, women's magazines had become too entrenched as catalogs to help women learn how to use it. The main function was to create a desire for products, teach how to use products, and make products a crucial part of gaining social approval, pleasing a husband, and performing as a homemaker. Some unrelated articles and short stories were included to persuade women to pay for these catalogs. But articles were neither consumerist nor rebellious. Even fiction was usually subject to formula: if a woman had any sexual life outside marriage, she was supposed to come to a bad end.

In 1965, Helen Gurley Brown began to change part of that formula by bringing "the sexual revolution" to women's magazines—but in an ad-oriented way. Attracting multiple men required even more consumerism, as the Cosmo Girl made clear, than finding one husband.

In response to the workplace revolution of the 1970s, traditional women's magazines—that is, "trade books" for women working at home—were joined by *Savvy, Working Woman,* and other trade books for women working in offices. But by keeping the fashion/beauty/entertaining articles necessary to get traditional ads and then adding career articles besides, they inadvertently produced the antifeminist stereotype of Super Woman. The male-imitative, dress-for-success woman carrying a briefcase became the media image of a woman worker, even though a blue-collar woman's salary was often higher than her glorified secretarial sister's, and though women at a real briefcase level are statistically rare. Needless to say, these dress-for-success women were also thin, white, and beautiful.

40

In recent years, advertisers' control over the editorial content of women's magazines has become so institutionalized that it is written into "insertion orders" or dictated to ad salespeople as official policy. The following are recent typical orders to women's magazines:

- Dow's Cleaning Products stipulates that ads for its Vivid and Spray 'n Wash products should be adjacent to "children or fashion editorial"; ads for Bathroom Cleaner Should be next to "home furnishing/family" features; and so on for other brands. "If a magazine fails for 1/2 the brands or more," the Dow order warns, "it will be omitted from further consideration."

- Bristol-Myers, the parent of Clairol, Windex, Drano, Bufferin, and much more, stipulates that ads be placed next to "a full page of compatible editorial."

- S.C. Johnson & Son, makers of Johnson Wax, lawn and laundry products, insect sprays, hair sprays, and so on, orders that its ads "should not *be opposite extremely controversial features or material antithetical to the nature/copy of the advertised product.*" (Italics theirs.)

- Maidenform, manufacturer of bras and other apparel, leaves a blank for the particular product and states: "The creative concept of the _____ campaign, and the very nature of the product itself appeal to the positive emotions of the reader/consumer. Therefore, it is imperative that all editorial adjacencies reflect that same Positive tone. The editorial must not be negative in content or lend itself contrary to the product imagery/message (*e.g. editorial relating to illness, disillusionment, large size fashion*, etc.)." (Italics mine.)

- The De Beers diamond company a big seller of engagement rings, prohibits magazines from placing its ads with "adjacencies to hard news or anti/love-romance themed editorial."

- Procter & Gamble, one of this country's most powerful and diversified advertisers, stands out in the memory of Anne Summers and Sandra Yates (no mean feat in this context): its products were not to be placed in *any* issue that included *any* material on gun control, abortion, the occult, cults, or the disparagement of religion. Caution was also demanded in any issue covering sex or drugs, even for educational purposes.

Those are the most obvious chains around women's magazines. There are also rules so clear they needn't be written down: for instance, an overall "look" compatible with beauty and fashion ads. Even "real" nonmodel women photographed for a woman's magazine are usually made up, dressed in credited clothes, and retouched out of all reality. When editors do include articles on less-than-cheerful subjects (for instance, domestic violence), they tend to keep them short and unillustrated. The Point is to be "upbeat." Just as women in the street are asked, "Why don't you smile, honey?" women's magazines acquire an institutional smile.

Within the text itself, praise for advertisers' products has become so ritualized that fields like "beauty writing" have been invented. One of its frequent practitioners explained seriously that "It's a difficult art. How many new adjectives can you find? How much greater can you make a lipstick sound? The FDA restricts what companies can say on labels, but we create illusion. And ad agencies are on the phone all the time pushing you to get their product in. A lot of them keep the business based on how many editorial clippings they produce every month. The worst are products," like Lauder's as the writer confirmed, "with their own name involved. It's all ego."

Often, editorial becomes one giant ad. Last November, for instance, *Lear's* featured an elegant woman executive on the cover. On the contents page, we learned she was wearing Guerlain makeup and Samsara, a new fragrance by Guerlain. Inside were full-page ads for Samsara and Guerlain antiwrinkle cream. In the cover profile, we learned that this executive was responsible for launching Samsara and is Guerlam's director of public relations. When the *Columbia Journalism Review* did one of the few articles to include women's magazines in coverage of the influence of ads, editor Frances Lear was quoted as defending her magazine because "this kind of thing is done all the time."

Often, advertisers also plunge odd-shaped ads into the text, no matter what the cost to the readers. At *Woman's Day*, a magazine originally founded by a supermarket chain, editor in chief Ellen Levine said, "The day the copy had to rag around a chicken leg was not a happy one." 45

Advertisers are also adamant about where in a magazine their ads appear. When Revlon was not placed as the first beauty ad in one Hearst magazine, for instance, Revlon pulled its ads from *all* Hearst magazines. Ruth Whitney editor in chief of *Glamour*, attributes some of these demands to "ad agencies wanting to prove to a client that they've squeezed the last drop of blood out of a magazine." She also is, she says, "sick and tired of hearing that women's magazines are controlled by cigarette ads." Relatively speaking, she's right. To be as censoring as are many advertisers for women's products, tobacco companies would have to demand articles in praise of smoking and expect glamorous photos of beautiful women smoking their brands.

I don't mean to imply that the editors I quote here share my objections to ads: most assume that women's magazines have to be the way they are. But it's also true that only former editors can be completely honest. "Most of the pressure came in the form of direct product mentions," explains Sey Chassler, who was editor in chief of *Redbook* from the sixties to the eighties. "We got threats from the big guys, the Revlons, blackmail threats. They wouldn't run ads unless we credited them."

"But it's not fair to single out the beauty advertisers because these pressures came from everybody. Advertisers want to know two things: What are you going to charge me? What *else* are you going to do for me? It's a holdup. For instance, management felt that fiction took up too much space. They couldn't put any advertising in that. For the last ten years, the number of fiction entries into the National Magazine Awards has declined.

"And pressures are getting worse. More magazines are more bottom-line oriented because they have been taken over by companies with no interest in publishing.

"I also think advertisers do this to women's magazines especially," he concluded, "because of the general disrespect they have for women." 50

Even media experts who don't give a damn about women's magazines are alarmed by the spread of this ad-edit linkage. In a climate the *Wall Street Journal* describes as an unacknowledged Depression for media, women's products are increasingly able to take their low standards wherever they go. For instance: newsweeklies publish uncritical stories on fashion and fitness. The *New York Times Magazine* recently ran an article on "firming creams," complete with mentions of advertisers. *Vanity Fair* published a profile of one major advertiser, Ralph Lauren, illustrated by the same photographer who does his ads, and turned the lifestyle of another, Calvin Klein, into a cover story Even the outrageous *Spy* has toned down since it began to go after fashion ads.

And just to make us really worry films and books, the last media that go directly to the public without having to attract ads first, are in danger, too. Producers are beginning to depend on payments for displaying products in movies, and books are now being commissioned by companies like Federal Express.

But the truth is that women's products — like women's magazines — have never been the subjects of much serious reporting anyway. News and general interest publications, including the "style" or "living" sections of newspapers, write about food and clothing as cooking and fashion, and almost never evaluate such products by brand name. Though chemical additives, pesticides, and animal fats are major health risks in the United States, and clothes, shoddy or not, absorb more consumer dollars than cars, this lack of information is serious. So is ignoring the contents of beauty products that are absorbed into our bodies through our skins, and that have profit margins so big they would make a loan shark blush.

## III.

What could women's magazines be like if they were as free as books? as realistic as newspapers? as creative as films? as diverse as women's lives? We don't know.

But we'll only find out if we take women's magazines seriously. 55 If readers were to act in a concerted way to change traditional practices of *all* women's magazines and the marketing of *all* women's products, we could do it. After all, they are operating on our consumer dollars; money that we now control. You and I could:

- write to editors and publishers (with copies to advertisers) that we're willing to pay *more* for magazines with editorial independence, but will *not* continue to pay for those that are just editorial extensions of ads;

- write to advertisers (with copies to editors and publishers) that we want fiction, political reporting, consumer reporting — whatever is, or is not, supported by their ads;

- put as much energy into breaking advertising's control over content as into changing the images in ads, or protesting ads for harmful products like cigarettes;

- support only those women's magazines and products that take us seriously as readers and consumers.

Those of us in the magazine world can also use the carrot-and-stick technique. For instance: pointing out that, if magazines were a regulated medium like television, the demands of advertisers would be against FCC rules. Payola and extortion could be punished. As it is, there are probably illegalities. A magazine's postal rates are determined by the ratio of ad to edit pages, and the former costs more than the latter. So much for the stick.

The carrot means appealing to enlightened self-interest. For instance: there are many studies showing that the greatest factor in determining an ad's effectiveness is the credibility of its surroundings. "The higher the rating of editorial believability" concluded a 1987 survey by the *Journal of Advertising Research*, "the higher the rating of the advertising." Thus, an impenetrable wall between edit and ads would also be in the best interest of advertisers.

Unfortunately, few agencies or clients hear such arguments. Editors often maintain the false purity of refusing to talk to them at all. Instead, they see ad salespeople who know little about editorial, are trained in business as usual, and are usually paid by commission. Editors might also band together to take on controversy. That happened once when all the major women's magazines did articles in the same month on the Equal Rights Amendment. It could happen again.

It's almost three years away from life between the grindstones of advertising pressures and readers' needs. I'm just beginning to realize how edges got smoothed down—in spite of all our resistance.

I remember feeling put upon when I changed "Porsche" to "car" in a piece about Nazi imagery in German pornography by Andrea Dworkin—feeling sure Andrea would understand that Volkswagen, the distributor of Porsche and one of our few supportive advertisers, asked only to be far away from Nazi subjects. It's taken me all this time to realize that Andrea was the one with a right to feel put upon. 60

Even as I write this, I get a call from a writer for *Elle*, who is doing a whole article on where women part their hair. Why, she wants to know, do I part mine in the middle?

It's all so familiar. A writer trying to make something of a nothing assignment; an editor laboring to think of new ways to attract ads; readers assuming that other women must want this ridiculous stuff; more women suffering for lack of information, insight, creativity, and laughter that could be on these same pages.

I ask you: Can't we do better than this?

## For Discussion and Writing

1. According to Steinem, what makes women's magazines different from other magazines?

2. "Sex, Lies, and Advertising" is full of strong examples, often images that capture exactly the idea that Steinem is trying to convey. Comb through the essay, make a list of ten examples that you find striking, and explain how each example works and why each is effective.

3. **connections**   Think about this essay in relation to David Sedaris's "I Like Guys" (p. 334). What are the similarities and differences between the attitudes about gender and sexuality examined in these two essays? Identify and compare the assumptions held by much of society in each — about women and gay men — and explain how they appear in the behavior of the people who hold these assumptions. Finally, explore the ways each author addresses these assumptions — head-on or indirectly, through scene or exposition, dispassionately or with great feeling — and compare their approaches. Is one approach more effective for you?

4. One of the ideas that Steinem depends on and promotes here is that advertising is a culturally significant practice — that it not only reflects what is going on in a culture but shapes it. What advertisements have you seen — in print, on TV, online — that you think are significant? Pick one advertisement and analyze it. How is it significant? What is it selling, and how? What assumptions about the world, our time, human nature, does it rely upon? What does it tell you about American culture?

5. **looking further**   Some people use the power of the boycott to attempt to shape the behavior of large corporations. For example, there are groups that have organized boycotts of companies who buy advertising on media outlets of which the groups do not approve. Do some research on this practice of employing the power of the wallet for political purposes and answer some basic questions: How widespread is this practice? What are some examples of it? Is it effective? Then reflect on this mode of protest: how do you feel about it as a use of the market and consumer power? Do you approve or disapprove? Would you do it? Why or why not?

JONATHAN SWIFT

# A Modest Proposal

*Born in 1667 in Ireland and raised there by English parents, Jonathan Swift was dean of St. Patrick's Cathedral in Dublin and a prolific poet, satirist, and pamphleteer. While he is best known today for his satiric novel* Gulliver's Travels *(1726) and for "A Modest Proposal," his political pamphlets and essays on behalf of Irish causes had great impact and are themselves masterpieces of political irony. Swift's work is thought by some to reveal a misanthropic, skeptical, and hopeless heart, but there always exists in his writing the possibility of alternatives, the hope for improvement. In "A Modest Proposal," Swift writes, "Therefore I repeat, let no man talk to me of these and the like expedients, till he has at least some glimpse of hope that there will be ever some hearty and sincere attempt to put them in practice" (par. 30). As you read this essay and try to tease out Swift's messages, keep this idea in mind.*

*In 1729, when "A Modest Proposal" was published, years of drought had been exacerbated by a crop failure that caused thousands of Irish to starve to death, and this suffering was essentially ignored by English landowners. "A Modest Proposal" is Swift's response to this tragedy.*

It is a melancholy object to those who walk through this great town or travel in the country, when they see the streets, the roads, and cabin doors, crowded with beggars of the female sex, followed by three, four, or six children, all in rags and importuning every passenger for an alms. These mothers instead of being able to work for their honest livelihood, are forced to employ all their time in strolling to beg sustenance for their helpless infants: who as they grow up either turn thieves for want of work, or leave their dear native country to fight for the pretender in Spain, or sell themselves to the Barbadoes.

I think it is agreed by all parties that this prodigious number of children in the arms, or on the backs, or at the heels of their mothers, and frequently of their fathers, is in the present deplorable state of the kingdom a very great additional grievance; and, therefore, whoever could find out a fair, cheap, and easy method of making these children sound, useful members of the commonwealth, would deserve so well of the public as to have his statue set up for a preserver of the nation.

But my intention is very far from being confined to provide only for the children of professed beggars; it is of a much greater extent, and shall take in the whole number of infants at a certain age who are born of parents in effect as little able to support them as those who demand our charity in the streets.

As to my own part, having turned my thoughts for many years upon this important subject, and maturely weighed the several schemes of our projectors, I have always found them grossly mistaken in their computation. It is true, a child just dropped from its dam may be supported by her milk for a solar year, with little other nourishment; at most not above the value of 2s., which the mother may certainly get, or the value in scraps, by her lawful occupation of begging; and it is exactly at one year old that I propose to provide for them in such a manner as instead of being a charge upon their parents or the parish, or wanting food and raiment for the rest of their lives, they shall on the contrary contribute to the feeding, and partly to the clothing, of many thousands.

There is likewise another great advantage in my scheme, that it will prevent those voluntary abortions, and that horrid practice of women murdering their bastard children, alas! too frequent among us! sacrificing the poor innocent babes I doubt more to avoid the expense than the shame, which would move tears and pity in the most savage and inhuman breast.

The number of souls in this kingdom being usually reckoned one million and a half, of these I calculate there may be about 200,000 couples whose wives are breeders; from which number I subtract 30,000 couples who are able to maintain their own children (although I apprehend there cannot be so many, under the present distress of the kingdom); but this being granted, there will remain 170,000 breeders. I again subtract 50,000 for those women who miscarry, or whose children die by accident or disease within the year. There only remain 120,000 children of poor parents annually born. The question therefore is, how this number shall be reared and provided for? which, as I have already said, under the present situation of affairs, is utterly impossible by all the methods hitherto proposed. For we can neither employ them in handicraft of agriculture; we neither build houses (I mean in the country) nor cultivate land; they can very seldom pick up a livelihood by stealing, till they arrive at six years old, except where they are of towardly parts, although I confess they learn the rudiments much earlier; during which time they can, however, be properly looked upon only as probationers; as I have been informed by a principal gentleman in the county of Cavan, who protested to me that he never knew above one or two instances under the age of six, even in a part of the kingdom so renowned for the quickest proficiency in that art.

I am assured by our merchants, that a boy or a girl before twelve years old is no salable commodity; and even when they come to this age they will not yield above 3£. or 3£. 2s. 6d. at most on the exchange; which cannot turn to account either to the parents or kingdom, the charge of nutriment and rags having been at least four times that value.

I shall now therefore humbly propose my own thoughts, which I hope will not be liable to the least objection.

I have been assured by a very knowing American of my acquaintance in London, that a young healthy child well nursed is at a year old a most delicious, nourishing, and wholesome food, whether stewed, roasted, baked, or broiled; and I make no doubt that it will equally serve in a fricassee or a ragout.

I do therefore humbly offer it to public consideration that of the 120,000 children already computed, 20,000 may be reserved for breed, whereof only one-fourth part to be males; which is more than we allow to sheep, black cattle, or swine; and my reason is, that these children are seldom the fruits of marriage, a circumstance not much regarded by our savages; therefore one male will be sufficient to serve four females. That the remaining 100,000 may, at a year old, be offered in sale to the persons of quality and fortune through the kingdom; always advising the mother to let them suck plentifully in the last month, so as to render them plump and fat for a good table. A child will make two dishes at an entertainment for friends; and when the family dines alone, the fore and hind quarter will make a reasonable dish, and seasoned with a little pepper or salt will be very good boiled on the fourth day, especially in winter.

I have reckoned upon a medium that a child just born will weigh 12 pounds, and in a solar year, if tolerably nursed, will increase to 28 pounds.

I grant this food will be somewhat dear, and therefore very proper for landlords, who, as they have already devoured most of the parents, seem to have the best title to the children.

Infants' flesh will be in season throughout the year, but more plentiful in March, and a little before and after: for we are told by a grave author, an eminent French physician, that fish being a prolific diet, there are more children born in Roman Catholic countries about nine months after Lent than at any other season; therefore, reckoning a year after Lent, the markets will be more glutted than usual, because the number of popish infants is at least three to one in this kingdom: and therefore it will have one other collateral advantage, by lessening the number of papists among us.

I have already computed the charge of nursing a beggar's child (in which list I reckon all cottagers, laborers, and four-fifths of the farmers) to be about 2s. per annum, rags included; and I believe no gentleman would repine to give 10s. for the carcass of a good fat child, which, as I have said, will make four dishes of excellent nutritive meat, when he has only some particular friend or his own family to dine with him. Thus the squire will learn to be a good landlord, and grow popular among the tenants; the mother will have 8s. net profit, and be fit for work till she produces another child.

Those who are more thrifty (as I must confess the times 15 require) may flay the carcass; the skin of which artificially dressed will make admirable gloves for ladies, and summer boots for fine gentlemen.

As to our city of Dublin, shambles may be appointed for this purpose in the most convenient parts of it, and butchers we may be assured will not be wanting: although I rather recommend buying the children alive, and dressing them hot from the knife as we do roasting pigs.

A very worthy person, a true lover of his country, and whose virtues I highly esteem, was lately pleased in discoursing on this matter to offer a refinement upon my scheme. He said that many gentlemen of this kingdom, having of late destroyed their deer, he conceived that the want of venison might be well supplied by the bodies of young lads and maidens, not exceeding fourteen years of age nor under twelve; so great a number of both sexes in every country being now ready to starve for want of work and service;

and these to be disposed of by their parents, if alive, or otherwise by their nearest relations. But with due deference to so excellent a friend and so deserving a patriot, I cannot be altogether in his sentiments; for as to the males, my American acquaintance assured me from frequent experience that their flesh was generally tough and lean, like that of our schoolboys by continual exercise, and their taste disagreeable; and to fatten them would not answer the charge. Then as to the females, it would, I think, with humble submission be a loss to the public, because they soon would become breeders themselves: and besides, it is not improbable that some scrupulous people might be apt to censure such a practice (although indeed very unjustly), as a little bordering upon cruelty; which, I confess, has always been with me the strongest objection against any project, how well soever intended.

But in order to justify my friend, he confessed that this expedient was put into his head by the famous Psalmanazar, a native of the island Formosa, who came from thence to London about twenty years ago: and in conversation told my friend, that in his country when any young person happened to be put to death, the executioner sold the carcass to persons of quality as a prime dainty; and that in his time the body of a plump girl of fifteen, who was crucified for an attempt to poison the emperor, was sold to his imperial majesty's prime minister of state, and other great mandarins of the court, in joints from the gibbet, at 400 crowns. Neither indeed can I deny, that if the same use were made of several plump young girls in this town, who without one single groat to their fortunes cannot stir abroad without a chair, and appear at the playhouse and assemblies in foreign fineries which they never will pay for, the kingdom would not be the worse.

Some persons of a desponding spirit are in great concern about the vast number of poor people, who are aged, diseased, or maimed, and I have been desired to employ my thoughts what course may be taken to ease the nation of so grievous an encumbrance. But I am not in the least pain upon that matter, because it is very well known that they are every day dying and rotting by cold and famine, and filth and vermin, as fast as can be reasonably expected. And as to the young laborers, they are now in as hopeful condition: They cannot get work, and consequently pine away for want of nourishment, to a degree that if at any time they are accidentally hired to common labor, they have not strength to perform it; and thus the country and themselves are happily delivered from the evils to come.

I have too long digressed, and therefore shall return to my sub-    20
ject. I think the advantages by the proposal which I have made are obvious and many, as well as of the highest importance.

For first, as I have already observed, it would greatly lessen the number of papists, with whom we are yearly overrun, being the principal breeders of the nation as well as our most danger-ous enemies; and who stay at home on purpose to deliver the kingdom to the Pretender, hoping to take their advantage by the absence of so many good Protestants, who have chosen rather to leave their country than stay at home and pay tithes against their conscience to an Episcopal curate.

Secondly, The poor tenants will have something valuable of their own, which by law may be made liable to distress and help to pay their landlord's rent, their corn and cattle being already seized, and money a thing unknown.

Thirdly, Whereas the maintenance of 100,000 children from two years old and upward, cannot be computed at less than ten shillings a-piece per annum, the nation's stock will be thereby increased £50,000 per annum, beside the profit of a new dish introduced to the tables of all gentlemen of fortune in the king-dom who have any refinement in taste. And the money will circu-late among ourselves, the goods being entirely of our own growth and manufacture.

Fourthly, The constant breeders beside the gain of 8s. sterling per annum by the sale of their children, will be rid of the charge of maintaining them after the first year.

Fifthly, This food would likewise bring great custom to tav-    25
erns, where the vintners will certainly be so prudent as to procure the best receipts for dressing it to perfection, and con-sequently have their houses frequented by all the fine gentlemen, who justly value themselves upon their knowledge in good eat-ing; and a skilful cook who understands how to oblige his guests, will contrive to make it as expensive as they please.

Sixthly, This would be a great inducement to marriage, which all wise nations have either encouraged by rewards or enforced by laws and penalties. It would increase the care and tender-ness of mothers toward their children, when they were sure of a settlement for life to the poor babes, provided in some sort by the public, to their annual profit instead of expense. We should see an honest emulation among the married women, which of them would bring the fattest child to the market. Men would become as fond of their wives during the time of their pregnancy as they are now of their mares in foal, their cows in calf, their sows when they are ready to farrow; nor offer to beat or kick them (as is too frequent a practice) for fear of a miscarriage.

Many other advantages might be enumerated. For instance, the addition of some thousand carcasses in our exportation of barreled beef, the propagation of swine's flesh, and improvement in the art of making good bacon, so much wanted among us by the great destruction of pigs, too frequent at our table; which are no way comparable in taste or magnificence to a well-grown, fat, yearling child, which roasted whole will make a considerable figure at a lord mayor's feast or any other public entertainment. But this and many others I omit, being studious of brevity.

Supposing that 1,000 families in this city would be constant customers for infants' flesh, besides others who might have it at merry-meetings, particularly at weddings and christenings, I compute that Dublin would take off annually about 20,000 carcasses; and the rest of the kingdom (where probably they will be sold somewhat cheaper) the remaining 80,000.

I can think of no one objection that will possibly be raised against this proposal unless it should be urged that the number of people will be thereby much lessened in the kingdom. This I freely own, and it was indeed one principal design in offering it to the world. I desire the reader will observe, that I calculate my remedy for this one individual kingdom of Ireland and for no other that ever was, is, or I think ever can be upon earth. Therefore let no man talk to me of other expedients: of taxing our absentees at 5s. a pound: of using neither clothes nor household furniture except what is of our own growth and manufacture: of utterly rejecting the materials and instruments that promote foreign luxury: of curing the expensiveness of pride, vanity, idleness, and gaming in our women: of introducing a vein of parsimony, prudence, and temperance: of learning to love our country, in the want of which we differ even from Laplanders and the inhabitants of Topinamboo: of quitting our animosities and factions, nor acting any longer like the Jews, who were murdering one another at the very moment their city was taken: of being a little cautious not to sell our country and conscience for nothing: of teaching landlords to have at least one degree of mercy toward their tenants: lastly, of putting a spirit of honesty, industry, and skill into our shopkeepers; who, if a resolution could now be taken to buy only our native goods, would immediately unite to cheat and exact upon us in the price the measure, and the goodness, nor could ever yet be brought to make one fair proposal of just dealing, though often and earnestly invited to it.

Therefore I repeat, let no man talk to me of these and the like expedients, till he has at least some glimpse of hope that there will be ever some hearty and sincere attempt to put them in practice. 30

But as to myself, having been wearied out for many years with offering vain, idle, visionary thoughts, and at length utterly despairing of success, I fortunately fell upon this proposal; which, as it is wholly new, so it has something solid and real, of no expense and little trouble, full in our own power, and whereby we can incur no danger in disobliging England. For this kind of commodity will not bear exportation, the flesh being of too tender a consistence to admit a long continuance in salt, although perhaps I could name a country which would be glad to eat up our whole nation without it.

After all, I am not so violently bent upon my own opinion as to reject any offer proposed by wise men, which shall be found equally innocent, cheap, easy, and effectual. But before something of that kind shall be advanced in contradiction to my scheme, and offering a better, I desire the author or authors will be pleased maturely to consider two points. First, as things now stand, how they will be able to find food and raiment for 100,000 useless mouths and backs. And secondly, there being a round million of creatures in human figure throughout this kingdom, whose subsistence put into a common stock would leave them in debt 2,000,000£. sterling, adding those who are beggars by profession to the bulk of farmers, cottagers, and laborers, with the wives and children who are beggars in effect; I desire those politicians who dislike my overture, and may perhaps be so bold as to attempt an answer, that they will first ask the parents of these mortals, whether they would not at this day think it a great happiness to have been sold for food at a year old in the manner

I prescribe, and thereby have avoided such a perpetual scene of misfortunes as they have since gone through by the oppression of landlords, the impossibility of paying rent without money or trade, the want of common sustenance, with neither house nor clothes to cover them from the inclemencies of the weather, and the most inevitable prospect of entailing the like or greater miseries upon their breed for ever.

I profess, in the sincerity of my heart, that I have not the least personal interest in endeavoring to promote this necessary work, having no other motive than the public good of my country, by advancing our trade, providing for infants, relieving the poor, and giving some pleasure to the rich. I have no children by which I can propose to get a single penny; the youngest being nine years old, and my wife past childbearing.

### For Discussion and Writing

1. List the ways in which the proposal is presented that make it appear rational.

2. If there exists a "typical" method for making an argument, Swift's method here is not it. What is the real point Swift is arguing, and how does it relate to the apparent point the speaker makes?

3. **connections** Swift's use of a persona — here, the "projector" who makes this proposal — involves the use of irony to make a political point, while Thomas Jefferson's Declaration of Independence (p. 218) is straightforward. Why might these texts' differing strategies be appropriate for their political goals?

4. Write a short response to "A Modest Proposal" focusing on the experience of reading it. How do your responses — to the beginning, to the moment when the proposal is laid out, to the handling of objections — change?

5. **looking further** Read up on conditions in Ireland at the time this essay was written. What different factors contributed to Ireland's dire state? Think about the contemporary world, and perhaps do a little more research on places where poverty and hunger are rampant. Do you see parallels? Are there ways in which Swift's non-ironic suggestions for improving Ireland's situation might be applicable?

AMY TAN

# Mother Tongue

*Amy Tan, born in 1952, was raised in northern California. Formerly a
business writer, Tan is now a novelist. She is best known for her first
book,* The Joy Luck Club *(1989), but has also written* The Kitchen
God's Wife *(1991),* The Bonesetter's Daughter *(2001),* Saving Fish
from Drowning *(2005), and* The Valley of Amazement *(2013). Her
fiction is rooted in her experiences as the child of Chinese immigrants
growing up and living in American culture.*

*In "Mother Tongue," Tan describes the variety of Englishes she uses.
In doing so, she addresses the connections between languages and
cultures, but in her writing she also demonstrates what she says about
herself in the essay: "I am a writer. And by that definition, I am someone who has always loved language" (par. 2). As you read, note the
ways in which this love for language manifests itself.*

I am not a scholar of English or literature. I cannot give you
much more than personal opinions on the English language and
its variations in this country or others.

I am a writer. And by that definition, I am someone who has
always loved language. I am fascinated by language in daily life.
I spend a great deal of my time thinking about the power of language — the way it can evoke an emotion, a visual image, a complex idea, or a simple truth. Language is the tool of my trade.
And I use them all — all the Englishes I grew up with.

Recently, I was made keenly aware of the different Englishes
I do use. I was giving a talk to a large group of people, the same
talk I had already given to half a dozen other groups. The nature
of the talk was about my writing, my life, and my book, *The Joy
Luck Club.* The talk was going along well enough, until I remembered one major difference that made the whole talk sound
wrong. My mother was in the room. And it was perhaps the first
time she had heard me give a lengthy speech, using the kind
of English I have never used with her. I was saying things like

"The intersection of memory upon imagination" and "There is an aspect of my fiction that relates to thus-and-thus"—a speech filled with carefully wrought grammatical phrases, burdened, it suddenly seemed to me, with nominalized forms, past perfect tenses, conditional phrases, all the forms of standard English that I had learned in school and through books, the forms of English I did not use at home with my mother.

Just last week, I was walking down the street with my mother, and I again found myself conscious of the English I was using, the English I do use with her. We were talking about the price of new and used furniture and I heard myself saying this: "Not waste money that way." My husband was with us as well, and he didn't notice any switch in my English. And then I realized why. It's because over the twenty years we've been together I've often used that same kind of English with him, and sometimes he even uses it with me. It has become our language of intimacy, a different sort of English that relates to family talk, the language I grew up with.

So you'll have some idea of what this family talk I heard sounds like, I'll quote what my mother said during a recent conversation which I videotaped and then transcribed. During this conversation, my mother was talking about a political gangster in Shanghai who had the same last name as her family's, Du, and how the gangster in his early years wanted to be adopted by her family, which was rich by comparison. Later, the gangster became more powerful, far richer than my mother's family, and one day showed up at my mother's wedding to pay his respects. Here's what she said in part:

"Du Yusong having business like fruit stand. Like off the street kind. He is Du like Du Zong—but not Tsung-ming Island people. The local people call putong, the river east side, he belong to that side local people. That man want to ask Du Zong father take him in like become own family. Du Zong father wasn't look down on him, but didn't take seriously, until that man big like become a mafia. Now important person, very hard to inviting him. Chinese way, came only to show respect, don't stay for dinner. Respect for making big celebration, he shows up. Mean gives lots of respect. Chinese custom. Chinese social life that way. If too important won't have to stay too long. He come to my wedding. I didn't see, I heard it. I gone to boy's side, they have YMCA dinner. Chinese age I was nineteen."

You should know that my mother's expressive command of English belies how much she actually understands. She reads the *Forbes* report, listens to *Wall Street Week*, converses daily with her stockbroker, reads all of Shirley MacLaine's books with ease—all kinds of things I can't begin to understand. Yet some of my friends tell me they understand 50 percent of what my mother says. Some say they understand 80 to 90 percent. Some say they understand none of it, as if she were speaking pure Chinese. But to me, my mother's English is perfectly clear, perfectly natural. It's my mother tongue. Her language, as I hear it, is vivid, direct, full of observation and imagery. That was the language that helped shape the way I saw things, expressed things, made sense of the world.

Lately, I've been giving more thought to the kind of English my mother speaks. Like others, I have described it to people as "broken" or "fractured" English. But I wince when I say that. It has always bothered me that I can think of no other way to describe it other than "broken," as if it were damaged and needed to be fixed, as if it lacked a certain wholeness and soundness. I've heard other terms used, "limited English," for example. But they seem just as bad, as if everything is limited, including people's perceptions of the limited English speaker.

I know this for a fact, because when I was growing up, my mother's "limited" English limited *my* perception of her. I was ashamed of her English. I believed that her English reflected the quality of what she had to say. That is, because she expressed them imperfectly her thoughts were imperfect. And I had plenty of empirical evidence to support me: the fact that people in department stores, at banks, and at restaurants did not take her seriously, did not give her good service, pretended not to understand her, or even acted as if they did not hear her.

My mother has long realized the limitations of her English as well. When I was fifteen, she used to have me call people on the phone to pretend I was she. In this guise, I was forced to ask for information or even to complain and yell at people who had been rude to her. One time it was a call to her stockbroker in New York. She had cashed out her small portfolio and it just so happened we were going to go to New York the next week, our very first trip outside California. I had to get on the phone and say in an adolescent voice that was not very convincing, "This is Mrs. Tan."

10

And my mother was standing in the back whispering loudly, "Why he don't send me check, already two weeks late. So mad he lie to me, losing me money."

And then I said in perfect English, "Yes, I'm getting rather concerned. You had agreed to send the check two weeks ago, but it hasn't arrived."

Then she began to talk more loudly. "What he want, I come to New York tell him front of his boss, you cheating me?" And I was trying to calm her down, make her be quiet, while telling the stockbroker, "I can't tolerate any more excuses. If I don't receive the check immediately, I am going to have to speak to your manager when I'm in New York next week." And sure enough, the following week there we were in front of this astonished stockbroker, and I was sitting there red-faced and quiet, and my mother, the real Mrs. Tan, was shouting at his boss in her impeccable broken English.

We used a similar routine just five days ago, for a situation that was far less humorous. My mother had gone to the hospital for an appointment, to find out about a benign brain tumor a CAT scan had revealed a month ago. She said she had spoken very good English, her best English, no mistakes. Still, she said, the hospital did not apologize when they said they had lost the CAT scan and she had come for nothing. She said they did not seem to have any sympathy when she told them she was anxious to know the exact diagnosis, since her husband and son had both died of brain tumors. She said they would not give her any more information until the next time and she would have to make another appointment for that. So she said she would not leave until the doctor called her daughter. She wouldn't budge. And when the doctor finally called her daughter, me, who spoke in perfect English—lo and behold—we had assurances the CAT scan would be found, promises that a conference call on Monday would be held, and apologies for any suffering my mother had gone through for a most regrettable mistake.

I think my mother's English almost had an effect on limiting 15 my possibilities in life as well. Sociologists and linguists probably will tell you that a person's developing language skills are more influenced by peers. But I do think that the language spoken in the family, especially in immigrant families which are more insular, plays a large role in shaping the language of the child. And I believe that it affected my results on achievement tests, IQ tests, and the SAT. While my English skills were never judged as poor, compared to math, English could not be considered my strong suit. In grade school I did moderately well, getting perhaps B's, sometimes B-pluses, in English and scoring perhaps in the six-tieth or seventieth percentile on achievement tests. But those scores were not good enough to override the opinion that my true abilities lay in math and science, because in those areas I achieved A's and scored in the ninetieth percentile or higher.

This was understandable. Math is precise; there is only one correct answer. Whereas, for me at least, the answers on English tests were always a judgment call, a matter of opinion and per-sonal experience. Those tests were constructed around items like fill-in-the-blank sentence completion, such as "Even though Tom was _____, Mary thought he was _____." And the correct answer always seemed to be the most bland combinations of thoughts, for example, "Even though Tom was shy, Mary thought he was charming," with the grammatical structure "even though" limiting the correct answer to some sort of semantic opposites, so you wouldn't get answers like, "Even though Tom was foolish, Mary thought he was ridiculous." Well, according to my mother, there were very few limitations as to what Tom could have been and what Mary might have thought of him. So I never did well on tests like that.

The same was true with word analogies, pairs of words in which you were supposed to find some sort of logical, semantic relationship—for example, "*Sunset* is to *nightfall* as _____ is to _____." And here you would be presented with a list of four possible pairs, one of which showed the same kind of relation-ship: *red* is to *stoplight, bus* is to *arrival, chills* is to *fever, yawn* is to *boring*. Well, I could never think that way. I knew what the tests were asking, but I could not block out of my mind the images already created by the first pair, "*sunset* is to *nightfall*" —and I would see a burst of colors against a darkening sky, the moon rising, the lowering of a curtain of stars. And all the other pairs of words—red, bus, stoplight, boring—just threw up a mass of con-fusing images, making it impossible for me to sort out something as logical as saying: "A sunset precedes nightfall" is the same as "a chill precedes a fever." The only way I would have gotten that answer right would have been to imagine an associative situation, for example, my being disobedient and staying out past sunset, catching a chill at night, which turns into feverish pneumonia as punishment, which indeed did happen to me.

I have been thinking about all this lately, about my mother's English, about achievement tests. Because lately I've been asked, as a writer, why there are not more Asian Americans represented in American literature. Why are there few Asian Americans enrolled in creative writing programs? Why do so many Chinese students go into engineering? Well, these are broad sociological questions I can't begin to answer. But I have noticed in surveys—in fact, just last week—that Asian students, as a whole, always do significantly better on math achievement tests than in English. And this makes me think that there are other Asian-American students whose English spoken in the home might also be described as "broken" or "limited." And perhaps they also have teachers who are steering them away from writing and into math and science, which is what happened to me.

Fortunately, I happen to be rebellious in nature and enjoy the challenge of disproving assumptions made about me. I became an English major my first year in college, after being enrolled as pre-med. I started writing nonfiction as a freelancer the week after I was told by my former boss that writing was my worst skill and I should hone my talents toward account management.

But it wasn't until 1985 that I finally began to write fiction.    20
And at first I wrote using what I thought to be wittily crafted sentences, sentences that would finally prove I had mastery over the English language. Here's an example from the first draft of a story that later made its way into *The Joy Luck Club*, but without this line: "That was my mental quandary in its nascent state." A terrible line, which I can barely pronounce.

Fortunately, for reasons I won't get into today, I later decided I should envision a reader for the stories I would write. And the reader I decided upon was my mother, because these were stories about mothers. So with this reader in mind—and in fact she did read my early drafts—I began to write stories using all the Englishes I grew up with: the English I spoke to my mother, which for lack of a better term might be described as "simple"; the English she used with me, which for lack of a better term might be described as "broken"; my translation of her Chinese, which could certainly be described as "watered down"; and what

I imagined to be her translation of her Chinese if she could speak in perfect English, her internal language, and for that I sought to preserve the essence, but neither an English nor a Chinese structure. I wanted to capture what language ability tests can never reveal: her intent, her passion, her imagery, the rhythms of her speech, and the nature of her thoughts.

Apart from what any critic had to say about my writing, I knew I had succeeded where it counted when my mother finished reading my book and gave me her verdict: "So easy to read."

## For Discussion and Writing

1. List the different Englishes Tan describes, defining each.

2. Of her mother's English, Tan writes, "That was the language that helped shape the way I saw things, expressed things, made sense of the world" (par. 7). How was the effect of her mother's English positive, and how was it negative?

3. **connections**    Gloria Anzaldúa, in "How to Tame a Wild Tongue" (p. 30), expresses a complicated set of feelings about her linguistic inheritances and what they mean to her and to the world around her. Compare her feelings to Tan's as expressed in "Mother Tongue." How does each deal with the way the world thinks of their language(s)?

4. Do you use different Englishes yourself? Even if English is your sole language, consider how your use of it changes depending on circumstances and audience. Write an essay in which you describe the different ways you speak and the meaning of these differences.

5. **looking further**    When literary writing — particularly fiction — attempts literal representation of accented or region-, race-, ethnicity-, or class-inflected English speech in dialogue, it is often said to be "doing dialect." At times in U.S. history, this practice has been seen not as an attempt at realism but rather as the product of prejudice, or at least as a means of unintentionally confirming stereotypes about people who don't speak Standard English. Read up on this practice and check out some examples. What do you think about it? Is it possible to make any kind of blanket judgment? Are there some cases where you think this technique is acceptable, and others you think are offensive?

# HENRY DAVID THOREAU

# Civil Disobedience

*Henry David Thoreau was born in 1817 and raised in Concord, Massachusetts, living there for most of his life. Along with Ralph Waldo Emerson, Thoreau was one of the most important thinkers of his time in America and is still widely read today.* Walden *(1854), the work for which he is best known, is drawn from the journal he kept during his two-year-long stay in a cabin on Walden Pond. In* Walden, *Thoreau explores his interests in naturalism, individualism, and self-sufficiency.*

*Thoreau is also remembered for his essay "Civil Disobedience" (1849), an early, influential statement of this tactic of protest later practiced by Mahatma Gandhi and, under the leadership of Martin Luther King Jr., by many in the civil rights movement. As you work your way through this essay, keep an eye out not just for the arguments Thoreau makes in support of his larger point but the well-crafted ways in which he makes them.*

I heartily accept the motto—"That government is best which governs least,"[1] and I should like to see it acted up to more rapidly and systematically. Carried out, it finally amounts to this, which also I believe—"That government is best which governs not at all"; and when men are prepared for it, that will be the kind of government which they will have. Government is at best but an expedient; but most governments are usually, and all governments are sometimes, inexpedient. The objections which have been brought against a standing army, and they are many and weighty, and deserve to prevail, may also at last be brought against a standing government. The standing army is only an arm of the standing government. The government itself, which is only the mode which the people have chosen to execute their will, is equally liable to

1. **governs least:** Possibly a reference to "The best government is that which governs least," the motto of the *United States Magazine and Democratic Review* (1837–1859), or "the less government we have, the better," from Ralph Waldo Emerson's "Politics" (1844). [Ed.]

be abused and perverted before the people can act through it. Witness the present Mexican war,[2] the work of comparatively a few individuals using the standing government as their tool; for in the outset the people would not have consented to this measure.

This American government—what is it but a tradition, a recent one, endeavoring to transmit itself unimpaired to posterity but each instant losing some of its integrity? It has not the vitality and force of a single living man; for a single man can bend it to his will. It is a sort of wooden gun to the people themselves. But it is not the less necessary for this; for the people must have some complicated machinery or other, and hear its din, to satisfy that idea of government which they have. Governments show thus how successfully men can be imposed on, even impose on themselves, for their own advantage. It is excellent, we must all allow. Yet this government never of itself furthered any enterprise but by the alacrity with which it got out of its way. *It* does not keep the country free. *It* does not settle the West. *It* does not educate. The character inherent in the American people has done all that has been accomplished; and it would have done somewhat more if the government had not sometimes got in its way. For government is an expedient by which men would fain succeed in letting one another alone; and, as has been said, when it is most expedient the governed are most let alone by it. Trade and commerce, if they were not made of India-rubber, would never manage to bounce over the obstacles which legislators are continually putting in their way; and, if one were to judge these men wholly by the effects of their actions and not partly by their intentions, they would deserve to be classed and punished with those mischievous persons who put obstructions on the railroads.

But to speak practically and as a citizen, unlike those who call themselves no-government men,[3] I ask for, not at once no government, but *at once* a better government. Let every man make known what kind of government would command his respect, and that will be one step toward obtaining it.

After all, the practical reason why, when the power is once in the hands of the people, a majority are permitted, and for a long

---

2. **the present Mexican war:** Abolitionists considered the U.S.–Mexican War (1846–1848) an effort to extend slavery into former Mexican territory. [Ed.]
3. **no-government men:** Anarchists. [Ed.]

period continue, to rule is not because they are most likely to be in the right, nor because this seems fairest to the minority but because they are physically the strongest. But a government in which the majority rule in all cases cannot be based on justice, even as far as men understand it. Can there not be a government in which majorities do not virtually decide right and wrong but conscience?—in which majorities decide only those questions to which the rule of expediency is applicable? Must the citizen ever for a moment, or in the least degree, resign his conscience to the legislator? Why has every man a conscience then? I think that we should be men first and subjects afterward. It is not desirable to cultivate a respect for the law, so much as for the right. The only obligation which I have a right to assume is to do at any time what I think right. It is truly enough said that a corporation has no conscience; but a corporation of conscientious men is a corporation *with* a conscience. Law never made men a whit more just; and, by means of their respect for it, even the well-disposed are daily made the agents of injustice. A common and natural result of an undue respect for law is that you may see a file of soldiers, colonel, captain, corporal, privates, powder-monkeys,[4] and all, marching in admirable order over hill and dale to the wars, against their wills, ay, against their common sense and consciences, which makes it very steep marching indeed and produces a palpitation of the heart. They have no doubt that it is a damnable business in which they are concerned; they are all peaceably inclined. Now, what are they? Men at all? or small movable forts and magazines at the service of some unscrupulous man in power? Visit the Navy-Yard, and behold a marine, such a man as an American government can make, or such as it can make a man with its black arts—a mere shadow and reminiscence of humanity, a man laid out alive and standing, and already, as one may say, buried under arms with funeral accompaniments, though it may be —

> Not a drum was heard, not a funeral note,
> As his corse to the rampart we hurried;
> Not a soldier discharged his farewell shot
> O'er the grave where our hero we buried.[5]

4. **powder monkeys:** The boys who carried gunpowder for soldiers. [Ed.]

5. From "The Burial of Sir John Moore at Corunna" by Charles Wolfe (1791–1823). [Ed.]

The mass of men serve the state thus, not as men mainly, but as machines, with their bodies. They are the standing army, and the militia, jailers, constables, posse comitatus,[6] &c. In most cases there is no free exercise whatever of the judgment or of the moral sense; but they put themselves on a level with wood and earth and stones; and wooden men can perhaps be manufactured that will serve the purpose as well. Such command no more respect than men of straw or a lump of dirt. They have the same sort of worth only as horses and dogs. Yet such as these even are commonly esteemed good citizens. Others—as most legislators, politicians, lawyers, ministers, and office-holders—serve the state chiefly with their heads; and, as they rarely make any moral distinctions, they are as likely to serve the Devil, without *intending* it, as God. A very few, as heroes, patriots, martyrs, reformers in the great sense, and *men*, serve the state with their consciences also and so necessarily resist it for the most part; and they are commonly treated as enemies by it. A wise man will only be useful as a man and will not submit to be "clay" and "stop a hole to keep the wind away,"[7] but leave that office to his dust at least:

> I am too high-born to be propertied,
> To be a secondary at control,
> Or useful serving-man and instrument
> To any sovereign state throughout the world.[8]

He who gives himself entirely to his fellow-men appears to them useless and selfish; but he who gives himself partially to them is pronounced a benefactor and philanthropist.

How does it become a man to behave toward this American government today? I answer, that he cannot without disgrace be associated with it. I cannot for an instant recognize that political organization as *my* government which is the *slave's* government also.

All men recognize the right of revolution; that is, the right to refuse allegiance to, and to resist the government when its tyranny or its inefficiency are great and unendurable. But almost all say that such is not the case now. But such was the case, they think, in the Revolution of '75. If one were to tell me that this was a bad

---

6. **posse comitatus:** Literally, "the power of the county"; a sheriff's posse. [Ed.]

7. From Hamlet, V.i.226–227. [Ed.]

8. From King John, V.ii.79–82. [Ed.]

government because it taxed certain foreign commodities brought to its ports, it is most probable that I should not make an ado about it, for I can do without them. All machines have their friction; and possibly this does enough good to counterbalance the evil. At any rate, it is a great evil to make a stir about it. But when the friction comes to have its machine, and oppression and robbery are organized, I say let us not have such a machine any longer. In other words, when a sixth of the population of a nation which has undertaken to be the refuge of liberty are slaves, and a whole country is unjustly overrun and conquered by a foreign army and subjected to military law, I think that it is not too soon for honest men to rebel and revolutionize. What makes this duty the more urgent is the fact that the country so overrun is not our own, but ours is the invading army.

Paley,[9] a common authority with many on moral questions, in his chapter on the "Duty of Submission to Civil Government," resolves all civil obligation into expediency; and he proceeds to say, "that so long as the interest of the whole society requires it, that is, so long as the established government cannot be resisted or charged without public inconveniency, it is the will of God that the established government be obeyed, and no longer. . . . This principle being admitted, the justice of every particular case of resistance is reduced to a computation of the quantity of the danger and grievance on the one side, and of the probability and expense of redressing it on the other." Of this, he says, every man shall judge for himself. But Paley appears never to have contemplated those cases to which the rule of expediency does not apply, in which a people, as well as an individual, must do justice, cost what it may. If I have unjustly wrested a plank from a drowning man, I must restore it to him though I drown myself. This, according to Paley, would be inconvenient. But he that would save his life, in such a case, shall lose it. This people must cease to hold slaves and to make war on Mexico, though it cost them their existence as a people.

In their practice, nations agree with Paley; but does anyone think    10
that Massachusetts does exactly what is right at the present crisis?

> A drab of state, a cloth-o'-silver slut,
> To have her train borne up, and her soul trail in the dirt.[10]

9. **Paley:** William Paley (1743–1805), an English theologian and philosopher. [Ed.]

10. From Cyril Tourneur's *The Revenger's Tragedy* (1607). [Ed.]

Practically speaking, the opponents to a reform in Massachusetts are not a hundred thousand politicians at the South but a hundred thousand merchants and farmers here, who are more interested in commerce and agriculture than they are in humanity, and are not prepared to do justice to the slave and to Mexico, cost what it may. I quarrel not with far-off foes but with those who, near at home, co-operate with, and do the bidding of, those far away, and without whom the latter would be harmless. We are accustomed to say that the mass of men are unprepared; but improvement is slow because the few are not materially wiser or better than the many. It is not so important that many should be as good as you as that there be some absolute goodness somewhere; for that will leaven the whole lump. There are thousands who are in opinion opposed to slavery and to the war who yet in effect do nothing to put an end to them; who, esteeming themselves children of Washington and Franklin, sit down with their hands in their pockets and say that they know not what to do, and do nothing; who even postpone the question of freedom to the question of free trade, and quietly read the prices-current along with the latest advices from Mexico after dinner and, it may be, fall asleep over them both. What is the price-current of an honest man and patriot today? They hesitate and they regret and sometimes they petition; but they do nothing in earnest and with effect. They will wait, well-disposed, for others to remedy the evil, that they may no longer have it to regret. At most, they give only a cheap vote, and a feeble countenance and God-speed, to the right, as it goes by them. There are nine hundred and ninety-nine patrons of virtue to one virtuous man. But it is easier to deal with the real possessor of a thing than with the temporary guardian of it.

All voting is a sort of gaming, like checkers or backgammon, with a slight moral tinge to it, a playing with right and wrong, with moral questions; and betting naturally accompanies it. The character of the voters is not staked. I cast my vote, perchance, as I think right; but I am not vitally concerned that that right should prevail. I am willing to leave it to the majority. Its obligation, therefore, never exceeds that of expediency. Even voting *for the right* is *doing* nothing for it. It is only expressing to men feebly your desire that it should prevail. A wise man will not leave the right to the mercy of chance, nor wish it to prevail through the power of the majority. There is but little virtue in the action of masses of men. When the majority shall at length vote for the abolition of slavery, it will be because they are indifferent to slavery, or because there is but little slavery left to be abolished by their vote. *They* will then be the only slaves. Only *his* vote can hasten the abolition of slavery who asserts his own freedom by his vote.

I hear of a convention to be held at Baltimore, or elsewhere, for the selection of a candidate for the Presidency, made up chiefly of editors, and men who are politicians by profession; but I think, what is it to any independent, intelligent, and respectable man what decision they may come to? Shall we not have the advantage of his wisdom and honesty nevertheless? Can we not count upon some independent votes? Are there not many individuals in the country who do not attend conventions? But no: I find that the responsible man, so called, has immediately drifted from his position, and despairs of his country when his country has more reason to despair of him. He forthwith adopts one of the candidates thus selected as the only *available* one, thus proving that he is himself *available* for any purposes of the demagogue. His vote is of no more worth than that of any unprincipled foreigner or hireling native who may have been bought. O for a man who is a *man* and, as my neighbor says has a bone in his back which you cannot pass your hand through! Our statistics are at fault: the population has been returned too large. How many *men* are there to a square thousand miles in this country? Hardly one. Does not America offer any inducement for men to settle here? The American has dwindled into an Odd Fellow[11] — one who may be known by the development of his organ of gregariousness and a manifest lack of intellect and cheerful self-reliance; whose first and chief concern, on coming into the world, is to see that the Almshouses are in good repair; and, before yet he has lawfully donned the virile garb, to collect a fund for the support of the widows and orphans that may be; who, in short, ventures to live only by the aid of the Mutual Insurance Company, which has promised to bury him decently.

It is not a man's duty, as a matter of course, to devote himself to the eradication of any, even the most enormous wrong; he

---

11. **Odd Fellow:** A member of the Independent Order of Odd Fellows, a fraternal organization originating in England in the mid-1700s. [Ed.]

may still properly have other concerns to engage him; but it is his duty, at least, to wash his hands of it and, if he gives it no thought longer, not to give it practically his support. If I devote myself to other pursuits and contemplations, I must first see, at least, that I do not pursue them sitting upon another man's shoulders. I must get off him first, that he may pursue his contemplations too. See what gross inconsistency is tolerated. I have heard some of my townsmen say, "I should like to have them order me out to help put down an insurrection of the slaves, or to march to Mexico—see if I would go"; and yet these very men have each directly by their allegiance and so indirectly, at least, by their money, furnished a substitute. The soldier is applauded who refuses to serve in an unjust war by those who do not refuse to sustain the unjust government which makes the war; is applauded by those whose own act and authority he disregards and sets at naught; as if the State were penitent to that degree that it hired one to scourge it while it sinned, but not to that degree that it left off sinning for a moment. Thus, under the name of Order and Civil Government, we are all made at last to pay homage to and support our own meanness. After the first blush of sin comes its indifference; and from immoral it becomes, as it were, *un*moral, and not quite unnecessary to that life which we have made.

The broadest and most prevalent error requires the most disinterested virtue to sustain it. The slight reproach to which the virtue of patriotism is commonly liable, the noble are most likely to incur. Those who, while they disapprove of the character and measures of a government, yield to it their allegiance and support, are undoubtedly its most conscientious supporters, and so frequently the most serious obstacles to reform. Some are petitioning the State to dissolve the Union, to disregard the requisitions of the President. Why do they not dissolve it themselves—the union between themselves and the State—and refuse to pay their quota into its treasury? Do not they stand in the same relation to the State that the State does to the Union? And have not the same reasons prevented the State from resisting the Union which have prevented them from resisting the State?

How can a man be satisfied to entertain an opinion merely, and enjoy *it*? Is there any enjoyment in it if his opinion is that he is aggrieved? If you are cheated out of a single dollar by your neighbor, you do not rest satisfied with knowing that you are 15

cheated, or with saying that you are cheated, or even with petitioning him to pay you your due; but you take effectual steps
at once to obtain the full amount and see that you are never
cheated again. Action from principle, the perception and the performance of right, changes things and relations; it is essentially
revolutionary and does not consist wholly with anything which
was. It not only divides states and churches, it divides families;
ay, it divides the *individual*, separating the diabolical in him from
the divine.

Unjust laws exist: shall we be content to obey them, or shall
we endeavor to amend them and obey them until we have succeeded, or shall we transgress them at once? Men generally,
under such a government as this, think that they ought to wait
until they have persuaded the majority to alter them. They think
that if they should resist the remedy would be worse than the evil.
*It* makes it worse. Why is it not more apt to anticipate and provide for reform? Why does it not cherish its wise minority? Why
does it cry and resist before it is hurt? Why does it not encourage
its citizens to be on the alert to point out its faults and *do* better
than it would have them? Why does it always crucify Christ and
excommunicate Copernicus and Luther[12] and pronounce Washington and Franklin rebels?

One would think that a deliberate and practical denial of its
authority was the only offense never contemplated by government; else why has it not assigned its definite, its suitable and
proportionate penalty? If a man who has no property refuses but
once to earn nine shillings for the State, he is put in prison for
a period unlimited by any law that I know, and determined only
by the discretion of those who placed him there; but if he should
steal ninety times nine shillings from the State, he is soon permitted to go at large again.

If the injustice is part of the necessary friction of the machine
of government, let it go, let it go: perchance it will wear
smooth — certainly the machine will wear out. If the injustice
has a spring or a pulley or a rope or a crank exclusively for itself,
then perhaps you may consider whether the remedy will not be

---

12. **Copernicus and Luther:** Nicolaus Copernicus (1473–1543) was the Polish
founder of modern astronomy; Martin Luther (1483–1546) was a German monk
who was integral to the Protestant Reformation. [Ed.]

worse than the evil; but if it is of such a nature that it requires you to be the agent of injustice to another, then I say break the law. Let your life be a counter friction to stop the machine. What I have to do is to see, at any rate, that I do not lend myself to the wrong which I condemn.

As for adopting the ways which the State has provided for remedying the evil, I know not of such ways. They take too much time, and a man's life will be gone. I have other affairs to attend to. I came into this world, not chiefly to make this a good place to live in, but to live in it, be it good or bad. A man has not everything to do, but something; and because he cannot do *everything*, it is not necessary that he should do *something* wrong. It is not my business to be petitioning the Governor or the Legislature any more than it is theirs to petition me; and if they should not hear my petition what should I do then? But in this case the State has provided no way: its very Constitution is the evil. This may seem to be harsh and stubborn and unconciliatory; but it is to treat with the utmost kindness and consideration the only spirit that can appreciate or deserves it. So is all change for the better, like birth and death, which convulse the body.

I do not hesitate to say that those who call themselves Abolitionists should at once effectually withdraw their support, both in person and property, from the government of Massachusetts, and not wait till they constitute a majority of one before they suffer the right to prevail through them. I think that it is enough if they have God on their side, without waiting for that other one. Moreover, any man more right than his neighbors constitutes a majority of one already. 20

I meet this American government or its representative, the State government, directly and face to face once a year — no more — in the person of its tax-gatherer; this is the only mode in which a man situated as I am necessarily meets it; and it then says distinctly, Recognize me; and the simplest, the most effectual and, in the present posture of affairs, the indispensablest mode of treating with it on this head, of expressing your little satisfaction with and love for it, is to deny it then. My civil neighbor, the tax-gatherer, is the very man I have to deal with — for it is, after all, with men and not with parchment that I quarrel — and he has voluntarily chosen to be an agent of the government. How shall he ever know well what he is and does as an officer of the government, or as a man, until he is obliged to consider whether he shall treat me, his neighbor, for whom he has respect, as a neighbor and well-disposed man, or as a maniac and disturber of the peace, and see if he can get over this obstruction to his neighborliness without a ruder and more impetuous thought or speech corresponding with his action. I know this well, that if one thousand, if one hundred, if ten men whom I could name—if ten *honest* men only—ay, if *one* HONEST man in this State of Massachusetts, *ceasing to hold slaves*, were actually to withdraw from this copartnership and be locked up in the county jail therefore, it would be the abolition of slavery in America. For it matters not how small the beginning may seem to be: what is once well done is done forever. But we love better to talk about it: that we say is our mission. Reform keeps many scores of newspapers in its service but not one man. If my esteemed neighbor,[13] the State's ambassador, who will devote his days to the settlement of the question of human rights in the Council Chamber, instead of being threatened with the prisons of Carolina, were to sit down the prisoner of Massachusetts, that State which is so anxious to foist the sin of slavery upon her sister—though at present she can discover only an act of inhospitality to be the ground of a quarrel with her—the Legislature would not wholly waive the subject the following winter.

Under a government which imprisons any unjustly, the true place for a just man is also a prison. The proper place today, the only place which Massachusetts has provided for her freer and less desponding spirits is in her prisons, to be put out and locked out of the State by her own act, as they have already put themselves out by their principles. It is there that the fugitive slave and the Mexican prisoner on parole and the Indian come to plead the wrongs of his race should find them; on that separate but more free and honorable ground where the State places those who are not *with* her but *against* her—the only house in a slave State in which a free man can abide with honor. If any think that their influence would be lost there, and their voices

---

13. **esteemed neighbor:** Thoreau is referring to Samuel Hoar, a Massachusetts congressman who was sent to South Carolina to protest the seizure and enslavement of black sailors. He was threatened and forced out of the state without securing the justice he sought. [Ed.]

no longer afflict the ear of the State, that they would not be as an enemy within its walls, they do not know by how much truth is stronger than error, nor how much more eloquently and effectively he can combat injustice who has experienced a little in his own person. Cast your whole vote, not a strip of paper merely, but your whole influence. A minority is powerless while it conforms to the majority; it is not even a minority then; but it is irresistible when it clogs by its whole weight. If the alternative is to keep all just men in prison or give up war and slavery, the State will not hesitate which to choose. If a thousand men were not to pay their tax-bills this year, that would not be a violent bloody measure, as it would be to pay them, and enable the State to commit violence and shed innocent blood. This is, in fact, the definition of a peaceable revolution, if any such is possible. If the tax-gatherer or any other public officer asks me, as one has done, "But what shall I do?" my answer is, "If you really wish to do anything, resign your office." When the subject has refused allegiance and the officer has resigned his office, then the revolution is accomplished. But even suppose blood should flow. Is there not a sort of blood shed when the conscience is wounded? Through this wound a man's real manhood and immortality flow out, and he bleeds to an everlasting death. I see this blood flowing now.

I have contemplated the imprisonment of the offender rather than the seizure of his goods—though both will serve the same purpose—because they who assert the purest right, and consequently are most dangerous to a corrupt State, commonly have not spent much time in accumulating property. To such the State renders comparatively small service, and a slight tax is wont to appear exorbitant, particularly if they are obliged to earn it by special labor with their hands. If there were one who lived wholly without the use of money, the State itself would hesitate to demand it of him. But the rich man—not to make any invidious comparison—is always sold to the institution which makes him rich. Absolutely speaking, the more money, the less virtue; for money comes between a man and his objects and obtains them for him; and it was certainly no great virtue to obtain it. It puts to rest many questions which he would otherwise be taxed to answer; while the only new question which it puts is the hard but superfluous one, how to spend it. Thus his moral ground is taken from under his feet. The opportunities of living are diminished in proportion as what are called the "means" are increased. The best thing a man can do for his culture when he is rich is to endeavor to carry out those schemes which he entertained when he was poor. Christ answered the Herodians according to their condition. "Show me the tribute-money," said he—and one took a penny out of his pocket—if you use money which has the image of Caesar on it, and which he has made current and valuable, that is, if *you are men of the State* and gladly enjoy the advantages of Caesar's government, then pay him back some of his own when he demands it; "Render therefore to Caesar that which is Caesar's, and to God those things which are God's"[14]—leaving them no wiser than before as to which was which; for they did not wish to know.

When I converse with the freest of my neighbors, I perceive that whatever they may say about the magnitude and seriousness of the question, and their regard for the public tranquillity, the long and the short of the matter is that they cannot spare the protection of the existing government, and they dread the consequences to their property and families of disobedience to it. For my own part, I should not like to think that I ever rely on the protection of the State. But if I deny the authority of the State when it presents its tax-bill, it will soon take and waste all my property and so harass me and my children without end. This is hard. This makes it impossible for a man to live honestly, and at the same time comfortably, in outward respects. It will not be worth the while to accumulate property; that would be sure to go again. You must hire or squat somewhere and raise but a small crop and eat that soon. You must live within yourself and depend upon yourself always tucked up and ready for a start, and not have many affairs. A man may grow rich in Turkey even, if he will be in all respects a good subject of the Turkish government. Confucius said: "If a state is governed by the principles of reason, poverty and misery are subjects of shame; if a state is not governed by the principles of reason, riches and honors are the subjects of shame." No; until I want the protection of Massachusetts to be extended to me in some distant Southern port, where my liberty is endangered, or until I am bent solely on building up an

---

14. **"Render therefore . . . which are God's":** Matthew 22:19–22. [Ed.]

estate at home by peaceful enterprise, I can afford to refuse allegiance to Massachusetts and her right to my property and life. It costs me less in every sense to incur the penalty of disobedience to the State than it would to obey. I should feel as if I were worth less in that case.

Some years ago the State met me in behalf of the Church and commanded me to pay a certain sum toward the support of a clergyman whose preaching my father attended, but never I myself. "Pay," it said, "or be locked up in the jail." I declined to pay. But, unfortunately, another man saw fit to pay it. I did not see why the schoolmaster should be taxed to support the priest, and not the priest the schoolmaster; for I was not the State's schoolmaster, but I supported myself by voluntary subscription. I did not see why the lyceum[15] should not present its tax-bill and have the State to back its demand, as well as the Church. However, at the request of the selectmen, I condescended to make some such statement as this in writing:— "Know all men by these presents, that I, Henry Thoreau, do not wish to be regarded as a member of any incorporated society which I have not joined." This I gave to the town clerk; and he has it. The State, having thus learned that I did not wish to be regarded as a member of that church, has never made a like demand on me since; though it said that it must adhere to its original presumption that time. If I had known how to name them, I should then have signed off in detail from all the societies which I never signed on to; but I did not know where to find a complete list.

I have paid no poll-tax for six years. I was put into a jail once on this account, for one night; and, as I stood considering the walls of solid stone, two or three feet thick, the door of wood and iron, a foot thick, and the iron grating which strained the light, I could not help being struck with the foolishness of that institution which treated me as if I were mere flesh and blood and bones, to be locked up. I wondered that it should have concluded at length that this was the best use it could put me to and had never thought to avail itself of my services in some way. I saw that if there was a wall of stone between me and my townsmen, there was a still more difficult one to climb or break through before they could get to be as free as I was. I did not for

25

---

15. **lyceum:** A hall where public lectures are held. [Ed.]

a moment feel confined, and the walls seemed a great waste of stone and mortar. I felt as if I alone of all my townsmen had paid my tax. They plainly did not know how to treat me but behaved like persons who are underbred. In every threat and in every compliment there was a blunder; for they thought that my chief desire was to stand on the other side of that stone wall. I could not but smile to see how industriously they locked the door on my meditations, which followed them out again without let or hindrance, and *they* were really all that was dangerous. As they could not reach me, they had resolved to punish my body; just as boys, if they cannot come at some person against whom they have a spite, will abuse his dog. I saw that the State was half-witted, that it was timid as a lone woman with her silver spoons, and that it did not know its friends from its foes, and I lost all my remaining respect for it and pitied it.

Thus the State never intentionally confronts a man's sense, intellectual or moral, but only his body, his senses. It is not armed with superior wit or honesty but with superior physical strength. I was not born to be forced. I will breathe after my own fashion. Let us see who is the strongest. What force has a multi-tude? They only can force me who obey a higher law than I. They force me to become like themselves. I do not hear of *men* being *forced* to live this way or that by masses of men. What sort of life were that to live? When I meet a government which says to me, "Your money or your life," why should I be in haste to give it my money? It may be in a great strait and not know what to do: I cannot help that. It must help itself; do as I do. It is not worth the while to snivel about it. I am not responsible for the success-ful working of the machinery of society. I am not the son of the engineer. I perceive that, when an acorn and a chestnut fall side by side, the one does not remain inert to make way for the other, but both obey their own laws and spring and grow and flourish as best they can till one, perchance, overshadows and destroys the other. If a plant cannot live according to its nature, it dies; and so a man.

The night in prison was novel and interesting enough. The prisoners in their shirt-sleeves were enjoying a chat and the evening air in the doorway when I entered. But the jailer said, "Come, boys, it is time to lock up"; and so they dispersed, and I heard the sound of their steps returning into the hollow apartments. My room-mate was introduced to me by the jailer as "a first-rate fellow and a clever man." When the door was locked, he showed me where to hang my hat and how he managed matters there. The rooms were whitewashed once a month; and this one, at least, was the whitest, most simply furnished, and probably the neatest apartment in the town. He naturally wanted to know where I came from and what brought me there; and when I had told him, I asked him in my turn how he came there, presuming him to be an honest man, of course; and, as the world goes, I believe he was. "Why," said he, "they accuse me of burning a barn; but I never did it." As near as I could discover, he had probably gone to bed in a barn when drunk and smoked his pipe there; and so a barn burnt. He had the reputation of being a clever man, had been there some three months waiting for his trial to come on, and would have to wait as much longer; but he was quite domesticated and contented, since he got his board for nothing and thought that he was well treated.

He occupied one window, and I the other; and I saw that if one stayed there long, his principal business would be to look out the window. I had soon read all the tracts that were left there and examined where former prisoners had broken out and where a grate had been sawed off and heard the history of the various occupants of that room; for I found that even here there was a history and a gossip which never circulated beyond the walls of the jail. Probably this is the only house in the town where verses are composed, which afterward printed in a circular form but not published. I was shown quite a long list of verses which were composed by some young men who had been detected in an attempt to escape, who avenged themselves by signing them.

I pumped my fellow-prisoner as dry as I could, for fear I should never see him again; but at length he showed me which was my bed and left me to blow out the lamp.

It was like travelling into a far country, such as I had never expected to behold, to lie there for one night. It seemed to me that I never had heard the town-clock strike before, nor the evening sounds of the village; for we slept with the windows open, which were inside the grating. It was to see my native village in the light of the Middle Ages, and our Concord was turned into a Rhine stream, and visions of knights and castles passed before me. They were the voices of old burghers that I heard in the streets. I was

402   HENRY DAVID THOREAU

an involuntary spectator and auditor of whatever was done and said in the kitchen of the adjacent village-inn—a wholly new and rare experience to me. It was a closer view of my native town. I was fairly inside of it. I never had seen its institutions before. This is one of its peculiar institutions; for it is a shire town.[16] I began to comprehend what its inhabitants were about.

In the morning our breakfasts were put through the hole in the door, in small oblong-square tin pans, made to fit, and holding a pint of chocolate, with brown bread and an iron spoon. When they called for the vessels again, I was green enough to return what bread I had left; but my comrade seized it and said that I should lay that up for lunch or dinner. Soon after he was let out to work at haying in a neighboring field, whither he went every day, and would not be back till noon; so he bade me good-day, saying that he doubted if he should see me again.

When I came out of prison—for someone interfered and paid that tax—I did not perceive that great changes had taken place on the common, such as he observed who went in a youth and emerged a tottering and gray-headed man; and yet a change had to my eyes come over the scene—the town and State and country—greater than any that mere time could effect. I saw yet more distinctly the State in which I lived. I saw to what extent the people among whom I lived could be trusted as good neighbors and friends; that their friendship was for summer weather only; that they did not greatly propose to do right; that they were a distinct race from me by their prejudices and superstitions, as the Chinamen and Malays are; that, in their sacrifices to humanity, they ran no risks, not even to their property; that, after all, they were not so noble but they treated the thief as he had treated them and hoped, by a certain outward observance and a few prayers, and by walking in a particular straight though useless path from time to time, to save their souls. This may be to judge my neighbors harshly; for I believe that many of them are not aware that they have such an institution as the jail in their village.

It was formerly the custom in our village, when a poor debtor came out of jail, for his acquaintances to salute him, looking through their fingers, which were crossed to represent the grating of a jail window, "How do ye do?" My neighbors did not thus

---

16. **shire town:** A town with a court, county offices, and jails. [Ed.]

salute me but first looked at me and then at one another as if I had returned from a long journey. I was put into jail as I was going to the shoemaker's to get a shoe which was mended. When I was let out the next morning I proceeded to finish my errand, and having put on my mended shoe, joined a huckleberry party who were impatient to put themselves under my conduct; and in half an hour—for the horse was soon tackled—was in the midst of a huckleberry field on one of our highest hills two miles off, and then the State was nowhere to be seen.

This is the whole history of "My Prisons."                    35

I have never declined paying the highway tax, because I am as desirous of being a good neighbor as I am of being a bad subject; and as for supporting schools I am doing my part to educate my fellow countrymen now. It is for no particular item in the tax-bill that I refuse to pay it. I simply wish to refuse allegiance to the State, to withdraw and stand aloof from it effectually. I do not care to trace the course of my dollar, if I could, till it buys a man or a musket to shoot one with—the dollar is innocent—but I am concerned to trace the effects of my allegiance. In fact, I quietly declare war with the State, after my fashion, though I will still make what use and get what advantage of her I can, as is usual in such cases.

If others pay the tax which is demanded of me from a sympathy with the State, they do but what they have already done in their own case, or rather they abet injustice to a greater extent than the State requires. If they pay the tax from a mistaken interest in the individual taxed, to save his property, or prevent his going to jail, it is because they have not considered wisely how far they let their private feelings interfere with the public good.

This, then, is my position at present. But one cannot be too much on his guard in such a case, lest his action be biased by obstinacy or an undue regard for the opinions of men. Let him see that he does only what belongs to himself and to the hour.

I think sometimes, Why, this people mean well; they are only ignorant; they would do better if they knew how: why give your neighbors this pain to treat you as they are not inclined to? But I think again, this is no reason why I should do as they do or permit others to suffer much greater pain of a different kind. Again, I sometimes say to myself, When many millions of men, without heat, without ill will, without personal feeling of any kind, demand of you a few shillings only, without the possibility, such is their constitution, of retracting or altering their present demand, and without the possibility, on your side, of appeal to any other millions, why expose yourself to this overwhelming brute force? You do not resist cold and hunger, the winds and the waves, thus obstinately; you quietly submit to a thousand similar necessities. You do not put your head into the fire. But just in proportion as I regard this as not wholly a brute force but partly a human force, and consider that I have relations to those millions as to so many millions of men, and not of mere brute or inanimate things, I see that appeal is possible, first and instantaneously, from them to the Maker of them, and secondly, from them to themselves. But if I put my head deliberately into the fire, there is no appeal to fire or to the Maker of fire, and I have only myself to blame. If I could convince myself that I have any right to be satisfied with men as they are, and to treat them accordingly, and not according, in some respects, to my requisitions and expectations of what they and I ought to be, then, like a good Mussulman[17] and fatalist, I should endeavor to be satisfied with things as they are and say it is the will of God. And, above all, there is this difference between resisting this and a purely brute or natural force, that I can resist this with some effect; but I cannot expect, like Orpheus,[18] to change the nature of the rocks and trees and beasts.

I do not wish to quarrel with any man or nation. I do not wish to split hairs, to make fine distinctions, or set myself up as better than my neighbors. I seek rather, I may say, even an excuse for conforming to the laws of the land. I am but too ready to conform to them. Indeed, I have reason to suspect myself on this head; and each year, as the tax-gatherer comes round, I find myself disposed to review the acts and position of the general and State governments, and the spirit of the people, to discover a pretext for conformity.   40

> We must affect our country as our parents;
> And if at any time we alienate
> Our love or industry from doing it honor,
> We must respect effects and teach the soul
> Matter of conscience and religion,
> And not desire of rule or benefit.[19]

17. **Mussulman:** A Muslim. [Ed.]

18. **Orpheus:** In Greek mythology, Orpheus's music was so affecting that his songs could charm rocks, trees, and animals. [Ed.]

19. From George Peele's *Battle of Alcazar* (acted 1588–1589; printed 1594). [Ed.]

I believe that the State will soon be able to take all my work of this sort out of my hands, and then I shall be no better a patriot than my fellow-countrymen. Seen from a lower point of view, the Constitution, with all its faults, is very good; the law and the courts are very respectable; even this State and this American government are, in many respects, very admirable and rare things, to be thankful for, such as a great many have described them; but seen from a point of view a little higher, they are what I have described them; seen from a higher still, and the highest, who shall say what they are, or that they are worth looking at or thinking of at all?

However, the government does not concern me much, and I shall bestow the fewest possible thoughts on it. It is not many moments that I live under a government, even in this world. If a man is thought-free, fancy-free, imagination-free, that which *is not* never for a long time appearing *to be* to him, unwise rulers or reformers cannot fatally interrupt him.

I know that most men think differently from myself; but those whose lives are by profession devoted to the study of these or kindred subjects content me as little as any. Statesmen and legislators, standing so completely within the institution, never distinctly and nakedly behold it. They speak of moving society but have no resting-place without it. They may be men of a certain experience and discrimination and have no doubt invented ingenious and even useful systems, for which we sincerely thank them; but all their wit and usefulness lie within certain not very wide limits. They are wont to forget that the world is not governed by policy and expediency. Webster[20] never goes behind government and so cannot speak with authority about it. His words are wisdom to those legislators who contemplate no essential reform in the existing government; but for thinkers, and those who legislate for all time, he never once glances at the subject. I know of those whose serene and wise speculations on this theme would soon reveal the limits of his mind's range and hospitality. Yet, compared with the cheap professions of most reformers, and the still cheaper wisdom and eloquence of politicians in general, his are almost the only sensible and valuable words, and we thank Heaven for him. Comparatively, he is always strong,

---

20. **Webster:** Daniel Webster, the secretary of state from 1841 to 1843. [Ed.]

original, and, above all, practical. Still his quality is not wisdom but prudence. The lawyer's truth is not Truth but consistency, or a consistent expediency. Truth is always in harmony with herself and is not concerned chiefly to reveal the justice that may consist with wrong-doing. He well deserves to be called, as he has been called, the Defender of the Constitution. There are really no blows to be given by him but defensive ones. He is not a leader but a follower. His leaders are the men of '87.[21] "I have never made an effort," he says, "and never propose to make an effort; I have never countenanced an effort, and never mean to countenance an effort, to disturb the arrangement as originally made, by which the various States came into the Union." Still thinking of the sanction which the Constitution gives to slavery, he says, "Because it was a part of the original compact—let it stand." Notwithstanding his special acuteness and ability, he is unable to take a fact out of its merely political relations and behold it as it lies absolutely to be disposed of by the intellect—what, for instance, it behooves a man to do here in America today with regard to slavery but ventures, or is driven, to make some such desperate answer as the following, while professing to speak absolutely, and as a private man—from which what new and singular code of social duties might be inferred? "The manner," says he, "in which the governments of those States where slavery exists are to regulate it, is for their own consideration, under their responsibility to their constituents, to the general laws of propriety, humanity, and justice, and to God. Associations formed elsewhere, springing from a feeling of humanity, or any other cause, have nothing whatever to do with it. They have never received any encouragement from me, and they never will."

They who know of no purer sources of truth, who have traced up its stream no higher, stand, and wisely stand, by the Bible and the Constitution, and drink at it there with reverence and humility; but they who behold where it comes trickling into this lake or that pool gird up their loins once more and continue their pilgrimage toward its fountain-head.

No man with a genius for legislation has appeared in America. They are rare in the history of the world. There are orators,   45

---

21. **men of '87:** The men who wrote the Constitution in 1787. [Ed.]

politicians, and eloquent men by the thousand; but the speaker has not yet opened his mouth to speak who is capable of settling the much-vexed questions of the day. We love eloquence for its own sake and not for any truth which it may utter or any heroism it may inspire. Our legislators have not yet learned the comparative value of free-trade and of freedom, of union, and of rectitude, to a nation. They have no genius or talent for comparatively humble questions of taxation and finance, commerce and manufacturers and agriculture. If we were left solely to the wordy wit of legislators in Congress for our guidance, uncorrected by the seasonable experience and the effectual complaints of the people, America would not long retain her rank among the nations. For eighteen hundred years, though perchance I have no right to say it, the New Testament has been written; yet where is the legislator who has wisdom and practical talent enough to avail himself of the light which it sheds on the science of legislation?

The authority of government, even such as I am willing to submit to — for I will cheerfully obey those who know and can do better than I, and in many things even those who neither know nor can do so well — is still an impure one: to be strictly just, it must have the sanction and consent of the governed. It can have no pure right over my person and property but what I concede to it. The progress from an absolute to a limited monarchy, from a limited monarchy to a democracy, is a progress toward a true respect for the individual. Even the Chinese philosopher[22] was wise enough to regard the individual as the basis of the empire. Is a democracy such as we know it the last improvement possible in government? Is it not possible to take a step further towards recognizing and organizing the rights of man? There will never be a really free and enlightened State until the State comes to recognize the individual as a higher and independent power, from which all its own power and authority are derived, and treats him accordingly. I please myself with imagining a State at last which can afford to be just to all men and to treat the individual with respect as a neighbor; which even would not think it inconsistent with its own repose if a few were to live aloof from

---

22. **the Chinese philosopher:** Most likely Confucius. [Ed.]

it, not meddling with it, nor embraced by it, who fulfilled all the duties of neighbors and fellow-men. A State which bore this kind of fruit and suffered it to drop off as fast as it ripened would prepare the way for a still more perfect and glorious State, which also I have imagined but not yet anywhere seen.

## For Discussion and Writing

1. What two specific situations is Thoreau most unhappy about?
2. For a document that has proven so important in world history, "Civil Disobedience" seems quite personal. What about the way that Thoreau presents himself and the way he addresses his readers makes it feel this way?
3. **connections**   Thoreau begins from the premise "that government is best which governs least" (par. 1), and says he even believes that the best government would be one that doesn't govern at all. Compare this belief to that implied by Swift's indirectly made argument in "A Modest Proposal" (p. 370). What exactly do you think Swift believes government's role could be in correcting the dire situation of the Irish poor? What do you think Thoreau would think of it? If you had to pick one of the two men's positions, which would you pick? Why?
4. Thoreau's writing has been remembered not only because its ideas remain appealing but because he states them memorably. Write about what you think it is that makes his writing stylistically memorable. Look at the way he sometimes uses mottoes or aphorisms, and think about how they work in terms of word choice and structure. Look also at the way he strings his thoughts together, how he builds his argument, how he strikes emotional chords.
5. **looking further**   While "Civil Disobedience" was important to Mahatma Gandhi and Martin Luther King Jr., it was also inspirational for many in the Vietnam-era antiwar movement. Do a little research into contemporary protest movements at home and abroad. Was this essay important to members of these movements, too? If not explicitly read by them, do you see evidence that the principles championed by Thoreau had some influence? How? If not, were other statements of protest influential to them, or other principles?

CALVIN TRILLIN

# Last Days of the Rickshaw

*Calvin Trillin was born and raised in Kansas City, Missouri. He attended Yale University and served in the U.S. Army. Trillin was a reporter at* Time *magazine until he went to work for the* New Yorker *in 1963, for which he wrote dispatches from the South on the civil rights movement and from all over the country on all sorts of subjects in his "U.S. Journal" column, which ran for fifteen years. He also authored a long-running column in* The Nation *and for syndication called "Uncivil Liberties." Trillin is perhaps most well-known as a food writer, but he is also known for his writing on politics, including a long-running series of doggerel poems, and for his personal writing on subjects ranging from his late wife Alice to his father. Trillin's work has ranged far and wide in search of subjects, but in all of them his keen observational eye, dry humor, and interest in the variety of arrangements of human life are all evident. As you read "Last Days of the Rickshaw," remember to look for evidence of these qualities.*

The strategy of drivers in Kolkata—drivers of private cars and taxis and buses and the enclosed three-wheel scooters used as jitneys and even pedicabs—is simple: Forge ahead while honking. There are no stop signs to speak of. To a visitor, the signs that say, in large block letters, OBEY TRAFFIC RULES come across as a bit of black humor. During a recent stay in Kolkata, the method I devised for crossing major thoroughfares was to wait until I could attach myself to more pedestrians than I figured a taxi was willing to knock down. In the narrow side streets known as the lanes, loud honking is the signal that a taxi or even a small truck is about to round the corner and come barreling down a space not meant for anything wider than a bicycle. But occasionally, during a brief lull in the honking, I'd hear the tinkling of a bell behind me. An American who has watched too many Hallmark Christmas specials might turn around half expecting to see a pair of draft horses pulling a sleigh through snowy woods. But what came into view was a rickshaw. Instead of being pulled by a horse, it was being pulled by a man—usually a skinny, bedraggled, barefoot man who didn't look quite up to the task. Hooked around his finger was a single bell that he shook continuously, producing what is surely the most benign sound to emanate from any vehicle in Kolkata.

Among the great cities of the world, Kolkata, the capital of West Bengal and the home of nearly 15 million people, is often mentioned as the only one that still has a large fleet of hand-pulled rickshaws. As it happens, that is not a distinction treasured by the governing authorities. Why? It's tempting, of course, to blame Mother Teresa. A politician in Kolkata told me that the city is known for the three m's: Marxism, *mishti*, and Mother Teresa. (West Bengal has had a government dominated by the Communist Party for 30 years. Mishti is a sweetened yogurt that Kolkatans love, though they're also partial to a sweet called *rossogolla*.) There is no doubt that the international attention given to Mother Teresa's work among the wretched and the dying firmly linked Kolkata in the Western mind with squalor—no matter how often Kolkatans point out that Mumbai, for example, has more extensive slums, and that no other city in India can match the richness of Kolkata's intellectual and cultural life.

The most loyal booster of Kolkata would acknowledge that the city has had some genuinely trying times in the 60 years since India became independent, starting well before the emergence of Mother Teresa. The partition that accompanied independence meant that, without substantial help from the central government, Kolkata had to absorb several million refugees from what became East Pakistan. There were times in the 1970s and '80s when it seemed Kolkata would never recover from the trauma of those refugees, followed by another wave of refugees who came during the war that turned East Pakistan into Bangladesh. Those were years marked by power outages and labor unrest and the flight of industry and the breathtaking violence unleashed by the Naxalite movement, which began with peasants demanding land redistribution in rural West Bengal and was transformed by college students into urban guerrilla warfare. In 1985 India's own prime minister, then Rajiv Gandhi, called Kolkata "a dying city."

There are still a lot of people sleeping on the streets in Kolkata, but there have been great changes in recent years. After decades of concentrating on its base among the rural poor and disdaining outside investment, the Communist Party of West Bengal has fiercely embraced capitalism and modernity. Although the government's symbols remain what might be expected from a party that still has a politburo — street-name changes have resulted in an American consulate with the address 5/1 Ho Chi Minh Road — the city regularly courts Western delegations looking for investment opportunities. Kolkata now has modern shopping malls and modern overpasses. Walking around the city recently for a week or so, often as the only Westerner in sight, I was approached by precisely two beggars.

Still, the image of any city has a half-life of many years. 5 (So does its name, officially changed in 2001 from Calcutta to Kolkata, which is closer to what the word sounds like in Bengali. Conversing in English, I never heard anyone call the city anything but Calcutta.) To Westerners, the conveyance most identified with Kolkata is not its modern subway — a facility whose spacious stations have art on the walls and cricket matches on television monitors — but the hand-pulled rickshaw. Stories and films celebrate a primitive-looking cart with high wooden wheels, pulled by someone who looks close to needing the succor of Mother Teresa. For years the government has been talking about eliminating hand-pulled rickshaws on what it calls humanitarian grounds — principally on the ground that, as the mayor of Kolkata has often said, it is offensive to see "one man sweating and straining to pull another man." But these days politicians also lament the impact of 6,000 hand-pulled rickshaws on a modern city's traffic and, particularly, on its image. "Westerners try to associate beggars and these rickshaws with the Calcutta landscape, but this is not what Calcutta stands for," the chief minister of West Bengal, Buddhadeb Bhattacharjee, said in a press conference in 2006. "Our city stands for prosperity and development." The chief minister — the equivalent of a state governor — went on to announce that hand-pulled rickshaws soon would be banned from the streets of Kolkata.

Rickshaws are not there to haul around tourists. (Actually, I saw almost no tourists in Kolkata, apart from the young backpackers on Sudder Street, in what used to be a red-light district and is now said to be the single place in the city where the services a rickshaw *wallah* offers may include providing female company to a gentleman for the evening.) It's the people in the lanes who most regularly use rickshaws—not the poor but people who are just a notch above the poor. They are people who tend to travel short distances, through lanes that are sometimes inaccessible to even the most daring taxi driver. An older woman with marketing to do, for instance, can arrive in a rickshaw, have the rickshaw wallah wait until she comes back from various stalls to load her purchases, and then be taken home. People in the lanes use rickshaws as a 24-hour ambulance service. Proprietors of cafés or corner stores send rickshaws to collect their supplies. (One morning I saw a rickshaw wallah take on a load of live chickens—tied in pairs by the feet so they could be draped over the shafts and the folded back canopy and even the axle. By the time he trotted off, he was carrying about a hundred upside-down chickens.) The rickshaw pullers told me their steadiest customers are schoolchildren. Middle-class families contract with a puller to take a child to school and pick him up; the puller essentially becomes a family retainer.

From June to September Kolkata can get torrential rains, and its drainage system doesn't need torrential rain to begin backing up. Residents who favor a touch of hyperbole say that in Kolkata "if a stray cat pees, there's a flood." During my stay it once rained for about 48 hours. Entire neighborhoods couldn't be reached by motorized vehicles, and the newspapers showed pictures of rickshaws being pulled through water that was up to the pullers' waists. When it's raining, the normal customer base for rickshaw wallahs expands greatly, as does the price of a journey. A writer in Kolkata told me, "When it rains, even the governor takes rickshaws."

While I was in Kolkata, a magazine called *India Today* published its annual ranking of Indian states, according to such measurements as prosperity and infrastructure. Among India's 20 largest states, Bihar finished dead last, as it has for four of the past five years. Bihar, a couple hundred miles north of Kolkata, is where the vast majority of rickshaw wallahs come from. Once in Kolkata, they sleep on the street or in their rickshaws or in a *dera*—a combination garage and repair shop and dormitory managed by someone called a *sardar*. For sleeping privileges in a dera, pullers pay 100 rupees (about $2.50) a month, which sounds like a pretty good deal until you've visited a dera. They gross between 100 and 150 rupees a day, out of which they have to pay 20 rupees for the use of the rickshaw and an occasional 75 or more for a payoff if a policeman stops them for, say, crossing a street where rickshaws are prohibited. A 2003 study found that rickshaw wallahs are near the bottom of Kolkata occupations in income, doing better than only the ragpickers and the beggars. For someone without land or education, that still beats trying to make a living in Bihar.

There are people in Kolkata, particularly educated and politically aware people, who will not ride in a rickshaw, because they are offended by the idea of being pulled by another human being or because they consider it not the sort of thing people of their station do or because they regard the hand-pulled rickshaw as a relic of colonialism. Ironically, some of those people are not enthusiastic about banning rickshaws. The editor of the editorial pages of Kolkata's *Telegraph*—Rudrangshu Mukherjee, a former academic who still writes history books—told me, for instance, that he sees humanitarian considerations as coming down on the side of keeping hand-pulled rickshaws on the road. "I refuse to be carried by another human being myself," he said, "but I question whether we have the right to take away their livelihood." Rickshaw supporters point out that when it comes to demeaning occupations, rickshaw wallahs are hardly unique in Kolkata.

When I asked one rickshaw wallah if he thought the government's plan to rid the city of rickshaws was based on a genuine interest in his welfare, he smiled, with a quick shake of his head—a gesture I interpreted to mean, "If you are so naive as to ask such a question, I will answer it, but it is not worth wasting words on." Some rickshaw wallahs I met were resigned to the imminent end of their livelihood and pin their hopes on being offered something in its place. As migrant workers, they don't have the political clout enjoyed by, say, Kolkata's sidewalk hawkers, who, after supposedly being scaled back at the beginning of the modernization drive, still clog the sidewalks, selling absolutely everything—or, as I found during the 48 hours of rain, absolutely everything but umbrellas. "The government was the government of the poor people," one sardar told me. "Now they shake hands with the capitalists and try to get rid of poor people."

But others in Kolkata believe that rickshaws will simply be confined more strictly to certain neighborhoods, out of the view of World Bank traffic consultants and California investment delegations—or that they will be allowed to die out naturally as they're supplanted by more modern conveyances. Buddhadeb Bhattacharjee, after all, is not the first high West Bengal official to say that rickshaws would be off the streets of Kolkata in a matter of months. Similar statements have been made as far back as 1976. The ban decreed by Bhattacharjee has been delayed by a court case and by a widely held belief that some retraining or social security settlement ought to be offered to rickshaw drivers. It may also have been delayed by a quiet reluctance to give up something that has been part of the fabric of the city for more than a century. Kolkata, a resident told me, "has difficulty letting go." One day a city official handed me a report from the municipal government laying out options for how rickshaw wallahs might be rehabilitated.

"Which option has been chosen?" I asked, noting that the report was dated almost exactly a year before my visit.

"That hasn't been decided," he said.

"When will it be decided?"

"That hasn't been decided," he said.                                    15

### For Discussion and Writing

1. Why might it be, in the title's words, the last days of the rickshaw?

2. While much of Trillin's substantial output as a writer has been humorous, from his many comic essays to his hundreds of political limericks, this essay couldn't be said to have as its main purpose the evoking of laughter. It does, however, use humor. Reread the essay and identify places where the author uses humor. How does each use work? What makes each funny? How does Trillin use these bits of humor in service of his larger points?

3. **connections**   Compare "Last Days of the Rickshaw" to Barbara Ehrenreich's "Serving in Florida" (p. 134). While both focus on low-wage work, the relationships between the two authors and their specific subjects are quite different, as are the subjects themselves and the social context in which they exist. What does work mean to the people in each of these jobs? What does it mean to the people around them? What does it mean to the authors? How much of the difference between these two pieces can be ascribed to the different social contexts? How much is similar across these contexts?

4. Write an essay from the point of view of a *wallah*. If you want, imagine yourself as one of the rickshaw operators Trillin observes, or imagine that you are a *wallah* who has just read this article. What

might you say? Might your understanding of things differ from Trillin's? How? Might you agree with the essay but have a different way of talking about what you do for a living, the place where you do it, and the way the people of Kolkata see you?

5. **looking further**    Trillin wrote this essay for *National Geographic* magazine. Research this magazine. What is its history? What has it become famous for? Has it become infamous for anything? Try to connect this history to Trillin's essay. How does it fit into the history of the magazine in which it appears?

MARK TWAIN

# The Lowest Animal

*Mark Twain is the nom de plume of writer Samuel Clemens (1835–1910), one of the best-known writers in U.S. history. Born in 1835 and raised in Hannibal, Missouri, he left school at age twelve to apprentice for a printer. At fifteen he worked as a typesetter and wrote for his brother's newspaper; he left Hannibal at nineteen to work as a printer in New York City, Philadelphia, St. Louis, and Cincinnati, returning to the Midwest to work as a steamboat pilot on the Mississippi River. After working as a miner in Nevada, Twain turned to journalism, setting off for good on a career that would see him write humorous regional tales such as those collected in* The Celebrated Jumping Frog of Calaveras County *(1867), travel literature such as* Innocents Abroad *(1869),* Roughing It *(1872), and* Life on the Mississippi *(1883), and novels such as* The Gilded Age *(1873),* The Adventures of Tom Sawyer *(1876),* The Adventures of Huckleberry Finn *(1884), and* Pudd'nhead Wilson *(1894), as well as many other works, both short and long. Later in his life, amid money troubles, Twain wrote and published many shorter nonfiction pieces that confirmed what could be gleaned of his views from his fiction, including his stances on the slavery he grew up with in his Missouri youth, on American imperialism, on the organization of labor, and on religion, though it wasn't until after his death that much of his commentary on that subject was published, in works such as* Letters from the Earth *(1962) and his autobiography, which appeared in 2010, 100 years after his death.*

*"The Lowest Animal" was written around the turn of the century and appeared in* Letters from the Earth, *which contained works suppressed by the family until Twain's daughter Clara reversed her position. As you read it, consider what it is about the essay that caused it to go unpublished for so long. Who might it have offended? Who might it still?*

In August, 1572,[1] similar things were occurring in Paris and elsewhere in France. In this case it was Christian against Christian. The Roman Catholics, by previous concert, sprang a surprise upon the unprepared and unsuspecting Protestants, and butchered them by thousands—both sexes and all ages. This was the memorable St. Bartholomew's Day. At Rome the Pope and the Church gave public thanks to God when the happy news came.

During several centuries hundreds of heretics were burned at the stake every year because their religious opinions were not satisfactory to the Roman Church.

In all ages the savages of all lands have made the slaughtering of their neighboring brothers and the enslaving of their women and children the common business of their lives.

Hypocrisy, envy, malice, cruelty, vengefulness, seduction, rape, robbery, swindling, arson, bigamy, adultery, and the oppression and humiliation of the poor and the helpless in all ways have been and still are more or less common among both the civilized and uncivilized peoples of the earth.

For many centuries "the common brotherhood of man" has 5 been urged—on Sundays—and "patriotism" on Sundays and weekdays both. Yet *patriotism contemplates the opposite of a common brotherhood.*

Woman's equality with man has never been conceded by any people, ancient or modern, civilized or savage.

I have been studying the traits and dispositions of the "lower animals" (so-called), and contrasting them with the traits and dispositions of man. I find the result humiliating to me. For it obliges me to renounce my allegiance to the Darwinian theory of the Ascent of Man from the Lower Animals; since it now seems plain to me that that theory ought to be vacated in favor of a new and truer one, this new and truer one to be named the *Descent* of Man from the Higher Animals.

In proceeding toward this unpleasant conclusion I have not guessed or speculated or conjectured, but have used what is commonly called the scientific method. That is to say, I have subjected every postulate that presented itself to the crucial test of actual experiment, and have adopted it or rejected it according to

1. This was to have been prefaced by newspaper clippings which, apparently, dealt with religious persecutions in Crete. The clippings have been lost. They probably referred to the Cretan revolt of 1897.

the result. Thus I verified and established each step of my course in its turn before advancing to the next. These experiments were made in the London Zoological Gardens, and covered many months of painstaking and fatiguing work.

Before particularizing any of the experiments, I wish to state one or two things which seem to more properly belong in this place than further along. This in the interest of clearness. The massed experiments established to my satisfaction certain generalizations, to wit:

1. That the human race is of one distinct species. It exhibits slight variations—in color, stature, mental caliber, and so on—due to climate, environment, and so forth; but it is a species by itself, and not to be confounded with any other.
2. That the quadrupeds are a distinct family, also. This family exhibits variations—in color, size, food preferences and so on; but it is a family by itself.
3. That the other families—the birds, the fishes, the insects, the reptiles, etc.—are more or less distinct, also. They are in the procession. They are links in the chain which stretches down from the higher animals to man at the bottom.

Some of my experiments were quite curious. In the course    10
of my reading I had come across a case where, many years ago, some hunters on our Great Plains organized a buffalo hunt for the entertainment of an English earl—that, and to provide some fresh meat for his larder. They had charming sport. They killed seventy-two of those great animals; and ate part of one of them and left the seventy-one to rot. In order to determine the difference between an anaconda and an earl—if any—I caused seven young calves to be turned into the anaconda's cage. The grateful reptile immediately crushed one of them and swallowed it, then lay back satisfied. It showed no further interest in the calves, and no disposition to harm them. I tried this experiment with other anacondas; always with the same result. The fact stood proven that the difference between an earl and an anaconda is that the earl is cruel and the anaconda isn't; and that the earl wantonly destroys what he has no use for, but the anaconda doesn't. This seemed to suggest that the anaconda was not descended from the earl. It also seemed to suggest that

the earl was descended from the anaconda, and had lost a good deal in the transition.

I was aware that many men who have accumulated more millions of money than they can ever use have shown a rabid hunger for more, and have not scrupled to cheat the ignorant and the helpless out of their poor servings in order to partially appease that appetite. I furnished a hundred different kinds of wild and tame animals the opportunity to accumulate vast stores of food, but none of them would do it. The squirrels and bees and certain birds made accumulations, but stopped when they had gathered a winter's supply, and could not be persuaded to add to it either honestly or by chicane. In order to bolster up a tottering reputation the ant pretended to store up supplies, but I was not deceived. I know the ant. These experiments convinced me that there is this difference between man and the higher animals: he is avaricious and miserly, they are not.

In the course of my experiments I convinced myself that among the animals man is the only one that harbors insults and injuries, broods over them, waits till a chance offers, then takes revenge. The passion of revenge is unknown to the higher animals.

Roosters keep harems, but it is by consent of their concubines; therefore no wrong is done. Men keep harems, but it is by brute force, privileged by atrocious laws which the other sex were allowed no hand in making. In this matter man occupies a far lower place than the rooster.

Cats are loose in their morals, but not consciously so. Man, in his descent from the cat, has brought the cat's looseness with him but has left the unconsciousness behind—the saving grace which excuses the cat. The cat is innocent, man is not.

Indecency, vulgarity, obscenity—these are strictly confined to man; he invented them. Among the higher animals there is no trace of them. They hide nothing; they are not ashamed. Man, with his soiled mind, covers himself. He will not even enter a drawing room with his breast and back naked, so alive are he and his mates to indecent suggestion. Man is "The Animal that Laughs." But so does the monkey, as Mr. Darwin pointed out; and so does the Australian bird that is called the laughing jackass. No—Man is the Animal that Blushes. He is the only one that does it—or has occasion to.

At the head of this article we see how "three monks were burnt to death" a few days ago, and a prior "put to death with atrocious cruelty." Do we inquire into the details? No; or we should find out that the prior was subjected to unprintable mutilations. Man—when he is a North American Indian—gouges out his prisoner's eyes; when he is King John, with a nephew to render untroublesome, he uses a red-hot iron; when he is a religious zealot dealing with heretics in the Middle Ages, he skins his captive alive and scatters salt on his back; in the first Richard's time he shuts up a multitude of Jew families in a tower and sets fire to it; in Columbus's time he captures a family of Spanish Jews and—but that is not printable; in our day in England a man is fined ten shillings for beating his mother nearly to death with a chair, and another man is fined forty shillings for having four pheasant eggs in his possession without being able to satisfactorily explain how he got them. Of all the animals, man is the only one that is cruel. He is the only one that inflicts pain for the pleasure of doing it. It is a trait that is not known to the higher animals. The cat plays with the frightened mouse; but she has this excuse, that she does not know that the mouse is suffering. The cat is moderate—unhumanly moderate: she only scares the mouse, she does not hurt it; she doesn't dig out its eyes, or tear off its skin, or drive splinters under its nails—man-fashion; when she is done playing with it she makes a sudden meal of it and puts it out of its trouble. Man is the Cruel Animal. He is alone in that distinction.

The higher animals engage in individual fights, but never in organized masses. Man is the only animal that deals in that atrocity of atrocities, War. He is the only one that gathers his brethren about him and goes forth in cold blood and with calm pulse to exterminate his kind. He is the only animal that for sordid wages will march out, as the Hessians did in our Revolution, and as the boyish Prince Napoleon did in the Zulu war, and help to slaughter strangers of his own species who have done him no harm and with whom he has no quarrel.

Man is the only animal that robs his helpless fellow of his country—takes possession of it and drives him out of it or destroys him. Man has done this in all the ages. There is not an acre of ground on the globe that is in possession of its rightful owner, or that has not been taken away from owner after owner, cycle after cycle, by force and bloodshed.

Man is the only Slave. And he is the only animal who enslaves. He has always been a slave in one form or another, and has always held other slaves in bondage under him in one way or another. In our day he is always some man's slave for wages, and does that man's work; and this slave has other slaves under him for minor wages, and they do *his* work. The higher animals are the only ones who exclusively do their own work and provide their own living.

Man is the only Patriot. He sets himself apart in his own country, under his own flag, and sneers—at the other nations, and keeps multitudinous uniformed assassins on hand at heavy expense to grab slices of other people's countries, and keep *them* from grabbing slices of *his*. And in the intervals between campaigns he washes the blood off his hands and works for "the universal brotherhood of man"—with his mouth.

20

Man is the Religious Animal. He is the only Religious Animal. He is the only animal that has the True Religion—several of them. He is the only animal that loves his neighbor as himself, and cuts his throat if his theology isn't straight. He has made a graveyard of the globe in trying his honest best to smooth his brother's path to happiness and heaven. He was at it in the time of the Caesars, he was at it in Mahomet's time, he was at it in the time of the Inquisition, he was at it in France a couple of centuries, he was at it in England in Mary's day, he has been at it ever since he first saw the light, he is at it today in Crete—as per the telegrams quoted above—he will be at it somewhere else tomorrow. The higher animals have no religion. And we are told that they are going to be left out, in the Hereafter. I wonder why? It seems questionable taste.

Man is the Reasoning Animal. Such is the claim. I think it is open to dispute. Indeed, my experiments have proven to me that he is the Unreasoning Animal. Note his history, as sketched above. It seems plain to me that whatever he is he is not a reasoning animal. His record is the fantastic record of a maniac. I consider that the strongest count against his intelligence is the fact that with that record back of him he blandly sets himself up as the head animal of the lot: whereas by his own standards he is the bottom one.

In truth, man is incurably foolish. Simple things which the other animals easily learn, he is incapable of learning. Among my experiments was this. In an hour I taught a cat and a dog to be friends. I put them in a cage. In another hour I taught them to be friends with a rabbit. In the course of two days I was able to add a fox, a goose, a squirrel and some doves. Finally a monkey. They lived together in peace; even affectionately.

Next, in another cage I confined an Irish Catholic from Tipperary, and as soon as he seemed tame I added a Scotch Presbyterian from Aberdeen. Next a Turk from Constantinople; a Greek Christian from Crete; an Armenian; a Methodist from the wilds of Arkansas; a Buddhist from China; a Brahman from Benares. Finally, a Salvation Army Colonel from Wapping. Then I stayed away two whole days. When I came back to note results, the cage of Higher Animals was all right, but in the other there was but a chaos of gory odds and ends of turbans and fezzes and plaids and bones and flesh—not a specimen left alive. These Reasoning Animals had disagreed on a theological detail and carried the matter to a Higher Court.

One is obliged to concede that in true loftiness of character, 25 Man cannot claim to approach even the meanest of the Higher Animals. It is plain that he is constitutionally incapable of approaching that altitude; that he is constitutionally afflicted with a Defect which must make such approach forever impossible, for it is manifest that this defect is permanent in him, indestructible, ineradicable.

I find this Defect to be *the Moral Sense*. He is the only animal that has it. It is the secret of his degradation. It is the quality *which enables him to do wrong*. It has no other office. It is incapable of performing any other function. It could never have been intended to perform any other. Without it, man could do no wrong. He would rise at once to the level of the Higher Animals.

Since the Moral Sense has but the one office, the one capacity—to enable man to do wrong—it is plainly without value to him. It is as valueless to him as is disease. In fact, it manifestly is a disease. *Rabies* is bad, but it is not so bad as this disease. Rabies enables a man to do a thing which he could not do when in a healthy state: kill his neighbor with a poisonous bite. No one is the better man for having rabies. The Moral Sense enables a man to do wrong. It enables him to do wrong in a thousand ways. Rabies is an innocent disease, compared to the Moral Sense. No one, then, can be the better man for having the Moral Sense. What, now, do we find the Primal Curse to have been? Plainly what it was in the beginning: the infliction upon man of the Moral Sense; the ability to distinguish good from evil; and with it, necessarily, the ability to *do* evil; for there can be no evil act without the presence of consciousness of it in the doer of it.

And so I find that we have descended and degenerated, from some far ancestor — some microscopic atom wandering at its pleasure between the mighty horizons of a drop of water perchance — insect by insect, animal by animal, reptile by reptile, down the long highway of smirchless innocence, till we have reached the bottom stage of development — namable as the Human Being. Below us — nothing. Nothing but the Frenchman.

There is only one possible stage below the Moral Sense; that is the Immoral Sense. The Frenchman has it. Man is but little lower than the angels. This definitely locates him. He is between the angels and the French.

Man seems to be a rickety poor sort of a thing, any way you take him; a kind of British Museum of infirmities and inferiorities. He is always undergoing repairs. A machine that was as unreliable as he is would have no market. On top of his specialty — the Moral Sense — are piled a multitude of minor infirmities; such a multitude, indeed, that one may broadly call them countless. The higher animals get their teeth without pain or inconvenience. Man gets his through months and months of cruel torture; and at a time of life when he is but ill able to bear it. As soon as he has got them they must all be pulled out again, for they were of no value in the first place, not worth the loss of a night's rest. The second set will answer for a while, by being reinforced occasionally with rubber or plugged up with gold; but he will never get a set which can really be depended on till a dentist makes him one. This set will be called "false" teeth — as if he had ever worn any other kind.

In a wild state — a natural state — the Higher Animals have a few diseases; diseases of little consequence; the main one is old age. But man starts in as a child and lives on diseases till the end, as a regular diet. He has mumps, measles, whooping cough, croup, tonsillitis, diphtheria, scarlet fever, almost as a matter of course. Afterward, as he goes along, his life continues to be threatened at every turn: by colds, coughs, asthma, bronchitis, itch, cholera, cancer, consumption, yellow fever, bilious fever, typhus fevers, hay fever, ague, chilblains, piles, inflammation of the entrails, indigestion, toothache, earache, deafness, dumbness, blindness, influenza, chicken pox, cowpox, smallpox, liver complaint, constipation, bloody flux, warts, pimples, boils, carbuncles, abscesses, bunions, corns, tumors, fistulas, pneumonia, softening of the brain, melancholia and fifteen other kinds of insanity; dysentery, jaundice, diseases of the heart, the bones, the skin, the scalp, the spleen, the kidneys, the nerves, the brain, the blood; scrofula, paralysis, leprosy, neuralgia, palsy, fits, headache, thirteen kinds of rheumatism, forty-six of gout, and a formidable supply of gross and unprintable disorders of one sort and another. Also—but why continue the list? The mere names of the agents appointed to keep this shackly machine out of repair would hide him from sight if printed on his body in the smallest type known to the founder's art. He is but a basket of pestilent corruption provided for the support and entertainment of swarming armies of bacilli—armies commissioned to rot him and destroy him, and each army equipped with a special detail of the work. The process of waylaying him, persecuting him, rotting him, killing him, begins with his first breath, and there is no mercy, no pity, no truce till he draws his last one.

Look at the workmanship of him, in certain of its particulars. What are his tonsils for? They perform no useful function; they have no value. They have no business there. They are but a trap. They have but the one office, the one industry: to provide tonsillitis and quinsy and such things for the possessor of them. And what is the vermiform appendix for? It has no value; it cannot perform any useful service. It is but an ambuscaded enemy whose sole interest in life is to lie in wait for stray grapeseeds and employ them to breed strangulated hernia. And what are the male's mammals for? For business, they are out of the question; as an ornament, they are a mistake. What is his beard for? It performs no useful function; it is a nuisance and a discomfort; all nations hate it; all nations persecute it with the razor. And because it is a nuisance and a discomfort, Nature never allows the supply of it to fall short, in any man's case, between puberty and the grave. You never see a man bald-headed on his chin. But his hair! It is a graceful ornament, it is a comfort, it is the best of all protections against certain perilous ailments, man prizes it above emeralds and rubies. And because of these things Nature puts it on, half the time, so that it won't stay. Man's sight, smell, hearing, sense of locality—how inferior they are. The condor sees a corpse at five miles; man has no telescope that can do it. The bloodhound follows a scent that is two days old. The robin hears the earthworm burrowing his course under the ground. The cat, deported in a closed basket, finds its way home again through twenty miles of country which it has never seen.

Certain functions lodged in the other sex perform in a lamentably inferior way as compared with the performance of the same functions in the Higher Animals. In the human being, menstruation, gestation and parturition are terms which Stand for horrors. In the Higher Animals these things are hardly even inconveniences.

For style, look at the Bengal tiger—that ideal of grace, beauty, physical perfection, majesty. And then look at Man—that poor thing. He is the Animal of the Wig, the Trepanned Skull, the Ear Trumpet, the Glass Eye, the Pasteboard Nose, the Porcelain Teeth, the Silver Windpipe, the Wooden Leg—a creature that is mended and patched all over, from top to bottom. If he can't get renewals of his bric-a-brac in the next world, what will he look like?

He has just one stupendous superiority. In his intellect he is 35 supreme. The Higher Animals cannot touch him there. It is curious, it is noteworthy, that no heaven has ever been offered him wherein his one sole superiority was provided with a chance to enjoy itself. Even when he himself has imagined a heaven, he has never made provision in it for intellectual joys. It is a striking omission. It seems a tacit confession that heavens are provided for the Higher Animals alone. This is matter for thought; and for serious thought. And it is full of a grim suggestion: that we are not as important, perhaps, as we had all along supposed we were.

### For Discussion and Writing

1. What is the point of Twain's comparisons of human behavior to the behavior of other animals? How does he make this point?

2. Twain argues here that "Man" should be called not "the Animal that Laughs" but rather "the Animal that Blushes" (par. 15). What does he mean by this? And how does he himself use humor, perhaps paradoxically, to prove his point? More broadly, examine his use of humor

generally. How does he create it, and to what ends does he use it? And how does he balance it with the distinctly unfunny moments in the essay, some of which are quite shocking?

3. **connections**   Read Twain's essay next to Carl Sagan's "Does Truth Matter?" (p. 310), both of which refer to the scientific method and both of which are concerned with the question of truth and with human behavior. How do their uses of the concept in these two essays compare? What is the ultimate goal of each author in invoking it? In the end, what does each think about reason and human use of it?

4. What do you think of Twain's opinion of humans? How much of what he says, once you analyze his statements and separate the ironic from the direct, do you agree with? Why?

5. **looking further**   Research controversy over Darwin's theory of evolution around the time of Twain's writing "The Lowest Animal." Describe the different positions held at the time. How does Twain's commentary here fit into this landscape?

AI WEIWEI

# The Refugee Crisis Isn't About Refugees. It's About Us.

*Ai Weiwei was born in 1957 in Beijing. His father was a well-known poet who was denounced by the government and sent, with his family, to a labor camp; Ai Weiwei was one year old at the time, and he and his family were not allowed to return to Beijing until 1976, after Mao Zedong's death and the end of the Cultural Revolution. After their return and two years of studying at the Beijing Film Academy, Ai lived in the United States for twelve years, studying art, working odd jobs, and becoming an expert professional blackjack player in Atlantic City. Returning to China when his father became ill, he established a career as an artist in many media including architecture, documentary, visual art, installations, and music and music video, and a chronicler of Beijing's art scene. He also established a blog for his political commentary, moving to Twitter when the government shut down the blog. In 2011, after years of activism, he was arrested and held for 81 days; he has lived abroad since being allowed to leave China in 2015. Ai's essay begins with the story of his childhood. As you read, think about the effect of his having chosen to start in this way.*

I was born in 1957, the same year China purged more than 300,000 intellectuals, including writers, teachers, journalists and whoever dared to criticize the newly established communist government. As part of a series of campaigns led by what was known as the anti—rightist movement, these intellectuals were sent to labour camps for "re-education."

Because my father, Ai Qing, was the most renowned poet in China then, the government made a symbolic example of him. In 1958, my family was forced from our home in Beijing and banished to the most remote area of the country—we had no idea that this was the beginning of a very dark, long journey that would last for two decades.

In the years that followed, my father was sentenced to hard labour cleaning latrines in a work camp in north-west China. He was also forced to criticize himself publicly.

From my youth, I experienced inhumane treatment from society. At the camp we had to live in an underground dugout and were subjected to unexplainable hatred, discrimination, unprovoked insults and assaults, all of which aimed to crush the basic human spirit rooted in my father's beliefs. As a result, I remember experiencing what felt like endless injustice. In such circumstances, there is no place to hide and there is no way to escape. You feel like your life is up against a wall, or that life itself is a dimming light, on the verge of being completely extinguished. Coping with the humiliation and suffering became the only way to survive.

I share this personal background because it sheds light on my emotional connection to the current global refugee condition, which I documented in the film *Human Flow*. My experience clarifies why I identify so deeply with all these unfortunate people who are pushed into extreme conditions by outside forces they are powerless to resist. 5

During two years of filming, we traveled to 23 nations and 40 refugee camps. Some of the camps are relatively new, coping with those who have fled from the war in Syria. Other camps — such as the Ain al-Hilweh camp in Lebanon — have existed for decades and have now sheltered three generations of refugees.

In the months since the film's release, some of the areas we covered have deteriorated even further. The Rohingya refugee situation in Myanmar, for example, has erupted in a wave of more than half a million newly displaced people, adding to the already existing 65 million refugees worldwide.

Observing and researching recent and historical refugee events makes some conclusions abundantly clear. Not a single refugee we met had willingly left their home, even when home was impoverished and undeveloped. The promise of economic prosperity is not more important than place. People left their homes because they were forced to by violence which caused the deaths of family members, relatives and fellow citizens. Often it is not just a single house that is destroyed, but entire villages vanish under indiscriminate bombing. There is simply no way for them to stay. Fleeing is the only choice they have to preserve their own lives and the lives of those they love.

A common argument is that many of the people who try to reach the west are economic migrants who wish to take unfair advantage of its prosperity. However, this view ignores the contradiction between today's physical borders and the real political and economic boundaries of our globalized world. Also implicit is a refusal to acknowledge that through globalization, certain states, institutions and individuals have greatly profited at the direct expense of those in many parts of the world who are vulnerable and increasingly exploited.

At this moment, the west—which has disproportionately benefited from globalization—simply refuses to bear its responsibilities, even though the condition of many refugees is a direct result of the greed inherent in a global capitalist system. If we map the 70-plus border walls and fences built between nations in the past three decades—increasing from roughly a dozen after the fall of the Berlin Wall—we can see the extent of global economic and political disparities. The people most negatively affected by these walls are the poorest and most desperate of society.

10

In nature there are two approaches to dealing with flooding. One is to build a dam to stop the flow. The other is to find the right path to allow the flow to continue. Building a dam does not address the source of the flow—it would need to be built higher and higher, eventually holding back a massive volume. If a powerful flood were to occur, it could wipe out everything in its path. The nature of water is to flow. Human nature too seeks freedom and that human desire is stronger than any natural force.

Can physical borders stop refugees? Instead of building walls, we should look at what is causing people to become refugees and work to solve those conditions to stem the flow at its source. To do so will require the most powerful nations in the world to adjust how they are actively shaping the world, how they are using political and economic ideology—enforced by overwhelming military power—to disrupt entire societies. How do we think the poor, displaced or occupied can exist when their societies are destroyed? Should they simply disappear? Can we recognize that their continued existence is an essential part of our shared humanity? If we fail to recognize this, how can we speak of "civilized" development?

The refugee crisis is not about refugees, rather, it is about us. Our prioritization of financial gain over people's struggle for the necessities of life is the primary cause of much of this crisis. The west has all but abandoned its belief in humanity and support for the precious ideals contained in declarations on universal human rights. It has sacrificed these ideals for short-sighted cowardice and greed.

Establishing the understanding that we all belong to one humanity is the most essential step for how we might continue to coexist on this sphere we call Earth. I know what it feels like to be a refugee and to experience the dehumanization that comes with displacement from home and country. There are many borders to dismantle, but the most important are the ones within our own hearts and minds—these are the borders that are dividing humanity from itself.

## For Discussion and Writing

1. Ai writes, "The refugee crisis is not about refugees, rather it is about us" (par. 13). What does he mean by this? Who is "us"? How is it "about us"?

2. One rhetorical device Ai makes use of is the rhetorical question. Where does he use this device? List each example. How does each work? Answer each of them. What do you think the desired effect was? Do you think that effect is achieved?

3. **connections**   Read this essay next to Mark Twain's "The Lowest Animal" (p. 416). Though these essays were written over a hundred years apart and take very different approaches to their topics, there are some notable parallels in their arguments and their subject matter. The differences are obvious, including tone and degree of directness. Name some of the parallels, both in terms of the kinds of events and historical phenomena each focuses on and in terms of the deeper, more universal human tendencies that arise in looking at these things.

4. The author writes that because of his childhood experiences as a displaced person, he has "an emotional connection to the current global refugee situation" (par. 5). Most of us have not had the kind of childhood Ai had, and so we do not know "what it feels like to be a refugee" (par. 14) in the way that he does. Because one way to try to understand others' experience is to imagine one's way into it, try to write a short narrative from the point of view of the author or someone who has become a refugee in another particular, specific historical situation. Tell the story of your imagined childhood as a refugee. What might it feel like to be displaced? What might it feel like to experience the loss of place of familiar surroundings, friends, and

family? (If you have experienced this kind of life and feel comfortable writing about it, please do.)

5. **looking further**   Write a researched version of the assignment in Question 4. Whether it is Ai's experience or another, imagined version, read up on the historical and political situation, on the geography, on the travel and living conditions particular to your imagined narrator's specific experience. Afterwards, reflect on your revision. What does adding the facts do for the narrative? How does it change both the writing and reading experience? Do you think your feelings about the global refugee crisis have changed at all, or did beefing up your narrative with research serve to confirm your opinions?

# E. B. WHITE

# Once More to the Lake

*Born in Mount Vernon, New York, in 1899, E. B. White was an editor, essayist, and writer of children's books.* He is identified in some circles as the writer of sketches, poems, editorials, and essays for the young New Yorker *magazine and in others as the author of the children's books* Stuart Little *(1945) and* Charlotte's Web *(1952). He is also known for his revision of William Strunk Jr.'s* The Elements of Style *(1959).*

*White's involvement with* The Elements of Style *highlights what is for many the most important element of his writing—his style. As you read "Once More to the Lake," look for telling details in his descriptions and take note of the kinds of words he chooses.*

One summer, along about 1904, my father rented a camp on a lake in Maine and took us all there for the month of August. We all got ringworm from some kittens and had to rub Pond's Extract on our arms and legs night and morning, and my father rolled over in a canoe with all his clothes on; but outside of that the vacation was a success and from then on none of us ever thought there was any place in the world like that lake in Maine. We returned summer after summer—always on August 1 for one month. I have since become a salt-water man, but sometimes in summer there are days when the restlessness of the tides and the fearful cold of the sea water and the incessant wind that blows across the afternoon and into the evening make me wish for the placidity of a lake in the woods. A few weeks ago this feeling got so strong I bought myself a couple of bass hooks and a spinner and returned to the lake where we used to go, for a week's fishing and to revisit old haunts.

I took along my son, who had never had any fresh water up his nose and who had seen lily pads only from train windows. On the journey over to the lake I began to wonder what it would be like. I wondered how time would have marred this unique, this holy spot—the coves and streams, the hills that the sun set behind, the camps and the paths behind the camps. I was sure that the tarred road would have found it out, and I wondered in what other ways it would be desolated. It is strange how much you can remember about places like that once you allow your mind to return into the grooves that lead back. You remember one thing, and that suddenly reminds you of another thing. I guess I remembered clearest of all the early mornings, when the lake was cool and motionless, remembered how the bedroom smelled of the lumber it was made of and of the wet woods whose scent entered through the screen. The partitions in the camp were thin and did not extend clear to the top of the rooms, and as I was always the first up I would dress softly so as not to wake the others, and sneak out into the sweet outdoors and start out in the canoe, keeping close along the shore in the long shadows of the pines. I remembered being very careful never to rub my paddle against the gunwale for fear of disturbing the stillness of the cathedral.

The lake had never been what you would call a wild lake. There were cottages sprinkled around the shores, and it was in farming country although the shores of the lake were quite heavily wooded. Some of the cottages were owned by nearby farmers, and you would live at the shore and eat your meals at the farmhouse. That's what our family did. But although it wasn't wild, it was a fairly large and undisturbed lake and there were places in it that, to a child at least, seemed infinitely remote and primeval.

I was right about the tar: it led to within half a mile of the shore. But when I got back there, with my boy, and we settled into a camp near a farmhouse and into the kind of summertime I had known, I could tell that it was going to be pretty much the same as it had been before — I knew it, lying in bed the first morning, smelling the bedroom and hearing the boy sneak quietly out and go off along the shore in a boat. I began to sustain the illusion that he was I, and therefore, by simple transposition, that I was my father. This sensation persisted, kept cropping up all the time we were there. It was not an entirely new feeling, but in this setting it grew much stronger. I seemed to be living a dual existence. I would be in the middle of some simple act, I would be picking up a bait box or laying down a table fork, or I would be saying something, and suddenly it would be not I but my father who was saying the words or making the gesture. It gave me a creepy sensation.

We went fishing the next morning. I felt the same damp moss ⁵
covering the worms in the bait can, and saw the dragonfly alight
on the tip of my rod as it hovered a few inches from the surface of the water. It was the arrival of this fly that convinced me
beyond any doubt that everything was as it always had been, that
the years were a mirage and that there had been no years. The
small waves were the same, chucking the rowboat under the chin
as we fished at anchor, and the boat was the same boat, the same
color green and the ribs broken in the same places, and under
the floorboards the same fresh-water leavings and débris—the
dead helgramite, the wisps of moss, the rusty discarded fish-
hook, the dried blood from yesterday's catch. We stared silently
at the tips of our rods, at the dragonflies that came and went. I
lowered the tip of mine into the water, tentatively, pensively dis-
lodging the fly, which darted two feet away, poised, darted two
feet back, and came to rest again a little farther up the rod. There
had been no years between the ducking of this dragonfly and the
other one—the one that was part of memory. I looked at the boy,
who was silently watching his fly, and it was my hands that held
his rod, my eyes watching. I felt dizzy and didn't know which rod
I was at the end of.

We caught two bass, hauling them in briskly as though they
were mackerel, pulling them over the side of the boat in a busi-
nesslike manner without any landing net, and stunning them
with a blow on the back of the head. When we got back for
a swim before lunch, the lake was exactly where we had left it,
the same number of inches from the dock, and there was only the
merest suggestion of a breeze. This seemed an utterly enchanted
sea, this lake you could leave to its own devices for a few hours
and come back to, and find that it had not stirred, this constant
and trustworthy body of water. In the shallows, the dark, water-
soaked sticks and twigs, smooth and old, were undulating in clusters on the bottom against the clean ribbed sand, and the track of
the mussel was plain. A school of minnows swam by, each min-
now with its small individual shadow, doubling the attendance,
so clear and sharp in the sunlight. Some of the other campers
were in swimming, along the shore, one of them with a cake of
soap, and the water felt thin and clear and unsubstantial. Over
the years there had been this person with the cake of soap, this
cultist, and here he was. There had been no years.

Up to the farmhouse to dinner through the teeming, dusty field, the road under our sneakers was only a two-track road. The middle track was missing, the one with the marks of the hooves and the splotches of dried, flaky manure. There had always been three tracks to choose from in choosing which track to walk in; now the choice was narrowed down to two. For a moment I missed terribly the middle alternative. But the way led past the tennis court, and something about the way it lay there in the sun reassured me; the tape had loosened along the backline, the alleys were green with plantains and other weeds, and the net (installed in June and removed in September) sagged in the dry noon, and the whole place steamed with midday heat and hunger and emptiness. There was a choice of pie for dessert, and one was blueberry and one was apple, and the waitresses were the same country girls, there having been no passage of time, only the illusion of it as in a dropped curtain—the waitresses were still fifteen; their hair had been washed, that was the only difference—they had been to the movies and seen the pretty girls with the clean hair.

Summertime, oh, summertime, pattern of life indelible, the fade-proof lake, the woods unshatterable, the pasture with the sweetfern and the juniper forever and ever, summer without end; this was the background, and the life along the shore was the design, the cottages with their innocent and tranquil design, their tiny docks with the flagpole and the American flag floating against the white clouds in the blue sky, the little paths over the roots of the trees leading from camp to camp and the paths leading back to the outhouses and the can of lime for sprinkling, and at the souvenir counters at the store the miniature birch-bark canoes and the postcards that showed things looking a little better than they looked. This was the American family at play, escaping the city heat, wondering whether the newcomers in the camp at the head of the cove were "common" or "nice," wondering whether it was true that the people who drove up for Sunday dinner at the farmhouse were turned away because there wasn't enough chicken.

It seemed to me, as I kept remembering all this, that those times and those summers had been infinitely precious and worth saving. There had been jollity and peace and goodness. The arriving (at the beginning of August) had been so big a business

in itself, at the railway station the farm wagon drawn up, the
first smell of the pine-laden air, the first glimpse of the smiling
farmer, and the great importance of the trunks and your father's
enormous authority in such matters, and the feel of the wagon
under you for the long ten-mile haul, and at the top of the last
long hill catching the first view of the lake after eleven months
of not seeing this cherished body of water. The shouts and cries
of the other campers when they saw you, and the trunks to be
unpacked, to give up their rich burden. (Arriving was less exciting nowadays, when you sneaked up in your car and parked it
under a tree near the camp and took out the bags and in five
minutes it was all over, no fuss, no loud wonderful fuss about
trunks.)

   Peace and goodness and jollity. The only thing that was wrong    10
now, really, was the sound of the place, an unfamiliar nervous
sound of the outboard motors. This was the note that jarred,
the one thing that would sometimes break the illusion and set
the years moving. In those other summertimes all motors were
inboard; and when they were at a little distance, the noise they
made was a sedative, an ingredient of summer sleep. They
were one-cylinder and two-cylinder engines, and some were
make-and-break and some were jump-spark, but they all made a
sleepy sound across the lake. The one-lungers throbbed and flut-
tered, and the twin-cylinder ones purred and purred, and that
was a quiet sound, too. But now the campers all had outboards.
In the daytime, in the hot mornings, these motors made a petu-
lant, irritable sound; at night, in the still evening when the after-
glow lit the water, they whined about one's ears like mosquitoes.
My boy loved our rented outboard, and his great desire was to
achieve single-handed mastery over it, and authority, and he soon
learned the trick of choking it a little (but not too much), and the
adjustment of the needle valve. Watching him I would remember
the things you could do with the old one-cylinder engine with the
heavy flywheel, how you could have it eating out of your hand
if you got really close to it spiritually. Motorboats in those days
didn't have clutches, and you would make a landing by shutting
off the motor at the proper time and coasting in with a dead rud-
der. But there was a way of reversing them, if you learned the
trick, by cutting the switch and putting it on again exactly on the
final dying revolution of the flywheel, so that it would kick back

against compression and begin reversing. Approaching a dock in a strong following breeze, it was difficult to slow up sufficiently by the ordinary coasting method, and if a boy felt he had complete mastery over his motor, he was tempted to keep it running beyond its time and then reverse it a few feet from the dock. It took a cool nerve, because if you threw the switch a twentieth of a second too soon you would catch the flywheel when it still had speed enough to go up past center, and the boat would leap ahead, charging bull-fashion at the dock.

We had a good week at the camp. The bass were biting well and the sun shone endlessly, day after day. We would be tired at night and lie down in the accumulated heat of the little bedrooms after the long hot day and the breeze would stir almost imperceptibly outside and the smell of the swamp drift in through the rusty screens. Sleep would come easily and in the morning the red squirrel would be on the roof, tapping out his gay routine. I kept remembering everything, lying in bed in the mornings—the small steamboat that had a long rounded stern like the lip of a Ubangi, and how quietly she ran on the moonlight sails, when the older boys played their mandolins and the girls sang and we ate doughnuts dipped in sugar, and how sweet the music was on the water in the shining night, and what it had felt like to think about girls then. After breakfast we would go up to the store and the things were in the same place—the minnows in a bottle, the plugs and spinners disarranged and pawed over by the youngsters from the boys' camp, the Fig Newtons and the Beeman's gum. Outside, the road was tarred and cars stood in front of the store. Inside, all was just as it had always been, except there was more Coca-Cola and not so much Moxie and root beer and birch beer and sarsaparilla. We would walk out with the bottle of pop apiece and sometimes the pop would backfire up our noses and hurt. We explored the streams, quietly, where the turtles slid off the sunny logs and dug their way into the soft bottom; and we lay on the town wharf and fed worms to the tame bass. Everywhere we went I had trouble making out which was I, the one walking at my side, the one walking in my pants.

One afternoon while we were there at that lake a thunderstorm came up. It was like the revival of an old melodrama that I had seen long ago with childish awe. The second-act climax of the drama of the electrical disturbance over a lake in America had not changed in any important respect. This was the big scene, still the big scene. The whole thing was so familiar, the first feeling of oppression and heat and a general air around camp of not wanting to go very far away. In midafternoon (it was all the same) a curious darkening of the sky, and a lull in everything that had made life tick; and then the way the boats suddenly swung the other way at their moorings with the coming of a breeze out of the new quarter, and the premonitory rumble. Then the kettle drum, then the snare, then the bass drum and cymbals, then crackling light against the dark, and the gods grinning and licking their chops in the hills. Afterward the calm, the rain steadily rustling in the calm lake, the return of light and hope and spirits, and the campers running out in joy and relief to go swimming in the rain, their bright cries perpetuating the deathless joke about how they were getting simply drenched, and the children screaming with delight at the new sensation of bathing in the rain, and the joke about getting drenched linking the generations in a strong indestructible chain. And the comedian who waded in carrying an umbrella.

When the others went swimming, my son said he was going in, too. He pulled his dripping trunks from the line where they had hung all through the shower and wrung them out. Languidly, and with no thought of going in, I watched him, his hard little body, skinny and bare, saw him wince slightly as he pulled up around his vitals the small, soggy, icy garment. As he buckled the swollen belt, suddenly my groin felt the chill of death.

*For Discussion and Writing*

1. Why does White describe the lake as "fade-proof" and the woods as "unshatterable" (par. 8)?

2. White uses description to give a fairly simple story great richness. Note and explain the effectiveness of five descriptive moments in the essay.

3. **connections**   As long as there has been writing, the natural world has served writers as a subject in its own right and as vehicle for expressing other things. Read "Once More to the Lake" next to Eli Clare's "Clearcut: Explaining the Distance" (p. 95) with this idea in mind. How does each writer use the natural world? How does each essay use nature as topic? How does each use it as vehicle?

4. Describe a childhood trip you remember well. Try to borrow descriptive devices from White.

5. **looking further**   White reads the changes on and around the lake in terms of his own mortality. How else might they be read? Literary critics with ecological concerns sometimes read works of art for what they reveal about our attitudes toward the natural world and our place in it. Try to read "Once More to the Lake" in this way. What can you say about the way "nature" is thought of and treated by people within the essay as well as by its author?

WALT WHITMAN

# Slang in America

*Walt Whitman (1819–1892) was born and raised in New York state; he was born and lived in Huntington, on Long Island, and from the age of four, lived in Brooklyn. He left school at age eleven and worked in a law office; he later worked as a typesetter, writer, and editor at various newspapers, taught, and founded his own short-lived news-paper, all while writing fiction and poetry for various publications. Whitman's* Leaves of Grass *(1855), a collection of poetry that would continue to grow and be revised by the author for the rest of his life, is one of the best-known and most influential works of American poetry, containing important poems such as "Song of Myself" and "Crossing Brooklyn Ferry." At the time of its publication,* Leaves of Grass *was generally positively received including by Ralph Waldo Emerson, but was condemned as obscene by others. During the Civil War, Whitman worked in the Army paymaster's office and volunteered as a nurse. He wrote the poetry collection* Drum Taps *(1865) during this period, seeing it to publication a month after the end of the war. While revis-ing his masterpiece* Leaves of Grass *up to just before his death in 1892, Whitman also produced* Democratic Vistas *(1871), a book on American history, politics, and culture;* Memoranda During the War *(1876), a book on his time in army hospitals during the war; and a collection of nonfiction pieces,* Specimen Days *(1882).*

*"Slang in America," first published in 1885, is the culminating com-mentary on language use by a poet who was as deeply interested in democ-racy and human diversity as he was fascinated by everyday American speech. As you read it, think about the ways our attitudes about language can be connected to our attitudes about people and society.*

View'd freely, the English language is the accretion and growth of every dialect, race, and range of time, and is both the free and compacted composition of all. From this point of view, it stands for Language in the largest sense, and is really the great-est of studies. It involves so much; is indeed a sort of universal absorber, combiner, and conqueror. The scope of its etymologies is the scope not only of man and civilization, but the history of Nature in all departments, and of the organic Universe, brought up to date; for all are comprehended in words, and their backgrounds. This is when words become vitaliz'd, and stand for things, as they unerringly and soon come to do, in the mind that enters on their study with fitting spirit, grasp, and appreciation.

Slang, profoundly consider'd, is the lawless germinal element, below all words and sentences, and behind all poetry, and proves a certain perennial rankness and protestantism in speech. As the United States inherit by far their most precious possession—the language they talk and write—from the Old World, under and out of its feudal institutes, I will allow myself to borrow a simile, even of those forms farthest removed from American Democracy. Considering Language then as some mighty potentate, into the majestic audience-hall of the monarch ever enters a personage like one of Shakspere's clowns, and takes position there, and plays a part even in the stateliest ceremonies. Such is Slang, or indirection, an attempt of common humanity to escape from bald literalism, and express itself illimitably, which in highest walks produces poets and poems, and doubtless in pre-historic times gave the start to, and perfected, the whole immense tangle of the old mythologies. For, curious as it may appear, it is strictly the same impulse-source, the same thing. Slang, too, is the wholesome fermentation or eructation of those processes eternally active in language, by which froth and specks are thrown up, mostly to pass away; though occasionally to settle and permanently chrystallize.

To make it plainer, it is certain that many of the oldest and solidest words we use, were originally generated from the daring and license of slang. In the processes of word-formation, myriads die, but here and there the attempt attracts superior meanings, becomes valuable and indispensable, and lives forever. Thus the term *right* means literally only straight. *Wrong* primarily meant twisted, distorted. *Integrity* meant oneness. *Spirit* meant breath, or flame. A *supercilious* person was one who rais'd his eyebrows. To *insult* was to leap against. If you *influenc'd* a man, you but flow'd into him. The Hebrew word which is translated *prophesy* meant to bubble up and pour forth as a fountain. The enthusiast bubbles up with the Spirit of God within him, and it pours forth from him like a fountain. The word *prophecy* is misunderstood. Many suppose that it is limited to mere prediction; that is but the lesser portion of prophecy. The greater work is to reveal God. Every true religious enthusiast is a prophet.

Language, be it remember'd, is not an abstract construction of the learn'd, or of dictionary-makers, but is something arising out of the work, needs, ties, joys, affections, tastes, of long generations of humanity, and has its bases broad and low, close to the ground. Its final decisions are made by the masses, people nearest the concrete, having most to do with actual land and sea. It impermeates all, the Past as well as the Present, and is the grandest triumph of the human intellect. "Those mighty works of art," says Addington Symonds, "which we call languages, in the construction of which whole peoples unconsciously co-operated, the forms of which were determin'd not by individual genius, but by the instincts of successive generations, acting to one end, inherent in the nature of the race — Those poems of pure thought and fancy, cadenced not in words, but in living imagery, fountainheads of inspiration, mirrors of the mind of nascent nations, which we call Mythologies — these surely are more marvellous in their infantine spontaneity than any more mature production of the races which evolv'd them. Yet we are utterly ignorant of their embryology; the true science of Origins is yet in its cradle."

Daring as it is to say so, in the growth of Language it is certain that the retrospect of slang from the start would be the recalling from their nebulous conditions of all that is poetical in the stores of human utterance. Moreover, the honest delving, as of late years, by the German and British workers in comparative philology, has pierc'd and dispers'd many of the falsest bubbles of centuries; and will disperse many more. It was long recorded that in Scandinavian mythology the heroes in the Norse Paradise drank out of the skulls of their slain enemies. Later investigation proves the word taken for skulls to mean *horns* of beasts slain in the hunt. And what reader had not been exercis'd over the traces of that feudal custom, by which *seigneurs* warm'd their feet in the bowels of serfs, the abdomen being open'd for the purpose? It now is made to appear that the serf was only required to submit his unharm'd abdomen as a foot cushion while his lord supp'd, and was required to chafe the legs of the *seigneur* with his hands.

5

It is curiously in embryons and childhood, and among the illit-
erate, we always find the groundwork and start, of this great science, and its noblest products. What a relief most people have
in speaking of a man not by his true and formal name, with
a "Mister" to it, but by some odd or homely appellative. The pro-
pensity to approach a meaning not directly and squarely, but
by circuitous styles of expression, seems indeed a born quality
of the common people everywhere, evidenced by nick-names,
and the inveterate determination of the masses to bestow sub-
titles, sometimes ridiculous, sometimes very apt. Always among
the soldiers during the Secession War, one heard of "Little
Mac" (Gen. McClellan), or of "Uncle Billy" (Gen. Sherman).
"The old man" was, of course, very common. Among the rank
and file, both armies, it was very general to speak of the differ-
ent States they came from by their slang names. Those from
Maine were call'd Foxes; New Hampshire, Granite Boys; Mas-
sachusetts, Bay Staters; Vermont, Green Mountain Boys; Rhode
Island, Gun Flints; Connecticut, Wooden Nutmegs; New York,
Knickerbockers; New Jersey, Clam Catchers; Pennsylvania,
Logher Heads; Delaware, Muskrats; Maryland, Claw Thumpers;
Virginia, Beagles; North Carolina, Tar Boilers; South Carolina,
Weasels; Georgia, Buzzards; Louisiana, Creoles; Alabama,
Lizards; Kentucky, Corn Crackers; Ohio, Buckeyes; Michigan,
Wolverines; Indiana, Hoosiers; Illinois, Suckers; Missouri, Pukes;
Mississippi, Tad Poles; Florida, Fly up the Creeks; Wisconsin,
Badgers; Iowa, Hawkeyes; Oregon, Hard Cases. Indeed I am not
sure but slang names have more than once made Presidents.
"Old Hickory," (Gen. Jackson) is one case in point. "Tippecanoe,
and Tyler too," another.

I find the same rule in the people's conversations everywhere.
I heard this among the men of the city horse-cars, where the conductor is often call'd a "snatcher" (i.e., because his characteristic
duty is to constantly pull or snatch the bell-strap, to stop or go
on). Two young fellows are having a friendly talk, amid which,
says 1st conductor, "What did you do before you was a snatcher?"
Answer of 2d conductor, "Nail'd." (Translation of answer: "I
work'd as carpenter.") What is a "boom"? says one editor to
another. "Esteem'd contemporary," says the other, "a boom is a
bulge." "Barefoot whiskey" is the Tennessee name for the undiluted stimulant. In the slang of the New York common restaurant

waiters a plate of ham and beans is known as "stars and stripes," codfish balls as "sleeve-buttons," and hash as "mystery."

The Western States of the Union are, however, as may be supposed, the special areas of slang, not only in conversation, but in names of localities, towns, rivers, etc. A late Oregon traveller says:

> On your way to Olympia by rail, you cross a river called the Shookum-Chuck; your train stops at places named Newaukum, Tumwater, and Toutle; and if you seek further you will hear of whole counties labell'd Wahkiakum, or Snohomish, or Kitsar, or Klikatat; and Cowlitz, Hookium, and Nenolelops greet and offend you. They complain in Olympia that Washington Territory gets but little immigration; but what wonder? What man, having the whole American continent to choose from, would willingly date his letters from the county of Snohomish or bring up his children in the city of Nenolelops? The village of Tumwater is, as I am ready to bear witness, very pretty indeed; but surely an emigrant would think twice before he establish'd himself either there or at Toutle. Seattle is sufficiently barbarous; Stelicoom is no better; and I suspect that the Northern Pacific Railroad terminus has been fixed at Tacoma because it is one of the few places on Puget Sound whose name does not inspire horror.

Then a Nevada paper chronicles the departure of a mining party from Reno: "The toughest set of roosters, that ever shook the dust off any town left Reno yesterday for the new mining district of Cornucopia. They came here from Virginia. Among the crowd were four New York cock-fighters, two Chicago murderers, three Baltimore bruisers, one Philadelphia prize-fighter, four San Francisco hoodlums, three Virginia beats, two Union Pacific roughs, and two check guerrillas." Among the far-west newspapers, have been, or are, *The Fairplay* (Colorado) *Flume, The Solid Muldoon,* of Ouray, *The Tombstone Epitaph,* of Nevada, *The Jimplecute,* of Texas, and *The Bazoo,* of Missouri. Shirttail Bend, Whiskey Flat, Puppytown, Wild Yankee Ranch, Squaw Flat, Rawhide Ranch, Loafer's Ravine, Squitch Gulch, Toenail Lake, are a few of the names of places in Butte county, Cal.

Perhaps indeed no place or term gives more luxuriant illustrations of the fermentation processes I have mention'd, and their froth and specks, than those Mississippi and Pacific coast regions, at the present day. Hasty and grotesque as are some of the names, others are of an appropriateness and originality unsurpassable. This applies to the Indian words, which are often perfect. Oklahoma is proposed in Congress for the name 10 of one of our new Territories. Hog-eye, Lick-skillet, Rake-pocket and Steal-easy are the names of some Texan towns. Miss Bremer found among the aborigines the following names: Men's, Hornpoint; Round-Wind; Stand-and-look-out; The-Cloud-that-goes-aside; Iron-toe; Seek-the-sun; Iron-flash; Red-bottle; White-spindle; Black-dog; Two-feathers-of-honor; Gray-grass; Bushy-tail; Thunder-face; Go-on-the-burning-sod; Spirits-of-the-dead. Women's, Keep-the-fire; Spiritual-woman; Second-daughter-of-the-house; Blue-bird.

Certainly philologists have not given enough attention to this element and its results, which, I repeat, can probably be found working everywhere to-day, amid modern conditions, with as much life and activity as in far-back Greece or India, under prehistoric ones. Then the wit—the rich flashes of humor and genius and poetry—darting out often from a gang of laborers, railroadmen, miners, drivers or boatmen! How often have I hover'd at the edge of a crowd of them, to hear their repartees and impromptus! You get more real fun from half an hour with them than from the books of all "the American humorists."

The science of language has large and close analogies in geological science, with its ceaseless evolution, its fossils, and its numberless submerged layers and hidden strata, the infinite go-before of the present. Or, perhaps Language is more like some vast living body, or perennial body of bodies. And slang not only brings the first feeders of it, but is afterward the start of fancy, imagination and humor, breathing into its nostrils the breath of life.

## For Discussion and Writing

1. How is the study of language like geological science, as Whitman says it is?

2. Whitman's form is endlessly interesting, if you are interested in form (and we hope you are). One element of Whitman's style here is his diction—the words he chooses to use. Of particular note is his use of a wide range of kinds of words, from the most everyday, two-syllable words to the rare, multisyllabic, Latinate words—perhaps fittingly for an essay about his love of all kinds of words. Read through the essay and identify five words you did not know. Look them up (as you always should when you encounter a word you don't know), write down the definition in your own words, and reflect on what you produce. Why do you think Whitman chose these words? Were there

simpler words he could have chosen? Do other words exist that he could have used instead, or are these the only words for the meaning he's trying to convey? What's the effect of these choices on the reader? (Feel free to include "eructation" in your list.)

3. **connections**   Compare Whitman's essay to Maria Michela Sassi's "The Sea Was Never Blue" (p. 325) on the topic of language. How do their subjects compare? How do the ways they explore them compare? How does each author discuss the power of language? Where do they differ in their conclusions and assumptions?

4. Whitman more than once uses metaphors involving life-giving to describe colloquial language in this essay: words are "vitaliz'd" (par. 1), slang "breathe the breath of life" into language. We are taught in primary and secondary school that the kinds of words we use in our writing for school should be proper and correct, and so should not contain slang. But linguists and students of composition know, as Whitman did, that everyday language brings writing to life; this doesn't mean that "proper" or academic English doesn't have value, and isn't required in certain settings, but it's not better in any meaningful sense. In "proper" English, write a substantial paragraph about yourself, or your day, or a movie you just saw—the subject doesn't really matter—and then rewrite it in less proper, colloquial, colorful, slang-ridden English. Then reflect on what you've written. Was one easier or more fun to write than the other? Rereading your two paragraphs, is one easier or more entertaining or more informative than the other? Is there a way to write that combines these two registers?

5. **looking further**   Do a little research into "proper English." What can you find out about how people define it, where it comes from, how it is used, and how it is valued? Summarize these findings and reflect on the conventions we follow in our school and work lives, not only in writing but also in speaking. What does the existence of these conventions tell you about the organization of society? What does speaking "proper English" or not speaking it mean in your community? In your school? In your workplace?

# VIRGINIA WOOLF

# Professions for Women

*Born Adeline Virginia Stephen in London in 1882, Virginia Woolf is one of the most important writers not just of her time but of all literary history. A modernist, Woolf, along with contemporaries such as James Joyce, T. S. Eliot, Ezra Pound, and Gertrude Stein, revolutionized literature by inventing new forms that explored the rich inner lives of their subjects. She is known especially for the novels* Mrs. Dalloway *(1925) and* To the Lighthouse *(1927) but also for the nonfiction and feminist* A Room of One's Own *(1929).*

*One section of* A Room of One's Own *is devoted to the imagining of a sister of William Shakespeare, equally talented but, because of the possibilities available to women of her time and place, unable to create masterpieces as he had. Woolf imagines this counterfactual in order to argue for expanded possibilities for women. As you read "Professions for Women," think of it (as Woolf did) as a sequel to* A Room of One's Own, *and consider the ways it further reflects on its concerns but also raises some new ones of its own.*

When your secretary invited me to come here, she told me that your Society is concerned with the employment of women and she suggested that I might tell you something about my own professional experiences. It is true I am a woman; it is true I am employed; but what professional experiences have I had? It is difficult to say. My profession is literature; and in that profession there are fewer experiences for women than in any other, with the exception of the stage — fewer, I mean, that are peculiar to women. For the road was cut many years ago — by Fanny Burney, by Aphra Behn, by Harriet Martineau, by Jane Austen, by George Eliot — many famous women, and many more unknown and forgotten, have been before me, making the path smooth, and regulating my steps. Thus, when I came to write, there were very few material obstacles in my way. Writing was a reputable and harmless occupation. The family peace was not broken by the scratching of a pen. No demand was made upon the family purse. For ten and sixpence one can buy paper enough to write all the plays of Shakespeare—if one has a mind that way. Pianos and models, Paris, Vienna and Berlin, masters and mistresses, are not needed by a writer. The cheapness of writing paper is, of course, the reason why women have succeeded as writers before they have succeeded in the other professions.

But to tell you my story—it is a simple one. You have only got to figure to yourselves a girl in a bedroom with a pen in her hand. She had only to move that pen from left to right—from ten o'clock to one. Then it occurred to her to do what is simple and cheap enough after all—to slip a few of those pages into an envelope, fix a penny stamp in the corner, and drop the envelope into the red box at the corner. It was thus that I became a journalist; and my effort was rewarded on the first day of the following month—a very glorious day it was for me—by a letter from an editor containing a cheque for one pound ten shillings and sixpence. But to show you how little I deserve to be called a professional woman, how little I know of the struggles and difficulties of such lives, I have to admit that instead of spending that sum upon bread and butter, rent, shoes and stockings, or butcher's bills, I went out and bought a cat—a beautiful cat, a Persian cat, which very soon involved me in bitter disputes with my neighbours.

What could be easier than to write articles and to buy Persian cats with the profits? But wait a moment. Articles have to be about something. Mine, I seem to remember, was about a novel by a famous man. And while I was writing this review, I discovered that if I were going to review books I should need to do battle with a certain phantom. And the phantom was a woman, and when I came to know her better I called her after the heroine of a famous poem, The Angel in the House. It was she who used to come between me and my paper when I was writing reviews. It was she who bothered me and wasted my time and so tormented me that at last I killed her. You who come of a younger and happier generation may not have heard of her—you may not know what I mean by the Angel in the House. I will describe her as shortly as I can. She was intensely sympathetic. She was immensely charming. She was utterly unselfish. She excelled in the difficult arts of family life. She sacrificed herself daily.

If there was chicken, she took the leg; if there was a draught she sat in it—in short she was so constituted that she never had a mind or a wish of her own, but preferred to sympathize always with the minds and wishes of others. Above all—I need not say it—she was pure. Her purity was supposed to be her chief beauty—her blushes, her great grace. In those days—the last of Queen Victoria—every house had its Angel. And when I came to write I encountered her with the very first words. The shadow of her wings fell on my page; I heard the rustling of her skirts in the room. Directly, that is to say, I took my pen in my hand to review that novel by a famous man, she slipped behind me and whispered: "My dear, you are a young woman. You are writing about a book that has been written by a man. Be sympathetic; be tender; flatter; deceive; use all the arts and wiles of our sex. Never let anybody guess that you have a mind of your own. Above all, be pure." And she made as if to guide my pen. I now record the one act for which I take some credit to myself, though the credit rightly belongs to some excellent ancestors of mine who left me a certain sum of money—shall we say five hundred pounds a year?—so that it was not necessary for me to depend solely on charm for my living. I turned upon her and caught her by the throat. I did my best to kill her. My excuse, if I were to be had up in a court of law, would be that I acted in self-defence. Had I not killed her she would have killed me. She would have plucked the heart out of my writing. For, as I found, directly I put pen to paper, you cannot review even a novel without having a mind of your own, without expressing what you think to be the truth about human relations, morality, sex. And all these questions, according to the Angel of the House, cannot be dealt with freely and openly by women; they must charm, they must conciliate, they must—to put it bluntly—tell lies if they are to succeed. Thus, whenever I felt the shadow of her wing or the radiance of her halo upon my page, I took up the inkpot and flung it at her. She died hard. Her fictitious nature was of great assistance to her. It is far harder to kill a phantom than a reality. She was always creeping back when I thought I had despatched her. Though I flatter myself that I killed her in the end, the struggle was severe; it took much time that had better have been spent upon learning Greek grammar; or in roaming the world in search of adventures. But it was a real experience; it was an experience that was bound to befall all women writers at that time. Killing the Angel in the House was part of the occupation of a woman writer.

But to continue my story. The Angel was dead; what then remained? You may say that what remained was a simple and common object—a young woman in a bedroom with an inkpot. In other words, now that she had rid herself of falsehood, that young woman had only to be herself. Ah, but what is "herself"? I mean, what is a woman? I assure you, I do not know. I do not believe that you know. I do not believe that anybody can know until she has expressed herself in all the arts and professions open to human skill. That indeed is one of the reasons why I have come here out of respect for you, who are in process of showing us by your experiments what a woman is, who are in process of providing us, by your failures and successes, with that extremely important piece of information.

But to continue the story of my professional experiences. I made one pound ten and six by my first review; and I bought a Persian cat with the proceeds. Then I grew ambitious. A Persian cat is all very well, I said; but a Persian cat is not enough. I must have a motor car. And it was thus that I became a novelist—for it is a very strange thing that people will give you a motor car if you will tell them a story. It is a still stranger thing that there is nothing so delightful in the world as telling stories. It is far pleasanter than writing reviews of famous novels. And yet, if I am to obey your secretary and tell you my professional experiences as a novelist, I must tell you about a very strange experience that befell me as a novelist. And to understand it you must try first to imagine a novelist's state of mind. I hope I am not giving away professional secrets if I say that a novelist's chief desire is to be as unconscious as possible. He has to induce in himself a state of perpetual lethargy. He wants life to proceed with the utmost quiet and regularity. He wants to see the same faces, to read the same books, to do the same things day after day, month after month, while he is writing, so that nothing may break the illusion in which he is living—so that nothing may disturb or disquiet the mysterious nosings about, feelings round, darts, dashes and sudden discoveries of that very shy and illusive spirit, the imagination. I suspect that this state is the same both for men and women. Be that as it may, I want you to imagine me writing a novel in a state of trance. I want you to figure to yourselves a girl sitting with a pen in her hand, which for minutes, and indeed for hours, she never dips into the inkpot. The image that comes to my mind when I think of this girl is the image of a fisherman lying sunk in dreams on the verge of a deep lake with a rod held out over the water. She was letting her imagination sweep unchecked round every rock and cranny of the world that lies submerged in the depths of our unconscious being. Now came the experience, the experience that I believe to be far commoner with women writers than with men. The line raced through the girl's fingers. Her imagination had rushed away. It had sought the pools, the depths, the dark places where the largest fish slumber. And then there was a smash. There was an explosion. There was foam and confusion. The imagination had dashed itself against something hard. The girl was roused from her dream. She was indeed in a state of the most acute and difficult distress. To speak without figure she had thought of something, something about the body, about the passions which it was unfitting for her as a woman to say. Men, her reason told her, would be shocked. The consciousness of—what men will say of a woman who speaks the truth about her passions had roused her from her artist's state of unconsciousness. She could write no more. The trance was over. Her imagination could work no longer. This I believe to be a very common experience with women writers—they are impeded by the extreme conventionality of the other sex. For though men sensibly allow themselves great freedom in these respects, I doubt that they realize or can control the extreme severity with which they condemn such freedom in women.

These then were two very genuine experiences of my own. These were two of the adventures of my professional life. The first—killing the Angel in the House—I think I solved. She died. But the second, telling the truth about my own experiences as a body, I do not think I solved. I doubt that any woman has solved it yet. The obstacles against her are still immensely powerful—and yet they are very difficult to define. Outwardly, what is simpler than to write books? Outwardly, what obstacles are there for a woman rather than for a man? Inwardly, I think, the case is very different; she has still many ghosts to fight, many prejudices to overcome. Indeed it will be a long time still, I think, before a woman can sit down to write a book without finding a phantom to be slain, a rock to be dashed against. And if this is so in literature, the freest of all professions for women, how is it in the new professions which you are now for the first time entering?

Those are the questions that I should like, had I time, to ask you. And indeed, if I have laid stress upon these professional experiences of mine, it is because I believe that they are, though in different forms, yours also. Even when the path is nominally open — when there is nothing to prevent a woman from being a doctor, a lawyer, a civil servant — there are many phantoms and obstacles, as I believe, looming in her way. To discuss and define them is I think of great value and importance; for thus only can the labour be shared, the difficulties be solved. But besides this, it is necessary also to discuss the ends and the aims for which we are fighting, for which we are doing battle with these formidable obstacles. Those aims cannot be taken for granted; they must be perpetually questioned and examined. The whole position, as I see it — here in this hall surrounded by women practising for the first time in history I know not how many different professions — is one of extraordinary interest and importance. You have won rooms of your own in the house hitherto exclusively owned by men. You are able, though not without great labour and effort, to pay the rent. You are earning your five hundred pounds a year. But this freedom is only a beginning — the room is your own, but it is still bare. It has to be furnished; it has to be decorated; it has to be shared. How are you going to furnish it, how are you going to decorate it? With whom are you going to share it, and upon what terms? These, I think are questions of the utmost importance and interest. For the first time in history you are able to ask them; for the first time you are able to decide for yourselves what the answers should be. Willingly would I stay and discuss those questions and answers — but not to-night. My time is up; and I must cease.

## For Discussion and Writing

1. What is the Angel in the House?
2. Think about narrative form in this essay. Woolf claims early in it that her story "is a simple one" (par. 2). Is it? If not, how does she complicate it? Why does she claim early on that it is?
3. **connections**  Woolf asks, "[W]hat is a woman?" (par. 4) not in isolation but as part of her story of becoming a writer. Read this essay alongside Joan Didion's "On Keeping a Notebook" (p. 118). How is

Didion's essay in part implicitly about the explicit subject of Woolf's essay? Where do you think Didion's exploration of the story of her writing life touches on the same concerns as Woolf's? Is there an Angel in Didion's house?

4. On one of her motivations for becoming a novelist, Woolf writes, "[I]t is a very strange thing that people will give you a motor car if you will tell them a story" (par. 5). While it is a luxury to do work that you love, if you could choose a profession purely out of interest, while being realistic (e.g., no professional basketball players) and selecting something that would pay (give you a motor car), what would it be? Why? Do you think you will end up doing it? Why, or why not?

5. **looking further**   Find one or two examples of people who have successfully built careers in the field you would like to work in. They can be famous enough to have online biographies you can consult or they can be people you interview. How did they get there? What did they have to do in terms of schooling, training, and other work to prepare themselves and gain entry into their field? What obstacles did they encounter, and how did they overcome them?

HANYA YANAGIHARA

# A Pet Tortoise Who Will Outlive Us All

*Hanya Yanagihara was born in Los Angeles, California, and raised in many places, including California, New York, Maryland, Texas, and Hawaii; she is a fourth generation Hawaiian, and attended high school there. Yanagihara attended Smith College and worked in publicity in New York after college. She was a writer and editor at* Conde Nast Traveler *until she became editor-in-chief of* The New York Times Style Magazine. *She is the author of two novels,* The People in the Trees *(2013) and* A Little Life *(2015).*

Every morning, Fred takes a walk around my parents' yard in suburban Honolulu. The yard, though small, around 600 square feet, is beautiful, green and cool and jungly, densely planted with lacy native ferns and heavy-headed crimson heliconia and fragrant with white flowers: gardenia, plumeria, ginger, night-blooming jasmine. Fred is 15 years old and 80 pounds, and since my parents adopted him two years ago, he has never left this yard. When he is dozing in the shade, the old shower trees outside the picket fence that surrounds the yard rain their pink and yellow petals down on him.

People get up early in Hawaii—by 6:30, kids are being dropped off at school and adults are driving to work—and yet Fred doesn't start moving until 8 or, sometimes, 9. By the time he does, the neighborhood is silent. Everyone else has already begun the day.

But exceptions are made for Fred, because Fred has nowhere to go and nothing to do, and my parents expect nothing from him. This is because Fred is not a human, but a sulcata tortoise, an impulse purchase ($250, from a man living a few minutes drive away, near Waikiki) whose consequences—as with all impulse purchases—were not quite fully imagined. Every morning, Fred must be fed: a mixture of timothy hay, romaine and protein-rich kibble, which is spread across a baking tray so he can see it easily. As Fred is eating, his turds—wet, cold, fat as hand-rolled cigars and strafed with undigested hay and grass—must be collected and the lawn around them doused with water. Some five hours later, lunch must be provided. Then, at around 6 in the evening, someone has to check that Fred has put himself to bed in his wooden house, where he spends at least 20 minutes bumping and scraping against the walls and the floor: the sulcata, which is native to sub-Saharan Africa, is like most tortoises a burrower by nature; in those arid climates, tortoises will dig deep tunnels in order to access damper, cooler earth. My parents' neighborhood is humid—it rains every morning and every evening, a light, brief mist that makes the air smell loamy and slightly feral—but Fred is conditioned to dig regardless, his stumpy back legs chafing against the flagstones beneath his house. By 8 p.m., he is silent, sluggish; like all reptiles, Fred is coldblooded, and he will remain in his house until the morning and the return of the sun and its heat.

Fred is not rare: not as a species (the sulcata is one of the largest species of tortoise in the world) and not even as a pet, not in Hawaii, at least, where there is a largely Asian population, which associates them with good fortune, wisdom and long life. And yet when the occasional passer-by looks over the fence and sees Fred marching across the yard, his legs churning with the same steady, hardy energy of a toddler delighting in his newfound ability to walk, they are always startled. The surprise is attributable to his size, as well as his shape and color; at first glance, you might mistake him for a large rock, only to then realize that the rock is moving.

But I think the other surprise of Fred has less to do with his 5 unexpected presence and more to do with what he represents. To be in the company of a tortoise is to be reminded—instantly, inarticulably—of the oldness of the world and the newness of us (humans, specifically, but also mammals in general). Nature has created thousands of creatures, but most of us have been redrawn over the millenniums: Our heads have grown larger, our teeth smaller, our legs longer, our jaws weaker. But tortoises, some varieties of which are 300 million years old, older than the dinosaurs, are a rough draft that was never refined, because they never needed to be. They are proof of nature's genius and of our own imperfection, our fragility and brevity in a world that existed long before us and will exist long after we're gone. They are older than we are in all ways, as a tribe and as individuals—they can live 150 years (and can grow to be 200 pounds). As such, you cannot help feeling a sort of humility around them: They may be slow and ungainly and lumpily fashioned, but they are, in their durability and unchangeability, perfect in a way we aren't. It is all this that makes them unique and unsettling animals to live with, for to be around them is to be reminded, incessantly, of our own vulnerability—and our own imminent deaths.

Last July, I went to Honolulu to meet Fred and to spend the summer with my parents. My parents and I have a warm relationship, even though, or perhaps because, I don't speak to or visit them frequently; until my most recent trip there, the previous July, I hadn't seen them in six years. I live in New York, and they live in Hawaii, and while it's true that traveling to the islands requires a certain commitment of time, the real reason I stayed away is that there were other places I wanted to go and other things I wanted to see. Of all the gifts and advantages my parents have given me, one of the greatest is their understanding of this desire, their conviction that it is the duty of children to leave and do what they want, and the duty of parents to not just accept this but to encourage it. When I was 14 and first leaving my parents—then living in East Texas—to attend high school in Honolulu, my father told me that any parent who expected anything from his child (he was speaking of money and accomplishment, but he also meant love, devotion and caretaking) was bound to be disappointed, because it was foolish and selfish to raise children in the hope that they might someday repay the debt of their existence; he has maintained this ever since. It is, in a culture that cherishes familial proximity, a radical way of thinking by people who otherwise pride themselves on their conventionality (though, lovably, their idea of the conventional tends to not actually be so at all).

This philosophy explains and contradicts their attachment to a pet that, in many ways, defies what we believe a pet should be. Those of us with animals in our lives don't like to think of ourselves as having expectations for them, but we do: We want their loyalty and dedication, and we want these things to be expressed in a way that we can understand; we want the bird chirping when we walk in the door, the dog trotting toward us, drooling and hopeful, the cat rumbling with pleasure as she butts her head against our fist, the horse nickering and shuffling in his stall as he hears our footfall.

Fred, however, provides none of these things. Other than a series of grunts when he's defecating, he can't make noises. Although he'll let you stroke the top of his cool, leathery head, he's literally unhuggable. Although he is, in his way, friendly or, less generously, un-shy—every deliveryman or neighbor who enters the yard is approached and inspected—he is not a creature who, you feel, has any particular fondness for you.

Owning a pet is often an act of assumed, albeit unacknowledged, reciprocity; when people speak of their pet's unconditional love, they are in fact revealing the unspoken, highly one-sided exchange of pet ownership: I, the human, will provide you with food and shelter, and you, the pet, will give me endless affection and acceptance, no matter how crummy a person I may be. Children, being humans and therefore manipulable only to a certain extent, may disappoint; a pet is not allowed to disappoint, or else it won't remain a pet for long.

Much as the role of a child has changed in the past century—from 10 undersize workers to creatures to spoil and cherish—so, too, have the animals in our lives come to fulfill a certain need. Many of us in the developed world have easier lives than our forebears had: There is less arduous labor; there is less labor in general. But it can often feel that the luxury of time has been accompanied by a heightened, commensurate craving for love: Part of the modern condition is wondering who might love us and how that love might be more perfectly expressed, and animals' new duty is to answer both of those problems, to make this loneliest of ages feel a little less lonely.

Being with Fred, therefore, makes me re-evaluate why we keep pets at all. Along with his inability to behave as a modern pet ought, his appeal as an animate being is of a specific and subtle kind: He is stolid and implacable, neither of which are traits we typically value in any species we hope to employ as companions. Then there is the fact of the amount of care he demands, which is accompanied by the contradictory suspicion that he might be perfectly content on his own, without us: As much as he may enjoy them, Fred doesn't actually need company, or water, or even food; were he at home in Sudan, he would be eating (dry grasses; shrubbery) only every few days. To own a turtle, then, means accepting that you will be seen as the neighborhood eccentrics, people who have chosen a secondary position in their own households. If people who love cats are self-assured (but self-absorbed), and people who love dogs are self-satisfied (but insecure), then it might be said that people who love turtles are, to some degree, fatalistic: Loving a turtle means pouring endless amounts of affection into a bucket that will never fill because it has a hole cut in its bottom.

And yet Fred's presence in my parents' life seemed to be an expression of something beyond mere eccentricity: As the days passed, I couldn't help seeing him as a late-in-life yank of the parental tether. My parents are 71 and 69; I am 42. Fred, therefore, will most likely outlive not only my father and mother but me as well. In the midafternoon, when Fred was at his most alert, I would sit and watch him: his asplike face, his determined, plucky trudge, which made his head bounce a little with every step, his piggy nostrils, each the size and shape of a watermelon seed, the faint, coin-size indentations on the side of his head where his ears lay. As I watched him, I wondered: Why would my parents assume such a responsibility? Why would they bring into their—my; our—lives something so disruptive?

The easy explanation was that they had simply chosen not to consider it: My parents are young enough and unsentimental enough that death (how, when, where) was still sufficiently distant to be an abstraction, a dinner-table conversation. But though they claimed to be ready to die at any moment—they had reached an age in which they viewed life as a contractor's punch list, a series of tasks that had been satisfactorily, or at least competently, completed—Fred's arrival belied those claims. Their adoption of him suggested that they might actually have expected something from my brother and me after all. My parents weren't upset when we left home (they were in fact pretty gleeful), and yet here, in Fred, was a collective problem, a challenge that would force a reunion of our small family. For what, after all, makes adult children remain in contact with their parents? Fondness, of course; love. But in the absence of or in addition to those, there is inheritance, the stuff (and quarrels and resentments) that will be left behind when the parents die.

In a post-industrialized country and era, there are fewer and fewer practical reasons for a family to stay together once its children are grown. We do so out of tradition, but tradition isn't an imperative. Fred, however, was his own imperative, a difficulty that demanded a response, a legacy that, unlike a car or a house, needed a caretaker, an animal who was both a repository of a surplus of parental love and an announcement of parental need: Come home. See what we've taken on. When you see him, will you remember us? Fred was a way of requesting devotion without having to literally ask.

I wish I could say that we had decided what to do with Fred 15 by the time I left Hawaii, but we hadn't. Instead, we watched Fred circle the yard, speaking of him with the same affectionate bewilderment we would a precocious child. I had already told my parents that I wouldn't take Fred when they died; my brother said he wouldn't, either. Our refusal seemed to provide them with a curious, even paradoxical contentment — my brother and I might not need them to stay alive (we would like them to, but like is not the same as need), but Fred did, or so they could believe. And so, for him, they would. If one of pets' great gifts is their ability to make us feel loved, their greater gift is how they make us feel necessary.

In the months after my return home, my parents sent me messages: Fred was getting bigger. He had broken through one of the metal gates and tried to escape. He was having diarrhea. He liked only red hibiscus, not pink. He had rejected the Swiss chard they tried to feed him. He was a whim that was becoming a burden. And yet they couldn't imagine letting him go. He was their pet, and they were going to take care of him, even if they didn't truly understand what that might entail. But what person who's responsible for another living creature ever really understands what care entails? You may think you know, or have some sense. But you never truly know until you are doing the actual work of caring, in particular for something that may not care for you in return but to whom you have sworn your allegiance.

Sometimes, after reading these messages, I found myself slipping into a daydream, imagining Fred's life — and, by extension, my own — years into the future. I imagined a day in which my parents were dead and still no one had determined what to do with Fred: where he would live, who would talk to him.

I imagined Fred edging out of his wooden house to find something to eat, a young specimen of an old species on a young island in an old world. I imagined him sitting, and waiting, for someone to come feed him. And when no one did? Maybe he would start eating the grass. And then when the grass was gone, he might eat the petals from the shower trees. And then the ferns. And then the ti leaves. And then the gardenia bushes. He would eat and eat, and when the yard had been denuded of anything green, he would wait until the lawn turned green once more. A tortoise knows how to wait. It is another piece of wisdom that comes from being a member of a species that is so very old.

He was, I always thought, an unattractive animal: his eyes might kindly be called beady, his mouth a puckered seam—the writer Jane Gardam once described a tortoise as having "an old man's mean little mouth"—but over my summer with my parents, I also realized that I was mesmerized by him—even that I respected him. How could I not? An animal that demands so little and craves even less? An animal so unlike the animal I am, one with such a developed sense of self-possession? What secret did Fred know that I did not?

In those daydreams, I would think of how, when the light was winy and golden, I liked to sit on the porch steps and watch Fred trundle across the lawn. A few weeks into my stay, we'd grown familiar enough that he would toddle right up to me and stretch out his neck, its skin sagging into crepey pleats, and let me pat his head, closing his little black eyes as I did. In those moments, I found myself talking to him, usually about banal things: asking if he'd enjoyed the hibiscus flowers I'd snapped off a neighbor's bush; if he could feel the myna birds that occasionally perched on his back. This time, though, I asked him something else, something more intimate, something about what it was like to be the creature he was, what it was like to live without a sense of obligation or pity or guilt—all the things that make being a human so sad and so mysterious and so wondrously rich.

He didn't answer, of course. But for a moment, he held his position, his head motionless beneath my hand, a short pause in his very long life. And then he moved on—and I stood and watched him go.

20

## For Discussion and Writing

1. Why is the author puzzled by her parents' choice of a pet?

2. This essay about a tortoise is in fact an essay about many different things. One of its author's tasks, then, was to bring all of these different things together into a coherent whole. Reread the essay and mark the primary subject of each paragraph. Invent a way to visually map the essay's structure—try balloons, arrows, flow charts, whatever works. When you are done, reflect on the essay's structure. How many different topics are there? How does the author connect them? How does Yanagihara make it work?

3. **connections**   Read this essay with Verlyn Klinkenborg's "Our Vanishing Night" (p. 237). These two essays—one on light pollution, one on a tortoise—have in common observations about the fact that something valuable that we used to have is slowly being lost. For Klinkenborg, what exactly is the valuable thing about human experience that is being lost as we lose the darkness of light? For Yanagihara, what valuable thing is lost in our experience when the tradition of families staying together once children are grown is less dominant? What does it mean that we can't see the stars and we can't see our parents or children?

4. Toward the end of the essay, Yanagihara asks, "What secret did Fred know that I did not?" (par. 18) and she even tries to talk to him. Write a short piece from Fred's point of view. Be as literal and scientific or as imaginative and whimsical as you wish, but try to imagine yourself into his shell and ask serious questions. What might his experience of life be like? How does it feel to move so slowly and live so long? Does he feel alone? Does he feel connected to the author's parents? Does he think about her the way she thinks about him?

5. **looking further**   Research the subject of animal consciousness. There is a range of scientific and nonscientific opinion on the questions of how or whether animals feel, think, and communicate. What do you think of what you find in your research? Does your dog love you? Are dolphins smart? Are we as different from the other animals as we think, or are we more different?

DAVE ZIRIN

# Pre-Game

*Dave Zirin is an American sportswriter. He writes about the politics of professional and college sports for the magazine the* Nation. *He also hosts one podcast called* Edge of Sports *and cohosts another. Zirin is the author of eight books on the history and politics of sports, including books on John Carlos, Muhammad Ali, and the economics of team ownership.*

*"Pre-Game" is drawn from Zirin's 2013 book* Game Over: How Politics Has Turned the Sports World Upside Down. *As you read, keep that subtitle in mind, in particular the historical narrative it implies—that things are changing in sports—and watch for how that narrative appears in the essay.*

In March 2012, the Miami Heat chose to put down their basketballs and put on their hoodies. As a team, they stood shoulder to shoulder and did what we are told athletes no longer do: made a conscious political stand for justice. The entire Heat roster—from stars LeBron James, Dwyane Wade, and Chris Bosh to South Dakota's Mike Miller to the nearly forty-year-old reserve Juwan Howard—stood as one for seventeen-year-old Trayvon Martin, who had been recently killed by armed self-appointed "neighborhood watch leader" George Zimmerman. While Martin's killer had a nine-millimeter, the teenager had nothing but a pack of Skittles and a can of Arizona iced tea in his pocket. Trayvon was wearing a hoodie when he died, which some pundits in their infinite wisdom believed made him "suspicious" and worthy of being pursued.

Of all the teams in the league, the Heat were the most shocking yet also most appropriate to step up and be heard. It was shocking because the Heat are often painted as being a collection of prima donnas, as allegedly superficial as the town they call home. It was also appropriate because this was Trayvon's favorite team, and he was killed after leaving his house during halftime of the NBA All-Star Game, where he was watching James and Wade perform.

Given the outrage over Trayvon Martin's death, particularly in southern Florida, the Heat's powerful gesture hardly came out of the blue. What may be surprising for many fans is that "the King" himself, LeBron James, drove the effort. The March 2012 team photo was reportedly James's idea and was first posted to his personal Twitter account with the hashtag #WeWantJustice.

James later said, "It was very emotional, an emotional day for all of us. Taking that picture, we're happy that we're able to shed light on the situation that we feel is unjust." His teammate Wade commented to the Associated Press, "This situation hit home for me because last Christmas, all my oldest son wanted as a gift was hoodies. So when I heard about this a week ago, I thought of my sons. I'm speaking up because I feel it's necessary that we get past the stereotype of young, black men."

Since he was a teenager, "King James" has been pegged as     5
potentially the greatest basketball player alive. He's a Fortune 500 company with legs and, thus far, has a very carefully crafted apolitical image. He is also someone who was raised by a single mother in Akron, Ohio, at times so poor that they were living in a car. He has everything, as well as memories of having had nothing. Perhaps this is why he once said that his dream is to be "a global icon like Muhammad Ali." We've rarely seen evidence of his efforts to achieve this dream, but the hoodie photo could be a result of the Ali in him straining to be heard.

At the Heat's home game the following Friday night, James and several of his teammates took the floor with messages such as "RIP Trayvon Martin" and "We want justice" scrawled on their sneakers. Their actions inspired others across the NBA. Players spanning the gamut—from stars, like Steve Nash and Carmelo Anthony, to less famous jocks, such as Will Bynum and Brandon Knight—spoke out to raise awareness. Anthony, the high-profile star of the New York Knicks, changed his own Twitter picture to show him in a hoodie with "I am Trayvon Martin" superimposed over his body.

Detroit Pistons center Greg Monroe explained to the *Detroit Free Press* why so many players wanted to say something. "These kids come from the same neighborhoods we walked—or worse. And we see the same news everybody sees. When we turn on CNN, we don't have a special CNN channel. When we get pulled over, there's no special millionaire cops. We're just paid to play basketball."

To put it a different way, athletes aren't cartoon characters or robots. They are a part of this world. We are often told that today's athletes have no stake, as their forebears did, in fighting for change. At one time, athletes, particularly athletes of color and women athletes, had a self-interest in broader struggles against discrimination, but no longer. The argument goes that we are now somehow a "postracial, postpolitical" society. But while there are more people than ever telling us that the world has changed, injustice, discrimination, and inequality of opportunity still rule the land.

In the real world, any change at all has been incremental and hard-won. In the sports world, there's been a different kind of change and it couldn't be more dramatic. Over the last thirty years, the athletic-industrial complex has transformed itself into a trillion-dollar, global entity. One way it's done this is by making its product and its players as explicitly apolitical as possible. From Peyton Manning to Derek Jeter to Danica Patrick, the dominant message projected by athletes has been that it's far more important to be a brand than an individual, and that a modern jock should never sacrifice commercial concerns for political principle. This credo echoes Jesse Owens, the great Olympic star, who once said, "The only time the black fist has significance is when there's money inside."

ESPN, twenty-four-hour talk radio, and a seemingly bottom- 10
less appetite for distraction have exploded the size of our sports world—and its profits—into the stratosphere. In conjunction with this expansion, politics has also been actively discouraged by management and slammed by sports columnists. Legendary sportscaster Howard Cosell toward the end of his life dubbed it rule number one of "the jockocracy": sports and politics just don't mix.

Yet over the last several years, the specter of politics has been haunting sports. Cosell's Golden Rule has been repeatedly and flagrantly breached. More athletes are speaking out across the political spectrum as a series of revolutions, occupations, and protests has defined the global landscape. The real world is gaining on the sports world and the sports world is starting to look over its shoulder. . . . As I hope to show, whether we see ourselves as sports fans or not, we all have a stake in understanding why the sports page is insufficient for understanding sports.

# THE WALL BETWEEN SPORTS
# AND POLITICS IS BREACHED

On Cinco de Mayo in 2010, the NBA's Phoenix Suns went where no American sports team had gone before. In their playoff game against the San Antonio Spurs, the squad took to the court wearing jerseys that read simply "Los Suns." They were coming out as one against Arizona's Senate Bill 1070, which critics said would codify racial profiling by criminalizing anyone suspected of being an undocumented immigrant. This was the first time in U.S. sports history that an entire team—from owner to general manager to players—had expressed any kind of unified political stance. This audacious move by the Suns was perhaps the most publicized moment of a low-frequency sea change in the world of sports.

There were the members of the Green Bay Packers who stood—and continue to stand—behind the workers of Wisconsin under attack by the state's Governor Scott Walker.

There were the soccer players and clubs in the Middle East who played a leading role in the Arab Spring and, with unprecedented impact, are helping shape their revolutions.

There were the two NFL players—Pro Bowler Brendon Ayanbadejo and New Orleans Saints Super Bowl hero Scott Fujita—who spoke out in favor of LGBT marriage equality in the fall of 2009. (They have been joined by basketball star Steve Nash, New England Patriot Rob Gronkowski, New York Giant Michael Strahan, New York Ranger Sean Avery, Charles Barkley, Michael Irvin, and other players willing to speak out on what was recently a taboo locker room subject.)

Other political explosions have recently detonated inside the world of sports. Labor lockouts in the NFL and NBA have brought a taste of the broader economic crisis that provoked the Occupy movement into this supposedly privileged space. The explosive child-molestation charges at Penn State University and broader issues of corruption in the NCAA have raised political questions that speak to the very role we expect our universities to play. College athletes in the "revenue-producing" sports of football and basketball have signed petitions to form organizations and unshackle themselves from an ugly, utterly corrupt system.

Discussions about Tim Tebow, Jeremy Lin, Caster Semenya, and many others have created a buzz and a dialogue beyond the

15

confines of sports radio. When Boston Bruins goalie Tim Thomas turned down the team's invitation to go to the White House after they won the 2011 Stanley Cup, he wasn't content with quiet protest and instead posted a Tea Party–influenced monologue on his Facebook page. When Joel Ward, a black player for the Washington Capitals, scored a playoff-clinching goal on Thomas in 2012, the racist bile on Twitter was so intense that players and the media felt compelled to respond.

The more recent political eruptions are in many respects a hangover from the 2008 elections, when an unprecedented number of athletes went public in support of Barack Obama's candidacy and the efforts to elect an African American president. Some of the most commercially successful—and therefore some of the most commercially vulnerable—jocks became involved in the campaign. LeBron James wore Obama T-shirts to games and all-star players like Baron Davis and Chauncey Billups vocally supported his candidacy. Boston Celtics star Kevin Garnett wore sneakers with "Vote for Change" scrawled on their sides. Then Denver Nuggets star Carmelo Anthony pledged that he would score forty-four points in a game in honor of the future forty-fourth president (he only scored twenty-eight, which was, one can assume, not a tribute to Woodrow Wilson). When Billups was asked if he was concerned that his public support of Obama would hurt his endorsement chances, he said, "Like I give a shit."

As it turns out, a whole new generation of "Jocks for Justice" is rejecting the yoke of apathy and speaking out about the world. NBA players like Nash, Etan Thomas, and Joakim Noah, as well as NFL players Scott Fujita and Adalius Thomas, raised objections against the U.S. war in Iraq. Even Ultimate Fighting champion Jeff "the Snowman" Monson took to distributing antiwar pamphlets on his way to the "Octagon" and was arrested protesting at the 2008 Republican National Convention. As Martina Navratilova said to *Sports Illustrated* in 2008, "It's like athletes have woken up to what actors and musicians have known forever: I have this amazing platform—why not use it?"

These small acts of solidarity may seem negligible—but they      20
matter. Whether we like it or not, athletes are role models; it's worth asking, then, what are they in fact modeling?

While not every athlete acts like his life's ambition off the playing field is to be featured on MTV Cribs, the media loves to highlight the salacious and scandalous. It's not just the worst examples, like football player Ben Roethlisberger, who was investigated twice for rape, or Adam "Pac Man" Jones getting in trouble with the law at "gentleman's clubs." As a rule, the pro athletes who engage in the most mindless conspicuous consumption are the ones who tend to be highlighted.

If, instead of modeling crass materialism, more athletes chose to display a broader sense of community awareness—no matter the issue or politics—we'd all be better off. Even when I personally disagree with the politics of an athlete (see Tim Tebow), the mere fact that he is saying anything has the potential to initiate a dialogue more full and involving than anything we get from Capitol Hill.

Having athletes risk their prime perch in society for the greater good also becomes a kind of weather vane, a crackling signal that we have entered a new era. In 1968, political struggle was part of the oxygen of the sports world. The people and the games we watched were shaped by the struggles in the streets.

In a time that has seen revolts from the Middle East to the Midwest, we can look at the facts on the ground and note that the citadel of American sports has also been breached. The apolitical 1990s were dubbed the "vacation from history." Well, vacation is over and history has returned with a vengeance—severe enough to cross the moat and enter the locker room.

Why are more athletes speaking out? Some point to social media as a critical delivery system for a generation of athletes who don't trust "old school" reporters. Hundred-and-forty-character bursts and Facebook posts offer the ability to speak without a filter directly to fans.

Another theory is that players are now actually encouraged, for commercial reasons, to "define their own brand." I spoke at a seminar for NBA rookies where the dominant theme was how players could distinguish themselves and create a memorable persona for their audience. Just repeating clichés by rote, like "We give 150 percent and play one game at a time," is now seen as a liability. But the most compelling reason is simply, as Greg Monroe said, that the world is changing and athletes are a part of that world.

But speaking out still has a cost. We saw this in May 2011, after al-Qaeda leader and "9/11 mastermind" Osama bin Laden was killed by U.S. Navy SEALs. In the aftermath of his assassination, the sports world embraced the public eruption of patriotism. From the spontaneous cheers of forty thousand fans in Philadelphia to amped "Military Appreciation Night" celebrations at stadiums around the country, the sports world exulted in the euphoria of bin Laden's dramatic demise.

Yet some athletes dared to buck the trend—and, in the process, learned a tough lesson about the limits of free speech in the jockocracy. Chris Douglas-Roberts, former Memphis basketball all-American and Milwaukee Buck, responded to bin Laden's death with a litany of reasons why he wasn't joining the party, tweeting, among other things, "It took 919,967 deaths to kill that one guy. It took 10 years & 2 Wars to kill that guy. It cost us (USA) roughly $1,188,263,000,000 to kill that guy. But we winning though. Haaaa. (Sarcasm)."

Profanity, threats, and the general belief that he was "stupid" and a "moron" who should shut his "dumb [expletive] mouth" because he is "not intelligent" came rolling in. Douglas-Roberts tried to hit back, tweeting: "What I'm sayin has nothing to do with 9/11 or that guy (Bin Laden). I still feel bad for the 9/11 families but I feel EQUALLY bad for the war families. . . . People are telling me to get out of America now b/c I'm against MORE INNOCENT people dying everyday? B/c I'm against a 10 year WAR? Whatever happened to our freedom of speech? What I've learned tonight, athletes shouldn't have perspectives. But I don't care. We feel certain ways about things TOO."

Rashard Mendenhall, the Pro Bowl running back for the Pittsburgh Steelers, raised eyebrows even higher with his comments, writing, "[For] those of you who said you want to see Bin Laden burn in hell and piss on his ashes, I ask how would God feel about your heart? . . . What kind of person celebrates death?" Mendenhall then took it further and voiced his doubts about the official story of the 9/11 attacks, causing *Sports Illustrated*'s senior football writer Don Banks to write a piece titled "Mendenhall Just the Latest NFL Player to Spout Utter Nonsense."

The outrage intensified to the point where Steelers president Art Rooney II, a big money bundler for President Obama and the U.S. ambassador to Ireland, had to actually issue a formal statement about a tweet, writing, "I have not spoken with Rashard so it is hard to explain or even comprehend what he meant with

30

his recent Twitter comments. The entire Steelers' organization is very proud of the job our military personnel have done and we can only hope this leads to our troops coming home soon."

Whether or not you supported some or all the wars of the last decade, it should be clear that the guardians of jock culture are trying to teach athletes a lesson: you have signed away your right to have an opinion beyond your choice of sneaker or sports drink. This is something that runs very deeply in the marrow of our sports world: the idea that athletes, particularly athletes of color, should just "shut up and play."

Douglas-Roberts and Mendenhall also unintentionally exposed the most bizarre contradiction of this no-politics rule. Players are strongly encouraged by management, family, and the media to follow the rules and "never talk politics"—but whether we choose to acknowledge it or not, a politically charged atmosphere pervades all of professional sports. I don't just say that because I live in a town where people root for a team called the Redskins. I say so because at every sporting event we are encouraged to collectively celebrate the displays of nationalism, patriotism, and military might that festoon every corner. In addition, the politics of big business and big sponsorship deals saturate sports arenas. At one point, baseball owners wanted to put ads for *Spider-Man 2* on every second base, and only backed away when fans erupted in outrage. Even college football players, so-called amateurs, are trussed in ads to a degree that would shame NASCAR. If only the owners of pro sports teams could create a red, white, and blue beer, they might collectively keel over in joy.

But throughout history, we've also seen athletes take this setup and stand it on its head. This has happened when they have used their exalted, hypercommercialized platform to say something about the world and then dare those in power to shut them up. There is a reason we associate people like Jackie Robinson with the civil rights movement; Muhammad Ali with the 1960s; Billie Jean King with the women's movement; or 1968 Olympian Tom Waddell, the founder of the Gay Games, with LGBT rights. This history indicates that sports is never just a spectacle—that it has a potential to tap into sentiments for social change.

Our sports culture shapes societal attitudes, relationships, and power arrangements. It is where cultural meanings—our very notions of who we are and how we see each other, not only as 35

Americans but also as individuals—play out. It frames the ways in which we understand and discuss issues of gender, race, and class. And, as ever, it is crucial for understanding how these norms and power structures have been negotiated, struggled with, and resisted.

### For Discussion and Writing

1. What does Zirin mean when he claims that athletes "are a part of this world" (par. 8)? In what way could people think athletes are not a part of this world? What does it mean for Zirin that they are?

2. Rather than presenting both sides disinterestedly, Zirin takes a strong position in "Pre-Game." How does he take that position? List five or six ways in which he presses his point. Does he argue from evidence and proof or through use of rhetoric, or some combination of the two?

3. **connections**   The surge in political awareness and political speech among the athletes Zirin describes in "Pre-Game" is significant, but what does Zirin have to say about its effect? Think about this question in the light of Malcolm Gladwell's "Small Change" (p. 180). Social media play a role in many of the moments of protest Zirin discusses; would they have had the same impact without the Internet? How might Zirin respond to Gladwell?

4. College and professional sports in the United States are billion-dollar industries. In 2013, networks paid a total of $20.4 billion for the broadcast rights to National Football League games. How do you feel about the place of sports in society that this fact reflects? Are you a fan, do you question national priorities, or do you not care? Do you think there are positive or negative ramifications for the place sports hold in our economy and culture?

5. **looking further**   Zirin alludes to the controversy over the name of the Washington, DC, National Football League team. Research this issue, summarizing the arguments on both sides and listing the positions taken for and against. Based on your research, where do you stand? Why?

# Glossary of Writing Terms

**Allusion**   A reference to an artistic work, person, place, or event about which readers are assumed to already know. The relevance of the reference is also not usually explained: Readers are assumed to understand the connection between the writer's subject and the thing referred to. As a result of these assumptions, allusion is an economical way of making a point, as it crams a lot of information into a few words. When Judith Ortiz Cofer, in "The Myth of the Latin Woman: I Just Met a Girl Named Maria" (p. 110), refers to popular songs (as she does in her title, to a song from the musical *West Side Story*), she is making allusions—assuming that we will be familiar with her references and that we will understand the connections she is trying to make between popular songs and stereotypes.

**Analogy**   An extended comparison. An analogy explains features of one thing by reference to features shared with something more commonly known and understood. In "A Modest Proposal" (p. 370), Jonathan Swift makes an analogy between the treatment of the poor in Ireland and a hypothetical, imagined treatment that would be unthinkable and impossible, but, if considered in a certain way, is not far from what is actually happening to them. Swift presents the analogy indirectly—it may not be until you are far into the essay that you realize what he's doing—but the power of the connection is the greater for it.

**Argument**   Writing that attempts to prove a point through reasoning. Argument presses its case by using logic and by supporting its logic with examples and **evidence**. When Thomas Jefferson, in "The Declaration of Independence" (p. 218), makes his case for why the American colonies should be given their independence, he introduces his list like this: "The history of the present King of Great Britain is a history of repeated injuries and usurpations, all having in direct object the establishment of an absolute Tyranny over these States. To prove this, let Facts be submitted to a candid world" (par. 6). Making a **claim** and then making the transition to supporting examples, Jefferson's writing is argument.

**Audience**   As actors have audiences who can see and hear them, writers have readers. Having a sense of audience is important in writing because we write differently depending on who we think will be reading our work. If the audience is specific, we write in such a way that will appeal to a small group; if it is general, we write in such a way that as many people as possible will listen to, and be able to hear, what we have to say. It is especially easy to see considerations of

471

audience in speeches, as in public documents such as Thomas Jefferson's Declaration of Independence (p. 218), but it can also be seen in works in which writers are trying to explain their experiences to readers who might not have had such experiences themselves, as in Brent Staples's "Just Walk on By: Black Men and Public Space" (p. 345).

**Cause and effect**    Analysis of events or situations in which reasons are sought and effects are considered. Writers tracing the chain of events leading to a present situation or arguing the consequences of a future decision are doing cause and effect writing. In "Why Don't We Complain?" (p. 69), William F. Buckley Jr. makes his focus on cause and effect explicit: he is asking what the cause of a particular phenomenon is—"why" it exists. Over the course of his essay, he describes the phenomenon, offers examples of it, and attempts to venture some possible explanations of the cause of it, as many cause and effect essays do. In this case, the cause of a behavior—failure or reluctance to complain—is explained by a larger cultural development: an increased sense of helplessness. He then goes on to explain *that* phenomenon as the product of even larger historical developments: technologization and centralization of political and economic power. To take exception to Buckley's argument, one thus has to refute at least two layers of cause and effect explanations.

**Claim**    What an argument tries to prove; often called a **thesis**. In "The Paranoid Style of American Policing" (p. 106), Ta-Nehisi Coates makes an argument that police violence against the community delegitimizes the police force in the eyes of the people. His claim is straightforward: when citizens cannot trust the police, the system is broken. Supporting that claim requires evidence and the well-reasoned addressing of opposing viewpoint, but the claim itself remains simple and clear.

**Classification and division**    The sorting out of elements into classes or groups, or the separation of something into its parts. Classification and division are used when a writer wants to break something down into its elements or group a number of things in order to analyze them. When Mike Rose talks about different kinds of teachers and students in "I Just Wanna Be Average" (p. 295), he is classifying; when Amy Tan in "Mother Tongue" (p. 379) breaks down her language use into the various Englishes she uses, she is dividing.

**Cliché**    An old, tired expression that writers should avoid like the plague. "Like the plague" is an example of cliché. When drafting and especially when revising, writers scan their work for words and phrases that have that less-than-fresh feeling and strike them out. "Like the plague," for example, can be replaced with a new, concrete image, which "like the plague" must have been at one time (closer to the time of the plague itself, perhaps). The uniqueness of a writer's voice comes in part from the words chosen. Using well-worn, often-chosen phrases can be thought of, then, as a lost opportunity.

**Comparison and contrast**    Examination of similarities and differences. One usually but not always appears with the other. Bharati Mukherjee's "Two Ways to

Belong in America" (p. 267) shows in its first sentence that differences often arise between similar things, and so that comparison and contrast often go together: "This is a tale of two sisters from Calcutta, Mira and Bharati, who have lived in the United States for some 35 years, but who find themselves on different sides in the current debate over the status of immigrants" (par. 1).

**Conclusion**   The ending of an **essay**, which should bring the writer's point home in a few sentences or even a **paragraph** or two. Good conclusions do more than repeat a **thesis**, and they can even sometimes point the way to extensions of the thesis, but they should not introduce entirely new thoughts. Conclusions can also be funny, as when Swift, at the end of "A Modest Proposal" (p. 370), insists he has no personal interest at stake in his **ironic** proposal that the people of Ireland eat their infants as, in his words, "I have no children by which I can propose to get a single penny; the youngest being nine years old, and my wife past childbearing" (par. 33).

**Definition**   Explanation of the nature of a word, thing, or idea. **Essays** that define may use many other kinds of writing, such as **description**, **exposition**, and **narration**. Definition essays often are really redefinition essays: they attempt to make us understand something we thought we already understood. When Nancy Mairs writes, in "On Being a Cripple" (p. 247), "As a cripple, I swagger" (par. 2), she is embracing a label that others have tried not to use and she is redefining what it means.

**Description**   Depiction through sensory evidence. Description is not just visual: it can use details of touch, smell, taste, and hearing. These concrete details can support a specific **argument**, give the reader a sense of immediacy, or establish a mood. Description, while tied to the concrete, can also use **metaphor**, as when Verlyn Klinkenborg writes in "Our Vanishing Night" (p. 237), "And yet above the city's pale ceiling lies the rest of the universe, utterly undiminished by the light we waste—a bright shoal of stars and planets and galaxies, shining in seemingly infinite darkness" (par. 5).

**Diction**   Word choice. Diction can be characterized in terms of level of formality (formal or informal), concreteness (specific or abstract), and other choices that reflect a level appropriate to the writer's subject and **audience**. Diction is a central vehicle by which a writer makes her meaning clear, and it is a major element of a writer's style as well, and so of her tone. "The Declaration of Independence" (p. 218) is an excellent example of careful word choice. In this important document, Thomas Jefferson had to make every word count, and in his choice of words, some repeated, such as *equal, usurpations, tyrant,* and *independent,* Jefferson made his meaning very clear indeed.

**Draft**   An unfinished **essay**. A draft may have a **conclusion**, but it has not been completely revised, edited, and proofread. When still in the draft stage, writers can rethink not just the structure of their essay but their ideas as well.

**Essay**   A short nonfiction piece of writing. A writer should present one main idea in an essay. There are different kinds of essays—scholarly and personal, formal and informal—and many that mix these different kinds of writing.

**Evidence**   The facts that support an **argument**. Evidence takes different forms depending on the kind of writing in which it appears, but it generally is concrete, agreed-on information that can be pointed to as example or proof. In "Serving in Florida" (p. 134), Barbara Ehrenreich supports the narrative of her experiences living as a low-income worker with both a detailed survey of the living conditions of her coworkers and statistical support gleaned from research. Ehrenreich's argument is strengthened by inclusion of these different kinds of evidence.

**Exemplification**   Providing specific instances in support of general ideas. In "On Compassion" (p. 43), Barbara Lazear Ascher tells a number of anecdotes that serve as examples of encounters between the less fortunate and those who offer help.

**Exposition**   Writing that explains. Rather than showing, as in **narrative**, exposition tells. A majority of **essays** contain some exposition because they need to convey information, give background, or tell how events occurred or processes work. Lars Eighner uses exposition in "On Dumpster Diving" (p. 144) to explain who scavenges from Dumpsters, how they do it, how things in Dumpsters get there, and many other things related to Dumpster diving.

**Fallacy**   A logical error. Fallacies weaken an argument. They include the making of false choices, the false assigning of cause (as in saying that because something happened after something else, the first event caused the second), the making of false generalizations, and many others.

**Five-paragraph essay**   You should be familiar with this format from high school. It is taught because it provides an easy template for composition: an introductory **paragraph**, which contains your **thesis statement**; three body paragraphs laying out three **arguments**, pieces of **evidence**, or other kinds of support for your **thesis**; and a final concluding paragraph restating the thesis and summarizing the material in the body. While it can be a useful tool for beginning writers, it is confining and tends to encourage uninspiring, unimaginative writing. You will notice that none of the authors in this book use that format, and you shouldn't either. It is the **cliché** of writing essays, and, like actual clichés, should be avoided—like the plague.

**Introduction**   The beginning of an **essay**; it should generally state a writer's main point. An introduction can include a **thesis statement** and can even begin to develop the **thesis**, but it can also simply pose a question, the answer to which will be the essay's thesis, or it can begin with a **story**, out of which the thesis will come. William F. Buckley Jr.'s "Why Don't We Complain?" (p. 69) is a good example of this kind of introduction.

**Irony**   Verbal irony is writing that says one thing while it means something else, often the opposite of what it says (sarcasm is one form of verbal irony). The difference between literal meaning and implicit meaning is often used to suggest the difference between what a situation or person seems or pretends to be and what it or he really is. This use of irony is the reason irony often appears in satirical writing (writing that mocks a situation or idea). Jonathan Swift's "A Modest

Proposal" (p. 370) is entirely ironic; the difficulty lies in figuring out what meaning Swift intends, since the literal meaning is certainly not his message. When something occurs that is counter to what is expected (what people often refer to when they say something is ironic), it is sometimes called situational irony. An example of this latter form of irony can be seen in the conclusion of Langston Hughes's "Salvation" (p. 210).

**Metaphor**   Metaphor can be understood as a figure of speech (a nonliteral use of language) that says one thing *is* another or, in the form of simile, as a figure of speech that says one thing is *like* another. In both cases, the writer is trying to explain one thing by means of comparing it to another, more familiar thing. One example of the metaphor that makes a comparison by saying one thing is another comes from E. B. White's "Once More to the Lake" (p. 432): "It took a cool nerve, because if you threw the switch a twentieth of a second too soon you would catch the flywheel when it still had speed enough to go up past center, and the boat would leap ahead, charging bull-fashion at the dock" (par. 10). Note that this metaphor does not say explicitly that the boat is a bull; rather it says that the boat would *leap* and *charge bull-fashion.*

**Narration**   Telling a **story**, or giving an account of an event. Narration is a part of many different kinds of writing. Writers often tell an anecdote, or short narrative often told to make a point, as support for an **argument**. Some **essays** are almost entirely narration, but usually the events of the story lead to some kind of **conclusion**. George Orwell's "Shooting an Elephant" (p. 279) is largely narration and leads him to a very specific conclusion, as can be seen when he writes, of the story he tells, "It was a tiny incident in itself, but it gave me a better glimpse than I had had before of the real nature of imperialism—the real motives for which despotic governments act" (par. 3).

**Paragraph**   A series of sentences, set off by an initial indentation or a blank line, that develop a main idea. Paragraphs often have **topic sentences** that state that main idea, followed by sentences that offer support.

**Paraphrase**   A rephrasing of a section of a work into one's own words. A paraphrase is different from a **summary** in that it includes the details of a work and so is of similar length to the original; a paraphrase is similar to a summary in that both attempt to give some sense of another work without using its words.

**Plagiarism**   Using another person's words or ideas in one's own work without acknowledgment.

**Point of view**   The angle from which a writer sees his or her subject. No matter how objective or impartial a writer claims to be, he or she is always writing from a point of view influenced by age, race, gender, and economic and social status, to name just a few factors. In the personal essay "How It Feels to Be Colored Me" (p. 213), Zora Neale Hurston acknowledges writing from her own point of view.

**Prewriting**   Writing that happens before drafting. Prewriting is an early stage in the writing process during which writers brainstorm, come up with topics and theses, and begin to work on ways to develop them.

**Process analysis**   Explaining how to do something, how others do it, or how certain things occur. Often process analysis supports another aim—to make a point or to tell one's own **story**, for example. When Frederick Douglass tells the story of his early reading in "Learning to Read and Write" (p. 127), for example, he explains how he managed to get poor white children to help him and how in doing so he learned things that would help him argue for the abolition of slavery.

**Quotation**   The inclusion of the words of another in one's own work, indicated by surrounding quotation marks. Used to convey a sense of the person who wrote or spoke those words, to reproduce a phrase or sentence or more that perfectly captures some meaning the writer wishes also to convey, or to borrow some authority from an expert or eyewitness. Gloria Anzaldúa's "How to Tame a Wild Tongue" (p. 30) demonstrates a number of uses of quotation.

**Revision**   The stage in the process of writing after a first **draft** is written when writers reexamine their work and try to improve it. This improvement consists of more than editing and proofreading—it also includes reevaluating the structure, the supporting **evidence**, the **thesis**, and even the topic. All good writers revise their work.

**Rhetoric**   The effective use of language; also, the study of effective language use. The term can also be used negatively, as when it is said that a particular argument is really just using rhetoric, that is, using words persuasively (perhaps by making emotional appeals) without actually making a solid **argument**.

**Story**   A **narrative**. The term is used in a number of different senses—to indicate a narrative within a nonfiction piece, to label a news article in a newspaper or magazine, or to name the genre of short fiction. Many, perhaps most, effective essays tell some kind of story.

**Style**   The way a writer writes. Any of the choices writers make while writing—about **diction**, sentence length, structure, rhythm, and figures of speech—that make their work sound like them. The **tone** of a particular work can be due in part to a writer's style. James Baldwin is known for his distinctive style, one aspect of which is the mixing of formal, sometimes biblical, language and an everyday, conversational style, as in this sentence from "Notes of a Native Son" (p. 47): "I had declined to believe in that apocalypse which had been central to my father's vision; very well, life seemed to be saying, here is something that will certainly pass for an apocalypse until the real thing comes along" (par. 2).

**Summary**   A condensation, in one's own words, of a work. Summaries consist of the main points of the work; supporting points, examples, and other kinds of support are left out.

**Synthesis**   The use of outside sources to gather information and opinions, in order to develop ideas, amass evidence, and support arguments. Synthesis enables writers to do more than simply express their opinion—it enables them to enter the conversation about their topic already being held in the wider world. It also allows them to complicate their ideas, to see more than one side, and to marshal information and logical arguments in the service of their position.

**Thesis**   The main idea in a piece of writing, which the work is trying to argue or explore. Also sometimes known as the **claim**, a term that also has a more specific meaning related to argumentation. The thesis can be explicit, as in essays that make an argument (as in Henry David Thoreau's "Civil Disobedience" (p. 386) or implicit or even secondary, as in some narrative essays (as in George Orwell's "Shooting an Elephant," p. 279).

**Thesis statement**   A sentence or group of sentences, usually appearing early in a piece of writing, that announce the thesis. The thesis statement often states plainly what the work as a whole is to be about, but it can take many forms, as in the following from Stephanie Ericsson's "The Ways We Lie" (p. 157), in which she makes an assertion and follows with a question: "We lie. We all do. We exaggerate, we minimize, we avoid confrontation, we spare people's feelings, we conveniently forget, we keep secrets, we justify lying to the big-guy institutions. Like most people, I indulge in small falsehoods and still think of myself as an honest person. Sure I lie, but it doesn't hurt anything. Or does it?" (par. 3).

**Tone**   Attitude toward subject, readers, and even the writer and work itself; also sometimes mood or atmosphere more generally. Achieved through **style** as well as content. In his indictment of King George III in "The Declaration of Independence" (p. 218), Thomas Jefferson writes, "He has abdicated Government here, by declaring us out of his Protection and waging War against us. He has plundered our seas, ravaged our Coasts, burnt our towns, and destroyed the lives of our people" (pars. 20–21). His tone in this passage comes from his choice of words, the shape of his sentences, and his imagery.

**Topic sentence**   The sentence in which the writer states a **paragraph**'s main idea. The topic sentence often appears at or near the beginning of the paragraph. When Gloria Anzaldúa in "How to Tame a Wild Tongue" (p. 30) begins a paragraph, "Chicanos, after 250 years of Spanish/Anglo colonization, have developed significant differences in the Spanish we speak" (par. 18), we should suspect the rest of the paragraph will develop that idea, perhaps with examples of these differences (and we would be right).

**Transitions**   The connective tissue among sentences, ideas, and **paragraphs**. Transitions help readers follow writers through their ideas and see the connections among the parts of an **argument** or the relation between scenes in a **narrative**. Through the use of transitional words (*therefore, nonetheless, then*), phrases (*on the other hand, as a result, in the same way*), effects (such as repetition or parallel sentence structures), and even whole paragraphs, good writers include signposts to show readers the direction the argument or story is going. Nancy Mairs in "On Being a Cripple" (p. 247) begins many of her paragraphs with transitions that help readers follow the line of her thought. Some examples: "Lest I begin to sound like Pollyanna, however, let me say that I don't like having MS" (par. 9); "Along with this fear that people are secretly accepting shoddy goods comes a relentless pressure to please" (par. 18); "This gentleness is part of the reason that I'm not sorry to be a cripple" (par. 32).

# Acknowledgments *(continued from p. ii)*

Maya Angelou, "Chapter 23" from *I Know Why the Caged Bird Sings* by Maya Angelou, copyright © 1969 and renewed 1997 by Maya Angelou. Used by permission of Random House, an imprint and division of Penguin Random House LLC. All rights reserved.

Gloria Anzaldúa, "How to Tame a Wild Tongue," from *Borderlands/La Frontera: The New Mestiza*, copyright © 1987, 1999, 2007, 2012 by Gloria Anzaldúa. Reprinted by permission of Aunt Lute Books. www.auntlute.com.

Barbara Lazear Ascher, "On Compassion" from *The Habit of Loving* by Barbara Lazear Ascher, copyright © 1986, 1987, 1989 by Barbara Lazear Ascher. Used by permission of Random House, an imprint and division of Penguin Random House LLC. All rights reserved.

James Baldwin, "Notes of a Native Son" by James Baldwin, copyright © 1955, renewed 1983, by James Baldwin. Reprinted by permission of Beacon Press, Boston.

Willam F. Buckley, Jr., "Why Don't We Complain?" from *Miles Gone By* by William F. Buckley, Jr., copyright © 1960, 2004 by William F. Buckley, Jr. Reprinted by permission of The Wallace Literary Agency.

Danny Chau, "The Burning Desire for Hot Chicken," *The Ringer*, August 31, 2016. Used with permission.

Sandra Cisneros, "Only Daughter." Copyright © 1990 by Sandra Cisneros. First published in GLAMOUR, November 1990. By permission of Susan Bergholz Literary Services, New York, NY and Lamy, NM. All rights reserved.

Eli Clare, "Clearcut: Explaining the Distance," in *Exile and Pride*, by Eli Clare, pp. 17–30. Copyright © 2015, Eli Clare. All rights reserved. Republished by permission of the copyright holder and the publisher, Duke University Press. www.dukeupress.edu.

Ta-Nehisi Coates, "The Paranoid Style of American Policing," *The Atlantic*, December 30, 2015. Copyright © 2015, The Atlantic Media Co., as first published in *The Atlantic Magazine*. All rights reserved. Distributed by Tribune Content Agency, LLC. Used with permission.

Judith Ortiz Cofer, "The Myth of the Latin Woman: I Just Met a Girl Named María," from *The Latin Del: Prose and Poetry*, copyright © 1993. Reprinted with permission from The University of Georgia Press.

Joan Didion, "On Keeping a Notebook," from *Slouching Towards Bethlehem*, copyright © 1966, 1968, renewed 1996 by Joan Didion. Reprinted by permission of Farrar, Straus and Giroux.

Barbara Ehrenreich, "Serving in Florida" from *Nickel and Dimed: On (Not) Getting By in America* by Barbara Ehrenreich, copyright © 2001 by Barbara Ehrenreich. Reprinted by permission of ICM Partners and Henry Holt and Company, LLC.

Lars Eighner, "On Dumpster Diving," from *Travels with Lizbeth: Three Years On the Road and On the Streets*, copyright © 1993 by Lars Eighner. Reprinted by permission of St. Martin's Press. All rights reserved.

Stephanie Ericsson, "The Ways We Lie," Copyright © 1992 by Stephanie Ericsson. Originally published by *The Utne Reader*. Reprinted by the permission of Dunham Literary Inc., as agent for the author.

Jen Gann, "Wrongful Birth," *The Cut*, November 27, 2017. Copyright © 2017 by New York Media LLC. Used with permission.

Malcolm Gladwell, "Small Change: Why the Revolution Will Not Be Tweeted," *New York Magazine*, 2010. Reprinted with the permission of the author.

Jonathan Gold, "What Is a Burrito? A Primer," *LA Weekly*, October 21, 2009. Copyright © 2009 by L.A. Weekly. Used with permission.

Rahawa Haile, "Going It Alone," *Outside*, May 1, 2017. Copyright © 2017 by Rahawa Haile. Reprinted by permission of HSG Agency.

Jenine Holmes, "When Pink Ballet Slippers Won't Do," *The New York Times*, July 13, 2018. © 2018 by The New York Times. All rights reserved. Used under license.

Langston Hughes, "Salvation," from *The Big Sea*, copyright © 1940 by Langston Hughes. Copyright renewed 1968 by Arna Bontemps and George Houston Bass. Reprinted by permission of Hill and Wang, a division of Farrar, Straus and Giroux.

Jamaica Kincaid, excerpt from "The Ugly Tourist," from *A Small Place*, copyright © by Jamaica Kincaid. Reprinted by permission of Farrar, Straus and Giroux.

Stephen King, "Reading to Write," from *On Writing: A Memoir of the Craft* by Stephen King, copyright © 2000 by Stephen King. Reprinted with the permission of Scribner, a division of Simon & Schuster, Inc. All rights reserved.

Verlyn Klinkenborg, "Our Vanishing Night," *National Geographic Magazine*, 2008. Reprinted with permission of the publisher.

Audre Lorde, "The Fourth of July" from *Zami: A New Spelling of My Name* — published by Crossing Press, copyright © 1982, 2006 by Audre Lorde. Used herewith by permission of the Charlotte Sheedy Literary Agency.

Nancy Mairs, "On Being a Cripple," from *Plaintext* by Nancy Mairs, copyright © 1986 by The Arizona Board of Regents. Reprinted by permission of the University of Arizona Press.

Matthew J. X. Malady, "The Ghosts in Our Machines," *The New Yorker*. Copyright © Condé Nast. Used with permission.

Bharati Mukherjee, "Two Ways to Belong in America," by Bharati Mukherjee. Copyright © 1996 by Bharati Mukherjee. Originally Published in *The New York Times*. Reprinted by permission of the author.

Tommy Orange, "Indian Heads," excerpt(s) from *There There: A Novel* by Tommy Orange, copyright © 2018 by Tommy Orange. Used by permission of Alfred A. Knopf, an imprint of the Knopf Doubleday Publishing Group, a division of Penguin Random House LLC. All rights reserved.

Mike Rose, "'I Just Wanna Be Average,'" From *Lives on the Boundary: The Struggles and Achievements of America's Underprepared* by Mike Rose, copyright © 1989 by Mike Rose. Reprinted with the permission of The Free Press, a division of Simon & Schuster, Inc. All rights reserved.

Carol Sagan, "Does Truth Matter?" Copyright © 1996 by Democritus Properties, LLC. Originally published in *Skeptical Inquirer*. Reprinted with permission from Democritus Properties, LLC.

Maria Michela Sassi, "The Sea Was Never Blue," *Aeon*, July 13, 2017. This essay was originally published in Aeon (aeon.co). Used with permission.

David Sedaris, "I Like Guys," from *Naked* by David Sedaris, copyright © 1997 by David Sedaris. Reprinted with permission of Little, Brown and Company and Don Congdon Associates, Inc. All rights reserved.

Brent Staples, "Just Walk on By: Black Men and Public Space." Copyright © 1986. Reprinted with permission from the author.

Gloria Steinem, "Sex, Lies, and Advertising," *Ms.* Magazine, 1990, pp. 18–28. Reprinted with permission of the author.

Amy Tan, "Mother Tongue," Copyright © 1989 by Amy Tan. First appeared in *The Threepenny Review*. Reprinted by permission of the author and the Sandra Dijkstra Literary Agency.

Calvin Trillin, "Last Days of the Rickshaw," first published in the *National Geographic*, 2008. Copyright © 2008 by Calvin Trillin. Used by permission of William Morris Endeavor Entertainment, LLC.

Ai Weiwei, "The Refugee Crisis Isn't About Refugees. It's About Us," *The Guardian*, February 2, 2018. Copyright Guardian News & Media Ltd 2018. Used with permission.

E. B. White, "Once More to the Lake." Copyright © 1941 by E. B. White. Reprinted by permission of ICM Partners.

Hanya Yanagihara, "A Pet Tortoise Who Will Outlive Us All," *The New York Times*, May 17, 2017. Copyright © 2017 by The New York Times. All rights reserved. Used under license.

Dave Zirin, excerpt from *Game Over: How Politics Has Turned the Sports World Upside Down*. Copyright © 2013 by Dave Zirin. Reprinted by permission of The New Press. www.thenewpress.com.

# Index of Authors and Titles